TO BELIEVE

or

NOT TO BELIEVE

*READINGS IN THE PHILOSOPHY
OF RELIGION*

○

TO BELIEVE *or* NOT TO BELIEVE

READINGS IN THE PHILOSOPHY OF RELIGION

○

E. D. KLEMKE
Iowa State University

*Under the general editorship of
Robert J. Fogelin,
Dartmouth College*

HARCOURT BRACE JOVANOVICH COLLEGE PUBLISHERS
Fort Worth   Philadelphia   San Diego   New York
Orlando   Austin   San Antonio
Toronto   Montreal   London   Sydney   Tokyo

Acquisitions Editor: Bill McLane
Manuscript Editor: Debbie Hardin
Production Editor: Tracey Engel
Designer: James Hughes
Production Manager: Mary Kay Yearin
Permissions Editor: Eleanor Garner

To

Steven and Pattie Stamy,

David Hauser,

and

Bryan Walker

Preface

○

With some exceptions, I have been teaching an intermediate level course and several upper level courses and seminars in the philosophy of religion for over 25 years. In the intermediate level course, I have experimented with many approaches, both in terms of course format and in terms of textbooks, assigned readings, and so on. While the course was always satisfactory and had high enrollments, I always felt somewhat dissatisfied.

About six years ago I decided to make a major change. Rather than offering a course that included from six to ten topics, approached sequentially, I decided to organize the course around one *major* question, and then examine via readings (and some lectures) various answers to that question. The question I chose was: Is religious belief (the belief in theism) a viable option for our time? The reasons for having selected this as the major question are given in the last section of the Introduction to this volume.

The course proceeded in this order. We began with the classical case for theism, using the traditional arguments for the existence of God, formulated by the classical theists. I then distinguished three main attacks on or critiques of theism that have been made in the past three centuries. In the second part of the course we examined, again through readings, the first two attacks and responses by twentieth-century theists. In the third part of the course, we examined the third, newer attack and (again) responses by contemporary theists. At the end of the course we returned to the main question, now seen in the light of several severe critiques of theism and some serious responses to those critiques. Of course, as time permitted, attention was given to topics related to the main question.

The first time I taught the course with this approach and revised format, the class became alive! It was an amazing experience, which gets better every year. Students were highly motivated. They did their homework diligently and came to class, ready to discuss, criticize, and argue. And argue they did—but always in an atmosphere of friendliness, relaxation, and even warmth. Both in terms of participation and in terms of written assignments (exams and short papers), the work by the students in the class each year was exceptional. This became my favorite class to teach.

When an Executive Editor at Harcourt Brace Jovanovich asked me to submit a proposal for an anthology in the philosophy of religion, I accepted. A glance at the Contents will reveal that I used essentially this same format. The only change occurs in the fourth part of the book where I have included a fairly large number of topics and readings that are not all contained within what I referred to as the main question but that are closely related to it.

I would like to express my deep gratitude to all those who helped in making this book a reality. I am especially indebted to the former chair of my department, A. David

Kline, and to my colleagues at Iowa State University, especially Gary Comstock, David Roochnik, and R. J. Van Iten. I would also like to thank the reviewers of the book, David Conway, University of Missouri, St. Louis; Frank B. Dilley, University of Delaware; John L. Hammond, Portland State University; and Delos B. McKown, Auburn University. I am especially grateful to Robert J. Fogelin who also reviewed the manuscript. Finally, I would like to express my deep gratitude to Bill McLane, my editor at Harcourt Brace Jovanovich, and to Eleanor R. Garner, permissions editor. Both helped me in ways that surely went far beyond the call of duty. Similarly, I would like to express my appreciation to Debbie Hardin, manuscript editor, and to Tracey Engel, production editor. Both were very helpful and patient.

I also wish to extend my thanks to all those who in various ways helped with the task of preparing the manuscript itself. Among these are: Edna Wiser, Bernice Power, Barbara Larson, Gretchen Binhammer, Mark T. Barnes, Michael D. Bolte, and Brian Luce.

Further, I want to express my abiding gratitude to the many students who were enrolled in my philosophy of religion classes over the years and who participated so magnificently and responded so favorably, and thereby enriched my life.

Finally, I want to express my abiding gratitude to my friends to whom this book is dedicated for their constant kindness, affection, and help.

—E. D. KLEMKE

Contents

○

The Main Problem
of the Philosophy
# of Religion

○

I N THIS INTRODUCTION, I want to focus on the topic of the subtitle: the main problem of the philosophy of religion. First, however, I will give some attention to two preliminary issues before I turn to the main issue. Also, since there are many other problems that fall within the scope of the philosophy of religion, I will need to devote some attention to these as well.

Hence I shall take up the following questions:

1. What is philosophy?
2. What is the philosophy of religion?
3. What is the main problem of the philosophy of religion; why is it the main problem?
4. What are some of the other closely related topics that are within the philosophy of religion?

In this book, I have emphasized the third question: what is the main problem of the philosophy of religion, and why is it so? The first three parts of the book focus on this question. The last part focuses on a number of the closely related topics referred to in the fourth question. Hence I will be brief with regard to the first two questions, and then I will discuss the third question at length. Finally, I will give some consideration to the fourth question.

1. What Is Philosophy?

The term "philosophy" is used in two main senses. I refer to these as the common sense of the term, and the technical sense. By the common sense of the term, I mean the one often used in everyday discourse, as when someone says: "My philosophy on that is so and so." What such a person refers to is a set of fundamental beliefs and cherished convictions. Often these are held in a naive, unexamined manner. At some point in life, we all develop our own such philosophies, or at least we start forming them. However, this common sense of the term "philosophy" is not what we will be concerned with in this book.

"Philosophy" in the second sense, the technical sense of the term, is not just a set of beliefs. Rather, philosophy consists in the effort to critically examine beliefs, to consider alternatives, to weigh pros and cons, to bring in factors like grounds, evidence, and to come up with arguments on behalf of those beliefs. Philosophy is an exacting discipline, with certain problems it is concerned with solving.

What, then, is philosophy in the technical sense? There are two ways to answer this question. The first way is to give a classification of the chief divisions of philosophy, and perhaps the subdivisions. The second way is to articulate the main aims or goals of philosophy—in other words, to specify the main tasks of philosophy.

Most of the main problems or questions with which philosophy is concerned may be thought of as falling into three categories: problems pertaining to reality, problems pertaining to knowledge, and problems pertaining to value. The three areas are: metaphysics (or ontology), epistemology, and axiology.[1]

Metaphysics (Ontology): What Is Real?

Let us begin with a discussion of what is meant by the term "reality" in the philosophical sense. In one very broad sense of the term, "reality" may mean *whatever* is. But in this broad sense, *anything* is— a ghost as well as a tree, an object of illusion as well as an object of veridical perception. In the philosophical sense of the term, "reality" designates what is *real*, not merely as opposed to what is unreal, but rather whatever is real in the sense of being *ultimately* real. It is difficult to explicate this definition to anyone who has no familiarity with philosophical works. Its meaning can best be apprehended by examples, that is, by reading philosophical works in which philosophers distinguish, and give grounds for the distinction, between those kinds of things that merely have a surface reality from those that have a more fundamental or underlying reality. But as a start, one might say that in the philosophical sense, the term "reality" refers to whatever is real rather than whatever is merely apparent. In fact, this problem of *appearance* versus *reality* has often been considered one of the main problems of philosophy. Metaphysics deals with the nature of reality.

Besides the general questions of, "What is the nature of reality?" or "What are the ultimate constituents of the universe?" there are also some specific problems that metaphysics seeks to address. To talk about the universe leads to the question "How did the universe originate and develop?" The subdivision of metaphysics (ontology) that deals with such questions is often referred to as philosophical cosmology. Some cosmologists would answer the preceding question by saying "A transcendent God created the universe." This leads to a host of questions that make up a second subdivision of metaphysics, that is, philosophy of religion. A third subdivision, philosophical anthropology deals with questions pertaining to humanity. For example, "Who or what are we—just material, just bodies, or are we more?"

Epistemology: What Is Knowledge?

Let us turn now to a consideration of what is meant by the term "knowledge." The philosophical sense of the term has its roots in the ordinary sense of the term but constitutes a refinement of it. We commonly contrast knowledge with ignorance. And we commonly think of knowledge as possessing some characteristics, whatever they may be, that are lacking in mere opinion or belief. Philosophers accept and insist on these distinctions. However, with regard to the province of knowledge, as distinguished from belief, philosophers also ask additional questions and make additional distinctions. Some of these distinctions are: knowledge that is absolutely certain as opposed to probable knowledge; knowledge that is significant and informative as opposed to knowledge that is trivial (such as "*A* is *A*"). Epistemology pertains to the study of knowledge.

We may distinguish two main types of knowledge: derived and nonderived. Sometimes we come to know that something is the case because we logically infer it from other things we know. Such claims are thus *derived* from others. A subdivision of epistemology, logic, studies such questions as "What are the principles by which to distinguish when our inferences (both deductive and inductive) are correct?" If all knowledge-claims were derived, we would argue in circles. Hence some of them must be nonderived. For example, claims about what we directly perceive, "The book is red," and so on, are non-derived. A second subdivision of epistemology deals with claims having to do with perception, memory, and so forth. Since epistemology is closely related to philosophy of science, some would consider the latter to be a third subdivision of epistemology.

Axiology: What Is of Value?

The term "value" in philosophy also has its roots in the ordinary sense of the term. However, philosophers often make additional distinctions and refinements by asking such questions as: "Are any values more ultimate than others (the latter being merely apparent or on-the-surface)?" "Are any values of greater importance to human life than others? If so, what are they?" Axiology is the study of value.

Axiology has two main subdivisions: ethics and aesthetics. As we have seen, axiology is concerned with questions that pertain to the nature of value judgments—some of which are specifically ethical in character, some of which are specifically aesthetic in character, and some of which are both. Among the chief problems of ethics are: "What is the correct standard of conduct by which to distinguish right from wrong behavior?" "What sorts of things are good rather than bad?" "What is the nature of ethical judgments? Are they mere expressions of subjective feelings or taste, or are they objective?" Axiology is the study of questions like these.

Now let us consider the second way of answering the question "What is philosophy?" by examining the chief aims of philosophy. Among them let us consider five that are relevant to humanity at large, as well as to professional philosophers. These are: (1) the critical scrutiny of our beliefs and convictions; (2) the bringing to light of our hidden assumptions or presuppositions; (3) the quest for a geniunely worthwhile life; (4) the effort to keep alive our sense of wonder about the world; and (5) the posing of certain questions that are not dealt with by other disciplines, and the attempt to answer them. I maintain that pursuing these aims constitutes a good reason both for philosophizing and for studying philosophy. In fact, these two activities are interconnected, for one cannot adequately study philosophy without doing some philosophizing.

So my answer to the question "What is philosophy" can now be given in one sentence: Philosophy is the enterprise that has the three main divisions mentioned in terms of subject matter, and in terms of goals, seeks to fulfill the five aims mentioned. Whichever way you approach it, philosophy seeks to solve certain problems that are not the province of science or any other discipline. Philosophers try to get answers to questions. And how does philosophy attempt to solve the problems (or get answers to the questions)? By the two-fold rigorous method of analysis and argumentation: (1) Before we can answer any question, we must understand it. We need to get clear as to meaning of the terms. We must make necessary distinctions and thereby arrive at clarity. (2) Once we have done that, we try to answer the question— that is, to find the best answer. We do that by means of arguments.

Many of the selections in this book are devoted to appraising arguments. There are people who think they can dismiss this emphasis on analysis and argumentation when evaluating an issue. They think that one can solve a problem on the basis of how one *feels* about it. This is irrational. Feelings are important, but they are not a basis for solving problems. There is only one way to solve them, and that is through reason. Therefore, the fundamental tools of reason — analysis and argumentation—will be vital when evaluating the readings in this book.

2. What Is the Philosophy of Religion?

Sometimes the best way to explain what something *is* is to start with what it is *not*. So first: *What philosophy of religion is not.* It is not a medium or instrument of religious teaching. It need not be pursued with any religious standpoint at all. The atheist and the agnostic, as well as the believer, can and do pursue the philosophy of religion. Philosophy of religion is not theology or a branch of theology, if by "theology" one means the systematic formulation of religious beliefs accepted on faith, or beliefs that are taken to be a revelation from God. (However, theology is defined in a second sense, often referred to as natural theology. Natural (or rational) theology asks: What, if anything, can we know about God and other matters through our "natural light" of reason alone, without appeal to revelation? In this sense, natural theology and philosophy of religion may be identical, or at least overlap greatly.)

So much for what philosophy of religion is *not*. What, then, *is* it? It is a branch of philosophy that has as its subject matter something concerning religion and theology, much as the term itself suggests. But religion and theology encompass a lot. More specifically, philosophy of religion consists of an analysis of religious and theological concepts and propositions, and an appraisal of the reasons and arguments put forth on behalf of those concepts and propositions. Among the chief concepts are: "God," "eternal life," "salvation," and so on. Among the chief propositions are: "God exists," "God has such and such a nature," "God was in Christ," "The saved shall have eternal life," and so on.

It is clear that, considered as an activity, the philosophy of religion, as the noted philosopher of religion John Hick has said, is a *second-order* activity that is one step above or apart from its subject matter. It is not itself a part of the domain of religion or theology, but has a certain relation to it.[2] If we consider religion and theology to be (in part) talk about God, then philosophy of religion is talk about such talk. Hence, it is not a first-order activity, on a plane with religion and theology, but a second-order activity. It is not itself religion or theology, but it has a certain relation to them.

John Hick has expressed that relation nicely: It is the same relation that philosophy of art (aesthetics) has to artistic phenomena and to the concepts and forms of aesthetic discussion. It is the same relation that philosophy of science has to the concepts, activities, and so forth of the specific sciences. In that same way, philosophy of religion is related to the religions and theologies of the world.[3] It seeks to analyze the basic concepts and propositions of religion and theology, and to critically examine the assertions made by religion and theology. Thus, just as:

I. Philosophy of Science	-is comprised of-	2nd-order discourse, which refers to ↓
Sciences	-are comprised of-	1st-order discourse, which refers to ↓
Reality	-is comprised of-	objects, processes, events, etc. in the natural universe.

So:

II. Philosophy of Religion	-is comprised of-	2nd-order discourse, which refers to ↓
Religion and Theology	-are comprised of-	1st-order discourse, which refers to

nations that claimed that religious belief stems from things like infantile dependency. Other writers claimed that religious belief is one of many ways in which ruling classes dominate over less fortunate classes. Frazier, Freud, and Marx were among the many who began such attacks — and, of course, Nietzsche.

The first two attacks on and rejections of theism were different in one respect. The first was more philosophical in nature—a critique of the arguments to prove the claims of theism. The second was more historical, psychological, and sociological—a critique to show that theism was the result of certain historical, cultural, and psychological factors. But both of them shared one thing in common—namely their end or goal. Both tried to show either that (1) theism is false; or (2) theism cannot be supported. In other words, both attacks accepted the claims of theism as significant and interesting claims, but, alas, false or insupportable ones.

The third, newer form of attack on and rejection of theism goes much further. It purports to show, *not* that theism is a meaningful but false view, but rather to show that the main claims of theism—there exists a transcendent God, and so on—are *meaningless* (in the cognitive sense). Assertions like "God exists" *look* like significant assertions. But, according to critics of the third kind, in fact, all such assertions are cognitively meaningless, and hence say nothing at all. They may have *emotive* meaning to weak souls, but cognitively they are utterly devoid of meaning, and hence say nothing.

In the eyes of many, this attack on theism is far more devastating than either of the first two attacks. After all, it is bad enough if someone shows that what you hold is false, or even unsupportable. But it is much worse if this person shows that what you believe is utterly meaningless!

In our time, all three of these attacks have been and are being made on theism. And many thinkers—philosophers, scientists, historians, and so on—engage in these attacks, or at least take them seriously. So do many "ordinary" people who are not academics, but who are reflective and sensitive. Hence since theism is under vigorous attack (and has been for centuries), and since many thinkers hold that theism is false, or in-supportable, or meaningless, it follows that our main question is and must be: "*Is* religious belief (in theism) a viable option for our time?"

Our approach to dealing with this question will consist in (1) examining the case for theism; (2) examining the three attacks on theism; and (3) examining responses by theists to those attacks.

There are three possibile answers to the question: "Is religious belief—the belief in theism, the acceptance of theological doctrines—a viable option for our time?" The three *possible answers are*:

1. *Yes*, religious belief is a viable option because theological assertions are both meaningful and true.

2. *No*, religious belief is not a viable option because theological assertions are false, or at least unsupportable. There are two forms of this answer:

2a. Theological assertions must be rejected because the arguments on behalf of them are fallacious.

2b. Theological assertions must be rejected because historical and scientific evidence shows that they stem from primitive mythology, infantile personality, and so forth.

3. *No*, religious belief is not a viable option because theological assertions are cognitively meaningless.

In this book we will consider *all* of these possible answers.

1. Most readers have some understanding of the first answer, and why it has been given. They are no doubt familiar with some of the arguments that have been given to prove that God exists. We shall examine this answer in the Introduction to and selections in Part I of this volume.

2. Many readers no doubt have some understanding of either or both forms of the second answer, and why these have been given. They may be aware of the fact that the traditional arguments for theism have been severely criticized, and they may have read some of the criticisms in an Introduction to Philosophy class. Similarly, some readers may be aware of the fact that historians, anthropologists, psychologists, and others have put forth explanations of how and why religious beliefs arose. For example, they may be aware of the fact that anthropologists of religion have claimed that religious beliefs are remnants of primitive myths and superstition. Or they may be aware of Freud's explanation that religious belief arose because of man's infantile insecurity and need for dependency. Or they may be aware of Marx's account that religion is but another way in which the masses have been enslaved by those in power. So even if one does not agree with the critics, one can see why the first two classical attacks on theism have been made. We shall examine this answer to our question, in both forms, in the Introduction to and selections in Part II of this volume.

3. But many readers may not quite understand the third answer to our main question. Hence they may not understand just what the third newer attack on theism is, or why it has been and is made. (Recall the third is the rejection of theism on the grounds that its claims are meaningless.) Because of this, it may be helpful for me to elaborate on this third, newer attack on theism, and how it has led to the third answer. This I shall do in the Introduction to Part III, and the selections in that part contain both the critique and numerous responses to it.

4. What Are Some of the Other Related Topics in the Philosophy of Religion?

As I mentioned, there are many other issues and problems in the philosophy of religion, in addition to the one that I have designated as the main one. Briefly, here are some of those that deserve attention:

- The Problem of Evil
- Belief and Faith
- Miracles
- Life after Death
- Religion and Ethics
- Religion and the Meaning of Life

These issues are discussed in the Introduction to and in the selections in Part IV of this volume.

Endnotes

1. For further study of the basics of philosophy, please refer to E. D. Klemke et al., *Philosophy: The Basic Issues*, 3rd ed. (New York: St. Martin's Press, 1990).
2. John Hick, *Philosophy of Religion*, 3rd ed. Englewood Cliffs, New Jersey: Prentice Hall, 1983, pp. 1–2.
3. *Ibid.*, p. 2.

PART I

The Classical Case for Theism

○

A S INDICATED IN the Introduction, the main question in the philosophy of religion is: "Is religious belief (in theism) a viable option for our time?" We shall begin our study of the philosophy of religion and this question by examining the classical case for theism. This will consist of two parts.

First (Chapter One), we will examine the classical arguments that have been put forth for the existence of God, mainly by writers who go as far back as the Middle Ages (Anselm, Aquinas) and into the seventeenth and eighteenth centuries (Descartes, Paley, Kant). Second (Chapter Two), we will consider some objections to those arguments that were put forth by the theists themselves (Guanilo, Aquinas, Kant, Hume). That is, these objections were made by writers who were theists but who found problems with some of the classical arguments. There are two exceptions to what I have said. First, it is perhaps doubtful whether Hume was really a theist. Hence his criticisms could be put into Chapter Four. Hume can be considered one of the first major philosophers who rigorously attacked theism. But at times he writes things (maybe tongue in cheek) that sound like he has some belief in theism or in religion. Second, Kierkegaard did not reject merely *some* arguments for the existence of God but *all* arguments. He also rejected the whole procedure of using arguments to try to prove God's existence. Nevertheless, he was a committed Christian theist.

The reader will perhaps be familiar with some or all of these arguments—even if in more contemporary formulations—but perhaps it would be best for us to have a synoptic review of the main arguments. Then we can turn to a study of the specific and detailed arguments in the original versions written by the philosophers and theologians who devised them.

The main classical arguments for God's existence are:

1. The Ontological Argument (A Priori Argument)
2. The First-Cause Argument (Cosmological Argument)
3. The Argument from Contingency (A Variant of the Cosmological Argument)
4. The Design Argument (Teleological Argument)
5. The Moral Argument
6. The Argument from Religious Experience
7. The Natural Law Argument

Of these arguments the main ones are numbers 1, 2, 3, 4, 5, and 6. Number 3, however, is a variant of 2, and I include 7 for the sake of completeness.

1. The Ontological Argument (A Priori Argument)

We have an idea of an all-perfect being, and that is what we mean by God. God is "that than which nothing greater can be conceived."* That is, God is a being who contains or possesses all conceivable perfections, among these qualities such as being all-powerful, all-knowing, and so on. Now, if this being "existed" merely as an idea in our minds, if this being did not actually possess existence, then it would be less perfect than if it actually existed. In fact, it would not be as great as a being who actually existed. But this would contradict our definition of God: a being who is all-perfect. Hence God must exist.

2. The First-Cause Argument (Cosmological Argument)

First Version   Every event must have a cause, and that cause, in turn, must have a cause, and so on. If there were no end to this backward progression of causes and effects, then their succession would be infinite. But an infinite series of causes and events is unintelligible. Hence, there must be a first cause that is itself uncaused. Such a being we call God. Therefore, God exists.

Second Version   Every event must have a cause. If we trace the succession of causes and effects within the universe backward to infinity, we find that we have two altenatives. Either there is no ultimate first cause, or there is such a cause that is itself uncaused. But if there were no ultimate first cause, then although there would be a cause for every event within the succession, there would be no cause for the entire succession as a whole. But there must be a cause for the whole succession. Therefore, there must exist a being that is the first or ultimate cause and is itself uncaused. Such a being we call God. Therefore, God exists.

3. The Argument from Contingency (A Variant of the Cosmological Argument)

Everything that exists has either contingent or necessary existence. To say that anything has contingent existence is to say that its existence is dependent on the existence of something else. It cannot be the ground of its own existence. To say that anything has necessary existence is to say that its existence is not dependent on the existence of something else. It is self-sufficient, the ground of its own existence. Since the existence of contingent beings is not self-sufficient, it is impossible that

---

* See the first selection, by St. Anselm.

only contingent beings exist. Therefore, there must exist a necessary being. This being we call God. Therefore, God exists.

4. The Design Argument (Teleological Argument)

The universe exhibits orderliness and purpose. Many things occur in an orderly fashion, for example, the behavior of the planets in our solar system. Many other things are correlated with one another in a way that is purposeful. Among these there is an adaptation of means to ends, as in the intricate structure of the human eye. These things that are of the second sort—the purposive features of living organisms, and life itself—require an explanation. They could not have come about by accident or by chance. They must be a result of some greater plan. Just as the existence of a watch indicates that a designer/creator (an intelligent mind) must have planned it and brought it into being, so the existence of the universe and various phenomena within the universe indicate that an even greater designer/creator must have planned it and brought it into being. Such a being is what we mean by God. Therefore, God exists.

5. The Moral Argument

First Form   People have a sense of moral obligation. This claim of obedience to a moral law is felt as coming from outside of themselves. No naturalistic account of this sense of obligation in terms of human needs or behavior can explain it. It can be explained only by the existence of a moral lawgiver outside of the natural universe. Hence, such a lawgiver must exist. Such a being we call God. Therefore, God exists.

Second Form   In the effort to fulfill our obligation, our pursuit of the good sometimes gets frustrated. If this constantly occurred, the world would not be really good. So the world in which this happens cannot be ultimately real. There must be a real world of genuine moral value, under the control of a supreme mind. Therefore such a mind, God, must exist.

Or: We have a duty to fulfill the highest good. For the world to be just, there must be agreement between our acting in accordance with our duty and the achievement of happiness. But in this world, that does not always happen. Therefore, there must be a guarantor that the virtuous will receive their reward in some other world. Such a guarantor, God, must exist. Therefore, God exists.

6. The Argument from Religious Experience

Many people claim to have experience in which they have immediate and direct knowledge of God. Therefore, God exists. (Strictly speaking, this is not an argument in behalf of God's existence. The advocate of this claim maintains that because one has a direct experience of God it is not necessary to infer the existence of God by drawing a conclusion from a set of premises.)

7. The Natural Law Argument

There exist natural laws (laws of nature). Where there are laws, there must be a lawgiver. Therefore, such a lawgiver, God, exists.

Let us turn now to the actual arguments as they were put forth by the classical writers (Chapter One). In the case of the selections by James and Stace, the authors did not invent either the argument from religious experience or mysticism. But James refers in great detail to many writers who make claims to have encountered God through religious experience or to have had a mystical experience of oneness with the universe, and Stace is sympathetic to mysticism. Then after we have become familiar with the arguments, in Chapter Two we will look at the specific criticisms of some of those arguments that were made by some of the classical theists themselves.

CHAPTER ONE

The Classical Theistic Arguments

○   ○   ○   **1**

The Ontological Argument for the Existence of God[1]

(The Proslogion, Chapters II–IV)
St. Anselm

CHAPTER II

I.   That God Truly Is

O LORD, YOU who give understanding to faith, so far as you know it to be beneficial, give me to understand that you are as we believe, and that you are what we believe.

We believe that you are something than which nothing greater can be conceived.[2]

But is there any such nature, since "the fool has said in his heart: God is not"?

However, when this same fool hears what I say, when he hears of this something than which nothing greater can be conceived, he at least understands what he hears.

What he understands stands in relation to his understanding, even if he does not understand that it exists.[3] For it is one thing for a thing to stand in relation to our understanding; it is another thing for us to understand that it really exists. For instance, when a painter imagines what he is about to paint, he has it in relation to his understanding. However, he does not yet understand that it exists, because he has not yet made it. After he paints it, then he both has it in relation to his understanding and understands that it exists. Therefore even the fool is convinced that something than which nothing greater can be conceived at least stands in relation to his understanding, because when he hears of it he understands it, and whatever he understands stands in relation to his understanding.[4]

---

[1] Anselm has two forms of the argument. The first is contained in this section, the second in the next section.—E.D.K.

[2] This sentence is meant to be a definition of "God." Thus it can be read: "God *is* that than which nothing greater can be conceived (the greatest conceivable being).—E.D.K.

[3] That is: What he understands must be (something) in his understanding (or thought), even if he does not understand that it actually exists (outside of his understanding).—E.D.K.

[4] The meaning of Anselm's phrase *esse in intellectu* has been the subject of much discussion. I have found little evidence that the word *intellectus* ever suggested to Anselm, as it does to us, an organ (such as the mind) or a faculty (such as the intellect). It was chiefly the noun form of the verb *intelligere*, and signified the act of understanding. "To be *in intellectu*" therefore does not mean to be located "in the intellect," inside the human head, as if this were a place, but to be located in relation to human thinking, to be present to the human act of understanding. See Adolf Kolping, *Anselm's Proslogion—Beweis der Existenz Gottes* (Bonn, 1939), pp. 114f. In moving from *intelligere* to *esse in intellectu*, Anselm is simply shifting the focus from the human activity, as related to some object, to the presence of that object to the human activity, still without prejudicing the question of the object's actual existence one way or the other. To avoid the peculiar modern overtones associated with the phrase "to be in the understanding," *esse in intellectu* is here translated "to stand in relation to the understanding."—TRANS.

However, that than which a greater cannot be conceived can certainly not stand only in relation to the understanding. For if it at least stood only in relation to the understanding, it could be conceived to be also in reality, and this would be something greater. Therefore, if that than which a greater cannot be conceived only stood in relation to the understanding, then that than which a greater cannot be conceived would be something than which a greater can be conceived. Obviously this is impossible.

Therefore, something than which a greater cannot be conceived undoubtedly both stands in relation to the understanding and exists in reality.[5]

CHAPTER III

II. That It Is Impossible to Conceive That God Is Not

This so truly is that it is impossible to think of it as not existing.

It can be conceived to be something such that we cannot conceive of it as not existing.

This is greater than something which we can conceive of as not existing.

Therefore, if that than which a greater cannot be conceived could be conceived not to be, we would have an impossible contradiction: that than which a greater cannot be conceived would not be that than which a greater cannot be conceived.

Therefore something than which a greater cannot be conceived so truly is that it is impossible even to conceive of it as not existing.

This is you, O Lord our God. You so truly are that you cannot be thought not to be. And rightly so.

For if some mind could conceive of something better than you, the creature would become superior to its Creator and would judge its Creator.

This is obviously absurd. Indeed, whatever else there is, except for you alone, can be conceived not to be.

Therefore you alone, of all things, exist in the truest and greatest way (*verissime et maxime esse*), for nothing else so truly exists and therefore everything else has less being.

Why, then, did the fool say in his heart: "God is not," since it is so obvious to the rational mind that you exist supremely above all things? Why, because he is a dim-witted fool.

CHAPTER IV

III. How the Fool Said in His Heart What Cannot Be Conceived

How was the fool able to "say in his heart" what he was unable to conceive? Or how was it that he could not conceive what he said in his heart? For to "say in one's heart" and to "conceive" are the same thing.

However, if—or rather because—he really did conceive of it (since he said it in his heart) and yet did not really say it in his heart (since he was unable to conceive of it), then there must be more than one way for something to be said in one's heart, or to be conceived.

Indeed, a thing is conceived of in one way when the word signifying it is thought; in another way when the very thing itself is understood. Accordingly God can be conceived not to be in the first way, but not at all in the second.

---

[5] That is: That something exists both in our understanding and in reality (outside of our understanding). —E.D.K.

[For no one who understands what fire and water are]⁶ can think that the reality of fire is the reality of water. At the level of the words, however, this confusion is possible.

No one, therefore, who understands what God is can think that God is not. It is possible, however, for him to say this word in his heart, while giving it either no meaning at all or some alien meaning. God is that than which a greater cannot be conceived. Whoever understands this correctly at least understands that he exists in such a way that even for thought he cannot not exist.

Therefore whoever understands that God is so cannot even conceive that He is not.

My thanksgiving to you, good Lord, my thanksgiving to you. For what I first believed through your giving I now understand through your illumination, so that now, even if I did not want to believe that you exist, I would be unable not to understand it.⁷

---

⁶ Recent manuscript investigations have established that these words in square brackets were not part of Anselm's text, but were interpolated later.—TRANS.

⁷ For Gaunilo's criticisms and Anselm's replies, see selection 8 in this volume. For Aquinas' criticism, see the last part of the first section of selection 2.—E.D.K.

∘ ∘ ∘ *2*

Five Ways to Prove
the Existence of God
St. Thomas Aquinas

FIRST ARTICLE

I.   *Whether the Existence of God Is Self-Evident?*

WE PROCEED THUS to the First Article: —

Objection 1. It seems that the existence of God is self-evident. For those things are said to be self-evident to us the knowledge of which exists naturally in us, as we can see in regard to first principles. But as Damascene says, "the knowledge of God is naturally implanted in all." Therefore the existence of God is self-evident.

Objection 2. Further, those things are said to be self-evident which are known as soon as the terms are known, which the Philosopher [Aristotle] says is true of the first principles of demonstration. Thus, when the nature of a whole and of a part is known, it is at once recognized that every whole is greater than its part. But as soon as the signification of the name *God* is understood, it is at once seen that God exists. For by this name is signified that thing than which nothing greater can be conceived. But that which exists actually and mentally is greater than that which exists only mentally. Therefore, since as soon as the name *God* is understood it exists mentally, it also follows that it exists actually. Therefore the proposition *God exists* is self-evident.[1]

Objection 3. Further, the existence of truth is self-evident. For whoever denies the existence of truth grants that truth does not exist: and, if truth does not exist, then the proposition *Truth does not exist* is true: and if there is anything true, there must be truth. But God is truth itself: "I am the way, the truth, and the life" (John, 14:6). Therefore *God exists* is self-evident.

On the contrary, No one can mentally admit the opposite of what is self-evident, as the Philosopher states concerning the first principles of demonstration. But the opposite of the proposition *God is* can be mentally admitted: "The fool said in his heart, There is no God" (Ps. 52:1). Therefore, that God exists is not self-evident.

I answer that, A thing can be self-evident in either of two ways: on the one hand, self-evident in itself, though not to us; on the other, self-evident in itself, and to us. A proposition is self-evident because the predicate is included in the essence of the subject: e.g., *Man is an animal,* for animal is contained in the essence of man. If, therefore, the essence of the predicate and subject be known to all, the proposition will be self-evident

---

[1] This is a modified restatement of Anselm's argument. Aquinas' criticism of this argument appears in his reply to Objection 2.—E.D.K.

to all; as is clear with regard to the first principles of demonstration, the terms of which are certain common notions that no one is ignorant of, such as being and non-being, whole and part, and the like. If, however, there are some to whom the essence of the predicate and subject is unknown, the proposition will be self-evident in itself, but not to those who do not know the meaning of the predicate and subject of the proposition. Therefore, it happens, as Boethius[2] says, that there are some notions of the mind which are common and self-evident only to the learned, as that incorporeal substances are not in space. Therefore I say that this proposition, *God exists*, of itself is self-evident, for the predicate is the same as the subject, because God is His own existence as will be hereafter shown. Now because we do not know the essence of God, the proposition is not self-evident to us, but needs to be demonstrated by things that are more known to us, though less known in their nature—namely, by His effects.

Reply Objection 1. To know that God exists in a general and confused way is implanted in us by nature, inasmuch as God is man's beatitude. For man naturally desires happiness, and what is naturally desired by man is naturally known by him. This, however, is not to know absolutely that God exists; just as to know that someone is approaching is not the same as to know that Peter is approaching, even though it is Peter who is approaching; for there are many who imagine that man's perfect good, which is happiness, consists in riches, and others in pleasures, and others in something else.

Reply Objection 2. Perhaps not everyone who hears this name *God* understands it to signify something than which nothing greater can be thought, seeing that some have believed God to be a body. Yet, granted that everyone understands that by this name *God* is signified something than which nothing greater can be thought, nevertheless, it does not therefore follow that he understands that what the name signifies exists actually, but only that it exists mentally. Nor can it be argued that it actually exists, unless it be admitted that there actually exists something than which nothing greater can be thought; and this precisely is not admitted by those who hold that God does not exist. [3]

Reply Objection 3. The existence of truth in general is self-evident, but the existence of a Primal Truth is not self-evident to us.

SECOND ARTICLE

II.   Whether It Can Be Demonstrated That God Exists?

We proceed thus to the Second Article: —

Objection 1. It seems that the existence of God cannot be demonstrated. For it is an article of faith that God exists. But what is of faith cannot be demonstrated, because a demonstration produces scientific knowledge, whereas faith is of the unseen, as is clear from the Apostle (Heb. 11:1). Therefore it cannot be demonstrated that God exists.

Objection 2. Further, essence is the middle term of demonstration. But we cannot know in what God's essence consists, but solely in what it does not consist, as Damascene says. Therefore we cannot demonstrate that God exists.

---

[2] A medieval religious thinker.—E.D.K.
[3] This paragraph is Aquinas' criticism of Anselm's argument.—E.D.K.

Objection 3. Further, if the existence of God were demonstrated, this could only be from His effects. But His effects are not proportioned to Him, since He is infinite and His effects are finite, and between the finite and infinite there is no proportion. Therefore, since a cause cannot be demonstrated by an effect not proportioned to it, it seems that the existence of God cannot be demonstrated.

On the contrary, The Apostle says: "The invisible things of Him are clearly seen, being understood by the things that are made" (Rom. 1:20). But this would not be unless the existence of God could be demonstrated through the things that are made; for the first thing we must know of anything is whether it exists.

I answer that, Demonstration can be made in two ways: One is through the cause, and is called *propter quid,* and this is to argue from what is prior absolutely. The other is through the effect, and is called a demonstration *quia;* this is to argue from what is prior relatively only to us. When an effect is better known to us than its cause, from the effect we proceed to the knowledge of the cause. And from every effect the existence of its proper cause can be demonstrated, so long as its effects are better known to us; because, since every effect depends upon its cause, if the effect exists, the cause must preexist. Hence the existence of God, insofar as it is not self-evident to us, can be demonstrated from those of His effects which are known to us.

Reply Objection 1. The existence of God and other like truths about God, which can be known by natural reason, are not articles of faith, but are preambles to the articles; for faith presupposes natural knowledge, even as grace presupposes nature and perfection the perfectible. Nevertheless, there is nothing to prevent a man, who cannot grasp a proof, from accepting, as a matter of faith, something which in itself is capable of being scientifically known and demonstrated.

Reply Objection 2. When the existence of a cause is demonstrated from an effect, this effect takes the place of the definition of the cause in proving the cause's existence. This is especially the case in regard to God, because, in order to prove the existence of anything, it is necessary to accept as a middle term the meaning of the name, and not its essence, for the question of its essence follows on the question of its existence. Now the names given to God are derived from His effects, as will be later shown. Consequently, in demonstrating the existence of God from His effects, we may take for the middle term the meaning of the name *God.*

Reply Objection 3. From effects not proportioned to the cause no perfect knowledge of that cause can be obtained. Yet from every effect the existence of the cause can be clearly demonstrated, and so we can demonstrate the existence of God from His effects; though from them we cannot know God perfectly as He is in His essence.

THIRD ARTICLE

III.   Whether God Exists?

We proceed thus to the Third Article: —

Objection 1. It seems that God does not exist; because if one of two contraries be infinite, the other would be altogether destroyed. But the name *God* means that He is infinite goodness. If, therefore, God existed, there would be no evil discoverable; but there is evil in the world. Therefore God does not exist.

Objection 2. Further, it is superfluous to suppose that what can be accounted for by a few principles has been produced by many. But it seems that everything we see in the world can be accounted for by other principles, supposing God did not exist. For all natural things can be reduced to one principle, which is nature; and all voluntary things can be reduced to one principle, which is human reason, or will. Therefore there is no need to suppose God's existence.

On the contrary, it is said in the person of God: "I am Who am" (Exod. 3:14).

I answer that, The existence of God can be proved in five ways.[4]

The first and more manifest way is the argument from motion. It is certain, and evident to our senses, that in the world some things are in motion. Now whatever is moved is moved by another, for nothing can be moved except it is in potentiality to that towards which it is moved; whereas a thing moves inasmuch as it is in act. For motion is nothing else than the reduction of something from potentiality to actuality. But nothing can be reduced from potentiality to actuality, except by something in a state of actuality. Thus that which is actually hot, as fire, makes wood, which is potentially hot, to be actually hot, and thereby moves and changes it. Now it is not possible that the same thing should be at once in actuality and potentiality in the same respect, but only in different respects. For what is actually hot cannot simultaneously be potentially hot; but it is simultaneously potentially cold. It is therefore impossible that in the same respect and in the same way a thing should be both mover and moved, i.e., that it should move itself. Therefore, whatever is moved must be moved by another. If that by which it is moved be itself moved, then this also must needs be moved by another, and that by another again. But this cannot go on to infinity, because then there would be no first mover, and, consequently, no other mover, seeing that subsequent movers move only inasmuch as they are moved by the first mover; as the staff moves only because it is moved by the hand. Therefore it is necessary to arrive at a first mover, moved by no other; and this everyone understands to be God.

The second way is from the nature of efficient cause.[5] In the world of sensible things we find there is an order of efficient causes. There is no case known (neither is it, indeed, possible) in which a thing is found to be the efficient cause of itself; for so it would be prior to itself, which is impossible. Now in efficient causes it is not possible to go on to infinity, because in all efficient causes following in order, the first is the cause of the intermediate cause, and the intermediate is the cause of the ultimate cause, whether the intermediate cause be several, or one only. Now to take away the cause is to take away the effect. Therefore, if there be no first cause among efficient causes, there will be no ultimate, nor any intermediate, cause. But if in efficient causes it is possible to go on to infinity, there will be no first efficient cause, neither will there be an ultimate effect, nor any intermediate efficient causes; all of which is plainly false. Therefore it is necessary to admit a first efficient cause, to which everyone gives the name of God.

The third way is taken from possibility and necessity, and runs thus. We find in nature things that are possible to be and not to be, since they are found to be generated, and to be corrupted, and consequently, it is possible for them to be and not to be. But it is impossible for these always to exist, for that which can not-be at some time is not.

---

[4] The first three ways (arguments) are variants of the cosmological argument. Perhaps the fourth, also. The fifth is a rudimentary version of the design argument.—E.D.K.

[5] That is, what we now simply call *cause*.—E.D.K.

Therefore, if everything can not-be, then at one time there was nothing in existence. Now if this were true, even now there would be nothing in existence, because that which does not exist begins to exist only through something already existing. Therefore, if at one time nothing was in existence, it would have been impossible for anything to have begun to exist; and thus even now nothing would be in existence—which is absurd. Therefore, not all beings are merely possible, but there must exist something the existence of which is necessary. But every necessary thing either has its necessity caused by another, or not. Now it is impossible to go on to infinity in necessary things which have their necessity caused by another, as has been already proved in regard to efficient causes. Therefore we cannot but admit the existence of some being having of itself its own necessity, and not receiving it from another, but rather causing in others their necessity. This all men speak of as God.

The fourth way is taken from the gradation to be found in things. Among beings there are some more and some less good, true, noble, and the like. But *more* and *less* are predicated of different things according as they resemble in their different ways something which is the maximum, as a thing is said to be hotter according as it more nearly resembles that which is hottest; so that there is something which is truest, something best, something noblest, and, consequently, something which is most being, for those things that are greatest in truth are greatest in being, as it is written in *Metaphysics* II.[6] Now the maximum in any genus is the cause of all in that genus, as fire, which is the maximum of heat, is the cause of all hot things, as is said in the same book. Therefore there must also be something which is to all beings the cause of their being, goodness, and every other perfection; and this we call God.

The fifth way is taken from the governance of the world. We see that things which lack knowledge, such as natural bodies, act for an end, and this is evident from their acting always, or nearly always, in the same way, so as to obtain the best result. Hence it is plain that they achieve their end, not fortuitously, but designedly. Now whatever lacks knowledge cannot move towards an end, unless it be directed by some being endowed with knowledge and intelligence; as the arrow is directed by the archer. Therefore some intelligent being exists by whom all natural things are directed to their end; and this being we call God.

Reply Objection 1. As Augustine[7] says: "Since God is the highest good, He would not allow any evil to exist in His works, unless His omnipotence and goodness were such as to bring good even out of evil" (*Enchiridion*, XI). This is part of the infinite goodness of God, that He should allow evil to exist, and out of it produce good.

Reply Objection 2. Since nature works for a determinate end under the direction of a higher agent, whatever is done by nature must be traced back to God as to its first cause. So likewise whatever is done voluntarily must be traced back to some higher cause other than human reason and will, since these can change and fail; for all things that are changeable and capable of defect must be traced back to an immovable and self-necessary first principle, as has been shown.[8]

---

[6] A work by the ancient Greek philosopher, Aristotle.—E.D.K.

[7] An early medieval theologian.—E.D.K.

[8] For Kant's criticisms of the ontological, cosmological, and teleological arguments, see selection 11. For Hume's criticisms, see selections 9 and 10.—E.D.K.

The Ontological Argument Restated
René Descartes

BUT NOW, IF just because I can draw the idea of something from my thought, it follows that all which I know clearly and distinctly as pertaining to this object does really belong to it, may I not derive from this an argument demonstrating the existence of God? It is certain that I no less find the idea of God, that is to say, the idea of a supremely perfect Being, in me, than that of any figure or number whatever it is; and I do not know any less clearly and distinctly that an [actual and] eternal existence pertains to this nature than I know that all that which I am able to demonstrate of some figure or number truly pertains to the nature of this figure or number, and therefore, although all that I concluded in the preceding Meditations were found to be false, the existence of God would pass with me as at least as certain as I have ever held the truths of mathematics (which concern only numbers and figures) to be.

This indeed is not at first manifest, since it would seem to present some appearance of being a sophism. For being accustomed in all other things to make a distinction between existence and essence, I easily persuade myself that the existence can be separated from the essence of God, and that we can thus conceive God as not actually existing. But, nevertheless, when I think of it with more attention, I clearly see that existence can no more be separated from the essence of God than can its having its three angles equal to two right angles be separated from the essence of a [rectilinear] triangle, or the idea of a mountain from the idea of a valley; and so there is not any less repugnance to our conceiving a God (that is, a Being supremely perfect) to whom existence is lacking (that is to say, to whom a certain perfection is lacking), than to conceive of a mountain which has no valley.

But although I cannot really conceive of a God without existence any more than a mountain without a valley, still from the fact that I conceive of a mountain with a valley, it does not follow that there is such a mountain in the world; similarly although I conceive of God as possessing existence, it would seem that it does not follow that there is a God which exists; for my thought does not impose any necessity upon things, and just as I may imagine a winged horse, although no horse with wings exists, so I could perhaps attribute existence to God, although no God existed.

But a sophism is concealed in this objection; for from the fact that I cannot conceive a mountain without a valley, it does not follow that there is any mountain or any valley in existence, but only that the mountain and the valley, whether they exist or do not exist, cannot in any way be separated one from the other. While from the fact that I cannot conceive God without existence, it follows that existence is inseparable from Him, and hence that He really exists; not that my thought can bring this to pass, or impose any necessity on things, but, on the contrary, because the necessity which lies in the thing itself, i.e., the necessity of the existence of God, determines me to think in this way. For it is not within my power to think of God without existence (that is, of a supremely perfect Being devoid of a supreme perfection) though it is in my power to imagine a horse either with wings or without wings.

And we must not here object that it is in truth necessary for me to assert that God exists after having presupposed that He possesses every sort of perfection, since existence is one of these, but that as a matter of fact my original supposition was not necessary, just as it is not necessary to consider that all quadrilateral figures can be inscribed in the circle; for supposing I thought this, I should be constrained to admit that the rhombus might be inscribed in the circle since it is a quadrilateral figure, which, however, is manifestly false. [We must not, I say, make any such allegations because] although it is not necessary that I should at any time entertain the notion of God, nevertheless whenever it happens that I think of a first and a sovereign Being, and, so to speak, derive the idea of Him from the storehouse of my mind, it is necessary that I should attribute to Him every sort of perfection, although I do not get so far as to enumerate them all, or to apply my mind to each one in particular. And this necessity suffices to make me conclude (after having recognized that existence is a perfection) that this first and sovereign Being really exists; just as though it is not necessary for me ever to imagine any triangle, yet, whenever I wish to consider a rectilinear figure composed only of three angles, it is absolutely essential that I should attribute to it all those properties which serve to bring about the conclusion that its three angles are not greater than two right angles, even although I may not then be considering this point in particular. But when I consider which figures are capable of being inscribed in the circle, it is in no wise necessary that I should think that all quadrilateral figures are of this number; on the contrary, I cannot even pretend that this is the case, so long as I do not desire to accept anything which I cannot conceive clearly and distinctly. And in consequence there is a great difference between the false suppositions such as this, and the true ideas born within me, the first and principal of which is that of God. For really I discern in many ways that this idea is not something factitious, and depending solely on my thought, but that it is the image of a true and immutable nature; first of all, because I cannot conceive anything but God Himself to whose essence existence [necessarily] pertains; in the second place because it is not possible for me to conceive two or more Gods in this same position; and, granted that there is one such God who now exists, I see clearly that it is necessary that He should have existed from all eternity, and that He must exist eternally; and finally, because I know an infinitude of other properties in God, none of which I can either diminish or change.

For the rest, whatever proof or argument I avail myself of, we must always return to the point that it is only those things which we conceive clearly and distinctly that have the power of persuading me entirely. And although amongst the matters which I conceive of in this way, some indeed are manifestly obvious to all, while others only manifest themselves to those who consider them closely and examine them attentively; still, after they have once been discovered, the latter are not esteemed as any less certain than the former. For example, in the case of every right-angled triangle, although it does not so manifestly appear that the square of the base is equal to the squares of the two other sides as that this base is opposite to the greatest angle; still, when this has once been apprehended, we are just as certain of its truth as of the truth of the other. And as regards

God, if my mind were not preoccupied with prejudices, and if my thought did not find itself on all hands diverted by the continual pressure of sensible things, there would be nothing which I could know more immediately and more easily than Him. For is there anything more manifest than that there is a God, that is to say, a Supreme Being, to whose essence alone existence pertains?[1]

And although for a firm grasp of this truth I have need of a strenuous application of mind, at present I not only feel myself to be as assured of it as of all that I hold as most certain, but I also remark that the certainty of all other things depends on it so absolutely, that without this knowledge it is impossible ever to know anything perfectly.

For although I am of such a nature that as long as[2] I understand anything very clearly and distinctly, I am naturally impelled to believe it to be true, yet because I am also of such a nature that I cannot have my mind constantly fixed on the same object in order to perceive it clearly, and as I often recollect having formed a past judgment without at the same time properly recollecting the reasons that led me to make it, it may happen meanwhile that other reasons present themselves to me, which would easily cause me to change my opinion, if I were ignorant of the facts of the existence of God, and thus I should have no true and certain knowledge, but only vague and vacillating opinions. Thus, for example, when I consider the nature of a [rectilinear] triangle, I who have some little knowledge of the principles of geometry recognize quite clearly that the three angles are equal to two right angles, and it is not possible for me not to believe this so long as I apply my mind to its demonstration; but so soon as I abstain from attending to the proof, although I still recollect having clearly comprehended it, it may easily occur that I come to doubt its truth, if I am ignorant of there being a God. For I can persuade myself of having been so constituted by nature that I can easily deceive myself even in those matters which I believe myself to apprehend with the greatest evidence and certainty, especially when I recollect that I have frequently judged matters to be true and certain which other reasons have afterwards impelled me to judge to be altogether false.

But after I have recognized that there is a God—because at the same time I have also recognized that all things depend upon Him, and that He is not a deceiver, and from that have inferred that what I perceive clearly and distinctly cannot fail to be true—although I no longer pay attention to the reasons for which I have judged this to be true, provided that I recollect having clearly and distinctly perceived it no contrary reason can be brought forward which could ever cause me to doubt of its truth; and thus I have a true and certain knowledge of it. And this same knowledge extends likewise to all other things which I recollect having formerly demonstrated, such as the truths of geometry and the like; for what can be alleged against them to cause me to place them in doubt? Will it be said that my nature is such as to cause me to be frequently deceived? But I already know that I cannot be deceived in the judgment whose grounds I know clearly. Will it be said that I formerly held many things to be true and certain which I have afterwards recognized to be false? But I had not had any clear and distinct knowledge of these things, and not as yet knowing the rule whereby I assure myself of the truth, I had been impelled to give my assent from reasons which I have since recognized to be less strong than I had at the time imagined them to be. What further objection can then be raised? That

---

[1] "in the idea of whom alone necessary or external existence is comprised." French version.—TRANS.

[2] "from the moment that." French version.—TRANS.

possibly I am dreaming (an objection I myself made a little while ago), or that all the thoughts which I now have are no more true than the phantasies of my dreams? But even though I slept the case would be the same, for all that is clearly present to my mind is absolutely true.

And so I very clearly recognize that the certainty and truth of all knowledge depends alone on the true God, insomuch that, before I knew Him, I could not have a perfect knowledge of any other thing. And now that I know Him I have the means of acquiring a perfect knowledge of an infinitude of things, not only of those which relate to God Himself and other intellectual matters, but also of those which pertain to corporeal nature insofar as it is the object of pure mathematics [which have no concern with whether it exists or not].

○ ○ ○ **4**

The Watch and the Human Eye
(The Design Argument)[1]
William Paley

I.   *A Watch Implies a Watchmaker*

IN CROSSING A heath, suppose I pitched my foot against a *stone*, and were asked how the stone came to be there; I might possibly answer, that, for anything I knew to the contrary, it had lain there forever: nor would it perhaps be very easy to show the absurdity of this answer. But suppose I had found a *watch* upon the ground, and it should be inquired how the watch happened to be in that place: I should hardly think of the answer which I had before given, that, for anything I knew, the watch might have always been there. Yet why should not this answer serve for the watch as well as for the stone? Why is it not as admissible in the second case, as in the first? For this reason, and for no other, viz. that, when we come to inspect the watch, we perceive (what we could not discover in the stone) that its several parts are formed and adjusted as to produce motion, and that motion so regulated, as to point out the hour of the day; that if the different parts had been differently shaped from what they are, of a different size from what they are, or placed after any other manner, or in any other order, than that in which they are placed, either no motion at all would have been carried on in the machine, or none which would have answered the use that is now served by it. . . . This mechanism being observed (it requires indeed an examination of the instrument, and perhaps some previous knowledge of the subject, to perceive and understand it; but being once, as we have said, observed and understood,) the inference, we think, is inevitable; that the watch must have had a maker; that there must have existed, at sometime, and at some place or other, an artificer or artificers, who formed it for the purpose which we find it actually to answer; who comprehended its construction, and designed its use.

Nor would it, I apprehend, weaken the conclusion, that we had never seen a watch made, that we had never known an artist capable of making one; that we were altogther incapable of executing such a piece of workmanship ourselves, or of understanding in what manner it was performed; all this being no more than what is true of some exquisite remains of ancient art, of some lost arts, and, to the generality of mankind, of the more curious productions of modern manufacture. Does one man in a million know how oval frames are turned? Ignorance of this kind exalts our opinion of the artist's skill, if he be

---

[1] Paley's argument is an argument by analogy. It is roughly of the form: "Just as (the existence of) A implies (the existence of) B, so in the *same* way (the existence of) A' implies (the existence of) B'."
—E.D.K.

unseen and unknown, but raises no doubt in our minds of the existence and agency of such an artist, at some former time, and in some place or other. Nor can I perceive that it varies at all the inference, whether the question arise concerning a human agent, or concerning an agent of different species, or an agent possessing, in some respects, a different nature.

Neither, secondly, would it invalidate our conclusion, that the watch sometimes went wrong, or that it seldom went exactly right. The purpose of the machinery, the design and the designer, might be evident, and in the case supposed would be evident, in whatever way we accounted for the irregularity of the movement, or whether we could account for it or not. It is not necessary that a machine be perfect, in order to show with what design it was made: still less necessary, where the only question is, whether it were made with any design at all.

Nor, thirdly, would it bring any uncertainty into the argument, if there were a few parts of the watch, concerning which we could not discover, or had not yet discovered, in what manner they conducted to the general effect; or even some parts, concerning which we could not ascertain whether they conducted to that effect in any manner whatever. For, as to the first branch of the case; if by the loss, or disorder, or decay of the parts in question; the movement of the watch were found in fact to be stopped, or disturbed, or retarded, no doubt would remain in our minds as to the utility or intention of these parts, although we should be unable to investigate the manner according to which, or the connexion by which, the ultimate effect depended upon their action or assistance; and the more complex is the machine, the more likely is this obscurity to arise. Then, as to the second thing supposed, namely, that there were parts which might be spared, without prejudice to the movement of the watch, and that we had proved this by experiment—these superfluous parts, even if we were completely assured that they were such, would not vacate the reasoning which we had instituted concerning other parts. The indication of contrivance remained, with respect to them, nearly as it was before.

Nor, fourthly, would any man in his senses think the existence of the watch, with its various machinery, accounted for, by being told that is was one out of possible combinations of material forms; that whatever he had found in the place where he found the watch, must have contained some internal configuration or other; and that this configuration might be the structure now exhibited, viz. of the works of a watch, as well as a different structure.

Nor, fifthly, would it yield to his inquiry more satisfaction to be answered, that there existed in things a principle of order, which had disposed the parts of the watch into their present form and situation. He never knew a watch made by the principle of order; nor can he even form to himself an idea of what is meant by a principle of order distinct from the intelligence of the watchmaker.

Sixthly, he would be surprised to hear that the mechanism of the watch was no proof of contrivance, only a motive to induce the mind to think so. . . .

Neither, lastly, would our observer be driven out of his conclusion, or from his confidence in its truth, by being told that he knew nothing at all about the matter. He knows enough for his argument. He knows the utility of the end: he knows the subserviency and adaptation of the means to the end. These points being known, his ignorance of other points, affect not the certainty of his reasoning. The consciousness of knowing little need not beget a distrust of that which he does know.

II. Even a "Self-Reproducing" Watch Implies a Watchmaker

Suppose, in the next place, that the person who found the watch, should, after sometime, discover, that, in addition to all the properties which he had hitherto observed in it, it possessed the unexpected property of producing, in the course of its movement, another watch like itself (the thing is conceivable), that it contained within it a mechanism, a system of parts, a mould for instance, or a complex adjustment of lathes, files, and other tools, evidently and separately calculated for this purpose; let us inquire, what effect ought such a discovery to have upon his former conclusion.

The first effect would be to increase his admiration of the contrivance, and his conviction of the consummate skill of the contriver. Whether he regarded the object of the contrivance, the distinct apparatus, the intricate, yet in many parts intelligible mechanism, by which it was carried on, he would perceive in this new observation, nothing but an additional reason for doing what he had already done,—for referring the construction of the watch to design, and to supreme art. If that construction *without* this property, or which is the same thing, before this property had been noticed, proved intention and art to have been employed about it, still more strong would the proof appear, when he came to the knowledge of this farther property, the crown and perfection of all the rest.

He would reflect, that though the watch before him were, *in some sense*, the maker of the watch which was fabricated in the course of its movements, yet it was in a very different sense from that in which a carpenter, for instance, is the maker of a chair; the author of its contrivance, the cause of the relation of its parts to their use. With respect to these, the first watch was no cause at all to the second: in no such sense as this was it the author of the constitution and order, either of the parts which the new watch contained, or of the parts by the aid and instrumentality of which it was produced. We might possibly say, but with great latitude of expression, that a stream of water ground corn; but no latitude of expression would allow us to say, no stretch of conjecture could lead us to think, that the stream of water built the mill, though it were too ancient for us to know who the builder was. What the stream of water does in the affair, is neither more nor less than this; by the application of an unintelligent impulse to a mechanism previously arranged, arranged independently of it, and *arranged by intelligence*, an effect is produced, viz. the corn is ground. But the effect results from the arrangement. The force of the stream cannot be said to be the cause or author of the effect, still less of the arrangement. Understanding and plan in the formation of the mill were not the less necessary, for any share which the water has in grinding the corn; yet is this share the same as that which the watch would have contributed to the production of the new watch, upon the supposition assumed in the last section. Therefore:

Though it be now no longer probable, that the individual watch which our observer had found was made immediately by the hand of an artificer, yet doth not this alteration in anywise affect the inference, that an artificer had been originally employed and concerned in the production. The argument from design remains as it was. Marks of design and contrivance are no more accounted for now than they were before. In the same thing, we may ask for the cause of different properties. We may ask for the cause of the color of a body, of its hardness, of its heat; and these causes may be all different. We are now asking for the cause of that subserviency to a case, that relation to an end, which we have remarked in the watch before us. No answer is given to this question by telling us that a preceding watch produced it. There cannot be design without a designer; contrivance, without a contriver; order, without choice; arrangement, without anything capable of arranging; subserviency and relation to a purpose without that which could intend a purpose; *means suitable to an end*, and executing their office in accomplishing that end, without the end ever having been contemplated, or the means accommodated to it. Arrangement, disposition of parts, *subserviency of means to an end*, relation of instruments to a use, imply the presence of intelligence and mind. No one, therefore, can rationally believe, that the insensible, inanimate watch, from which the watch before us issued, was the proper cause of the mechanism we so much admire in it;—could be truly said to have constructed the instrument, disposed its parts, assigned their office, determined their order, action, and mutual dependency, combined their several motions into one result, and that also a result connected with the utilities of other beings. All these properties, therefore, are as much unaccounted for as they were before.

III.   Impossibility of an Infinite Regress

Nor is anything gained by running the difficulty farther back, i.e., by supposing the watch before us to have been produced from another watch, that from a former, and so on indefinitely. Our going back ever so far brings us no nearer to the least degree of satisfaction upon the subject. *Contrivance* is still unaccounted for. We still want a *contriver*. A *designing mind* is neither supplied by this supposition, nor dispensed with. If the difficulty were diminished the farther we went back, by going back indefinitely we might exhaust it. And this is the only case to which this sort of reasoning applies. Where there is a tendency, or, as we increase the number of terms, a continual approach towards a limit, *there*, by supposing the number of terms to be what is called infinite, we may conceive the limit to be attained: but where there is no such tendency, or approach, nothing is effected by lengthening the series. There is no difference, as to the point in question (whatever there may be as to many points), between one series and another; between a series which is finite, and a series which is infinite. A chain, composed of an infinite number of links, can no more support itself, than a chain composed of a finite number of links. And of this we are assured (though we never *can* have tried the experiment), because, by increasing the number of links, from ten, for instance, to a hundred, from a hundred to a thousand, etc. we make not the smallest approach, we observe not the smallest tendency, towards self-support. There is no difference in this respect (yet there may be a great difference in several respects) between a chain of a greater or less length, between one chain and another, between one that is finite and one that is infinite. This very much resembles the case before us. The machine which we are inspecting demonstrates, by its construction, contrivance and design. *Contrivance* must have had a *contriver*; design, a *designer*; whether the machine immediately proceeded from another machine or not. That circumstance alters not the case. That other machine may, in like manner, have proceeded from a former machine: nor does that alter the case; contrivance must have had a contriver. That former one from one preceding it: no alteration still; a contriver is still necessary. No tendency is perceived, no approach towards a diminution of this necessity. It is the same with any and every succession of these machines; a succession of ten, of a hundred, of a thousand; with one series as with another; a series which is finite, as with a series which is infinite. In whatever other respects they may differ, in this they do not. In all, equally, contrivance and design are unaccounted for.

The question is not simply, How came the first watch into existence? which question, it may be pretended, is done away by supposing the series of watches thus produced from one another to have been infinite, and consequently to have had no such *first*, for which it was necessary to provide a cause. This, perhaps, would have been nearly the state of the question, if nothing had been before us but an unorganized, unmechanized substance, without mark or indication of contrivance. It might be difficult to show that such substance could not have existed from eternity, either in succession (if it were possible, which I think it is not, for unorganized bodies to spring from one another) or by individual perpetuity. But that is not the question now. To suppose it to be so, is to suppose that it made no difference whether we had found a watch or a stone. As it is, the metaphysics of that question have no place; for, in the watch which we are examining, are seen *contrivance, design; an end, a purpose; means for the end, adaptation to the purpose.* And the question which irresistibly presses upon our thoughts, is, whence this *contrivance* and *design?* The thing required is the intending mind, the adapting hand, the intelligence by which the hand was directed. This question, this demand, is not shaken off, by increasing a number or succession of substances, destitute of these properties; nor the more, by increasing that number to infinity. If it be said, that upon the supposition of one watch being produced from another in the course of that other's movements, and by means of the mechanism within it, we have a cause for the watch in my hand, viz. the watch from which it proceeded: I deny, that for the design, the *contrivance, the suitableness of means to an end*, the adaptation of instruments to a use (all means which we discover in a watch), we have any cause whatever. It is in vain, therefore, to assign a series of such causes, or to allege that a series may be carried back to infinity; for I do not admit that we have yet any cause at all of the phenomena, still less any series of causes either finite or infinite. Here is contrivance, but no contriver: proofs of design, but no designer.

Our observer would farther also reflect, that the maker of the watch before him, was, in truth and reality, the maker of every watch produced from it; there being no difference (except that the latter manifests a more exquisite skill) between the making of another watch with his own hands, by the mediation of files, lathes, chisels, etc. and the disposing, fixing, and inserting of these instruments, or of others equivalent to them, in the body of the watch already made, in such a manner as to form a new watch in the course of the movements which he had given to the old one. It is only working by one set of tools instead of another.

The conclusion which the *first* examination of the watch, of its works, construction, and movement, suggested, was, that it must have had, for the cause and author of that construction, an *artificer*, who *understood* its mechanism, and *designed* its use. This conclusion is invincible. A *second* examination presents us with a new discovery. The watch is found, in the course of its movement, to produce another watch, similar to itself: and not only so, but we perceive in it a system or organization, separately calculated for that *purpose*. What effect would this discovery have or ought it to have, upon our former inference? What, as hath already been said, but to increase, beyond measure, our admiration of the skill which had been employed in the formation of such a machine! Or shall it, instead of this, all at once turn us round to an opposite conclusion viz. that no art or skill whatever has been concerned in the business, although all other evidences of art and skill remain as they were, and this last and supreme piece of art be now added to the rest? Can this be maintained without absurdity? Yet this is atheism.

This is atheism: for every indication of contrivance, every manifestation of design, which existed in the watch, exists in the works of nature; with the difference, on the side of nature, of being greater and more, and that in a degree which exceeds all computation. I mean, that the contrivances of nature surpass the contrivances of art, in the complexity, subtlety, and curiosity of the mechanism; and still more, if possible, do they go beyond them in number and variety: yet, in a multitude of cases, are not less evidently mechanical, not less evidently contrivances, not less evidently accommodated to their end, or suited to their office, than are the most perfect productions of human ingenuity.

IV.   The Eye and the Telescope

I know no better method of introducing so large a subject, than that of comparing a single thing with a single thing; an eye, for example, with a telescope. As far as the examination of the instrument goes, there is precisely the same proof that the eye was made for vision, as there is that the telescope was made for assisting it. They are made upon the same principles; both being adjusted to the laws by which the transmission and reflection of rays of light are regulated. I speak not of the origin of the laws themselves; but such laws being fixed, the construction in both cases, is *adapted* to them. For instance; these laws require, in order to produce the same effect, that the rays of light, in passing from water into the eye, should be refracted by a more convex surface than when it passes out of air into the eye. Accordingly we find, that the eye of a fish, in that part of it called the crystalline lens, is much rounder than the eye of terrestrial animals. What plainer manifestation of design can there be than this difference? What could a mathematical instrument-maker have done more, to show his knowledge, of his principle, his application of knowledge, *his suiting of his means to his end*; I will not say to display the compass or excellence of his skill and art, for in these all comparison is indecorous, but to testify counsel, choice, consideration, purpose?

To some it may appear a difference sufficient to destroy all similitude between the eye and the telescope, that the one is a perceiving organ, the other an unperceiving instrument. The fact is, that they are both instruments. And as to the mechanism, at least as to mechanism being employed, and even as to the kind of it, this circumstance varies not the analogy at all. . . . The lenses of the telescope, and the humours of the eye, bear a complete resemblance to one another, in their figure, their position, and in their power over the rays of light, viz. in bringing each pencil to a point at the right distance from the lens; namely, in the eye, at the exact place where the membrane is spread to receive it. How is it possible, under circumstances of such close affinity, and under the operation of equal evidence, to exclude contrivance from the one, yet to acknowledge the proof of contrivance having been employed, as the plainest and clearest of all propositions, in the other?

The resemblance between the two cases is still more accurate, and obtains in more points that we have yet represented, or than we are, on the first view of the subject, aware off. In dioptric telescopes there is an imperfection of this nature. Pencils of light, in passing through glass lenses, are separated into different colors, thereby tinging the object, especially the edges of it, as if it were viewed through a prism. To correct this inconvenience had been long a desideratum in the art. At last it came into the mind of a sagacious optician, to inquire how this matter was managed in the eye; in which there was exactly the same difficulty to contend with as in the telescope. His observation taught him, that, in the eye, the evil was cured by combining lenses composed of different substances, i.e. of substances which possessed different refracting powers. Our artist borrowed thence his hint; and produced a correction of the defect by imitating, in glasses made from different materials, the effects of the different humours though which the rays of light pass before they reach the bottom of the eye. Could this be in the eye without purpose, which suggested to the optician the only effectual means of attaining that purpose?

But farther; there are other points, not so much perhaps of strict resemblance between the two, as of superiority of the eye over the telescope, which being found in the laws that regulate both, may furnish topics of fair and just comparison. . . .

V.   Further Evidence of Design in the Eye

In considering vision as achieved by the means of an image formed at the bottom of the eye, we can never reflect without wonder upon the smallness, yet correctness, of the picture, the subtility of the touch, the fineness of the lines. A landscape of five or six square leagues is brought into a space of half an inch diameter; yet the multitude of objects which it contains, are all preserved; are all discriminated in their magnitudes, positions, figures, colors. The prospect from Hampstead-hill is compressed into the compass of a sixpence, yet circumstantially represented. A stage-coach, travelling at its ordinary speed for half an hour, passes, in the eye, only over one-twelfth of an inch, yet is this change of place in the image distinctly perceived throughout its whole progress; for it is only by means of that perception that the motion of the coach itself is made sensible to the eye. If anything can abate our admiration of the smallness of the visual tablet compared with the extent of vision, it is a reflection, which the view of nature leads us, every hour, to make, viz. that in the hand of the Creator, great and little or nothing.

Sturmius held, that the examination of the eye was a cure for atheism. Besides that conformity to optical principles which its internal constitution displays, and which alone amounts to a manifestation of *intelligence* having been exerted in the structure; besides this, which forms no doubt, the leading character of the organ, there is to be seen, in everything belonging to it and about it, an extraordinary degree of care, and anxiety for its preservation, due, if we may so speak, to its value and its tenderness. It is lodged in a strong, deep, bony socket, composed by the junction of seven different bones, hollowed out at their edges. In some few species, as that of the coatimondi, the orbit is not bony throughout; but whenever this is the case, the upper, which is the deficient part, is supplied by a cartilaginous ligament; a substitution which shows the same care. Within this socket it is embedded in fat, of all animal substances the best adapted both to its repose and motion. It is sheltered by the eyebrows; an arch of hair, which like a thatched penthouse, prevents the sweat and moisture of the forehead from running down into it.

But it is still better protected by its lid. Of the superficial parts of the animal frame, I know none which, in its office and structure, is more deserving of attention than the eyelid. It defends the eye; it wipes it; it closes it in sleep. Are there, in any work of art whatever, purposes more evident than those which this organ fulfills? or an apparatus for executing those purposes more intelligible, more appropriate, or more mechanical? If it be overlooked by the observer of nature, it can only be because it is obvious and familiar. This is a tendency to be guarded against. We pass by the plainest instances, whilst we are exploring those which are rare and curious; by which conduct of the understanding, we sometimes neglect the strongest observations, being taken up with others, which though more recondite and scientific, are, as solid arguments, entitled to much less consideration.

In order to keep the eye moist and clean (which qualities are necessary to its brightness and its use), a wash is constantly supplied by a secretion for the purpose; and the superfluous brine is conveyed to the nose through a perforation in the bone as large as a goosequill. When once the fluid has entered the nose, it spreads itself upon the inside of the nostril, and is evaporated by the current of warm air, which, in the course of respiration, is continually passing over it. Can any pipe or outlet for carrying off the waste liquor from a dye-house or a distillery, be more mechanical than this is? It is easily perceived, that the eye must want moisture: but could the want of the eye generate the gland which produces the tear, or bore the hole by which it is discharged,—a hole through a bone? . . .

∘ ∘ ∘ **5**

God and Immortality as Postulates of Practical Reason[1]

(Chapter II: The Dialectic of Pure Reason in Defining the Concept of the Highest Good)

Immanuel Kant

THE CONCEPT OF the "highest" contains an ambiguity which, if not attended to, can occasion unnecessary disputes. The "highest" can mean the "supreme" (*supremum*) or the "perfect" (*consummatum*). The former is the unconditional condition, i.e., the condition which is subordinate to no other (*originarium*); the latter is that whole which is no part of a yet larger whole of the same kind (*perfectissimum*). That virtue (as the worthiness to be happy) is the supreme condition of whatever appears to us to be desirable and thus of all our pursuit of happiness and, consequently, that it is the supreme good have been proved in the Analytic.[2] But these truths do not imply that virtue is the entire and perfect good as the object of the faculty of desire of rational finite beings. For this, happiness is also required, and indeed not merely in the partial eyes of a person who makes himself his end but even in the judgment of an impartial reason, which impartially regards persons in the world as ends-in-themselves. For to be in need of happiness and also worthy of it and yet not to partake of it could not be in accordance with the complete volition of an omnipotent rational being, if we assume such only for the sake of the argument. Inasmuch as virtue and happiness together constitute the possession of the highest good for one person, and happiness in exact proportion to morality (as the worth of a person and his worthiness to be happy) constitutes that of a possible world, the highest good means the whole, the perfect good, wherein virtue is always the supreme good, being the condition having no condition superior to it, while happiness, though something always pleasant to him who possesses it, is not of itself absolutely good in every respect by always presupposes conduct in accordance with the moral law as its condition. . . .

I.   The Immortality of the Soul as a Postulate[3] of Pure Practical Reason

The achievement of the highest good in the world is the necessary object of a will determinable by the moral law. In such a will, however, the complete fitness of intentions

---

[1] Kant holds that there are two forms of reason: pure speculative and pure practical. The first is concerned with more theoretical issues of metaphysics, etc.; the second with more practical issues in ethics, etc.—E.D.K

[2] An earlier part of Kant's book.—E.D.K.

[3] A postulate (or posit) is a proposition assumed as true.—E.D.K

to the moral law is the supreme comdition of the highest good. This fitness, therefore, must be just as possible as its object, because it is contained in the command that requires us to promote the latter. But complete fitness of the will to the moral law is holiness, which is a perfection of which no rational being in the world of sense is at any time capable. But since it is required as practically necessary, it can be found only in an endless progress to that complete fitness; on principles of pure practical reason, it is necessary to assume such a practical progress as the real object of our will.

This infinite progress is possible, however, only under the presupposition of an infinitely enduring existence and personality of the same rational being; this is called the immortality of the soul. Thus the highest good is practically possible only on the supposition of the immortality of the soul, and the latter, as inseparably bound to the moral law, is postulate of pure practical reason. By a postulate of pure practical reason, I understand a theoretical proposition which is not as such demonstrable, but which is an inseparable corollary of an a priori unconditionally valid practical law.

The thesis of the moral destiny of our nature, viz., that it is able only in an infinite progress toward complete fitness to the moral law, is of great use, not merely for the present purpose of supplementing the impotence of speculative reason, but also with respect to religion. Without it, either the moral law is completely degraded from its holiness, by being made out as lenient (indulgent) and thus compliant to our convenience, or its call and its demands are strained to an unattainable destination, i.e., a hoped-for complete attainment of holiness of will, and are lost in fanatical theosophical dreams which completely contradict our knowledge of ourselves. In either case, we are only hindered in the unceasing striving toward the precise and persistent obedience to a command of reason which is stern, unindulgent, truly commanding, really and not just ideally possible.

Only endless progress from lower to higher stages of moral perfection is possible to a rational but finite being. The Infinite Being, to whom the temporal condition is nothing, sees in this series, which is for us without end, a whole conformable to the moral law; holiness, which His law inexorably commands in order to be true to His justice in the share He assigns to each in the highest good, is to be found in a single intellectual intuition of the existence of rational beings. All that can be granted to a creature with respect to hope for this share is consciousness of his tried character. And on the basis of his previous progress from the worse to the morally better, and of the immutability of intention which thus becomes known to him, he may hope for a further uninterrupted continuance of this progress, however long his existence may last, even beyond this life.[4] But he cannot hope here or at any foreseeable point of his future existence to be fully adequate to God's will,

---

[4] The conviction of the immutability of character in progress toward the good may appear to be impossible for a creature. For this reason, Christian doctrine lets it derive from the same Spirit which works sanctification, i.e., this firm intention and therewith the consciousness of steadfastness in moral progress. But naturally one who is conscious of having persisted, from legitimate moral motives, to the end of a long life in a progress to the better may very well have the comforting hope, though not the certainty, that he will be steadfast in these principles in an existence continuing beyond this life. Though he can never be justified in his own eyes either here or in the hoped-for increase of natural perfection together with an increase of his duties, nevertheless in this progress toward a goal infinitely remote (a progress which in God's sight is regarded as equivalent to possession) he can have prospect of a blessed future. For "blessed" is the word which reason uses to designate a perfect well-being independent of all contingent causes in the world. Like holiness, it is an idea which can be contained only in an infinite progress and its totality and thus is never fully reached by any creature.—I.K.

without indulgence or remission which would not harmonize with justice. This he can do only in the infinity of his duration which God alone can survey.

II.   *The Existence of God as a Postulate[5] of Pure Practical Reason*

The moral law led, in the foregoing analysis, to a practical problem which is assigned solely by pure reason and without any concurrence of sensuous incentives. It is the problem of the completeness of the first and principal part of the highest good, viz., morality; since this problem can be solved only in eternity, it led to the postulate of immorality. The same law must also lead us to affirm the possibility of the second element of the highest good, i.e., happiness proportional to that morality; it must do so just as disinterestedly as heretofore, by a purely impartial reason. This it can do on the supposition of the existence of a cause adequate to this effect, i.e., it must postulate the existence of God as necessarily belonging to the possibility of the highest good (the object of our will which is necessarily connected with the moral legislation of pure reason). We proceed to exhibit this connection in a convincing manner.

Happiness is the condition of a rational being in the world, in whose whole existence everything goes according to wish and will. It thus rests on the harmony of nature with his entire end and with the essential determining ground of his will. But the moral law commands as a law of freedom through motives wholly independent of nature and of its harmony with our faculty of desire (as incentives). Still, the acting rational being in the world is not at the same time the cause of the world and of nature itself. Hence there is not the slightest ground in the moral law for a necessary connection between the morality and proportionate happiness of a being which belongs to the world as one of its parts and as thus dependent of it. Not being nature's cause, his will cannot by its own strength bring nature, as it touches on his happiness, into complete harmony with his practical principles. Nevertheless, in the practical task of pure reason, i.e., in the necessary endeavor after the highest good, such a connection is postulated as necessary: we *should* seek to further the highest good (which therefore must be at least possible). Therefore also the existence is postulated of a cause of the whole of nature, itself distinct from nature, which contains the ground of the exact coincidence of happiness with morality. This supreme cause, however, must contain the ground of the agreement of nature not merely with a law of the will of rational beings but with the idea of this law so far as they make it the supreme ground of determination of the will. Thus it contains the ground of the agreement of nature not merely with actions moral in their form but also with their morality as the motives to such actions, i.e., with their moral intention. Therefore, the highest good is possible in the world only on the supposition of a supreme cause of nature which has a causality corresponding to the moral intention. Now a being which is capable of actions by the idea of laws is an intelligence (a rational being), and the causality of such a being according to this idea of laws is his will. Therefore, the supreme cause of nature, insofar as it must be presupposed for the highest good, is a being which is the cause (and consequently the author) of nature through understanding and will, i.e., God. As a consequence, the postulate of the possibility of a highest derived good (the best world) is at the same time the postulate of the reality of a highest original good,

---

[5] See note 3.—E.D.K.

namely, the existence of God. Now it was our duty to promote the highest good; and it is not merely our privilege but a necessity connected with duty as a requisite to presuppose the possibility of this highest good. This presupposition is made only under the condition of the existence of God, and this condition inseparably connects this supposition with duty. Therefore, it is morally necessary to assume the existence of God.

It is well to notice here that this moral necessity is subjective, i.e., a need, and not objective, i.e., duty itself. For there cannot be any duty to assume the existence of a thing, because such a supposition concerns only the theoretical use of reason. It is also not to be understood that the assumption of the existence of God is necessary as a ground of all obligation in general (for this rests, as has been fully shown, solely on the autonomy of reason itself). All that here belongs to duty is the endeavor to produce and to further the highest good in the world, the existence of which may thus be postulated though our reason cannot conceive it except by presupposing a highest intelligence. To assume its existence is thus connected with the consciousness of our duty, though this assumption itself belongs to the realm of theoretical reason. Considered only in reference to the latter, it is a hypothesis, i.e., a ground of explanation. But in reference to the comprehensibility of an object (the highest good) placed before us by the moral law, and thus as a practical need, it can be called *faith* and even pure *rational faith*, because pure reason alone (by its theoretical as well as practical employment) is the source from which it springs.

From this deduction it now becomes clear why the Greek schools could never succeed in solving their problem of the practical possibility of the highest good. It was because they made the rule of the use which the human will makes of its freedom the sole and self-sufficient ground of its possibility, thinking that they had no need of the existence of God for this purpose. They were certainly correct in establishing the principle of morals by itself, independently of this postulate and merely from the relation of reason to the will, thus making the principle of morality the *supreme* practical condition of the highest good; but this principle was not the *entire* condition of its possibility. The Epicureans had indeed raised a wholly false principle of morality, i.e., that of happiness, into the supreme one, and for law had substituted a maxim of arbitrary choice of each according to his inclination. But they proceeded consistently enough, in that they degraded their highest good in proportion to the baseness of their principle and expected no greater happiness than that which could be attained through human prudence (wherein both temperance and the moderation of inclinations belong), though everyone knows prudence to be scarce enough and to produce diverse results according to circumstances, not to mention the exceptions which their maxims continually had to admit and which made them worthless as laws. The Stoics, on the other hand, had chosen their supreme practical principle, virtue, quite correctly as the condition of the highest good. But as they imagined the degree of virtue which is required for its pure law as completely attainable in this life, they not only exaggerated the moral capacity of man, under the name of "sage," beyond all the limits of his nature, making it into something which is contradicted by all our knowledge of men; they also refused to accept the second component of the highest good, i.e., happiness, as a special object of human desire. Rather, they made their sage like a god in a consciousness of the excellence of his person, wholly independent of nature (as regards his own contentment), exposing him to the evils of life but not subjecting him to them. (They also represented him as free from everything morally evil.) Thus they really left out of the highest good the second element (personal happiness), since they placed the highest good only in acting in contentment with one's own personal worth, including it in the consciousness of moral character. But the voice of their own nature could have sufficiently refuted this.

The doctrine of Christianity, [6] even when not regarded as a religious doctrine, gives at this point a concept of the highest good (the Kingdom of God) which is alone sufficient to the strictest demand of practical reason. The moral law is holy (unyielding) and demands holiness of morals, although all moral perfection to which man can attain is only virtue, i.e., a law-abiding disposition resulting from respect for the law and thus implying consciousness of a continuous propensity to transgress it or at least to a defilement, i.e., to an admixture of many spurious (not moral) motives to obedience to the law; consequently, man can achieve only a self-esteem combined with humility. And thus with respect to the holiness required by the Christian law, nothing remains to the creature but endless progress, though for the same reason hope of endless duration is justified. The worth of a character completely accordant with the moral law is infinite, because of posssible happiness in the judgment of a wise and omnipotent dispenser of happiness has no other limitation than the lack of fitness of rational beings to their duty. But the moral law does not of itself promise happiness, for the latter is not, according to concepts of any order of nature, necessarily connected with obedience to the law. Christian ethics supplies this defect of the second indispensable component of the highest good by presenting a world wherein reasonable beings single-mindedly devote themselves to the moral law; this is the Kingdom of God, in which nature and morality come into a harmony, which is foreign to each as such, through a holy Author of the world, who makes possible the derived highest good. The holiness of morals is prescribed to them even in this life as a guide to conduct, but the well-being proportionate to this, which is bliss, is thought of as attainable only in eternity. This is due to the fact that the former must always be the pattern of their conduct in every state, and

---

[6] The view is commonly held that the Christian precept of morals has no advantage over the moral concept of the Stoics in respect to its purity; but the difference between them is nevertheless obvious. The Stoic system makes the consciousness of strength of mind the pivot around which all moral intentions should turn; and, if the followers of this system spoke of duties and even defined them accurately, they nevertheless placed the incentives and the real determining gound of the will in an elevation of character above the base incentives of the senses which have their power only through weakness of the mind. Virtue was, therefore, for them a certain heroism of the sage who, raising himself above the animal nature of man, was sufficient to himself, subject to no temptation to transgress the moral law, and elevated above duties though he propounded duties to others. But all this they could not have done had they conceived this law in the same purity and rigor as does the precept of the Gospel. If I understand by "idea" a perfection to which the senses can give nothing adequate, the moral ideas are not transcendent, i.e., of such a kind that we cannot even sufficiently define the concept or of which we are uncertain whether there is a corresponding object (as are the ideas of speculative reason); rather, they serve as models of practical perfection, as an indispensable rule of moral conduct, and as a standard for comparison. If I now regard Christian morals from their philosophical side, it appears in comparison with the ideas of the Greek schools as follows: the ideas of the Cynics, Epicureans, Stoics, and Christians are, respectively, the simplicity of nature, prudence, wisdom, and holiness. In respect to the way they achieve them, the Greek schools differ in that the Cynics found common sense sufficient, while the others found it in the path of science, and thus all held it to lie in the mere use of man's natural powers. Christian ethics, because it formulated its precept as pure and uncompromising (as befits a moral precept), destroyed man's confidence of being wholly adequate to it, at least in this life; but it re-established it by enabling us to hope that, if we act as well as lies in our power, what is not in our power will come to our aid from another source, whether we know in what way or not. Aristotle and Plato differed only as to the origin of our moral concepts.—I.K.

progressing toward it is even in this life possible and necessary, whereas the latter, under the happiness, cannot (as far as our own capacity is concerned) be reached in this life and therefore is made only an object of hope. Nevertheless, the Christian principle of morality is not theological and thus heteronomous, being rather the autonomy of pure practical reason itself, because it does not make the knowledge of God and His will the basis of these laws but makes such knowledge the basis only of succeeding to the highest good on condition of obedience to these laws; it places the real incentive for obedience to the law not in the desired consequences of obedience but in the conception of duty alone, in true observance of which the worthiness to attain the latter alone consists.

In this manner, through the concept of the highest good as the object and final end of pure practical reason, the moral law leads to religion. Religion is the recognition of all duties as divine commands, not as sanctions, i.e., arbitrary and contingent ordinances of a foreign will, but as essential laws of any free will as such. Even as such, they must be regarded as commands of the Supreme Being because we can hope for the highest good (to strive for which is our duty under the moral law) only from a morally perfect (holy and beneficent) and omnipotent will; and, therefore, we can hope to attain it only through harmony with this will. But here again everything remains disinterested and based only on duty, without being based on fear or hope as incentives, which, if they became principles, would destroy the entire moral worth of the actions. The moral law commands us to make the highest possible good in a world the final object of all our conduct. This I cannot hope to effect except through the agreement of my will with that of a holy and beneficent Author of the world. And although my own happiness is included in the concept of the highest good as a whole wherein the greatest happiness is thought of as connected in exact proportion to the greatest degree of moral law (which, in fact, sternly places restricting conditions upon my boundless longing for happiness) which is proved to be the ground determining the will to further the highest good.

Therefore, morals is not really the doctrine of how to make ourselves happy but of how we are to be *worthy* of happiness. Only if religion is added to it can the hope arise of someday participating in happiness in proportion as we endeavored not to be unworthy of it.

One is worthy of possessing a thing or a state when his possession is harmonious with the highest good. We can easily see not that all worthiness is a matter of moral conduct, because this constitutes the condition of everything else (which belongs to one's state) in the concept of the highest good, i.e., participation in happiness. From this there follows that one must never consider morals itself as a doctrine of happiness, i.e., as an instruction in how to acquire happiness. For morals has to do only with the rational condition (*conditio sine qua non*)[7] of happiness and not with means of achieving it. But when morals (which imposes only duties instead of providing rules for selfish wishes) is completely expounded, and a moral wish has been awakened to promote the highest good (to bring the Kingdom of God to us), which is a wish based on law and one to which no selfish mind could have aspired, and when for the sake of this wish the step to religion has been taken—then only can ethics be called a doctrine of happiness, because the *hope* for it first arises with religion.

---

[7] Necessary condition. Literally: that without which not.—E.D.K.

From this it can also be seen that, if we inquire into God's final end in creating the world, we must name not the happiness of rational beings in the world but the highest good, which adds a further condition to the wish of rational beings to be happy, viz., the condition of being worthy of happiness, which is the morality of these beings, for this alone contains the standard by which they can hope to participate in happiness at the hand of a *wise* creator. For since wisdom, theoretically regarded, means the knowledge of the highest good and, practically, the suitability of the will to the highest good, one cannot ascribe to a supreme independent wisdom an end based merely on benevolence. For we cannot conceive the action of this benevolence (with respect to the happiness of rational beings) except as conformable to the restrictive conditions of harmony with the holiness[8] of His will as the highest original good. Then perhaps those who have placed the end of creation in the glory of God, provided this is not thought of anthropomorphically as an inclination to be esteemed, have found the best term. For nothing glorifies God more than what is the most estimable thing in the world, namely, respect for His command, the observance of sacred duty which His law imposes on us, when there is added to this His glorious plan of crowning such an excellent order with corresponding happiness. If the latter, to speak in human terms, makes Him worthy of love, by the former He is an object of adoration. Human beings can win love by doing good, but by this alone even they never win respect; the greatest well-doing does them honor only by being exercised according to worthiness.

It follows of itself that, in the order of ends, man (and every rational being) is an end-in-himself, i.e., he is never to be used merely as a means for someone (even for God) without at the same time being himself an end, and that thus the humanity in our person must itself be holy to us, because man is subject to the moral law and therefore subject to that which is of itself holy, and it is only on account of this and in agreement with this that anything can be called holy. For this moral law is founded on the autonomy of his will as a free will, which by its universal laws must necessarily be able to agree with that to which it subjects itself.

---

[8] Incidentally, and in order to make the peculiarity of this concept clear, I make the following remark. Since we ascribe various attributes to God, whose quality we find suitable also to creatures (e.g., power, knowledge, presence, goodness, etc.), though in God they are present in a higher degree under such names as omnipotence, omniscience, omnipresence, and perfect goodness, etc., there are three which exclusively and without qualification of magnitude are ascribed to God, and they are all moral. He is the only holy, the only blessed, and the only wise being, because these concepts of themselves imply unlimitedness. By the arrangement of these He is thus the holy lawgiver (and creator), the beneficient ruler (and sustainer), and the just judge. These three attributes contain everything whereby God is the object of religion, and in conformity to them the metaphysical perfections of themselves arise in reason.—I.K.

○ ○ ○ **6**

Mysticism and Religious Experience[1]
William James

· I ·

ONE MAY SAY truly, I think, that personal religious experience has its root and centre in mystical states of consciousness; so for us, who in these lectures are treating personal experience as the exclusive subject of our study, such states of consciousness ought to form the vital chapter from which the other chapters get their light. Whether my treatment of mystical states will shed more light or darkness, I do not know, for my own constitution shuts me out from their enjoyment almost entirely, and I can speak of them only at second hand. But though forced to look upon the subject so externally, I will be as objective and receptive as I can; and I think I shall at least succeed in convincing you of the reality of the states in question, and of the paramount importance of their function.

· II ·

First of all, then, I ask, What does the expression "mystical states of consciousness" mean? How do we part off mystical states from other states?

The words "mysticism" and "mystical" are often used as terms of mere reproach, to throw at any opinion which we regard as vague and vast and sentimental, and without a base in either facts or logic. For some writers a "mystic" is any person who believes in thought-transference, or spirit-return. Employed in this way the word has little value: there are too many less ambiguous synonyms. So, to keep it useful by restricting it, I will . . . simply propose to you four marks which, when an experience has them, may justify us in calling it mystical for the purpose of the present lectures. In this way we shall save verbal disputation, and the recriminations that generally go therewith.

1. *Ineffability.* The handiest of the marks by which I classify a state of mind as mystical is negative. The subject of it immediately says that it defies expression, that no adequate report of its contents can be given in words. It follows from this that its quality must be directly experienced; it cannot be imparted or transferred to others. In this peculiarity mystical states are more like states of feeling than like states of intellect. No one can make clear to another who has never had a certain feeling in what the quality or worth of it consists. One must have musical ears to know the value of a symphony; one

---

[1] The more philosophical parts of this selection are found in sections I, II, VI, and VIII.—E.D.K.

must have been in love oneself to understand a lover's state of mind. Lacking the heart or ear, we cannot interpret the musician or the lover justly, and are even likely to consider him weak-minded or absurd. The mystic finds that most of us accord to his experiences an equally incompetent treatment.

2. *Noetic*[2] *quality*. Although so similar to states of feeling, mystical states seem to those who experience them to be also states of knowledge. They are states of insight into depths of truth unplumbed by the discursive intellect. They are illuminations, revelations, full of significance and importance, all inarticulate though they remain; and as a rule they carry with them a curious sense of authority for after-time.

These two characters will entitle any state to be called mystical, in the sense in which I use the word. Two other qualities are less sharply marked, but are usually found. These are:

3. *Transiency*. Mystical states cannot be sustained for long. Except in rare instances, half an hour, or at most an hour or two, seems to be the limit beyond which they fade into the light of common day. Often, when faded, their quality can but imperfectly be reproduced in memory; but when they recur it is recognized; and from one recurrence to another it is susceptible of continuous development in what is felt as inner richness and importance.

4. *Passivity*. Although the oncoming of mystical states may be facilitated by preliminary voluntary operations, as by fixing the attention, or going through certain bodily performances, or in other ways which manuals of mysticism prescribe; yet when the characteristic sort of consciousness once has set in, the mystic feels as if his own will were in abeyance, and indeed sometimes as if he were grasped and held by a superior power. This latter peculiarity connects mystical states with certain definite phenomena of secondary or alternative personality, such as prophetic speech, automatic writing, or the mediumistic trance. When these latter conditions are well pronounced, however, there may be no recollection whatever of the phenomenon, and it may have no significance for the subject's usual inner life, to which, as it were, it makes a mere interruption. Mystical states, strictly so called, are never merely interruptive. Some memory of their content always remains, and a profound sense of their importance. They modify the inner life of the subject between the times of their recurrence. Sharp divisions in this region are, however, difficult to make, and we find all sorts of gradations and mixtures.

These four characteristics are sufficient to mark out a group of states of consciousness peculiar enough to deserve a special name and to call for careful study. Let it then be called the mystical group.

· III ·

Our next step should be to gain acquaintance with some typical examples. Professional mystics at the height of their development have often elaborately organized experiences and a philosophy based thereupon. But . . . phenomena are best understood when placed within their series, studied in their germ and in their over-ripe decay, and compared with their exaggerated and degenerated kindred. The range of mystical experience is very

---

[2] Pertaining to or yielding knowledge.—E.D.K.

wide, much too wide for us to cover in the time at our disposal. Yet the method of serial study is so essential for interpretation that if we really wish to reach conclusions we must use it. I will begin, therefore, with phenomena which claim no special religious significance, and end with those of which the religious pretensions are extreme.

The simplest rudiment of mystical experience would seem to be that deepened sense of the significance of a maxim or formula which occasionally sweeps over one. "I've heard that said all my life," we exclaim, "but I never realized its full meaning until now." "When a fellow-monk," said Luther, "one day repeated the words of the Creed: 'I believe in the forgiveness of sins,' I saw the Scripture in an entirely new light; and straightway I felt as if I were born anew. It was as if I had found the door of paradise thrown wide open." This sense of deeper significance is not confined to rational propositions. Single words, and conjunctions of words, effects of light on land and sea, odors and musical sounds, all bring it when the mind is tuned aright. Most of us can remember the strangely moving power of passages in certain poems read when we were young, irrational doorways as they were through which the mystery of fact, the wildness and the pang of life, stole into our hearts and thrilled them. The words have now perhaps become mere polished surfaces for us; but lyric poetry and music are alive and significant only in proportion as they fetch these vague vistas of a life continuous with our own, beckoning and inviting, yet ever eluding our pursuit. We are alive or dead to the eternal inner message of the arts according as we have kept or lost this mystical susceptibility.

A more pronounced step forward on the mystical ladder is found in an extremely frequent phenomenon, that sudden feeling, namely, which sometimes sweeps over us, of having "been here before," as if at some indefinite past time, in just this place, with just these people, we were already saying just these things. As Tennyson writes [in "The Two Voices"]:

> Moreover, something is or seems,
> That touches me with mystic gleams,
> Like glimpses of forgotten dreams —
> Of something felt, like something here;
> Of something done, I know not where;
> Such as no language may declare.

Sir James Crichton-Browne has given the technical name of "dreamy states" to these sudden invasions of vaguely reminiscent consciousness. They bring a sense of mystery and of the metaphysical duality of things, and the feeling of an enlargement of perception which seems imminent but which never completes itself. In Dr. Crichton-Browne's opinion they connect themselves with the perplexed and scared disturbances of self-consciousness which occasionally precede epileptic attacks. I think that this learned alienist takes a rather absurdly alarmist view of an intrinsically insignificant phenomenon. He follows it along the downward ladder, to insanity; our path pursues the upward ladder chiefly. The divergence shows how important it is to neglect no part of a phenomenon's connections, for we make it appear admirable or dreadful according to the context by which we set it off.

Somewhat deeper plunges into mystical consciousness are met with in yet other dreamy states. Such feelings as these which Charles Kingsley describes are surely far from being uncommon, especially in youth:

When I walk the fields, I am oppressed now and then with an innate feeling that everything I see has a meaning, if I could but understand it. And this feeling of being surrounded with truths which I cannot grasp amounts to indescribable awe sometimes. . . . Have you not felt that your real soul was imperceptible to your mental vision, except in a few hallowed moments?[3]

A much more extreme state of mystical consciousness is described by J. A. Symonds; and probably more persons than we suspect could give parallels to it from their own experience.

Suddenly at church, or in company, or when I was reading, and always, I think, when my muscles were at rest, I felt the approach of the mood. Irresistibly it took possession of my mind and will, lasted what seemed an eternity, and disappeared in a series of rapid sensations which resembled the awakening from anaesthetic influence. One reason why I disliked this kind of trance was that I could not describe it to myself. I cannot even now find words to render it intelligible. It consisted in a gradual but swiftly progressive obliteration of space, time, sensation, and the multitudinous factors of experience which seem to qualify what we are pleased to call our Self. In proportion as these conditions of ordinary consciousness were subtracted, the sense of an underlying or essential consciousness acquired intensity. At last nothing remained but a pure, absolute, abstract Self. The universe became without form and void of content. But Self persisted, formidable in its vivid keenness, feeling the most poignant doubt about reality, ready, as it seemed, to find existence break as breaks a bubble round about it. And what then? The apprehension of a coming dissolution, the grim conviction that this state was the last state of the conscious Self, the sense that I had followed the last threat of being to the verge of the abyss, and had arrived at demonstration of eternal Maya or illusion, stirred or seemed to stir me up again. The return to ordinary conditions of sentient existence began by my first recovering the power of touch, and then by the gradual though rapid influx of familiar impressions and diurnal interests. At last I felt myself once more a human being; and though the riddle of what is meant by life remained unsolved, I was thankful for this return from the abyss—this deliverance from so awful an initiation into the mysteries of skepticism.

This trance recurred with diminishing frequency until I reached the age of twenty-eight. It served to impress upon my growing nature the phantasmal unreality of all the circumstances which contribute to a merely phenomenal consciousness. Often have I asked myself with anguish, on waking from that formless state of denuded, keenly sentient being, "Which is the unreality?"—the trance of fiery, vacant, apprehensive, skeptical Self from which I issue, or these surrounding phenomena and habits which veil that inner Self and build a self of flesh-and-blood conventionality? Again, are men the factors of some dream, the dream-like unsubstantiality of which they comprehend at such eventful moments? What would happen if the final stage of the trance were reached?[4]

In a recital like this there is certainly something suggestive of pathology. The next step into mystical states carries us into a realm that public opinion and ethical philosophy have long since branded as pathological, though private practice and certain lyric strains of poetry seem still to bear witness to its ideality. I refer to the consciousness produced by intoxicants and anaesthetics, especially by alcohol. The sway of alcohol over mankind

---

[3] Quoted in Inge, *Christian Mysticism* (London: Methuen & Co., Ltd., 1899), p. 341.—W.J.

[4] H. F. Brown, *J. A. Symonds: A Biography* (London, 1895), pp. 29–31.—W.J.

is unquestionably due to its power to stimulate the mystical faculties of human nature, usually crushed to earth by the cold facts and dry criticisms of the sober hour. Sobriety diminishes, discriminates, and says no; drunkenness expands, unites, and says yes. It is in fact the great exciter of the *Yes* function in man. It brings its votary from the chill periphery of things to the radiant core. It makes him for the moment one with truth. Not through mere perversity do men run after it. To the poor and the unlettered it stands in the place of symphony concerts and of literature; and it is part of the deeper mystery and tragedy of life that whiffs and gleams of something that we immediately recognize as excellent should be vouchsafed to so many of us only in the fleeting earlier phases of what in its totality is so degrading a poisoning. The drunken consciousness is one bit of the mystic consciousness, and our total opinion of it must find its place in our opinion of that larger whole.

Nitrous oxide and ether, especially nitrous oxide, when sufficiently diluted with air, stimulate the mystical consciousness in an extraordinary degree. Depth beyond depth of truth seems revealed to the inhaler. This truth fades out, however, or escapes, at the moment of coming to; and if any words remain over in which it seemed to clothe itself, they prove to be the veriest nonsense. Nevertheless, the sense of a profound meaning having been there persists; and I know more than one person who is persuaded that in the nitrous oxide trance we have a genuine metaphysical revelation.

Some years ago I myself made some observations on this aspect of nitrous oxide intoxication, and reported them in print. One conclusion was forced upon my mind at that time, and my impression of its truth has ever since remained unshaken. It is that our normal waking consciousness, rational consciousness as we call it, is but one special type of consciousness, whilst all about it, parted from it by the filmiest of screens, there lie potential forms of consciousness entirely different. We may go through life without suspecting their existence; but apply the requisite stimulus, and at a touch they are there in all their completeness, definite types of mentality which probably somewhere have their field of application and adaptation. No account of the universe in its totality can be final which leaves these other forms of consciousness quite disregarded. How to regard them is the question—for they are so discontinuous with ordinary consciousness. Yet they may determine attitudes though they cannot furnish formulas, and open a region though they fail to give a map. At any rate, they forbid a premature closing of our accounts with reality. Looking back on my own experiences, they all converge towards a kind of insight to which I cannot help ascribing some metaphysical significance. The keynote of it is invariably a reconciliation. It is as if the opposites of the world, whose contradictoriness and conflict make all our difficulties and troubles, were melted into unity. Not only do they, as contrasted species, belong to one and the same genus, but *one of the species*, the nobler and better one, *is itself the genus, and so soaks up and absorbs its opposite into itself.* This is a dark saying, I know, when thus expressed in terms of common logic, but I cannot wholly escape from its authority. I feel as if it must mean something, something like what the Hegelian philosophy means, if one could only lay hold of it more clearly. Those who have ears to hear, let them hear; to me the living sense of its reality only comes in the artificial mystic state of mind.

I just now spoke of friends who believe in the anaesthetic revelation. For them too it is a monistic insight, in which the *other* in its various forms appears absorbed into the One. [Writes one of them:]

Into this pervading genius we pass, forgetting and forgotten, and thenceforth each is all, in God. There is no higher, no deeper, no other, than the life in which we are founded. "The One remains, the many change and pass"; and each and every one of us *is* the One that remains. . . . This is the ultimatum. . . . As sure as being—whence is all our care—so sure is content, beyond duplexity, antithesis, or trouble, where I have triumphed in a solitude that God is not above.[5]

This has the genuine religious mystic ring! I just now quoted J. A. Symonds. He also records a mystical experience with chloroform, as follows:

After the choking and stifling had passed away, I seemed at first in a state of utter blankness; then came flashes of intense light, alternating with blackness, and with a keen vision of what was going on in the room around me, but no sensation of touch. I thought that I was near death; when, suddenly, my soul became aware of God, who was manifestly dealing with me, handling me, so to speak, in an intense personal present reality. I felt him streaming in like light upon me. . . . I cannot describe the ecstasy I felt. Then, as I gradually awoke from the influence of the anaesthetics, the old sense of my relation to the world began to return, the new sense of my relation to God began to fade. I suddenly lept to my feet on the chair where I was sitting, and shrieked out, "It is too horrible, it is too horrible, it is too horrible," meaning that I could not bear this disillusionment. Then I flung myself on the ground, and at last awoke covered with blood, calling to the two surgeons (who were frightened), "Why did you not kill me? Why would you not let me die?" Only think of it. To have felt for that long dateless ecstasy of vision the very God, in all purity and tenderness and truth and absolute love, and then to find that I had after all had no revelation, but that I had been tricked by the abnormal excitement of my brain.

Yet, this question remains, Is it possible that the inner sense of reality which succeeded, when my flesh was dead to impressions from without, to the ordinary sense of physical relations, was not a delusion but an actual experience? Is it possible that I, in that moment, felt what some of the saints have said they always felt, the undemonstrable but irrefragable certainty of God?[6]

With this we make connection with religion mysticism pure and simple. ". . . [The] sudden realization of the immediate presence of God . . . in one shape or another is not uncommon," writes Mr. Ralph Waldo Trine:

I know an officer on our police force who has told me that many times when off duty, and on his way home in the evening, there comes to him such a vivid and vital realization of his oneness with this Infinite Power, and this Spirit of Infinite Peace so takes hold of and so fills him, that it seems as if his feet could hardly keep to the pavement, so buoyant and so exhilarated does he become by reason of this inflowing tide.[7]

Certain aspects of nature seem to have a peculiar power of awakening such mystical moods. Most of the striking cases which I have collected occured out of doors. Literature has commemorated this fact in many passages of great beauty—this extract, for example, from Amiel's *Journal Intime*:

---

[5] Benjamin Paul Blood, *The Anaesthetic Revelation and the Gist of Philosophy* (Amsterdam, N.Y., 1874), pp. 35, 36.—w.j.

[6] Brown, *op. cit.*, pp. 78–80.—w.j.

[7] Ralph Waldo Trine, *In Tune with the Infinite* (London, 1900), p. 137.—w.j.

Shall I ever again have any of those prodigious reveries which sometimes came to me in former days? One day, in youth, at sunrise, sitting in the ruins of the castle of Faucigny; and again in the mountains, under the noonday sun, above Lavey, lying at the foot of a tree and visited by three butterflies; once more at night upon the shingly shore of the Northern Ocean, my back upon the sand and my vision ranging through the milky way—such grand and spacious, immortal, cosmogonic reveries, when one reaches to the stars, when one owns the infinite! Moments divine, ecstatic hours; in which our thought flies from world to world, pierces the great enigma, breathes with a respiration broad, tranquil, and deep as the respiration of the ocean, serene and limitless as the blue firmament; . . . instants of irresistible intuition in which one feels oneself great as the universe, and calm as a god. . . .What hours, what memories! The vestiges they leave behind are enough to fill us with belief and enthusiasm, as if they were visits of the Holy Ghost.[8]

Here is a similar record from the memoirs of that interesting German idealist, Malwida von Meysenbug:

I was alone upon the seashore as all these thoughts flowed over me, liberating and reconciling; and now again, as once before in distant days in the Alps of Dauphiné, I was impelled to kneel down, this time before the illimitable ocean, symbol of the Infinite. I felt that I prayed as I had never prayed before, and knew now what prayer really is: to return from the solitude of individuation into the consciousness of unity with all that is, to kneel down as one that passes away, and to rise up as one imperishable. Earth, heaven, and sea resounded as in one vast world-encircling harmony. It was as if the chorus of all the great who had ever lived were about me. I felt myself one with them, and it appeared as if I heard their greeting: "Thou too belongest to the company of those who overcome."[9]

The well-known passage from Walt Whitman is a classical expression of this sporadic type of mystical experience.

I believe in you, my Soul . . .
Loaf with me on the grass, loose the stop from your throat; . . .
Only the lull I like, the hum of your valved voice.
I mind how once we lay, such a transparent summer morning.
Swiftly arose and spread around me the peace and knowledge that pass all the
    argument of the earth,
And I know that the hand of God is the promise of my own,
And I know that the spirit of God is the brother of my own,
And that all the men ever born are also my brothers and the women my sisters and
    lovers,
And that a kelson of the creation is love.

I could easily give more instances, but one will suffice. I take it from the Autobiography of J. Trevor.

One brilliant Sunday morning, my wife and boys went to the Unitarian Chapel in Macclesfield. I felt it impossible to accompany them—as though to leave the sunshine on the hills, and go down there to the chapel, would be for the time an act of spiritual

---

[8] *Op. cit.*, pp. 43–44.—w.j.
[9] *Memoiren einer Idealistin*, 5th ed. (1900, Vol. III, 166).—w.j.

suicide. And I felt such need for new inspiration and expansion in my life. So, very reluctantly and sadly, I left my wife and boys to go down into the town, while I went further up into the hills with my stick and my dog. In the loveliness of the morning, and the beauty of the hills and valleys, I soon lost my sense of sadness and regret. For nearly an hour I walked along the road to the "Cat and Fiddle," and then returned. On the way back, suddenly, without warning, I felt that I was in Heaven—an inward state of peace and joy and assurance indescribably intense, accompanied with a sense of being bathed in a warm glow of light, as though the external condition had brought about the internal effect—a feeling of having passed beyond the body, though the scene around me stood out more clearly and as if nearer to me than before, by reason of the illumination in the midst of which I seemed to be placed. This deep emotion lasted, though with decreasing strength, until I reached home, and for some time after, only gradually passing away.[10]

The writer adds that having had further experiences of a similar sort, he now knows them well.

The spiritual life justifies to those who live it; but what can we say to those who do not understand? This, at least, we can say, that it is a life whose experiences are proved real to their possessor, because they remain with him when brought closest into contact with the objective realities of life. Dreams cannot stand this test. We wake from them to find that they are but dreams. Wanderings of an overwrought brain do not stand this test. These highest experiences that I have had of God's presence have been rare and brief— flashes of consciousness which have compelled me to exclaim with surprise—God is *here!*—or conditions of exaltation and insight, less intense, and only gradually passing away. I have severely questioned the worth of these moments. To no soul have I named them, lest I should be building my life and work on mere phantasies of the brain. But I find that, after every questioning and test, they stand out today as the most real experiences of my life, and experiences which have explained and justified and unified all past experiences and all past growth. Indeed, their reality and their far-reaching significance are ever becoming more clear and evident. When they came, I was living the fullest, strongest, sanest, deepest life. I was not seeking them. What I was seeking, with resolute determination, was to live more intensely my own life, as against what I knew would be the adverse judgment of the world. It was in the most real seasons that the Real Presence came, and I was aware that I was immersed in the infinite ocean of God.[11]

Even the least mystical of you must by this time be convinced of the existence of mystical moments as states of consciousness of an entirely specific quality, and of the deep impression which they make on those who have them. A Canadian psychiatrist, Dr. R. M. Bucke, gives to the more distinctly characterized of these phenomena the name of cosmic consciousness. "Cosmic consciousness in its more striking instances is not," Dr. Bucke says, " simply an expansion or extension of the self-conscious mind with which we are all familiar, but the superaddition of a function as distinct from any possessed by the average man as *self*-consciousness is distinct from any function possessed by one of the higher animals."

The prime characteristic of cosmic consciousness is a consciousness of the cosmos, that is, of the life and order of the universe. Along with the consciousness of the cosmos there occurs an intellectual enlightenment which alone would place the individual on a new

---

[10] *My Quest for God* (London, 1897), pp. 268–69.—w.j.
[11] *Ibid.*, pp. 256–57.—w.j.

plane of existence—would make him almost a member of a new species. To this is added a state of moral exaltation, an indescribable feeling of elevation, elation, and joyousness, and a quickening of the moral sense, which is fully as striking, and more important than is the enhanced intellectual power. With these come what may be called a sense of immortality, a consciousness of eternal life, not a conviction that he shall have this, but the consciousness that he has it already.[12]

It was Dr. Bucke's own experience of a typical onset of cosmic consciousness in his own person which led him to investigate it in others. He has printed his conclusions in a highly interesting volume, from which I take the following account of what occurred to him:

I had spent the evening in a great city, with two friends, reading and discussing poetry and philosophy. We parted at midnight. I had a long drive in a hansom to my lodging. My mind, deeply under the influence of the ideas, images, and emotions called up by the reading and talk, was calm and peaceful. I was in a state of quiet, almost passive enjoyment, not actually thinking, but letting ideas, images, and emotions flow of themselves, as it were, through my mind. All at once, without warning of any kind, I found myself wrapped in a flame-colored cloud. For an instant I thought of fire, an immense conflagration somewhere close by in that great city; the next, I knew that the fire was within myself. Directly afterward there came upon me a sense of exultation, of immense joyousness accompanied or immediately followed by an intellectual illumination impossible to describe. Among other things, I did not merely come to believe, but I saw that the universe is not composed of dead matter, but is, on the contrary, a living Presence; I became conscious in myself of eternal life. It was not a conviction that I would have eternal life, but a consciousness that I possessed eternal life then; I saw that all men are immortal; that the cosmic order is such that without any peradventure all things work together for the good of each and all; that the foundation principle of the world, of all the worlds, is what we call love, and that the happiness of each and all is in the long run absolutely certain. The vision lasted a few seconds and was gone; but the memory of it and the sense of the reality of what it taught has remained during the quarter of a century which has since elapsed. I knew that what the vision showed was true. I had attained to a point of view from which I saw that it must be true. That view, that conviction, I may say that consciousness, has never, even during periods of the deepest depression, been lost.[13]

· IV ·

We have now seen enough of this cosmic or mystic consciousness, as it comes sporadically. We must next pass to its methodical cultivation as an element of the religious life. Hindus, Buddhists, Mohammedans, and Christians all have cultivated it methodically.

In India, training in mystical insight has been known from time immemorial under the name of yoga. Yoga means the experimental union of the individual with the divine. It is based on persevering exercise; and the diet, posture, breathing, intellectual concentration, and moral discipline vary slightly in the different systems which teach it. The yogi, or disciple, who has by these means overcome the obscurations of his lower

---

[12] *Cosmic Consciousness: A Study in the Evolution of the Human Mind* (Philadelphia, 1901), p. 2.—w.j.
[13] *Ibid.*, pp. 7–8.—w.j.

nature sufficiently, enters into the condition termed *samadhi*, "and comes face to face with facts which no instinct or reason can ever know." He learns —

> That the mind itself has a higher state of existence, beyond reason, a superconscious state, and that when the mind gets to that higher state, then this knowledge beyond reasoning comes. . . . All the different steps in yoga are intended to bring us scientifically to the superconscious state or samadhi. . . . Just as unconscious work is beneath consciousness, so there is another work which is above consciousness, and which, also, is not accompanied with the feeling of egoism. . . . There is no feeling of *I*, and yet the mind works, desireless, free from effulgence, and we know ourselves—for samadhi lies potential in us all—for what we truly are, free, immortal, omnipotent, loosed from the finite, and its contrasts of good and evil altogether, and identical with the Atman or Universal Soul.[14]

The Vedantists say that one may stumble into superconsciousness sporadically, without the previous discipline, but it is then impure. Their test of its purity, like our test of religion's value, is empirical: its fruits must be good for life. When a man comes out of samadhi, they assure us that he remains "enlightened, a sage, a prophet, a saint, his whole character changed, his life changed, illumined."

The Buddhists use the word "samadhi" as well as the Hindus; but "dhyana" is their special word for higher states of contemplation. There seem to be four stages recognized in dhyana. The first stage comes through concentration of the mind upon one point. It excludes desire, but not discernment or judgment: it is still intellectual. In the second stage the intellectual functions drop off, and the satisfied sense of unity remains. In the third stage the satisfaction departs, and indifference begins, along with memory and self-consciousness. In the fourth stage the indifference, memory, and self-consciousness are perfected. (Just what "memory" and "self-consciousness" mean in this connection is doubtful. They cannot be the faculties familiar to us in the lower life.) Higher stages still of contemplation are mentioned—a region where there exists nothing, and where the meditator says: "There exists absolutely nothing," and stops. Then he reaches another region where he says: "There are neither ideas nor absence of ideas," and stops again. Then another region where, "having reached the end of both idea and perception, he stops finally." This would seem to be, not yet Nirvana, but as close an approach to it as this life affords.[15]

In the Mohammedan world the Sufi sect and various dervish bodies are the possessors of the mystical tradition. The Sufis have existed in Persia from the earliest times, and as their pantheism is so at variance with the hot and rigid monotheism of the Arab mind, it has been suggested that Sufism must have been inoculated into Islam by Hindu influences. We Christians know little of Sufism, for its secrets are disclosed only to those initiated. To give its existence a certain liveliness in your minds, I will quote a Moslem document, and pass away from the subject.

Al-Ghazzali, a Persian philosopher and theologian, who flourished in the eleventh century, and ranks as one of the greatest doctors of the Moslem church, has left us one

---

[14] My quotations are from Vivekananda, *Raja Yoga* (London, 1896). The completest source of information on Yoga is the work translated by Vihari Lala Mitra, *Yoga Vasishta Maha Ramayana*, 4 vols. (Calcutta, 1891–1899).—W.J.

[15] I follow the account in C. F. Koeppen, *Die Religion des Buddha* (Berlin, 1857), Vol. I, 585 ff.—W.J.

of the few autobiographies to be found outside of Christian literature. Strange that a species of book so abundant among ourselves should be so little represented elsewhere—the absence of strictly personal confessions is the chief difficulty to the purely literary student who would like to become acquainted with the inwardness of religions other than the Christian.

M. Schmölders has translated a part of Al-Ghazzali's autobiography into French:

The Science of the Sufis aims at detaching the heart from all that is not God, and at giving to it for sole occupation the meditation of the divine being. Theory being more easy for me than practice, I read [certain books] until I understood all that can be learned by study and hearsay. Then I recognized that what pertains most exclusively to their method is just what no study can grasp, but only transport, ecstasy, and the transformation of the soul. How great, for example, is the difference between knowing the definitions of health, of satiety, with their causes and conditions, and being really healthy or filled. How different to know in what drunkenness consists—as being a state occasioned by a vapor that rises from the stomach—and *being* drunk effectively. Without doubt, the drunken man knows neither the definition of drunkenness nor what makes it interesting for science. Being drunk, he knows nothing; whilst the physician, although not drunk, knows well in what drunkenness consists, and what are its predisposing conditions. Similarly there is a difference between knowing the nature of abstinence, and *being* abstinent or having one's soul detached from the world. Thus I had learned what words could teach of Sufism, but what was left could be learned neither by study nor through the ears, but solely by giving oneself up to ecstasy and leading a pious life.

Reflecting on my situation, I found myself tied down by a multitude of bonds—temptations on every side. Considering my teaching, I found it was impure before God. I saw myself struggling with all my might to achieve glory and to spread my name. [Here follows an account of his six months' hesitation to break away from the conditions of his life at Baghdad, at the end of which he fell ill with a paralysis of the tongue.] Then, feeling my own weakness, and having entirely given up my own will, I repaired to God like a man in distress who has no more resources. He answered, as he answers the wretch who invokes him. My heart no longer felt any difficulty in renouncing glory, wealth, and my children. So I quitted Baghdad, and reserving from my fortune only what was indispensable for my subsistence, I distributed the rest. I went to Syria, where I remained about two years, with no other occupation than living in retreat and solitude, conquering my desires, combating my passions, training myself to purify my soul, to make my character perfect, to prepare my heart for meditating on God—all according to the methods of the Sufis, as I had read of them.

This retreat only increased my desire to live in solitude, and to complete the purification of my heart and fit it for meditation. But the vicissitudes of the times, the affairs of the family, the need of subsistence, changed in some respects my primitive resolve, and interfered with my plans for a purely solitary life. I had never yet found myself completely in ecstasy, save in a few single hours; nevertheless, I kept the hope of attaining this state. Every time that the accidents led me astray, I sought to return; and in this situation I spent ten years. During this solitary state things were revealed to me which it is impossible either to describe or to point out. I recognized for certain that the Sufis are assuredly walking in the path of God. Both in their acts and in their inaction, whether internal or external, they are illumined by the light which proceeds from the prophetic source. The first condition for a Sufi is to purge his heart entirely of all that is not God. The next key of the contemplative life consists in the humble prayers which escape from the fervent soul, and in the meditations on God in which the heart is swallowed up entirely. But in reality this is only the beginning of the Sufi life, the end of Sufism being total absorption in God. The intuitions and all that precede are, so to speak, only the threshold for those who enter. From the beginning, revelations take place in so flagrant a shape that the Sufis see before them, whilst wide awake, the angels and the souls of the prophets. They hear their voices and obtain their favors. Then the transport rises from the perception of forms and figures to a degree which escapes all expression, and which no man may seek to give an account of without his words involving sin.

Whoever has had no experience of the transport knows of the true nature of prophetism nothing but the name. He may meanwhile be sure of its existence, both by experience and by what he hears the Sufis say. As there are men endowed only with the sensitive faculty who reject what is offered them in the way of objects of the pure understanding, so there are intellectual men who reject and avoid the things perceived by the prophetic faculty. A blind man can understand nothing of colors save what he has learned by narration and hearsay. Yet God has brought prophetism near to men in giving them all a state analogous to it in its principal characters. This state is sleep. If you were to tell a man who was himself without experience of such a phenomenon that there are people who at times swoon away so as to resemble dead men, and who [in dreams] yet perceive things that are hidden, he would deny it [and give his reasons]. Nevertheless, his arguments would be refuted by actual experience. Wherefore, just as the understanding is a stage of human life in which an eye opens to discern various intellectual objects uncomprehended by sensation; just so in the prophetic the sight is illumined by a light which uncovers hidden things and objects which the intellect fails to reach. The chief properties of prophetism are perceptible only during the transport, by those who embrace the Sufi life. The prophet is endowed with qualities to which you possess nothing analogous, and which consequently you cannot possibly understand. How should you know their true nature, since one knows only what one can comprehend? But the transport which one attains by the method of the Sufis is like an immediate perception, as if one touched the objects with one's hand.[16]

This incommunicableness of the transport is the keynote of all mysticism. Mystical truth exists for the individual who has the transport, but for no one else. In this, as I have said, it resembles the knowledge given to us in sensations more than that given by conceptual thought. Thought, with its remoteness and abstractness, has often enough in the history of philosophy been contrasted unfavorably with sensation. It is a commonplace of metaphysics that God's knowledge cannot be discursive but must be intuitive, that is, must be constructed more after the pattern of what in ourselves is called immediate feeling, than after that of proposition and judgment. But *our* immediate feelings have no content but what the five senses supply; and we have seen and shall see again that mystics may emphatically deny that the senses play any part in the very highest type of knowledge which their transports yield.

· V ·

In the Christian church there have always been mystics. Although many of them have been viewed with suspicion, some have gained favor in the eyes of the authorities. The experiences of these have been treated as precedents, and a codified system of mystical theology has been based upon them, in which everything legitimate finds its place. The basis of the system is "orison" or meditation, the methodical elevation of the soul towards God. Through the practice of orison the higher levels of mystical experience may be attained. It is odd that Protestantism, especially evangelical Protestantism, should seemingly have abandoned everything methodical in this line. Apart from what prayer

---

[16] A. Schmölders, *Essai sur les écoles philosophiques chez les Arabes* (Paris, 1842), pp. 54–68, abridged.—W.J.

may lead to, Protestant mystical experience appears to have been almost exclusively sporadic. It has been left to our mind-curers to reintroduce methodical meditation into our religious life.

The first thing to be aimed at in orison is the mind's detachment from outer sensations, for these interfere with its concentration upon ideal things. Such manuals as Saint Ignatius' *Spiritual Exercises* recommend the disciple to expel sensations by a graduated series of efforts to imagine holy scenes. The acme of this kind of discipline would be a semi-hallucinatory mono-ideism—an imaginary figure of Christ, for example, coming fully to occupy the mind. Sensorial images of this sort, whether literal or symbolic, play an enormous part in mysticism. But in certain cases imagery may fall away entirely, and in the very highest raptures it tends to do so. The state of consciousness becomes then insusceptible of any verbal description. Mystical teachers are unanimous as to this. Saint John of the Cross, for instance, one of the best of them, thus describes the condition called the "union of love," which, he says, is reached by "dark contemplation." In this the Deity compenetrates the soul, but in such a hidden way that the soul —

> . . . finds no terms, no means, no comparison whereby to render the sublimity of the wisdom and the delicacy of the spiritual feeling with which she is filled. . . . We receive this mystical knowledge of God clothed in none of the kinds of images, in none of the sensible representations, which our mind makes use of in other circumstances. Accordingly in this knowledge, since the sense and the imagination are not employed, we get neither form not impression, nor can we give any account or furnish any likeness, although the mysterious and sweet-tasting wisdom comes home so clearly to the inmost parts of our soul. Fancy a man seeing a certain kind of thing for the first time in his life. He can understand it, use and enjoy it, but he cannot apply a name to it, nor communicate any idea of it, even though all the while it be a mere thing of sense. How much greater will be his powerlessness when it goes beyond the senses! This is the peculiarity of the divine language. The more infused, intimate, spiritual, and supersensible it is, the more does it exceed the senses, both inner and outer, and impose silence upon them. . . . The soul then feels as if placed in a vast and profound solitude, to which no created thing has access, in an immense and boundless desert, desert the more delicious the more solitary it is. There, in this abyss of wisdom, the soul grows by what it drinks in from the well-springs of the comprehension of love, . . . and recognizes, however sublime and learned may be the terms we employ, how utterly vile, insignificant, and improper they are, when we seek to discourse of divine things by their means.[17]

I cannot pretend to detail to you the sundry stages of the Christian mystical life. Our time would not suffice, for one thing; and moreover, I confess that the subdivisions and names which we find in the Catholic books seem to me to represent nothing objectively distinct. So many men, so many minds: I imagine that these experiences can be as infinitely varied as are the idiosyncrasies of individuals.

The cognitive aspects of them, their value in the way of revelation, is what we are directly concerned with, and it is easy to show by citation how strong an impression they leave of being revelations of new depths of truth. Saint Teresa is the expert of experts in describing such conditions, so I will turn immediately to what she says of one of the highest of them, the "orison of union."

---

[17] Saint John of the Cross, *The Dark Night of the Soul*, Bk. II, Chap. 17, in *Vie et Œuvres*, 3rd ed. (Paris, 1893), pp. 428-32.—w.j.

In the orison of union, the soul is fully awake as regards God, but wholly asleep as regards things of this world and in respect of herself. During the short time the union lasts, she is as it were deprived of every feeling, and even if she would, she could not think of any single thing. Thus she needs to employ no artifice in order to arrest the use of her understanding: it remains so stricken with inactivity that she neither knows what she loves, nor in what manner she loves, nor what she wills. In short, she is utterly dead to the things of the world and lives solely in God. . . . I do not even know whether in this state she has enough life left to breathe. It seems to me she has not; or at least that if she does breathe, she is unaware of it. Her intellect would fain understand something of what is going on within her, but it has so little force now that it can act in no way whatsoever. So a person who falls into a deep faint appears as if dead. . . .

Thus does God, when he raises a soul to union with himself, suspend the natural action of all her faculties. She neither sees, hears, nor understands, so long as she is united with God. But this time is always short, and it seems even shorter than it is. God establishes himself in the interior of this soul in such a way, that when she returns to herself, it is wholly impossible for her to doubt that she has been in God, and God in her. This truth remains so strongly impressed on her that, even though many years should pass without the condition returning, she can neither forget the favor she received, nor doubt of its reality. If you, nevertheless, ask how it is possible that the soul can see and understand that she has been in God, since during the union she has neither sight nor understanding, I reply that she does not see it then, but that she sees it clearly later, after she has returned to herself, not by any vision, but by a certitude which abides with her and which God alone can give her. I knew a person who was ignorant of the truth that God's mode of being in everything must be either by presence, by power, or by essence, but who, after having received the grace of which I am speaking, believed this truth in the most unshakable manner. So much so that, having consulted a half-learned man who was as ignorant on this point as she had been before she was enlightened, when he replied that God is in us only by "grace," she disbelieved his reply, so sure she was of the true answer; and when she came to ask wiser doctors, they confirmed her in her belief, which much consoled her. . . .

But how, you will repeat, *can* one have such certainty in respect to what one does not see? This question, I am powerless to answer. These are secrets of God's omnipotence which it does not appertain to me to penetrate. All that I know is that I tell the truth; and I shall never believe that any soul who does not possess this certainty has ever been really united to God.[18]

The kinds of truth communicable in mystical ways, whether these be sensible or supersensible, are various. Some of them relate to this world—visions of the future, the reading of hearts, the sudden understanding of texts, the knowledge of distant events, for example—but the most important revelations are theological or metaphysical.

Saint Ignatius confessed one day to Father Laynez that a single hour of meditation at Manresa had taught him more truths about heavenly things than all the teachings of all the doctors put together could have taught him. . . . One day in orison, on the steps of the choir of the Dominican church, he saw in a distinct manner the plan of divine wisdom in the creation of the world. On another occasion, during a procession, his spirit was ravished in God, and it was given him to contemplate, in a form and images fitted to the weak understanding of a dweller on the earth, the deep mystery of the holy Trinity. This

---

[18] *The Interior Castle*, Fifth Abode, Chap. 1, in *Œuvres*, translated by Bouix, pp. 421–24.—W.J.

last vision flooded his heart with such sweetness, that the mere memory of it in after times made him shed abundant tears.[19]

Similarly with Saint Teresa. "One day, being in orison," she writes, "it was granted me to perceive in one instant how all things are seen and contained in God. I did not perceive them in their proper form, and nevertheless the view I had of them was of a sovereign clearness, and has remained vividly impressed upon my soul. It is one of the most signal of all the graces which the Lord has granted me. . . . The view was so subtle and delicate that the understanding cannot grasp it.[20]

She goes on to tell how it was as if the Deity were an enormous and sovereignly limpid diamond, in which all our actions were contained in such a way that their full sinfulness appeared evident as never before. On another day, she relates, while she was reciting the Athanasian Creed—

> Our Lord made me comprehend in what way it is that one God can be in three Persons. He made me see it so clearly that I remained as extremely surprised as I was comforted, . . . and now, when I think of the holy Trinity, or hear It spoken of, I understand how the three adorable Persons form only one God and I experience an unspeakable happiness.

On still another occasion, it was given to Saint Teresa to see and understand in what wise the Mother of God had been assumed into her place in Heaven.[21]

The deliciousness of some of these states seems to be beyond anything known in ordinary consciousness. It evidently involves organic sensibilities, for it is spoken of as something too extreme to be borne, and as verging on bodily pain. But it is too subtle and piercing a delight for ordinary words to denote. God's touches, the wounds of his spear, references to ebriety and to nuptial union have to figure in the phraseology by which it is shadowed forth. Intellect and sense both swoon away in these highest states of ecstasy. "If our understanding comprehends," says Saint Teresa, "it is in a mode which remains unknown to it, and it can understand nothing of what it comprehends. For my own part, I do not believe that it does comprehend, because, as I said, it does not understand itself to do so. I confess that it is all a mystery in which I am lost."[22] In the condition called *raptus* or ravishment by theologians, breathing and circulation are so depressed that it is a question among the doctors whether the soul be or be not temporarily dissevered from the body. One must read Saint Teresa's descriptions and the very exact distinctions which she makes, to persuade oneself that one is dealing, not with imaginary experiences, but with phenomena which, however rare, follow perfectly definite psychological types.

· VI ·

To the medical mind these ecstasies signify nothing but suggested and imitated hypnoid states, on an intellectual basis of superstition, and a corporeal one of degeneration and hysteria. Undoubtedly these pathological conditions have existed in many and possibly

---

[19] Bartoli-Michel, *Vie de Saint Ignace of Loyola*, pp. 34–36.—w.j.

[20] *Vie*, pp. 581–82.—w.j.

[21] *Ibid.*, p. 574.—w.j.

[22] *Ibid.*, p. 198.—w.j.

in all the cases, but that fact tells us nothing about the value for knowledge of the consciousness which they induce. To pass a spiritual judgment upon these states, we must not content ourselves with superficial medical talk, but inquire into their fruits for life.

Their fruits appear to have been various. Stupefaction, for one thing, seems not to have been altogether absent as a result. . . . Many . . . ecstatics would have perished but for the care taken of them by admiring followers. The "other-worldliness" encouraged by the mystical consciousness makes this over-abstraction from practical life peculiarly liable to befall mystics in whom the character is naturally passive and the intellect feeble; but in natively strong minds and characters we find quite opposite results. The great Spanish mystics, who carried the habit of ecstasy as far as it has often been carried, appear for the most part to have shown indomitable spirit and energy, and all the more so for the trances in which they indulged.

Saint Ignatius was a mystic, but his mysticism made him assuredly one of the most powerfully practical human engines that ever lived. Saint John of the Cross, writing of the intuitions and "touches" by which God reaches the substance of the soul, tells us that —

> They enrich it marvelously. A single one of them may be sufficient to abolish at a stroke certain imperfections of which the soul during its whole life had vainly tried to rid itself, and to leave it adorned with virtues and loaded with supernatural gifts. A single one of these intoxicating consolations may reward it for all the labors undergone in its life— even were they numberless. Invested with an invincible courage, filled with an impassioned desire to suffer for its God, the soul then is seized with a strange torment—that of not being allowed to suffer enough.[23]

Saint Teresa is as emphatic, and much more detailed. . . . Where in literature is a more evidently veracious account of the formation of a new centre of spiritual energy, than is given in her description of the effects of certain ecstasies which in departing leave the soul upon a higher level of emotional excitement?

> Often, infirm and wrought upon with dreadful pains before the ecstasy, the soul emerges from it full of health and admirably disposed for action . . . as if God had willed that the body itself, already obedient to the soul's desires, should share in the soul's happiness. . . . The soul after such a favor is animated with a degree of courage so great that if at that moment its body should be torn to pieces for the cause of God, it would feel nothing but the liveliest comfort. Then it is that promises and heroic resolutions spring up in profusion in us, soaring desires, horror of the world, and the clear perception of our proper nothingness. . . . What empire is comparable to that of a soul who, from this sublime summit to which God has raised her, sees all the things of earth beneath her feet, and is captivated by no one of them? How ashamed she is of her former attachments! How amazed at her blindness! What lively pity she feels for those whom she recognizes still shrouded in the darkness! . . . She groans at having ever been sensitive to points of honor, at the illusion that made her ever see as honor what the world calls by that name. Now she sees in this name nothing more than an immense lie of which the world remains a victim. She discovers, in the new light from above, that in genuine honor there is nothing spurious, that to be faithful to this honor is to give our respect to what deserves to be respected really, and to consider as nothing, or as less than nothing, whatsoever perishes and is not agreeable to God. . . . She laughs when she sees grave person, persons of orison, caring for points of honor for which she now feels profoundest contempt. It

---

[23] *Œuvres, op. cit.*, p. 320.—W.J.

is suitable to the dignity of their rank to act thus, they pretend, and it makes them more useful to others. But she knows that in despising the dignity of their rank for the pure love of God they would do more good in a single day than they would effect in ten years by preserving it. . . . She laughs at herself that there should ever have been a time in her life when she made any case of money, when she ever desired it. . . . Oh! if human beings might only agree together to regard it as so much useless mud, what harmony would then reign in the world! With what friendship we would all treat each other if our interest in honor and in money could but disappear from earth! For my own part, I feel as if it would be a remedy for all our ills.[24]

· VII ·

Mystical conditions may, therefore, render the soul more energetic in the lines which their inspiration favors. But this could be reckoned an advantage only in case the inspiration were a true one. If the inspiration were erroneous, the energy would be all the more mistaken and misbegotten. So we stand once more before that problem of truth which confronted us at the end of the lectures on saintliness. You will remember that we turned to mysticism precisely to get some light on truth. Do mystical states establish the truth of those theological affections in which the saintly life has its root?

In spite of their repudiation of articulate self-description, mystical states in general assert a pretty distinct theoretic drift. It is possible to give the outcome of the majority of them in terms that point in definite philosophical directions. One of these directions is optimism, and the other is monism. We pass into mystical states from out of ordinary consciousness as from a less into a more, as from a smallness into a vastness, and at the same time as from an unrest to a rest. We feel them as reconciling, unifying states. They appeal to the yes-function more than to the no-function in us. In them the unlimited absorbs the limits and peacefully closes the account. Their very denial of every adjective you may propose as applicable to the ultimate truth—He, the Self, the Atman, is to be described by "No! no!" only, say the Upanishads[25]—though it seems on the surface to be a no-function, is a denial made on behalf of a deeper yes. Whoso calls the Absolute anything in particular, or says that it is *this*, seems implicitly to shut it off from being *that*—it is as if he lessened it. So we deny the "this," negating the negation which it seems to us to imply, in the interests of the higher affirmative attitude by which we are possessed. The fountainhead of Christian mysticism is Dionysius the Areopagite. He describes the absolute truth by negatives exclusively.

> The cause of all things is neither soul nor intellect; nor has it imagination, opinion, or reason, or intelligence; nor is it reason or intelligence; nor is it spoken or thought. It is neither number, nor order, nor magnitude, nor littleness, nor equality, nor inequality, nor similarity, nor dissimilarity. It neither stands, nor moves, nor rests. . . . It is neither essence, nor eternity, nor time. Even intellectual contact does not belong to it. It is neither science nor truth. It is not even royalty or wisdom; not one; not unity; not divinity or goodness; nor even spirit as we know it. . . .[26]

---

[24] *Vie, op. cit.*, pp. 200, 229, 231–33, 243.—w.j.

[25] Müller's translation, Part II, p. 180.—w.j.

[26] T. Davidson's translation, in *Journal of Speculative Philosophy* (1893), Vol. XXII, 339.—w.j.

But these qualifications are denied by Dionysius, not because the truth falls short of them, but because it so infinitely excels them. It is above them. It is *super*-lucent, *super*-splendent, *super*-essential, *super*-sublime, *super* everything that can be named. Like Hegel in his logic, mystics journey towards the positive pole of truth only by the *Methode der Absoluten Negativität.*[27]

Thus come the paradoxical expressions that so abound in mystical writings. As when Eckhart tells of the still desert of the Godhead, "where never was seen difference, neither Father, Son, nor Holy Ghost, where there is no one at home, yet where that spark of the soul is more at peace than in itself."[28] As when Boehme writes of the Primal Love, that "it may fitly be compared to Nothing, for it is deeper than any Thing, and is as nothing with respect to all things, forasmuch as it is not comprehensible by any of them. And because it is nothing respectively, it is therefore free from all things, and is that only good, which a man cannot express or utter what it is, there being nothing to which it may be compared, to express it by."[29] Or as when Angelus Silesius sings:

> *Gott ist ein lauter Nichts, ihn rührt kein Nun noch Hier;*
> *je mehr du nach ihm greifst, je mehr entwind er dir.*[30]

To this dialectical use, by the intellect, of negation as a mode of passage towards a higher kind of affirmation, there is correlated the subtlest of moral counterparts in the sphere of the personal will. Since denial of the finite self and its wants, since asceticism of some sort, is found in religious experience to be the only doorway to the larger and more blessed life, this moral mystery intertwines and combines with the intellectual mystery in all mystical writings.

> Love [is Nothing, for] when thou art gone forth wholly from the Creature and from that which is visible, and art become Nothing to all that is Nature and Creature, then thou art in that eternal One, which is God himself, and then thou shalt feel within thee the highest virtue of Love. . . . The treasure of treasures for the soul is where she goeth out of the Somewhat into that Nothing out of which all things may be made. The soul here saith, *I have nothing*, for I am utterly stripped and naked; *I can do nothing*, for I have no manner of power, but am as water poured out; *I am nothing*, for all that I am is no more than an image of Being, and only God is to me I AM; and so, sitting down in my own Nothingness, I give glory to the eternal Being, and *will nothing* of myself, that so God may will all in me, being unto me my God and all things.[31]

In Paul's language, I live, yet not I, but Christ liveth in me. Only when I become as nothing can God enter in and no difference between his life and mine remain outstanding.

This overcoming of all the usual barriers between the individual and the Absolute is the great mystic achievement. In mystic states we both become one with the Absolute

---

[27] The method of absolute negation.—E.D.K.

[28] J. Royce, *Studies in Good and Evil*, p. 282.—W.J.

[29] Jacob Behmen, *Dialogues on the Supersensual Life*, translated by Bernard Holland, London, 1901, p. 48.—W.J.

[30] *Cherubinischer Wandersmann*, Strophe 25. [God is a mere Nothing, no now or here touches Him; the more you grasp at Him the more He evades you.]—W.J.

[31] *Op. cit.*, pp. 42, 74.—W.J.

and we become aware of our oneness. This is the everlasting and triumphant mystical tradition, hardly altered by differences of clime or creed. In Hinduism, in Neoplatonism, in Sufism, in Christian mysticism, in Whitmanism, we find the same recurring note, so that there is about mystical utterances an eternal unanimity which ought to make a critic stop and think, and which brings it about that the mystical classics have, as has been said, neither birthday nor native land. Perpetually telling of the unity of man with God, their speech antedates languages, and they do not grow old.

"That art Thou!" say the Upanishads, and the Vedantists add: "Not a part, not a mode of That, but identically That, that absolute Spirit of the World." "As pure water poured into pure water remains the same, thus, O Gautama, is the Self of a thinker who knows. Water in water, fire in fire, ether in ether, no one can distinguish them; likewise a man whose mind has entered into the Self."[32] "Every man," says the Sufi Gulshan-Raz, "whose heart is no longer shaken by any doubt, knows with certainty that there is no being save only One. . . . In his divine majesty the *me*, the *we*, the *thou*, are not found, for in the One there can be no distinction. Every being who is annulled and entirely separated from himself, hears resound outside of him this voice and this echo: *I am God*: he has an eternal way of existing, and is no longer subject to death."[33] In the vision of God, says Plotinus, "what sees is not our reason, but something prior and superior to our reason. . . . He who thus sees does not properly see, does not distinguish or imagine two things. He changes, he ceases to be himself, preserves nothing of himself. Absorbed in God, he makes but one with him, like a centre of a circle coinciding with another centre."[34] "Here," writes Suso, "the spirit dies, and yet is all alive in the marvels of the Godhead . . . and is lost in the stillness of the glorious dazzling obscurity and of the naked simple unity. It is in this modeless *where* that the highest bliss is to be found."[35] *"Ich bin so gross als Gott,"* sings Angelus Silesius again, *"Er ist als ich so klein; Er kann nicht über mich, ich unter ihm nicht sein."*[36]

In mystical literature such self-contradictory phrases as "dazzling obscurity," "whispering silence," "teeming desert," are continually met with. They prove that not conceptual speech, but music rather, is the element through which we are best spoken to by mystical truth. Many mystical scriptures are indeed little more than musical compositions.

> He who would hear the voice of Nada, "the Soundless Sound," and comprehend it, he has to learn the nature of Dharana. . . . When to himself his form appears unreal, as do on waking all the forms he sees in dreams; when he has ceased to hear the many, he may discern the ONE—the inner sound which kills the outer. . . . For then the soul will hear, and will remember. And then to the inner ear will SPEAK THE VOICE OF THE SILENCE. . . . And now thy *Self* is lost in SELF, *thyself* unto THYSELF, merged in that SELF from which thou first didst radiate. . . . Behold! thou has become the Light, thou hast become the

---

[32] *Upanishads, op. cit.,* pp. 17, 334.—W.J.

[33] Schmölders, *op. cit.,* p. 210—W.J.

[34] *Enneads,* Bouillier's translation, Paris, 1861, Vol. III, 561. Compare pp. 473–77, and Vol. I, 27.—W.J.

[35] *Autobiography,* pp. 309–10.—W.J.

[36] *Op. cit.,* Strophe 10 [I am as great as God. He is as small as me; He cannot exceed me, nor am I beneath Him].—W.J.

Sound, thou art thy Master and thy God. Thou art THYSELF the object of thy search: the VOICE unbroken, that resounds throughout eternities, exempt from change, from sin exempt, the seven sounds in one, the VOICE OF THE SILENCE. *Om tat Sat.*[37]

These words, if they do not awaken laughter as you receive them, probably stir chords within you which music and language touch in common. Music gives us ontological messages which non-musical criticism is unable to contradict, though it may laugh at our foolishness in minding them. There is a verge of the mind which these things haunt; and whispers therefrom mingle with the operations of our understanding, even as the waters of the infinite ocean send their waves to break among the pebbles that lie upon our shores.

Here begins the sea that ends not till the world's end. Where we stand,
Could we know the next high sea-mark set beyond these waves that gleam,
We should know what never man hath known, nor eye of man hath scanned. . . .
Ah, but here man's heart leaps, yearning towards the gloom with venturous glee,
From the shore that hath no shore beyond it, set in all the sea.[38]

That doctrine, for example, that eternity is timeless, that our "immortality," if we live in the eternal, is not so much future as already now and here, which we find so often expressed today in certain philosophic circles, finds its support in a "hear, hear!" or an "amen," which floats up from that mysteriously deeper level. We recognize the passwords to the mystical region as we hear them, but we cannot use them ourselves; it alone has the keeping of "the password primeval."

I have now sketched with extreme brevity and insufficiency, but as fairly as I am able in the time allowed, the general traits of the mystic range of consciousness. *It is on the whole pantheistic and optimistic, or at least the opposite of pessimistic. It is anti-naturalistic, and harmonizes best with twice-bornness and so-called other-worldly states of mind.*

· VIII ·

My next task is to inquire whether we can invoke it as authoritative. Does it furnish any *warrant for the truth* of the twice-bornness and super-naturality and pantheism which it favors? I must give my answer to this question as concisely as I can.

In brief my answer is this—and I will divide it into three parts:

1. Mystical states, when well developed, usually are, and have the right to be, absolutely authoritative over the individuals to whom they come.

2. No authority emanates from them which should make it a duty for those who stand outside of them to accept their revelations uncritically.

3. They break down the authority of the non-mystical or rationalistic consciousness, based upon the understanding and the senses alone. They show it to be only one kind of consciousness. They open out the possibility of other orders of truth, in which, so far as anything in us vitally responds to them, we may freely continue to have faith.

---

[37] H. P. Blavatsky, *The Voice of the Silence.*—W.J.
[38] Swinburne, "On the Verge," in *A Midsummer Vacation.*—W.J.

I will take up these points one by one.

1. As a matter of psychological fact, mystical states of a well-pronounced and emphatic sort *are* usually authoritative over those who have them. They have been "there," and know. It is vain for rationalism to grumble about this. If the mystical truth that comes to a man proves to be a force that he can live by, what mandate have we of the majority to order him to live in another way? We can throw him into a prison or a madhouse, but we cannot change his mind—we commonly attach it only the more stubbornly to its beliefs. It mocks our utmost efforts, as a matter of fact, and in point of logic it absolutely escapes our jurisdiction. Our own more "rational" beliefs are based on evidence exactly similar in nature to that which mystics quote for theirs. Our senses, namely, have assured us of certain states of fact; but mystical experiences are as direct perceptions of fact for those who have them as any sensations ever were for us. The records show that even though the five senses be in abeyance in them, they are absolutely sensational in their epistemological quality, if I may be pardoned the barbarous expression—that is, they are face-to-face presentations of what seems immediately to exist.

The mystic is, in short, *invulnerable*, and must be left, whether we relish it or not, in undisturbed enjoyment of his creed. Faith, says Tolstoy, is that by which men live. And faith state and mystic state are practically convertible terms.

2. But I now proceed to add that mystics have no right to claim that we ought to accept the deliverance of their peculiar experiences, if we are ourselves outsiders and feel no private call thereto. The utmost they can ever ask of us in this life is to admit that they establish a presumption. They form a consensus and have an unequivocal outcome; and it would be odd, mystics might say, if such a unanimous type of experience should prove to be altogether wrong. At bottom, however, this would only be an appeal to numbers, like the appeal of rationalism the other way; and the appeal to numbers has no logical force. If we acknowledge it, it is for "suggestive," not for logical reasons: we follow the majority because to do so suits our life.

But even this presumption from the unanimity of mystics is far from being strong. In characterizing mystic states as pantheistic, optimistic, etc., I am afraid I over-simplified the truth. I did so for expository reasons, and to keep the closer to the classic mystical tradition. The classic religious mysticism, it now must be confessed, is only a "privileged case." It is an *extract*, kept true to type by the selection of the fittest specimens and their preservation in "schools." It is carved out from a much larger mass; and if we take the larger mass as seriously as religious mysticism has historically taken itself, we find that the supposed unanimity largely disappears. To begin with, even religious mysticism itself, the kind that accumulates traditions and makes schools, is much less unanimous than I have allowed. It has been both ascetic and antinomianly self-indulgent within the Christian church. It is dualistic in Sankhya, and monistic in Vedanta philosophy. I called it pantheistic; but the great Spanish mystics are anything but pantheists. They are with few exception non-metaphysical minds, for whom "the category of personality" is absolute. The "union" of man with God is for them much more like an occasional miracle than like an original identity. How different again, apart from the happiness common to all, is the mysticism of Walt Whitman, Edward Carpenter, Richard Jefferies, and other naturalistic pantheists, from the more distinctively Christian sort. The fact is that the mystical feeling of enlargement, union, and emancipation has no specific intellectual content whatever of its own. It is capable of forming matrimonial alliances with material furnished by the most diverse philosophies and theologies, provided only they can find a place in their framework for its peculiar emotional mood. We have no right, therefore, to invoke its prestige as distinctively in favor of any special belief, such as that in absolute idealism, or in the absolute monistic identity, or in the absolute goodness, of the world. It is only relatively in favor of all these things—it passes out of common human consciousness in the direction in which they lie.

So much for religious mysticism proper. But more remains to be told, for religious mysticism is only one half of mysticism. The other half has no accumulated traditions except those which the textbooks on insanity supply. Open any one of these, and you will find abundant cases in which "mystical ideas" are cited as characteristic symptoms of enfeebled or deluded states of mind. In delusional insanity, paranoia, as they sometimes call it, we may have a *diabolical* mysticism, a sort of religious mysticism turned upside down. The same sense of ineffable importance in the smallest events, the same texts and words coming with new meanings, the same voices and visions and leadings and missions, the same controlling by extraneous powers; only this time the emotion is pessimistic: instead of consolations we have desolations; the meanings are dreadful; and the powers are enemies to life. It is evident that from the point of view of their psychological mechanism, the classic mysticism and these lower mysticisms spring from the same mental level, from that great subliminal or transmarginal region of which science is beginning to admit the existence, but of which so little is really known. That region contains every kind of matter: "seraph and snake" abide there side by side. To come from thence is no infallible credential. What comes must be sifted and tested, and run the gauntlet of confrontation with the total context of experience, just like what comes from the outer world of sense. Its value must be ascertained by empirical methods, so long as we are not mystics ourselves.

Once more, then, I repeat that non-mystics are under no obligation to acknowledge in mystical states a superior authority conferred on them by their intrinsic nature.

3. Yet, I repeat once more, the existence of mystical states absolutely overthrows the pretension of non-mystical states to be the sole and ultimate dictators of what we may believe. As a rule, mystical states merely add a supersensuous meaning to the ordinary outward data of consciousness. They are excitements like the emotions of love or ambition, gifts to our spirit by means of which facts already objectively before us fall into a new expressiveness and make a new connection with our active life. They do not contradict these facts as such, or deny anything that our senses have immediately seized. It is the rationalistic critic rather who plays the part of denier in the controversy, and his denials have no strength, for there never can be a state of facts to which new meaning may not truthfully be added, provided the mind ascend to a more enveloping point of view. It must always remain an open question whether mystical states may not possibly be such superior points of view, windows through which the mind looks out upon a more extensive and inclusive world. The difference of the views seen from the different mystical windows need not prevent us from entertaining this supposition. The wider world would in that case prove to have a mixed constitution like that of this world, that is all. It would have its celestial and its infernal regions, its tempting and its saving moments, its valid experiences and its counterfeit ones, just as our world has them; but it would be a wider world all the same. We should have to use its experiences by selecting and subordinating and substituting just as is our custom in this ordinary naturalistic

world; we should be liable to error just as we are now; yet the counting in of that wider world of meanings, and the serious dealing with it, might, in spite of all the perplexity, be indispensable stages in our approach to the final fullness of the truth.

· *IX* ·

In this shape, I think, we have to leave the subject. Mystical states indeed wield no authority due simply to their being mystical states. But the higher ones among them point in directions to which the religious sentiments even of non-mystical men incline. They tell of the supremacy of the ideal, of vastness, of union, of safety, and of rest. They offer us *hypotheses*, hypotheses which we may voluntarily ignore, but which as thinkers we cannot possible upset. The supernaturalism and optimism to which they would persuade us may, interpreted in one way or another, be after all the truest of insights into the meaning of this life. . . .

○ ○ ○ 7

The Teachings of the Mystics
W. T. Stace

(1.) A New Kind of Consciousness

IN HIS BOOK *The Varieties of Religious Experience* William James suggests, as a result of his psychological researches, that "our normal consciousness, rational consciousness as we call it, is but one special type of consciousness, whilst all about it, parted from it by the filmiest of screens, there lie potential forms of consciousness entirely different." This statement exactly fits mystical consciousness. It is entirely unlike our everyday consciousness and is wholly incommensurable with it. What are the fundamental characteristics or elements of our ordinary consciousness? We may think of it as being like a building with three floors. The ground floor consists of physical sensations—sights, sounds, smells, tastes, touch sensations, and organic sensations. The second floor consists of images, which we tend to think of as mental copies of sensations. The third floor is the level of the intellect, which is the faculty of concepts. On this floor we find abstract thinking and reasoning processes. This account of the mind may be open to cavil. Some philosophers think that colors, sounds, and so on, are not properly called "sensations"; others that images are not "copies" of sensations. These fine points, however, need not seriously concern us. Our account is sufficiently clear to indicate what we are referring to when we speak of sensations, images, and concepts as being the fundamental elements of the cognitive aspects of our ordinary consciousness. Arising out of these basic cognitive elements and dependent upon them are emotions, desires, and volitions. In order to have a name for it we may call this whole structure—including sensations, images, concepts, and their attendant desires, emotions, and volitions—our *sensory-intellectual consciousness.*

Now the mystical consciousness is quite different from this. It is not merely that it involves different kinds of sensation, thought, or feeling. We are told that some insects or animals can perceive ultraviolet color and infrared color; and that some animals can hear sounds which are inaudible to us; even that some creatures may have a sixth sense quite different from any of our five senses. These are all, no doubt, kinds of sensations different from any we have. But they are still sensations. And the mystical consciousness is destitute of any sensations at all. Nor does it contain any concepts or thoughts. It is not a sensory-intellectual consciousness at all. Accordingly, it cannot be described or analyzed in terms of any of the elements of the sensory-intellectual consciousness, with which it is wholly incommensurable.

This is the reason why mystics always say that their experiences are "ineffable." All words in all languages are the products of our sensory-intellectual consciousness and express or describe its elements or some combination of them. But as these elements (with the doubtful exception of emotions) are not found in the mystical consciousness, it is felt to be impossible to describe it in any words whatever. In spite of this the mystics do describe their experiences in roundabout ways, at the same time telling us that the words they use are inadequate. This raises a serious problem for the philosophy of mysticism, but it is not possible for us to dwell on it here.

The incommensurability of the mystical with the sensory-intellectual consciousness is also the ultimate reason why we have to exclude visions and voices, telepathy, precognition, and clairvoyance from the category of the mystical. Suppose someone sees a vision of the Virgin Mary. What he sees has shape, the shape of a woman, and color— white skin, blue raiment, a golden halo, and so on. But these are all images or sensations. They are therefore composed of elements of our sensory-intellectual consciousness. The same is true of voices. Or suppose one has a precognition of a neighbor's death. The components one is aware of—a dead man, a coffin, etc.—are composed of elements of our sensory-intellectual consciousness. The only difference is that these ordinary elements are arranged in unfamiliar patterns which we have come to think cannot occur, so that if they do occur they seem supernormal. Or the fact that such elements are combined in an unusual way so as to constitute the figure of a woman up in the clouds, perhaps surrounded by other humanlike figures with wings added to them—all this does not constitute a different *kind* of consciousness at all. And just as sensory elements of any sort are excluded from the mystical consciousness, so are conceptual elements. It is not that the thoughts in the mystical consciousness are different from those we are accustomed to. It does not include any thoughts at all. The mystic, of course, expresses thoughts about his experience after that experience is over, and he remembers it when he is back again in his sensory-intellectual consciousness. But there are no thoughts *in* the experience itself.

If anyone thinks that a kind of consciousness without either sensations, images, or thoughts, because it is totally unimaginable and inconceivable to most of us, cannot exist, he is surely being very stupid. He supposes that the possibilities of this vast universe are confined to what can be imagined and understood by the brains of average human insects who crawl on a minute speck of dust floating in illimitable space.

On the other hand, there is not the least reason to suppose that the mystical consciousness is miraculous or supernatural. No doubt it has, like our ordinary consciousness, been produced by the natural processes of evolution. Its existence in a few men is psychological fact of which there is abundant evidence. To deny or doubt that it exists as a psychological fact is not a reputable opinion. It is ignorance. Whether it has any value or significance beyond itself, and if so what—these, of course, are matters regarding which there can be legitimate differences of opinion. Owing to the comparative rarity of this kind of consciousness, it should no doubt be assigned to the sphere of abnormal psychology.

(2.) The Core of Mysticism

I shall, for the present, treat it as an hypothesis that although mystical experience may in certain respects have different characteristics in different parts of the world, in different ages, and in different cultures, there are nevertheless a number of fundamental common characteristics. I shall also assume that the agreements are more basic and important, the differences more superficial and relatively less important. This hypothesis can only be fully justified by an elaborate empirical survey of the descriptions of their experiences given by mystics and collected from all over the world. But I believe that enough of the evidence for it will appear in the following pages to convince any reasonable person.

The most important, the central characteristics in which all *fully developed* mystical experiences agree, and which in the last analysis is definitive of them and serves to mark them off from other kinds of experiences, is that they involve the apprehension of *an ultimate nonsensuous unity in all things*, a oneness or a One to which neither the senses nor the reason can penetrate. In other words, it entirely transcends our sensory-intellectual consciousness.

It should be carefully noted that only fully developed mystical experiences are necessarily apprehensive of the One. Many experiences have been recorded which lack this central feature but yet possess other mystical characteristics. These are borderline cases, which may be said to shade off from the central core of cases. They have to the central core the relation which some philosophers like to call "family resemblance."

We should also note that although at this stage of our exposition we speak of mystical experience as an apprehension *of* the Unity, the mystics of the Hindu and Buddhist cultures, as well as Plotinus and many others, generally insist that this is incorrect since it supposes a division between subject and object. We should rather say that the experience *is* the One. Thus Plotinus writes: "We should not speak of seeing, but instead of seen or seer, speak boldly of a simple Unity for in this seeing we neither distinguish nor are there two." But we will leave the development of this point till later. And often for convenience' sake we shall speak of the experience *of* the unity.

(3.) Extrovertive Mysticism

There appear to be two main distinguishable types of mystical experience, both of which may be found in all the higher cultures. One may be called extrovertive mystical experience, the other introvertive mystical experience. Both are apprehensions of the One, but they reach it in different ways. The extrovertive way looks outward and through the physical senses into the external world and finds the One there. The introvertive way turns inward, introspectively, and finds the One at the bottom of the self, at the bottom of the human personality. The latter far outweighs the former in importance both in the history of mysticism and in the history of human thought generally. The introvertive way is the major strand in the history of mysticism, the extrovertive way a minor strand. I shall only briefly refer to extrovertive mysticism and then pass on, and shall take introvertive mysticism as the main subject of this book.

The extrovertive mystic with his physical senses continues to perceive the same world of trees and hills and tables and chairs as the rest of us. But he sees these objects transfigured in such manner that the Unity shines through them. Because it includes ordinary sense perceptions, it only partially realizes the description given in section (1). For the full realization of this we have to wait for the introvertive experience. I will give two brief historical instances of extrovertive experience. The great Catholic mystic Meister Eckhart (circa 1260–1329) wrote as follows: "Here [i.e., in this experience] all blades of grass, wood, and stone, all things are One. . . . When is a man in mere understanding? When he sees one thing separated from another. And when is he above mere understanding? When he sees all in all, then a man stands above mere understanding."

In this quotation we note that according to Eckhart seeing a number of things as separate and distinct, seeing the grass and the wood and the stone as three different things, is the mark of the sensory-intellectual consciousness. For Eckhart's word "understanding" means the conceptual intellect. But if one passes beyond the sensory-intellectual consciousness into the mystical consciousness, then one sees these three things as being "all one." However, it is evident that in this extrovertive experience the distinctions between things have not wholly disappeared. There is no doubt that what Eckhart means is that he sees the three things as distinct and separate and yet at the same time as not distinct but identical. The grass is identical with the stone, and the stone with the wood, although they are all different. Rudolph Otto, commenting on this, observes that it is as if one said that black is the same as white, white the same as black, although at the same time white remains white and black remains black. Of course this is a complete paradox. It is in fact contradictory. But we shall find that paradoxicality is one of the common characteristics of all mysticism. And it is no use saying that this is all logically impossible, and that no consciousness of this kind can exist, unless we wish, on these a priori grounds, to refuse to study the evidence—which is overwhelming.

What some mystics simply call the One other mystics often identify with God. Hence we find Jakob Böhme (1575–1624) saying much the same thing about the grass and the trees and the stones as Eckhart does, but saying that they are all God instead of just all One. The following is a statement of one of his experiences: "In this light my spirit saw through all things and into all creatures and I recognized God in grass and plants."

It is suggested that the extrovertive type of experience is a kind of halfway house to the introvertive. For the introvertive experience is wholly nonsensuous and nonintellectual. But the extrovertive experience is sensory-intellectual in so far as it still perceives physical objects but is nonsensuous and nonintellectual in so far as it perceives them as "all one."

We may sum up this short account of the extrovertive consciousness by saying that it is a perception of the world as transfigured and unified in one ultimate being. In some cultures the one being is identified with God; and since God is then perceived as the inner essence of all objects, this type of experience tends toward pantheism. But in some cultures—for example, Buddhism—the unity is not interpreted as God at all.

(4.) Introvertive Mysticism

Suppose that one could shut all physical sensations out of one's consciousness. It may be thought that this would be easy as regards some of the senses, namely sight, hearing, taste, and smell. One can shut one's eyes, stop up one's ears, and hold one's nose. One can avoid taste sensations by keeping one's mouth empty. But one cannot shut off tactual sensations in any simple way of this kind. And it would be even more difficult to get rid of organic sensations. However, one can perhaps suppose it possible somehow to thrust tactual and organic sensations out of conscious awareness—perhaps into the unconscious. Mystics do not, as far as I know, descend to the ignominious level of holding their noses and stopping their ears. My only point is that it is possible to conceive of getting rid of all sensations, and in one way or other mystics claim that they do this.

Suppose now, after this has been done, we next try to get rid of all sensuous *images* from our minds. This is very difficult. Most people, try as they will not to picture anything at all, will find vague images floating about in consciousness. Suppose, however, that it is possible to suppress all images. And suppose finally that we manage to stop all thinking and reasoning. Having got rid of the whole empirical content of sensations, images, and thoughts, presumably all emotions and desires and volitions would also disappear, since they normally exist only as attachments to the cognitive content. What, then, would be left of consciousness? What would happen? It is natural to suppose that with all the elements of consciousness gone consciousness itself would lapse and the subject would fall asleep or become *un*conscious.

Now it happens to be the case that this total suppression of the whole empirical content of consciousness is precisely what the introvertive mystic claims to achieve. And he claims that what happens is not that all consciousness disappears but that only the ordinary sensory-intellectual consciousness disappears and is replaced by an entirely new kind of consciousness, the mystical consciousness. Naturally we now ask whether any description of this new consciousness can be given. But before trying to answer that difficult question, I propose to turn aside for a brief space to speak about the methods which mystics use to suppress sensuous images, and thinking, so as to get rid of their sensory-intellectual consciousness. There are the Yoga techniques of India; and Christian mystics in Catholic monasteries also evolved their own methods. The latter usually call their techniques "prayers," but they are not prayers in the vulgar sense of asking God for things; they are much more like the "meditation" and "concentration" of Yogis than may be commonly supposed. This is too vast a subject to be discussed in detail here. But I will give two elementary illustrations.

Everyone has heard of the breathing exercises undertaken by the yogins of India seeking samadhi—samadhi being the Indian name for mystical consciousness. What is this special method of breathing, and what is it supposed to accomplish? The theory of the matter is, I understand, something like this: It is practically impossible, or at least very difficult, to stop all sensing, imaging, and thinking by a forcible act of the will. What comes very near to it, however, is to concentrate one's attention on some single point or object so that all other mental content falls away and there is left nothing but the single point of consciousness. If this can be done, then ultimately that single point will itself disappear because contrast is necessary for our ordinary consciousness, and if there is only one point of consciousness left, there is nothing to form a contrast to it.

The question then is: On what single thing should one concentrate? A simple way is to concentrate on the stream of one's own breath. Simple instructions which I have heard given are these. One first adopts a suitable physical position with spine and neck perfectly erect. Then breathe in and out slowly, evenly, and smoothly. Concentrate your attention on this and nothing else. Some aspirants, I believe, count their breaths, 1, 2, 3, . . . up to 10, and then begin the count again. Continue this procedure till you attain the desired results.

A second method is to keep repeating in one's mind some short formula of words over and over again till the words lose all meaning. So long as they carry meaning, of course, the mind is still occupied with the thought of this meaning. But when the words become meaningless there is nothing left of consciousness except the monotonous sound-image, and that too, like the consciousness of one's breath, will in the end disappear. There is an interesting connection between this method and a remark made by the poet Tennyson. From childhood up Tennyson had frequent mystical experiences. They came to him spontaneously, without effort, and unsought. But he mentions the curious fact that he could induce them at will by the odd procedure of repeating his own name over and over again to himself. I know of no evidence that he studied mysticism enough to understand the theory of his own procedure, which would presumably be that the constantly repeated sound image served as the focus of the required one-pointed attention.

This leads to another curious reflection. Mystics who follow the procedure of constantly repeating a verbal formula often, I believe, tend to choose some religious set of words, for instance a part of the Lord's Prayer or a psalm. They probably imagine that these uplifting and inspirational words will carry them upwards toward the divine. But Tennyson's procedure suggests that any nonsense words would probably do as well. And this seems to agree with the general theory of concentration. It doesn't seem to matter what is chosen as the single point of concentration, whether it be one's breathing, or the sound of one's own name, or one's navel, or anything else, provided only it serves to shut off all other mental content.

Another point on which mystics usually insist in regard to spiritual training is what they call "detachment." Emphasis on this is found just as much in Hinduism and Buddhism as in Christianity. What is sought is detachment from desire, the uprooting of desire, or at any rate of all self-centered desires. The exact psychology of the matter presents great difficulties. In Christian mysticism the idea of detachment is usually given a religious and moral twist by insisting that it means the destruction of self-will or any kind of self-assertiveness, especially the rooting out of pride and the attainment of absolute humility. In non-Christian mysticism detachment does not usually get this special slant. But in the mysticism of all cultures detachment from desires for sensations and sensory images is emphasized.

We will now return to the main question. Supposing that the sensory-intellectual consciousness has been successfully supplanted by the mystical consciousness, can we find in the literatures of the subject any descriptions of this consciousness that will give us any idea of what it is like? The answer is that although mystics frequently say that their experiences are ineffable and indescribably, they nevertheless do often in fact describe them, and one can find plenty of such descriptive statements in the literature. They are usually extremely short—perhaps only three or four lines. And frequently they are indirect and not in the first person singular. Mystics more often than not avoid direct references to themselves.

I will give here a famous description which occurs in the Mandukya Upanishad. The Upanishads are supposed to have been the work of anonymous forest seers in India who lived between three thousand and twenty-five hundred years ago. They are among the oldest records of mysticism in the world. But they are of an unsurpassable depth of spirituality. For long ages and for countless millions of men in the East they have been, and they remain, the supreme source of the spiritual life. Of the introvertive mystical consciousness the Mandukya says that it is "beyond the senses, beyond the understanding, beyond all expression. . . . It is the pure unitary consciousness, wherein awareness of the world and of multiplicity is completely obliterated. It is ineffable peace. It is the Supreme Good. It is One without a second. It is the Self."

It will repay us, not to just slur over this passage, but to examine it carefully clause by clause. The first sentence is negative, telling us only what the experience is *not*. It is "beyond the senses, beyond the understanding." That is to say, it is beyond the sensory-intellectual consciousness; and there are in it no elements of sensation or sensuous imagery and no elements of conceptual thought. After these negatives there comes the statement that "it is the unitary consciousness, wherein all awareness of multiplicity has been obliterated." The core of the experience is thus described as an undifferentiated unity—a oneness or unity in which there is no internal division, no multiplicity.

I happen to have quoted a Hindu source. But one can find exactly the same thing in Christian mysticism. For instance the great Flemish mystic Jan van Ruysbroeck (1293–1381) says of what he calls "the God-seeing man" that "his spirit is undifferentiated and without distinction, and therefore it feels nothing but the unity." We see that the very words of the faithful Catholic are almost identical with those of the ancient Hindu, and I do not see how it can be doubted that they are describing the same experience. Not only in Christianity and Hinduism but everywhere else we find that the essence of the experience is that it is an *undifferentiated unity*, though each culture and each religion interprets this undifferentiated unity in terms of its own creeds or dogmas.

It may be objected that "undifferentiated unity" is a conceptual thought, and this is inconsistent with our statement that the experience is wholly nonintellectual. The answer is that concepts such as "one," "unity," "undifferentiated," "God," "Nirvana," etc., are only applied to the experience *after* it has passed and when it is being *remembered*. None can be applied during the experience itself.

The passage of the Upanishad goes on to say that the undifferentiated unity "is the Self." Why is this? Why is the unity now identified with the Self? The answer is plain. We started with the full self or mind of our ordinary everyday consciousness. What was it full of? It was full of the multiplicity of sensations, thoughts, desires, and the rest. But the mind was not merely this multiplicity. These disparate elements were held together in a unity, the unity of the single mind or self. A multiplicity without a unity in which the multiple elements are together is inconceivable—e.g., many objects in one space. Now when we emptied all the multiple contents out of this unity of the self what is left, according to the Upanishad, is the unity of the self, the original unity minus its contents. And this is the self. The Upanishads go further than this. They always identify this individual self with the Universal Self, the soul of the world. [. . . But] for the moment we may continue to think in terms of the individual self, the pure ego of you or me. The undifferentiated unity is thought to be the pure ego.

I must draw the reader's attention to several facts about this situation. In the first place it flatly contradicts what David Hume said in a famous passage about the self. He said that when he looked introspectively into himself and searched for the I, the self, the ego, all he could ever introspect was the multiplicity of the sensations, images, thoughts, and feelings. He could never observe any I, and pure self apart from its contents, and he inferred that the I is a fiction and does not really exist. But now a vast body of empirical evidence, that of the mystics from all over the world, affirms that Hume was simply mistaken on a question of psychological fact, and that it is possible to get rid of all the mental contents and find the pure self left over and to experience this. This evidence need not mean that the self is a thing or a "substance," but can be taken as implying that it is a pure unity, the sort of being which Kant called the "transcendental unity" of the self.

The next thing to note is that the assertion of this new kind of consciousness is completely paradoxical. One way of bringing out the paradox is to point out that what we are left with here, when the contents of consciousness are gone, is a kind of consciousness which has no objects. It is not a consciousness *of* anything, but yet it is still consciousness. For the contents of our ordinary daily consciousness, the colors, sounds, wishes, thoughts are the same as the objects of consciousness, so that when the contents are gone the objects are gone. This consciousness of the mystics is not even a consciousness of consciousness, for then there would be a duality which is incompatible with the idea of an undifferentiated unity. In India it is called *pure* consciousness. The word "pure" is used in somewhat that same sense as Kant used it—meaning "without any empirical contents."

Another aspect of the paradox is that this pure consciousness is simultaneously both positive and negative, something and nothing, a fullness and an emptiness. The positive side is that it is an actual and positive consciousness. Moreover, all mystics affirm that it is pure peace, beatitude, joy, bliss, so that it has a positive affective tone. The Christians call it "the peace of God which passeth all understanding." The Buddhists call it Nirvana. But although it has this positive character, it is quite correct to say also that when we empty out all objects and contents of the mind *there is nothing whatever left*. That is the negative side of the paradox. What is left is sheer Emptiness. This is fully recognized in all mystical literature. In Mahayan Buddhism this total emptiness of the mystical consciousness is called the Void. In Christian mysticism the experience is identified with God. And this cases Eckhart and others to say that God, or the Godhead, is pure Nothingness, is a "desert," or "wilderness," and so on. Usually the two sides of the paradox are expressed in metaphors. The commonest metaphor for the positive side is light and for the negative side darkness. This is the darkness of God. It is called darkness because all distinctions disappear in it just as all distinctions disappear in a physical darkness.

We must not say that what we have here is a light *in* the darkness. For that would be no paradox. The paradox is that the light *is* the darkness, and the darkness *is* the light. This statement can be well documented from the literature of different cultures. I will give two examples, one from Christianity, one from Buddhism—and from the Buddhism of Tibet of all place in the world. Dionysius the Areopagite, a Christian, speaks of God as "the dazzling obscurity which outshines all brilliance with the intensity of its darkness." And the Tibetan book of the Dead puts the same paradox in the words, "the clear light of the Void." In Dionysius we see that the obscurity, or the darkness, *is* the brilliance, and in the Tibetan book we see that the Void itself *is* a clear light.

(5.) *Mysticism and Religion*

Most writers on mysticism seem to take it for granted that mystical experience is a religious experience, and that mysticism is necessarily a religious phenomenon. They seem to think that mysticism and religious mysticism are one and the same thing. But this is far from being correct. It is true that there is an important connection between mysticism and religion, but it is not nearly so direct and immediate as most writers have seemed to think, nor can it be simply taken for granted as an obvious fact.

There are several grounds for insisting that intrinsically and in itself mystical experience is not a religious phenomenon at all and that its connection with religions is subsequent and even adventitious. In the first place, it seems to be clear that if we strip the mystical experience of all intellectual interpretation such as that which identifies it with God, or with the Absolute, or with the soul of the world, what is left is simply the undifferentiated unity. Now what is there that is religious about an undifferentiated unity? The answer seems to be, in the first instance, "Nothing at all." There seems to be nothing religious about an undifferentiated unity as such.

In the theistic religions of the West, in Christianity, Judaism, and Islam, the experience of the undifferentiated unity is interpreted as "union with God." But this is an interpretation and is not the experience itself. It is true that some Christian mystics, such as St. Teresa of Avila, invariably speak simply of having experienced "union with God," and do not talk about an undifferentiated unity. St. Teresa did not have a sufficiently analytical mind to distinguish between experience and its interpretation. But other Christian mystics who are more analytically minded, such as Eckhart and Ruysbroeck, do speak of the undifferentiated unity.

These considerations are further underlined by the fact that quite different interpretations of the same experience are given in different cultures. The undifferentiated unity is interpreted by Eckhart and Ruysbroeck in terms of the Trinitarian conception of God, but by Islamic mystics as the Unitarian God of Islam, and by the leading school of Vedantists as a more impersonal Absolute. And when we come to Buddhism we find that the experience is not interpreted as any kind of God at all. For the Buddhist it becomes the Void or Nirvana. Buddha denied the existence of a Supreme Being altogether. It is often said that Buddhism is atheistic. And whether this description of Buddhism is true or not, it is certainly the case that there can exist an atheistic mysticism, a mystical experience naked and not clothed in any religious garb.

In view of these facts, we have a problem on our hands. Why is it that, in spite of exceptions, mysticism *usually* takes on some religious form and is usually found in connection with a definitely religious culture and as being a part of some definite religion? The following are, I think, the main reasons.

First, there is a very important feature of the introvertive mystical experience which I have not mentioned yet. I refer to the experience of the "melting away" into the Infinite of one's own individuality. Such phrases as "melting away," "fading away," "passing away" are found in the mystical literature of Christianity, Islam, Hinduism, and Buddhism. Among the Sufis of Islam there is a special technical term for it. It is called fanä. It must be insisted that this is not an inference or an interpretation or a theory or a speculation. It is an actual experience. The individual, as it were, directly experiences the disappearance of his own individuality, its fading away into the Infinite. To document this, one could quote from Eckhart, or from the Upanishads or the Sufis. But I believe I can bring home the point to a modern reader better by quoting a modern author. I referred earlier to the fact that Tennyson had frequent mystical experiences. His account of them is quoted by William James in his *The Varieties of Religious Experience*. Tennyson wrote, "All at once, as it were out of the intensity of the consciousness of individuality, individuality itself seemed to dissolve and fade away into boundless being. . . . the loss of personality, if such it were, seeming no extinction but the only true life." "Boundless being" seems to have the same meaning as "the Infinite." The Infinite is in most minds identified with the idea of God. We are finite beings, God is the only Infinite Being. Once can see at once, therefore, how this experience of the dissolution of one's own individuality, its being merged into the Infinite, takes on a religious meaning. In theistic cultures the experience of melting away into boundless being is interpreted as union with God.

A second reason for the connection between mysticism and religion is that the undifferentiated unity is necessarily thought of by the mystics as being *beyond space and beyond time*. For it is without any internal division or multiplicity of parts, whereas the essence of time is its division into an endless multitude of successive parts, and the essence of space is its division into a multitude of parts lying side by side. Therefore the undifferentiated unity, being without any multiplicity of parts, is necessarily spaceless and timeless. Being timeless is the same as being eternal. Hence Eckhart is constantly telling us that the mystical experience transcends time and is an experience of "the Eternal Now." But in religious minds the Eternal, like the Infinite, is another name for God. Hence the mystical experience is thought of as an experience of God.

A third reason for this identification of the undifferentiated unity with God lies in the emotional side of the experience. It is the universal testimony of the mystics that their kind of consciousness brings feelings of an exalted peace, blessedness, and joy. It becomes identified with the peace of God, the gateway of the Divine, the gateway of salvation. This is also why in Buddhism, though the experience is not personified or called God, it nevertheless becomes Nirvana which is the supreme goal of the Buddhist religious life.

Thus we see that mysticism naturally, though not necessarily, becomes intimately associated with whatever is the religion of the culture in which it appears. It is, however, important to realize that it does not favor any particular religion. Mystical experience in itself does not have any tendency to make a man a Christian or a Buddhist. Into the framework of what creed he will fit his experience will tend to depend mostly on the culture in which he lives. In a Buddhist country the mystic interprets his experience as a glimpse of Nirvana, in a Christian country he may interpret it as union with God or even (as in Eckhart) as penetrating into the Godhead which is beyond God. Or if he is a highly sophisticated modern individual, who has been turned by his education into a religious skeptic, he may remain a skeptic as regards the dogma of the different religions; he may allow his mystical experience to remain naked without any clothing of creeds or dogmas; but he is likely at the same time to feel that in that experience he has found something *sacred*. And this feeling of the sacred may quite properly be called "religious" feeling though it does not clothe itself in any dogmas. And this alone may be enough to uplift his ideals and to revolutionize his life and to give it meaning and purpose.

(6.) The Ethical Aspects of Mysticism

It is sometimes asserted that mysticism is merely an escape from life and from its duties and responsibilities. The mystics, it is said, retreats into a private ecstasy of bliss, turns his back on the world, and forgets not only his own sorrows but the needs and sorrows of his fellow-men. In short, his life is essentially selfish.

It is possible that there have been mystics who deserved this kind of condemnation. To treat the bliss of the mystical consciousness as an end in itself is certainly a psychological possibility. And no doubt there have been men who have succumbed to this temptation. But this attitude is not the mystic ideal, and it is severely condemned by those who are most representative of the mystics themselves. For instance, St. John of the Cross condemns it as "spiritual gluttony." Eckhart tells us that if a man were in mystical ecstasy and knew of a poor man who needed his help, he should leave his ecstasy in order to go and serve the poor man. The Christian mystics especially have always emphasized that mystical union with God brings with it an intense and burning love of God which must needs overflow into the world in the form of love for our fellow-men; and that this must show itself in deeds of charity, mercy, and self-sacrifice, and not merely in words.

Some mystics have gone beyond this and have insisted that the mystical consciousness is the secret fountain of all love, human as well as divine; and that since love in the
end is the only source of true moral activity, therefore mysticism is the source from which
ethical values ultimately flow. For all selfishness and cruelty and evil result from the
separateness of one human being from another. This separateness of individuals breeds
egoism and the war of all against all. But in the mystical consciousness all distinctions
disappear and therefore the distinction between "I" and "you" and "he" and "she." This
is the mystical and metaphysical basis of love, namely the realization that my brother and
I are one, and that therefore his sufferings are my sufferings and his happiness is my
happiness. This reveals itself dimly in the psychological phenomena of sympathy and
more positively in actual love. For one who had no touch of the mystical vision all men
would be islands. And in the end it is because of mysticism that it is possible to say that
"no man is an island" and that on the contrary every man is "a part of the main.'

(7.) Alternative Interpretations of Mysticism

We have seen that the same experience may be interpreted in terms of different religious
creeds. There is also another set of alternative interpretations which we ought to
mention. We may believe that the mystic really is in touch, as he usually claims, with
some being greater than himself, some spiritual Infinite which transcends the temporal
flux of things. Or we may, on the other hand, adopt the alternative solution of the skeptic
who will think that the mystical consciousness is entirely subjective and imports nothing
outside itself. My own vote would be cast for the former solution. I would agree with the
words of Arthur Koestler [. . . when] he speaks of a higher order of reality which for us
is like a text written in invisible ink. "I also liked to think," he says, "that the founders of
religions, prophets, saints and seers had at moments been able to read a fragment of the
invisible text; after which they had so much padded, dramatised and ornamented it, that
they themselves could no longer tell what parts of it were authentic."

But I wish to point out that even if one should choose the skeptical alternative and
suppose that the mystical consciousness reveals no reality outside its owner's brain, one
is far from having disposed of mysticism as some worthless delusion which ought to be
got rid of. Even if it is wholly subjective, it still reveals something which is supremely
great in human life. It is still the peace which passeth all understanding. It is still the
gateway to salvation—not, I mean, in a future life, but as the highest beatitude that a man
can reach in this life, and out of which the greatest deeds of love can flow. But it must
be added, of course, that it belongs among those things of which Spinoza wrote in those
famous words: "If the road which I have shown is very difficult, it yet can be discovered.
And clearly it must be very hard if it is so rarely found. For how could it be that it is
neglected by practically all, if salvation . . . could be found without difficulty. But all
excellent things are as difficult as they are rare."

Classical Criticisms of Some of the Arguments for the Existence of God

○

○ ○ ○ *8*

The Ontological Arguments[1]
Gaunilo and Anselm—Criticism and Reply[2]
Gaunilo
St. Anselm

AGAINST THE REASONING that if "That Than Which Nothing Greater Can Be Conceived" Is Understood It Must Also Exist.

1. Gaunilo argues that for something to stand in relation to the understanding cannot establish its real existence, if that something is doubted.

Gaunilo
PARA. 5 (p. 127.25–p. 128.13)

That this exists necessarily in reality is proved to me in this way: if this does not exist, whatever is in reality will be greater than it, in which case that which has just been proved at least to stand in relation to my understanding will not be greater than all things.

To this I reply. If it is said that this stands in relation to the understanding as something which cannot be conceived on the basis of the truth of any real thing, I do not deny that it does stand in relation to the understanding in this way. However, because it cannot possess real existence simply by standing in relation to the understanding, I certainly do not concede that it really exists—at least not until it is proved to me by an indubitable argument.

He who says that this exists because otherwise that which is greater than all would not be greater than all, does not sufficiently attend to what is being said. I do not yet say—on the contrary I deny or doubt—that this is greater than any real thing. I concede to it no other reality (if this can be called "reality") than of something which is absolutely unknown to the mind, but which the mind tries to conceive of on the basis of a word merely heard. Therefore, how is it proved to me that this "greater" exists in reality,

---

[1] The reader may wish to read this selection in conjunction with selection 1 in Chapter One.—E.D.K.

[2] Of the extant manuscripts which contain Chapters II–IV of the *Proslogion*, almost half also contain a criticism of Anselm's argument written by one of his contemporaries, and his own reply. Two manuscripts attribute the criticism to a monk Gaunilo of the French cloister at Marmoutiere.

   Anselm's reply is not a sustained discussion [but] a series of notes, each in answer to a particular point made by Gaunilo. . . . The page references below refer to Dom Schmitt's Latin edition.—A.C. MCGILL AND JOHN HICK.

simply because it is held to be greater than all things, when I deny or doubt that this is to be held at all? I deny or doubt it so completely, in fact, that in my view this "greater" does not stand in relation to my understanding or to conception, except in the way in which many doubtful and uncertain things stand there.

It first must be made certain to me that this "greater" is actually somewhere, and only then, from the fact that it is greater than all things, will there be no doubt that it subsists in itself.

Anselm

I said that, even if it only stood in relation to the understanding, it could at least be conceived to be also in reality, and that this is greater. Therefore, if it only stood in relation to the understanding, then "that than which a greater cannot be conceived" would be that than which a greater can be conceived. What, I ask, could be more logical? For if it only stood in relation to the understanding, could it not be conceived to be in reality also? And if so, then does not anyone who conceives of this existing also in reality conceive of something greater than that which only stands in relation to the understanding? What therefore could be more logical than this: if "that than which a greater cannot be conceived" only stands in relation to the understanding, then it is that than which a greater can be conceived? But certainly "that than which a greater can be conceived" does not stand in relation to any understanding as "that than which a greater cannot be conceived."

Does it not therefore follow that if "that than which a greater cannot be conceived" stands in relation to *any* understanding, it does not only stand in relation to the understanding? For if it only stood in relation to the understanding alone, it would then be that than which a greater can be conceived, which is a contradiction (Chap. II, p. 132.22–133.2).

* * *

"That which cannot possibly not be" is obviously something that can be conceived and understood. He who conceives of this conceives of something greater than he who conceives of that which has the possibility of not being. Therefore, while he is conceiving of "that than which a greater cannot be conceived," if he conceives that it has the possibility of not being, he is obviously not conceiving of that than which a greater cannot be conceived. However, the same thing cannot be conceived and not be conceived at the same time. Therefore he who conceives of "that than which a greater cannot be conceived" is not conceiving of what can, but of what cannot possibly not be. For that reason what he is conceiving of must necessarily exist, because whatever is able not to exist is not that of which he is conceiving (Chap. IX, p. 138.19–27).

2. Gaunilo argues that if in the case of God "to be the best conceivable" entails "to exist," then it can also be demonstrated that the best conceivable island must exist.

Gaunilo
PARA. 6 (p. 128.14–32)

Consider this example. Certain people say that somewhere in the ocean there is an island which they call the "Lost Island," because of the difficulty or, rather, the impossibility of finding what does not exist. They say that it is more abundantly filled with inestimable riches and delights than the Isles of the Blessed, and that although it has no owner or inhabitant, it excels all the lands that men inhabit taken together in the unceasing abundance of its fertility.

When someone tells me that there is such an island, I easily understand what is being said, for there is nothing difficult here. Suppose, however, as a consequence of this, he then goes on to say: you cannot doubt that this island, more excellent than all lands, actually exists somewhere in reality, because it undoubtedly stands in relation to your understanding. Since it is more excellent, not simply to stand in relation to the understanding, but to be in reality as well, therefore this island must necessarily be in reality. Otherwise any other land that exists in reality would be more excellent than this island, and this island, which you understood to be the most excellent of all lands, would then not be the most excellent.

If, I repeat, someone should wish by this argument to demonstrate to me that this island truly exists and is no longer to be doubted, I would think he were joking; or, if I accepted the argument, I do not know whom I would regard as the greater fool, me for accepting it or him for supposing that he had proved the existence of this island with any kind of certainty. He should first show that this excellent island exists as a genuine and undeniably real thing, and not leave it standing in relation to my understanding as a false or uncertain something.

Anselm

My reasoning, you claim, is as if someone should say that there is an island in the ocean, which surpasses the whole earth in its fertility, but which is called a "Lost Island" because of the difficulty, or even impossibility, of finding something that does not exist, and as if he should then argue that no one can doubt that it actually does exist because the words describing it are easily understood.

I can confidently say that if anyone discovers for me something existing either in fact or in thought alone, other than "that than which a greater cannot be thought," and is able to apply the logic of my argument to it, I shall find that lost island for him and shall give it to him as something which he will never lose again (Chap. III, p. 133.3–9).

3. *Gaunilo argues that since the existence of "that than which nothing greater can be conceived" has not been proved, it can be conceived not to exist.*

Gaunilo
PARA. 7 (p. 129.1–10)

When it is asserted to the fool [in *Pros*. III] that this "greater than all things" is such that even to thought it cannot not be, and yet when this is proved to him on no other grounds than that otherwise this greater than all things would not be greater than all things, he can give the same answer and reply: When did *I* ever say that such a being, one that is "greater than all things," exists in reality, so that from this you could prove to me that it exists so fully in reality that it cannot be conceived not to be? First of all it should be proved by some most certain argument that some superior reality, that is, a nature which is greater and better than everything that is, actually exists. From this we can then prove all the other qualities which must not be lacking from that which is greater and better than all things.

Anselm [3]

It is now obvious, however, that "that than which a greater cannot be conceived" cannot be conceived not to be, because its existing has such manifest truthfulness. Otherwise, it would not exist at all.

Let us suppose that there is someone who says that he does conceive that this does not exist. In my view, when he is conceiving in this way, he is either conceiving of that than which a greater cannot be conceived, or he is not conceiving of it. If he is not conceiving of it, then it is not this which he thinks does not exist. On the other hand, if he is really conceiving of it, he at least conceives of something which cannot be conceived not to be. For if it could be conceived not to be, it could also be conceived to have a beginning and an end. But this is impossible [for "that than which a greater cannot be conceived"]. Therefore whoever really conceives of this conceives of something which cannot be conceived not to be. Whoever really conceives of it, then, does not in fact conceive that it is not. Otherwise he would be conceiving of something which cannot be conceived. Therefore "that than which a greater cannot be conceived" cannot be conceived not to be (Chap. III, p. 133.10–20).

4. Gaunilo argues that it should be said that God's existence cannot be "understood," not that it cannot be "conceived."

Gaunilo
PARA. 7 (p. 129.10–19)

When it is said that this supreme reality cannot be "conceived" *(cogitari)* not to be, it would probably be better to say that it cannot be "understood" *(intelligi)* not to be, or even that it cannot be "understood" to be capable of not being.

According to the proper meaning of this word "understand," false matters cannot be understood, though they can certainly be conceived, just as the fool conceived that God is not. I "know" *(scio)* most certainly that I am, but I also know nonetheless than I am capable of not being. I "understand" without any doubt that the greatest reality which is God both is and cannot not be. However, I do not know whether I can "conceive" of my not existing at the time when I "know" most certainly that I do exist. If I can do this, why can I not also "conceive" as not existing whatever else I "know" to exist with the same certainty [including God]? If I cannot do this, however, then the impossibility of being conceived not to exist will not be the property of God alone.

Anselm

Further still you say: while it is said that this greatest reality cannot be "conceived" not to be, it would probably be better to say that its nonexistence, or even the possibility of its non-existence, cannot be "understood."

It is more correct, however, to say that this cannot be "conceived." For you yourself say that according to the proper meaning of this word nothing false can be "understood." Therefore, if I had said that this supreme reality itself could not be "understood" not to

---

[3] In the manuscripts, this passage immediately follows Anselm's remarks on the Lost Island, and in the view of some thinkers it applies to this objection.—A.C. MCGILL AND JOHN HICK.

be, you would probably have made three objections: that nothing which is can be "understood" not to be, for the non-being of that which is is something false [and therefore not a proper object of "understanding"]; that the impossibility of being understood not to be is therefore not a property peculiar to God [but is characteristic of every object of "understanding"]; and finally, that *if* something which most certainly exists can be "understood" not to be, in the same way other certain things can also be "understood" not to be.

If one examines the matter closely, these objections cannot be made against "conceiving." For even if there is nothing existing which can be "understood" not to be, nevertheless *everything* can be "conceived" not to be, except that which is the highest. In fact all those things—and only those things—can be conceived not to be which have a beginning, or an end, or a combination of parts, and, as I have already said, which do not exist completely everywhere and always. But that alone cannot be conceived not to be which has neither beginning nor end nor combination of parts, and which thought finds existing completely always and everywhere.

You must realize that even though you know with complete certainty that you exist, you can "conceive" of yourself as not existing. It surprises me that you say that you do not know this. For we "conceive" of the nonexistence of many things which we "know" to exist, and we "conceive" of the existence of many things which we "know" not to exist. We do this, not by making a real judgment, but by imagining that these things are as we conceive of them. In this sense, we can "conceive" that something is not when we "know" that it is, because at one and the same time we can "conceive" of the former and "know" the latter. In another sense, we cannot "conceive" that something is not when we "know" that it is, because we cannot conceive of something as both existing and not existing at the same time.

Therefore, if anyone distinguished between these two meanings [of "conceive"— conceiving within the limits of what he knows to be actual (meaning A), and conceiving by his own imaginative effort (meaning B)], he will understand that whenever something is "known" to be, it cannot be "conceived" not to be [in the sense of meaning A]; and yet that whatever is, except that than which a greater cannot be conceived, even if it is "known" to be, can still be "conceived" not to be [in the sense of meaning B]. Therefore it is the peculiar property of God that he cannot be "conceived" not to be [in the sense of meaning B], while many things, so far as they exist, cannot be "conceived" not to be [in the sense of meaning A].

○　○　○　*9*

The Cosmological Argument
Dialogues: Part IX [1]
David Hume

BUT IF SO many difficulties attend the argument *a posteriori*,[2] said DEMEA; had we not better adhere to that simple and sublime argument *a priori*,[3] which, by offering to us infallible demonstration, cuts off at once all doubt and difficulty? By this argument, too, we may prove the INFINITY of the divine attributes, which, I am afraid, can never be ascertained with certainty from any other topic. For how can an effect, which either is finite, or, for aught we know, may be so; how can such an effect, I say, prove an infinite cause? The unity too of the divine nature, it is very difficult, if not absolutely impossible, to deduce merely from contemplating the works of nature; nor will the uniformity alone of the plan, even were it allowed, give us any assurance of that attribute. Whereas the argument *a priori*. . . .

You seem to reason, DEMEA, interposed CLEANTHES, as if those advantages and conveniences in the abstract argument were full proofs of its solidity. But it is first proper, in my opinion, to determine what argument of this nature you choose to insist on; and we shall afterwards, from itself, better than from its *useful* consequences, endeavour to determine what value we ought to put upon it.

The argument, replied DEMEA, which I would insist on is the common one. Whatever exists must have a cause or reason of its existence; it being absolutely impossible for any thing to produce itself, or be the cause of its own existence. In mounting up, therefore, from effects to causes, we must either go on in tracing an infinite succession, without any ultimate cause at all, or must at last have recourse to some ultimate cause, that is *necessarily* existent: Now that the first supposition is absurd may be thus proved. In the infinite chain or succession of causes and effects, each single effect is determined to exist by the power and efficacy of that cause which immediately preceded; but the whole eternal chain or succession, taken together, is not determined or caused by any thing: And yet it is evident that it requires a cause or reason, as much as any particular object, which begins to exist in time. The question is still reasonable, why this particular succession of causes existed from eternity, and not any other succession, or no succession at all. If there be no necessarily existent Being, any supposition, which can be formed,

---

[1] This selection and selection 10 are from Hume's *Dialogues Concerning Natural Religion*. Part numbers refer to this book.—E.D.K

[2] Design (Teleological) Argument.—E.D.K

[3] First Cause (Cosmological) Argument.—E.D.K

is equally possible; nor is there any more absurdity in nothing's having existed from eternity, than there is in that succession of causes, which constitutes the universe. What was it, then, which determined something to exist rather than nothing, and bestowed being on a particular possibility, exclusive of the rest? *External causes*, there are supposed to be none. *Chance* is a word without a meaning. Was it *nothing*? But that can never produce any thing. We must, therefore, have recourse to a necessarily existent Being, who carries the REASON of his existence in himself; and who cannot be supposed not to exist without an express contradiction. There is consequently such a Being, that is, there is a Deity.

I shall not leave it to PHILO, said CLEANTHES (thought I know that the starting objections is his chief delight), to point out the weakness of this metaphysical reasoning. It seems to me so obviously ill-grounded, and at the same time of so little consequence to the cause of true piety and religion, that I shall myself venture to show the fallacy of it.

· (1) ·

I shall begin with observing, that there is an evident absurdity in pretending to demonstrate a matter of fact, or to prove it by any arguments *a priori*. Nothing is demonstrable, unless the contrary implies a contradiction. Nothing, that is distinctly conceivable, implies a contradiction. Whatever we conceive as existent, we can also conceive as non-existent. There is no Being, therefore, whose non-existence implies a contradiction. Consequently there is no Being, whose existence is demonstrable. I propose this argument as entirely decisive, and am willing to rest the whole controversy upon it.

· (2) ·

It is pretended that the Deity is a necessarily existent Being; and this necessity of his existence is attempted to be explained by asserting, that, if we knew his whole essence or nature, we should perceive it to be as impossible for him not to exist as for twice two not to be four. But it is evident, that this can never happen, while our faculties remain the same as at present. It will still be possible for us, at any time, to conceive the non-existence of what we formerly conceived to exist; nor can the mind ever lie under a necessity of supposing any object to remain always in being; in the same manner as we lie under a necessity of always conceiving twice two to be four. The words, therefore, *necessary existence*, have no meaning; or, which is the same thing, none that is consistent.

· (3) ·

But farther; why may not the material universe be the necessarily existent Being, according to this pretended explication of necessity? We dare not affirm that we know all the qualities of matter; and for aught we can determine, it may contain some qualities, which, were they known, would make its non-existence appear as great a contradiction as that twice two is five. I find only one argument employed to prove, that the material world is not the necessarily existent Being; and this argument is derived from the contingency both of the matter and the form of the world. "Any particle of matter," it is said,[4] "may be *conceived* to be annihilated; and any form may be *conceived* to be altered. Such an annihilation or alteration, therefore, is not impossible." But it seems a great partiality not to perceive, that the same argument extends equally to the Deity, so far as we have any conception of him; and that the mind can at least imagine[5] him to be non-existent, or his attributes to be altered. It must be some unknown, inconceivable qualities, which can make his non-existence appear impossible, or his attributes unalterable: And no reason can be assigned, why these qualities may not belong to matter. As they are altogether unknown and inconceivable, they can never be proved incompatible with it.

· *(4)* ·

Add to this, that in tracing an eternal succession of objects, it seems absurd to inquire for a general cause or first Author. How can any thing, that exists from eternity, have a cause, since that relation implies a priority in time and a beginning of existence?

In such a chain too, or succession of objects, each part is caused by that which preceded it, and causes that which succeeds it. Where then is the difficulty? But the WHOLE, you say, wants a cause. I answer, that the uniting of these parts into a whole, like the uniting of several distinct counties into one kingdom, or several distinct members into one body, is performed merely by an arbitrary act of the mind, and has no influence on the nature of things. Did I show you the particular causes of each individual in a collection of twenty particles of matter, I should think it very unreasonable, should you afterwards ask me, what was the cause of the whole twenty. This is sufficiently explained in explaining the cause of the parts.

---

[4] Dr. Clarke

[5] [or conceive]

○   ○   ○   **10**

The Design Argument[1]
David Hume

• *I* •

(PART II)

I MUST OWN, Cleanthes, said Demea, that nothing can more surprise me than the light in which you have all along put this argument. By the whole tenor of your discourse, one would imagine that you were maintaining the Being of a God against the cavils of atheists and infidels, and were necessitated to become a champion for that fundamental principle of all religion. But this, I hope, is not by any means a question among us. No man, no man at least of common sense, I am persuaded, ever entertained a serious doubt with regard to a truth so certain and self-evident. The question is not concerning the *being* but the *nature* of God.[2] This I affirm, from the infirmities of human understanding, to be altogether incomprehensible and unknown to us. The essence of that supreme Mind, His attributes, the manner of His existence, the very nature of His duration—these and every particular which regards so divine a Being are mysterious to men. Finite, weak, and blind creatures, we ought to humble ourselves in His august presence, and, conscious of our frailties, adore in silence His infinite perfections which eye hath not seen, ear hath not heard, neither hath it entered into the heart of man to conceive. They are covered in a deep cloud from human curiosity; it is profaneness to attempt penetrating through these sacred obscurities, and, next to the impiety of denying His existence, is the temerity of prying into His nature and essence, decrees and attributes.

But lest you should think that my *piety* has here got the better of my *philosophy*, I shall support my opinion, if it needs any support, by a very great authority. I might cite all the divines, almost from the foundation of Christianity, who have ever treated of this or any other theological subject; but I shall confine myself, at present, to one equally celebrated for piety and philosophy. It is Father Malebranche who, I remember, thus expresses himself.[3] "One ought not so much," says he, "to call God a spirit in order to express positively what He is, as in order to signify that He is not matter. He is a Being infinitely perfect—of this we cannot doubt. But in the same manner as we ought not to imagine, even supposing Him corporeal, that He is clothed with a human body, as the anthropomorphites asserted, under colour that that figure was the most perfect of any,

---

[1] *Dialogues Concerning Natural Religion*, Parts II, IV–VIII.—E.D.K.

[2] This is not strictly true. Cleanthes' argument and Philo's criticisms pertain to both the existence (being) and nature of God.—E.D.K.

[3] *Recherche de la Vérité*, Bk. III, Chap. 9.—E.D.K.

so neither ought we to imagine that the spirit of God has human ideas or bears any resemblance to our spirit, under colour that we know nothing more perfect than a human mind. We ought rather to believe that as He comprehends the perfections of matter without being material . . . He comprehends also the perfections of created spirits without being spirit, in the manner we conceive spirit: that His true name is *He that is,* or, in other words, Being without restriction, All Being, the Being infinite and universal."

After so great an authority, Demea, replied Philo, as that which you have produced, and a thousand more which you might produce, it would appear ridiculous in me to add my sentiment or express my approbation of your doctrine. But surely, where reasonable men treat these subjects, the question can never be concerning the *being* but only the *nature* of the Deity.[4] The former truth, as you well observe, is unquestionable and self-evident. Nothing exists without a cause; and the original cause of this universe (whatever it be) we all God, and piously ascribe to Him every species of perfection. Whoever scruples this fundamental truth deserves every punishment which can be inflicted among philosophers, to wit, the greatest ridicule, contempt, and disapprobation. But as all perfection is entirely relative, we ought never to imagine that we comprehend the attributes of this divine Being, or to suppose that his perfections have any analogy or likeness to the perfections of a human creature. Wisdom, thought, design, knowledge— these we justly ascribe to Him because these words are honourable among men, and we have no other language or other conceptions by which we can express our adoration of Him. But let us beware lest we think that our ideas anywise correspond to His perfections, or that His attributes have any resemblance to these qualities among men. He is infinitely superior to our limited view and comprehension, and is more the object of worship in the temple than of disputation in the schools.

In reality, Cleanthes, continued he, there is no need of having recourse to that affected skepticism so displeasing to you in order to come at this determination. Our ideas reach no farther than our experience. We have no experience of divine attributes and operations. I need not conclude my syllogism, can draw the inference yourself. And it is a pleasure to me (and I hope to you, too) that just reasoning and sound piety here concur in the same conclusion, and both of them establish the adorably mysterious and incomprehensible nature of the Supreme Being.

Not to lose any time in circumlocutions, said Cleanthes, addressing himself to Demea, much less in replying to the pious declamations of Philo, I shall briefly explain how I conceive this matter.[5] Look round the world, contemplate the whole and every part of it: you will find it to be nothing but one great machine, subdivided into an infinite number of lesser machines, which again admit of subdivisions to a degree beyond what human senses and faculties can trace and explain. All these various machines, and even their most minute parts, are adjusted to each other with an accuracy which ravishes into admiration all men who have ever contemplated them. The curious adapting of means to ends, throughout all nature, resembles exactly, though it much exceeds, the productions of human contrivance—of human design, thought, wisdom, and intelligence. Since therefore the effects resemble each other, we are led to infer, by all the rules of analogy, that the causes also resemble, and that the Author of nature is somewhat similar to the mind of man,

---

[4] See footnote 2.—E.D.K.

[5] The argument begins here.—E.D.K.

though possessed of much larger faculties, proportioned to the grandeur of the work which He has executed. By this argument a posteriori, and by this argument alone, do we prove at once the existence of a Deity and His similarity to human mind and intelligence.

I shall be so free, Cleanthes, said Demea, as to tell you that from the beginning I could not approve of your conclusion concerning the similarity of the Deity to men, still less can I approve of the mediums by which you endeavour to establish it. What! No demonstration of the Being of God! No abstract arguments! No proofs a priori! Are these which have hitherto been so much insisted on by philosophers all fallacy, all sophism? Can we reach no farther in this subject than experience and probability? I will not say that this is betraying the cause of a Deity; but surely, by this affected candour, you give advantages to atheists which they never could obtain by the mere dint of argument and reasoning.

What I chiefly scruple in this subject, said Philo, is not so much that all religious arguments are by Cleanthes reduced to experience, as that they appear not to be even the most certain and irrefragable of that inferior kind. That a stone will fall, that fire will burn, that the earth has solidity, we have observed a thousand and a thousand times; and when any new instance of this nature is presented, we draw without hesitation the accustomed inference. The exact similarity of the cases gives us a perfect assurance of a similar event, and a stronger evidence is never desired nor sought after. But wherever you depart, in the least, from the similarity of the cases, you diminish proportionably the evidence, and may at last bring it to a very weak *analogy*, which is confessedly liable to error and uncertainty. After having experienced the circulation of the blood in human creatures, we make no doubt that it takes place in Titius and Maevius; but from its circulation in frogs and fishes it is only a presumption, though a strong one, from analogy that it takes place in men and other animals. The analogical reasoning is much weaker when we infer the circulation of the sap in vegetables from our experience that the blood circulates in animals; and those who hastily followed that imperfect analogy are found, by more accurate experiments, to have been mistaken.

If we see a house, Cleanthes, we conclude, with the greatest certainty, that it had an architect or builder because this is precisely that species of effect which we have experienced to proceed from that species of cause. But surely you will not affirm that the universe bears such a resemblance to a house that we can with the same certainty infer a similar cause, or that the analogy is here entire and perfect. The dissimiltude is so striking that the utmost you can here pretend to is a guess, a conjecture, a presumption concerning a similar cause; and how that pretension will be received in the world, I leave you to consider.

It would surely be very ill received, replied Cleanthes; and I should be deservedly blamed and detested did I allow that the proofs of a Deity amounted to no more than a guess or conjecture. But is the whole adjustment of means to ends in a house and in the universe so slight a resemblance? the economy of final causes? the order, proportion, and arrangement of every part? Steps of a stair are plainly contrived that human legs may use them in mounting; and this inference is certain and infallible. Human legs are also contrived for walking and mounting; and this inference, I allow, is not altogether so certain because of the dissimilarity which you remark; but does it, therefore, deserve the name only of presumption or conjecture?

Good God! cried Demea, interrupting him, where are we? Zealous defenders of religion allow that the proofs of a Deity fall short of perfect evidence! And you, Philo, on whose assistance I depended in proving the adorable mysteriousness of the Divine Nature, do you assent to all these extravagant opinions of Cleanthes? For what other name can I give them? or, why spare my censure when such principles are advanced, supported by such an authority. . . .

You seem not to apprehend, replied Philo, that I argue with Cleanthes in his own way, and, by showing him the dangerous consequences of his tenets, hope at last to reduce him to our opinion. But what sticks most with you, I observe, is the representation which Cleanthes has made of the argument a posteriori; and, finding that that argument is likely to escape your hold and vanish into air, you think it so disguised that you can scarcely believe it to be set in its true light. Now, however much I may dissent, in other respects, from the dangerous principle of Cleanthes, I must allow that he has fairly represented that argument, and I shall endeavour so to state the matter to you that you will entertain no further scruples with regard to it.

Were a man to abstract from everything which he knows or has seen, he would be altogether incapable, merely from his own ideas, to determine what kind of scene the universe must be, or to give the preference to one state or situation of things above another. For as nothing which he clearly conceives could be esteemed impossible or implying a contradiction, every chimera of his fancy would be upon an equal footing; nor could he assign any just reason why he adheres to one idea or system, and rejects the others which are equally possible.

Again, after he opens his eyes and contemplates the world as it really is, it would be impossible for him at first to assign the cause of any one event, much less of the whole of things, or of the universe. He might set his fancy a-rambling, and she might bring him in an infinite variety of reports and representations. These would all be possible, but, being all equally possible, he would never of himself give a satisfactory account for his preferring one of them to the rest. Experience alone can point out to him the true cause of any phenomenon.

Now, according to this method of reasoning, Demea, it follows (and is, indeed, tacitly allowed by Cleanthes himself) that order, arrangement, or the adjustment of final causes, is not of itself any proof of design, but only so far as it has been experienced to proceed from that principle. For aught we can know a priori, matter may contain the source or spring of order originally within itself, as well as mind does; and there is no more difficulty in conceiving that the several elements, from an internal unknown cause, may fall into the most exquisite arrangement, than to conceive that their ideas, in the great universal mind, from a like internal unknown cause, fall into that arrangement. The equal possibility of both these suppositions is allowed. But, by experience, we find (according to Cleanthes) that there is a difference between them. Throw several pieces of steel together, without shape or form, they will never arrange themselves so as to compose a watch. Stone and mortar and wood, without an architect, never erect a house. But the ideas in a human mind, we see, by an unknown, inexplicable economy, arrange themselves so as to form the plan of a watch or house. Experience, therefore, proves that there is an original principle of order in mind, not in matter. From similar effects we infer similar causes. The adjustment of means to ends is alike in the universe, as in a machine of human contrivance. The causes, therefore, must be resembling.

I was from the beginning scandalized, I must own, with this resemblance which is asserted between the Deity and human creatures, and must conceive it to imply such a degradation of the Supreme Being as no sound theist could endure. With your assistance, therefore, Demea, I shall endeavor to defend what you justly call the adorable mysteriousness of the Divine Nature, and shall refute this reasoning of Cleanthes, provided he allows that I have made a fair representation of it.

When Cleanthes had assented, Philo, after a short pause, proceeded in the following manner.

That all inferences, Cleanthes, concerning fact are founded on experience, and that all experimental reasonings are founded on the supposition that similar causes prove similar effects, and similar effects similar causes, I shall not at present much dispute with you. But observe, I entreat you, with what extreme caution all just reasoners proceed in the transferring of experiments to similar cases. Unless the cases be exactly similar, they repose no perfect confidence in applying their past observation to any particular phenomenon. Every alternation of circumstances occasions a doubt concerning the event; and it requires new experiments to prove certainly that the new circumstances are of no moment or importance. A change in bulk, situation, arrangement, age, disposition of the air, or surrounding bodies—any of these particulars may be attended with the most unexpected consequences. And unless the objects be quite familiar to us, it is the highest temerity to expect with assurance, after any of these changes, an event similar to that which before fell under our observation. The slow and deliberate steps of philosophers here, if anywhere, are distinguished from the precipitate march of the vulgar, who, hurried on by the smallest similitude, are incapable of all discernment or consideration.

[1. FIRST MAJOR CRITICISM OF THE ARGUMENT.][6]

But can you think, Cleanthes, that your usual phlegm and philosophy have been preserved in so wide a step as you have taken when you compared to the universe houses, ships, furniture, machines, and, from their similarity in some circumstances, inferred a similarity in their causes? Thought, design, intelligence, such as we discover in men and other animals, is no more than one of the springs and principles of the universe, as well as heat or cold, attraction or repulsion, and a hundred others which fall under daily observation. It is an active cause by which some particular parts of nature, we find, produce alterations on other parts. But can a conclusion, with any propriety, be transferred from parts to the whole? Does not the great disproportion bar all comparison and inference? From observing the growth of a hair, can we learn anything concerning the generation of a man? Would the manner of a leaf's blowing, even though perfectly known, afford us any instruction concerning the vegetation of a tree?

But allowing that we were to take the *operations* of one part of nature upon another for the foundation of our judgment concerning the *origin* of the whole (which never can be admitted), yet why select so minute, so weak, so bounded a principle as the reason and design of animals is found to be upon this planet? What peculiar privilege has this little agitation of the brain which we call *thought*, that we must thus make it the model of the whole universe? Our partiality in our own favour does indeed present it on all occasions, but sound philosophy ought carefully to guard against so natural an illusion.

So far from admitting, continued Philo, that the operations of a part can afford us any just conclusion concerning the origin of the whole, I will not allow any one part to

---

[6] Note that this first criticism has four parts.—E.D.K.

form a rule for another part if the latter be very remote from the former. Is there any reasonable ground to conclude that the inhabitants of other planets possess thought, intelligence, reason, or anything similar to these faculties in men? When nature has so extremely diversified her manner of operation in this small globe, can we imagine that she incessantly copies herself throughout so immense a universe? And if thought, as we may well suppose, be confined merely to this narrow corner and his even there so limited a sphere of action, with what propriety can we assign it for the original cause of all things? The narrow views of a peasant who makes his domestic economy the rule for the government of kingdoms is in comparison a pardonable sophism.

But were we ever so much assured that a thought and reason resembling the human were to be found throughout the whole universe, and were its activity elsewhere vastly greater and more commanding than it appears in this globe, yet I cannot see why the operations of a world constituted, arranged, adjusted, can with propriety be extended to a world which is in its embryo state, and is advancing towards that constitution and arrangement. By observation we know somewhat of the economy, action, and nourishment of a finished animal, but we must transfer with great caution that observation to the growth of a fetus in the womb, and still more to the formation of an animalcule in the loins of its male parent. Nature, we find, even from our limited experience, possesses an infinite number of springs and principles which incessantly discover themselves on every change of her position and situation. And what new and unknown principles would actuate her in so new and unknown a situation as that of the formation of a universe, we cannot, without the utmost temerity, pretend to determine.

A very small part of this great system during a very short time, is very imperfectly discovered to us; and do we thence pronounce decisively concerning the origin of the whole?

Admirable conclusion! Stone, wood, brick, iron, brass, have not, at this time, in this minute globe of earth, an order or arrangement without human art and contrivance; therefore, the universe could not originally attain its order and arrangement without something similar to human art. But is a part of nature a rule for another part very wide of the former? Is it a rule for the whole? Is a very small part a rule for the universe? Is nature in one situation a certain rule for nature in another situation vastly different from the former?

And can you blame me, Cleanthes, if I here imitate the prudent reserve of Simonides, who, according to the noted story, being asked by Hiero what God was, desired a day to think of it, and then two days more; and after that manner continually prolonged the term, without ever bringing in his definition or description? Could you even blame me if I had answered, at first, *that I did not know*, and was sensible that this subject lay vastly beyond the reach of my faculties? You might cry out skeptic and rallier, as much as you pleased; but, having found in so many other subjects much more familiar the imperfections and even contradictions of human reason, I never should expect any success from its feeble conjectures in a subject so sublime and so remote from the sphere of our observation. When two species of objects have always been observed to be conjoined together, I can *infer*, by custom, the existence of one wherever I *see* the existence of the other; and this I call an argument from experience. But how this argument can have place where the objects, as in the present case, are single, individual, without parallel or specific resemblance, may be difficult to explain. And will any man tell me with a serious countenance that an orderly universe must arise from some thought and art like the human because we have experience of it? To ascertain this reasoning it were requisite that we had experience of the origin of worlds; and it is not sufficient, surely, that we have seen ships and cities arise from human art and contrivance.

Philo was proceeding in this vehement manner, somewhat between jest and earnest, as it appeared to me, when he observed some signs of impatience in Cleanthes, and then immediately stopped short. What I had to suggest, said Cleanthes, is only that you would not abuse terms, or make use of popular expressions to subvert philosophical reasonings. You know that the vulgar often distinguish reason from experience, even where the question relates only to matter of fact and existence, though it is found, where that reason is properly analyzed, that it is nothing but a species of experience. To prove by experience the origin of the universe from mind is not more contrary to common speech than to prove the motion of the earth from the same principle. And a caviller might raise all the same objections to the Copernican system which you have urged against my reasonings. Have you other earths, might he say, which you have seen to move? Have. . . .

Yes! cried Philo, interrupting him, we have other earths. Is not the moon another earth, which we see to turn round its center? Is not Venus another earth, where we observe the same phenomenon? Are not the revolutions of the sun also a confirmation, from analogy, of the same theory? All the planets, are they not earths which revolve about the sun? Are not the satellites moons which move round Jupiter and Saturn, and along with these primary planets round the sun? These analogies and resemblances, with others which I have not mentioned, are the sole proofs of the Copernican system; and to you it belongs to consider whether you have any analogies of the same kind to support your theory.

In reality, Cleanthes, continued he, the modern system of astronomy is now so much received by all inquirers, and has become so essential a part even of our earliest education, that we are not commonly very scrupulous in examining the reasons upon which it is founded. It is now become a matter of mere curiosity to study the first writers on that subject who had the full force of prejudice to encounter, and were obliged to turn their arguments on every side in order to render them popular and convincing. But if we peruse Galileo's famous *Dialogues* concerning the system of the world, we shall find that the great genius, one of the sublimest that ever existed, first bent all his endeavours to prove that there was no foundation for the distinction commonly made between elementary and celestial substances. The schools, proceeding from the illusions of sense, had carried this distinction very far; and had established the latter substances to be ingenerable, incorruptible, unalterable, impassible; and had assigned all the opposite qualities to the former. But Galileo, beginning with the moon, proved its similarity in every particular to the earth: its convex figure, its natural darkness when not illuminated, its density, its distinction into solid and liquid, the variations of its phases, the mutual illuminations of the earth and moon, their mutual eclipses, the inequalities of the lunar surface, etc. After many instances of this kind, with regard to all the planets, men plainly saw that the similarity of their nature enabled us to extend the same arguments and phenomena from one to the other.

In this cautious proceeding of the astronomers you may read your own condemnation, Cleanthes, or rather may see that the subject in which you are engaged exceeds all human reason and inquiry. Can you pretend to show any such similarity between the fabric of a house and the generation of a universe? Have you ever seen nature in any such situation as resembles the first arrangement of the elements? Have worlds ever been formed under your eye, and have you had leisure to observe the whole progress of the phenomenon, from the first appearance of order to its final consummation? If you have, then cite your experience and deliver your theory. . . .

· *II* ·

(PART IV)

It seems strange to me, said Cleanthes, that you, Demea, who are so sincere in the cause of religion, should still maintain the mysterious, incomprehensible nature of the Deity, and should insist so strenuously that He has no manner of likeness or resemblance to human creatures. The Deity, I can readily allow, possesses many powers and attributes of which we can have no comprehension; but, if our ideas, so far as they go, be not just and adequate and correspondent to His real nature, I know not what there is in this subject worth insisting on. Is the name, without any meaning, of such mighty importance? Or how do you mystics, who maintain the absolute incomprehensibility of the Deity, differ from skeptics or atheists, who assert that the first cause of all is unknown and unintelligible? Their temerity must be very great if, after rejecting the production by a mind—I mean a mind resembling the human (for I know of no other)—they pretend to assign, with certainty, any other specific intelligible cause; and their conscience must be very scrupulous, indeed, if they refuse to call the universal unknown cause a God or Deity, and to bestow on Him as many sublime eulogies and unmeaning epithets as you shall please to require of them.

Who could imagine, replied Demea, that Cleanthes, the calm philosophical Cleanthes, would attempt to refute his antagonists by affixing a nickname to them, and, like the common bigots and inquisitors of the age, have recourse to invective and declamation instead of reasoning? Or does he not perceive that these topics are easily retorted, and that *anthropomorphite* is an appellation as invidious, and implies as dangerous consequences, as the epithet of *mystic* with which he has honoured us? In reality, Cleanthes, consider what it is you assert when you represent the Deity as similar to a human mind and understanding. What is the soul of man? A composition of various faculties, passions, sentiments, ideas—united, indeed, into one self or person, but still distinct from each other. When it reasons, the ideas which are the parts of its discourse arrange themselves in a certain form or order which is not preserved entire for a moment, but immediately gives place to another arrangement. New opinions, new passions, new affections, new feelings arise which continually diversify the mental scene and produce in it the greatest variety and most rapid succession imaginable. How is this compatible with that perfect immutability and simplicity which all true theists ascribe to the Deity? By the same act, say they, He sees past, present, and future; His love and hatred, His mercy and justice, are one individual operation; He is entire in every point of space, and complete in every instant of duration. No succession, no change, no acquisition, no diminution. What He is implies not in it any shadow of distinction or diversity. And what He is this moment He ever has been and ever will be, without any new judgment, sentiment, or operation. He stands fixed in one simple, perfect state; nor can you ever say, with any propriety, that this act of His is different from that other, or that this judgment or idea has been lately formed and will give place, by succession, to any different judgment or idea.

I can readily allow, said Cleanthes, that those who maintain the perfect simplicity of the Supreme Being, to the extent in which you have explained it, are complete mystics, and chargeable with all the consequences which I have drawn from their opinion. They are, in a word, atheists, without knowing it. For though it be allowed that the Deity possesses attributes of which we have no comprehension, yet ought we never to ascribe to Him any attributes which are absolutely incompatible with that intelligent nature essential to Him. A mind whose acts and sentiments and ideas are not distinct and successive, one that is wholly simple and totally immutable, is a mind which has no thought, no reason, no will, no sentiment, no love, no hatred; or, in a word, is no mind at all. It is an abuse of terms to give it that appellation, and we may as well speak of limited extension without figure, or of number without composition.

Pray consider, said Philo, whom you are at present inveighing against. You are honouring with the appellation of *atheist* all the sound, orthodox divines, almost, who have treated of this subject; and you will at last be, yourself, found, according to your reckoning, the only sound theist in the world. But if idolaters be atheists, as, I think, may justly be asserted, and Christian theologians the same, what becomes of the argument, so much celebrated, derived from the universal consent of mankind?

But, because I know you are not much swayed by names and authorities, I shall endeavour to show you, a little more distinctly, the inconveniences of that anthropomorphism which you have embraced, and shall prove that there is no ground to suppose a plan of the world to be formed in the Divine mind, consisting of distinct ideas, differently arranged, in the same manner as an architect forms in his head the plan of a house which he intends to execute.

It is not easy, I own, to see what is gained by this supposition, whether we judge of the matter by *reason* or by *experience*. We are still obliged to mount higher in order to find the cause of this cause which you has assigned as satisfactory and conclusive.

If *reason* (I mean abstract reason derived from inquiries a priori) be not alike mute with regard to all questions concerning cause and effect, this sentence at least it will venture to pronounce: that a mental world or universe of ideas requires a cause as much as does a material world or universe of objects, and, if similar in its arrangement, must require a similar cause. For what is there in this subject which should occasion a different conclusion or inference? In an abstract view, they are entirely alike; and no difficulty attends the one supposition which is not common to both of them.

Again, when we will needs force *experience* to pronounce some sentence, even on these subjects which lie beyond her sphere, neither can she perceive any material difference in this particular between these two kinds of worlds, but finds them to be governed by similar principles, and to depend upon an equal variety of causes in their operations. We have specimens in miniature of both of them. Our own mind resembles the one; a vegetable or animal body the other. Let experience, therefore, judge from these samples. Nothing seems more delicate, with regard to its causes, than thought; and as these causes never operate in two persons after the same manner, so we never find two persons who think exactly alike. Nor indeed does the same person think exactly alike at any two different periods of time. A different of age, of the disposition of his body, of weather, of food, of company, of books, of passions—any of these particulars, or others more minute, are sufficient to alter the curious machinery of thought and communicate to it very different movements and operations. As far as we can judge, vegetables and animal bodies are not more delicate in their motions, nor depend upon a greater variety or more curious adjustment of springs and principles.

How, therefore, shall we satisfy ourselves concerning the cause of that Being whom you suppose the Author of nature, or, according to your system of anthropomorphism, the ideal world into which you trace the material? Have we not the same reason to trace that ideal world into another ideal world or new intelligent principle? But if we stop and go no farther, why go so far? why not stop at the material world? How can we satisfy ourselves without going on *in infinitum*? And, after all, what satisfaction is there in that infinite progression? Let us remember the story of the Indian philosopher and his elephant. It was never more applicable than to the present subject. If the material world rests upon a similar ideal world, this ideal world must rest upon some other, and so on without end. It were better, therefore, never to look beyond the present material world. By supposing it to contain the principle of its order within itself, we really assert it to be God; and the sooner we arrive at that Divine Being, so much the better. When you go one step beyond the mundane system, you only excite an inquisitive humour which it is impossible ever to satisfy.

To say that the different ideas which compose the reason of the Supreme Being fall into order of themselves and by their own nature is really to talk without any precise meaning. If it has a meaning, I would fain know why it is not as good sense to say that the parts of the material world fall into order of themselves and by their own nature. Can the one opinion be intelligible, while the other is not so?

We have, indeed, experience of ideas which fall into order of themselves and without any *known* cause. But, I am sure, we have a much larger experience of matter which does the same, as in all instances of generation and vegetation where the accurate analysis of the cause exceeds all human comprehension. We have also experience of particular systems of thought and of matter which have no order; of the first in madness, of the second in corruption. Why, then, should we think that order is more essential to one than the other? And if it requires a cause in both, what do we gain by your system, in tracing the universe of objects into a similar universe of ideas? The first step which we make leads us on forever. It were, therefore, wise in us to limit all our inquiries to the present world, without looking farther. No satisfaction can ever be attained by these speculations which so far exceed the narrow bounds of human understanding.

It was usual with the Peripatetics, you know, Cleanthes, when the cause of any phenomenon was demanded, to have recourse to their *faculties* or *occult qualities*, and to say, for instance, that bread nourished by its nutritive faculty, and senna purged by its purgative. But it has been discovered that this subterfuge was nothing but the disguise of ignorance, and that these philosophers, though less ingenuous, really said the same thing with the skeptics or the vulgar who fairly confessed that they knew not the cause of these phenomena. In like manner, when it is asked what cause produces order in the ideas of the Supreme Being, can any other reason be assigned by you, anthropomorphites, than that it is a *rational* faculty, and that such is the nature of the Deity? But why a similar answer will not be equally satisfactory in accounting for the order of the world, without having recourse to any such intelligent Creator as you insist on, may be difficult to determine. It is only to say that *such* is the nature of material objects, and that they are all originally possessed of a *faculty* of order and proportion. These are only more learned and elaborate ways of confessing our ignorance; nor has the one hypothesis any real advantage above the other, except in its greater conformity to vulgar prejudices.

You have displayed this argument with great emphasis, replied Cleanthes: You seem not sensible how easy it is to answer it. Even in common life, if I assign a cause for any event, is it any objection, Philo, that I cannot assign the cause of that cause, and answer every new question which may incessantly be started? And what philosophers could possibly submit to so rigid a rule?—philosophers who confess ultimate causes to be totally unknown, and are sensible that the most refined principles into which they trace the phenomena are still to them as inexplicable as these phenomena themselves are to the vulgar. The order and arrangement of nature, the curious adjustment of final causes, the plain use of intention of every part and organ—all these bespeak in the clearest language an intelligent cause or author. The heavens and the earth join in the same testimony; The whole chorus of nature raises one hymn to the praises of its Creator. You alone, or almost alone, disturb this general harmony. You start abstruse doubts, cavils, and objections; you ask me what is the cause of this cause? I know not; I care not; that concerns not me. I have found a Deity; and here I stop my inquiry. Let those go farther who are wiser or more enterprising.

I pretend to be neither, replied Philo; and for that very reason I should never, perhaps, have attempted to go so far, especially when I am sensible that I must at last be contented to sit down with the same answer which, without further trouble, might have satisfied me from the beginning. If I am still to remain in utter ignorance of causes and can absolutely give an explication of nothing, I shall never esteem it any advantage to shove off for a moment a difficulty which you acknowledge must immediately, in its full force, recur upon me. Naturalists indeed very justly explain particular effects by more general causes, though these general causes themselves should remain in the end totally inexplicable, but they never surely thought it satisfactory to explain a particular effect by a particular cause which was no more to be accounted for than the effect itself. An ideal system, arranged of itself, without a precedent design, is not a whit more explicable than a material one which attains its order in a like manner; nor is there any more difficulty in the latter supposition than in the former.

· III ·

(PART V)

[2. SECOND CRITICISM.]

But to show you still more inconveniences, continued Philo, in your anthropomorphism, please to take a new survey of your principle. *Like effects prove like causes.* This is the experimental argument; and this, you say too, is the sole theological argument. Now it is certain that the liker the effects are which are seen and the liker the causes which are inferred, the stronger is the argument. Every departure on either side diminishes the probability and renders the experiment less conclusive. You cannot doubt of the principle; neither ought you to reject its consequences.

All the new discoveries in astronomy which prove the immense grandeur and magnificence of the works of nature are so many additional arguments for a Deity, according to the true system of theism; but, according to your hypothesis of experimental theism, they become so many objections, by removing the effect still farther from all resemblance to the effects of human art and contrivance. For if Lucretius, even following the old system of the world, could exclaim:

> Quis regere immensi summam, quis habere profundi
> Indu manu validas potis est moderanter habenas?
> Quis pariter cœlos omnes convertere? et omnes

Ignibus ætheriis terras suffire feraces?
Omnibus inve locis esse omni tempore præsto?[7]

If Tully [Cicero] esteemed this reasoning so natural as to put it into the mouth of his Epicurean:

Quibus enim oculis animi intueri potuit vester Plato fabricam illam tanti operis, qua construi a Deo atque ædificari mundum facit? quæ molitio? quæ ferramenta? qui vectes? quæ machinæ? qui ministri tanti muneris fuerunt? quemadmodum autem obedire et parere voluntati architecti aer, ignis, aqua, terra potuerunt?[8]

If this argument, I say, had any force in former ages, how much greater must it have at present when the bounds of nature are so infinitely enlarged and such a magnificent scene is opened to us? It is still more unreasonable to form our idea of so unlimited a cause from our experience of the narrow production of human design and invention.

The discoveries by microscopes, as they open a new universe in miniature, are still objections, according to you, arguments, according to me. The further we push our researches of this kind, we are still led to infer the universal cause of all to be vastly different from mankind, or from any object of human experience and observation.

And what say you to the discoveries in anatomy, chemistry, botany? . . . These surely are no objections, replied Cleanthes; they only discover new instances of art and contrivance. It is still the image of mind reflected on us from innumerable objects. Add a mind *like the human*, said Philo. I know of no other, replied Cleanthes. And the liker, the better, insisted Philo. To be sure, said Cleanthes.

Now, Cleanthes, said Philo, with an air of alacrity and triumph, mark the consequences. *First*, by this method of reasoning you renounce all claim to infinity in any of the attributes of the Deity. For, as the cause ought only to be proportioned to the effect, and the effect, so far as it falls under our cognizance, is not infinite, what pretensions have we, upon your suppositions, to ascribe that attribute to the Divine Being? You will still insist that, by removing Him so much from all similarity to human creatures, we give in to the most arbitrary hypothesis, and at the same time weaken all proofs of His existence.

Secondly, you have no reason, on your theory, for ascribing perfection to the Deity, even in His finite capacity, or for supposing Him free from every error, mistake, or incoherence, in His undertakings. There are many inexplicable difficulties in the works of nature which, if we allow a perfect Author to be proved a priori, are easily solved, and become only seeming difficulties from the narrow capacity of man, who cannot trace infinite relations. But according to your method of reasoning, these difficulties become all real, and, perhaps,

---

[7] *De Rerum Natura*, Bk. XI, Chap. 2. "Who can rule the sum, who hold in his hand with controlling force the strong reins, of the immeasurable deep? Who can at once make all the different heavens to roll and warm with ethereal fires all the fruitful earths, or be present in all places at all times?" (Munro's translation).—D.H.

[8] *De Natura Deorum*, Bk. I, Chap. 8. "For with what eyes of the mind could your Plato see the construction of so vast a work which, according to him, God was putting together and building? What materials, what tools, what bars, what machines, what servants were employed in such gigantic work? How could the air, fire, water, and earth pay obedience and submit to the will of the architect?"—D.H.

will be insisted on as new instances of likeness to human art and contrivance. At least, you must acknowledge that it is impossible for us to tell, from our limited views, whether this system contains any great faults or deserves any considerable praise if compared to other possible and even real systems. Could a peasant, if the *Æneid* were read to him, pronounce that poem to be absolutely faultless, or even assign to it its proper rank among the productions of human wit, he who had never seen any other production?

But were this world ever so perfect a production, it must still remain uncertain whether all the excellences of the work can justly be ascribed to the workman. If we survey a ship, what an exalted idea must we form of the ingenuity of the carpenter who framed so complicated, useful, and beautiful a machine? And what surprise must we feel when we find him a stupid mechanic who imitated others, and copied an art which, through a long succession of ages, after multiplied trials, mistakes, corrections, deliberations, and con-troversies, had been gradually improving? Many worlds might have been botched and bungled, throughout an eternity, ere this system was struck out; much labour lost, many fruitless trials made, and a slow but continued improvement carried on during infinite ages in the art of world-making. In such subjects, who can determine where the truth, nay, who can conjecture where the probability, lies, amidst a great number of hypotheses which may be proposed, and a still greater which may be imagined?

And what shadow of an argument, continued Philo, can you produce from your hypothesis to prove the unity of the Deity? A great number of men join in building a house or ship, in rearing a city, in framing a commonwealth; why may not several deities combine in contriving and framing a world? This is only so much greater similarity to human affairs. By sharing the work among several, we may so much further limit the attributes of each, and get rid of that extensive power and knowledge which must be supposed in one deity, and which, according to you, can only serve to weaken the proof of his existence. And if such foolish, such vicious creatures as man can yet often unite in framing and executing one plan, how much more those deities or demons, whom we may suppose several degrees more perfect!

To multiply causes without necessity is indeed contrary to true philosophy, but this principle applies not to the present case. Were one deity antecedently proved by your theory who were possessed of every attribute requisite to the production of the universe, it would be needless, I own (though not absurd), to suppose any other deity exist. But while it is still a question whether all these attributes are united in one subject or dispersed among several independent beings, by what phenomena in nature can we pretend to decide the controversy? Where we see a body raised in a scale, we are sure that there is in the opposite scale, however concealed from sight, some counterpoising weight equal to it; but it is still allowed to doubt whether that weight be an aggregate of several distinct bodies or one uniform united mass. And if the weight requisite very much exceeds anything which we have ever seen conjoined in any single body, the former supposition becomes still more probable and natural. An intelligent being of such vast powers and capacity as is necessary to produce the universe, or, to speak in the language of ancient philosophy, so prodigious an animal exceeds all analogy and even comprehension.

But further, Cleanthes: men are mortal, and renew their species by generation; and this is common to all living creatures. The two great sexes of male and female, says Milton, animate the world. Why must this circumstance, so universal, so essential, be excluded from those numerous and limited deities? Behold, then, the theogeny of ancient times brought back upon us.

And why not become a perfect anthropomorphite? Why not assert the deity or deities to be corporeal, and to have eyes, a nose, mouth, ears, etc.? Epicurus maintained that no man had ever seen reason but in a human figure; therefore, the gods must have a human figure. And this argument, which is deservedly so much ridiculed by Cicero, becomes, according to you, solid and philosophical.

In a word, Cleanthes, a man who follows your hypothesis is able, perhaps, to assert or conjecture that the universe sometime arose from something like design; but beyond that position he cannot ascertain one single circumstance, and is left afterwards to fix every point of his theology by the utmost license of fancy and hypothesis. This world, for aught he knows, is very faulty and imperfect, compared to a superior standard, and was only the first rude essay of some infant deity who afterwards abandoned it, ashamed of his lame performance; it is the work only of some dependent, inferior deity, and is the object of derision to his superiors; it is the production of old age and dotage in some superannuated deity, and ever since his death has run on at adventures, from the first impulse and active force which it received from him. You justly give signs of horror, Demea, at these strange suppositions; but these, and a thousand more of the same kin, are Cleanthes' suppositions, not mine. From the moment the attributes of the Deity are supposed finite, all these have place. And I cannot, for my part, think that so wild and unsettled a system of theology is, in any respect, preferable to none at all.

These suppositions I absolutely disown, cried Cleanthes: they strike me, however, with no horror, especially when proposed in that rambling way in which they drop from you. On the contrary, they give me pleasure when I see that, by the utmost indulgence of your imagination, you never get rid of the hypothesis of design in the universe, but are obliged at every turn to have recourse to it. To this concession I adhere steadily; and this I regard as a sufficient foundation for religion.

· *IV* ·

(PART VI)

[3. THIRD CRITICISM.]

It must be a slight fabric, indeed, said Demea, which can be erected on so tottering a foundation. While we are uncertain whether there is one deity or many, whether the deity or deities, to whom we owe our existence, be perfect or imperfect, subordinate or supreme, dead or alive, what trust or confidence can we repose in them? What devotion or worship address to them? What veneration or obedience pay them? To all the purposes of life the theory of religion becomes altogether useless; and even with regard to speculative consequences its uncertainty, according to you, must render it totally precarious and unsatisfactory.

To render it still more unsatisfactory, said Philo, there occurs to me another hypothesis which must acquire an air of probability from the method of reasoning so much insisted on by Cleanthes. That like effects arise from like causes—this principle he supposes the foundation of all religion. But there is another principle of the same kind, no less certain and derived from the same source of experience, that, where several known circumstances are observed to be similar, the unknown will also be found similar. Thus, if we see the limbs of a human body, we conclude that it is also attended with a human head, though hid from us. Thus, if we see, through a chink in a wall, a small part of the sun, we conclude that were the wall removed we should see the whole body. In short, this method of reasoning is so obvious and familiar that no scruple can ever be made with regard to its solidity.

Now, if we survey the universe, so far as it falls under our knowledge, it bears a great resemblance to an animal or organized body, and seems actuated with a like principle of life and motion. A continual circulation of matter in it produces no disorder; a continual waste in every part is incessantly repaired; the closest sympathy is perceived throughout the entire system; and each part or member, in performing its proper offices, operates both to its own preservation and to that of the whole. The world, therefore, I infer, is an animal; and the Deity is the *soul* of the world, actuating it, and actuated by it.

You have too much learning, Cleanthes, to be at all surprised at this opinion which, you know, was maintained by almost all the theists of antiquity, and chiefly prevails in their discourses and reasoning. For though, sometimes, the ancient philosophers reason from final causes, as if they thought the world the workmanship of God, yet it appears rather their favorite notion to consider it as His body whose organization renders it subservient to Him. And it must be confessed that, as the universe resembles more a human body that it does the works of human art and contrivance, if our limited analogy could ever, with any propriety, be extended to the whole of nature, the inference seems juster in favour of the ancient than the modern theory.

There are many other advantages, too, in the former theory which recommended it to the ancient theologians. Nothing more repugnant to all their notions because nothing more repugnant to common experience than mind without body, a mere spiritual substance which fell not under their senses nor comprehension, and of which they had not observed one single instance throughout all nature. Mind and body they knew because they felt both; an order, arrangement, organization, or internal machinery, in both they likewise knew, after the same manner; and it could not but seem reasonable to transfer this experience to the universe, and to suppose the divine mind and body to be also coeval and to have, both of them, order and arrangement naturally inherent in them and inseparable from them.

Here, therefore, is a new species of anthropomorphism, Cleanthes, on which you may deliberate, and a theory which seems not liable to any considerable difficulties. You are too much superior, surely, to *systematical prejudices* to find any more difficulty in supposing an animal body to be, originally, of itself or from unknown causes, possessed of order and organization, than in supposing a similar order to belong to mind. But the *vulgar prejudice* that body and mind ought always to accompany each other ought not, one should think, to be entirely neglected; since it is founded on *vulgar experience*, the only guide which you profess to follow in all these theological inquiries. And if you assert that our limited experience is an unequal standard by which to judge of the unlimited extent of nature, you entirely abandon your own hypothesis, and must thenceforward adopt our mysticism, as you call it, and admit of the absolute incomprehensibility of the Divine Nature.[9]

This theory, I own, replied Cleanthes, has never before occurred to me, though a pretty natural one; and I cannot readily, upon so short an examination and reflection,

---

[9] From here to the end of the selection there are objections and replies.—E.D.K.

deliver any opinion with regard to it. You are very scrupulous, indeed, said Philo, were I to examine any system of yours, I should not have acted with half that caution and reserve, in starting objections and difficulties to it. However, if anything occur to you, you will oblige us by proposing it.

Why then, replied Cleanthes, it seems to me that, though the world does, in many circumstances, resemble an animal body, yet is the analogy also defective in many circumstances the most material: no organs of sense; no seat of thought or reason; no one precise origin of motion and action. In short, it seems to bear a stronger resemblance to a vegetable than to an animal, and your inference would be so far inconclusive in favour of the soul of the world.

But, in the next place, your theory seems to imply the eternity of the world; and that is a principle which, I think, can be refuted by the strongest reasons and probabilities. I shall suggest an argument to this purpose which, I believe, has not been insisted on by any writer. Those who reason from the late origin of arts and sciences, though their inference wants not force, may perhaps be refuted by considerations derived from the nature of human society, which is in continual revolution between ignorance and knowledge, liberty and slavery, riches and poverty; so that it is impossible for us, from out limited experience, to foretell with assurance what events may or may not be expected. Ancient learning and history seem to have been in great danger of entirely perishing after the inundation of the barbarous nations; and had these convulsions continued a little longer or been a little more violent, we should not probably have now known what passed in the world a few centuries before us. Nay, were it not for the superstition of the popes, who preserved a little jargon of Latin in order to support the appearance of an ancient and universal church, that tongue must have been utterly lost; in which case the Western world, being totally barbarous, would not have been in a fit disposition for receiving the Greek language and learning, which was conveyed to them after the sacking of Constantinople. When learning and books had been extinguished, even the mechanical arts would have fallen considerably to decay; and it is easily imagined that fable or tradition might ascribe to them a much later origin than the true one. This vulgar argument, therefore, against the eternity of the world seems a little precarious.

But here appears to be the foundation of a better argument. Lucullus was the first that brought cherry trees from Asia to Europe, though that tree thrives so well in many European climates that it grows in the woods without any culture. Is it possible that, throughout a whole eternity, no European had ever passed into Asia and thought of transplanting so delicious a fruit into his own country? Or if the tree was once transplanted and propagated, how could it ever afterwards perish? Empires may rise and fall, liberty and slavery succeed alternately, ignorance and knowledge give place to each other; but the cherry tree will still remain in the woods of Greece, Spain, and Italy, and will never be affected by the revolutions of human society.

It is not two thousand years since vines were transplanted into France, though there is no climate in the world more favourable to them. It is not three centuries since horses, cows, sheep, swine, dogs, corn, were known in America. Is it possible that during the revolutions of a whole eternity there never arose a Columbus who might open the communication between Europe and that continent? We may as well imagine that all men would wear stockings for ten thousand years, and never have the sense to think of garters to tie them. All these seem convincing proofs of the youth or rather infancy of the world, as being founded on the operation of principles more constant and steady than those by which human society is governed and directed. Nothing less than a total convulsion of the elements will ever destroy all the European animals and vegetables which are now to be found in the Western world.

And what argument have you against such convulsions? replied Philo. Strong and almost incontestable proofs may be traced over the whole earth that every part of this globe has continued for many ages entirely covered with water. And though order were supposed inseparable from matter, and inherent in it, yet may matter be susceptible of many and great revolutions, through the endless periods of eternal duration. The incessant changes to which every part of it is subject seem to intimate some such general transformations; though, at the same time, it is observable that all the changes and corruptions of which we have ever had experience are but passages from one state of order to another; nor can matter ever rest in total deformity and confusion. What we see in the parts, we may infer in the whole; at least, that is the method of reasoning on which you rest your whole theory. And were I obliged to defend any particular system of this nature, which I never willingly should do, I esteem none more plausible than that which ascribes an eternal inherent principle of order to the world, though attended with great and continual revolutions and alterations. This at once solves all difficulties; and if the solution, by being so general, is not entirely complete and satisfactory, it is at least a theory that we must sooner or later have recourse to, whatever system we embrace. How could things have been as they are, were there not an original inherent principle of order somewhere, in thought or in matter? And it is very indifferent to which of these we give the preference. Chance has no place, on any hypothesis, skeptical or religious. Everything is surely governed by steady, inviolable laws. And were the inmost essence of things laid open to us, we should then discover a scene of which, at present, we can have no idea. Instead of admiring the order of natural beings, we should clearly see that it was absolutely impossible for them, in the smallest article, ever to admit of any other disposition.

Were anyone inclined to revive the ancient pagan theology which maintained, as we learn from Hesiod, that this globe was governed by 30,000 deities, who arose from the unknown powers of nature, you would naturally object, Cleanthes, that nothing is gained by this hypothesis; and that it is as easy to suppose all men and animals, beings more numerous but less perfect, to have sprung immediately from a like origin. Push the same inference a step further, and you will find a numerous society of deities as explicable as one universal deity who possesses within himself the powers and perfections of the whole society. All these systems, then, of skepticism, polytheism, and theism, you must allow, on your principles, to be on a like footing, and that no one of them has any advantage over the others. You may thence learn the fallacy of your principles.

. *V* .

(PART VII)

But here, continued Philo, in examining the ancient system of the soul of the world there strikes me, all of a sudden, a new idea which, if just, must go near to subvert all your reasoning, and destroy even your first inferences on which you repose such confidence. If the universe bears a greater likeness to animal bodies and to vegetables than to the works of human art, it is more probable that its cause resembles the cause of the former than that of the latter, and its origin ought rather to be ascribed to generation or vegetation than to reason or design. Your conclusion, even according to your own principles, is therefore lame and defective.

Pray open up this argument a little further, said Demea, for I do not rightly apprehend it in that concise manner in which you have expressed it.

Our friend Cleanthes, replied Philo, as you have heard, asserts that, since no question of fact can be proved otherwise than by experience, the existence of a Deity admits not of proof from any other medium. The world, says he, resembles the works of human contrivance; therefore its cause must also resemble that of the other. Here we may remark that the operation of one very small part of nature, to wit, man, upon another very small part, to wit, that inanimate matter lying within his reach, is the rule by which Cleanthes judges of the origin of the whole; and he measures objects, so widely disproportioned, by the same individual standard. But to waive all objections drawn from this topic, I affirm that there are other parts of the universe (besides the machines of human invention) which bear still a greater resemblance to the fabric of the world, and which, therefore, afford a better conjecture concerning the universal origin of this system. These parts are animals and vegetables. The world plainly resembles more an animal or a vegetable than it does a watch or a knitting-loom. Its cause, therefore, it is more probable, resembles the cause of the former. The cause of the former is generation or vegetation. The cause, therefore, of the world we may infer to be something similar or analogous to generation or vegetation.

But how is it conceivable, said Demea, that the world can arise from anything similar to vegetation or generation?

Very easily, replied Philo. In like manner as a tree sheds its seed into the neighbouring fields and produces other trees, so the great vegetable, the world, or this planetary system, produces within itself certain seeds which, being scattered into the surrounding chaos, vegetate into new worlds. A comet, for instance, is the seed of a world; and after it has been fully ripened, by passing from sun to sun, and star to star, it is, at last, tossed into the unformed elements which everywhere surround this universe, and immediately sprouts up into a new system.

Or if, for the sake of variety (for I see no other advantage), we should suppose this world to be an animal: a comet is the egg of this animal; and in like manner as an ostrich lays its egg in the sand, which, without any further care, hatches the egg and produces a new animal, so. . . . I understand you, says Demea. But what wild, arbitrary suppositions are these! What data have you for such extraordinary conclusions? And is the slight, imaginary resemblance of the world to a vegetable or an animal sufficient to establish the same inference with regard to both? Objects which are in general so widely different, ought they to be a standard for each other?

Right, cries Philo: This is the topic on which I have all along insisted. I have still asserted that we have no data to establish any system of cosmogony. Our experience, so imperfect in itself and so limited both in extent and duration, can afford us no probable conjecture concerning the whole of things. But if we must needs fix on some hypothesis, by what rule, pray, ought we to determine our choice? Is there any other rule than the greater similarity of the objects compared? And does not a plant or an animal, which springs from vegetation or generation, bear a stronger resemblance to the world than does any artificial machine, which arises from reason and design?

But what is this vegetation and generation of which you talk? said Demea. Can you explain their operations, and anatomize that fine internal structure on which they depend?

As much, at least, replied Philo, as Cleanthes can explain the operations of reason, or anatomize that internal structure on which it depends. But without any such elaborate disquisitions, when I see an animal, I infer that it sprang from generation; and that with as great certainty as you conclude a house to have been reared by design. These words *generation*, *reason* mark only certain powers and energies in nature whose effects are known, but whose essence is incomprehensible; and one of these principles, more than the other, has no privilege for being made a standard to the whole of nature.

In reality, Demea, it may reasonably be expected that the larger the views are which we take of things, the better will they conduct us in our conclusions concerning such extraordinary and such magnificent subjects. In this little corner of the world alone, there are four principles, *reason*, *instinct*, *generation*, *vegetation*, which are similar to each other, and are the causes of similar effects. What a number of other principles may we naturally suppose in the immense extent and variety of the universe could we travel from planet to planet, and from system to system, in order to examine each part of this mighty fabric? Any one of these four principles above mentioned (and a hundred others which lie open to our conjecture) may afford us a theory by which to judge of the origin of the world; and it is a palpable and egregious partiality to confine our view entirely to that principle by which our own minds operate. Were this principle more intelligible on that account, such a partiality might be somewhat excusable; but reason, in its internal fabric and structure, is really as little known to us as instinct or vegetation; and, perhaps, even that vague, undeterminate word *nature* to which the vulgar refer everything is not at the bottom more inexplicable. The effects of these principles are all known to us from experience; but the principles themselves and their manner of operation are totally unknown; nor is it less intelligible or less conformable to experience to say that the world arose by vegetation, from a seed shed by another world, than to say that it arose from a divine reason or contrivance, according to the sense in which Cleanthes understands it.

But methinks, said Demea, if the world has a vegetative quality and could sow the seeds of new worlds into the infinite chaos, this power would be still an additional argument for design in its Author. For whence could arise so wonderful a faculty but from design? Or how can order spring from anything which perceives not that order which it bestows?

You need only look around you, replied Philo, to satisfy yourself with regard to this question. A tree bestows order and organization on that tree which springs from it, without knowing the order; an animal in the same manner on its offspring; a bird on its nest; and instances of this kind are even more frequent in the world than those of order which arise from reason and contrivance. To say that all this order in animals and vegetables proceeds ultimately from design is begging the question; nor can that great point be ascertained otherwise than by proving, a priori, both that order is, from its nature, inseparably attached to thought and that it can never of itself or from original unknown principles belong to matter.

But further, Demea, this objection which you urge can never be made use of by Cleanthes, without renouncing a defence which he has already made against one of my objections. When I inquired concerning the cause of that supreme reason and intelligence into which he resolves everything, he told me that the impossibility of satisfying such inquiries could never be admitted as an objection in any species of philosophy. "We must stop somewhere," says he; "nor is it ever within the reach of human capacity to explain ultimate causes or show the last connections of any objects. It is sufficient if any steps, so far as we go, are supported by experience and observation." Now that vegetation and generation, as well as reason, are experienced to be principles of order in nature is undeniable. If I rest my system of cosmogony on the former, preferably to the latter, it is at my choice. The matter seems entirely arbitrary. And when Cleanthes asks me what is the cause of my great vegetative or generative faculty, I am equally entitled to ask him the cause of his great reasoning principle. These questions we have agreed to forbear on both sides; and it is chiefly his interest on the present occasion to stick to this agreement. Judging by our limited and imperfect experience, generation has some privileges above reason; for we see everyday the latter arise from the former, never the former from the latter.

Compare, I beseech you, the consequences on both sides. The world, say I, resembles an animal; therefore it is an animal, therefore it arose from generation. The steps, I confess, are wide, yet there is some small appearance of analogy in each step. The world, says Cleanthes, resembles a machine; therefore it is a machine, therefore it arose from design. The steps are here equally wide, and the analogy less striking. And if he pretends to carry on *my* hypothesis a step further, and to infer design or reason from the great principle of generation on which I insist, I may, with better authority, use the same freedom to push further *his* hypothesis, and infer a divine generation or theogony from his principle of reason. I have at least some faint shadow of experience, which is the utmost that can ever be attained in the present subject. Reason, in innumerable instances, is observed to arise from the principle of generation, and never to arise from any other principle.

Hesiod and all the ancient mythologists were so struck with this analogy that they universally explained the origin of nature from an animal birth, and copulation. Plato, too, so far as he is intelligible, seems to have adopted some such notion in his *Timœus*.

The Brahmins assert that the world arose from an infinite spider, who spun this whole complicated mass from his bowels, and annihilates afterwards the whole or part of it, by absorbing it again and resolving it into his own essence. Here is a species of cosmogony which appears to us ridiculous because a spider is a little, contemptible animal whose operations we are never likely to take for a model of the whole universe. But still here is a new species of analogy, even in our globe. And were there a planet wholly inhabited by spiders (which is very possible), this inference would there appear as natural and irrefragable as that which in our planet ascribes the origin of all things to design and intelligence, as explained by Cleanthes. Why an orderly system may not be spun from the belly as well as from the brain, it will be difficult for him to give a satisfactory reason.

I must confess, Philo, replied Cleanthes, that, of all men living, the task which you have undertaken, of raising doubts and objections, suits you best and seems, in a manner, natural and unavoidable to you. So great is your fertility of invention that I am not ashamed to acknowledge myself unable, on a sudden, to solve regularly such out-of-the-way difficulties as you incessantly start upon me, thought I clearly see, in general, their fallacy and error. And I question not, but you are yourself, at present, in the same case, and have not the solution so ready as the objection, while you must be sensible that common sense and reason are entirely against you, and that such whimsies as you have delivered may puzzle but never can convince us.

· *VI* ·

(PART VIII)

What you ascribe to the fertility of my invention, replied Philo, is entirely owing to the nature of the subject. In subjects adapted to the narrow compass of human reason there is commonly but one determination which carries probability or conviction with it; and to a man of sound judgment all other supposition but that one appear entirely absurd and chimerical. But in such questions as the present, a hundred contradictory views may preserve a kind of imperfect analogy, and invention has here full scope to exert itself. Without any great effort of thought, I believe that I could, in an instant, propose other systems of cosmogony which would have some faint appearance of truth, though it is a thousand, a million to one if either yours or anyone of mine be the true system.

For instance, what if I should revive the old Epicurean hypothesis? This is commonly, and I believe justly, esteemed the most absurd system that has yet been proposed; yet I know not whether, with a few alterations, it might not be brought to bear a faint appearance of probability. Instead of supposing matter infinite, as Epicurus did, let us suppose it finite. A finite number of particles is only susceptible of finite transpositions; and it must happen, in an eternal duration, that every possible order or position must be tried an infinite number of times. This world, therefore, with all its events, even the most minute, has before been produced and destroyed, and will again be produced and destroyed, without any bounds and limitations. No one who has a conception of the powers of infinite, in comparison of finite, will ever scruple this determination.

But this supposes, said Demea, that matter can acquire motion without any voluntary agent or first mover.

And where is the difficulty, replied Philo, of that supposition? Every event, before experience, is equally difficult and incomprehensible; and every event, after experience, is equally easy and intelligible. Motion, in many instances, from gravity, from elasticity, from electricity, begins in matter, without any known voluntary agent; and to suppose always, in these cases, an unknown, voluntary agent is mere hypothesis and hypothesis attended with no advantages. The beginning of motion in matter itself is as conceivable a priori as its communication from mind and intelligence.

Besides, why may not motion have been propagated by impulse through all eternity, and the same stock of it, or nearly the same, be still upheld in the universe? As much is lost by the composition of motion, as much is gained by its resolution. And whatever the causes are, the fact is certain that matter is and always has been in continual agitation, as far as human experience or tradition reaches. There is not probably, at present, in the whole universe, one particle of matter at absolute rest.

And this very consideration, too, continued Philo, which we have stumbled on in the course of the argument suggests a new hypothesis of cosmogony that is not absolutely absurd and improbable. Is there a system, an order, an economy of things, by which matter can preserve that perpetual agitation which seems essential to it, and yet maintain a constancy in the forms which it produces? There certainly is such an economy, for this is actually the case with the present world. The continual motion of matter, therefore, in less than infinite transpositions, must produce this economy or order, and, by its very nature, that order, when once established, supports itself for many ages if not to eternity. But wherever matter is so poised, arranged, and adjusted as to continue in perpetual motion, and yet preserve a constancy in the forms, its situation must, of necessity, have all the same appearance of art and contrivance which we observe at present. All the parts of each form must have a relation to each other and to the whole; and the whole itself must have a relation to the other parts of the universe, to the element in which the form subsists, to the materials with which it repairs its waste and decay, and to every other form which is hostile or friendly. A defect in any of these particulars destroys the form, and the matter of which it is composed is again set loose, and is thrown into irregular motions and fermentations till it unite itself to some other regular form. If no such form be prepared to receive it, and if there be a great quantity of this corrupted matter in the universe, the universe itself is entirely disordered, whether it be the feeble embryo of a world in its first beginnings that is thus destroyed or the rotten carcass of one languishing in old age and infirmity. In either case, a chaos ensues till finite though innumerable revolutions produce, at last, some forms whose parts and organs are so adjusted as to support the forms amidst a continued succession of matter.

Suppose (for we shall endeavour to vary the expression) that matter were thrown into any position by a blind, unguided force; it is evident that this first position must, in all probability, be the most confused and most disorderly imaginable, without any resemblance to those works of human contrivance which, along with a symmetry of parts, discover an adjustment of means to ends and a tendency to self-preservation. If the actuating force cease after this operation, matter must remain forever in disorder and continue an immense chaos, without any proportion of activity. But suppose that the actuating force, whatever it be, still continues in matter, this first position will immediately give place to a second which will likewise, in all probability, be as disorderly as the first, and so on through many successions of changes and revolutions. No particular order or position ever continues a moment unaltered. The original force, still remaining in activity, gives a perpetual restlessness to matter. Every possible situation is produced, and instantly destroyed. If a glimpse or dawn of order appears for a moment, it is instantly hurried away and confounded by that never-ceasing force which actuates every part of matter.

Thus the universe goes on for many ages in a continued succession of chaos and disorder. But is it not possible that it may settle at last, so as not to lose its motion and active force (for that we have supposed inherent in it), yet so as to preserve an uniformity of appearance, amidst the continual motion and fluctuation of its parts? This we find to be the case with the universe at present. Every individual is perpetually changing, and every part of every individual; and yet the whole remains, in appearance, the same. May we not hope for such a position or rather be assured of it from the eternal revolutions of unguided matter; and may not this account for all the appearing wisdom and contrivance which is in the universe? Let us contemplate the subject a little, and we shall find that this adjustment if attained by matter of a seeming stability in the forms, with a real and perpetual revolution or motion of parts, affords a plausible, if not a true, solution of the difficulty.

It is in vain, therefore, to insist upon the uses of the parts in animals or vegetables, and their curious adjustment to each other. I would fain know how an animal could subsist unless its parts were so adjusted. Do we not find that it immediately perishes whenever this adjustment ceases, and that its matter, corrupting, tries some new form? It happens indeed that the parts of the world are so well adjusted that some regular form immediately lays claim to this corrupted matter; and if it were not so, could the world subsist? Must it not dissolve, as well as the animal, and pass through new positions and situations till in great but finite succession it fall, at last, into the present or some such order?

It is well, replied Cleanthes, you told us that this hypothesis was suggested on a sudden, in the course of the argument. Had you had leisure to examine it, you would soon have perceived the insuperable objections to which it is exposed. No form, you say, can subsist unless it possess those powers and organs requisite for its subsistence; some new order or economy must be tried, and so on, without intermission, till at last some order which can support and maintain itself is fallen upon. But according to this hypothesis, whence arise the many conveniences and advantages which men and all animals possess? Two eyes, two ears are not absolutely necessary for the subsistence of the species. Human race might have been propagated and preserved without horses, dogs, cows, sheep, and those innumerable fruits and products which serve to our satisfaction and enjoyment. If no camels had been created for the use of man in the sandy deserts of Africa and Arabia, would the world have been dissolved? If no loadstone had been framed to give that wonderful and useful direction to the needle, would human society and the humankind have been immediately extinguished? Though the maxims of nature be in general very frugal, yet instances of this kind are far from being rare; and any one of them is a sufficient proof of design—and of a benevolent design—which gave rise to the order and arrangement of the universe.

At least, you may safely infer, said Philo, that the foregoing hypothesis is so far incomplete and imperfect, which I shall not scruple to allow. But can we ever reasonably expect greater success in any attempts of this nature? Or can we ever hope to erect a system of cosmogony that will be liable to no exceptions, and will contain no circumstance repugnant to our limited and imperfect experience of the analogy of nature? Your theory itself cannot surely pretend to any such advantage, even though you have run into anthropomorphism, the better to preserve a conformity to common experience. Let us once more put it to trial. In all instances which we have ever seen, ideas are copied from real objects, and are ectypal, not archetypal, to express myself in learned terms. You reverse this order and give thought the precedence. In all instances which we have ever seen, thought has no influence upon matter except where that matter is so conjoined with it as to have an equal reciprocal influence upon it. No animal can move immediately anything but the members of its own body; and, indeed, the equality of action and reaction seems to be an universal law of nature; but your theory implies a contradiction to this experience. These instances, with many more which it were easy to collect (particularly the supposition of a mind or system of thought that is eternal or, in other words, an animal ingenerable and immortal)—these instances, I say, may teach all of us sobriety in condemning each other, and let us see that as no system of this kind ought ever to be received from a slight analogy, so neither ought any to be rejected on account of a small incongruity. For that is an inconvenience from which we can justly pronounce no one to be exempted.

All religious systems, it is confessed, are subject to great and insuperable difficulties. Each disputant triumphs in his turn, while he carries on an offensive war, and exposes the absurdities, barbarities, and pernicious tenets of his antagonist. But all of them, on the whole, prepare a complete triumph for the *skeptic*, who tells them that no system ought ever to be embraced with regard to such subjects: for this plain reason that no absurdity ought ever to be assented to with regard to any subject. A total suspense of judgment is here our only reasonable resource. And if every attack, as is commonly observed, and no defence among theologians is successful, how complete must be *his* victory who remains always, with all mankind, on the offensive, and has himself no fixed station or abiding city which he is ever, on any occasion, obliged to defend?

∘ ∘ ∘ *11*

The Ontological, Cosmological, and Design Arguments
Immanuel Kant

THERE ARE ONLY three possible ways of proving the existence of God by means of speculative reason.
All the paths leading to this goal begin either from determinate experience and the specific constitution of the world of sense as thereby known, and ascend from it, in accordance with laws of causality, to the supreme cause outside the world; or they start from experience which is purely indeterminate, that is, from experience of existence in general; or finally they abstract from all experience, and argue completely a priori, from mere concepts, to the existence of supreme cause. The first proof is the *physico-theological*,[1] the second the *cosmological*, the third the *ontological*. There are, and there can be, no others.

I propose to show that reason is as little able to make progress on the one path, the empirical, as on the other path, the transcendental, and that it stretches its wings in vain in thus attempting to soar above the world of sense by the mere power of speculation. As regards the order in which these arguments should be dealt with, it will be exactly the reverse of that which reason takes in the progress of its own development, and therefore of that which we have ourselves followed in the above account. For it will be shown that, although experience is what first gives occasion to this enquiry, it is the *transcendental concept* which in all such endeavours marks out the goal that reason has set itself to attain, and which is indeed its sole guide in its efforts to achieve that goal. I shall therefore begin with the examination of the transcendental proof, and afterwards enquire what effect the addition of the empirical factor can have in enhancing the force of the argument.

I. The Impossibility of an Ontological Proof of the Existence of God
CHAPTER III, SECTION 4:

It is evident, from what has been said, that the concept of an absolutely necessary being is a concept of pure reason, that is, a mere idea the objective reality of which is very far from being proved by the fact that reason requires it. For the idea instructs us only in regard to a certain unattainable completeness, and so serves rather to limit the understanding than to extend it to new objects. But we are here faced by what is indeed strange and perplexing, namely, that while the inference from a given existence in

---

[1] That is, the teleological (design) argument.—E.D.K.

general to some absolutely necessary being seems to be both imperative and legitimate, all those conditions under which alone the understanding can form a concept of such a necessity are so many obstacles in the way of our doing so.

In all ages men have spoken of an *absolutely necessary* being, and in so doing have endeavoured, not so much to understand whether and how a thing of this kind allows even of being thought, but rather to prove its existence. There is, of course, no difficulty in giving a verbal definition of the concept, namely, that it is something the non-existence of which is impossible. But this yields no insight into the conditions which make it necessary to regard the non-existence of a thing as absolutely unthinkable. It is precisely these conditions that we desire to know, in order that we may determine whether or not, in resorting to this concept, we are thinking anything at all. The expedient of removing all those conditions which the understanding indispensably requires in order to regard something as necessary, simply through the introduction of the word *unconditioned*, is very far from sufficing to show whether I am still thinking anything in the concept of the unconditionally necessary, or perhaps rather nothing at all.

Nay more, this concept, at first ventured upon blindly, and now become so completely familiar, has been supposed to have its meaning exhibited in a number of examples; and on this account all further inquiry into its intelligibility has seemed to be quite needless. Thus the fact that every geometrical proposition, as, for instance, that a triangle has three angles, is absolutely necessary, has been taken as justifying us in speaking of an object which lies entirely outside the sphere of our understanding as if we understood perfectly what it is that we intend to convey by the concept of that object.

All the alleged examples are, without exception, taken from *judgments*, not from *things* and their existence. But the unconditioned necessity of judgments is not the same as an absolute necessity of things. The absolute necessity of the judgment is only a conditioned necessity of the thing, or of the predicate in the judgment. The above proposition does not declare that three angles are absolutely necessary, but that, under the condition that there is a triangle (that is, that a triangle is given), three angles will necessarily be found in it. So great, indeed, is the deluding influence exercised by this logical necessity that, by the simple device of forming an a priori concept of a thing in such a manner as to include existence within the scope of its meaning, we have supposed ourselves to have justified the conclusion that because existence necessarily belongs to the object of this concept—always under the condition that we posit the thing as given (as existing)—we are also of necessity, in accordance with the law of identity,[2] required to posit the existence of its object, and that this being is therefore itself absolutely necessary—and this, to repeat, for the reason that the existence of this being has already been thought in a concept which is assumed arbitrarily and on condition that we posit its object.

If, in an identical proposition, I reject the predicate while retaining the subject, contradiction results; and I therefore say that the former belongs necessarily to the latter. But if we reject subject and predicate[3] alike, there is no contradiction; for nothing is then left that can be contradicted. To posit a triangle, and yet to reject its three angles, is self-contradictory; but there is no contradiction in rejecting the triangle together with its three angles. The same holds true of the concept of an absolutely necessary being. If its existence is rejected, we reject the thing itself with all its predicates; and no question of

[2] The logical law that for anything x, x=x, or for propositions: For any proposition *p*, if *p*, then *p*.—E.D.K.
[3] In "All *As* are *Bs*" *As* is the subject, *Bs* the predicate.—E.D.K.

contradiction can then arise. There is nothing outside it that would then be contradicted, since the necessity of the thing is not supposed to be derived from anything external; nor is there anything internal that would be contradicted, since in rejecting the thing itself we have at the same time rejected all its internal properties. "God is omnipotent" is a necessary judgment. The omnipotence cannot be rejected if we posit a Deity, that is, an infinite being; for the two concepts are identical. But if we say, "There is no God," neither the omnipotence nor any other of its predicates is given; they are one and all rejected together with the subject, and there is therefore not the least contradiction in such a judgment.[4]

We have thus seen that if the predicate of a judgment is rejected together with the subject, no internal contradiction can result, and that this holds no matter what the predicate may be. The only way of evading this conclusion is to argue that there are subjects which cannot be removed, and must always remain. That, however, would only be another way of saying that there are absolutely necessary subjects; and that is the very assumption which I have called in question, and the possibility of which the above argument professes to establish. For I cannot form the least concept of a thing which, should it be rejected with all its predicates, leaves behind a contradiction; and in the absence of contradiction I have, through pure a priori concepts alone, no criterion of impossibility.

Notwithstanding all these general considerations, in which everyone must concur, we may be challenged with a case which is brought forward as proof that in actual fact the contrary holds, namely, that there is one concept, and indeed only one, in reference to which the not-being or rejection of its object is in itself contradictory, namely, the concept of the *ens realissimum*.[5] It is declared that it possesses all reality, and that we are justified in assuming that such a being is possible (the fact that a concept does not contradict itself by no means proves the possibility of its object: but the contrary assertion I am for the moment willing to allow).[6] Now [the argument proceeds] "all reality" includes existence; existence is therefore contained in the concept of a thing that is possible. If, then, this thing is rejected the internal possibility of the thing is rejected— which is self-contradictory.

My answer is as follows. There is already a contradiction in introducing the concept of existence—no matter under what title it may be disguised—into the concept of a thing which we profess to be thinking solely in reference to its possibility. If that be allowed as legitimate, a seeming victory has been won; but in actual fact nothing at all is said: the assertion is a mere tautology.[7] We must ask: Is the proposition that *this or that thing* (which, whatever is may be is allowed as possible) *exists*, an analytic[8] or a synthetic

---

[4] Proposition, assertion.—E.D.K.

[5] Supreme reality, the greatest being (God), most real being.—E.D.K.

[6] A concept is always possible if it is not self-contradictory. This is the logical criterion of possibility, and by it the object of the concept is distinguishable from the *nihil negativum*. But it may nonetheless be an empty concept, unless the objective reality of the synthesis through which the concept is generated has been specifically proved; and such proof, as we have shown above, rests on principles of possible experience, and not on the principle of analysis (the law of contradiction). This is a warning against arguing directly from the logical possibility of concepts to the real possibility of things.—I.K.

[7] Any statement of the form "*A* is *A*" (or "If *p*, then *p*") or any that is reducible to that form via definitions. Hence a trivially true statement.—E.D.K.

[8] Any statement that is an identity or definition or true by identities or definitions, and hence uninformative.—E.D.K.

proposition?[9] If it is analytic, the assertion of the existence of the thing adds nothing to the thought of the thing; but in that case either the thought, which is in us, is the thing itself, or we have presupposed an existence as belonging to the realm of the possible, and have then, on that pretext, inferred its existence from its internal possibility—which is nothing but a miserable tautology. The word "reality,"which in the concept of the thing sounds other than the word "existence" in the concept of the predicate, is of no avail in meeting this objection. For if all positing (no matter what it may be that is posited) is entitled reality, the thing with all its predicates is already posited in the concept of the subject, and is assumed as actual; and in the predicate this is merely repeated. But if, on the other hand, we admit, as every reasonable person must, that all existential propositions[10] are synthetic, how can we profess to maintain that the predicate of existence cannot be rejected without contradiction? This is a feature which is found only in analytic propositions, and is indeed precisely what constitutes their analytic character.

I should have hoped to put an end to these idle and fruitless disputations in a direct manner, by an accurate determination of the concept of existence, had I not found that the illusion which is caused by the confusion of a logical with a real predicate (that is, with a predicate which determines a thing) is almost beyond correction. Anything we please can be made to serve as a logical predicate; the subject can even be predicated of itself; for logic abstracts from all content. But a *determining* predicate is a predicate which is added to the concept of the subject and enlarges it. Consequently, it must not be already contained in the concept.

Being is obviously not a real predicate; that is, it is not a concept of something which could be added to the concept of a thing. It is merely the positing of a thing, or of certain determinations, as existing in themselves. Logically, it is merely the copula[11] of a judgment. The proposition, "God is omnipotent," contains two concepts, each of which has its object—God and omnipotence. The small word "is" adds no new predicate, but only serves to posit the predicate *in its relation* to the subject. If, now, we take the subject (God) with all its predicates (among which is omnipotence), and say "God is," or "There is a God," we attach no new predicate to the concept of God, but only posit the subject in itself with all its predicates, and indeed posit it as being an *object* that stands in relation to my *concept*. The content of both must be one and the same; nothing can have been added to the concept, which expresses merely what is possible, by my thinking its object (through the expression "it is") as given absolutely. Otherwise stated, the real contains no more than the merely possible. A hundred real thalers[12] do not contain the least coin more than a hundred possible thalers. For as the latter signify the concept, and the former the object and the positing of the object, should the former contain more than the latter, my concept would not, in that case, express the whole object, and would not therefore be an adequate concept of it. My financial position is, however, affected very differently by a hundred real thalers than it is by the mere concept of them (that is, of their possibility). For the object, as it actually exists, is not analytically contained in my concept, but is added to my concept (which is a determination of my state) synthetically;

---

[9] Non-analytic statement, and hence substantive and informative.—E.D.K.

[10] One that asserts or denies the existence of a thing or class of things.—E.D.K.

[11] The "is" in a statement "*A* is *B*" (or "are" for plural).—E.D.K.

[12] Unit of German currency in Kant's time.—E.D.K.

and yet the conceived hundred thalers are not themselves in the least increased through thus acquiring existence outside my concept.

By whatever and by however many predicates we may think a thing—even if we completely determine it—we do not make the least addition to the thing when we further declare that this thing *is*. Otherwise, it would not be exactly the same thing that exists, but something more than we had thought in the concept; and we could not, therefore, say that the exact object of my concept exists. If we think in a thing every feature of reality except one, the missing reality is not added by my saying that this defective thing exists. On the contrary, it exists with the same defect with which I have thought it, since otherwise what exists would be something different from what I thought. When, therefore, I think a being as the supreme reality, without any defect, the question still remains whether it exists or not. For though, in my concept, nothing may be lacking of the possible real content of a thing in general, something is still lacking in its relation to my whole state of thought, namely, [insofar as I am unable to assert] that knowledge of this object is also possible a posteriori. And here we find the source of our present difficulty. Were we dealing with an object of the senses, we could not confound the existence of the thing with the mere concept of it. For through the concept the object is thought only as conforming to the *universal conditions* of possible empirical knowledge in general, whereas through its existence it is thought as belonging to the context of experience as a whole. In being thus connected with the *content* of experience as a whole, the concept of the object is not, however, in the least enlarged; all that has happened is that our thought has thereby obtained an additional possible perception. It is not, therefore, surprising that, if we attempt to think existence through the pure category alone, we cannot specify a single mark distinguishing it from mere possibility.

Whatever, therefore, and however much, our concept of an object may contain, we must go outside it, if we are to ascribe existence to the object. In the case of objects of the senses, this takes place through their connection with some one of our perceptions, in accordance with empirical laws. But in dealing with objects of pure thought, we have no means whatsoever of knowing their existence, since it would have to be known in a completely a priori manner. Our consciousness of all existence (whether immediately through perception, or mediately through inferences which connect something with perception) belongs exclusively to the unity of experience; any [alleged] existence outside this field, while not indeed such as we can declare to be absolutely impossible, is of the nature of an assumption which we can never be in a position to justify.

The concept of a supreme being is in many respects a very useful idea; but just because it is a mere idea, it is altogether incapable, by itself alone, of enlarging our knowledge in regard to what exists. It is not even competent to enlighten us as to the *possibility* of any existence beyond that which is known in and through experience. The analytic criterion of possibility, as consisting in the principle that bare positives (realities) give rise to no contradiction, cannot be denied to it. But since the realities are not given to us in their specific characters; since even if they were, we should still not be in a position to pass judgment; since the criterion of the possibility of synthetic knowledge is never to be looked for save in experience, to which the object of an idea cannot belong, the connection of all real properties in a thing is a synthesis, the possibility of which we are unable to determine a priori. And thus the celebrated Leibniz is far from having succeeded in what he plumed himself on achieving—the comprehension a priori of the possibility of this sublime ideal being.

The attempt to establish the existence of a supreme being by means of the famous ontological argument of Descartes is therefore merely so much labour and effort lost; we can no more extend our stock of [theoretical] insight by mere ideas, than a merchant can better his position by adding a few noughts to his cash account.

II. The Impossibility of a Cosmological Proof of the Existence of God
CHAPTER III, SECTION 5:

To attempt to extract from a purely arbitrary idea the existence of an object corresponding to it is a quite unnatural procedure and a mere innovation of scholastic subtlety. Such an attempt would never have been made if there had not been antecedently, on the part of our reason, the need to assume as a basis of existence in general something necessary (in which our regress may terminate); and if, since this necessity must be unconditioned and certain a priori, reason had not, in consequence, been forced to seek a concept which would satisfy, if possible, such a demand, and enable us to know an existence in a completely a priori manner. Such a concept was supposed to have been found in the idea of an *ens realissimum*; and that idea was therefore used only for the more definite knowledge of that necessary being, of the necessary existence of which we were already convinced, or persuaded, on other grounds. This natural procedure of reason was, however, concealed from view, and instead of ending with this concept, the attempt was made to begin with it, and so to deduce from it that necessity of existence which it was only fitted to supplement. Thus arose the unfortunate ontological proof, which yields satisfaction neither to the natural and healthy understanding not to the more academic demands of strict proof.

The *cosmological proof*, which we are now about to examine, retains the connection of absolute necessity with the highest reality, but instead of reasoning, like the former proof, from the highest reality to necessity of existence, it reasons from the previously given unconditioned necessity of some being to the unlimited reality of that being. It thus enters upon a course of reasoning which, whether rational or only pseudo-rational, is at any rate natural, and the most convincing not only for common sense but even for speculative understanding. It also sketches the first outline of all the proofs in natural theology, an outline which has always been and always will be followed, however much embellished and disguised by superfluous additions. This proof, termed by Leibniz the proof *a contingentia mundi*,[13] we shall now proceed to expound and examine.

It runs thus: If anything exists, an absolutely necessary being must also exist. Now I, at least, exist. Therefore an absolutely necessary being exists. The minor premise contains an experience, the major premise the inference from there being any experience at all to the existence of the necessary.[14] The proof therefore really begins with experience, and is not wholly a priori or ontological. For this reason, and because the object

---

[13] From the contingency of the world (universe).—E.D.K.

[14] This inference is too well known to require a detailed statement. It depends on the supposedly transcendental law of natural causality: that everything contingent has a cause, which, if itself contingent, must likewise have a cause, till the series of subordinate causes ends with an absolutely necessary cause, without which it would have no completeness.—I.K.

of all possible experience is called the world, it is entitled the *cosmological* proof. Since, in dealing with the objects of experience, the proof abstracts from all special properties through which this world may differ from any other possible world, the title also serves to distinguish it from the physico-theological proof, which is based upon observations of the particular properties of the world disclosed to us by our senses.

The proof then proceeds as follows: The necessary being can be determined in one way only, that is, by one out of each possible pair of opposed predicates. It must therefore be *completely* determined through its own concept. Now there is only one possible concept which determines a thing completely a priori, namely, the concept of the *ens realissimum*.[15] The concept of the *ens realissimum* is therefore the only concept through which a necessary being can be thought. In other words, a supreme being necessarily exists.

In this cosmological argument there are combined so many pseudorational principles that speculative reason seems in this case to have brought to bear all the resources of its dialectical skill to produce the greatest possible transcendental illusion. The testing of the argument may meantime be postponed while we detail in order the various devices whereby an old argument is disguised as a new one, and by which appeal is made to the agreement of two witnesses, the one with credentials of pure reason and the other with those of experience. In reality the only witness is that which speaks in the name of pure reason; in the endeavour to pass as a second witness it merely changes its dress and voice. In order to lay a secure foundation for itself, this proof takes its stand on experience, and thereby makes profession of being distinct from the ontological proof, which puts its entire trust in pure a priori concepts. But the cosmological proof uses this experience only for a single step in the argument, namely, to conclude the existence of a necessary being. What properties this being may have, the empirical premise cannot tell us. Reason therefore abandons experience altogether, and endeavours to discover from mere concepts what properties an absolutely necessary being must have, that is, which among all possible things contains in itself the conditions (*requisita*) essential to absolute necessity. Now these, it is supposed, are nowhere to be found save in the concept of an *ens realissimum*; and the conclusion is therefore drawn that the *ens realissimum* is the absolutely necessary being. But it is evident that we are here presupposing that the concept of the highest reality is completely adequate to the concept of absolute necessity of existence; that is, that the latter can be inferred from the former. Now this is the proposition maintained by the ontological proof; it is here being assumed in the cosmological proof, and indeed made the basis of the proof; and yet it is an assumption with which this latter proof has professed to dispense. For absolute necessity is an existence determined from mere concepts. If I say, the concept of the *ens realissimum* is a concept, and indeed the only concept, which is appropriate and adequate to necessary existence, I must also admit that necessary existence can be inferred from this concept. Thus the so-called cosmological proof really owes any cogency which it may have to the ontological proof from mere concepts. The appeal to experience is quite superfluous; experience may perhaps lead us to the concept of absolute necessity, but is unable to demonstrate this necessity as belonging to any determinate thing. For immediately we endeavour to do so, we must abandon all experience and search among pure concepts to discover whether any one of them contains the conditions of the possibility of an

---

[15] See note 5.—E.D.K.

absolutely necessary being. If in this way we can determine the possibility of a necessary being, we likewise establish its existence. For what we are then saying is this: that of all possible beings there is one which carries with it absolute necessity, that is, that this being exists with absolute necessity.

Fallacious and misleading arguments are most easily detected if set out in correct syllogistic form. This we now proceed to do in the instance under discussion.

If the proposition, that every absolutely necessary being is likewise the most real of all beings, is correct (and this is the *nervus probandi*[16] of the cosmological proof), it must, like all affirmative judgments, be convertible, at least *per accidens*.[17] It therefore follows that some *entia realissima*[18] are likewise absolutely necessary beings. But one *ens realissimum* is in no respect different from another, and what is true of *some* under this concept is true also of *all*. In this case, therefore, I can convert the proposition *simpliciter*,[19] not only *per accidens*, and say that every *ens realissimum* is a necessary being. But since this proposition is determined from its a priori concepts alone, the mere concept of the *ens realissimum* must carry with it the absolute necessity of that being; and this is precisely what the ontological proof has asserted and what the cosmological proof has refused to admit, although the conclusions of the latter are indeed covertly based on it.

Thus the second path upon which speculative reason enters in its attempt to prove the existence of a supreme being is not only as deceptive as the first, but has this additional defect, that it is guilty of an *ignoratio elenchi*.[20] It professes to lead us by a new path, but after a short circuit brings us back to the very path which we had deserted at its bidding.

I have stated that in this cosmological argument there lies hidden a whole nest of dialectical assumptions, which the transcendental critique can easily detect and destroy. These deceptive principles I shall merely enumerate, leaving to the reader, who by this time will be sufficiently expert in these matters, the task of investigating them further, and of refuting them.

We find, for instance, (1) the transcendental principle whereby from the contingent we infer a cause. This principle is applicable only in the sensible world; outside that world it has no meaning whatsoever. For the mere intellectual concept of the contingent cannot give rise to any synthetic proposition, such as that of causality. The principle of causality[21] has no meaning and no criterion for its application save only in the sensible world. But in the cosmological proof it is precisely in order to enable us to advance beyond the sensible world that it is employed. (2) The inference to a first cause, from the impossibility of an infinite series of causes, given one after the other, in the sensible world. The principles of the employment of reason do not justify this conclusion even within the world of experience, still less beyond this world in a realm into which this series can never be extended. (3) The unjustified self-satisfaction of reason in respect of the completion of this series. The removal of all the conditions without which no concept of necessity is possible is taken by reason to be a completion of the concept of the series,

---

[16] Roughly, "heart"; main nerve; force.—E.D.K.

[17] By accident.—E.D.K.

[18] Greatest realities.—E.D.K.

[19] As such; simply.—E.D.K.

[20] Irrelevant conclusion (a logical fallacy).—E.D.K.

[21] The principle that every event has a cause.—E.D.K.

on the ground that we can then conceive nothing further. (4) The confusion between the logical possibility of a concept of all reality united into one (without inner contradiction) and the transcendental possibility of such a reality. In the case of the latter there is needed a principle to establish the practicability of such a synthesis, a principle which itself, however, can apply only to the field of possible experiences, etc.

The procedure of the cosmological proof is artfully designed to enable us to escape having to prove the existence of a necessary being a priori through mere concepts. Such proof would require to be carried out in the ontological manner, and that is an enterprise for which we feel ourselves to be altogether incompetent. Accordingly, we take as the starting-point of our inference an actual existence (an experience in general), and advance, in such manner as we can, to some absolutely necessary condition of this existence. We have then no need to show the possibility of this condition. For if it has been proved to exist, the question as to its possibility is entirely superfluous. If now we want to determine more fully the nature of this necessary being, we do not endeavour to do so in the manner that would be really adequate, namely, by discovering from its concept the necessity of its existence. For could we do that, we should be in no need of an empirical starting-point. No, all we seek is the negative condition (*conditio sine qua non*),[22] without which a being would not be absolutely necessary. And in all other kinds of reasoning from a given consequence to its ground this would be legitimate; but in the present case it unfortunately happens that the condition which is needed for absolute necessity is only to be found in one single being. This being must therefore contain in its concept all that is required for absolute necessity, and consequently it enables me to infer this absolute necessity a priori. I must therefore be able also to reverse the inference, and to say: Anything to which this concept (of supreme reality) applies is absolutely necessary. If I cannot make this inference (as I must concede, if I am to avoid admitting the ontological proof), I have come to grief in the new way that I have been following, and am back again at my starting-point. The concept of the supreme being satisfies all questions a priori which can be raised regarding the inner determinations of a thing, and is therefore an ideal that is quite unique, in that the concept, while universal, also at the same time designates an individual as being among the things that are possible. But it does not give satisfaction concerning the question of its own existence—though this is the real purpose of our enquiries—and if anyone admitted the existence of a necessary being but wanted to know which among all [existing] things is to be identified with that being, we could not answer: "This, not that, is the necessary being."

We may indeed be allowed to *postulate* the existence of an all-sufficient being, as the cause of all possible effects, with a view to lightening the task of reason in its search for the unity of the grounds of explanation. But in presuming so far as to say that such a being *necessarily exists*, we are no longer giving modest expression to an admissible hypothesis, but are confidently laying claim to apodeictic[23] certainty. For the knowledge of what we profess to know as absolutely necessary must itself carry with its absolute necessity.

The whole problem of the transcendental ideal amounts to this: either, given absolute necessity, to find a concept which possesses it, or, given the concept of something, to find that something to be absolutely necessary. If either task be possible,

---

[22] Necessary condition.—E.D.K.
[23] Necessary.—E.D.K.

so must the other; for reason recognizes that only as absolutely necessary which follows of necessity from its concept. But both tasks are quite beyond our utmost efforts to *satisfy* our understanding in this matter; and equally unavailing are all attempts to induce it to acquiesce in its incapacity.

Unconditioned necessity, which we so indispensably require as the last bearer of all things, is for human reason the veritable abyss. Eternity itself, in all its terrible sublimity, as depicted by a Haller,[24] is far from making the same overwhelming impression on the mind; for it only *measures* the duration of things, it does not *support* them. We cannot put aside, and yet also cannot endure the thought, that a being, which we represent to ourselves as supreme amongst all possible beings, should, as it were, say to itself: "I am from eternity to eternity, and outside me there is nothing save what is through my will, *but whence then am I?*" All support here fails us; and the *greatest* perfection, no less than the *least* perfection, is unsubstantial and baseless for the merely speculative reason, which makes not the least effort to retain either the one or the other, and feels indeed no loss in allowing them to vanish entirely.

Many forces in nature, which manifest their existence through certain effects, remain for us inscrutable; for we cannot track them sufficiently far by observation. Also, the transcendental object lying at the basis of appearances (and with it the reason why our sensibility is subject to certain supreme conditions rather than to others) is and remains for us inscrutable. The thing itself is indeed given, but we can have no insight into its nature. But it is quite otherwise with an ideal of pure reason; it can never be said to be inscrutable. For since it is not required to give any credentials of its reality save only the need on the part of reason to complete all synthetic unity by means of it; and since, therefore, it is in no wise given as thinkable *object*, it cannot be inscrutable in the manner in which an object is. On the contrary it must, as a mere idea, find its place and its solution in the nature of reason, and must therefore allow of investigation. For it is of the very essence of reason that we should be able to give an account of all our concepts, opinions, and assertions, either upon objective or, in the case of mere illusion, upon subjective grounds. . . .

III. The Impossibility of the Physico, Theological Proof [25]
CHAPTER III SECTION 6:

If, then, neither the concept of things in general nor the experience of any *existence in general* can supply what is required, it remains only to try whether a *determinate experience*, the experience of the things of the present world, and the constitution and order of these, does not provide the basis of a proof which may help us to attain to an assured conviction of a supreme being. Such proof we propose to entitle the *physico-theological*. Should this attempt also fail, it must follow that no satisfactory proof of the existence of a being corresponding to our transcendental idea can be possible by pure speculative reason.

In view of what has already been said, it is evident that we can count upon a quite easy and conclusive answer to this enquiry. For how can any experience ever be adequate to an idea? The peculiar nature of the latter consists just in the fact that no experience

---

[24] Albrecht von Haller (1708–1777), a writer on medical and kindred subjects, author of *Die Alpen* and other poems.—TRANS.

[25] The teleological (design) argument.—E.D.K.

can ever be equal to it. The transcendental idea of a necessary and all-sufficient original being is so overwhelmingly great, so high above everything empirical, the latter being always conditioned, that it leaves us at a loss, partly because we can never find in experience material sufficient to satisfy such a concept, and partly because it is always in the sphere of the conditioned that we carry out our search, seeking there ever vainly for the unconditioned—no law of any empirical synthesis giving us an example of any such unconditioned or providing the least guidance in its pursuit.

If the supreme being should itself stand in this chain of conditions, it would be a member of the series, and like the lower members which it precedes, would call for further enquiry as to the still higher ground from which it follows. If, on the other hand, we propose to separate it from the chain, and to conceive it as a purely intelligible being, existing apart from the series of natural causes, by what bridge can reason contrive to pass over to it? For all laws governing the transition from effects to causes, all synthesis and extension of our knowledge, refer to nothing but possible experience, and therefore solely to objects of the sensible world, and apart from them can have no meaning whatsoever.

This world presents to us so immeasurable a stage of variety, order, purposiveness, and beauty, as displayed alike in its infinite extent and in the unlimited divisibility of its parts, that even with such knowledge as our weak understanding can acquire of it, we are brought face to face with so many marvels immeasurably great, that all speech loses its force, all numbers their power to measure, our thoughts themselves all definiteness, and that our judgment of the whole resolves itself into an amazement which is speechless, and only the more eloquent on that account. Everywhere we see a chain of effects and causes, of ends and means, a regularity in origination and dissolution. Nothing has of itself come into the condition in which we find it to exist, but always points to something else as its cause, while this in turn commits us to repetition of the same enquiry. The whole universe must thus sink into the abyss of nothingness, unless, over and above this infinite chain of contingencies, we assume something to support it—something which is original and independently self-subsistent, and which as the cause of the origin of the universe secures also at the same time its continuance. What magnitude are we to ascribe to this supreme cause—admitting that it is supreme in respect of all things in the world? We are not acquainted with the whole content of the world, still less do we know how to estimate its magnitude by comparison with all that is possible. But since we cannot, as regards causality, dispense with an ultimate and supreme being, what is there to prevent us ascribing to it a degree of perfection that sets it *above everything else that is possible?* This we can easily do—though only through the slender outline of an abstract concept—by representing this being to ourselves as combining in itself all possible perfection, as in a single substance. This concept is in conformity with the demand of our reason for parsimony of principles; it is free from self-contradiction, and is never decisively contradicted by any experience; and it is likewise of such a character that it contributes to the extension of the employment of reason within experience, through the guidance which it yields in the discovery of order and purposiveness.

This proof always deserves to be mentioned with respect. It is the oldest, the clearest, and the most accordant with the common reason of mankind. It enlivens the study of nature, just as it itself derives its existence and gains ever new vigour from that source. It suggests ends and purposes, where our observation would not have detected them by itself, and extends our knowledge of nature by means of the guiding concept of a special unity, the principle of which is outside nature. This knowledge again reacts on its cause, namely, upon the idea which has led to it, and so strengthens the belief in a supreme Author [of nature] that the belief acquires the force of an irresistible conviction.

It would therefore not only be uncomforting but utterly vain to attempt to diminish in any way the authority of this argument. Reason, constantly upheld by this ever-increasing evidence, which, though empirical, is yet so powerful, cannot be so depressed through doubts suggested by subtle and abstruse speculation, that it is not at once aroused from the indecision of all melancholy reflection, as from a dream, by one glance at the wonders of nature and the majesty of the universe—ascending from height to height up to the all-highest, from the conditioned to its conditions, up to the supreme and unconditioned Author [of all conditioned being].

But although we have nothing to bring against the rationality and utility of this procedure, but have rather to commend and to further it, we still cannot approve the claims, which this mode of argument would fain advance, to apodeictic certainty and to an assent founded on no special favour or support from other quarters. It cannot hurt the good cause, if the dogmatic language of the overweening sophist be toned down to the more moderate and humble requirements of a belief adequate to quiet our doubts, though not to command unconditional submission. I therefore maintain that the physico-theological proof can never by itself establish the existence of a supreme being, but must always fall back upon the ontological argument to make good its deficiency. It only serves as an introduction to the ontological argument; and the latter therefore contains (insofar as a speculative proof is possible at all) *the one possible ground of proof* with which human reason can never dispense.

The chief points of the physico-theological proof are as follows: (1) In the world we everywhere find clear signs of an order in accordance with a determinate purpose, carried out with great wisdom; and this in a universe which is indescribably varied in content and unlimited in extent. (2) This purposive order is quite alien to the things of the world, and only belongs to them contingently; that is to say, the diverse things could not of themselves have cooperated, by so great a combination of diverse means, to the fulfilment of determinate final purposes, had they not been chosen and designed for these purposes by an ordering rational principle in conformity with underlying ideas. (3) There exists, therefore, a sublime and wise cause (or more than one), which must be the cause of the world not merely as a blindly working all-powerful nature, by *fecundity*, but as intelligence, through *freedom*. (4) The unity of this cause may be inferred from the unity of the reciprocal relations existing between the parts of the world, as members of an artfully arranged structure—inferred with certainty insofar as our observation suffices for its verification, and beyond these limits with probability, in accordance with the principles of analogy.

We need not here criticize natural reason too strictly in regard to its conclusion from the analogy between certain natural products and what our human art produces when we do violence to nature, and constrain it to proceed not according to its own ends but in conformity with ours—appealing to the similarity of these particular natural products with houses, ships, watches. Nor need we here question its conclusion that there lies at the basis of nature a causality similar to that responsible for artificial products, namely, an understanding and a will; and that the inner possibility of a self-acting nature (which is what makes all art, and even, it may be, reason itself, possible) is therefore derived from another, though superhuman, art—a mode of reasoning which could not perhaps withstand a searching transcendental criticism. But at any rate we must admit that, if we are to specify a cause at all, we cannot here proceed more securely than by analogy with those purposive productions of which alone the cause and mode of action are fully known to us. Reason could never be justified in abandoning the causality which it knows for grounds of explanation which are obscure, of which it does not have any knowledge, and which are incapable of proof.

On this method of argument, the purposiveness and harmonious adaptation of so much in nature can suffice to prove the contingency of the form merely, not of the matter, that is, not of the substance in the world. To prove the latter we should have to demonstrate that the things in the world would not of themselves be capable of such order and harmony, in accordance with universal laws, if they were not *in their substance* the product of supreme wisdom. But to prove this we should require quite other grounds of proof than those which are derived from the analogy with human art. The utmost, therefore, that the argument can prove is an *architect* of the world who is always very much hampered by the adaptability of the material in which he works, not a *creator* of the world to whose idea everything is subject. This, however, is altogether inadequate to the lofty purpose which we have before our eyes, namely, the proof of an all-sufficient primordial being. To prove the contingency of matter itself, we should have to resort to a transcendental argument, and this is precisely what we have here set out to avoid.

The inference, therefore, is that the order and purposiveness everywhere observable throughout the world may be regarded as a completely contingent arrangement, and that we may argue to the existence of a cause *proportioned* to it. But the concept of this cause must enable us to know something quite *determinate* about it, and can therefore be no other than the concept of a being who possesses all might, wisdom, etc., in a word, all the perfection which is proper to an all-sufficient being. For the predicates—"very great," "astounding," "immeasurable" in power and excellence— give no determinate concept at all, and do not really tell us what the thing is in itself. They are only relative representations of the magnitude of the object, which the observer, in contemplating the world, compares with himself and with his capacity of comprehension, and which are equally terms of eulogy whether we be magnifying the object or be depreciating the observing subject in relation to that object. Where we are concerned with the magnitude (or the perfection) of a thing, there is no determinate concept except that which comprehends all possible perfection; and in that concept only the allness (*omnitudo*) of the reality is completely determined.

Now no one, I trust, will be so bold as to profess that he comprehends the relation of the magnitude of the world as he has observed it (alike as regards both extent and content) to omnipotence, of the world order to supreme wisdom, of the world unity to the absolute unity of its Author, etc. Physico-theology is therefore unable to give any determinate concept of the supreme cause of the world, and cannot therefore serve as the foundation of a theology which is itself in turn to form the basis of religion.

To advance to absolute totality by the empirical road is utterly impossible. Nonetheless this is what is attempted in the physico-theological proof. What, then, are the means which have been adopted to bridge this wide abyss?

The physico-theological argument can indeed lead us to the point of admiring the greatness, wisdom, power, etc., of the Author of the world, but can take us no further. Accordingly, we then abandon the argument from empirical grounds of proof, and fall back upon the contingency which, in the first steps of the argument, we had inferred from the order and purposiveness of the world. With this contingency as our sole premise, we then advance, by means of transcendental concepts alone, to the existence of an absolutely necessary being, and [as a final step] from the concept of the absolute necessity of the first cause to the completely determinate or determinable concept of that necessary being, namely, to the concept of an all-embracing reality. Thus the physico-theological proof, failing in its undertaking, has in face of this difficulty suddenly fallen back upon the cosmological proof; and since the latter is only a disguised ontological proof, it has really achieved its purpose by pure reason alone—although at the start it disclaimed all kinship with pure reason and professed to establish its conclusions on convincing evidence derived from experience.

Those who propound the physico-theological argument have therefore no ground for being so contemptuous in their attitude to the transcendental mode of proof, posing as clear-sighted students of nature, and complacently looking down upon that proof as the artificial product of obscure speculative refinements. For were they willing to scrutinize their own procedure, they would find that, after advancing some considerable way on the solid ground of nature and experience, and finding themselves just as far distant as ever from the object which discloses itself to their reason, they suddenly leave this ground, and pass over into the realm of mere possibilities, where they hope upon the wings of ideas to draw near to the object—the object that has refused itself to all their *empirical* enquiries. For after this tremendous leap, when they have, as they think, found firm ground, they extend their concept—the *determinate* concept, into the possession of which they have now come, they know not how—over the whole sphere of creation. And the ideal [which this reasoning thus involves, and] which is entirely a product of pure reason, they then elucidate by reference to experience, though inadequately enough, and in a manner far below the dignity of its object; and throughout they persist in refusing to admit that they have arrived at this knowledge or hypothesis by a road quite other than that of experience.

Thus the physico-theological proof of the existence of an original or supreme being rests upon the cosmological proof, and the cosmological upon the ontological. And since, beside these three, there is no other path open to speculative reason, the ontological proof from pure concepts of reason is the only possible one, if indeed any proof of a proposition so far exalted above all empirical employment of the understanding is possible at all.

∘ ∘ ∘ *12*

Against Proofs of God
Søren Kierkegaard

BUT WHAT IS this unknown something with which the Reason collides when inspired by its paradoxical passion, with the result of unsettling even man's knowledge of himself? It is the Unknown. It is not a human being, insofar as we know what man is; nor is it any other known thing. So let us call this unknown something: *God*. It is nothing more than a name we assign to it. The idea of demonstrating that this unknown something (God) exists could scarcely suggest itself to the Reason, For if God does not exist it would of course be impossible to prove it; and if he does exist it would be folly to attempt it. For at the very outset, in beginning my proof, I will have presupposed it, not as doubtful but as certain (a presupposition is never doubtful, for the very reason that it is a presupposition), since otherwise I would not begin, readily understanding that the whole would be impossible if he did not exist. But if when I speak of proving God's existence I mean that I propose to prove that the Unknown, which exists, is God, then I express myself unfortunately. For in that case I do not prove anything, least of all an existence, but merely develop the content of a conception. Generally speaking, it is a difficult matter to prove that anything exists; and what is still worse for the intrepid souls who undertake the venture, the difficulty is such that fame scarcely awaits those who concern themselves with it. The entire demonstration always turns into something very different from what it assumes to be, and becomes an additional development of the consequences that flow from [our] having assumed that the object in question exists. Thus I always reason from existence, not toward existence, whether I move in the sphere of palpable sensible fact or in the realm of thought. I do not, for example, prove that a stone exists, but that some existing thing is a stone. The procedure in a court of justice does not prove that a criminal exists, but that the accused, whose existence is given, is a criminal. Whether we call existence an *accessorium*[1] or the eternal *prius*,[2] it is never subject to demonstration. Let us take ample time for consideration. We have no such reason for haste as have those who from concern for themselves or for God or for some other thing, must make haste to get its existence demonstrated. Under such circumstances there may indeed be need for haste, especially if the prover sincerely seeks to appreciate the danger that he himself, or the thing in question, may be non-existent unless the proof is finished; and does not surreptitiously entertain the thought that it exists whether he succeeds in proving it or not.

If it were proposed to prove Napoleon's existence from Napoleon's deeds, would it not be a most curious proceeding? His existence does indeed explain his deeds, but the

---

[1] Addition.—E.D.K.

[2] Presupposition.—E.D.K.

deeds do not prove his existence, unless I have already understood the word "his" so as thereby to have assumed his existence. But Napoleon is only an individual, and insofar there exists no absolute relationship between him and his deeds; some other person might have performed the same deeds. Perhaps this is the reason why I cannot pass from the deeds to existence. If I call these deeds the deeds of Napoleon, the proof becomes superfluous, since I have already named him; if I ignore this, I can never prove from the deeds that they are Napoleon's, but only in a purely ideal manner that such deeds are the deeds of a great general, and so forth. But between God and his works there exists an absolute relationship; God is not a name but a concept. Is this perhaps the reason that his *essentia involvit existentiam* [essence involves existence]? The works of God are such that only God can perform them. Just so, but where then are the works of God? The works from which I would deduce his existence are not immediately given. The wisdom of God in nature, his goodness, his wisdom in the governance of the world—are all these manifest, perhaps, upon the very face of things? Are we not here confronted with the most terrible temptations to doubt, and is it not impossible finally to dispose of all these doubts? But from such an order of things I will surely not attempt to prove God's existence; and even if I began I would never finish, and would in addition have to live constantly in suspense, lest something so terrible should suddenly happen that my bit of proof would be demolished. From what works then do I propose to derive the proof? From the works as apprehended through an ideal interpretation, i.e., such as they do not immediately reveal themselves. But in that case it is not from the works that I prove God's existence. I merely develop the ideality I have presupposed, and because of my confidence in *this* I make so bold as to defy all objections, even those that have yet been made. In beginning my proof I presuppose the ideal interpretation, and also that I will be successful in carrying it through; but what else is this but to presuppose that God exists, so that I really begin by virtue of confidence in him?

And how does God's existence emerge from the proof? Does it follow straightway, without any breach of continuity? Or have we not here an analogy to the behaviour of these toys, the little Cartesian dolls? As soon as I let go of the doll it stands on its head. As soon as I let it go—I must therefore let it go. So also with the proof for God's existence. As long as I keep my hold on the proof, i.e., continue to demonstrate, the existence does not come out, if for no other reason than that I am engaged in proving it; but when I let the proof go, the existence is there. But this act of letting go is surely also something; it is indeed a contribution of mine. Must not this also be taken into the account, this little moment, brief as it may be—it need not be long, for it is a *leap*. However brief this moment, if only an instantaneous now, this "now" must be included in the reckoning. If anyone wishes to have it ignored, I will use it to tell a little anecdote, in order to show that it really does exist. Chrysippus was experimenting with a sorites[3] to see if he could not bring about a break in its quality, either progressively or retrogressively. But Carneades could not get it in his head when the new quality actually emerged. Then Chrysippus told him to try making a little pause in the reckoning, and so—so it would be easier to understand. Carneades replied: "With the greatest pleasure, please do not hesitate on my account; you may not only pause, but

---

[3] A type of argument.—E.D.K.

even lie down to sleep, and it will help you just as little; for when you awake we will begin again where you left off. Just so; it boots as little to try to get rid of something by sleeping as to try to come into the possession of something in the same manner."

Whoever therefore attempts to demonstrate the existence of God (except in the sense of clarifying the concept, and without the *reservatio finalis*[4] noted above, that the existence emerges from the demonstration by a leap) proves in lieu thereof something else, something which at times perhaps does not need a proof, and in any case needs none better; for the fool says in his heart that there is no God, but whoever says in his heart or to men: "Wait just a little and I will prove it" —what a rare man of wisdom is he![5] If in the moment of beginning his proof it is not absolutely undetermined whether God exists or not, he does not prove it; and if it is thus undetermined in the beginning he will never come to begin, partly from fear of failure, since God perhaps does not exist, and partly because he has nothing with which to begin. A project of this kind would scarcely have been undertaken by the ancients. Socrates at least, who is credited with having put forth the physico-teleological proof for God's existence, did not go about it in any such manner. He always presupposes God's existence, and under this presupposition seeks to interpenetrate nature with the idea of purpose. Had he been asked why he pursued this method, he would doubtless have explained that he lacked the courage to venture out upon so perilous a voyage of discovery without having made sure of God's existence behind him. At the word of God he casts his net as if to catch the idea of purpose; for nature herself finds many means of frightening the inquirer, and distracts him by many a digression.

The paradoxical passion of the Reason thus comes repeatedly into collision with the Unknown, which does indeed exist, but is unknown, and insofar does not exist. The Reason cannot advance beyond this point, and yet it cannot refrain in its paradoxicalness from arriving at this limit and occupying itself therewith. It will not serve to dismiss its relation to it simply by asserting that the Unknown does not exist, since this itself involves a relationship. But what then is the Unknown, since the designation of it as God merely signifies for us that it is unknown? To say that it is the Unknown because it cannot be known, and even if it were capable of being known, it could not be expressed, does not satisfy the demands of passion, though it correctly interprets the Unknown as a limit; but a limit is precisely a torment for passion, though it also serves as an incitement. And yet the Reason can come no further, whether it risks an issue *via negationis* or *via eminentia*.[6]

What then is the Unknown? It is the limit to which the Reason repeatedly comes, and insofar, substituting a static form of conception for the dynamic, it is the different, the absolutely different. But because it is absolutely different, there is no mark by which it could be distinguished. When qualified as absolutely different it seems on the verge of disclosure, but this is not the case; for the Reason cannot even conceive an absolute unlikeness. The Reason cannot negate itself absolutely, but uses itself for the purpose, and thus conceives only such an unlikeness within itself as it can conceive by means of

---

[4] Ultimate reservation.—E.D.K.

[5] What an excellent subject for a comedy of the higher lunacy!—S.K.

[6] In other words, by the method of making negative statements about God or by the method of attributing human qualities to God in a higher degree.—E.D.K.

itself; it cannot absolutely transcend itself, and hence conceives only such a superiority over itself as it can conceive by means of itself. Unless the Unknown (God) remains a mere limiting conception, the single idea of difference will be thrown into a state of confusion, and become many ideas of many differences. The Unknown is then in a condition of dispersion (διασπορά), and the Reason may choose at pleasure from what is at hand and the imagination may suggest (the monstrous, the ludicrous, etc.).

But it is impossible to hold fast to a difference of this nature. Every time this is done it is essentially an arbitrary act, and deepest down in the heart of piety lurks the mad caprice which knows that it has itself produced its God. If no specific determination of difference can be held fast, because there is no distinguishing mark, like and unlike finally become identified with one another, thus sharing the fate of all such dialectical opposites. The unlikeness clings to the Reason and confounds it, so that the Reason no longer knows itself and quite consistently confuses itself with the unlikeness. On this point paganism has been sufficiently prolific in fantastic inventions. As for the last-named supposition, the self-irony of the Reason, I shall attempt to delineate it merely by a stroke or two, without raising any question of its being historical. There lives an individual whose appearance is precisely like that of other men; he grows up to manhood like others, he marries, he has an occupation by which he earns his livelihood, and he makes provision for the future as befits a man. For though it may be beautiful to live like the birds of the air, it is not lawful, and may lead to the sorriest of consequences: either starvation if one has enough persistence, or dependence on the bounty of others. This man is also God. How do I know? I cannot know it, for in order to know it I would have to know God, and the nature of the difference between God and man; and this I cannot know, because the Reason has reduced it to likeness with that from which it was unlike. Thus God becomes the most terrible of deceivers, because the Reason has deceived itself. The Reason has brought God as near as possible, and yet he is as far away as ever.

○ ○ ○ *13*

Eternal Happiness,
Subjectivity, and Truth
Søren Kierkegaard

I. The Eternal Happiness Promised by Christianity

OUR TREATMENT OF the problem merely deals with the question of the individual's relationship to Christianity. It has nothing whatever to do with the systematic zeal of the personally indifferent individual to arrange the truths of Christianity in paragraphs; it deals with the concern of the infinitely interested individual for his own relationship to such a doctrine. To put it as simply as possible, using myself by way of illustration: I, Johannes Climacus,[1] born in this city and now thirty years old, a common ordinary human being like most people, assume that there awaits me a highest good, an eternal happiness, in the same sense that such a good awaits a servant-girl or a professor. I have heard that Christianity proposes itself as a condition for the acquirement of this good, and now I ask how I may establish a proper relationship to this doctrine. "What extraordinary presumption," I seem to hear a thinker say, "what egotistical vanity to dare lay so much stress upon one's own petty self in this theocentric age, in the speculatively significant nineteenth century, which is entirely immersed in the great problems of universal history." I shudder at the reproof; and if I had not already hardened myself against a number of fearful things, I would no doubt slink quietly away, like a dog with his tail between his legs. But my conscience is quite clear in this matter; it is not I who have become so presumptuous of my own accord, but it is Christianity itself which compels me to ask the question in this manner. It puts quite an extraordinary emphasis upon my own petty self, and upon every other self however petty, in that it proposes to endow each self with an eternal happiness, provided a proper relationship is established.

Without having understood Christianity, since I merely present the problem, I have still understood enough to apprehend that it proposes to bestow an eternal happiness upon the individual man, thus presuming an infinite interest in his eternal happiness as *conditio sine qua non*; an interest by virtue of which the individual hates father and mother, and thus doubtless also snaps his fingers at speculative systems and outlines of universal history. Although I am only an outsider, I have at least understood so much, that the only unpardonable offense against the majesty of Christianity is for the individual to take his relationship to it for granted, treating it as a matter of course. However unassuming it

---

[1] *Concluding Unscientific Postscript*, was published under the pseudonym of Johannes Climacus. The title page lists Johannes Climacus as author and S. Kierkegaard as "responsible for publication."—E.D.K.

may seem to permit oneself this kind of a relationship to Christianity, Christianity judges it as insolence. I must therefore respectfully decline the assistance of all the theocentric helpers and helpers' helpers, in so far as they propose to help me into Christianity on such a basis. Then I rather prefer to remain where I am, with my infinite interest, with the problem, with the possibility.

It is not entirely impossible that one who is infinitely interested in his eternal happiness may sometime come into possession of it. But it is surely quite impossible for one who has lost a sensibility for it (and this can scarcely be anything else than the infinite interest), ever to enjoy an eternal happiness. If the sense for it is once lost, it may perhaps be impossible to recover it. . . .

The objective problem consists of an inquiry into the truth of Christianity. The subjective problem concerns the relationship of the individual to Christianity. To put it quite simply: How may I, Johannes Climacus, participate in the happiness promised by Christianity? . . .

II. *Faith and Historical Documentation*

When Christianity is viewed from the standpoint of its historical documentation, it becomes necessary to secure an entirely trustworthy account of what the Christian doctrine really is. If the inquirer were infinitely interested in behalf of his relationship to the doctrine he would at once despair; for nothing is more readily evident than that the greatest attainable certainty with respect to anything historical is merely an *approximation*. And an approximation, when viewed as a basis for an eternal happiness, is wholly inadequate, since the incommensurability makes a result impossible. But the interest of the inquiring subject being merely historical (whether he also has an infinite interest in Christianity in his capacity as believer, in which case the whole enterprise might readily come to involve him in several contradictions; or whether he stands aloof, yet without any passionate negative decision *qua* unbeliever), he begins upon the tremendous task of research, adding new contributions of his own, and continuing thus until his seventieth year. Just two weeks before his death he looks forward to the publication of a new work, which it is hoped will throw light upon one entire side of the inquiry. Such an objective temper is an epigram, unless its antithesis be an epigram over it, over the restless concern of the infinitely interested subject, who surely needs to have such a question answered, related as it is to his eternal happiness. And in any case he will not upon any consideration dare to relinquish his interest until the last moment.

When one raises the historical question of the truth of Christianity, or of what is and is not Christian truth, the Scriptures at once present themselves as documents of decisive significance. The historical inquiry therefore first concentrates upon the Bible.

Here it is necessary for the scholar to secure the maximum of dependability; for me, on the contrary, it is of importance not to make a display of learning, or to betray the fact that I have none. In the interest of my problem it is more important to have it understood and remembered that even with the most stupendous learning and persistence in research, and even if all the brains of all the critics were concentrated in one, it would still be impossible to obtain anything more than an approximation; and that an approximation is essentially incommensurable with an infinite personal interest in an eternal happiness.

When the Scriptures are viewed as a court of last resort for determining what is and is not Christian doctrine, it becomes necessary to make sure of the Scriptures historically and critically.

In this connection there are a number of topics that come up for consideration: the canonicity of the individual books, their authenticity, their integrity, the trustworthiness of their authors; and a dogmatic guaranty is posited: Inspiration. When one thinks of the labors which the English have devoted to digging the tunnel under the Thames,[2] the tremendous expenditure of energy involved, and then how a little accident may for a long time obstruct the entire enterprise, one will be able to form a fitting conception of this critical undertaking as a whole. How much time, what great industry, what splendid talents, what distinguished scholarship have been requisitioned from generation to generation in order to bring this miracle to pass. And yet a little dialectical doubt touching the presuppositions may suddenly arise, sufficient for a long time to unsettle the whole, closing the subterranean way to Christianity which one has attempted to construct objectively and scientifically, instead of letting the problem remain subjective, as it is.

One sometimes hears uneducated or half educated people, or conceited geniuses, speak with contempt of the labor of criticism devoted to ancient writings; one hears them foolishly deride the learned scholar's careful scrutiny of the most insignificant detail, which is precisely the glory of the scholar, namely, that he considers nothing insignificant that bears upon his science. No, philological scholarship is absolutely within its rights, and the present author yields to none in profound respect for that which science consecrates. But the scholarly critical theology makes no such clear and definite impression upon the mind; its entire procedure suffers from a certain conscious or unconscious ambiguity. It constantly seems as if this labor of criticism were suddenly about to yield a result for faith, issue in something relevant to faith. Here lies the difficulty. When a philologist prepares an edition of one of Cicero's writings, for example, and performs his task with great acumen, the scholarly apparatus held in beautiful subservience to the control of the spirit; when his ingenuity and his familiarity with the period, gained through formidable industry, combine with his instinct for discovery to overcome obstacles, preparing a clear way for the meaning through the obscure maze of the readings, and so forth—then it is quite safe to yield oneself in wholehearted admiration. For when he has finished, nothing follows except the wholly admirable result that an ancient writing has now through his skill and competence received its most accurate possible form. But by no means that I should now base my eternal happiness on this work; for in relation to my eternal happiness, his astonishing acumen seems, I must admit, inadequate. Aye, I confess that my admiration for him would be not glad but despondent, if I thought he had any such thing in mind. But this is precisely how the learned theologian goes to work; when he has completed his task (and until then he keeps us in suspense, but holds this prospect before us) he draws the conclusion: *ergo*, now you can base your eternal happiness on these writings.

---

[2] A work begun in 1825 but owing to many disasters not finished until 1845 (note supplied by Walter Lowrie).—WALTER LOWRIE

Anyone who posits inspiration, as a believer does, must consistently consider every critical deliberation, whether for or against, as a misdirection, a temptation for the spirit. And anyone who plunges into these critical inquiries without being a believer, cannot possibly intend to have inspiration emerge as a result. Who then really has any interest in the whole inquiry?

But the contradiction remains unnoticed because the mode of approach is purely objective; and then indeed the contradiction is no longer there. The inquirer forgets what he has up his sleeve, except in so far as he occasionally stimulates and encourages himself lyrically by referring to it; or indulges in lyrical polemics with the aid of eloquence. But let an individual approach this enterprise, let him propose in infinite personal passion to attach his eternal happiness to the result: he will readily perceive that there is no result, and that none is to be expected; and the contradiction will bring him to despair. Luther's rejection of the Epistle of James will alone suffice. In relation to an eternal happiness, and an infinite passionate interest in its behalf (in which latter alone the former can exist), an iota is of importance, of infinite importance; or rather, despair over the contradiction involved will teach him that there is no possibility of getting through along this road. . . .

I assume that the critics have succeeded in proving about the Bible everything that any learned theologian in his happiest moment has ever wished to prove about the Bible. These books and no others belong to the canon; they are authentic; they are integral; their authors are trustworthy—one may well say, that it is as if every letter were inspired. . . .

Well then, everything being assumed in order with respect to the Scriptures—what follows? Has anyone who previously did not have faith been brought a single step nearer to its acquisition? No, not a single step. Faith does not result simply from a scientific inquiry; it does not come directly at all. On the contrary, in this objectivity one tends to lose that infinite personal interestedness in passion which is the condition of faith, the *ubique et nusquam*[3] in which faith can come into being. Has anyone who previously had faith gained anything with respect to its strength and power? No, not in the least. Rather is it the case that in this voluminous knowledge, this certainty that lurks at the door of faith and threatens to devour it, he is in so dangerous a situation that he will need to put forth much effort in great fear and trembling, lest he fall a victim to the temptation to confuse knowledge with faith. While faith has hitherto had a profitable schoolmaster in the existing uncertainty, it would have in the new certainty its most dangerous enemy. For if passion is eliminated, faith no longer exists, and certainty and passion do not go together. Whoever believes that there is a God and an over-ruling providence finds it easier to preserve his faith, easier to acquire something that definitely is faith and not an illusion, in an imperfect world where passion is kept alive, than in an absolutely perfect world. In such a world faith is in fact unthinkable. Hence also the teaching that faith is abolished in eternity.

How fortunate then that this wishful hypothesis, this beautiful dream of critical theology, is an impossibility, because even the most perfect realization would still remain an approximation. And again how fortunate for the critics that the fault is by no means in them! If all the angels in heaven were to put their heads together, they could still bring

---

[3] Everywhere and nowhere.—E.D.K.

to pass only an approximation, because an approximation is the only certainty attainable for historical knowledge—but also an inadequate basis for an eternal happiness.

I assume now the opposite, that the opponents have succeeded in proving what they desire about the Scriptures, with a certainty transcending the most ardent wish of the most passionate hostility—what then? Have the opponents thereby abolished Christianity? By no means. Has the believer been harmed? By no means, not in the least. Has the opponent made good a right to be relieved of responsibility for not being a believer? By no means. Because these books are not written by these authors, are not authentic, are not in an integral condition, are not inspired (though this cannot be disproved, since it is an object of faith), it does not follow that these authors have not existed; and above all, it does not follow that Christ has not existed. In so far, the believer is equally free to assume it; equally free, let us note this well, for if he had assumed it by virtue of any proof, he would have been on the verge of giving up his faith. If matters ever come to this pass, the believer will have some share of guilt, in so far as he has himself invited this procedure, and begun to play into the hands of unbelief by proposing to demonstrate.

Here is the crux of the matter, and I come back to the case of the learned theology. For whose sake is it that the proof is sought? Faith does not need it; aye, it must even regard the proof as its enemy. But when faith begins to feel embarrassed and ashamed, like a young woman for whom her love is no longer sufficient, but who secretly feels ashamed of her lover and must therefore have it established that there is something remarkable about him—when faith thus begins to lose its passion, when faith begins to cease to be faith, then a proof becomes necessary so as to command respect from the side of unbelief. . . .

III. The Task of Becoming Subjective

Objectively we consider only the matter at issue, subjectively we have regard to the subject and his subjectivity; and behold, precisely this subjectivity is the matter at issue. This must constantly be borne in mind, namely, that the subjective problem is not something about an objective issue, but is the subjectivity itself. For since the problem in question poses a decision, and since all decisiveness, as shown above, inheres in subjectivity, it is essential that every trace of an objective issue should be eliminated. If any such trace remains, it is at once a sign that the subject seeks to shirk something of the pain and crisis of the decision; that is, he seeks to make the problem to some degree objective . . . Hence we do not here raise the question of the truth of Christianity in the sense that when this has been determined, the subject is assumed ready and willing to accept it. No, the question is as to the mode of the subject's acceptance; and it must be regarded as an illusion rooted in the demoralization which remains ignorant of the subjective nature of the decision, or as an evasion springing from the disingenuousness which seeks to shirk the decision by an objective mode of approach, wherein there can in all eternity be no decision by an objective mode of approach, wherein there can in all eternity be no decision, to assume that the transition from something objective to the subjective acceptance is a direct transition, following upon the objective deliberation as a matter of course. On the contrary, the subjective acceptance is precisely the decisive factor; and an objective acceptance of Christianity is paganism or thoughtlessness.

Christianity proposes to endow the individual with an eternal happiness, a good which is not distributed wholesale, but only to one individual at a time. Though

Christianity assumes that there inheres in the subjectivity of the individual, as being the potentiality of the appropriation of this good, the possibility for its acceptance, it does not assume that the subjectivity is immediately ready for such acceptance, or even has, without further ado, a real conception of the significance of such a good. The development or transformation of the individual's subjectivity, its infinite concentration in itself over against the conception of an eternal happiness, that highest good of the infinite—this constitutes the developed potentiality of the primary potentiality which subjectivity as such presents. In this way Christianity protests every form of objectivity; it desires that the subject should be infinitely concerned about himself. It is subjectivity that Christianity is concerned with, and it is only in subjectivity that its truth exists, if it exists at all; objectively, Christianity has absolutely no existence. If its truth happens to be in only a single subject, it exists in him alone; and there is greater Christian joy in heaven over this one individual than over universal history and the System, which as objective entities are incommensurable for that which is Christian.

It is commonly assumed that no art or skill is required in order to be subjective. To be sure, every human being is a bit of a subject, in a sense. But now to strive to become what one already is: who would take the pains to waste his time on such a task, involving the greatest imaginable degree of resignation? Quite so. But for this very reason alone it is a very difficult task, the most difficult of all tasks in fact, precisely because every human being has a strong natural bent and passion to become something more and different. And so its with all such apparently insignificant tasks, precisely their seeming insignificance makes them infinitely difficult. In such cases the task itself is not directly alluring, so as to support the aspiring individual; instead, it works against him, and it needs an infinite effort on his part merely to discover that his task lies here, that this is his task—an effort from which he is otherwise relieved. To think about the simple things of life, about what the plain man also knows about a fashion, is extremely forbidding; for the differential distinction attainable even through the utmost possible exertion is by no means obvious to the sensual man. No indeed, thinking about the high-falutin is very much more attractive and glorious.

When one overlooks this little distinction, humoristic from the Socratic standpoint and infinitely anxious from the Christian, between being something like a subject so called, and being a subject, or becoming one, or being what one is through having become what one is: then it becomes wisdom, the admired wisdom of our own age, that it is the task of the subject increasingly to divest himself of his subjectivity in order to become more and more objective. It is easy to see what this guidance understands by being a subject of a sort. It understands by it quite rightly the accidental, the angular, the selfish, the eccentric, and so forth, all of which every human being can have enough of. Nor does Christianity deny that such things should be gotten rid of; it has never been a friend of loutishness. But the difference is, that philosophy teaches that the way is to become objective, while Christianity teaches that the way is to become subjective, i.e., to become a subject in truth. Lest this should seem a mere dispute about words, let me say that Christianity wishes to intensify passion to it highest pitch; but passion is subjectivity, and does not exist objectively. . . .

The task of becoming subjective, then, may be presumed to be the highest task, and one that is proposed to every human being; just as, correspondingly, the highest reward, an eternal happiness, exists only for those who are subjective; or rather, comes into being for the individual who becomes subjective. . . .

IV. Truth Is Subjectivity

When the question of truth is raised in an objective manner, reflection is directed objectively to the truth, as an object to which the knower is related. Reflection is not focused upon the relationship, however, but upon the question of whether it is the truth to which the knower is related. If only the object to which he is related is the truth, the subject is accounted to be in the truth. When the question of the truth is raised subjectively, reflection is directed subjectively to the nature of the individual's relationship; if only the mode of this relationship is in the truth, the individual is in the truth even if he should happen to be thus related to what is not true. Let us take as an example the knowledge of God. Objectively, reflection is directed to the problem of whether this object is the true God; subjectively, reflection is directed to the question whether the individual is related to a something *in such a manner* that his relationship is in truth a God-relationship. . . .

The existing individual who chooses to pursue the objective way enters upon the entire approximation-process by which it is proposed to bring God to light objectively. But this is in all eternity impossible, because God is a subject, and therefore exists only for subjectivity in inwardness. The existing individual who chooses the subjective way apprehends instantly the entire dialectical difficulty involved in having to use some time, perhaps a long time, in finding God objectively; and he feels this dialectical difficulty in all its painfulness, because every moment is wasted in which he does not have God. That very instant he has God, not by virtue of any objective deliberation, but by virtue of the infinite passion of inwardness. The objective inquirer, on the other hand, is not embarrassed by such dialectical difficulties as are involved in devoting an entire period of investigation to finding God—since it is possible that the inquirer may die tomorrow; and if he lives he can scarcely regard God as something to be taken along if convenient, since God is precisely that which one takes *a tout prix*, which in the understanding of passion constitutes the true inward relationship to God.

It is at this point, so difficult dialectically, that the way swings off for everyone who knows what it means to think, and to think existentially; which is something very different from sitting at a desk and writing about what one has never done, something very different from writing *de omnibus dubitandum*[4] and at the same time being as credulous existentially as the most sensuous of men. Here is where the way swings off, and the change is marked by the fact that while objective knowledge rambles comfortably on by way of the long road of approximation without being impelled by the urge of passion, subjective knowledge counts every delay a deadly peril, and the decision so infinitely important and so instantly pressing that it is as if the opportunity had already passed.

Now when the problem is to reckon up on which side there is most truth, whether on the side of one who seeks the true God objectively, and pursues the approximate truth of the God-idea; or on the side of one who, driven by the infinite passion of his need of God, feels an infinite concern for his own relationship to God in truth (and to be at one and the same time on both sides equally, is as we have noted not possible for an existing individual, but is merely the happy delusion of an imaginary I-am-I): the answer cannot be in doubt for anyone who has not been demoralized with the aid of science. If one who lives in the midst of Christendom goes up to the house of God, the house of the true God, with the true conception of God in his knowledge, and prays, but prays in a false spirit;

---

[4] About everything there must be doubt.—E.D.K.

and one who lives in an idolatrous community prays with the entire passion of the infinite, although his eyes rest upon the image of an idol: where is there most truth? The one prays in truth to God though he worships an idol; the other prays falsely to the true God, and hence worships in fact an idol.

When one man investigates objectively the problem of immortality, and another embraces an uncertainty with the passion of the infinite: where is there most truth, and who has the greater certainty? The one has entered upon a never-ending approximation, for the certainty of immortality lies precisely in the subjectivity of the individual; the other is immortal, and fights for his immortality by struggling with the uncertainty. Let us consider Socrates. Nowadays everyone dabbles in a few proofs; some have several such proofs, other fewer. But Socrates! He puts the question objectively in a problematic manner: *if* there is an immortality. He must therefore be accounted a doubter in comparison with one of our modern thinkers with the three proofs? By no means. On this "if" he risks his entire life, he has the courage to meet death, and he has with the passion of the infinite so determined the pattern of his life that it must be found acceptable—*if* there is an immortality. Is any better proof capable of being given for the immortality of the soul? But those who have the three proofs do not at all determine their lives in conformity therewith; if there is an immortality it must feel disgust over their manner of life: can any better refutation be given of the three proofs? The bit of uncertainty that Socrates had, helped him because he himself contributed the passion of the infinite; the three proofs that the others have do not profit them at all, because they are dead to spirit and enthusiasm, and their three proofs, in lieu of proving anything else, prove just this. A young girl may enjoy all the sweetness of love on the basis of what is merely a weak hope that she is beloved, because she rests everything on this weak hope; but many a wedded matron more than once subjected to the strongest expressions of love, has in so far indeed had proofs, but strangely enough has not enjoyed *quod erat demonstrandum*.[5] The Socratic ignorance, which Socrates held fast with the entire passion of his inwardness, was thus an expression for the principle that the eternal truth is related to an existing individual, and that this truth must therefore be a paradox for him as long as he exists; and yet it is possible that there was more truth in the Socratic ignorance as it was in him, than in the entire objective truth of the System, which flirts with what the times demand and accommodates itself to *Privatdocents*.[6]

The objective accent falls on WHAT is said, the subjective accent on HOW it is said. This distinction holds even in the aesthetic realm, and receives definite expression in the principle that what is in itself true may in the mouth of such and such a person become untrue. In these times this distinction is particularly worthy of notice, for if we wish to express in a single sentence the difference between ancient times and our own, we should doubtless have to say: "In ancient times only an individual here and there knew the truth; now all know it, except that the inwardness of its appropriation stands in an inverse relationship to the extent of its dissemination. Aesthetically the contradiction that truth becomes untruth in this or that person's mouth, is best construed comically: In the ethicoreligious sphere, accent is again on the "how." But this is not to be understood as

---

[5] That which was to be proved.—E.D.K.

[6] Professors.—E.D.K.

referring to demeanor, expression, or the like; rather it refers to the relationship sustained by the existing individual, in his own existence, to the content of his utterance. Objectively the interest is focussed merely on the thought-content, subjectively on the inwardness. At its maximum this inward "how" is the passion of the infinite, and the passion of the infinite is the truth. But the passion of the infinite is precisely subjectivity, and thus subjectivity becomes the truth . . . Only in subjectivity is there decisiveness, to seek objectivity is to be in error. It is the passion of the infinite that is the decisive factor and not its content, for its content is precisely itself. In this manner subjectivity and the subjective "how" constitute the truth.

But the "how" which is thus subjectively accentuated precisely because the subject is an existing individual, is also subject to a dialectic with respect to time. In the passionate moment of decision, where the road swings away from objective knowledge, it seems as if the infinite decision were thereby realized. But in the same moment the existing individual finds himself in the temporal order, and the subject "how" is transformed into a striving, a striving which receives indeed its impulse and a repeated renewal from the decisive passion of the infinite, but is nevertheless a striving.

When subjectivity is the truth, the conceptual determination of the truth must include an expression for the antithesis to objectivity, a memento of the fork in the road where the way swings off; this expression will at the same time serve as an indication of the tension of the subjective inwardness. Here is such a definition of truth: *An objective uncertainty held fast in an appropriation-process of the most passionate inwardness is the truth*, the highest truth attainable for an *existing* individual. At the point where the way swings off (and where this is cannot be specified objectively, since it is a matter of subjectivity), there objective knowledge is placed in abeyance. Thus the subject merely has, objectively, the uncertainty; but it is this which precisely increases the tension of that infinite passion which constitutes his inwardness. The truth is precisely the venture which chooses an objective uncertainty with the passion of the infinite. I contemplate the order of nature in the hope of finding God, and I see omnipotence and wisdom; but I also see much else that disturbs my mind and excites anxiety. The sum of all this is an objective uncertainty. But it is for this very reason that the inwardness becomes as intense as it is, for it embraces this objective uncertainty with the entire passion of the infinite. In the case of a mathematical proposition the objectivity is given, but for this reason the truth of such a proposition is also an indifferent truth.

But the above definition of truth is an equivalent expression for faith. Without risk there is no faith. Faith is precisely the contradiction between the infinite passion of the individual's inwardness and the objective uncertainty. If I am capable of grasping God objectively, I do not believe, but precisely because I cannot do this I must believe. If I wish to preserve myself in faith I must constantly be intent upon holding fast the objective uncertainty, so as to remain out upon the deep, over seventy thousand fathoms of water, still preserving my faith.

V. Faith and the Absurd

. . . The Socratic ignorance gives expression to the objective uncertainty attaching to the truth, while his inwardness in existing is the truth. To anticipate here what will be developed later, let me make the following remark. The Socratic ignorance is an analogue to the category of the absurd, only that there is still less of objective certainty in the absurd, and in the repellent effect that the absurd exercises. It is certain only that it is absurd, and precisely on that account it incites to an infinitely greater tension in the corresponding inwardness. The Socratic inwardness in existing is an analogue to faith; only that the inwardness of faith, corresponding as it does, not to the repulsion of the Socratic ignorance, but to the repulsion exerted by the absurd, is infinitely more profound.

... Without risk there is no faith, and the greater the risk the greater the faith; the more objective security the less inwardness (for inwardness is precisely subjectivity), and the less objective security the more profound the possible inwardness. When the paradox is paradoxical in itself, it repels the individual by virtue of its absurdity, and the corresponding passion of inwardness is faith. ...

When Socrates believed that there was a God, he held fast to the objective uncertainty with the whole passion of his inwardness, and it is precisely in this contradiction and in this risk, that faith is rooted. Now it is otherwise. Instead of the objective uncertainty, there is here a certainty, namely, that objectively it is absurd; and this absurdity, held fast in the passion of inwardness, is faith. The Socratic ignorance is as a witty jest in comparison with the earnestness of facing the absurd; and the Socratic existential inwardness is as Greek light-mindedness in comparison with the grave strenuosity of faith.

... The absurd is precisely by its objective repulsion the measure of the intensity of faith in inwardness. Suppose a man who wishes to acquire faith; let the comedy begin. He wishes to have faith, but he wishes also to safeguard himself by means of an objective inquiry and its approximation-process. What happens? With the help of the approximation-process the absurd becomes something different; it becomes probable, it becomes increasingly probable, it becomes extremely and emphatically probable. Now he is ready to believe it, and he ventures to claim for himself that he does not believe as shoemakers and tailors and simple folk believe, but only after long deliberation. Now he is ready to believe it; and lo, now it has become precisely impossible to believe it. Anything that is almost probable, or probable, or extremely and emphatically probable, is something he can almost know, or as good as know, or extremely and emphatically almost *know*—but it is impossible to *believe*. For the absurd is the object of faith, and the only object that can be believed. ...

There has been said much that is strange, much that is deplorable, much that is revolting about Christianity; but the most stupid thing ever said about it is, that it is to a certain degree true. There has been said much that is strange, much that is deplorable, much that is revolting about enthusiasm; but the most stupid thing ever said about it is, that it is to a certain degree. There has been said much that is strange, much that is deplorable, much that is revolting about love, but the most stupid thing ever said about it is, that it is to a certain degree. And when a man has prostituted himself by speaking in this manner about enthusiasm and love, he has betrayed his stupidity, which in this case is not in the direction of intelligence, however, since it has its ground rather in the fact that the understanding has become too large, in the same sense as when a disease of the liver is caused by an enlargement of the liver, and hence, as another author has remarked, "is the flatness that salt takes on when it loses its savor": then there is still one phenomenon left, Christianity. If the sight of enthusiasm has not sufficed to help him break with the understanding, if love has not been able to emancipate him from his slavery: then let him consider Christianity. Let him be offended, he is still human; let him despair of ever himself becoming a Christian, he is yet perhaps nearer than he believes;

let him fight to the last drop of blood for the extermination of Christianity, he is still human—but if he is able here to say: it is true to a certain degree, then he is stupid.

Perhaps someone will think that I tremble to say this, that I must be prepared for a terrible castigation at the hands of speculative philosophy. By no means. The speculative philosopher will here again be quite consistent with himself, and say: "There is a certain degree of truth in what the man says, only we cannot stop there, but must advance beyond it." It would also be strange if my insignificance should succeed where even Christianity had failed, namely, in bringing the speculative philosopher to the point of passion; if so, then my little fragment of philosophy would suddenly take on a significance I had least of all dreamed of.

But whoever is neither cold nor hot is nauseating; and just as the hunter is ill-served by a weapon that misses fire at the crucial moment, so God is ill-served by misfiring individuals. Had not Pilate asked objectively what truth is, he would never have condemned Christ to be crucified. Had he asked subjectively, the passion of his inwardness respecting what in the decision facing him he had *in truth to do*, would have prevented him from doing wrong. It would then not have been merely his wife who was made anxious by the dreadful dream, but Pilate himself would have become sleepless. But when a man has something so infinitely great before his eyes as the objective truth, he can afford to set at naught his little bit of subjectivity, and what he as subject has to do. And the approximation-process of the objective truth is figuratively expressed in washing the hands, for objectively there is no decision, and the subjective decision shows that one was in error nevertheless, through not understanding that the decision inheres precisely in subjectivity.

Suppose, on the other hand, that subjectivity is the truth, and that subjectivity is an existing subjectivity, then, if I may so express myself, Christianity fits perfectly into the picture. Subjectivity culminates in passion, Christianity is the paradox, paradox and passion are a mutual fit, and the paradox is altogether suited to one whose situation is, to be in the extremity of existence. Aye, never in all the world could there be found two lovers so wholly suited to one another as paradox and passion, and the strife between them is like the strife between lovers, when the dispute is about whether he first aroused her passion, or she his. And so it is here; the existing individual has by means of the paradox itself come to be placed in the extremity of existence. And what can be more splendid for lovers than that they are permitted a long time together without any alteration in the relationship between them, except that it becomes more intensive in inwardness? And this is indeed granted to the highly unspeculative understanding between passion and the paradox, since the whole of life in time is vouchsafed, and the change comes first in eternity. . . .

Faith has in fact two tasks: to take care in every moment to discover the improbable, the paradox; and then to hold it fast with the passion of inwardness. The common conception is that the improbable, the paradoxical, is something to which faith is related only passively; it must provisionally be content with this relationship, but little by little things will become better, as indeed seems probable. O miraculous creation of confusions in speaking about faith! One is to begin believing, in reliance upon the probability that things will soon become better. In this way probability is after all smuggled in, and one is prevented from believing; so that it is easy to understand that the fruit of having been for a long time a believer is, that one no longer believes, instead of, as one might think, that the fruit is a more intensive inwardness in faith. No, faith is self-active in its relation to the improbable and the paradoxical, self-active in the discovery, and self-active in every moment holding it fast—in order to believe. Merely to lay hold of the improbable requires all the passion of the infinite and its concentration in itself; for the improbable and the paradoxical are not to be reached by the understanding's quantitative calculation of the more and more difficult. Where the understanding despairs, faith is already present in order to make the despair properly decisive, in order that the movement of faith may not become a mere exchange within the bargaining sphere of the understanding. But to believe against the understanding is martyrdom; to begin to get the understanding a little in one's favor, is temptation and retrogression. This martyrdom is something that the speculative philosopher is free from. That he must pursue his studies, and especially that he must read many modern books, I admit is burdensome; but the martyrdom of faith is not the same thing. What I therefore fear and shrink from, more than I fear to die and to lose my sweetheart, is to say about Christianity that it is to a certain degree true. If I lived to be seventy years old, if I shortened the night's sleep and increased the day's work from year to year, inquiring into Christianity—how insignificant such a little period of study, viewed as entitling me to judge in so lofty a fashion about Christianity! For to be so embittered against Christianity after a casual acquaintance with it, that I declared it to be false: that would be far more pardonable, far more human. But this lordly superiority seems to me the true corruption, making every saving relationship impossible—and it may possibly be the case, that Christianity is the truth. . . .

PART II

The Earlier Critiques of Theism

○

A s I MENTIONED in the Introduction, the critiques of and attacks on theism are of two main sorts: (1) philosophical critiques that attack and reject theism on the grounds that all of the classical arguments for theism are fallacious, and/or there are no other grounds for the beliefs in a god; (2) cultural critiques that focus on the historical, psychological, political, sociological, and so on, bases of religious belief and that attack theism on these grounds.

Although such critiques of theism (and not merely criticisms of specific arguments for theism) date back to ancient times, our study of them will focus mainly on the past three centuries. (1) The philosophical critiques, for our purposes, may be said to begin with writers such as Hume in the eighteenth century. But they have continued to this very day with writers such as Russell. (2) The cultural critiques began in full force in the nineteenth century and have also continued to the present. Since this is a book in the *philosophy* of religion, not the history of religion, we will focus on the more philosophical attacks on theism (Chapter Four, along with Hume, Chapter Two).

Before we do so, let us briefly look at some of the main cultural critiques of theism (Chapter Three). Of course, the distinction between philosophical and cultural critiques is not a sharp one. It is more a matter of emphasis. We shall examine some writings by mainly nineteenth-century and very early twentieth-century writers, including Feuerbach, Marx, Freud, Nietzsche, and Durkheim.

In Chapter Four we shall examine in somewhat more detail the writers who made critiques either of traditional theism or of all forms of theism. If we again include Hume, then we have one eighteenth-century critique represented, one nineteenth-century critique by Mill, and some twentieth-century critiques by Dewey, Nagel, and Russell.

But again I need to point out some exceptions. As we shall see, Mill's analysis/critique did not lead him to totally reject theism, but to reject *traditional* theism. Hence, he is perhaps more accurately described as a revisionary theist rather than a critic of theism in all forms. Also, one of the selections in this chapter consists of a debate between a traditional theist (Copleston) and an atheist (Russell).

After we have dealt with the philosophical critiques of theism made by Mill, Nagel, and Russell, in Chapter Five we shall turn to rejoinders to the philosophical critiques. All of these responses to the philosophical critiques are made by twentieth-century theists, most of whom are philosophers, including Taylor, Pratt, Alston, Lewis, and Malcolm. In some cases, the responding theists defend the classical arguments, but do so with a fresh approach. In other cases, the responding theists put forth new and original versions of one or two of the arguments.

CHAPTER THREE

Cultural Critiques

○

○   ○   ○   *14*

Religion as Illusion
Ludwig Feuerbach

WHAT WE HAVE hitherto been maintaining generally, even with regard to sensational impressions, of the relation between subject and object, applies especially to the relation between the subject and the religious object.

In the perceptions of the senses consciousness of the object is distinguishable from consciousness of self; but in religion, consciousness of the object and self-consciousness coincide. The object of the senses is out of man, the religious object is within him, and therefore as little forsakes him as his self-consciousness or his conscience; it is the intimate, the closest object. "God," says Augustine, for example, "is nearer, more related to us, and therefore more easily known by us, than sensible, corporeal things." The object of the senses is in itself indifferent—independent of the disposition or of the judgment; but the object of religion is a selected object; the most excellent, the first, the supreme being; it essentially presupposes a critical judgment, a discrimination between the divine and the non-divine, between that which is worthy of adoration and that which is not worthy. And here may be applied, without any limitation, the proposition: the object of any subject is nothing else than the subject's own nature taken objectively. Such as are a man's thoughts and dispositions, such is his God; so much worth as a man has, so much and no more has his God. Consciousness of God is self-consciousness, knowledge of God is self-knowledge. By his God thou knowest the man, and by the man his God; the two are identical. Whatever is God to a man, that is his heart and soul; and conversely, God is the manifested inward nature, the expressed self of a man—religion the solemn unveiling of a man's hidden treasures, the revelation of his intimate thoughts, the open confession of his love-secrets.[1]

But when religion—consciousness of God—is designated as the self-consciousness of man, this is not to be understood as affirming that the religious man is directly aware of this identity; for, on the contrary, ignorance of it is fundamental to the peculiar nature of religion. To preclude this misconception, it is better to say, religion is man's earliest and also indirect form of self-knowledge. Hence, religion everywhere precedes philosophy, as in the history of the race, so also in that of the individual. Man first of all sees his nature as if *out* of himself, before he finds it in himself. His own nature is in the first instance contemplated by him as that of another being. Religion is the childlike condition of humanity; but the child sees his nature—man—out of himself; in childhood a man is an object to himself, under the form of another man. Hence the historical

---

[1] In this paragraph and elsewhere, by "is" Feuerbach means "is identical with."

progress of religion consists in this: that what by an earlier religion was regarded as objective, is now recognized as subjective; that is, what was formerly contemplated and worshiped as God is now perceived to be something *human*. What was at first religion becomes at a later period idolatry; man is seen to have adored his own nature. Man has given objectivity to himself, but has not recognized the object as his own nature: a later religion takes this forward step; every advance in religion is therefore a deeper self-knowledge. But every particular religion, while it pronounces its predecessors idolatrous excepts itself—and necessarily so, otherwise it would no longer be religion—from the fate, the common nature of all religions: it imputes only to other religions what is the fault, if fault it be, of religion in general. Because it has a different object, a different tenor, because it has transcended the ideas of preceding religions, it erroneously supposes itself exalted above the necessary eternal laws which constitute the essence of religion—it fancies its objects, its ideas, to be superhuman. But the essence of religion, thus hidden from the religious, is evident to the thinker, by whom religion is viewed objectively, which it cannot be by its votaries. And it is our task to show that the antithesis of divine and human is altogether illusory, that it is nothing else than the antithesis between the human nature in general and the human individual; that, consequently, the object and contents of the Christian religion are altogether human.

Religion, at least the Christian, is the relation of man to himself, or more correctly to his own nature (i.e., his subjective nature); but a relation to it, viewed as a nature apart from his own. The divine being is nothing else than the human being, or, rather, the human nature purified, freed from the limits of the individual man, made objective—i.e., contemplated and revered as another, a distinct being. All the attributes of the divine nature are, therefore, attributes of the human nature.

In relation to the attributes, the predicates, of the Divine Being, this is admitted without hesitation, but by no means in relation to the subject of these predicates. The negation of the subject is held to be irreligion, nay, atheism; though not so the negation of the predicates. But that which has no predicates or qualities has no effect upon me; that which has no effect upon me has no existence for me. To deny all the qualities of a being is equivalent to denying the being himself. A being without qualities is one which cannot become an object to the mind, and such a being is virtually non-existent. Where man deprives God of all qualities, God is no longer anything more to him than a negative being. To the truly religious man, God is not a being without qualities, because to him he is a positive, real being. The theory that God cannot be defined, and consequently cannot be known by man, is therefore the offspring of recent times, a product of modern unbelief.

As reason is and can be pronounced finite only where man regards sensual enjoyment, or religious emotion, or aesthetic contemplation, or moral sentiment, as the absolute, the true; so the proposition that God is unknowable or undefinable, can only be enunciated and become fixed as a dogma, where this object has no longer any interest for the intellect; where the real, the positive, alone has any hold on man, where the real alone has for him the significance of the essential, of the absolute, divine object, but where at the same time, in contradiction with this purely worldly tendency, there yet exist some old remains of religiousness. On the ground that God is unknowable, man excuses himself to what is yet remaining of his religious conscience for his forgetfulness of God, his absorption in the world: he denies God practically by his conduct—the world has possession of all his thoughts and inclinations—but he does not deny him theoretically, he does not attack his existence; he lets that rest. But this existence does not affect or incommode him; it is a merely negative existence, an existence without existence, a self-contradictory exist-ence—a state of being which, as to its effects, is not distinguishable from nonbeing. The denial of determinate, positive predicates concerning the divine nature is nothing else than a denial of religion, with, however, an appearance of religion in its favour, so that it is not recognized as a denial; it is simply a subtle, disguised atheism. The alleged religious horror of limiting God by positive predicates is only the irreligious wish to know nothing more of God, to banish God from the mind. Dread of limitation is dread of existence. All real existence, i.e., all existence which is truly such, is qualitative, determinative existence. He who earnestly believes in the Divine existence is not shocked at the attributing even of gross sensuous qualities to God. He who dreads an existence that may give offence, who shrinks from the grossness of a positive predicate, may as well renounce existence altogether. A God who is injured by determinate qualities has not the courage and the strength to exist. Qualities are the fire, the vital breath, the oxygen, the salt of existence. An existence in general, an existence without qualities, is an insipidity, an absurdity. But there can be no more in God than is supplied by religion. Only where man loses his taste for religion, and thus religion itself becomes insipid, does the existence of God become an insipid existence—an existence without qualities.

There is, however, a still milder way of denying the divine predicates than the direct one just described. It is admitted that the predicates of the divine nature are finite, and, more particularly, human qualities, but their rejection is rejected; they are even taken under protection, because it is necessary to man to have a definite conception of God, and since he is man he can form no other than a human conception of him. In relation to God, it is said, these predicates are certainly without any objective validity; but to me, if he is to exist for me, he cannot appear otherwise than as he does appear to me, namely, as a being with attributes analogous to the human. But this distinction between what God is in himself, and what he is for me destroys the peace of religion, and is besides in itself an unfounded and untenable distinction. I cannot know whether the God is something else in himself or for himself than he is for me; what he is to me is to me all that he is. For me, there lies in these predicates under which he exists for me, what he is in himself, his very nature; he is for me what he can alone ever be for me. The religious man finds perfect satisfaction in that which God is in relation to himself; of any other relation he knows nothing, for God is to him what he can alone be to man. In the distinction above stated, man takes a point of view above himself, i.e., above his nature, the absolute measure of his being; but this transcendentalism is only an illusion; for I can make the distinction between the object as it is in itself, and the object as it is for me, only where an object can really appear otherwise to me, not where it appears to me such as the absolute measure of my nature determines it to appear—such as it must appear to me. It is true that I may have a merely subjective conception, i.e., one which does not arise out of the general constitution of my species; but if my conception is determined by the constitution of my species, the distinction between what an object is in itself, and what it is for me ceases; for this conception is itself an absolute one. The measure of the species is the absolute measure, law, and criterion of man. And, indeed, religion has the conviction that its conceptions, its predicates of God, are such as every man ought to have, and must have, if he would have the true ones—that they are the conceptions necessary to human nature; nay, further, that they are objectively true, representing God as he is. To every religion the gods of *other* religions are only notions concerning God, but its own conception of God is to it God himself, the true God—God such as he is in himself. Religion is satisfied only with a complete Deity, a God without reservation; it will not have a mere phantasm of God; it demands God himself. Religion gives up its own existence when it gives up the nature of God; it is no longer a truth when it renounces the possession of the true God. Skepticism is the arch-enemy of religion; but the distinction between object and conception—between God as he is in himself, and God as he is for me—is a skeptical distinction, and therefore an irreligious one.

That which is to man the self-existent, the highest being, to which he can conceive nothing higher—that is to him the Divine Being. How then should he inquire concerning this being, what he is in himself? If God were an object to the bird, he would be a winged being: the bird knows nothing higher, nothing more blissful, than the winged condition. How ludicrous would it be if this bird pronounced: To me God appears as a bird, but what he is in himself I know not. To the bird the highest nature is the bird-nature; take from him the conception of the highest being. How, then, could he ask whether God in himself what he is for me is to ask whether God in himself were winged? To ask whether God is in himself what he is for me is to ask whether God is God, is to lift oneself above one's God, to rise up against him.

Wherever, therefore, this idea, that the religious predicates are only anthropomorphisms, has taken possession of a man, there has doubt, has unbelief, obtained the mastery of faith. And it is only the inconsequence of faint-heartedness and intellectual imbecility which does not proceed from this idea to the formal negation of the predicates, and from thence to the negation of the subject to which they relate. If thou doubtest the objective truth of the predicates, thou must also doubt the objective truth of the subject whose predicates they are. If thy predicates are anthropomorphisms, the subject of them is an anthropomorphism too. If love, goodness, personality, etc., are human attributes, so also is the subject which thou presupposest, the existence of God, the belief that there is a God, an anthropomorphism—a presupposition purely human. Whence knowest thou that the belief in a God at all is not a limitation of man's mode of conception? Higher beings—and thou supposest such—are perhaps so blest in themselves, so at unity with themselves, that they are not hung in suspense between themselves and a yet higher being. To know God and not oneself to be God, to know blessedness and not oneself to enjoy it, is a state of disunity, of unhappiness. Higher beings know nothing of this unhappiness; they have no conception of that which they are not.

Thou believest in love as a divine attribute because thou thyself lovest; thou believest that God is a wise, benevolent being because thou knowest nothing better in thyself than benevolence and wisdom; and thou believest that God exists, that therefore he is a subject—whatever exists is a subject, whether it be defined as substance, person, essence, or otherwise—because thou thyself existest, art thyself a subject. Thou knowest no higher human good than to love, than to be good and wise; and even so thou knowest no higher happiness than to exist, to be a subject; for the consciousness of all reality, of all bliss, is for thee bound up in the consciousness of being a subject, of existing. God is an existence, a subject to thee, for the same reason that he is to thee a wise, a blessed, a personal being. The distinction between the divine predicates and the divine subject is only this, that to thee the subject, the existence, does not appear an anthropomorphism, because the conception of it is necessarily involved in thy own existence as a subject, whereas the predicates do appear anthropomorphisms, because their necessity—the necessity that God should be conscious, wise, good, etc.—is not an immediate necessity, identical with the being of man, but is evolved by his self-consciousness, by the activity of his thought. I am a subject, I exist, whether I be wise or unwise, good or bad. To exist is to man the first datum; it constitutes the very idea of the subject; it is presupposed by the predicates. Hence man relinquishes the predicates, but the existence of God is to him a settled, irrefragable, absolutely certain, objective truth. But, nevertheless, this distinction is merely an apparent one. The necessity of the subject lies only in the necessity of the predicate. Thou art a subject only insofar as thou art a human subject; the certainty and reality of thy existence lie only in the certainty and reality of thy human attributes. What the subject is lies only in the predicate; the predicate is the *truth* of the subject— the subject only the personified, existing predicate, the predicate conceived as existing. Subject and predicate are distinguished only as existence and essence. The negation of the predicates is therefore the negation of the subject. What remains of the human subject when abstracted from the human attributes? Even in the language of common life the divine predicates—providence, omniscience, omnipotence—are put for the divine subject.

The certainty of the existence of God, of which it has been said that it is as certain, nay, more certain to man than his own existence, depends only on the certainty of the qualities of God—it is in itself no immediate certainty. To the Christian the existence of the Christian God only is a certainty; to the heathen that of the heathen God only. The heathen did not doubt the existence of Jupiter, because he took no offence at the nature of Jupiter, because he could conceive of God under no other qualities, because to him these qualities were a certainty, a divine reality. The reality of the predicate is the sole guarantee of existence.

Whatever man conceives to be true, he immediately conceives to be real (that is, to have an objective existence), because, originally, only the real is true to him—true in opposition to what is merely conceived, dreamed, imagined. The idea of being, of existence, is the original idea of truth; or, originally, man makes truth dependent on existence, subsequently, existence dependent on truth. Now God is the nature of man regarded as absolute truth—the truth of man; but God, or, what is the same thing, religion, is as various as are the conditions under which man conceives this his nature, regards it as the highest being. These conditions, then, under which man conceives God, are to him the truth, and for that reason they are also the highest existence, or rather they are existence itself; for only the emphatic, the highest existence, is existence, and deserves this name. Therefore, God is an existent, real being, on the very same ground that he is a particular, definite being; for the qualities of God are nothing else than the essential qualities of man himself, and a particular man is what he is, has his existence, his reality, only in his particular conditions. Take away from the Greek the quality of being Greek, and you take away his existence. On this ground it is true that for a definite positive religion—that is, relatively—the certainty of the existence of God is *immediate*; for just as involuntarily, as necessarily, as the Greek was a Greek, so necessarily were his gods Greek beings, so necessarily were they real, existent beings. Religion is that conception of the nature of the world and of man which is essential to, i.e., identical with, a man's nature. But man does not stand above this his necessary conception; on the contrary, it stands above him; it animates, determines, governs him. The necessity of a proof, of a middle term to unite qualities with existence, the possibility of a doubt, is abolished. Only that which is apart from my own being is capable of being doubted by me. How then can I doubt of God, who is my being? To doubt of God is to doubt myself. Only when God is thought of abstractly, when his predicates are the result of philosophic abstraction, arises the distinction or separation between subject and predicate, existence and nature—arises the fiction that the existence or the subject is something else than the predicate, something immediate, indubitable, in distinction from the predicate, which is held to be doubtful. But this is only a fiction. A God who has abstract predicates has also an abstract existence. Existence, being, varies with varying qualities.

The identity of the subject and predicate is clearly evidenced by the progressive development of religion, which is identical with the progressive development of human culture. So long as man is in a mere state of nature, so long is his god a mere nature-god—a personification of some natural force. Where man inhabits houses, he also encloses his gods in temples. The temple is only a manifestation of the value which man attaches to beautiful buildings. Temples in honour of religion are in truth temples in honour of architecture. With the emerging of man from a state of savagery and wildness to one of culture, with the distinction between what is fitting for man and what is not fitting, arises simultaneously the distinction between that which is fitting and that which is not fitting for God. God is the idea of majesty, of the highest dignity: the religious sentiment is the sentiment of supreme fitness. The later, more cultured artists of Greece were the first to embody in the statues of the gods the ideas of dignity, of spiritual grandeur, of imperturbable repose and serenity. But why were these qualities in their view attributes, predicates of God? Because they were in themselves regarded by the Greeks as divinities. Why did those artists exclude all disgusting and low passions? Because they perceived them to be unbecoming, unworthy, unhuman, and consequently ungodlike. The Homeric gods eat and drink—that implies eating and drinking is a divine pleasure. Physical strength is an attribute of the Homeric gods: Zeus is the strongest of the gods. Why? Because physical strength, in and by itself, was regarded as something glorious, divine. To the ancient Germans the highest virtues were those of the warrior; therefore their supreme god was the god of war, Odin—war, "the original or oldest law." Not the attribute of the divinity, but the divineness or deity of the attribute, is the first true Divine Being. Thus what theology and philosophy have held to be God, the Absolute, the Infinite, is not God; but that which they have held not to be God is God: namely, the attribute, the quality, whatever has reality. Hence he alone is the true atheist to whom the predicates of the Divine Being—for example, love, wisdom, justice—are nothing; not he to whom merely the subject of these predicates is nothing. And in no wise is the negation of the subject necessarily also a negation of the predicates considered in themselves. These have an intrinsic, independent reality; they force their recognition upon man by their very nature; they are self-evident truths to him; they prove, they attest themselves. It does not follow that goodness, justice, wisdom, are chimæras because the existence of God is a chimæra, nor truths because this is a truth. The idea of God is dependent on the idea of justice, of benevolence; a God who is not benevolent, not just, not wise, is no God; but the converse does not hold. The fact is not that a quality is divine because God has it, but that God has it because it is in itself divine: because without it God would be a defective being. Justice, wisdom, in general every quality which constitutes the divinity of God, is determined and known by itself independently, but the idea of God is determined by the qualities which have thus been previously judged to be worthy of the divine nature; only in the case in which I identify God and justice, in which I think of God immediately as the reality of the idea of justice, is the idea of God self-determined. But if God as a subject is the determined, while the quality, the predicate, is the determining, then in truth the rank of the godhead is due not to the subject, but to the predicate.

Not until several, and those contradictory, attributes are united in one being, and this being is conceived as personal—the personality being thus brought into especial prominence—not until then is the origin of religion lost sight of, is it forgotten that what the activity of the reflective power has converted into a predicate distinguishable or separable from the subject, was originally the true subject. Thus the Greeks and Romans deified accidents as substances; virtues, states of mind, passions, as independent beings. Man, especially the religious man, is to himself the measure of all things, of all reality. Whatever strongly impresses a man, whatever produces an unusual effect on his mind, if it be only a peculiar, inexplicable sound or note, he personifies as a divine being. Religion embraces all the objects of the world: everything existing has been an object of religious reverence; in the nature and consciousness of religion there is nothing else than what lies in the nature of man and in his consciousness of himself and of the world. Religion has no material exclusively its own. In Rome even the passions of fear and terror had their temples. The Christians also made mental phenomena into independent beings, their own feelings into qualities of things, the passions which governed them into powers which governed the world, in short, predicates of their own nature, whether recognized as such or not, into independent subjective existences. Devils, cobolds, witches, ghosts, angels, were sacred truths as long as the religious spirit held undivided sway over mankind.

In order to banish from the mind the identity of the divine and human predicates, and the consequent identity of the divine and human nature, recourse is had to the idea that God, as the absolute, real Being, has an infinite fulness of various predicates, of which we here know only a part, and those such as are analogous to our own; while the rest, by virtue of which God must thus have quite a different nature from the human or that which is analogous to the human, we shall only know in the future—that is, after death. But an infinite plentitude or multitude of predicates which are really different, so different that the one does not immediately involve the other, is realized only in an infinite plentitude or multitude of different beings or individuals. Thus the human nature presents an infinite abundance of different predicates, and for that very reason it presents an infinite abundance of different individuals. Each new man is a new predicate, a new phasis of humanity. As many as are the men, so many are the powers, the properties of humanity. It is true that there are the same elements in every individual, but under such various conditions and modifications that they appear new and peculiar. The mystery of the inexhaustible fulness of the divine predicates is therefore nothing else than the mystery of human nature considered as an infinitely varied, infinitely modifiable, but, consequently, phenomenal being. Only in the realm of the senses, only in space and time, does there exist a being of really infinite qualities or predicates. Where there are really different predicates there are different times. One man is a distinguished musician, a distinguished author, a distinguished physician; but he cannot compose music, write books, and perform cures in the same moment of time. Time, and not the Hegelian dialectic, is the medium of uniting opposites, contradictories, in one and the same subject. But distinguished and detached from the nature of man, and combined with the idea of God, the infinite fulness of various predicates is a conception without reality, a mere phantasy, a conception derived from the sensible world, but without the essential conditions, without the truth of sensible existence, a conception which stands in direct contradiction with the Divine Being considered as a spiritual, i.e., an abstract, simple, single being; for the predicates of God are precisely of this character, that one involves all the others, because there is no real difference between them. If, therefore, in the present predicates I have not the future, in the present God not the future God, then the future God is not the present, but they are two distinct beings.[2] But this distinction is in contradiction with the unity and simplicity of the theological God. Why is a given predicate a predicate of God? Because it is divine in its nature, i.e., because it expresses no limitation, no defect. Why are other predicates applied to him? Because, however various in themselves, they agree in this, that they all alike express perfection, unlimitedness. Hence I can conceive innumerable predicates of God, because they must all agree with the abstract idea of the Godhead, and must have in common that which constitutes every single predicate a divine attribute. Thus it is in the system of Spinoza.[3] He speaks of an infinite number of attributes of the divine substance, but he specifies none except Thought and Extension. Why? Because it is a matter of indifference to know them? Nay, because they are in themselves indifferent, superfluous; for with all these innumerable predicates, I yet always mean to say the same thing as when I speak of Thought and Extension. Why is Thought an attribute of substance? Because, according to Spinoza, it is capable of being conceived by itself, because it expresses something indivisible, perfect, infinite. Why Extension or Matter? For the same reason. Thus, substance can have an indefinite number of predicates, because it is not their specific definition, their difference, but their identity, their equivalence, which makes them attributes of substance. Or rather, substance has innumerable predicates only because (how strange!) it has properly no predicate; that is, no definite, real predicate. The indefinite unity which is the product of thought completes itself by the indefinite multiplicity which is the product of the imagination. Because the predicate is not *multum*, it is *multa*. In truth, the positive predicates are Thought and Extension. In these two infinitely more is said than in the nameless innumerable predicates; for they express something definite—in them I have something. But substance is too indifferent, too apathetic to be *something*; that is, to have qualities and passions; that it may not be something; it is rather nothing.

Now, when it is shown that what the subject is lies entirely in the attributes of the subject; that is, that the predicate is the true subject; it is also proved that if the divine predicates are attributes of the human nature, the subject of those predicates is also of the human nature. But the divine predicates are partly general, partly personal. The general predicates are the metaphysical, but these serve only as external points of support to religion; they are not the characteristic definitions of religion. It is the personal predicates alone which constitute the essence of religion—in which the Divine Being is the object of religion. Such are, for example, that God is a Person, that his is the moral Lawgiver, the Father of mankind, the Holy One, the Just, the Good, the Merciful. It is, however, at once clear, or it will at least be clear in the sequel, with regard to these and other definitions, that, especially as applied to a personality, they are purely human definitions, and that consequently man in religion—in his relation to God—is in relation to his own nature; for to the religious sentiment these predicates are not mere conceptions, mere images, which man forms of God, to be distinguished from that

---

[2] For religious faith there is no other distinction between the present and future God than that the former is an object of faith, of conception, of imagination, while the latter is to be an object of immediate, that is, personal, sensible perception. In this life and in the next he is the same God; but in the one he is incomprehensible, in the other comprehensible.—L.F.

[3] A seventeenth-century philosopher who put forth a philosophical system with supposedly self-evident axioms and theorems deduced from them.—E.D.K.

which God is in himself, but truths, facts, realities. Religion knows nothing of anthropomorphisms; to it they are not anthropomorphisms. It is the very essence of religion that to it these definitions express the nature of God. They are pronounced to be images only by the understanding, which reflects on religion, and which while defending them yet before its own tribunal denies them. But to the religious sentiment God is a real Father, real Love and Mercy; for to it he is a real, living, personal being, and therefore his attributes are also living and personal. Nay, the definitions which are the most sufficing to the religious sentiment are precisely those which give the most offence to the understanding, and which in the process of reflection on religion it denies. Religion is essentially emotion; hence, objectively also, emotion is to it necessarily of a divine nature. Even anger appears to it an emotion not unworthy of God, provided only there be a religious motive at the foundation of this anger.

But here it is also essential to observe, and this phenomenon is an extremely remarkable one, characterizing the very core of religion, that in proportion as the divine subject is in reality human, the greater is the apparent difference between God and man; that is, the more, by reflection on religion, by theology, is the identity of the divine and human denied, and the human, considered as such, is depreciated. The reason of this is, that as what is positive in the conception of the divine being can only be human, the conception of man, as an object of consciousness, can only be negative. To enrich God, man must become poor; that God may be all, man must be nothing. But he desires to be nothing in himself, because what he takes from himself is not lost to him, since it is preserved in God. Man has his being in God; why then should he have it in himself? Where is the necessity of positing the same thing twice, of having it twice? What man withdraws from himself, what he renounces in himself, he only enjoys in an incomparably higher and fuller measure in God.

The monks made a vow of chastity to God; they mortified the sexual passion in themselves, but therefore they had in heaven, in the Virgin Mary, the image of woman—an image of love. They could the more easily dispense with the real woman in proportion as an ideal woman was an object of love to them. The greater the importance they attached to the denial of sensuality, the greater the importance of the heavenly virgin for them: she was to them in the place of Christ, in the stead of God. The more the sensual tendencies are renounced, the more sensual is the God to whom they are sacrificed. For whatever is made an offering to God has an especial value attached to it; in it God is supposed to have especial pleasure. That which is the highest in the estimation of man is naturally the highest in the estimation of his God; what pleases man pleases God also. The Hebrews did not offer to Jehovah unclean, ill-conditioned animals; on the contrary, those which they most highly prized, which they themselves ate, were also the food of God (Lev. 3:2). Wherever, therefore, the denial of the sensual delights is made a special offering, a sacrifice well-pleasing to God, there the highest value is attached to the senses, and the sensuality which has been renounced is unconsciously restored, in the fact that God takes the place of the material delights which have been renounced. The nun weds herself to God; she has a heavenly bridegroom, the monk a heavenly bride. But the heavenly virgin is only a sensible presentation of a general truth, having relation to the essence of religion. Man denies as to himself only what he attributes to God. Religion abstracts from man, from the world; but it can only abstract from the limitations, from the phenomena; in short, from the negative, not from the essence, the positive, of the world and humanity: hence, in the very abstraction and negation it must recover that from which it abstracts, or believes itself to abstract. And thus, in reality, whatever religion consciously denies—always supposing that what is denied by it is something essential, true, and consequently incapable of being ultimately denied—it unconsciously restores in God. Thus, in religion man denies his reason; of himself he knows nothing of God, his thoughts are only worldly, earthly; he can only believe what God reveals to him. But on this account the thoughts of God are human, earthly thoughts: like man, he has plans in his mind, he accommodates himself to circumstances and grades of intelligence, like a tutor with his pupils; he calculates closely the effect of his gifts and revelations; he observes man in all his doings; he knows all things, even the most earthly, the commonest, the most trivial. In brief, man in relation to God denies his own knowledge, his own thoughts, that he may place them in God. Man gives up his personality; but in return, God, the Almighty, infinite, unlimited being, is a person; he denies human dignity, the human ego; but in return God is to him a selfish, egoistical being, who in all things seeks only himself, his own honour, his own ends; he represents God as simply seeking the satisfaction of his own selfishness, while yet he frowns on that of every other being; his God is the very luxury of egoism. Religion further denies goodness as a quality of human nature; man is wicked, corrupt, incapable of good; but, on the other hand, God is only good—the Good Being. Man's nature demands as an object goodness, personified as God; but is it not hereby declared that goodness is an essential tendency of man? If my heart is wicked, my understanding perverted, how can I perceive and feel the holy to be holy, the good to be good? Could I perceive the beauty of a fine picture if my mind were æsthetically an absolute piece of perversion? Though I may not be a painter, though I may not have the power of producing what is beautiful myself, I must yet have æsthetic feeling, æsthetic comprehension, since I perceive the beauty that is presented to me externally. Either goodness does not exist at all for man, or, if it does exist, therein is revealed to the individual man the holiness and goodness of human nature. That which is absolutely opposed to my nature, to which I am united by no bond of sympathy, is not even conceivable or perceptible by me. The holy is in opposition to me only as regards the modifications of my personality, but as regards my fundamental nature it is in unity with me. The holy is a reproach to my sinfulness; in it I recognize myself as a sinner; but in so doing, while I blame myself, I acknowledge what I am not, but ought to be, and what, for that very reason, I, according to my destination, can be; for an "ought" which has no corresponding capability does not affect me, is a ludicrous chimæra without any true relation to my mental constitution. But when I acknowledge goodness as my destination, as my law, I acknowledge it, whether consciously or unconsciously, as my own nature. Another nature than my own, one different in quality, cannot touch me. I can perceive sin as sin, only when I perceive it to be a contradiction of myself with myself—that is, of my personality with my fundamental nature. As a contradiction of the absolute, considered as another being, the feeling of sin is inexplicable, unmeaning.

The distinction between Augustinianism and Pelagianism[4] consists only in this, that the former expresses after the manner of religion what the latter expresses after the

---

[4] Pelagius, a contemporary of Augustine, opposed Augustine's teaching that fallen man is wholly wicked and powerless to do good. As Feuerbach says in a footnote: "Augustinianism denies man; but, as a consequence of this, it reduces God to the level of man, even to the ignominy of the cross, for the sake of man. The former puts man in the place of God, the latter puts God in the place of man; both lead to the same result—the distinction is only apparent, a pious illusion. Augustinianism is only an inverted Pelagianism; what to the latter is a subject, is to the former an object."—TRANS.

manner of rationalism. Both say the same thing, both vindicate the goodness of man; but Pelagianism does it directly, in a rationalistic and moral form; Augustinianism indirectly, in a mystical, that is, a religious form. For that which is given to man's God is in truth given to man himself; what a man declares concerning God, he in truth declares concerning himself. Augustinianism would be a truth, and a truth opposed to Pelagianism, only if man had the devil for his God, and, with the consciousness that he was the devil, honoured, reverenced, and worshiped him as the highest being. But so long as man adores a good being as his God, so long does he contemplate in God the goodness of his own nature.

As with the doctrine of the radical corruption of human nature, so is it with the identical doctrine, that man can do nothing good—i.e., in truth, nothing of himself—by his own strength. For the denial of human strength and spontaneous moral activity to be true, the moral activity of God must also be denied; and we must say, with the Oriental nihilist or pantheist: the Divine Being is absolutely without will or action, indifferent, knowing nothing of the discrimination between evil and good. But he who defines God as an active being, and not only so, but as morally active and morally critical—as a being who loves, works, and rewards good, punishes, rejects, and condemns evil—he who thus defines God only in appearance denies human activity, in fact, making it the highest, the most real activity. He who makes God act humanly, declares human activity to be divine; he says: A god who is not active, and not morally or humanly active, is no god; and thus he makes the idea of the Godhead dependent on the idea of activity, that is, of human activity, for a higher he knows not.

Man—this is the mystery of religion—projects his being into objectivity, and then again makes himself an object to this projected image of himself thus converted into a subject; he thinks of himself as an object to himself, but as the object of an object, of another being than himself. Thus here. Man is an object to God. That man is good or evil is not indifferent to God; no! He has a lively, profound interest in man's being good; he will that man should be good, happy—for without goodness there is no happiness. Thus the religious man virtually retracts the nothingness of human activity, by making his dispositions and actions an object to God, by making man the end of God—for that which is an object to the mind is an end in action—by making the divine activity a means of human salvation. God acts, that man may be good and happy. Thus man, while he is apparently humiliated to the lowest degree, is in truth exalted to the highest. Thus, in and through God, man has in view himself alone. It is true that man places the aim of his action in God, but God has no other aim of action than the moral and eternal salvation of man: thus man has in fact no other aim than himself. The divine activity is not distinct from the human.

How could the divine activity work on me as its object, nay, work in me, if it were essentially different from me; how could it have a human aim, the aim of ameliorating and blessing man, if it were not itself human? Does not the purpose determine the nature of the act? When man makes his moral improvement an aim to himself, he has divine resolutions, divine projects; but also, when God seeks the salvation of man, he has human ends and a human mode of activity corresponding to these ends. Thus in God man has only his own activity as an object. But for the very reason that he regards his own activity as objective, goodness only as an object, he necessarily receives the impulse, the motive not from himself, but from this object. He contemplates his nature as external to himself, and this nature as goodness; thus it is self-evident, it is mere tautology to say that the impulse to good comes only from thence where he places the good.

God is the highest subjectivity of man abstracted from himself; hence man can do nothing of himself, all goodness comes from God. The more subjective God is, the more completely does man divest himself of his subjectivity, because God is, per se, his relinquished self, the possession of which he however again vindicates to himself. As the action of the arteries drives the blood into the extremities, and the action of the veins brings it back again, as life in general consists in a perpetual systole and diastole; so is it in religion. In the religious systole man propels his own nature from himself, he throws himself outward; in the religious diastole he receives the rejected nature into his heart again. God alone is the being who acts of himself—this is the force of repulsion in religion; God is the being who acts in me, with me, through me, upon me, for me, is the principle of my salvation, of my good dispositions and actions, consequently my own good principle and nature—this is the force of attraction in religion.

The course of religious development which has been generally indicated consists specifically in this, that man abstracts more and more from God, and attributes more and more to himself. This is especially apparent in the belief in revelation. That which to a later age or a cultured people is given by nature or reason, is to an earlier age, or to a yet uncultured people, given by God. Every tendency of man, however natural—even the impulse to cleanliness—was conceived by the Israelites as a positive divine ordinance. From this example we again see that God is lowered, is conceived more entirely on the type of ordinary humanity, in proportion as man detracts from himself. How can the self-humiliation of man go further than when he disclaims the capability of fulfilling spontaneously the requirements of common decency?[5] The Christian religion, on the other hand, distinguished the impulses and passions of man according to their quality, their character; it represented only good emotions, good dispositions, good thoughts, as revelations, operations—that is, as dispositions, feelings, thoughts—of God; for what God reveals is a quality of God himself: that of which the heart is full overflows the lips; as is the effect such is the cause; as the revelation, such the being who reveals himself. A God who reveals himself in good dispositions is a God whose essential attribute is only moral perfection. The Christian religion distinguishes inward moral purity from external physical purity; the Israelites identified the two.[6] In relation to the Israelitish religion, the Christian religion is one of criticism and freedom. The Israelite trusted himself to do nothing except what was commanded by God; he was without will even in external things; the authority of religion extended itself even to his food. The Christian religion, on the other hand, in all these external things made man dependent on himself, i.e., placed in man what the Israelite placed out of himself in God. Israel is the most complete presentation of Positivism in religion. In relation to the Israelite, the Christian is an *esprit fort*, a free-thinker. Thus do things change. What yesterday was still religion is no longer such today; and what today is atheism, tomorrow will be religion.

---

[5] Deut. 23:12–13.—L.F.

[6] See, for example, Gen. 35:2; Lev. 11:44; 20:26.—L.F.

○ ○ ○ *15*

The Opium of the People
Karl Marx

FOR GERMANY, THE *criticism of religion* has been largely completed; and the criticism of religion is the premise of all criticism.

The *profane* existence of error is compromised once its *celestial oratio pro aris et focis*[1] has been refuted. Man, who has found in the fantastic reality of heaven, where he sought a supernatural being, only his own reflection, will no longer be tempted to find only the *semblance* of himself—a non-human being—where he seeks and must seek his true reality.

The basis of irreligious criticism is this: *man makes religion*; religion does not make man. Religion is indeed man's self-consciousness and self-awareness so long as he has not found himself or has lost himself again. But *man* is not an abstract being, squatting outside the world. Man is *the human world*, the state, society. This state, this society, produce religion which is an *inverted world consciousness*, because they are an *inverted world*. Religion is the general theory of this world, its encyclopedic compendium, its logic in popular form, its spiritual point d'honneur, its enthusiasm, its moral sanction, its solemn complement, its general basis of consolation and justification. It is *the fantastic realization* of the human being inasmuch as the *human being* possesses no true reality. The struggle against religion is, therefore, indirectly a struggle against *that world* whose spiritual *aroma* is religion.

Religious suffering is at the same time an *expression* of real suffering and a *protest* against real suffering. Religion is the sigh of the oppressed creature, the sentiment of a heartless world, and the soul of soulless conditions. It is the *opium* of the people.

The abolition of religion as the *illusory* happiness of men, is a demand for their *real* happiness. The call to abandon their illusions about their condition is a *call to abandon a condition which requires illusions*. The criticism of religion is, therefore, *the embryonic criticism of this vale of tears* of which religion is the *halo*.

Criticism has plucked the imaginary flowers from the chain, not in order that man shall bear the chain without caprice or consolation but so that he shall cast off the chain and pluck the living flower. The criticism of religion disillusions man so that he will think, act and fashion his reality as a man who has lost his illusions and regained his reason; so that he will revolve about himself as his own true sun. Religion is only the illusory sun about which man revolves so long as he does not revolve about himself.

It is the *task of history*, therefore, once the *other-world of truth* has vanished, to establish the *truth of this world*. The immediate *task of philosophy*, which is in the service of

---

[1] Heavenly speech on behalf of alters and hearths.—E.D.K.

history, is to unmask human self-alienation in its *secular form* now that it has been unmasked in its *sacred form*. Thus the criticism of heaven is transformed into the criticism of earth, the *criticism of religion* into the *criticism of law*, and the *criticism of theology* into the criticism *of politics*.

The following exposition[2]—which is a contribution to this undertaking—does not deal directly with the original but with a copy, the German *philosophy* of the state and of right, for the simple reason that it deals with Germany.

• • •

It is clear that the arm of criticism cannot replace the criticism of arms. Material force can only be overthrown by material force; but theory itself becomes a material force when it has seized the masses. Theory is capable of seizing the masses when it demonstrates *ad hominem*, and it demonstrates *ad hominem* as soon as it becomes radical. To be radical is to grasp things by the root. But for man the root is himself. What proves beyond doubt the radicalism of German theory, and thus its practical energy, is that it begins from the resolute *positive* abolition of religion. The criticism of religion ends with the doctrine that *man is the supreme being for man*. It ends, therefore, with the *categorical imperative to overthrow all those conditions* in which man is an abased, enslaved, abandoned, contemptible being—conditions which can hardly be better described than in the exclamation of a Frenchman on the occasion of a proposed tax upon dogs: "Wretched dogs! They want to treat you like men!"

Even from the historical standpoint theoretical emancipation has a specific practical importance for Germany. In fact Germany's *revolutionary* past is theoretical—it is the *Reformation*. In that period the revolution originated in the brain of a monk, today in the brain of the philosopher.

Luther, without question, overcame servitude through devotion but only by substituting servitude through *conviction*. He shattered the faith in authority by restoring the authority of faith. He transformed the priests into laymen by turning laymen into priests. He liberated man from external religiosity by making religiosity the innermost essence of man. He liberated the body from its chains because he fettered the heart with chains.

But if Protestantism was not the solution it did at least pose the problem correctly. It was no longer a question, thereafter, of the layman's struggle against the priest outside himself, but of his struggle against his *own internal priest*, against his own *priestly nature*. And if the Protestant metamorphosis of German laymen into priests emancipated the lay popes— the *princes* together with their clergy, the privileged and the philistines— the philosophical metamorphosis of the priestly Germans into men will emancipate the *people*. But just as emancipation will not be confined to princes, so the *secularization* of property will not be limited to the *confiscation of church property*, which was practised especially by hypocritical Prussia. At that time, the Peasant War, the most radical event in German history, came to grief because of theology.

---

[2] Marx refers to his intentions to publish a critical study of Hegel's *Philosophy of Right*, to which this essay was an introduction. One of Marx's preliminary manuscripts for such a study has been published entitled "Aus der Kritik der Hegelschen Rechtsphilosophie. Kritik des Hegelschen Staatsrechts." (*MEGA* I₁₁, pp. 403–553). The "Economic and Philosophical Manuscripts" is another version of this study; *see* Marx's comment. . . . —T.B. BOTTOMORE

Today, when theology itself has come to grief, the most unfree phenomenon in German history—our *status quo*—will be shattered by philosophy. . . .

• • •

Where is there, then, a *real* possibility of emancipation in Germany?

This is our reply. A class must be formed which has *radical chains*, a class in civil society which is not a class of civil society, a class which is the dissolution of all classes, a sphere of society which has a universal character because its sufferings are universal, and which does not claim a *particular redress* because the wrong which is done to it is not a *particular wrong* but *wrong in general.* There must be formed a sphere of society which claims no *traditional* status but only a human status, a sphere which is not opposed to particular consequences but is totally opposed to the assumptions of the German political system; a sphere, finally, which cannot emancipate itself without emancipating itself from all the other spheres of society, without, therefore, emancipating all these other spheres, which is, in short, a *total loss* of humanity and which can only redeem itself by a *total redemption of humanity.* This dissolution of society, as a particular class, is the *proletariat.*

The proletariat is only beginning to form itself in Germany, as a result of the industrial movement. For what constitutes the proletariat is not *naturally existing* poverty, but poverty *artificially produced*, is not the mass of people mechanically oppressed by the weight of society, but the mass resulting from the *disintegration* of society and above all from the disintegration of the middle class. Needless to say, however, the numbers of the proletariat are also increased by the victims of natural poverty and of Christian-Germanic serfdom.

When the proletariat announces the *dissolution of the existing social order*, it only declares the *secret of its* own existence, for it *is* the *effective* dissolution of this order. When the proletariat demands the *negation of private property* it only lays down as a *principle for society* what society has already made a principle *for the proletariat*, and what the *latter* already involuntarily embodies as the negative result of society. Thus the proletarian has the same right, in relation to the new world which is coming into being, as the *German king* has in relation to the existing world when he calls the people *his* people or a horse *his* horse. In calling the people his private property the king simply declares that the owner of private property is king.

Just as philosophy finds its *material* weapons in the proletariat, so the proletariat finds its *intellectual* weapons in philosophy. And once the lightning of thought has penetrated deeply into this virgin soil of the people, the *Germans* will emancipate themselves and become *men.*

Let us sum up these results. The emancipation of Germany is only possible *in practice* if one adopts the point of view of that theory according to which man is the highest being for man. Germany will not be able to emancipate itself from the *Middle Ages* unless it emancipates itself at the same time from the *partial* victories over the Middle Ages. In Germany *no* type of enslavement can be abolished unless *all* enslavement is destroyed. Germany, which likes to get to the bottom of things, can only make a revolution which upsets *the whole order* of things. The *emancipation of Germany* will be an *emancipation of man.* *Philosophy* is the *head* of this emancipation and the *proletariat* is its *heart.* Philosophy can only be realized by the abolition of the proletariat, and the proletariat can only be abolished by the realization of philosophy.

∘ ∘ ∘ *16*

Religious Ideas as Illusions
Sigmund Freud

[I]

WE HAVE SPOKEN of the hostility of culture, produced by the pressure it exercises and the instinctual renunciations that it demands. If one imagined its prohibitions removed, then one could choose any woman who took one's fancy as one's sexual object, one could kill without hesitation one's rival or whoever interfered with one in any other way, and one could seize what one wanted of another man's goods without asking his leave: how splendid, what a succession of delights, life would be! True, one soon finds the first difficulty: everyone else has exactly the same wishes, and will treat one with no more consideration than one will treat him. And so in reality there is only one single person who can be made unrestrictedly happy by abolishing thus the restrictions imposed by culture, and that is a tyrant or dictator who has monopolized all the means of power; and even he has every reason to want the others to keep at least one cultural commandment: thou shalt not kill.

But how ungrateful, how short-sighted after all to strive for the abolition of culture! What would then remain would be the state of nature, and that is far harder to endure. It is true that natures does not ask us to restrain our instincts, she lets us do as we like; but she has her peculiarly effective mode of restricting us: she destroys us, coldly, cruelly, callously, as it seems to us, and possibly just through what has caused our satisfaction. It was because of these very dangers with which nature threatens us that we united together and created culture, which, amongst other things, is supposed to make our communal existence possible. Indeed, it is the principal task of culture, its real *raison d'etre*,[1] to defend us against nature.

One must confess that in many ways it already does this tolerably well, and clearly as time goes on it will be much more successful. But no one is under the illusion that natures has so far been vanquished; few dare to hope that she will ever be completely under man's subjection. There are the elements, which seem to mock at all human control: the earth, which quakes, is rent asunder, and buries man and all his works; the water, which in tumult floods and submerges all things; the storm, which drives all before it; there are the diseases, which we have only lately recognized as the attacks of other living creatures; and finally there is the painful riddle of death, for which no remedy at all has yet been found, nor probably every will be. With these forces nature rises up before us, sublime, pitiless, inexorable; thus she brings again to mind our weakness and helplessness, of which we thought the work of civilization had rid us. It is one of the few

---

[1] Reason for being.—E.D.K.

noble and gratifying spectacles that men can offer, when in the face of an elemental catastrophe they awake from their muddle and confusion, forget all their internal difficulties and animosities, and remember the great common task, the preservation of mankind against the supremacy of nature.

For the individual, as for mankind in general, life is hard to endure. The culture in which he shares imposes on him some measure of privation, and other men occasion him a certain degree of suffering, either in spite of the laws of this culture or because of its imperfections. Add to this the evils that unvanquished nature—he calls it Fate—inflicts on him. One would expect a permanent condition of anxious suspense and a severe injury to his innate narcissism to be the result of this state of affairs. We know already how the individual reacts to the injuries that culture and other men inflict on him: he develops a corresponding degree of resistance against the institutions of this culture, of hostility towards it. But how does he defend himself against the supremacy of nature, of fate, which threatens him, as it threatens all?

Culture relieves him of this task: it performs it in the same way for everyone. (It is also noteworthy that pretty well all cultures are the same in this respect.) It does not cry a halt, as it were, in its task of defending man against nature; it merely pursues it by other methods. This is a complex business; man's seriously menaced self-esteem craves for consolation, life and the universe must be rid of their terrors, and incidentally man's curiosity, reinforced, it is true, by the strongest practical motives, demands an answer.

With the first step, which is the humanization of nature, much is alreay won. Nothing can be made of impersonal forces and fates; they remain eternally remote. But if the elements have passions that rage like those in our own souls, if death itself is not something spontaneous, but the violent act of an evil Will, if everywhere in nature we have about us beings who resemble those of our own environment, then indeed we can "breathe freely, we can feel at home in face of the supernatural, and we can deal psychically with our frantic anxiety. We are perhaps still defenceless, but no longer helplessly paralysed; we can at least react; perhaps indeed we are not even defenceless, we can have recourse to the same methods against these violent supermen of the beyond that we make use of in our own community; we can try to exorcise them, to appease them, to bribe them, and so rob them of part of their power by thus influencing them. Such a substitution of psychology for natural science provides not merely immediate relief, it also points the way to a futher mastery of the situation.

For there is nothing new in this situation. It has an infantile prototype, and is really only the continuation of this. For once before one has been in such a state of helplessness: as a little child in one's relationship to one's parents. For one had reason to fear them, especially the father, though at the same time one was sure of his protection against the dangers then known to one. And so it was natural to assimilate and combine the two situations. Here, too, as in dream-life, the wish came into its own. The sleeper is seized by a presentiment of death, which seeks to carry him to the grave. But the dream-work knows how to select a condition that will turn even this dreaded event into a wish-fulfilment: the dreamer sees himself in an ancient Etruscan grave, into which he has descended, happy in the satisfaction it has given to his archaeological interests. Similarly man makes the forces of nature not simply in the image of men with whom he can associate as his equals—that would not do justice to the overpowering impression they make on him—but he gives them the characteristics of the father, makes them into gods, thereby following not only an infantile, but also, as I have tried to show, a phylogenetic prototype.

In the course of time the first observations of law and order in natural phenomena are made, and therewith the forces of nature lose their human traits. But men's helplessness remains, and with it their father-longing and the gods. The gods retain their threefold task: they must exorcise the terrors of nature, they must reconcile one to the cruelty of fate, particularly as shown in death, and they must make amends for the sufferings and privations that the communal life of culture has imposed on man.

But within these there is a gradual shifting of the accent. It is observed that natural phenomena develop of themselves from inward necessity; without doubt the gods are the lords of nature: they have arranged it thus and now they can leave it to itself. Only occasionally, in the so-called miracles, do they intervene in its course, as if to protest that they have surrendered nothing of their original sphere of power. As far as the vicissitudes of fate are concerned, an unpleasant suspicion persists that the perplexity and helplessness of the human race cannot be remedied. This is where the gods are most apt to fail us; if they themselves make fate, then their ways must be deemed inscrutable. The most gifted people of the ancient world dimly surmised that above the gods stands Destiny and that the gods themselves have their destinies. And the more autonomous nature becomes and the more earnestly are all expectations concentrated on the third task assigned to them and the more does morality become their real domain. It now becomes the business of the gods to adjust the defects and evils of culture, to attend to the sufferings that men inflict on each other in their communal life, and to see that the laws of culture, which men obey so ill, are carried out. The laws of culture themselves are claimed to be of divine origin, they are elevated to a position above human society, and they are extended over nature and the universe.

And so a rich store of ideas is formed, born of the need to make tolerable the helplessness of man, and built out of the material offered by memories of the helplessness of his own childhood and the childhood of the human race. It is easy to see that these ideas protect man in two directions; against the dangers to nature and fate, and against the evils of human society itself. What it amounts of is this: life in this world serves a higher purpose; true, it is not easy to guess the nature of this purpose, but certainly a perfecting of human existence is implied. Probably the spiritual part of man, the soul, which in the course of time has so slowly and unwillingly detached itself from the body, is to be regarded as the object of this elevation and exaltation. Everything that takes place in this world expresses the intentions of an Intelligence, superior to us, which in the end, though its devious ways may be difficult to follow, orders everything for good, that is, to our advantage. Over each one of us watches a benevolent, and only apparently severe, Providence, which will not suffer us to become the plaything of the stark and pitiless forces of nature; death itself is not annihilation, not a return to inorganic lifelessness, but the beginning of a new kind of existence, which lies on the road of development to something higher. And to turn to the other side of the question, the moral laws that have formed our culture govern also the whole universe, only they are upheld with incomparably more force and consistency by a supreme judicial court. In the end all good is rewarded, all evil is punished, if not actually in this life, then in the further existences that begin after death. And thus all the terrors, the sufferings, and the hardships of life are destined to be obliterated; the life after death, which continues our earthly existence as the invisible part of the spectrum adjoins the visible, brings all the perfection that perhaps we have missed here. And the superior wisdom that directs this issue, the supreme goodness that expresses itself thus, the justice that thus achieves its aim—these are the qualities of the divine beings who have fashioned us and the world in general; or rather of the one divine being into which in our culture all the gods of antiquity have been condensed. The race that first succeeded in thus concentrating the divine qualities was not a little proud of this advance. It has revealed the father nucleus which had always lain hidden behind every divine figure; fundamentally it was a return to the historical beginnings of the idea of God. Now that God was a single person, man's relations to him could recover the intimacy and intensity of the child's relation to the father. If one had done so much for the father, then surely one would be rewarded —at least the only beloved child, the chosen people, would be. More recently, pious America has laid claim to be "God's own country," and for one of the forms under which men worship the deity the claim certainly holds good.

The religious ideas that have just been summarized have of course gone through a long process of development, and have been held in various phases by various cultures. I have singled out one such phase of development, which more or less corresponds to the final form of our contemporary Christian culture in the west. It is easy to see that not all the parts of this whole tally equally well with each other, that not all the questions that press for an answer receive one, and that the contradiction of daily experience can only with difficulty be dismissed. But such as they are, these ideas—religious, in the broadest sense of the word—are prized as the most precious possession of culture, as the most valuable thing it has to offer its members; far more highly prized than all our devices for winning the treasures of the earth, for providing men with sustenance, or for preventing their diseases, and so forth; men suppose that life would be intolerable if they did not accord these ideas the value that is claimed for them. And now the question arises: what are these ideas in the light of psychology; whence do they derive the esteem in which they are held; and further, in all diffidence, what is their real worth?

[II]

Now to take up again the threads of our enquiry: what is the psychologoical significance of religious ideas and how can we classify them? The question is at first not at all easy to answer. Having rejected various formulas, I shall take my stand by this one: religion consists of certain dogmas, assertions about facts and conditions of external (or internal) reality, which tell one something that one has not oneself discovered and which claim that one should give them credence. As they give information about what are to us the most interesting and important things in life, they are particularly highly valued. He who knows nothing of them is ignorant indeed, and he who has assimilated them may consider himself enriched.

• • •

If we ask on what their claim to be believed is based, we receive three answers, which accord remarkably ill with one another. They deserve to be believed: firstly, because our primal ancestors already believed them; secondly, because we possess proofs, which have been handed down to us from this very period of antiquity; and thirdly, because it is forbidden to raise the question of their authenticity at all. Formerly this presumptuous act was visited with the very severest penalties, and even to-day society is unwilling to see anyone renew it.

This third point cannot but rouse our strongest suspicions. Such a prohibition can surely have only one motive: that society knows very well the uncertain basis of the claim it makes for its religious doctrines. If it were otherwise, the relevant material would certainly be placed most readily at the disposal of anyone who wished to gain conviction for himself. And so we proceed to test the other two arguments with a feeling of mistrust not easily allayed. We ought to believe because our forefathers believed. But these ancestors of ours were far more ignorant than we; they believed in things we could not possibly accept to-day; so the possibility occurs that religious doctrines may also be in this category. The proofs they have bequeathed to us are deposited in writings that themselves bear every trace of being untrustworthy. They are full of contradictions, revisions, and interpolations; where they speak of actual authentic proofs they are themselves of doubtful authenticity. It does not help much if divine revelation is asserted to be the origin of their text or only of their content, for this assertion is itself already a part of those doctrines whose authenticity is to be examined, and no statement can bear its own proof.

Thus we arrive at the singular conclusion that just what might be of the greatest significance for us in our cultural system, the information which should solve for us the riddles of the universe and reconcile us to the troubles of life, that just this has the weakest possible claim to authenticity. We should not be able to bring ourselves to accept anything of as little concern to us as the fact that whales bear young instead of laying eggs, if it were not capable of better proof than this.

This state of things is in itself a very remarkable psychological problem. Let no one think that the foregoing remarks on the impossibility of proving religious doctrines contain anything new. It has been felt at all times, assuredly even by the ancestors who bequeathed this legacy. Probably many of them nursed the same doubts as we, but the pressure imposed on them was too strong for them to have dared to utter them. And since then countless people have been tortured by the same doubts, which they would fain have suppressed because they held themselves in duty bound to believe, and since then many brilliant intellects have been wrecked upon this conflict and many characters have come to grief through the compromises by which they sought a way out.

• • •

One must now mention two attempts to evade the problem, which both convey the impression of frantic effort. One of them, high-handed in its nature, is old; the other is subtle and modern. The first is the *Credo quia absurdum*[2] of the early Fathers. It would imply that religious doctrines are outside reason's jurisdiction; they stand above reason. Their truth must inwardly be felt: one does not need to comprehend them. But this *Credo* is only of interest as a voluntary confession; as a decree it has no binding force. Am I to be obliged to believe every absurdity? And if not, why just this one? There is no appeal beyond reason. And if the truth of religious doctrines is dependent on an inner experience which bears witness to that truth, what is one to make of the many people who do not have that rare experience? One may expect all men to use the gift of reason that

---

[2] "I believe because it is absurd." Written in a work of Tertullian.—E.D.K.

they possess, but one cannot set up an obligation that shall apply to all on a basis that only exists for quite a few. Of what significance is it for other people that you have won from a state of ecstasy, which has deeply moved you, an imperturbable conviction of the real truth of the doctrines of religion?

The second attempt is that of the philosophy of "As If." It explains that in our mental activity we assume all manner of things, the groundlessness, indeed the absurdity, of which we fully realize. They are called "fictions," but from a variety of practical motives we are led to behave "as if" we believed in these fictions. This, it is argued, is the case with religious doctrines on account of their unequalled importance for the maintenance of human society. This argument is not far removed from the *Credo quia absurdum*. But I think that the claim of the philosophy of "As If" is such as only a philosopher could make. The man whose thinking is not influenced by the wiles of philosophy will never be able to accept it; with the confession of absurdity, of illogicality, there is no more to be said as far as he is concerned. He cannot be expected to forgo the guarantees he demands for all his usual activities just in the matter of his most important interests. I am reminded of one of my children who was distinguished at an early age by a peculiarly marked sense of reality. When the children were told a fairy tale, to which they listened with rapt attention, he would come forward and ask: Is that a true story? Having been told that it was not, he would turn away with an air of disdain. It is to be expected that men will soon behave in like manner towards the religious fairy tales, despite the advocacy of the philosophy of "As If."

But at present they still behave quite differently, and in past ages, in spite of their incontrovertible lack of authenticity, religious ideas have exercised the very strongest influence on mankind. This is a fresh psychological problem. We must ask where the inherent strength of these doctrines lies and to what circumstance they owe their efficacy, independent, as it is, of the acknowledgement of the reason.

[III]

I think we have sufficiently paved the way for the answer to both these questions. It will be found if we fix our attention on the psychical origin of religious ideas. These, which profess to be dogmas, are not the residue of experience or the final result of reflection; they are illusions, fulfilments of the oldest, strongest and most insistent wishes of mankind; the secret of their strength is the strength of these wishes. We know already that the terrifying effect of infantile helplessness aroused the need for protection—protection through love—which the father relieved, and that the discovery that this helplessness would continue through the whole of life made it necessary to cling to the existence of a father—but this time a more powerful one. Thus the benevolent rule of divine providence allays our anxiety in face of life's dangers, the establishment of a moral world order ensures the fulfilment of the demands of justice, which within human culture have so often remained unfulfilled and the prolongation of the earthly existence by a future life provides in addition the local and temporal setting for these wish-fulfilments. Answers to the questions that tempt human curiosity, such as the origin of the universe and the relation between the body and the soul, are developed in accordance with the underlying assumptions of this system; it betokens a tremendous relief for the individual psyche if it is released from the conflicts of childhood arising out of the father complex, which are never wholly overcome, and if these conflicts are afforded a universally accepted solution.

When I say that they are illusions, I must define the meaning of the word. An illusion is not the same as an error, it is indeed not necessarily an error. Aritstotle's belief that vermin are evolved out of dung, to which ignorant people still cling, was an error; so was the belief of a former generation of doctors that *tabes dorsalis*[3] was the result of sexual excess. It would be improper to call these errors illusions. On the other hand, it was an illusion on the part of Columbus that he had discovered a new sea-route to India. The part played by his wish in this error is very clear. One may describe as an illusion the statement of certain nationalists that the Indo-Germanic race is the only one capable of culture, or the belief, which only psycho-analysis destroyed, that the child is a being without sexuality. It is characteristic of the illusion that it is derived from men's wishes; in this respect it approaches the psychiatric delusion, but it is to be distinguished from this, quite apart from the more complicated structure of the latter. In the delusion we emphasize as essential the conflict with reality; the illusion need not be necessarily false, that is to say, unrealizable or incompatible with reality. For instance, a poor girl may have an illusion that a prince will come and fetch her home. It is possible; some such cases have occurred. That the Messiah will come and found a golden age is much less probable; according to one's personal attitude one will classify this belief as an illusion or as analogous to a delusion. Examples of illusions that have come true are not easy to discover, but the illusion of the alchemists that all metals can be turned into gold may prove to be one. The desire to have lots of gold, as much gold as possible, has been considerably damped by our modern insight into the nature of wealth, yet chemistry no longer considers a transmutation of metals into gold as impossible. Thus we call a belief an illusion when wish-fulfilment is a prominent factor in its motivation, while disregarding its relations to reality, just as the illusion itself does.

If after this survey we turn again to religious doctrines, we may reiterate that they are all illusions, they do not admit of proof, and no one can be compelled to consider them as true or to believe in them. Some of them are so improbable, so very incompatible with everything we have laboriously discovered about the reality of the world, that we may compare them—taking adequately into account the psychological differences—to delusions. Of the reality value of most of them we cannot judge; just as they cannot be proved, neither can they be refuted. We still know too little to approach them critically. The riddles of the universe only reveal themselves slowly to our enquiry, to many questions science can as yet give no answer; but scientific work is our only way to the knowledge of external reality.

• • •

It does not lie within the scope of this enquiry to estimate the value of religious doctrines as truth. It suffices that we have recognized them, psychologically considered, as illusions. But we need not conceal the fact that this discovery strongly influences our attitutde to what must appear to many the most important of questions. We know approximately at what periods and by what sort of men religious doctrines were formed. If we now learn from what motives this happened, our attitude to the problem of religion

---

[3] An illness or malfunction.—E.D.K.

will suffer an appreciable change. We say to ourselves: it would indeed be very nice if there were a God, who was both creator of the world and a benevolent providence, if there were a moral world order and a future life, but at the same time it is very odd that this is all just as we should wish it ourselves. And it would be still odder if our poor, ignorant, enslaved ancestors had succeeded in solving all these difficult riddles of the universe.

• • •

I know how difficult it is to avoid illusions. But I hold fast to one distinction. My illusions—apart from the fact that no penalty is imposed for not sharing them—are not, like the religious ones, incapable of correction, they have no delusional character. If experience should show—not to me, but to others after me who think as I do—that we are mistaken, then we shall give up our expectations. Take my endeavour for what it is. A psychologist, who does not deceive himself about the difficulty of finding his bearings in this world, strives to review the development of mankind in accord with what insight he has won from studying the mental processes of the individual during his development from childhood to manhood. In this connection the idea forces itself upon him that religion is comparable to a childhood neurosis, and he is optimistic enough to assume that mankind will overcome this neurotic phase, just as so many children grow out of their similar neuroses.

• • •

But science has shown us by numerous and significant successes that it is no illusion. Science has many open, and still more secret, enemies among those who cannot forgive it for having weakened religious belief and for threatening to overthrow it. People reproach it for the small amount it has taught us and the incomparably greater amount it has left in the dark. But then they forget how young it is, how difficult its beginnings, and how infinitesimally small the space of time since the human intellect has been strong enough for the tasks it sets it. Do we not all do wrong in that the periods of time which we make the basis of our judgements are of too short duration? We should take an example from the geologist. People complain of the unreliability of science, that she proclaims as a law to-day what the next generation will recognize to be an error and which will replace by a new law of equally short currency. But that is unjust and in part untrue. The transformation of scientific ideas is a process of development and progress, not of revolution. A law that was at first held to be universally valid proves to be a special case of a more comprehensive law, or else its scope is limited by another law not discovered until later; a rough approximation to the truth is replaced by one more carefully adjusted, which in turn awaits a further approach to perfection. In several spheres we have not yet surmounted a phase of investigation in which we test hypotheses that have soon to be rejected as inadequate; but in others we have already an assured and almost immutable core of knowledge. Finally an attempt has been made to discredit radically scientific endeavour on the ground that, bound as it is to the conditions of our own organization, it can yield nothing but subjective results, while the real nature of things outside us remains inaccessible to it. But this is to disregard several factors of decisive importance for the understanding of scientific work, Firstly, our organization, *i.e.* our mental apparatus, has been developed actually in the attempt to explore the outer world, and therefore it must have realized in its structure a certain measure of appropriateness; secondly, it itself is a constituent part of that world which we are to investigate, and readily admits of such investigation; thirdly, the task of science is fully circumscribed if we confine it to showing how the world must appear to us in consequence of the particular character of our organization; fourthly, the ultimate findings of science, just because of the way in which they are attained, are conditioned not only by our organization but also by that which has affected this organization; and, finally, the problem of the nature of the world irrespective of our perceptive mental apparatus is an empty abstraction without practical interest.

No, science is no illusion. But it would be an illusion to suppose that we could get anywhere else what it cannot give us.

Attack on Christianity
Friedrich Nietzsche

· 2 ·

WHAT IS GOOD? Everything that heightens the feeling of power in man, the will to power, power itself.

What is bad? Everything that is born of weakness.

What is happiness? The feeling that power it *growing*, that resistance is overcome.

Not contentedness but more power; not peace but war; not virtue but fitness (Renaissance virtue, *virtù*, virtue that is moraline-free).

The weak and the failures shall perish: first principle of *our* love of man. And they shall even be given every possible assistance.

What is more harmful than any vice? Active pity for all the failures and all the weak: Christianity. . . .

· 5 ·

Christianity should not be beautified and embellished: it has waged deadly war against this higher type of man; it has placed all the basic instincts of this type under the ban; and out of these instincts it has distilled evil and the Evil One: the strong man as the typically reprehensible man, the "reprobate." Christianity has sided with all that is weak and base, with all failures; it has made an ideal of whatever *contradicts* the instinct of the strong life to preserve itself; it has corrupted the reason even of those strongest in spirit by teaching men to consider the supreme values of the spirit as something sinful, as something that leads into error—as temptations. The most pitiful example: the corruption of Pascal, who believed in the corruption of his reason through original sin when it had in fact been corrupted only by his Christianity. . . .

· 7 ·

Christianity is called the religion of *pity*. Pity stands opposed to the tonic emotions which heighten our vitality: it has a depressing effect. We are deprived of strength when we feel pity. That loss of strength which suffering as such inflicts on life is still further increased and multiplied by pity. Pity makes suffering contagious. Under certain circumstances, it may engender a total loss of life and vitality out of all proportion to the magnitude of the cause (as in the case of the death of the Nazarene). That is the first consideration, but there is a more important one.

Suppose we measure pity by the value of the reactions it usually produces; then its perilous nature appears in an even brighter light. Quite in general, pity crosses the law of development, which is the law of *selection*. It preserves what is ripe for destruction; it defends those who have been disinherited and condemned by life; and by the abundance of the failures of all kinds which it keeps alive, it gives life itself a gloomy and questionable aspect.

Some have dared to call pity a virtue (in every *noble* ethic it is considered a weakness); and as if this were not enough, it has been made *the* virtue, the basis and source of all virtues. To be sure—and one should always keep this in mind—this was done by a philosophy that was nihilistic and had inscribed the *negation of life* upon its shield. Schopenhauer was consistent enough: pity negates life and renders it *more deserving of negation*.

Pity is the *practice* of nihilism. To repeat: this depressive and contagious instinct crosses those instincts which aim at the preservation of life and at the enhancement of its value. It multiplies misery and conserves all that is miserable, and is thus a prime instrument of the advancement of the decadence: pity persuades men to *nothingness*! Of course, one does not say "nothingness" but "beyond" or "God," or "*true* life," or Nirvana, salvation, blessedness.

This innocent rhetoric from the realm of the religious-moral idiosyncrasy appears much less innocent as soon as we realize which tendency it is that here shrouds itself in sublime words: *hostility against life*. Schopenhauer was hostile to life; therefore pity became a virtue for him. . . .

· 15 ·

In Christianity neither morality nor religion has even a single point of contact with reality. Nothing but imaginary *causes* ("God," "soul," "ego," "spirit," "free will"—for that matter, "unfree will"), nothing but imaginary *effects* ("sin," "redemption," "grace," "punishment," "forgiveness of sins"). Intercourse between imaginary *beings* ("God," "spirits," "souls"); an imaginary *natural* science (anthropocentric; no trace of any concept of natural causes); an imaginary *psychology* (nothing but self-misunderstandings, interpretations of agreeable or disagreeable general feelings—for example, of the states of the *nervus sympathicus*—with the aid of the sign language of the religio-moral idiosyncrasy: "repentance," "pangs of conscience," "temptation by the devil," "the presence of God"); an imaginary *teleology* ("the kingdom of God," "the Last Judgment," "eternal life").

This *world of pure fiction* is vastly inferior to the world of dreams insofar as the latter *mirrors* reality, whereas the former falsifies, devalues, and negates reality. Once the concept of "nature" had been invented as the opposite of "God," "natural" had to become a synonym of "reprehensible": this whole world of fiction is rooted in *hatred* of the natural (of reality!); it is the expression of a profound vexation at the sight of reality.

But this explains everything. Who alone has good reason to lie his way out of reality? He who suffers from it. But to suffer from reality is to be a piece of reality that has come to grief. The preponderance of feelings of displeasure over feelings of pleasure is the cause of this fictitious morality and religion; but such a preponderance provides the very formula for decadence.

· 16 ·

A critique of the *Christian conception of God* forces us to the same conclusion. A people that still believes in itself retains its own god. In him it reveres the conditions which let it prevail, its virtues: it projects its pleasure in itself, its feeling of power, into a being to whom one may offer thanks. Whoever is rich wants to give of his riches; a proud people needs a god: it wants to *sacrifice*. Under such conditions, religion is a form of thankfulness. Being thankful for himself, man needs a god. Such a god must be able to help and to harm, to be friend and enemy—he is admired whether good or destructive. The *anti-natural* castration of a god, to make him a god of the good alone, would here be contrary to everything desirable. The evil god is needed no less than the good one: after all, we do not owe our own existence to tolerance and humanitarianism.

What would be the point of a god who knew nothing of wrath, revenge, envy, scorn, cunning, and violence? who had perhaps never experienced the delightful *ardeurs* of victory and annihilation? No one would understand such a god: why have him then?

To be sure, when a people is perishing, when it feels how its faith in the future and its hope of freedom are waning irrevocably, when submission begins to appear to it as the prime necessity and it becomes aware of the virtues of the subjugated as the conditions of self-preservation, then its god *has* to change too. Now he becomes a sneak, timid and modest; he counsels "peace of soul," hate-no-more, forbearance, even "love" of friend and enemy. He moralizes constantly, he crawls into the cave of every private virtue, he becomes god for everyman, he becomes a private person, a cosmopolitan.

Formerly, he represented a people, the strength of a people, everything aggressive and power-thirsty in the soul of a people; now he is merely the good god.

Indeed, there is no other alternative for gods: *either* they are the will to power, and they remain a people's gods, *or* the incapacity for power, and then they necessarily become *good*. . . .

· 18 ·

The Christian conception of God—God as god of the sick, God as a spider, God as spirit— is one of the most corrupt conceptions of the divine ever attained on earth. It may even represent the low-water mark in the descending development of divine types. God degenerated into the *contradiction* of life, instead of being its transfiguration and eternal Yes! God as the declaration of war against life, against nature, against the will to live! God—the formula for every slander against "this world," for every lie about the "beyond"! God—the deification of nothingness, the will to nothingness pronounced holy! . . .

· 21 ·

In Christianity the instincts of the subjugated and oppressed come to the fore: here the lowest classes seek their salvation. The casuistry of sin, self-criticism, the inquisition of the conscience, are pursued as a *pastime*, as a remedy for boredom; the emotional reaction to one who has *power*, called "God," is constantly sustained (by means of prayer); and what is highest is considered unattainable, a gift, "grace." Public acts are precluded; the hiding-place, the darkened room, is Christian. The body is despised, hygiene repudiated as sensuality; the church even opposes cleanliness (the first Christian measure after the expulsion of the Moors was the closing of the public baths, of which there were two hundred and seventy in Cordova alone). Christian too is a certain sense of cruelty against oneself and against others; hatred of all who think differently; the will to persecute. Gloomy and exciting conceptions predominate; the most highly desired states, designated with the highest names, are epileptoid; the diet is so chosen as to favor morbid phenomena and overstimulate the nerves. Christian too is mortal enmity against the lords of the earth, against the "noble"—along with a sly, secret rivalry (one leaves them the "body," one wants *only* the "soul"). Christian, finally, is the hatred of the *spirit*, of pride, courage, freedom, liberty of the spirit; Christian is the hatred of the *senses*, of joy in the senses, of joy itself. . . .

· *24* ·

Here I merely touch on the problem of the *genesis* of Christianity. The *first* principle for its solution is: Christianity can be understood only in terms of the soil out of which it grew—it is *not* a counter-movement to the Jewish instinct, it is its very consequence, one inference more in its awe-inspiring logic. In the formula of the Redeemer: "Salvation is of the Jews." The *second* principle is: the psychological type of the Galilean is still recognizable; but only in its complete degeneration (which is at the same time a mutilation and an overloading with alien features) could it serve as that for which it has been used—as the type of a redeemer of mankind.

The Jews are the strangest people in world history because, confronted with the question whether to be or not to be, they chose, with a perfectly uncanny deliberateness, to be *at any price*: this price was the radical *falsification* of all nature, all naturalness, all reality, of the whole inner world as well as the outer. They defined themselves sharply *against* all the conditions under which a people had hitherto been able to live, been *allowed* to live; out of themselves they created a counter-concept to *natural* conditions: they turned religion, cult, morality, history, psychology, one after the other, into an incurable *contradiction to their natural values*. We encounter this same phenomenon once again and in immeasurably enlarged proportions, yet merely as a copy: the Christian church cannot make the slightest claim to originality when compared with the "holy people." That precisely is why the Jews are the *most catastrophic* people of world history: by their aftereffect they have made mankind so thoroughly false that even today the Christian can feel anti-Jewish without realizing that he himself is *the ultimate Jewish consequence*.

In my *Genealogy of Morals* I offered the first psychological analysis of the counter-concepts of a *noble* morality and a morality of *ressentiment*—the latter born of the No to the former: but this is the Judaeo-Christian morality pure and simple. So that it could say No to everything on earth that represents the ascending tendency of life, to that which has turned out well, to power, to beauty, to self-affirmation, the instinct of *ressentiment*, which had here become genius, had to invent *another* world from whose point of view this affirmation of life appeared as evil, as the reprehensible as such.

Psychologically considered, the Jewish people are a people endowed with the toughest vital energy, who, placed in impossible circumstances, voluntarily and out of the most profound prudence of self-preservation, take sides with all the instincts of decadence—*not* as mastered by them, but because they divined a power in these instincts with which one could prevail against "the world." The Jews are the antithesis of all decadents: they have had to *represent* decadents to the point of illusion; with a *non plus ultra* of histrionic genius they have known how to place themselves at the head of all movements of decadence (as the Christianity of *Paul*), in order to create something out of them which is stronger than any *Yes-saying* party of life. Decadence is only a *means* for the type of man who demands power in Judaism and Christianity, the *priestly* type: this type of man has a life interest in making mankind *sick* and in so twisting the concepts of good and evil, true and false, as to imperil life and slander the world. . . .

· 27 ·

On such utterly *false* soil, where everything natural, every natural value, every *reality* was opposed by the most profound instincts of the ruling class, *Christianity* grew up— a form of moral enmity against reality that has never yet been surpassed. The "holy people," who had retained only priestly values, only priestly words for all things and who, with awe-inspiring consistency, had distinguished all other powers on earth from themselves as "unholy," as "world," as "sin"—this people produced an ultimate formula for its instinct that was logical to the point of self-negation: as *Christianity*, it negated even the last form of reality, the "holy people," the "chosen people," the Jewish reality itself. This case is of the first rank: the little rebellious movement which is baptized with the name of Jesus of Nazareth represents the Jewish instinct *once more*— in other words, the priestly instinct which can no longer stand the priest as a reality: the invention of a still more abstract form of existence, of a still more unreal vision of the world than is involved in the organization of a church. Christianity *negates* the church.

Jesus has been understood, or *misunderstood* as the cause of a rebellion; and I fail to see against what this rebellion was directed, if it was not the Jewish church—"church" exactly in the sense in which we use the word today. It was a rebellion against "the good and the just," against "the saints of Israel," against the hierarchy of society—*not* against its corruption, but against caste, privilege, order, and formula; it was the *disbelief* in the "higher man," the No to all that was priest or theologian. But the hierarchy which was thus questioned, even though for just a moment, was the lake-dwelling on which alone the Jewish people could continue to exist amid the "water"—the hard-won *last* chance of survival, the residue of its independent political existence. An attack on this was an attack on the deepest instinct of a people, on the toughest life-will which has ever existed in any people on earth. That holy anarchist who summoned the people at the bottom, the outcasts and "sinners," the chandalas within Judaism, to opposition against the dominant order—using language, if the Gospels were to be trusted, which would lead to Siberia today too—was a political criminal insofar as political criminals were possible at all in an absurdly unpolitical community. This brought him to the cross: the proof for this is the inscription on the cross. He died for *his* guilt. All evident is lacking, however often it has been claimed, that he died for the guilt of others.

· 28 ·

It is a completely different question whether any such opposition ever entered his consciousness—whether he was not merely experienced by others as representing this opposition. And it is only at this point that I touch on the problem of the *psychology of the Redeemer*.

I confess that I read few books with as many difficulties as the Gospels. These difficulties are different from those whose demonstration has provided the scholarly curiosity of the German spirit with one of its most unforgettable triumphs. The time is long past when I too, like every young scholar, slowly drew out the savor of the work of the incomparable Strauss, with the shrewdness of a refined philologist. I was twenty years old then: now I am too serious for that. What do I care about the contradictions in the "tradition"? How can one call saints' legends "tradition" in the first place? The biographies of saints are the most ambiguous kind of literature there is: to apply scientific methods to them, *in the absence of any other documents*, strikes me as doomed to failure from the start—mere scholarly idleness.

· 29 ·

What concerns *me* is the psychological type of the Redeemer. After all, this could be contained in the Gospels despite the Gospels, however mutilated or overloaded with alien features: as Francis of Assisi is preserved in his legends, despite his legends. *Not* the truth concerning what he did, what he said, how he really died; but the question *whether* his type can still be exhibited at all, whether it has been "transmitted."

The attempts I know to read the *history* of a "soul" out of the Gospels seem to me proof of a contemptible psychological frivolity. M. Renan, that buffoon *in psychologicis*, has introduced the two most inappropriate concepts possible into his explanation of the Jesus type: the concept of *genius* and the concept of the *hero ("héros")*. But if anything is unevangelical it is the concept of the hero. Just the opposite of all wrestling, of all feeling-oneself-in-a-struggle, has here become instinct: the incapacity for resistance becomes morality here ("resist not evil"—the most profound word of the Gospels, their key in a certain sense), blessedness in peace, in gentleness, in not *being able* to be an enemy. What are the "glad tidings"? True life, eternal life, has been found—it is not promised, it is here, it is *in you*: as a living in love, in love without subtraction and exclusion, without regard for station. Everyone is the child of God—Jesus definitely presumes nothing for himself alone—and as a child of God everyone is equal to everyone. To make a *hero* of Jesus! And even more, what a misunderstanding is the word "genius"! Our whole concept, our cultural concept, of "spirit" has no meaning whatever in the world in which Jesus lives. Spoken with the precision of a physiologist, even an entirely different word would still be more nearly fitting here—the word *idiot*.

We know a state in which the *sense of touch* is pathologically excitable and shrinks from any contact, from grasping a solid object. One should translate such a physiological *habitus* into its ultimate consequence—an instinctive hatred of every reality, a flight into "what cannot be grasped," "the incomprehensible," an aversion to every formula, to every concept of time and space, to all that is solid, custom, institution, church; a being at home in a world which is no longer in contact with any kind of reality, a merely "inner" world, a "true" world, an "eternal" world. "The kingdom of God is *in you*." . . .

In the whole psychology of the "evangel" the concept of guilt and punishment is lacking; also the concept of reward. "Sin"—any distance separating God and man—is abolished: *precisely this is the "glad tidings."* Blessedness is not promised, it is not tied to conditions: it is the only reality—the rest is a sign with which to speak of it.

The consequence of such a state projects itself into a new practice, the genuine evangelical practice. It is not a "faith" that distinguishes the Christian: the Christian *acts*, he is distinguished by acting *differently*: by not resisting, either in words or in his heart, those who treat him ill; by making no distinction between foreigner and native, between Jew and not-Jew ("the neighbor"—really the coreligionist, the Jew); by not growing angry with anybody, by not despising anybody; by not permitting himself to be seen or involved at courts of law ("not swearing"); by not divorcing his wife under any circumstances, not even if his wife has been proved unfaithful. All of this, at bottom one principle; all of this, consequences of one instinct.

The life of the Redeemer was nothing other than *this* practice—nor was his death anything else. He no longer required any formulas, any rites for his intercourse with God—not even prayer. He broke with the whole Jewish doctrine of repentance and reconciliation; he knows that it is only in the *practice* of life that one feels "divine," "blessed," "evangelical," at all times a "child of God." Not "repentance," not "prayer for forgiveness," are the ways to God: *only the evangelical practice* leads to God, indeed, it *is* "God"! What was disposed of with the evangel was the Judaism of the concepts of "sin," "forgiveness of sin," "faith," "redemption through faith"—the whole Jewish *ecclesiastical* doctrine was negated in the "glad tidings."

The deep instinct for how one must *live*, in order to feel oneself "in heaven," to feel "eternal," while in all other behavior one decidedly does *not* feel oneself "in heaven"—this alone is the psychological reality of "redemption." A new way of life, *not* a new faith.

· 34 ·

If I understand anything about this great symbolist, it is that he accepted only *inner* realities as realities, as "truths"—that he understood the rest, everything natural, temporal, spatial, historical, only as signs, as occasions for parables. The concept of "the son of man" is not a concrete person who belongs in history, something individual and unique, but an "eternal" factuality, a psychological symbol redeemed from the concept of time. The same applies once again, and in the highest sense, to the *God* of this typical symbolist, to the "kingdom of God," to the "kingdom of heaven," to the "filiation of God." Nothing is more unchristian than the *ecclesiastical crudities* of a god as person, of a "kingdom of God" which is to come, of a "kingdom of heaven" beyond, of a "son of God" as the second person in the Trinity. All this is—forgive the expression—like a fist in the eye—oh, in what an eye!—of the evangel—a *world-historical cynicism* in the derision of symbols. But what the signs "father" and "son" refer to is obvious—not to everyone, I admit: the word "son" expresses the *entry* into the over-all feeling of the transfiguration of all things (blessedness); the word "father" expresses *this feeling itself*, the feeling of eternity, the feeling of perfection. I am ashamed to recall what the church has made of this symbolism: Has it not placed an Amphitryon story at the threshold of the Christian "faith"? And a dogma of "immaculate conception" on top of that? *But with that it has maculated conception.*

The "kingdom of heaven" is a state of the heart—not something that is to come "above the earth" or "after death." That whole concept of natural death is lacking in the evangel: death is no bridge, no transition; it is lacking because it belongs to a wholly different, merely apparent world, useful only insofar as it furnishes signs. The "hour of death" is *no* Christian concept—an "hour," time, physical life and its crises do not even exist for the teacher of the "glad tidings." The "kingdom of God" is nothing that one expects; it has no yesterday and no day after tomorrow, it will not come in "a thousand years"—it is an experience of the heart; it is everywhere, it is nowhere.

· 35 ·

This "bringer of glad tidings" died as he had lived, as he had taught—*not* to "redeem men" but to show how one must live. This practice is his legacy to mankind: his behavior before the judges, before the catchpoles, before the accusers and all kinds of slander and scorn—his behavior on the *cross*. He does not resist, he does not defend his right, he takes no step which might ward off the worst; on the contrary, he *provokes* it. And he begs, he suffers, he loves *with* those, *in* those, who do him evil. *Not* to resist, *not* to be angry, *not* to hold responsible—but to resist not even the evil one—to *love* him. . . .

· 39 ·

I go back, I tell the *genuine* history of Christianity. The very word "Christianity" is a misunderstanding: in truth, there was only *one* Christian, and he died on the cross. The "evangel" *died* on the cross. What has been called "evangel" from that moment was actually the opposite of that which *he* had lived: "*ill* tidings," a *dysangel*. It is false to the point of nonsense to find the mark of the Christian in a "faith," for instance, in the faith in redemption through Christ: only Christian *practice*, a life such as he *lived* who died on the cross, is Christian.

Such a life is still possible today, for certain people even necessary: genuine, original Christianity will be possible at all times.

Not a faith, but a doing; above all, a *not* doing of many things, another state of *being*. States of consciousness, any faith, considering something true, for example—every psychologist knows this—are fifth-rank matters of complete indifference compared to the value of the instincts: speaking more strictly, the whole concept of spiritual causality is false. To reduce being a Christian, Christianism, to a matter of considering something true, to a mere phenomenon of consciousness, is to negate Christianism. *In fact, there have been no Christians at all.* The "Christian," that which for the last two thousand years has been called a Christian, is merely a psychological self-misunderstanding. If one looks more closely, it was, in spite of all "faith," only the instincts that ruled in him—and *what instincts!*

"Faith" was at all times, for example, in Luther, only a cloak, a pretext, a *screen* behind which the instincts played their game—a shrewd *blindness* about the dominance of *certain* instincts. "Faith"—I have already called it the characteristic Christian *shrewdness*—one always *spoke* of faith, but one always *acted* from instinct alone.

In the Christian world of ideas there is nothing that has the least contact with reality—and it is in the instinctive hatred of reality that we have recognized the only motivating force at the root of Christianity. What follows from this? That *in psychologicis* too, the error here is radical, that it is that which determines the very essence, that it is the *substance*. One concept less, one single reality in its place—and the whole of Christianity hurtles down into nothing.

Viewed from high above, this strangest of all facts—a religion which is not only dependent on errors but which has its inventiveness and even its genius *only* in harmful errors, *only* in errors which poison life and the heart—is really a *spectacle for gods*, for those gods who are at the same time philosophers and whom I have encountered, for example, at those famous dialogues on Naxos. The moment *nausea* leaves them (*and* us!), they become grateful for the spectacle of the Christian: perhaps the miserable little star that is called earth deserves a divine glance, a divine sympathy, just because of *this* curious case. For let us not underestimate the Christian: the Christian, false *to the point of innocence*, is far above the ape—regarding Christians, a well-known theory of descent becomes a mere compliment.

· *40* ·

The catastrophe of the evangel was decided with the death—it was attached to the "cross." Only the death, this unexpected, disgraceful death, only the cross which was generally reserved for the rabble—only this horrible paradox confronted the disciples with the real riddle: "*Who was this? Who was this?*" Their profoundly upset and insulted feelings, and their suspicion that such a death might represent the *refutation* of their cause, the terrible question mark, "Why in this manner?"—this state is only too easy to understand. Here everything *had* to be necessary, had to have meaning, reason, the highest reason; a disciple's love knows no accident. Only now the cleft opened up: "*Who* killed him? *Who* was his natural enemy?" This question leaped forth like lightning. Answer: *ruling* Jewry, its highest class. From this moment one felt oneself in rebellion against the existing order, and in retrospect one understood Jesus to have been *in rebellion against the existing order*. Until then this warlike, this No-saying, No-doing trait had been *lacking* in his image; even more, he had been its opposite.

Evidently the small community did *not* understand the main point, the exemplary character of this kind of death, the freedom, the superiority over any feeling of *ressentiment*: a token of how little they understood him altogether! After all, Jesus could not intend anything with his death except to give publicly the strongest exhibition, the *proof* of his doctrine. But his disciples were far from *forgiving* this death—which would have been evangelic in the highest sense—or even from offering themselves for a like death in gentle and lovely repose of the heart. Precisely the most unevangelical feeling, *revenge*, came to the fore again. The matter could not possibly be finished with this death: "retribution" was needed, "judgment" (and yet, what could possibly be more unevangelical than "retribution," "punishment," "sitting in judgment"!). Once more the popular expectation of a Messiah came to the foreground; a historic moment was envisaged: the "kingdom of God" comes as a judgment over his enemies.

But in this way everything is misunderstood: the "kingdom of God" as the last act, as a promise! After all, the evangel had been precisely the presence, the fulfillment, the *reality* of this "kingdom." Just such a death was this very "kingdom of God." Now for the first time all the contempt and bitterness against the Pharisees and theologians were carried into the type of the Master—and in this way he himself was made into a Pharisee and theologian! On the other hand, the frenzied veneration of these totally unhinged souls no longer endured the evangelic conception of everybody's equal right to be a child of God, as Jesus had taught: it was their revenge to *elevate* Jesus extravagantly, to sever him from themselves—precisely as the Jews had formerly, out of revenge against their enemies, severed their God from themselves and elevated him. The one God and the one Son of God—both products of *ressentiment*.

· *41* ·

And from now on an absurd problem emerged: "How *could* God permit this?" To this the deranged reason of the small community found an altogether horribly absurd answer: God gave his son for the remission of sins, as a *sacrifice*. In one stroke, it was all over with the evangel! The *trespass sacrifice*—in its most revolting, most barbarous form at that, the sacrifice of the *guiltless* for the sins of the guilty! What gruesome paganism! Jesus had abolished the very concept of "guilt"—he had denied any cleavage between God and man; he *lived* this unity of God and man as his "glad tidings." And *not* as a prerogative! From now on there enters into the type of the Redeemer, step by step, the doctrine of judgment and return, the doctrine of death as a sacrificial death, the doctrine of the *resurrection* with which the whole concept of "blessedness," the whole and only actuality of the evangel, is conjured away—in favor of a state after death.

Paul, with the rabbinical impudence which distinguishes him in all things, logicalized this conception, this *obscenity* of a conception, in this way: "*If* Christ was not resurrected from the dead, then our faith is vain." And all at once the evangel became the most contemptible of all unfulfillable promises, the *impertinent* doctrine of personal immortality. Paul himself still taught it as a *reward*. . . .

· 47 ·

That we find no God—either in history or in nature or behind nature—is not what differentiates *us*, but that we experience what has been revered as God, not as "godlike" but as miserable, as absurd, as harmful, not merely as an error but as a *crime against life*. We deny God as God. If one were to *prove* this God of the Christians to us, we should be even less able to believe in him. In a formula: *deus, qualem, Paulus creavit, dei negatio*.[1]

A religion like Christianity, which does not have contact with reality at any point, which crumbles as soon as reality is conceded its rights at even a single point, must naturally be mortally hostile against the "wisdom of this world," which means *science*. It will applaud all means with which the discipline of the spirit, purity and severity in the spirit's matters of conscience, the noble coolness and freedom of the spirit, can be poisoned, slandered, brought into disrepute. "Faith" as an imperative is the *veto* against science—in practice, the lie at any price.

Paul comprehended that the lie—that "faith"—was needed; later the church in turn comprehended Paul. The "God" whom Paul invented, a god who "ruins the wisdom of the world" (in particular, philology and medicine, the two great adversaries of all superstition), is in truth merely Paul's own resolute *determination* to do this: to give the name of "God" to one's own will, *torah*, that is thoroughly Jewish. Paul *wants* to ruin the "wisdom of the world": his enemies are the good philologists and physicians with Alexandrian training—it is they against whom he wages war. Indeed, one cannot be a philologist or physician without at the same time being an *anti-Christian*. For as a philologist one sees *behind* the "holy books"; as a physician, *behind* the physiological depravity of the typical Christian. The physician says "incurable"; the philologist, "swindle." . . .

· 50 ·

At this point I do not let myself off without a psychology of "faith," of "believers"— precisely for the benefit of "believers," as is fitting. If today there is no lack of people who do not know in what way it is *indecent* to "believe"—*or* a sign of decadence, of broken will to life—tomorrow they will already know it. My voice reaches even the hard of hearing.

Unless I have heard wrong, it seems that among Christians there is a kind of criterion of truth that is called the "proof of strength." "Faith makes blessed: *hence* it is

---

[1] "God, as Paul created him, is the negation of God."—TRANS.

true." Here one might object first that it is precisely the making blessed which is not proved but merely *promised*: blessedness tied to the condition of "faith"—one *shall* become blessed *because* one believes. But whether what the priest promises the believer in fact occurs in a "beyond" which is not subject to any test—how is that proved? The alleged "proof of strength" is thus at bottom merely another faith, namely, that the effect one expects from faith will not fail to appear. In a formula: "I believe that faith makes blessed; consequently it is true." But with this we are already at the end. This "consequently" would be absurdity itself as the criterion of truth.

But let us suppose, with some leniency, that it was proved that faith makes blessed (not merely desired, not merely promised by the somewhat suspicious mouth of a priest): would blessedness—or more technically speaking, *pleasure*—ever be a proof of truth? This is so far from the case that it almost furnishes a counter-proof; in any event, the greatest suspicion of a "truth" should arise when feelings of pleasure enter the discussion of the question "What is true?" The proof of "pleasure" is a proof of "pleasure"—nothing else: how in all the world could it be established that true judgments should give greater delight than false ones and, according to a pre-established harmony, should necessarily be followed by agreeable feelings?

The experience of all severe, of all profoundly inclined, spirits teaches the *opposite*. At every step one has to wrestle for truth; one has had to surrender for it almost everything to which the heart, to which our love, our trust in life, cling otherwise. That requires greatness of soul: the service of truth is the hardest service. What does it mean, after all, to have *integrity* in matters of the spirit? That one is severe against one's heart, that one despises "beautiful sentiments," that one makes of every Yes and No a matter of conscience. Faith makes blessed: consequently it lies.

· *51* ·

That faith makes blessed under certain circumstances, that blessedness does not make of a fixed idea a *true* idea, that faith moves no mountains but *puts* mountains where there are none—a quick walk through a madhouse enlightens one sufficiently about this. *Not*, to be sure, a priest: for he denies instinctively that sickness is sickness, that madhouse is madhouse. Christianity *needs* sickness just as Greek culture needs a super-abundance of health—to *make* sick is the true, secret purpose of the whole system of redemptive procedures constructed by the church. And the church itself—is it not the catholic madhouse as the ultimate ideal? The earth altogether as a madhouse?

The religious man, as the church wants him, is a typical decadent; the moment when a religious crisis overcomes a people is invariably marked by epidemics of the nerves; the "inner world" of the religious man looks exactly like the "inner world" of the overexcited and the exhausted; the "highest" states that Christianity has hung over mankind as the value of all values are epileptoid forms—only madmen or great imposters have been pronounced holy by the church *in maiorem de honorem*. I once permitted myself to designate the whole Christian repentance and redemption training (which today is best studied in England) as a methodically produced *folie circulaire*, as is proper, on soil prepared for it, that is to say, thoroughly morbid soil. Nobody is free to become a Christian: one is not "converted" to Christianity—one has to be sick enough for it.

We others who have the *courage* to be healthy and also to despise—how may we despise a religion which taught men to misunderstand the body! which does not want to get rid of superstitious belief in souls! which turns insufficient nourishment into something "meritorious"! which fights health as a kind of enemy, devil, temptation! which fancies that one can carry around a "perfect soul" in a cadaver of a body, and which therefore found it necessary to concoct a new conception of "perfection"—a pale, sickly, idiotic-enthusiastic character, so-called "holiness." Holiness—merely a series of symptoms of an impoverished, unnerved, incurably corrupted body.

The Christian movement, as a European movement, has been from the start a collective movement of the dross and refuse elements of every kind (these want to get power through Christianity). It does *not* express the decline of a race, it is an aggregate of forms of decadence flocking together and seeking each other out from everywhere. It is *not*, as is supposed, the corruption of antiquity itself, of *noble* antiquity, that made Christianity possible. The scholarly idiocy which upholds such ideas even today cannot be contradicted harshly enough. At the very time when the sick, corrupt chandala strata in the whole *imperium* adopted Christianity, the *opposite type*, nobility, was present in its most beautiful and most mature form. The great number became master; the democratism of the Christian instincts *triumphed*. Christianity was not "national," not a function of a race—it turned to every kind of man who was disinherited by life, it had its allies everywhere. At the bottom of Christianity is the rancor of the sick, instinct directed *against* the healthy, *against* health itself. Everything that has turned out well, everything that is proud and prankish, beauty above all, hurts its ears and eyes. Once more I recall the inestimable words of Paul: "The *weak* things of the world, the *foolish* things of the world, the *base* and *despised* things of the world hath God chosen." This was the formula; *in hoc signo* decadence triumphed.

God on the cross—are the horrible secret thoughts behind this symbol not understood yet? All that suffers, all that is nailed to the cross, is *divine*. All of us are nailed to the cross, consequently *we* are divine. We alone are divine. Christianity was a victory, a nobler outlook perished of it—Christianity has been the greatest misfortune of mankind so far. . . .

· 53 ·

The *martyrs* prove anything about the truth of a matter is so far from true that I would deny that any martyr ever had anything whatsoever to do with truth. The tone with which a martyr throws his considering-something-true into the face of the world expresses such a low degree of intellectual integrity, such an *obtuseness* for the question of truth, that one never needs to refute a martyr. Truth is not something which one person might have and another not have: only peasants and peasant apostles like Luther can think that way about truth. One may be sure that modesty, *moderation* in this matter, becomes greater in proportion to the degree of conscientiousness in matters of the spirit. To have *knowledge* of five matters, and to refuse with a gentle hand to have *other* knowledge. . . .

· 62 ·

With this I am at the end and I pronounce my judgment. I *condemn* Christianity. I raise against the Christian church the most terrible of all accusations that any accuser ever uttered. It is to me the highest of all conceivable corruptions. It has had the will to the last corruption that is even possible. The Christian church has left nothing untouched by its corruption; it has turned every value into an un-value, every truth into a lie, every integrity into a vileness of the soul. Let anyone dare to speak to me of its "humanitarian" blessings! To *abolish* any distress ran counter to its deepest advantages: it lived on distress, it *created* distress to eternalize *itself*.

The worm of sin, for example: with this distress the church first enriched mankind. The "equality of souls before God," this falsehood, this *pretext* for the rancor of all the base-minded, this explosive of a concept which eventually became revolution, modern idea, and the principle of decline of the whole order of society—is *Christian* dynamite. "Humanitarian" blessings of Christianity! To breed out of *humanitas* a self-contradiction, an art of self-violation, a will to lie at any price, a repugnance, a contempt for all good and honest instincts! Those are some of the blessings of Christianity!

Parasitism as the *only* practice of the church; with its ideal of anemia, of "holiness," draining all blood, all love, all hope for life; the beyond as the will to negate every reality; the cross as the mark of recognition for the most subterranean conspiracy that ever existed—against health, beauty, whatever has turned out well, courage, spirit, *graciousness* of the soul, *against life itself*.

This eternal indictment of Christianity I will write on all walls, wherever there are walls—I have letters to make even the blind see.

I call Christianity the one great curse, the one great innermost corruption, the one great instinct of revenge, for which no means is poisonous, stealthy, subterranean, *small* enough—I call it the one immortal blemish of mankind. . . .

○ ○ ○ *18*

The Social Foundation
of Religion
Emile Durkheim

ALL KNOWN RELIGIOUS beliefs, whether simple or complex, present one common characteristic: they presuppose a classification of all the things, real and ideal, of which men think, into two classes or opposed groups, generally designated by two distinct terms which are translated well enough by words *profane* and *sacred (profane, sacré)*. This division of the world into two domains, the one containing all that is sacred, the other all that is profane, is the distinctive trait of religious thought; the beliefs, myths, dogmas and legends are either representations or systems of representations which express the nature of sacred things, the virtues and powers which are attributed to them, or their relations with each other and with profane things. But by sacred things one must not understand simply those personal beings which are called gods or spirits; a rock, a tree, a spring, a pebble, a piece of wood, a house, in a word, anything can be sacred. A rite can have this character; in fact, the rite does not exist which does not have it to a certain degree. There are words, expressions and formulae which can be pronounced only by the mouths of consecrated persons; there are gestures and movements which everybody cannot perform. If the Vedic sacrifice has had such an efficacy that, according to mythology, it was the creator of the gods, and not merely a means of winning their favor, it is because it possessed a virtue comparable to that of the most sacred beings. The circle of sacred objects cannot be determined, then, once for all. Its extent varies infinitely, according to the different religions. That is how Buddhism is a religion: in default of gods, it admits the existence of sacred things, namely, the four noble truths and the practices derived from them.

Up to the present we have confined ourselves to enumerating a certain number of sacred things as examples: we must now show by what general characteristics they are to be distinguished from profane things.

One might be tempted, first of all, to define them by the place they are generally assigned in the hierarchy of things. They are naturally considered superior in dignity and power to profane things, and particularly to man, when he is only a man and has nothing sacred about him. One thinks of himself as occupying an inferior and dependent position in relation to them; and surely this conception is not without some truth. Only there is nothing in it which is really characteristic of the sacred. It is not enough that one thing be subordinated to another for the second to be sacred in regard to the first. Slaves are inferior to their masters, subjects to their king, soldiers to their leaders, the miser to his gold, the man ambitious for power to the hands which keep it from him; but if it is sometimes said of a man that he makes a religion of those beings or things whose eminent value and superiority to himself he thus recognizes, it is clear that in any case the word is taken in a metaphorical sense, and that there is nothing in these relations which is really religious.

On the other hand it must not be lost to view that there are sacred things of every degree, and that there are some in relation to which a man feels himself relatively at his ease. An amulet has a sacred character, yet the respect which it inspires is nothing exceptional. Even before his gods, a man is not always in such a marked state of inferiority; for it very frequently happens that he exercises a veritable physical constraint upon them to obtain what he desires. He beats the fetish with which he is not contented, but only to reconcile himself with it again, if in the end it shows itself more docile to the wishes of its adorer. To have rain, he throws stones into the spring or sacred lake where the god of rain is thought to reside; he believes that by this means he forces him to come out and show himself. Moreover, if it is true that man depends upon his gods, this dependence is reciprocal. The gods also have need of man; without offerings and sacrifices they would die. We shall even have occasion to show that this dependence of the gods upon their worshippers is maintained even in the most idealistic religions.

But if a purely hierarchic distinction is a criterion at once too general and too imprecise, there is nothing left with which to characterize the sacred in its relation to the profane except their heterogeneity. However, this heterogeneity is sufficient to characterize this classification of things and to distinguish it from all others, because it is very particular: *it is absolute.* In all the history of human thought there exists no other example of two categories of things so profoundly differentiated or so radically opposed to one another. The traditional opposition of good and bad is nothing beside this; for the good and the bad are only two opposed species of the same class, namely morals, just as sickness and health are two different aspects of the same order of facts, life, while the sacred and the profane have always and everywhere been conceived by the human mind as two distinct classes, as two worlds between which there is nothing in common. The forces which play in one are not simply those which are met with in the other, but a little stronger; they are of a different sort. In different religions, this opposition has been conceived in different ways. Here, to separate these two sorts of things, it has seemed sufficient to localize them in different parts of the physical universe; there, the first have been put into an ideal and transcendental world, while the material world is left in full possession of the others. But howsoever much the forms of the contrast may vary,[1] the fact of the contrast is universal.

This is not equivalent to saying that a being can never pass from one of these worlds into the other: but the manner in which this passage is effected, when it does take place, puts into relief the essential duality of the two kingdoms. In fact, it implies a veritable metamorphosis. This is notably demonstrated by the initiation rites, such as they are practised by a multitude of peoples. This initiation is a long series of ceremonies with the object of introducing the young man into the religious life: for the first time, he leaves

---

[1] The conception according to which the profane is opposed to the sacred, just as the irrational is to the rational, or the intelligible is to the mysterious, is only one of the forms under which this opposition is expressed. Science being once constituted, it has taken a profane character, especially in the eyes of the Christian religions; from that it appears as though it could not be applied to sacred things.—L.F.

the purely profane world where he passed his first infancy, and enters into the world of sacred things. Now this change of state is thought of, not as a simple and regular development of pre-existent germs, but as a transformation *totius substantiae*[2]—of the whole being. It is said that at this moment the young man dies, that the person that he was ceases to exist, and that another is instantly substituted for it. He is reborn under a new form. Appropriate ceremonies are felt to bring about this death and rebirth, which are not understood in a merely symbolic sense, but are taken literally.[3] Does this not prove that between the profane being which he was and the religious being which he becomes, there is a break of continuity?

This heterogeneity is even so complete that it frequently degenerates into a veritable antagonism. The two worlds are not only conceived of as separate, but as even hostile and jealous rivals of each other. Since men cannot fully belong to one except on condition of leaving the other completely, they are exhorted to withdraw themselves completely from the profane world, in order to lead an exclusively religious life. Hence comes the monasticism which is artificially organized outside of and apart from the natural environment in which the ordinary man leads the life of this world, in a different one, closed to the first, and nearly its contrary. Hence comes the mystic asceticism whose object is to root out from man all the attachment for the profane world that remains in him. From that come all the forms of religious suicide, the logical working-out of this asceticism; for the only manner of fully escaping the profane life is, after all, to forsake all life.

The opposition of these two classes manifests itself outwardly with a visible sign by which we can easily recognize this very special classification, wherever it exists. Since the idea of the sacred is always and everywhere separated from the idea of the profane in the thought of men, and since we picture a sort of logical chasm between the two, the mind irresistably refuses to allow the two corresponding things to be confounded, or even to be merely put in contact with each other; for such a promiscuity, or even too direct a contiguity, would contradict too violently the dissociation of these ideas in the mind. The sacred thing is *par excellence* that which the profane should not touch, and cannot with impunity. To be sure, this interdiction cannot go so far as to make all communication between the two worlds impossible; for if the profane could in no way enter into relations with the sacred, this latter could be good for nothing. But, in addition to the fact that this establishment of relations is always a delicate operation in itself, demanding great precautions and a more or less complicated initiation, it is quite impossible, unless the profane is to lose its specific characteristics and become sacred after a fashion and to a certain degree itself. The two classes cannot even approach each other and keep their own nature at the same time.

Thus we arrive at the first criterion of religious beliefs. Undoubtedly there are secondary species within these two fundamental classes which, in their turn, are more or less incompatible with each other. But the real characteristic of religious phenomena is that they always suppose a bipartite division of the whole universe, known and knowable,

---

[2] See Frazer, "On some ceremonies of the Central Australian tribes" in *Australian Association for the Advancement of Science*, 1901, pp. 313ff. This conception is also of an extreme generality. In India, the simple participation in the sacrificial act has the same effects; the sacrificer, by the mere act of entering within the circle of sacred things, changes his personality. (See Hubert and Mauss, "Essai sur la nature et la fonction du sacrifice" in the *Année Sociologique*, vol. 2, 1899, p. 101.)—L.F.

[3] Of the whole substance or being.—E.D.K.

into two classes which embrace all that exists, but which radically exclude each other. Sacred things are those which the interdictions protect and isolate; profane things, those to which these interdictions are applied and which must remain at a distance from the first. Religious beliefs are the representations which express the nature of sacred things and the relations which they sustain, either with each other or with profane things. Finally, rites are the rules of conduct which prescribe how a man should comport himself in the presence of these sacred objects.

. . . We arrive at the following definition: *a religion is a unified system of beliefs and practices relative to sacred things, that is to say, things set apart and forbidden—beliefs and practices which unite into one single moral community called a Church, all those who adhere to them.* The second element which finds a place in our definition is no less essential than the first; for by showing that the idea of religion is inseparable from that of the Church, it makes it clear that religion should be an eminently collective thing. . . .

Our entire study rests upon the postulate that the unanimous sentiment of the believers of all times cannot be purely illusory.[4] Together with an apologist of the faith[5] we admit that these religious beliefs rest upon a specific experience whose demonstrative value is, in one sense, not one bit inferior to that of scientific experiments, though different from them. We, too, think that "a tree is known by its fruits,"[6] and that fertility is the best proof of "what the roots are worth." But from the fact that a "religious experience," if we choose to call it this, does exist and that it has a certain foundation—and, by the way, is there any experience which has none?—it does not follow that the reality which is its foundation conforms objectively to the idea which believers have of it. The very fact that the fashion in which it has been conceived has varied infinitely in different times is enough to prove that none of these conceptions express it adequately. If a scientist states it as an axiom that the sensations of heat and light which we feel correspond to some objective cause, he does not conclude that this is what it appears to the senses to be. Likewise, even if the impressions which the faithful feel are not imaginary, still they are in no way privileged intuitions; there is no reason for believing that they inform us better upon the nature of their object than do ordinary sensations upon the nature of bodies and their properties. In order to discover what this object consists of, we must submit them to an examination and elaboration analogous to that which has substituted for the sensuous idea of the world another which is scientific and conceptual.

This is precisely what we have tried to do, and we have seen that this reality, which mythologies have represented under so many different forms, but which is the universal and eternal objective cause of these sensations *sui generis* out of which religious experience is made, is society. We have shown what moral forces it develops and how it awakens this sentiment of a refuge, of a shield and of a guardian support which attaches the believer to his cult. It is that which raises him outside himself; it is even that which made him. For that which makes a man is the totality of the intellectual property which constitutes civilization, and civilization is the work of society. This is explained by the

---

[4] Durkheim refers here and subsequently to the details of his analysis of aboriginal religion in Australia.—J. SWAIN.

[5] William James, *The Varieties of Religious Experience.*—L.F.

[6] Quoted by James, op. cit., p. 20.—L.F.

preponderating role of the cult in all religions, whichever they may be. This is because society cannot make its influence felt unless it is in action, and it is not in action unless the individuals who compose it are assembled together and act in common. It is by common action that it takes consciousness of itself and realizes its position; it is before all else an active cooperation. The collective ideas and sentiments are even possible only owing to these exterior movements which symbolize them, as we have established. Then it is action which dominates the religious life, because of the mere fact that it is society which is its source.

In addition to all the reasons which have been given to justify this conception, a final one may be added here, which is the result of our whole work. As we have progressed, we have established the fact that the fundamental categories of thought, and consequently of science, are of religious origin. We have seen that the same is true for magic and consequently for the different processes which have issued from it. On the other hand, it has long been known that up until a relatively advanced moment of evolution, moral and legal rules have been indistinguishable from ritual prescriptions. In summing up, then, it may be said that nearly all the great social institutions have been born in religion. Now in order that these principal aspects of the collective life may have commenced by being only varied aspects of the religious life, it is obviously necessary that the religious life be the eminent form and, as it were, the concentrated expression of the whole collective life. If religion has given birth to all that is essential in society, it is because the idea of society is the soul of religion.

Religious forces are therefore human forces, moral forces. It is true that since collective sentiments can become conscious of themselves only by fixing themselves upon external objects, they have not been able to take form without adopting some of their characteristics from other things: they have thus acquired a sort of physical nature; in this way they have come to mix themselves with the life of the material world, and then have considered themselves capable of explaining what passes there. But when they are considered only from this point of view and in this role, only their most superficial aspect is seen. In reality, the essential elements of which these collective sentiments are made have been borrowed by the understanding. It ordinarily seems that they should have a human character only when they are conceived under human forms;[7] but even the most impersonal and the most anonymous are nothing else than objectified sentiments.

It is only by regarding religion from this angle that it is possible to see its real significance. If we stick closely to appearances, rites often give the effect of purely manual operations: they are anointings, washings, meals. To consecrate something, it is put in contact with a source of religious energy, just as today a body is put in contact with a source of heat or electricity to warm or electrize it; the two processes employed are not essentially different. Thus understood, religious technique seems to be a sort of mystic mechanics. But these material maneuvers are only the external envelope under which the mental operations are hidden. Finally, there is no question of exercising a physical constraint upon blind, and incidentally, imaginary forces, but rather of reaching individual consciousness of giving them a direction and of disciplining them. It is sometimes said that inferior religions are materialistic. Such an expression is inexact. All religions, even the crudest, are in a sense

---

[7] It is for this reason that Frazer and even Preuss set impersonal religious forces outside of, or at least on the threshold of religion, to attach them to magic.—L.F.

spiritualistic: for the powers they put in play are before all spiritual, and also the principal object is to act upon the moral life. Thus it is seen that whatever has been done in the name of religion cannot have been done in vain: for it is necessarily the society that did it, and it is humanity that has reaped the fruits.

But, it is said, what society is it that has thus made the basis of religion? Is it the real society, such as it is and acts before our very eyes, with the legal and moral organization which it has laboriously fashioned during the course of history? This is full of defects and imperfections. In it, evil goes beside the good, injustice often reigns supreme, and the truth is often obscured by error. How could anything so crudely organized inspire the sentiments of love, the ardent enthusiasm and the spirit of abnegation which all religions claim of their followers? These perfect beings which are gods could not have taken their traits from so mediocre, and sometimes even so base a reality.

But, on the other hand, does someone think of a perfect society, where justice and truth would be sovereign, and from which evil in all its forms would be banished for ever? No one would deny that this is in close relations with the religious sentiment; for, they would say, it is towards the realization of this that all religions strive. But that society is not an empirical fact, definite and observable; it is a fancy, a dream with which men have lightened their sufferings, but in which they have never really lived. It is merely an idea which comes to express our more or less obscure aspirations towards the good, the beautiful and the ideal.Now these aspirations have their roots in us; they come from the very depths of our being; then there is nothing outside of us which can account for them. Moreover, they are already religious in themselves; thus is would seem that the ideal society presupposes religion, far from being able to explain it.

But, in the first place, things are arbitrarily simplified when religion is seen only on its idealistic side: in its way, it is realistic. There is no physical or moral ugliness, there are no vices or evils which do not have a special divinity. There are gods of theft and trickery, of lust and war, of sickness and of death. Christianity itself, howsoever high the idea which it has made of the divinity may be, has been obliged to give the spirit of evil a place in its mythology. Satan is an essential piece of the Christian system; even if he is an impure being, he is not a profane one. The anti-god is a god, inferior and subordinated, it is true, but nevertheless endowed with extended powers; he is even the object of rites, at least of negative ones. Thus religion, far from ignoring the real society and making abstraction of it, is in its image; it reflects all its aspects, even the most vulgar and the most repulsive. All is to be found there, and if in the majority of cases we see the good victorious over evil, life over death, the powers of light over the powers of darkness, it is because reality is not otherwise. If the relation between these two contrary forces were reversed, life would be impossible; but, as a matter of fact, it maintains itself and even tends to develop.

But if, in the midst of these mythologies and theologies we see reality clearly appearing, it is none the less true that it is found there only in an enlarged, transformed and idealized form. In this respect, the most primitive religions do not differ from the most recent and the most refined. For example, we have seen how the Arunta place at the beginning of time a mythical society whose organization exactly reproduces that which still exists today; it includes the same clans and phratries, it is under the same matrimonial rules and it practises the same rites. But the personages who compose it are ideal beings, gifted with powers and virtues to which common mortals cannot pretend.

Their nature is not only higher, but it is different, since it is at once animal and human. The evil powers there undergo a similar metamorphosis: evil itself is, as it were, made sublime and idealized. The question now raises itself of whence this idealization comes.

Some reply that men have a natural faculty for idealizing, that is to say, of substituting for the real world another different one, to which they transport themselves by thought. But that is merely changing the terms of the problem; it is not resolving it or even advancing it. This systematic idealization is an essential characteristic of religions. Explaining them by an innate power of idealization is simply replacing one word by another which is the equivalent of the first; it is as if they said that men have made religions because they have a religious nature. Animals know only one world, the one which they perceive by experience, internal as well as external. Men alone have the faculty of conceiving the ideal, of adding something to the real. Now where does this singular privilege come from? Before making it an initial fact or a mysterious virtue which escapes science, we must be sure that it does not depend upon empirically determinable conditions.

The explanation of religion which we have proposed has precisely this advantage, that it gives an answer to this question. For our definition of the sacred is that it is something added to and above the real; now the ideal answers to this same definition; we cannot explain one without explaining the other. In fact, we have seen that if collective life awakens religious thought on reaching a certain degree of intensity, it is because it brings about a state of effervescence which changes the conditions of psychic activity. Vital energies are over-excited, passions more active, sensations stronger; there are even some which are produced only at this moment. A man does not recognize himself; he feels himself transformed and consequently he transforms the environment which surrounds him. In order to account for the very particular impressions which he receives, he attributes to the things with which he is in most direct contact properties which they have not, exceptional powers and virtues which the objects of everyday experience do not possess. In a word, above the real world where his profane life passes he has placed another which, in one sense, does not exist except in thought, but to which he attributes a higher sort of dignity than to the first. Thus, from a double point of view it is an ideal world.

The formation of the ideal world is therefore not an irreducible fact which escapes science; it depends upon conditions which observation can touch; it is a natural product of social life. For a society to become conscious of itself and maintain at the necessary degree of intensity the sentiments which it thus attains, it must assemble and concentrate itself. Now this concentration brings about an exaltation of the mental life which takes form in a group of ideal conceptions where is portrayed the new life thus awakened; they correspond to this new set of psychical forces which is added to those which we have at our disposition for the daily tasks of existence. A society can neither create itself nor recreate itself without at the same time creating an ideal. This creation is not a sort of work of supererogation for it, by which it would complete itself, being already formed; it is the act by which it is periodically made and remade. Therefore when some oppose the ideal society to the real society, like two antagonists which would lead us in opposite directions, they materialize and oppose abstractions. The ideal society is not outside of the real society; it is a part of it. Far from being divided between them as between two poles which mutually repel each other, we cannot hold to one without holding to the other. For a society is not made up merely of the mass of individuals who compose it, the ground which they occupy, the things which they use and the movements which they perform, but above all is the idea which it forms of itself. It is undoubtedly true that it hesitates over the manner in which it ought to conceive itself; it feels itself drawn in divergent directions. But these conflicts which break forth are not between the ideal and reality, but between two different ideals, that of yesterday and that of today, that which has the authority of tradition and that which has the hope of the future. There is surely a place for investigating whence these ideals evolve; but whatever solution may be given to this problem, it still remains that all passes in the world of the ideal.

Thus the collective ideal which religion expresses is far from being due to a vague innate power of the individual, but it is rather at the school of collective life that the individual has learned to idealize. It is in assimilating the ideals elaborated by society that he has become capable of conceiving the ideal. It is society which, by leading him within its sphere of action, has made him acquire the need of raising himself above the world of experience and has at the same time furnished him with the means of conceiving another. For society has constructed this new world in constructing itself, since it is society which this expresses. Thus both with the individual and in the group, the faculty of idealizing has nothing mysterious about it. It is not a sort of luxury which a man could get along without, but a condition of his very existence. He could not be a social being, that is to say, he could not be man, if he had not acquired it. It is true that in incarnating themselves in individuals, collective ideals tend to individualize themselves. Each understands them after his own fashion and marks them with his own stamp; he suppresses certain elements and adds others. Thus the personal ideal disengages itself from the social ideal in proportion as the individual personality develops itself and becomes an autonomous source of action. But if we wish to understand this aptitude, so singular in appearance, of living outside of reality, it is enough to connect it with the social conditions upon which it depends.

Therefore it is necessary to avoid seeing in this theory of religion a simple restatement of historical materialism: that would be misunderstanding our thought to an extreme degree. In showing that religion is something essentially social, we do not mean to say that it confines itself to translating into another language the material forms of society and its immediate vital necessities. It is true that we take it as evident that social life depends upon its material foundation and bears its mark, just as the mental life of an individual depends upon his nervous system and in fact his whole organism. But collective consciousness is something more than a mere epiphenomenon of its morphological basis, just as individual consciousness is something more than a simple efflorescence of the nervous system. In order that the former may appear, a synthesis *sui generis*[8] of particular consciousness is required. Now this synthesis has the effect of disengaging a whole world of sentiments, ideas and images which, once born, obey laws all their own. They attract each other, repel each other, unite, divide themselves and multiply, though these combinations are not commanded and necessitated by the condition of the underlying reality. The life thus brought into being even enjoys so great an independence that it sometimes indulges in manifestations with no purpose or utility of any sort, for the mere pleasure of affirming itself. We have shown that this is often precisely the case with ritual activity and mythological thought.

---

[8] Unique.—E.D.K.

CHAPTER FOUR

Philosophical Critiques

○

Evil and a Finite God
John Stuart Mill

· I ·

. . . GIVEN THE INDICATIONS of a Deity, what *sort* of a Deity do they point to? What attributes are we warranted, by the evidence which nature affords of a creative mind, in assigning to that mind?[1]

It needs no showing that the power, if not the intelligence, must be so far superior to that of man, as to surpass all human estimate. But from this to omnipotence and omniscience there is a wide interval. And the distinction is of immense practical importance.

It is not too much to say that every indication of design in the cosmos is so much evidence against the omnipotence of the Designer. For what is meant by design? Contrivance: the adaptation of means to an end. But the necessity for contrivance—the need of employing means—is a consequence of the limitation of power. Who would have recourse to means if to attain his end his mere word was sufficient? The very idea of means implies that the means have an efficacy which the direct action of the being who employs them has not. Otherwise they are not means, but an incumbrance. A man does not use machinery to move his arms. If he did, it could only be when paralysis had deprived him of the power of moving them by volition. But if the employment of contrivance is in itself a sign of limited power, how much more so is the careful and skillful choice of contrivances? Can any wisdom be shown in the selection of means, when the means have no efficacy but what is given them by the will of him who employs them, and when his will could have bestowed the same efficacy on any other means? Wisdom and contrivance are shown in overcoming difficulties, and there is no room for them in a Being for whom no difficulties exist. The evidences, therefore, of natural theology distinctly imply that the author of the cosmos worked under limitations; that he was obliged to adapt himself to conditions independent of his will, and to attain his ends by such arrangements as those conditions admitted of.

And this hypothesis agrees with what we have seen to be the tendency of the evidences in another respect. We found that the appearances in nature point indeed to an origin of the cosmos, or order in nature, and indicate that origin to be design but do not point to any commencement, still less creation, of the two great elements of the universe, the passive element and the active element, matter and force. There is in nature no reason whatever to suppose that either matter or force, or any of their properties, were made by the Being who was the author of the collocations by which the world is adapted

---

[1] In the opening pages of this essay, omitted here, Mill finds the design arguments to have some force. That is, he takes the design in nature to be evidence for the existence of some sort of creator-designer.—E.D.K.

to what we consider as its purposes; or that he has power to alter any of those properties. It is only when we consent to entertain this negative supposition that there arises a need for wisdom and contrivance in the order of the universe. The Deity had on this hypothesis to work out his ends by combining materials of a given nature and properties. Out of these materials he had to construct a world in which his designs should be carried into effect through given properties of matter and force, working together and fitting into one another. This did require skill and contrivance, and the means by which it is effected are often such as justly excite our wonder and admiration: but exactly because it requires wisdom, it implies limitation of power, or rather the two phrases express different sides of the same fact.

· *II* ·

If it be said that an omnipotent Creator, though under no necessity of employing contrivances such as man must use, thought fit to do so in order to leave traces by which man might recognize his creative hand, the answer is that this equally supposes a limit to his omnipotence. For if is was his will that men should know that they themselves and the world are his work, he, being omnipotent, had only to will that they should be aware of it. Ingenious men have sought for reasons why God might choose to leave his existence so far a matter of doubt that men should not be under an absolute necessity of knowing it, as they are of knowing that three and two make five. These imagined reasons are very unfortunate specimens of casuistry; but even did we admit their validity, they are of no avail on the supposition of omnipotence, since if it did not please God to implant in man a complete conviction of his existence, nothing hindered him from making the conviction fall short of completeness by any margin he chose to leave. It is usual to dispose of arguments of this description by the easy answer, that we do not know what wise reasons the Omniscient may have had for leaving undone things which he had the power to do. It is not perceived that this plea itself implies a limit to omnipotence. When a thing is obviously good and obviously in accordance with what all the evidences of creation imply to have been the Creator's design, and we say we do not know what good reason he may have had for not doing it, we mean that we do not know to what other, still better object—to what object still more completely in the line of his purposes—he may have seen fit to postpone it. But the necessity of postponing one thing to another belongs only to limited power. Omnipotence could have made the objects compatible. Omnipotence does not need to weigh one consideration against another. If the Creator, like a human ruler, had to adapt himself to a set of conditions which he did not make, it is as unphilosophical as presumptuous in us to call him to account for any imperfections in his work; to complain that he left anything in it contrary to what, if the indications of design prove anything, he must have intended. He must at least know more than we know, and we cannot judge what greater good would have had to be sacrificed, or what greater evil incurred, if he had decided to remove this particular blot. Not so if he be omnipotent. If he be that, he must himself have willed that the two desirable objects should be incompatible; he must himself have willed that the obstacle to his supposed design should be insuperable. It cannot therefore *be* his design. It will not do to say that it was, but that he had other designs which interfered with it; for no one purpose imposes necessary limitations on another in the case of a Being not restricted by conditions of possibility.

· III ·

Omnipotence, therefore, cannot be predicated of the Creator on grounds of natural theology. The fundamental principles of natural religion as deduced from the facts of the universe, negative his omnipotence. They do not, in the same manner, exclude omniscience: if we suppose limitation of power, there is nothing to contradict the supposition of perfect knowledge and absolute wisdom. But neither is there anything to prove it. The knowledge of the powers and properties of things necessary for planning and executing the arrangements of the cosmos is no doubt as much in excess of human knowledge as the power implied in creation is in excess of human power. And the skill, the subtlety of contrivance, the ingenuity as it would be called in the case of a human work, is often marvellous. But nothing obliges us to suppose that either the knowledge or the skill is infinite. We are not even compelled to suppose that the contrivances were always the best possible. If we venture to judge them as we judge the works of human artificers, we find abundant defects. The human body, for example, is one of the most striking instances of artful and ingenious contrivance which nature offers, but we may well ask whether so complicated a machine could not have been made to last longer, and not to get so easily and frequently out of order. We may ask why the human race should have been so constituted as to grovel in wretchedness and degradation for countless ages before a small portion of it was enabled to lift itself into the very imperfect state of intelligence, goodness and happiness which we enjoy. The divine power may not have been equal to doing more; the obstacles to a better arrangement of things may have been insuperable. But it is also possible that they were not. The skill of the Demiurge[2] was sufficient to produce what we see; but we cannot tell that this skill reached the extreme limit of perfection compatible with the material it employed and the forces it had to work with. I know not how we can even satisfy ourselves on grounds of natural theology, that the Creator foresees all the future; that he foreknows all the effects that will issue from his own contrivances. There may be great wisdom without the power of foreseeing and calculating everything: and human workmanship teaches us the possibility that the workman's knowledge of the properties of the things he works on may enable him to make arrangements admirably fitted to produce a given result, while he may have very little power of foreseeing the agencies of another kind which may modify or counteract the operation of the machinery he has made. Perhaps a knowledge of the laws of nature on which organic life depends, not much more perfect than the knowledge which man even now possesses of some other natural laws, would enable man, if he had the same power over the materials and the forces concerned which he had over some of those of inanimate nature, to create organized beings not less wonderful nor less adapted to their conditions of existence than those in nature.

Assuming then that while we confine ourselves to natural religion we must rest content with a Creator less than Almighty; the question presents itself, of what nature is the limitation of his power? Does the obstacle at which the power of the Creator stops, which says to it: Thus far shalt thou go and no further, lie in the power of other intelligent beings; or in the insufficiency and refractoriness of the materials of the universe; or must we resign ourselves to admitting the hypothesis that the author of the

---

[2] The artificer or fashioner of the Universe.—E.D.K.

cosmos, though wise and knowing, was not all-wise and all-knowing, and may not always have done the best that was possible under the conditions of the problem?

The first of these suppositions has until a very recent period been and in many quarters still is, the prevalent theory even of Christianity. Though attributing, and in a certain sense sincerely, omnipotence to the Creator, the received religion represents him as for some inscrutable reason tolerating the perpetual counteraction of his purposes by the will of another being of opposite character and of great though inferior power, the Devil. The only difference on this matter between popular Christianity and the religion of Ormuzd and Ahriman[3] is that the former pays its good Creator the bad compliment of having been the maker of the Devil and of being at all times able to crush and annihilate him and his evil deeds and counsels, which nevertheless he does not do. But, as I have already remarked, all forms of polytheism, and this among the rest, are with difficulty reconcilable with a universe governed by general laws. Obedience to law is the note of a settled government, and not of a conflict always going on. When powers are at war with one another for the rule of the world, the boundary between them is not fixed but constantly fluctuating. This may seem to be the case on our planet as between the powers of good and evil when we look only at the results; but when we consider the inner springs, we find that both the good and the evil take place in the common course of nature, by virtue of the same general laws originally impressed—the same machinery turning out now good, now evil things, and oftener still, the two combined. The division of power is only apparently variable, but really so regular that, were we speaking of human potentates, we should declare without hesitation that the share of each must have been fixed by previous consent. Upon that supposition indeed, the result of the combination of antagonist forces might be much the same as on that of a single creator with divided purposes.

But when we come to consider, not what hypothesis may be conceived, and possibly reconciled with known facts, but what supposition is pointed to by the evidences of natural religion; the case is different. The indications of design point strongly in one direction, the preservation of the creatures in whose structure the indications are found. Along with the preserving agencies there are destroying agencies, which we might be tempted to ascribe to the will of a different Creator: but there are rarely appearances of the recondite contrivance of means of destruction, except when the destruction of one creature is the means of preservation to others. Nor can it be supposed that the preserving agencies are wielded by one Being, the destroying agencies by another. The destroying agencies are a necessary part of the preserving agencies: the chemical compositions by which life is carried on could not take place without a parallel series of decompositions. The great agent of decay in both organic and inorganic substances is oxidation, and it is only by oxidation that life is continued for even the length of a minute. The imperfections in the attainment of the purposes which the appearances indicate, have not the air of having been designed. They are like the unintended results of accidents insufficiently guarded against, or of a little excess or deficiency in the quantity of some of the agencies by which the good purpose is carried on, or else they are consequences of the wearing out of a machinery

---

[3] Zoroastrianism, an ancient Persian religion held that there is a constant struggle between the good spirit of the universe, Ormuzd (or Ormadz), and an evil spirit, Ahriman.—E.D.K.

not made to last forever: they point either to shortcomings in the workmanship as regards its intended purpose, or to external forces not under the control of the workman, but which forces bear no mark of being wielded and aimed by any other and rival intelligence.

. *IV* .

We may conclude, then, that there is no ground in natural theology for attributing intelligence or personality to the obstacles which partially thwart what seem the purposes of the Creator. The limitation of his power more probably results either from the qualities of the material—the substances and forces of which the universe is composed not admitting of any arrangements by which his purposes could be more completely fulfilled—or else, the purposes might have been more fully attained, but the Creator did not know how to do it; creative skill, wonderful as it is, was not sufficiently perfect to accomplish his purposes more thoroughly.

∘ ∘ ∘ *20*

Religion versus the Religious
John Dewey

· *I* ·

NEVER BEFORE IN history has mankind been so much of two minds, so divided into two camps, as it is today. Religions have traditionally been allied with ideas of the supernatural, and often have been based upon explicit beliefs about it. Today there are many who hold that nothing worthy of being called religious is possible apart from the supernatural. Those who hold this belief differ in many respects. They range from those who accept the dogmas and sacraments of the Greek and Roman Catholic church as the only sure means of access to the supernatural to the theist or mild deist. Between them are the many Protestant denominations who think the Scriptures, aided by a pure conscience, are adequate avenues to supernatural truth and power. But they agree in one point: the necessity for a Supernatural Being and for an immortality that is beyond the power of nature.

The opposed group consists of those who think the advance of culture and science has completely discredited the supernatural and with it all religions that were allied with belief in it. But they go beyond this point. The extremists in this group believe that with elimination of the supernatural not only must historic religions be dismissed but with them everything of a religious nature. When historical knowledge has discredited the claims made for the supernatural character of the persons said to have founded historic religions; when the supernatural inspiration attributed to literatures held sacred has been riddled, and when anthropological and psychological knowledge has disclosed the all-too-human source from which religious beliefs and practices have sprung, everything religious must, they say, also go.

There is one idea held in common by these two opposite groups: identification of the religious with the supernatural. The question I shall raise in these chapters concerns the ground for and the consequences of this identification: its reasons and its value. In the discussion I shall develop another conception of the nature of the religious phase of experience, one that separates it from the supernatural and the things that have grown up about it. I shall try to show that these derivations are encumbrances and that what is genuinely religious will undergo an emancipation when it is relieved from them; that then, for the first time, the religious aspect of experience will be free to develop freely on its own account.

This view is exposed to attack from both the other camps. It goes contrary to traditional religions, including those that have the greatest hold upon the religiously minded today. The view announced will seem to them to cut the vital nerve of the religious element itself in taking away the basis upon which traditional religions and institutions have been founded. From the other side, the position I am taking seems like a timid halfway position, a concession and compromise unworthy of thought that is thoroughgoing. It is regarded as a view entertained from mere tendermindedness, as an emotional hangover from childhood indoctrination, or even as a manifestation of a desire to avoid disapproval and curry favor.

· II ·

The heart of my point, as far as I shall develop it in this first section, is that there is a difference between religion, *a* religion, and the religious; between anything that may be denoted by a noun substantive and the quality of experience that is designated by an adjective. It is not easy to find a definition of religion in the substantive sense that wins general acceptance. However, in the *Oxford Dictionary* I find the following: "Recognition on the part of man of some unseen higher power as having control of his destiny and as being entitled to obedience, reverence and worship."

A.   This particular definition is less explicit in assertion of the supernatural character of the higher unseen power than are others that might be cited. It is, however, surcharged with implications having their source in ideas connected with the belief in the supernatural, characteristic of historic religions. Let us suppose that one familiar with the history of religions, including those called primitive, compares the definition with the variety of known facts and by means of the comparison sets out to determine just what the definition means. I think he will be struck by three facts that reduce the terms of the definition to such a low common denominator that little meaning is left.

He will note that the "unseen powers" referred to have been conceived in a multitude of incompatible ways. Eliminating the differences, nothing is left beyond the bare reference to something unseen and powerful. This has been conceived as the vague and undefined Mana of the Melanesians; the Kami of primitive Shintoism; the fetish of the Africans; spirits, having some human properties, that pervade natural places and animate natural forces; the ultimate and impersonal principle of Buddhism; the unmoved mover of Greek thought; the gods and semidivine heroes of the Greek and Roman Pantheons; the personal and loving Providence of Christianity, omnipotent, and limited by a corresponding evil power; the arbitrary Will of Moslemism; the supreme legislator and judge of deism. And these are but a few of the outstanding varieties of ways in which the invisible power has been conceived.

There is no greater similarity in the ways in which obedience and reverence have been expressed. There has been worship of animals, of ghosts, of ancestors, phallic worship, as well as of a Being of dread power and of love and wisdom. Reverence has been expressed in the human sacrifices of the Peruvians and Aztecs; the sexual orgies of some Oriental religions; exorcisms and ablutions; the offering of the humble and contrite mind of the Hebrew prophet, the elaborate rituals of the Greek and Roman Churches. Not even sacrifice has been uniform; it is highly sublimated in Protestant denominations and in Moslemism. Where it has existed it has taken all kinds of forms and been directed to a great variety of powers and spirits. It has been used for expiation, for propitiation and for buying special favors. There is no conceivable purpose for which rites have not been employed.

Finally, there is no discernible unity in the moral motivations appealed to and utilized. They have been as far apart as fear of lasting torture, hope of enduring bliss in which sexual enjoyment has sometimes been a conspicuous element; mortification of the flesh and extreme asceticism; prostitution and chastity; wars to extirpate the unbeliever; persecution to convert or punish the unbeliever, and philanthropic zeal; servile acceptance of imposed dogma, along with brotherly love and aspiration for a reign of justice among men.

I have, of course, mentioned only a sparse number of the facts which fill volumes in any well-stocked library. It may be asked by those who do not like to look upon the darker side of the history of religions why the darker facts should be brought up. We all know that civilized man has a background of bestiality and superstition and that these elements are still with us. Indeed, have not some religions, including the most influential forms of Christianity, taught that the heart of man is totally corrupt? How could the course of religion in its entire sweep not be marked by practices that are shameful in their cruelty and lustfulness, and by beliefs that are degraded and intellectually incredible? What else than what we find could be expected, in the case of people having little knowledge and no secure method of knowing; with primitive institutions, and with so little control of natural forces that they lived in a constant state of fear?

I gladly admit that historic religions have been relative to the conditions of social culture in which peoples lived. Indeed, what I am concerned with is to press home the logic of this method of disposal of outgrown traits of past religions. Beliefs and practices in a religion that now prevails are by this logic relative to the present state of culture. If so much flexibility has obtained in the past regarding an unseen power, the way it affects human destiny, and the attitudes we are to take toward it, why should it be assumed that change in conception and action has now come to an end? The logic involved in getting rid of inconvenient aspects of past religions compels us to inquire how much in religions now accepted are survivals from outgrown cultures. It compels us to ask what conception of unseen powers and our relations to them would be consonant with the best achievements and aspirations of the present. It demands that in imagination we wipe the slate clean and start afresh by asking what would be the idea of the unseen, of the manner of its control over us and the ways in which reverence and obedience would be manifested, if whatever is basically religious in experience had the opportunity to express itself free from all historic encumbrances.

So we return to the elements of the definition that has been given. What boots it to accept, in defense of the universality of religion, a definition that applies equally to the most savage and degraded beliefs and practices that have related to unseen powers and to noble ideals of a religion having the greatest share of moral content? There are two points involved. One of them is that there is nothing left worth preserving in the notions of unseen powers, controlling human destiny to which obedience, reverence and worship are due, if we glide silently over the nature that has been attributed to the powers, the radically diverse ways in which they have been supposed to control human destiny, and in which submission and awe have been manifested. The other point is that when we begin to select, to choose, and say that some present ways of thinking about the unseen powers are better than others; that the reverence shown by a free and self-respecting human being is better than the servile obedience rendered to an arbitrary power by frightened men; that we should believe that control of human destiny is exercised by a wise and loving spirit rather than by madcap ghosts or sheer force—when I say, we begin to choose, we have entered upon a road that has not yet come to an end. We have reached a point that invites us to proceed farther.

For we are forced to acknowledge that concretely there is no such thing as religion in the singular. There is only a multitude of religions. "Religion" is a strictly collective term and the collection it stands for is not even of the kind illustrated in textbooks of logic. It has not the unity of a regiment or assembly but that of any miscellaneous aggregate. Attempts to prove the universality prove too much or too little. It is probable that religions have been universal in the sense that all the peoples we know anything about have had *a* religion. But the differences among them are so great and so shocking that any common element that can be extracted is meaningless. The idea that religion is universal proves too little in that the older apologists for Christianity seem to have been better advised than some modern ones in condemning every religion but one as an impostor, as at bottom some kind of demon worship or at any rate a superstitious figment. Choice among religions is imperative, and the necessity for choice leaves nothing of any force in the argument from universality. Moreover, when once we enter upon the road of choice, there is at once presented a possibility not yet generally realized.

B.   For the historic increase of the ethical and ideal content of religions suggests that the process of purification may be carried further. It indicates that further choice is imminent in which certain values and functions in experience may be selected. This possibility is what I had in mind in speaking of the difference between the religious and a religion. I am not proposing a religion, but rather the emancipation of elements and outlooks that may be called religious. For the moment we have a religion, whether that of the Sioux Indian or of Judaism or of Christianity, that moment the ideal factors in experience that may be called religious take on a load that is not inherent in them, a load of current beliefs and of institutional practices that are irrelevant to them.

I can illustrate what I mean by a common phenomenon in contemporary life. It is widely supposed that a person who does not accept any religion is thereby shown to be a non-religious person. Yet it is conceivable that the present depression in religion is closely connected with the fact that religions now prevent, because of their weight of historic encumbrances, the religious quality of experience from coming to consciousness and finding the expression that is appropriate to present conditions, intellectual and moral. I believe that such is the case. I believe that many persons are so repelled from what exists as a religion by its intellectual and moral implications, that they are not even aware of attitudes in themselves that if they came to fruition would be genuinely religious. I hope that this remark may help make clear what I mean by the distinction between "religion" as a noun substantive and "religious" as adjectival.

To be somewhat more explicit, a religion (and as I have just said there is no such thing as religion in general) always signifies a special body of beliefs and practices having some kind of institutional organization, loose or tight. In contrast, the adjective "religious" denotes nothing in the way of a specifiable entity, either institutional or as a system of beliefs. It does not denote anything to which one can specifically point as one can point to this and that historic religion or existing church. For it does not denote anything that can exist by itself or that can be organized into a particular and distinctive form of existence. It denotes attitudes that may be taken toward every object and every proposed end or ideal.

Before, however, I develop my suggestion that realization of the distinction just made would operate to emancipate the religious quality from encumbrances that now smother or limit it, I must refer to a position that in some respects is similar in words to the position I have taken, but that in fact is a whole world removed from it. I have several times used the phrase "religious elements of experience." Now at present there is much talk, especially in liberal circles, of religious experience as vouching for the authenticity of certain beliefs and the desirability of certain practices, such as particular forms of prayer and worship. It is even asserted that religious experience is the ultimate basis of religion itself. The gulf between this position and that which I have taken is what I am now concerned to point out.

Those who hold to the notion that there is a definite kind of experience which is itself religious, by that very fact make out of it something specific, as a kind of experience that is marked off from experience as aesthetic, scientific, moral, political; from experience as companionship and friendship. But "religious" as a quality of experience signifies something that may belong to all these experiences. It is the polar opposite of some type of experience that can exist by itself. The distinction comes out clearly when it is noted that the concept of this distinct kind of experience is used to validate a belief in some special kind of object and also to justify some special kind of practice.

For there are many religionists who are now dissatisfied with the older "proofs" of the existence of God, those that go by the name of ontological, cosmological and teleological. The cause of the dissatisfaction is perhaps not so much the arguments that Kant used to show the insufficiency of these alleged proofs, as it is the growing feeling that they are too formal to offer any support to religion in action. Anyway, the dissatisfaction exists. Moreover, these religionists are moved by the rise of the experimental method in other fields. What is more natural and proper, accordingly, than that they should affirm they are just as good empiricists as anybody else—indeed, as good as the scientists themselves? As the latter rely upon certain kinds of experience to prove the existence of certain kinds of objects, so the religionists rely upon a certain kind of experience to prove the existence of the object of religion, especially the supreme object, God.

The discussion may be made more definite by introducing, at this point, a particular illustration of this type of reasoning. A writer says: "I broke down from overwork and soon came to the verge of nervous prostration. One morning after a long and sleepless night . . . I resolved to stop drawing upon myself so continuously and begin drawing upon God. I determined to set apart a quiet time every day in which I could relate my life to its ultimate source, regain the consciousness that in God I live, move and have my being. That was thirty years ago. Since then I have had literally not one hour of darkness or despair."

This is an impressive record. I do not doubt its authenticity nor that of the experience related. It illustrates a religious aspect of experience. But it illustrates also the use of that quality to carry a superimposed load of a particular religion. For having been brought up in the Christian religion, its subject interprets it in the terms of the personal God characteristic of that religion. Taoists, Buddhists, Moslems, persons of no religion including those who reject all supernatural influence and power, have had experiences similar in their effect. Yet another author commenting upon the passage says: "The religious expert can be more sure that this God exists than he can of either the cosmological God of speculative surmise or the Christlike God involved in the validity of moral optimism," and goes on to add that such experiences "mean that God the savior, the power that gives victory over sin on certain conditions that man can fulfill, is an existent, accessible and scientifically knowable reality." It should be clear that this inference is sound only if the conditions, of whatever sort, that produce the effect are called "God." But most readers will take the inference to mean that the existence of a particular Being, of the type called "God" in the Christian religion, is proved by a method akin to that of experimental science.

In reality, the only thing that can be said to be "proved" is the existence of some complex of conditions that have operated to effect an adjustment in life, an orientation, that brings with it a sense of security and peace. The particular interpretation given to this complex of conditions is not inherent in the experience itself. It is derived from the culture with which a particular person has been imbued. A fatalist will give one name to it; a Christian Scientist another, and the one who rejects all supernatural being still another. The determining factor in the interpretation of the experience is the particular doctrinal apparatus into which a person has been inducted. The emotional deposit connected with prior teaching floods the whole situation. It may readily confer upon the experience such a peculiarly sacred preciousness that all inquiry into its causation is barred. The stable outcome is so invaluable that the cause to which it is referred is usually nothing but a reduplication of the thing that has occurred, plus some name that has acquired a deeply emotional quality.

The intent of this discussion is not to deny the genuineness of the result nor its importance in life. It is not, save incidentally, to point out the possibility of a purely naturalistic explanation of the event. My purpose is to indicate what happens when religious experience is already set aside as something *sui generis*.[1] The actual religious quality in the experience described is the *effect* produced, the better adjustment in life and its conditions, not the manner and cause of its production. The way in which the experience operated, its function, determines its religious value. If the reorientation actually occurs, it, and the sense of security and stability accompanying it, are forces on their own account. It takes place in different persons in a multitude of ways. It is sometimes brought about by devotion to a cause; sometimes by a passage of poetry that opens a new perspective; sometimes as was the case with Spinoza—deemed an atheist in his day—through philosophical reflection.

The difference between an experience having a religious force because of what it does in and to the processes of living and religious experience as a separate kind of thing gives me occasion to refer to a previous remark. If this function were rescued through emancipation from dependence upon specific types of beliefs and practices, from those elements that constitute a religion, many individuals would find that experiences having the force of bringing about a better, deeper and enduring adjustment in life are not so rare and infrequent as they are commonly supposed to be. They occur frequently in connection with many significant moments of living. The idea of invisible powers would take on the meaning of all the conditions of nature and human association that support and deepen the sense of values which carry one through periods of darkness and despair to such an extent that they lose their usual depressive character.

I do not suppose for many minds the dislocation of the religious from a religion is easy to effect. Tradition and custom, especially when emotionally charged, are a part of the habits that have become one with our very being. But the possibility of the transfer is demonstrated by its actuality. Let us then for the moment drop the term "religious," and ask what are the attitudes that lend deep and enduring support to the processes of living. I have, for example, used the words "adjustment" and "orientation." What do they signify?

---

[1] In a class by itself; unique.—E.D.K.

While the words "accommodation," "adaptation," and "adjustment" are frequently employed as synonyms, attitudes exist that are so different that for the sake of clear thought they should be discriminated. There are conditions we meet that cannot be changed. If they are particular and limited, we modify our own particular attitudes in accordance with them. Thus we accommodate ourselves to changes in weather, to alterations in income when we have no other recourse. When the external conditions are lasting we become inured, habituated, or, as the process is not often called, conditioned. The two main traits of this attitude, which I should like to call accommodation, are that it affects *particular* modes of conduct, not the entire self, and that the process is mainly *passive*. It may, however, become general and then it becomes fatalistic resignation or submission. There are other attitudes toward the environment that are also particular but that are more active. We re-act against conditions and endeavor to change them to meet our wants and demands. Plays in a foreign language are "adapted" to meet the needs of an American audience. A house is rebuilt to suit changed conditions of the household; the telephone is invented to serve the demand for speedy communication at a distance; dry soils are irrigated so that they may bear abundant crops. Instead of accommodating ourselves to conditions, we modify conditions so that they will be accommodated to our wants and purposes. This process may be called adaptation.

Now both of these processes are often called by the more general name of adjustment. But there are also changes in ourselves in relation to the world in which we live that are much more inclusive and deep-seated. They relate not to this and that want in relation to this and that condition of our surroundings, but pertain to our being in its entirety. Because of their scope, this modification of ourselves is enduring. It lasts through any amount of vicissitude of circumstances, internal and external. There is a composing and harmonizing of the various elements of our being such that, in spite of changes in the special conditions that surround us, these conditions are also arranged, settled, in relation to us. This attitude includes a note of submission. But it is voluntary, not externally imposed; and as voluntary it is something more than a mere Stoical resolution to endure unperturbed throughout the buffetings of fortune. It is more outgoing, more ready and glad, than the latter attitude, and it is more active than the former. And in calling it voluntary, it is not meant that it depends upon a particular resolve or volition. It is a change *of* will conceived as the organic plenitude of our being, rather than any special change *in* will.

It is the claim of religions that they effect this generic and enduring change in attitude. I should like to turn the statement around and say that whenever this change takes place there is a definitely religious attitude. It is not *a* religion that brings it about, but when it occurs, from whatever cause and by whatever means, there is a religious outlook and function. As I have said before, the doctrinal or intellectual apparatus and the institutional accretions that grow up are, in a strict sense, adventitious to the intrinsic quality of such experiences. For they are affairs of the traditions of the culture with which individuals are inoculated. Mr. Santayana[2] has connected the religious quality of experience with the imaginative, as that is expressed in poetry. "Religion and poetry," he says, "are identical in essence, and differ merely in the way in which they

---

[2] An early twentieth-century American philosopher.—E.D.K.

are attached to practical affairs. Poetry is called religion when it intervenes in life, and religion, when it merely supervenes upon life, is seen to be nothing but poetry." The difference between intervening *in* and supervening *upon* is as important as is the identity set forth. Imagination may play upon life or it may enter profoundly into it. As Mr. Santayana puts it, "poetry has a universal and a moral function," for "its highest power lies in its relevance to the ideals and purposes of life." Except as it intervenes, "all observation is observation of brute fact, all discipline is mere repression, until these facts digested and this discipline embodied in humane impulses become the starting point for a creative movement of the imagination, the firm basis for ideal constructions in society, religion, and art."

If I may make a comment upon this penetrating insight of Mr. Santayana, I would say that the difference between imagination that only supervenes and imagination that intervenes is the difference between one that completely interpenetrates all the elements of our being and one that is interwoven with only special and partial factors. There actually occurs extremely little observation of brute facts merely for the sake of the facts, just as there is little discipline that is repression and nothing but repression. Facts are usually observed with reference to some practical end and purpose, and that end is presented only imaginatively. The most repressive discipline has some end in view to which there is at least imputed an ideal quality; otherwise it is purely sadistic. But in such cases of observation and discipline imagination is limited and partial. It does not extend far; it does not permeate deeply and widely.

The connection between imagination and the harmonizing of the self is closer than is usually thought. The idea of a whole, whether of the whole personal being or of the world, is an imaginative, not a literal, idea. The limited world of our observation and reflection becomes the Universe only through imaginative extension. It cannot be apprehended in knowledge nor realized in reflection. Neither observation, thought, nor practical activity can attain that complete unification of the self which is called a whole. The *whole* self is an ideal, an imaginative projection. Hence the idea of a thoroughgoing and deep-seated harmonizing of the self with the Universe (as a name for the totality of conditions with which the self is connected) operates only through imagination—which is one reason why this composing of the self is not voluntary in the sense of an act of special volition or resolution. An "adjustment" possesses the will rather than is its express product. Religionists have been right in thinking of it as an influx from sources beyond conscious deliberation and purpose—a fact that helps explain, psychologically, why it has so generally been attributed to a supernatural source and that, perhaps, throws some light upon the reference of it by William James to unconscious factors. And it is pertinent to note that the unification of the self throughout the ceaseless flux of what it does, suffers, and achieves, cannot be attained in terms of itself. The self is always directed toward something beyond itself and so its own unification depends upon the idea of the integration of the shifting scenes of the world into the imaginative totality we call the Universe.

The intimate connection of imagination with ideal elements in experience is generally recognized. Such is not the case with respect to its connection with faith. The latter has been regarded as a substitute for knowledge, for sight. It is defined, in the Christian religion, as *evidence* of things not seen. The implication is that faith is a kind of anticipatory vision of things that are now invisible because of the limitations of our finite and erring nature. Because it is a substitute for knowledge, its material and object are intellectual in quality. As John Locke summed up the matter, faith is "assent to a proposition . . . on the credit of its proposer." Religious faith is then given to a body of propositions as true on the credit of their supernatural author, reason coming in to demonstrate the reasonableness of giving such credit. Of necessity there results the development of theologies, or bodies of systematic propositions, to make explicit in organized form the content of the propositions to which belief is attached and assent given. Given the point of view, those who hold that religion necessarily implies a theology are correct.

But belief or faith has also a moral and practical import. Even devils, according to the older theologians, believe—and tremble. A distinction was made, therefore, between "speculative" or intellectual belief and an act called "justifying" faith. Apart from any theological context, there is a difference between belief that is a conviction that some end should be supreme over conduct, and belief that some object or being exists as a truth for the intellect. Conviction in the moral sense signifies being conquered, vanquished, in our active nature by an ideal end; it signifies acknowledgment of its rightful claim over our desires and purposes. Such acknowledgment is practical, not primarily intellectual. It goes beyond evidence that can be presented to *any* possible observer. Reflection, often long and arduous, may be involved in arriving at the conviction, but the import of thought is not exhausted in discovery of evidence that can justify intellectual assent. The authority of an ideal over choice and conduct is the authority of an ideal, not of a fact, of a truth guaranteed to intellect, not of the status of one who propounds the truth.

Such moral faith is not easy. It was questioned of old whether the Son of Man should find faith on the earth in his coming. Moral faith has been bolstered by all sorts of arguments intended to prove that its object is not ideal and that its claim upon us is not primarily moral or practical, since the ideal in question is already embedded in the existent frame of things. It is argued that the ideal is already the final reality at the heart of things that exist, and that only our senses or the corruption of our natures prevent us from apprehending its prior existential being. Starting, say, from such an idea as that justice is more than a moral ideal because it is embedded in the very make-up of the actually existent world, men have gone on to build up vast intellectual schemes, philosophies, and theologies, to prove that ideals are real not as ideals but as antecedently existing actualities. They have failed to see that in converting moral realities into matters of intellectual assent they have evinced lack of *moral* faith. Faith that something should be in existence as far as lies in our power is changed into the intellectual belief that it is already in existence. When physical existence does not bear out the assertion, the physical is subtly changed into the metaphysical. In this way, moral faith has been inextricably tied up with intellectual beliefs about the supernatural.

The tendency to convert ends of moral faith and action into articles of an intellectual creed has been furthered by a tendency of which psychologists are well aware. What we ardently desire to have thus and so, we tend to believe is already so. Desire has a powerful influence upon intellectual beliefs. Moreover, when conditions are adverse to realization of the objects of our desire—and in the case of significant ideals they are extremely adverse—it is an easy way out to assume that after all they are already embodied in the ultimate structure of what is, and the appearances to the contrary are *merely* appearances. Imagination then merely supervenes and is freed from the responsibility for intervening. Weak natures take to reverie as a refuge as strong ones do to fanaticism. Those who dissent are mourned over by the first class and converted through the use of force by the second.

What has been said does not imply that all moral faith in ideal ends is by virtue of that fact religious in quality. The religious is "morality touched by emotion" only when the ends of moral conviction arouse emotions that are not only intense but are actuated and supported by ends so inclusive that they unify the self. The inclusiveness of the end in relation to both self and the "universe" to which an inclusive self is related is indispensable. According to the best authorities, "religion" comes from a root that means being bound or tied. Originally, it meant being bound by vows to a particular way of life—as *les religieux* were monks and nuns who had assumed certain vows. The religious attitude signifies something that is bound through imagination to a *general* attitude. This comprehensive attitude, moreover, is much broader than anything indicated by "moral" in its usual sense. The quality of attitude is displayed in art, science and good citizenship.

If we apply the conception set forth to the terms of the definition earlier quoted, these terms take on a new significance. An unseen power controlling our destiny becomes the power of an ideal. All possibilities, as possibilities, are ideal in character. The artist, scientist, citizen, parent, as far as they are actuated by the spirit of their callings, are controlled by the unseen. For all endeavor for the better is moved by faith in what is possible, not by adherence to the actual. Nor does this faith depend for its moving power upon intellectual assurance or belief that the things worked for must surely prevail and come into embodied existence. For the authority of the object to determine our attitude and conduct, the right that is given it to claim our allegiance and devotion is based on the intrinsic nature of the ideal. The outcome, given our best endeavor, is not with us. The inherent vice of all intellectual schemes of idealism is that they convert the idealism of action into a system of beliefs about antecedent reality. The character assigned this reality is so different from that which observation and reflection lead to and support that these schemes inevitably glide into alliance with the supernatural.

All religions, marked by elevated ideal quality, have dwelt upon the power of religion to introduce perspective into the piecemeal and shifting episodes of existence. Here too we need to reverse the ordinary statement and say that whatever introduces genuine perspective is religious, not that religion is something that introduces it. There can be no doubt (referring to the second element of the definition) of our dependence upon forces beyond our control. Primitive man was so impotent in the face of these forces that, especially in an unfavorable natural environment, fear became a dominant attitude, and, as the old saying goes, fear created the gods.

With increase of mechanisms of control, the element of fear has, relatively speaking, subsided. Some optimistic souls have even concluded that the forces about us are on the whole essentially benign. But every crisis, whether of the individual or of the community, reminds man of the precarious and partial nature of the control he exercises. When man, individually and collectively, has done his uttermost, conditions that at different times and places have given rise to the ideas of Fate and Fortune, of Chance and Providence, remain. It is the part of manliness to insist upon the capacity of mankind to strive to direct natural and social forces to humane ends. But unqualified absolutistic statements about the omnipotence of such endeavors reflect egoism rather than intelligent courage.

The fact that human destiny is so interwoven with forces beyond human control renders it unnecessary to suppose that dependence and the humility that accompanies it have to find the particular channel that is prescribed by traditional doctrines. What is especially significant is rather the form which the sense of dependence takes. Fear never gave stable perspective in the life of anyone. It is dispersive and withdrawing. Most religions have in fact added rites of communion to those of expiation and propitiation. For our dependence is manifested in those relations to the environment that support our undertakings and aspirations as much as it is in the defeats inflicted upon us. The essentially unreligious attitude is that which attributes human achievement and purpose to man in isolation from the world of physical nature and his fellows. Our successes are dependent upon the cooperation of nature. The sense of the dignity of human nature is as religious as is the sense of awe and reverence when it rests upon a sense of human nature as a cooperating part of a larger whole. Natural piety is not of necessity either a fatalistic acquiescence in natural happenings or a romantic idealization of the world. It may rest upon a just sense of nature as the whole of which we are parts, while it also recognizes that we are parts that are marked by intelligence and purpose, having the capacity to strive by their aid to bring conditions into greater consonance with what is humanly desirable. Such piety is an inherent constituent of a just perspective in life.

Understanding and knowledge also enter into a perspective that is religious in quality. Faith in the continued disclosing of truth through directed cooperative human endeavor is more religious in quality than is any faith in a complete revelation. It is of course now usual to hold that revelation is not completed in the sense of being ended. But religions hold that the essential framework is settled in its significant moral features at least, and that new elements that are offered must be judged by conformity to this framework. Some fixed doctrinal apparatus is necessary for *a* religion. But faith in the possibilities of continued and rigorous inquiry does not limit access to truth to any channel or scheme of things. It does not first say that truth is universal and then add there is but one road to it. It does not depend for assurance upon subjection to any dogma or item of doctrine. It trusts that the natural interactions between man and his environment will breed more intelligence and generate more knowledge provided the scientific methods that define intelligence in operation are pushed further into the mysteries of the world, being themselves promoted and improved in the operation. There is such a thing as faith in intelligence becoming religious in quality—a fact that perhaps explains the efforts of some religionists to disparage the possibilities of intelligence as a force. They properly feel such faith to be a dangerous rival.

Lives that are consciously inspired by loyalty to such ideals as have been mentioned are still comparatively infrequent to the extent of that comprehensiveness and intensity which arouse an ardor religious in function. But before we infer the incompetency of such ideals and of the actions they inspire, we should at least ask ourselves how much of the existing situation is due to the fact that the religious factors of experience have been drafted into supernatural channels and thereby loaded with irrelevant encumbrances. A body of beliefs and practices that are apart from the common and natural relations of mankind must, in the degree in which it is influential, weaken and sap the force of the possibilities inherent in such relations. Here lies one aspect of the emancipation of the religious from religion.

Any activity pursued in behalf of an ideal end against obstacles and in spite of threats of personal loss because of conviction of its general and enduring value is religious in quality. Many a person, inquirer, artist, philanthropist, citizen, men and women in the humblest walks of life, have achieved, without presumption and without display, such unification of themselves and of their relations to the conditions of existence. It remains to extend their spirit and inspiration to ever wider numbers. If I have said anything about religions and religion that seems harsh, I have said those things because of a firm belief that the claim on the part of religions to possess a monopoly of ideals and of the supernatural means by which alone, it is alleged, they can be furthered, stands in the way of the realization of distinctively religious value inherent in natural experience. For that reason, if for no other, I should be sorry if any were misled by the frequency with which I have employed the adjective "religious" to conceive of what I have said as a disguised apology for what have passed as religions. The opposition between religious values as I conceive them and religions is not to be bridged. Just because the release of these values is so important, their identification with the creeds and cults of religions must be dissolved.

∘ ∘ ∘ *21*

Philosophical Concepts
of Atheism

Ernest Nagel

· *I* ·

I MUST BEGIN by stating what sense I am attaching to the word "atheism," and how I am construing the theme of this paper. I shall understand by "atheism" a critique and a denial of the major claims of all varieties of theism.And by theism I shall mean the view which holds, as one writer has expressed it, "that the heavens and the earth and all that they contain owe their existence and continuance in existence to the wisdom and will of a supreme, self-consistent, omnipotent, omniscient, righteous, and benevolent being, who is distinct from, and independent of, what he has created." Several things immediately follow from these definitions.

In the first place, atheism is not necessarily an irreligious concept, for theism is just one among many views concerning the nature and origin of the world. The denial of theism is logically compatible with a religious outlook upon life, and is in fact characteristic of the great historical religions. . . . Early Buddhism is a religion which does not subscribe to any doctrine about a god; and there are pantheistic religions and philosophies which, because they deny that God is a being separate from and independent of the world, are not theistic in the sense of the word explained above.

The second point to note is that atheism is not to be identified with sheer unbelief, or with disbelief in some particular creed of a religious group. Thus, a child who has received no religious instruction and has never heard about God, is not an atheist—for he is not denying any theistic claims.Similarly, an adult who has withdrawn from the faith of his fathers without reflection or because of frank indifference to any theological issue is also not an atheist—for such an adult is not challenging theism and is not professing any views on the subject. Moreover, thought the term "atheist" has been used historically as an abusive label for those who do not happen to subscribe to some regnant orthodoxy (for example, the ancient Romans called the early Christians atheists, because the latter denied the Roman divinities), or for those who engage in conduct regarded as immoral, it is not in this sense that I am discussing atheism.

One final word of preliminary explanation. I propose to examine some *philosophic* concepts of atheism, and I am not interested in the slightest in the many considerations atheists have advanced against the evidences for some particular religious and theological doctrine—for example, against the truth of the Christian story. What I mean by "philosophical" in the present context is that the views I shall consider are directed against any form of theism, and have their origin and basis in a logical analysis of the theistic position, and in a comprehensive account of the world believed to be wholly intelligible without the adoption of a theistic hypothesis.

Theism as I conceive it is a theological proposition, not a statement of a position that belongs primarily to religion. On my view, religion as a historical and social phenomenon is primarily an institutionalized *cultus* or practice, which possesses identifiable social functions and which expresses certain attitudes men take toward their world. Although it is doubtful whether men ever engage in religious practices or assume religious attitudes without some more or less explicit interpretation of their ritual or some rationale for their attitude, it is still the case that it is possible to distinguish religion as a social and personal phenomenon from the theological doctrines which may be developed as justifications for religious practices. Indeed, in some of the great religions of the world the profession of a creed plays a relatively minor role. In short, religion is a form of social communion, a participation in certain kinds of ritual (whether it be a dance, worship, prayer, or the like), and a form of experience (sometimes, though not invariably, directed to a personal confrontation with divine and holy things). Theology is an articulated and, at its best, a rational attempt at understanding these feelings and practices in the light of their relation to other parts of human experience and in terms of some hypothesis concerning the nature of things entire.

· *II* ·

As I see it, atheistic philosophies fall into two major groups: (1) those which hold that the theistic doctrine is meaningful, but reject it either on the ground that (a) the positive evidence for it is insufficient or (b) the negative evidence is quite overwhelming; and (2) those who hold that the theistic thesis is not even meaningful, and reject it (a) as just nonsense or (b) as literally meaningless, but interpreting it as a symbolic rendering of human ideals, thus reading the theistic thesis in a sense that most believers in theism would disavow. It will not be possible in the limited space at my disposal to discuss the second category of atheistic critiques; and in any event, most of the traditional atheistic critiques of theism belong to the first group.

But before turning to the philosophical examination of the major classical arguments for theism, it is well to note that such philosophical critiques do not quite convey the passion with which atheists have often carried on their analyses of theistic views. For historically, atheism has been, and indeed continues to be, a form of social and political protest, directed as much against institutionalized religion as against theistic doctrine. Atheism has been, in effect, a moral revulsion against the undoubted abuses of the secular power exercised by religious leaders and religious institutions.

Religious authorities have opposed the correction of glaring injustices, and encouraged politically and socially reactionary policies. Religious institutions have been havens of obscurantist thought and centers for the dissemination of intolerance. Religious creeds have been used to set limits to free inquiry, to perpetuate inhumane treatment of the ill and the underprivileged, and to support moral doctrines insensitive to human suffering.

These indictments may not tell the whole story about the historical significance of religion; but they are at least an important part of the story. The refutation of theism has thus seemed to many an indispensable step not only toward liberating men's minds from supersition but also toward achieving a more equitable reordering of society. And no account of even the more philosophical aspects of atheistic thought is adequate which does not give proper recognition to the powerful social motives that actuate many atheistic arguments.

But however this may be, I want now to discuss three classical arguments for the existence of God, arguments which have constituted at least a partial basis for theistic commitments. As long as theism is defended simply as dogma, asserted as a matter of direct revelation or as the deliverance of authority, belief in the dogma is impregnable to rational argument. In fact, however, reasons are frequently advanced in support of the theistic creed, and these reasons have been the subject of acute philosophical critiques.

· *III* ·

One of the oldest intellectual defenses of theism is the cosmological argument, also known as the argument from a first cause. Briefly put, the argument runs as follows. Every event must have a cause. Hence an event A must have as cause some event B, which in turn must have a cause C, and so on. But if there is no end to this backward progression of causes, the progression will be infinite; and in the opinion of those who use this argument, an infinite series of actual events is unintelligible and absurd. Hence there must be a first cause, and this first cause is God, the initiator of all change in the universe.

The argument is an ancient one . . . and it has impressed many generations of exceptionally keen minds. The argument is nonetheless a weak reed on which to rest the theistic thesis. Let us waive any question concerning the validity of the principle that every event has a cause, for though the question is important its discussion would lead us far afield. However, if the principle is assumed, it is surely incongruous to postulate a first cause as a way of escaping from the coils of an infinite series. For if everything must have a cause, why does not God require one for His own existence? The standard answer is that He does not need any, because He is self-caused. But if God can be self-caused, why cannot the world be self-caused? Why do we require a God transcending the world to bring the world into existence and to initiate changes in it? On the other hand, the supposed inconceivability and absurdity of an infinite series of regressive causes will be admitted by no one who has competent familiarity with the modern mathematical analysis of infinity. The cosmological argument does not stand up under scrutiny.

· *IV* ·

The second "proof" of God's existence is usually called the ontological argument. It too has a long history going back to early Christian days, though it acquired great prominence only in medieval times. The argument can be stated in several ways, one of which is the following. Since God is conceived to be omnipotent, he is a perfect being. A perfect being is defined as one whose essence or nature lacks no attributes (or properties) whatsoever, one whose nature is complete in every respect. But it is evident that we have an idea of a perfect being, for we have just defined the idea; and since this is so, the argument continues, God who is the perfect being must exist. Why must he? Because his existence follows from his defined nature. For if God lacked the attribute of existence, he would be lacking at least one attribute, and would therefore not be perfect. To sum up, since we have an idea of God as a perfect being, God must exist.

There are several ways of approaching this argument, but I shall consider only one. The argument was exploded by the 18th century philosopher Immanuel Kant. The substance of Kant's criticism is that it is just a confusion to say that existence is an attribute, and that though the *word* "existence" may occur as the grammatical predicate in a sentence, no attribute is being predicated of a thing when we say that the thing exists or has existence. Thus, to use Kant's example, when we think of $100 we are thinking of the nature of this sum of money; but the nature of $100 remains the same whether we have $100 in our pockets or not. Accordingly, we are confounding grammar with logic if we suppose that some characteristic is being attributed to the nature of $100 when we say that a $100 bill exists in someone's pocket.

To make the point clearer, consider another example. When we say that a lion has a tawny color, we are predicating a certain attribute of the animal, and similarly when we say that the lion is fierce or is hungry. But when we say the lion exists, all that we are saying is that something is (or has the nature of) a lion; we are not specifying an attribute which belongs to the nature of anything that is a lion.In short, the word "existence" does not signify any attribute, and in consequence no attribute that belongs to the nature of anything. Accordingly, it does not follow from the assumption that we have an idea of a perfect being that such a being exists. For the idea of a perfect being does not involve the attribute of existence as a constituent of that idea, since there is no such attribute. The ontological argument thus has a serious leak, and it can hold no water.

. V .

The two arguments discussed thus far are purely dialectical, and attempt to establish God's existence without any appeal to empirical data. The next argument, called the argument from design, is different in character, for it is based on what purports to be empirical evidence. I wish to examine two forms of this argument.

One variant of it calls attention to the remarkable way in which different things and processes in the world are integrated with each other, and concludes that this mutual "fitness" of things can be explained only by the assumption of a divine architect who planned the world and everything in it. For example, living organisms can maintain themselves in a variety of environments, and do so in virtue of their delicate mechanisms which adapt the organisms to all sorts of environmental changes. There is thus an intricate pattern of means and ends throughout the animate world. But the existence of this pattern is unintelligible, so the argument runs, except on the hypothesis that the pattern has been deliberately instituted by a Supreme Designer. If we find a watch in some deserted spot, we do not think it came into existence by chance, and we do not hesitate to conclude that an intelligent creature designed and made it. But the world and all its contents exhibit mechanisms and mutual adjustments that are far more complicated and subtle than are those of a watch. Must we not therefore conclude that these things too have a Creator?

The conclusion of this argument is based on an inference from analogy: The watch and the world are alike in possessing a congruence of parts and an adjustment of means to ends; the watch has a watch-maker; hence the world has a world-maker. But is the analogy a good one? Let us once more waive some important issues, in particular the issue of whether the universe is the unified system such as the watch admittedly is. And let us concentrate on the question of what is the ground for our assurance that watches do not come into existence except through the operations of intelligent manufacturers.

nature. It has exerted an enormous influence on subsequent theological speculation. In barest outline, the argument is as follows. According to Kant, we are subject not only to physical laws like the rest of nature, but also to moral ones. These moral laws are categorical imperatives, which we must heed not because of their utilitarian consequences but simply because as autonomous moral agents it is our duty to accept them as binding. However, Kant was keenly aware that though virtue may be its reward, the virtuous man (that is, the man who acts out of a sense of duty and in conformity with the moral law) does not always receive his just desserts in this world; nor did he shut his eyes to the fact that evil men frequently enjoy the best things this world has to offer. In short, virtue does not always reap happiness. Nevertheless, the highest good is the realization of happiness commensurate with one's virtue; and Kant believed that it is a practical postulate of the moral life to promote this good. But what can guarantee that the highest good is realizable? Such a guarantee can be found only in God, who must therefore exist if the highest good is not to be a fatuous ideal. The existence of an omnipotent, omniscient, and omnibenevolent God is thus postulated as a necessary condition for the possibility of a moral life.

Despite the prestige this argument has acquired, it is difficult to grant it any force. It is enough to postulate God's existence. But as Bertrand Russell observed in another connection, postulation has all advantages of theft over honest toil. No postulation carries with it any assurance that what is postulated is actually the case. And though we may postulate God's existence as a means to guaranteeing the possibility of realizing happiness together with virtue, the postulation establishes neither the actual realizability of this ideal nor the fact of his existence. Moreover, the argument is not made more cogent when we recognize that it is based squarely on the highly dubious conception that considerations of utility and human happiness must not enter into the determination of what is morally obligatory. Having built his moral theory on a radical separation of means from ends, Kant was driven to the desperate postulation of God's existence in order to relate them again. The argument is thus at best a *tour de force*, contrived to remedy a fatal flaw in Kant's initial moral assumptions. It carries no conviction to anyone who does not commit Kant's initial blunder.

One further type of argument, pervasive in much Protestant theological literature, deserves brief mention. Arguments of this type take their point of departure from the psychology of religious and mystical experience. Those who have undergone such experiences often report that during the experience they feel themselves to be in the presence of the divine and holy, that they lose their sense of self-identity and become merged with some fundamental reality, or that they enjoy a feeling of total dependence upon some ultimate power. The overwhelming sense of transcending one's finitude, which characterizes such vivid periods of life, and of coalescing with some ultimate source of all existence, is then taken to be compelling evidence for the existence of a supreme being. In a variant form of this argument, other theologians have identified God as the object which satisfies the commonly experienced need for integrating one's scattered and conflicting impulses into a coherent unity, or as the subject which is of ultimate concern to us. In short, a proof of God's existence is found in the occurrence of certain distinctive experiences.

It would be flying in the face of well-attested facts were one to deny that such experiences frequently occur. But do these facts constitute evidence for the conclusion based on them? Does the fact, for example, that an individual experiences a profound

The answer is plain. We have never run across a watch which has not been deliberately made by someone. But the situation is nothing like this in the case of the innumerable animate and inanimate systems with which we are familiar. Even in the case of living organisms, though they are generated by their parent organisms, the parents do not "make" their progeny in the same sense in which watchmakers make watches. And once this point is clear, the inference from the existence of living organisms to the existence of a supreme designer no longer appears credible.

Moreover, the argument loses all its force if the facts which the hypothesis of a divine designer is supposed to explain can be understood on the basis of a better supported assumption. And indeed, such an alternative explanation is one of the achievements of Darwinian biology. For Darwin showed that one can account for the variety of biological species, as well as for their adaptations to their environments, without invoking a divine creator and acts of special creation. The Darwinian theory explains the diversity of biological species in terms of chance variations in the structure of organisms, and of a mechanism of selection which retains those variant forms that possess some advantages for survival. The evidence for these assumptions is considerable; and developments subsequent to Darwin have only strengthened the case for a thoroughly naturalistic explanation of the facts of biological adaptation. In any event, this version of the argument from design has nothing to recommend it.

A second form of this argument has been recently revived in the speculations of some modern physicists. No one who is familiar with the facts can fail to be impressed by the success with which the use of mathematical methods has enabled us to obtain intellectual mastery of many parts of nature. But some thinkers have therefore concluded that since the book of nature is ostensibly written in mathematical language, nature must be the creation of a divine mathematician. However, the argument is most dubious. For it rests, among other things, on the assumption that mathematical tools can be successfully used only if the events of nature exhibit some *special* kind of order, and on the further assumption that if the structure of things were different from what it is, mathematical language would be inadequate for describing such structure. But it can be shown that no matter what the world were like—even if it impressed us as being utterly chaotic—it would still possess some order, and would in principle be amenable to a mathematical description. In point of fact, it makes no sense to say that there is absolutely *no* pattern in any conceivable subject matter. To be sure, there are differences in complexities of structure, and if the patterns of events were sufficiently complex we might not be able to unravel them. But however that may be, the success of mathematical physics in giving us some understanding of the world around us does not yield the conclusion that only a mathematician could have devised the patters of order we have discovered in nature.

· VI ·

The inconclusiveness of the three classical arguments for the existence of God was already made evident by Kant, in a manner substantially not different from the above discussion. There are, however, other types of arguments for theism that have been influential in the history of thought, two of which I wish to consider, even if only briefly.

Indeed, though Kant destroyed the classical intellectual foundations for theism, he himself invented a fresh argument for it. Kant's attempted proof is not intended to be a purely theoretical demonstration, and is based on the supposed facts of our moral sense of direct contact with an alleged transcendent ground of all reality, constitute competent evidence for the claim that there is such a ground and that it is the immediate cause of the experience? If well-established canons for evaluating evidence are accepted, the answer is surely negative. No one will dispute that many men do have vivid experiences in which such things as ghosts or pink elephants appear before them; but only the hopelessly credulous will without further ado count such experiences as establishing the existence of ghosts and pink elephants. To establish the existence of such things, evidence is required that is obtained under controlled conditions and that can be confirmed by independent inquirers. Again, though a man's report that he is suffering pain may be taken at face value, one cannot take at face value the claim, were he to make it, that it is the food he ate which is the cause (or a contributory cause) of his felt pain—not even if the man were to report a vivid feeling of abdominal disturbance. And similarly, an overwhelming feeling of being in the presence of the Divine is evidence enough for admitting the genuineness of such feeling; it is no evidence for the claim that a supreme being with a substantial existence independent of the experience is the cause of the experience.

· *VII* ·

Thus far the discussion has been concerned with noting inadequacies in various arguments widely used to support theism. However, much atheistic criticism is also directed toward exposing incoherencies in the very thesis of theism. I want therefore to consider this aspect of the atheistic critique, though I will restrict myself to the central difficulty in the theistic position, which arises from the simultaneous attribution of omnipotence, omniscience, and omnibenevolence to the Deity. The difficulty is that of reconciling these attributes with the occurrence of evil in the world. Accordingly, the question to which I now turn is whether, despite the existence of evil, it is possible to construct a theodicy which will justify the ways of an infinitely powerful and just God to man.

Two main types of solutions have been proposed for this problem. One way that is frequently used is to maintain that what is commonly called evil is only an illusion, or at worst only the "privation" or absence of good. Accordingly, evil is not "really real," it is only the "negative" side of God's beneficence, it is only the product of our limited intelligence, which fails to plumb the true character of God's creative bounty. A sufficient comment on this proposed solution is that facts are not altered or abolished by rebaptizing them. Evil may indeed be only an appearance and not genuine. But this does not eliminate from the realm of appearance the tragedies, the sufferings, and the iniquities which men so frequently endure. And it raises once more, though on another level, the problem of reconciling the fact that there is evil in the realm of appearance with God's alleged omnibenevolence. In any event, it is small comfort to anyone suffering a cruel misfortune for which he is in no way responsible to be told that what he is undergoing is only the absence of good. It is a gratuitous insult to mankind, a symptom of insensitivity and indifference to human suffering, to be assured that all the miseries and agonies men experience are only illusory.

Another gambit often played in attempting to justify the ways of God to man is to argue that the things called evil are evil only because they are viewed in isolation; they are not evil when viewed in proper perspective and in relation to the rest of creation. Thus, if one attends to but a single instrument in an orchestra, the sounds issuing from it may indeed be harsh and discordant. But if one is placed at a proper distance from the whole orchestra, the sounds of that single instrument will mingle with the sounds issuing from the other players to produce a marvellous bit of symphonic music. Analogously, experiences we call painful undoubtedly occur and are real enough. But the pain is judged to be an evil only because it is experienced in a limited perspective—the pain is there for the sake of a more inclusive good, whose reality eludes us because our intelligences are too weak to apprehend things in their entirety.

It is an appropriate retort to this argument that of course we judge things to be evil in a human perspective, but that since we are not God this is the only proper perspective in which to judge them. It may indeed be the case that what is evil for us is not evil for some other part of creation. However, we are not this other part of creation, and it is irrelevant to argue that were we something other than what we are, our evaluations of what is good and bad would be different. Moreover, the worthlessness of the argument becomes even more evident if we remind ourselves that it is unsupported speculation to suppose that whatever is evil in a finite perspective is good from the purported perspective of the totality of things. For the argument can be turned around: What we judge to be a good is a good only because it is viewed in isolation; when it is viewed in proper perspective, and in relation to the entire scheme of things, it is an evil. This is in fact a standard form of the argument for a universal pessimism. Is it any worse than the similar argument for a universal optimism? The very raising of this question is a *reductio ad absurdum*[1] of the proposed solution to the ancient problem of evil.

I do not believe it is possible to reconcile the alleged omnipotence and omnibenevolence of God with the unvarnished facts of human existence. In point of fact, many theologians have concurred in this conclusion; for in order to escape from the difficulty which the traditional attributes of God present, they have assumed that God is not all-powerful, and that there are limits as to what He can do in his efforts to establish a righteous order in the universe. But whether such a modified theology is better off is doubtful; and in any event, the question still remains whether the facts of human life support the claim that an omnibenevolent Deity, though limited in power, is revealed in the ordering of human history. It is pertinent to note in this connection that though there have been many historians who have made the effort, no historian has yet succeeded in showing to the satisfaction of his professional colleagues that the hypothesis of a Divine Providence is capable of explaining anything which cannot be explained just as well without this hypothesis.

· VIII ·

This last remark naturally leads to the question whether, apart from their polemics against theism, philosophical atheists have not shared a common set of positive views, a common set of philosophical convictions which set them off from other groups of thinkers. In one very clear sense of this query the answer is indubitably negative. For there never has been what one might call a "school of atheism" in the way in which there has been a Platonic school or even a Kantian school. In point of fact, atheistic critics of theism can be found among many of the conventional groupings of philo-

---

[1] A reduction to absurdity.—E.D.K.

sophical thinkers—even, I venture to add, in recent years among professional theologians, who in effect preach atheism in the guise of language taken bodily from the Christian tradition.

Nevertheless, despite the variety of philosophic positions to which atheists have subscribed at one time or another in the history of thought, it seems to me that atheism is not simply a negative standpoint. At any rate, there is a certain quality of intellectual temper that has characterized, and continues to characterize, many philosophical atheists. (I am excluding from consideration the so-called village atheist, whose primary concern is to twit and ridicule those who accept some form of theism, or for that matter those who have any religious convictions.) Moreover, their rejection of theism is based not only on the inadequacies they have found in the arguments for theism but often also on the positive ground that atheism is a corollary to a better supported general outlook upon the nature of things. I want therefore to conclude this discussion with a brief enumeration of some points of positive doctrine to which by and large philosophical atheists seem to me to subscribe. These points fall into three major groups.

In the first place, philosophical atheists reject the assumption that there are disembodied spirits, or that incorporeal entities of any sort can exercise a causal agency. On the contrary, atheists are generally agreed that if we wish to achieve any understanding of what takes place in the universe, we must look to the operations of organized bodies. Accordingly, the various processes taking place in nature, whether animate or inanimate, are to be explained in terms of the properties and structures of identifiable and spatio-temporally located objects. Moreover, the present variety of systems and activities found in the universe is to be accounted for on the basis of the transformations things undergo when they enter into different relations with one another—transformations which often result in the emergence of novel kinds of objects. On the other hand, though things are in flux and undergo alteration, there is no all-encompassing unitary pattern of change. Nature is ineradicably plural, both in respect to the individuals occurring in it as well as in respect to the processes in which things become involved. Accordingly, the human scene and the human perspective are not illusory; and man and his works are no less and no more "real" than are other parts or phases of the cosmos. At the risk of using a possibly misleading characterization, all of this can be summarized by saying that an atheistic view of things is a form of materialism.

In the second place, atheists generally manifest a marked empirical temper, and often take as their ideal the intellectual methods employed in the contemporaneous empirical sciences. Philosophical atheists differ considerably on important points of detail in their account of how responsible claims to knowledge are to be established. But there is substantial agreement among them that controlled sensory observation is the court of final appeal in issues concerning matters of fact. It is indeed this commitment to the use of an empirical method which is the final basis of the atheistic critique of theism. For at bottom this critique seeks to show that we can understand whatever a theistic assumption is alleged to explain, through the use of the proved methods of the positive sciences and without the introduction of empirically unsupported *ad hoc* hypotheses about a Deity. It is pertinent in this connection to recall a familiar legend about the French mathematical physicist Laplace. According to the story, Laplace made a personal presentation of a copy of his now famous book on celestial mechanics to Napoleon. Napoleon glanced through the volume, and finding no reference to the Deity asked Laplace whether God's existence played any role in the analysis. "Sire, I have no need for that hypothesis," Laplace is reported to have replied. The dismissal of sterile hypotheses characterizes not only the work of Laplace; it is the uniform rule in scientific inquiry. The sterility of the theistic assumption is one of the main burdens of the literature of atheism both ancient and modern.

And finally, atheistic thinkers have generally accepted a utilitarian basis for judging moral issues, and they have exhibited a libertarian attitude toward human needs and impulses. The conceptions of the human good they have advocated are conceptions which are commensurate with the actual capacities of mortal men, so that it is the satisfaction of the complex needs of the human creature which is the final standard for evaluating the validity of a moral ideal or moral prescription.

In consequence, the emphasis of atheistic moral reflection has been this-worldly rather than other-worldly, individualistic rather than authoritarian. The stress upon a good life that must be consummated in this world has made atheists vigorous opponents of moral codes which seek to repress human impulses in the name of some unrealizable other-worldly ideal. The individualism that is so pronounced a strain in many philosophical atheists has made them tolerant of human limitations and sensitive to the plurality of legitimate moral goals. On the other hand, this individualism has certainly not prevented many of them from recognizing the crucial role which institutional arrangements can play in achieving desirable patterns of human living. In consequence, atheists have made important contributions to the development of a climate of opinion favorable to pursuing the values of a liberal civilization, and they have played effective roles in attempts to rectify social injustices.

Atheists cannot build their moral outlook on foundations upon which so many men conduct their lives. In particular, atheism cannot offer the incentives to conduct and the consolations for misfortune which theistic religions supply to their adherents. It can offer no hope of personal immortality, no threats of Divine chastisement, no promise of eventual recompense for injustices suffered, no blueprints to sure salvation. For on its view of the place of man in nature, human excellence and human dignity must be achieved within a finite life-span, or not at all, so that the rewards of moral endeavor must come from the quality of civilized living, and not from some source of disbursement that dwells outside of time. Accordingly, atheistic moral reflection at its best does not culminate in a quiescent ideal of human perfection, but is a vigorous call to intelligent activity—activity for the sake of realizing human potentialities and for eliminating whatever stands in the way of such realization. Nevertheless, though slavish resignation to remediable ills is not characteristic of atheistic thought, responsible atheists have never pretended that human effort can invariably achieve the heart's every legitimate desire. A tragic view of life is thus an uneliminable ingredient in atheistic thought. This ingredient does not invite or generally produce lugubrious lamentation. But it does touch the atheist's view of man and his place in nature with an emotion that makes the philosophical atheist a kindred spirit to those who, within the framework of various religious traditions, have developed a serenely resigned attitude toward the inevitable tragedies of the human estate.

○ ○ ○ **22**

The Existence of God
Bertrand Russell

TO COME TO this question of the existence of God: It is a large and serious question, and if I were to attempt to deal with it in any adequate manner I should have to keep you here until Kingdom Come, so that you will have to excuse me if I deal with it in a somewhat summary fashion. You know, of course, that the Catholic Church has laid it down as a dogma that the existence of God can be proven by the unaided reason. That is a somewhat curious dogma, but it is one of their dogmas. They had to introduce it because at one time the freethinkers adopted the habit of saying that there were such and such arguments which mere reason might urge against the existence of God, but of course they knew as a matter of faith that God did exist. The arguments and the reasons were set out at great length, and the Catholic Church felt that they must stop it. Therefore they laid it down that the existence of God can be proved by the unaided reason, and they have had to set up what they considered were arguments to prove it. There are, of course, a number of them, but I shall take only a few.

1. The First-Cause Argument / Perhaps the simplest and easiest to understand is the argument of the First Cause. It is maintained that everything we see in this world has a cause, and as you go back in the chain of causes further and further you must come to a First Cause, and to that First Cause you give the name of God. That argument, I suppose, does not carry very much weight nowadays, because, in the first place, cause is not quite what it used to be. The philosophers and the men of science have got going on cause, and it has not anything like the vitality it used to have; but, apart from that, you can see that the argument that there must be a First Cause is one that cannot have any validity. I may say that when I was a young man and was debating these questions very seriously in my mind, I for a long time accepted the argument of the First Cause, until one day, at the age of eighteen, I read John Stuart Mill's Autobiography, and I there found this sentence: "My father taught me that the question 'Who made me?' cannot be answered, since it immediately suggests the further question 'Who made God?' " That very simple sentence showed me, as I still think, the fallacy in the argument of the First Cause. If everything must have a cause, then God must have a cause. If there can be anything without a cause, it may just as well be the world as God, so that there cannot be any validity in that argument. It is exactly of the same nature as the Hindu's view that the world rested upon an elephant and the elephant rested upon a tortoise; and when they said, "How about the tortoise?" the Indian said, "Suppose we change the subject." The argument is really no better than that. There is no reason why the world could not have come into being without a cause; nor, on the other hand, is there any reason why it should not have always existed. There is no reason to suppose that the world had a beginning at all. The idea that things must have a beginning is really due to the poverty of our imagination. Therefore, perhaps, I need not waste any more time upon the argument about the First Cause.

2. The Natural-Law Argument / Then there is a very common argument from natural law. That was a favorite argument all through the eighteenth century, especially under the influence of Sir Isaac Newton and his cosmogony. People observed the planets going around the sun according to the law of gravitation, and they thought that God had given a behest to these planets to move in that particular fashion, and that was why they did so. That was, of course, a convenient and simple explanation that saved them the trouble of looking any further for explanations of the law of gravitation. Nowadays we explain the law of gravitation in a somewhat complicated fashion that Einstein has introduced. I do not propose to give you a lecture on the law of gravitation, as interpreted by Einstein, because that again would take some time; at any rate, you no longer have the sort of natural law that you had in the Newtonian system, where, for some reason that nobody could understand, nature behaved in a uniform fashion. We now find that a great many things we thought were natural laws are really human conventions. You know that even in the remotest depths of stellar space there are still three feet to a yard. That is, no doubt, a very remarkable fact, but you would hardly call it a law of nature. And a great many things that have been regarded as laws of nature are of that kind. On the other hand, where you can get down to any knowledge of what atoms actually do, you will find they are much less subject to law than people thought, and that the laws at which you arrive are statistical averages of just the sort that would emerge from chance. There is, as we all know, a law that if you throw dice you will get double sixes only about once in thirty-six times, and we do not regard that as evidence that the fall of the dice is regulated by design; on the contrary, if the double sixes came every time we should think that there was design. The laws of nature are of that sort as regards a great many of them. They are statistical averages such as would emerge from the laws of chance; and that makes this whole business of natural law much less impressive than it formerly was. Quite apart from that, which represents the momentary state of science that may change tomorrow, the whole idea that natural laws imply a lawgiver is due to a confusion between natural and human laws. Human laws are behests commanding you to behave a certain way, in which you may choose to behave, or you may choose not to behave; but natural laws are a description of how things do in fact behave, and being a mere description of what they in fact do, you cannot argue that there must be somebody who told them to do that, because even supposing that there were, you are then faced with the question, "Why did God issue just those natural laws and no others?" If you say that he did it simply from his own good pleasure, and without any reason, you then find that there is something which is not subject to law, and so your train of natural law is interrupted. If you say, as more orthodox theologians do, that in all the laws which God issues he had a reason for giving those laws rather than others—the reason, of course, being to create the best universe, although you would never think it to look at it—if there were a reason for the laws which God gave, then God himself was subject to law, and therefore you do not get any advantage by introducing God as an intermediary. You have really a law outside and anterior to the divine edicts, and God does not serve your purpose, because he is not the ultimate lawgiver. In short, this whole argument about natural law no longer has anything like the strength that it used to have. I am traveling on in time in my review of the arguments. The arguments that are used for the existence of God change their character as time goes on. They were at first hard intellectual arguments embodying certain quite definite fallacies. As we come to modern times they become less respectable intellectually and more and more affected by a kind of moralizing vagueness.

3. The Argument from Design / The next step in this process brings us to the argument from design. You all know the argument from design: Everything in the world is made just so that we can manage to live in the world, and if the world was ever so little different, we could not manage to live in it. That is the argument from design. It sometimes takes a rather curious form; for instance, it is argued that rabbits have white tails in order to be easy to shoot. I do not know how rabbits would view that application. It is an easy argument to parody. You all know Voltaire's remark, that obviously the nose was designed to be such as to fit spectacles. That sort of parody has turned out to be not nearly so wide of the mark as it might have seemed in the eighteenth century, because since the time of Darwin we understand much better why living creatures are adapted to their environment. It is not that their environment was made to be suitable to them but that they grew to be suitable to it, and that is the basis of adaptation. There is no evidence of design about it.

When you come to look into this argument from design, it is a most astonishing thing that people can believe that this world, with all the things that are in it, with all its defects, should be the best that omnipotence and omniscience have been able to produce in millions of years. I really cannot believe it. Do you think that, if you were granted omnipotence and omniscience and millions of years in which to perfect your world, you could produce nothing better than the Ku Klux Klan or the Fascists? Moreover, if you accept the ordinary laws of science, you have to suppose that human life and life in general on this planet will die out in due course: It is a stage in the decay of the solar system; at a certain stage of decay you get the sort of conditions of temperature and so forth which are suitable to protoplasm, and there is life for a short time in the life of the whole solar system. You see in the moon the sort of thing to which the earth is tending—something dead, cold, and lifeless.

I am told that that sort of view is depressing, and people will sometimes tell you that if they believed that, they would not be able to go on living. Do not believe it; it is all nonsense. Nobody really worries much about what is going to happen millions of years hence. Even if they think they are worrying much about that, they are really deceiving themselves. They are worried about something much more mundane, or it may merely be a bad digestion; but nobody is really seriously rendered unhappy by the thought of something that is going to happen to this world millions and millions of years hence. Therefore, although it is of course a gloomy view to suppose that life will die out—at least I suppose we may say so, although sometimes when I contemplate the things that people do with their lives I think it is almost a consolation—it is not such as to render life miserable. It merely makes you turn your attention to other things.

4. The Moral Arguments for Deity / Now we reach one stage further in what I shall call the intellectual descent that the theists have made in their argumentations, and we come to what are called the moral arguments for the existence of God. You all know, of course, that there used to be in the old days three intellectual arguments for the existence of God all of which were disposed of by Immanuel Kant in the *Critique of Pure Reason*; but no sooner had he disposed of those arguments than he invented a new one, a moral argument, and that quite convinced him. He was like many people: In intellectual matters he was skeptical, but in moral matters he believed implicitly in the maxims that he had imbibed at his mother's knee. That illustrates what the psychoanalysts so much emphasize—the immensely stronger hold upon us that our very early associations have than those of later times.

Kant, as I say, invented a new moral argument for the existence of God, and that in varying forms was extremely popular during the nineteenth century. It has all sorts of forms. One form is to say that there would be no right or wrong unless God existed. I am not for the moment concerned with whether there is a difference between right and wrong, or whether there is not: That is another question. The point I am concerned with it that, if you are quite sure there is a difference between right and wrong, you are then in this situation: Is that difference due to God's fiat or is it not? If it is due to God's fiat, then for God himself there is no difference between right and wrong, and it is no longer a significant statement to say that God is good. If you are going to say, as theologians do, that God is good, you must then say that right and wrong have some meaning which is independent of God's fiat, because God's fiats are good and not bad independently of the mere fact that he made them. If you are going to say that, you will then have to say that it is not only through God that right and wrong came into being, but that they are in their essence logically anterior to God. You could, of course, if you liked, say that there was a superior deity who gave orders to the God who made this world, or could take up the line that some of the gnostics took up—a line which I often thought was a very plausible one—that as a matter of fact this world that we know was made by the devil at a moment when God was not looking. There is a good deal to be said for that, and I am not concerned to refute it.

5. **The Argument for the Remedying of Injustice** / Then there is another very curious form of moral argument, which is this: They say that the existence of God is required in order to bring justice into the world. In the part of this universe that we know there is great injustice, and often the good suffer, and often the wicked prosper, and one hardly knows which of those is more annoying; but if you are going to have justice in the universe as a whole you have to suppose a future life to redress the balance of life here on earth. So they say that there must be a God, and there must be heaven and hell in order that in the long run there may be justice. That is a very curious argument. If you looked at the matter from a scientific point of view, you would say, "After all, I know only this world. I do not know about the rest of the universe, but so far as one can argue at all on probabilities one would say that probably this world is a fair sample, and if there is injustice here the odds are that there is injustice elsewhere also." Supposing you got a crate of oranges that you opened, and you found all the top layer of oranges bad, you would not argue, "The underneath ones must be good, so as to redress the balance." You would say, "Probably the whole lot is a bad consignment"; and that is really what a scientific person would argue about the universe. He would say, "Here we find in this world a great deal of injustice, and so far as that goes that is a reason for supposing that justice does not rule in the world; and therefore so far as it goes it affords a moral argument against deity and not in favor of one." Of course I know that the sort of intellectual arguments that I have been talking to you about are not what really moves people. What really moves people to believe in God is not any intellectual argument at all. Most people believe in God because they have been taught from early infancy to do it, and that is the main reason.

Then I think that the next most powerful reason is the wish for safety, a sort of feeling that there is a big brother who will look after you. That plays a very profound part in influencing people's desire for a belief in God.

○ ○ ○ *23*

The Existence of God—A Debate
(between Bertrand Russell and Father F. C. Copleston, S.J.)
Bertrand Russell and F. C. Copleston

COPLESTON: As we are going to discuss the existence of God, it might perhaps be as well to come to some provisional agreement as to what we understand by the term "God." I presume that we mean a supreme personal being—distinct from the world and creator of the world. Would you agree—provisionally at least—to accept this statement as the meaning of the term "God"?

RUSSELL: Yes, I accept this definition.

COPLESTON: Well, my position is the affirmative position that such a being actually exists, and that His existence can be proved philosophically. Perhaps you would tell me if your position is that of agnosticism or of atheism. I mean, would you say that the non-existence of God can be proved?

RUSSELL: No, I should not say that: my position is agnostic.

COPLESTON: Would you agree with me that the problem of God is a problem of great importance? For example, would you agree that if God does not exist, human beings and human history can have no other purpose than the purpose they choose to give themselves, which—in practice—is likely to mean the purpose which those impose who have the power to impose it?

RUSSELL: Roughly speaking, yes, though I should have to place some limitation on your last clause.

COPLESTON: Would you agree that if there is no God—no absolute Being—there can be no absolute values? I mean, would you agree that if there is no absolute good that the relativity of values results?

RUSSELL: No, I think these questions are logically distinct. Take, for instance, G.E. Moore's[1] *Principia Ethica*, where he maintains that there is a distinction of good and evil, that both of these are definite concepts. But he does not bring in the idea of God to support that contention.

COPLESTON: Well, suppose we leave the question of good till later, till we come to the moral argument, and I give first a metaphysical argument. I'd like to put the main weight on the metaphysical argument based on Leibniz's argument from "Contingency" and then later we might discuss the moral argument. Suppose I give a brief statement on the metaphysical argument and that then we go on to discuss it?

RUSSELL: That seems to me to be a very good plan.

---

[1] A prominent British philosopher of the first four decades of the twentieth century. —E.D.K.

I. The Argument from Contingency

COPLESTON: Well, for clarity's sake, I'll divide the argument into distinct stages. First of all, I should say, we know that there are at least some beings in the world which do not contain in themselves the reason for their existence. For example, I depend on my parents, and now on the air, and on food, and so on. Now, secondly, the world is simply the real or imagined totality or aggregate of individual objects, none of which contain in themselves alone the reason for their existence. There isn't any world distinct from the objects which form it, any more than the human race is something apart from the members. Therefore, I should say, since objects or events exist, and since no object of experience contains within itself the reason of its existence, this reason, the totality of objects, must have a reason external to itself. That reason must be an existent being. Well, this being is either itself the reason for its own existence, or it is not. If it is, well and good. If it is not, then we must proceed farther. But if we proceed to infinity in that sense, then there's no explanation of existence at all. So, I should say, in order to explain existence,we must come to a being which contains within itself the reason for its own existence, that is to say, which cannot not-exist.

RUSSELL: This raises a great many points and it is not altogether easy to know where to begin, but I think that, perhaps, in answering your argument, the best point at which to begin is the question of necessary being. The word "necessary" I should maintain, can only be applied significantly to propositions. And, in fact, only to such as are analytic—that is to say—such as it is self-contradictory to deny. I could only admit a necessary being if there were a being whose existence it is self-contradictory to deny. I should like to know whether you would accept Leibniz's division of propositions into truths of reason and truths of fact. The former—the truths of reason—being necessary.

COPLESTON: Well, I certainly should not subscribe to what seems to be Leibniz's[2] idea of truths of reason and truths of fact, since it would appear that, for him, there are in the long run only analytic propositions. It would seem that for Leibniz truths of fact are ultimately reducible to truths of reason. That is to say, to analytic propositions, at least for an omniscient mind. Well, I couldn't agree with that. For one thing, it would fail to meet the requirements of the experience of freedom. I don't want to uphold the whole philosophy of Leibniz. I have made use of his argument from contingent to necessary being, basing the argument on the principle of sufficient reason, simply because it seems to me a brief and clear formulation of what is, in my opinion, the fundamental metaphysical argument for God's existence.

RUSSELL: But, to my mind, "a necessary proposition" has got to be analytic. I don't see what else it can mean. And analytic propositions are always complex and logically somewhat late. "Irrational animals are animals" is an analytic proposition; but a proposition such as "This is an animal" can never be analytic. In fact, all the propositions that can be analytic are somewhat late in the build-up of propositions.

COPLESTON: Take the proposition "If there is a contingent being then there is a necessary being." I consider that that proposition hypothetically expressed is a necessary proposition. If you are going to call every necessary proposition an analytic proposition, then—in order to avoid a dispute in terminology—I would agree to call it analytic, though I don't consider it a tautological proposition. That there is a contingent being

---

[2] A seventeenth Century "rationalist" philosopher.—E.D.K.

actually existing has to be discovered by experience, and the proposition that there is a contingent being, is certainly not an analytic proposition, though once you know, I should maintain, that there is a contingent being, it follows of necessity that there is a necessary being.

RUSSELL: The difficulty of this argument is that I don't admit the idea of a necessary being and I don't admit that there is any particular meaning in calling other beings "contingent." These phrases don't for me have a significance except within a logic that I reject.

COPLESTON: Do you mean that you reject these terms because they won't fit in with what is called "modern logic"?

RUSSELL: Well, I can't find anything that they could mean. The word "necessary," it seems to me, is a useless word, except as applied to analytic propositions, not to things.

COPLESTON: In the first place, what do you mean by "modern logic"? As far as I know, there are somewhat differing systems. In the second place, not all modern logicians surely would admit the meaninglessness of metaphysics. We both know, at any rate, one very eminent modern thinker whose knowledge of modern logic was profound, but who certainly did not think that metaphysics are meaningless or, in particular, that the problem of God is meaningless. Again, even if all modern logicians held that metaphysical terms are meaningless, it would not follow that they were right. The proposition that metaphysical terms are meaningless seems to me to be a proposition based on an assumed philosophy. The dogmatic position behind it seems to be this: What will not go into my machine is non-existent, or it is meaningless; it is the expression of emotion. I am simply trying to point out that anybody who says that a particular system of modern logic is the sole criterion of meaning is saying something that is over dogmatic; he is dogmatically insisting that a part of philosophy is the whole of philosophy. After all, a "contingent" being is a being which has not in itself the complete reason for its existence, that's what I mean by a contingent being. You know, as well as I do, that the existence of neither of us can be explained without reference to something or somebody outside us, our parents, for example. A "necessary" being, on the other hand, means a being that must and cannot not-exist. You may say that there is no such being, but you will find it hard to convince me that you do not understand the terms I am using. If you do not understand them, then how can you be entitled to say that such a being does not exist, if that is what you do say?

RUSSELL: Well, there are points here that I don't propose to go into at length. I don't maintain the meaninglessness of metaphysics in general at all. I maintain the meaninglessness of certain particular terms—not on any general ground, but simply because I've not been able to see an interpretation of those particular terms. It's not a general dogma—it's a particular thing. But those points I will leave out for the moment. And I will say that what you have been saying brings us back, it seems to me, to the ontological argument that there is a being whose essence involves existence, so that his existence is analytic. That seems to me to be impossible, and it raises, of course, the question what one means by existence, and as to this, I think a subject named can never be significantly said to exist but only a subject described. And that existence, in fact, quite definitely is not a predicate.

COPLESTON: Well, you say, I believe, that it is bad grammar, or rather bad syntax to say for example "T.S. Eliot exists"; one ought to say, for example, "He, the author of *Murder in the Cathedral*, exists." Are you going to say that the proposition, "The cause of the world exists," is without meaning? You may say that the world has no cause; but I fail to see how you can say that the proposition that "the cause of the world exists" is meaningless. Put it in the form of a question: "Has the world a cause?" or "Does a cause of the world exist?" Most people surely would understand the question, even if they don't agree about the answer.

RUSSELL: Well, certainly the question "Does the cause of the world exist?" is a question that has meaning. But if you say "Yes, God is the cause of the world" you're using God as a proper name; then "God exists" will not be a statement that has meaning; that is the position that I'm maintaining. Because, therefore, it will follow that it cannot be an analytic proposition ever to say that this or that exists. For example, suppose you take as your subject "the existent round-square," it would look like an analytic proposition that "the existent round-square exists," but it doesn't exist.

COPLESTON: No, it doesn't, then surely you can't say it doesn't exist unless you have a conception of what existence is. As to the phrase "existent round-square," I should say that it has no meaning at all.

RUSSELL: I quite agree. Then I should say the same thing in another context in reference to a "necessary being."

COPLESTON: Well, we seem to have arrived at an impasse. To say that a necessary being is a being that must exist and cannot not-exist has for me a definite meaning. For you it has no meaning.

RUSSELL: Well, we can press the point a little, I think. A being that must exist and cannot not-exist, would surely, according to you, be a being whose essence involved existence.

COPLESTON: Yes, a being the essence of which is to exist. But I should not be willing to argue the existence of God simply from the idea of His essence because I don't think we have any clear intuition of God's essence as yet. I thing we have to argue from the world of experience to God.

RUSSELL: Yes, I quite see the distinction. But, at the same time, for a being with sufficient knowledge it would be true to say "Here is this being whose essence involves existence!"

COPLESTON: Yes, certainly if anybody saw God, he would see that God must exist.

RUSSELL: So that I mean there is a being whose essence involves existence although we don't know there is such a being.

COPLESTON: Yes, I should add we don't know the essence *a priori*. It is only *a posteriori* through our experience of the world that we come to a knowledge of the existence of that being. And then one argues, the essence and existence must be identical. Because if God's essence and God's existence was not identical, then some sufficient reason for this existence would have to be found beyond God.

RUSSELL: So it all turns on this question of sufficient reason, and I must say you haven't defined "sufficient reason" in a way that I can understand—what do you mean by sufficient reason? You don't mean cause?

COPLESTON: Not necessarily. Cause is a kind of sufficient reason. Only contingent being can have a cause. God is His own sufficient reason; and He is not cause of Himself. By sufficient reason in the full sense I mean an explanation adequate for the existence of some particular being.

RUSSELL: But when is an explanation adequate? Suppose I am about to make a flame with a match. You may say that the adequate explanation of that is that I rub it on the box.

COPLESTON: Well, for practical purposes—but theoretically, that is only a partial explanation. An adequate explanation must ultimately be a total explanation, to which nothing further can be added.

RUSSELL: Then I can only say that you're looking for something which can't be got, and which one ought not to expect to get.

COPLESTON: To say that one has not found it is one thing; to say that one should not look for it seems to me rather dogmatic.

RUSSELL: Well, I don't know. I mean, the explanation of one thing is another thing which makes the other thing dependent on yet another, and you have to grasp this sorry scheme of things entire to do what you want, and that we can't do.

COPLESTON: But are you going to say that we can't, or we shouldn't even raise the question of the existence of the whole of this sorry scheme of things—of the whole universe?

RUSSELL: Yes, I don't think there's any meaning in it at all. I think the word "universe" is a handy word in some connections, but I don't think it stands for anything that has a meaning.

COPLESTON: If the word is meaningless, it can't be so very handy. In any case, I don't say that the universe is something different from the objects which compose it (I indicated that in my brief summary of the proof), what I'm doing is to look for the reason, in this case the cause of the objects—the real or imagined totality of which constitute what we call the universe. You say, I think that the universe—or my existence if you prefer, or any other existence—is unintelligible?

RUSSELL: First may I take up the point that if a word is meaningless it can't be handy. That sounds well but isn't in fact correct. Take, say, such a word as "the" or "than." You can't point to any object that those words mean, but they are very useful words; I should say the same of "universe." But leaving that point, you ask whether I consider that the universe is unintelligible. I shouldn't say unintelligible—I think it is without explanation. Intelligible, to my mind, is a different thing. Intelligible has to do with the thing itself intrinsically and not with its relations.

COPLESTON: Well, my point is that what we call the world is intrinsically unintelligible, apart from the existence of God. You see, I don't believe that the infinity of the series of events—I mean a horizontal series, so to speak—if such an infinity could be proved, would be in the slightest degree relevant to the situation. If you add up chocolates you get chocolates after all and not a sheep. If you add up chocolates to infinity, you presumably get an infinite number of chocolates. So if you add up contingent beings to infinity, you still get contingent beings, not a necessary being. An infinite series of contingent beings will be, to my way of thinking, as unable to cause itself as one contingent being. However, you say, I think, that it is illegitimate to raise the question of what will explain the existence of any particular object?

RUSSELL: It's quite all right if you mean by explaining it, simply finding a cause for it.

COPLESTON: Well, why stop at one particular object? Why shouldn't one raise the question of the cause of the existence of all particular objects?

RUSSELL: Because I see no reason to think there is any. The whole concept of cause is one we derive from our observation of particular things; I see no reason whatsoever to suppose that the total has any cause whatsoever.

COPLESTON: Well, to say that there isn't any cause is not the same thing as saying that we shouldn't look for a cause. The statement that there isn't any cause should come, if it comes at all, at the end of the enquiry, not the beginning. In any case, if the total has no cause, then to my way of thinking it must be its own cause, which seems to me impossible. Moreover, the statement that the world is simply there, if in answer to a question, presupposes that the question has meaning.

RUSSELL: No, it doesn't need to be its own cause, what I'm saying is that the concept of cause is not applicable to the total.

COPLESTON: Then you would agree with Sartre[3] that the universe is what he calls "gratuitous"?

RUSSELL: Well, the word "gratuitous" suggests that it might be something else; I should say that the universe is just there, and that's all.

COPLESTON: Well, I can't see how you can rule out the legitimacy of asking the question how the total, or anything at all comes to be there. Why something rather than nothing, that is the question? The fact that we gain our knowledge of causality empirically, from particular causes, does not rule out the possibility of asking what the cause of the series is. If the word "cause" were meaningless or if it could be shown that Kant's view of the matter were correct, the question would be illegitimate I agree; but you don't seem to hold that the word "cause" is meaningless, and I do not suppose you are a Kantian.

RUSSELL: I can illustrate what seems to me your fallacy. Every man who exists has a mother, and it seems to me your argument is that therefore the human race must have a mother, but obviously the human race hasn't a mother—that's a different logical sphere.

COPLESTON: Well, I can't really see any parity. If I were saying "every object has a phenomenal cause, therefore, the whole series has a phenomenal cause," there would be a parity; but I'm not saying that; I'm saying, every object has a phenomenal cause if you insist on the infinity of the series—but the series of phenomenal causes is an insufficient explanation of the series. Therefore, the series has not a phenomenal cause but a transcendent cause.

RUSSELL: That's always assuming that not only every particular thing in the world, but the world as a whole must have a cause. For that assumption I see no ground whatever. If you'll give me a ground I'll listen to it.

COPLESTON: Well, the series of events is either caused or it's not caused. If it is caused, there must obviously be a cause outside the series. If it's not caused then it's sufficient to itself, and if it's sufficient to itself it is what I call necessary. But it can't be necessary since each member is contingent, and we've agreed that the total is no reality apart from its members, therefore, it can't be necessary. Therefore, it can't be uncaused, therefore it must have a cause. And I should like to observe in passing that the statement "the world is simply there and is inexplicable" can't be got out of logical analysis.

RUSSELL: I don't want to seem arrogant, but it does seem to me that I can conceive things that you say the human mind can't conceive. As for things not having a cause, the physicists assure us that individual quantum transition in atoms have no cause.

COPLESTON: Well, I wonder now whether that isn't simply a temporary inference.

RUSSELL: It may be, but it does show that physicists' minds can conceive it.

COPLESTON: Yes, I agree, some scientists—physicists—are willing to allow for indetermination within a restricted field. But very many scientists are not so willing. I think that Professor Dingle, of London University, maintains that the Heisenberg

---

[3] A twentieth century French existentialist philosopher, novelist, and playwrite.—E.D.K.

uncertainty principle tells us something about the success (or the lack of it) of the present atomic theory in correlating observations, but not about nature in itself, and many physicists would accept this view. In any case, I don't see how physicists can fail to accept the theory in practice, even if they don't do so in theory. I cannot see how science could be conducted on any other assumption than that of order and intelligibility in nature. The physicist presupposes, at least tacitly, that there is some sense in investigating nature and looking for the causes of events, just as the detective presupposes that there is some sense in looking for the cause of a murder. The metaphysician assumes that there is sense in looking for the reason or cause of phenomena, and, not being a Kantian, I consider that the metaphysician is as justified in his assumption as the physicist. When Sartre, for example, says that the world is gratuitous, I thing that he has not sufficiently considered what is implied by "gratuitous."

RUSSELL: I think—there seems to me a certain unwarrantable extension here; a physicist looks for causes; that does not necessarily imply that there are causes everywhere. A man may look for gold without assuming that there is gold everywhere; if he finds gold, well and good, if he doesn't he's had bad luck. The same is true when the physicists look for causes. As for Sartre, I don't profess to know what he means, and I shouldn't like to be thought to interpret him, but for my part, I do think the notion of the world having an explanation is a mistake. I don't see why one should expect it to have, and I think what you say about what the scientist assumes is an over-statement.

COPLESTON: Well, it seems to me that the scientist does make some such assumption. When he experiments to find out some particular truth, behind that experiment lies the assumption that the universe is not simply discontinuous. There is the possibility of finding out a truth by experiment. The experiment may be a bad one, it may lead to no result, or not to the result that he wants, but that at any rate there is the possibility, through experiment, of finding out the truth that he assumes. And that seems to me to assume an ordered and intelligible universe.

RUSSELL: I think you're generalising more than is necessary. Undoubtedly the scientist assumes that this sort of thing is likely to be found and will often be found. He does not assume that it will be found, and that's a very important matter in modern physics.

COPLESTON: Well, I think he does assume or is bound to assume it tacitly in practice. It may be that, to quote Professor Haldane, "when I light the gas under the kettle, some of the water molecules will fly off as vapour, and there is no way of finding out which will do so," but it doesn't follow necessarily that the idea of chance must be introduced except in relation to our knowledge.

RUSSELL: No it doesn't—at least if I may believe what he says. He's finding out quite a lot of things—the scientist is finding out quite a lot of things that are happening in the world, which are, at first, beginnings of causal chains—first causes which haven't in themselves got cause. He does not assume that everything has a cause.

COPLESTON: Surely that's a first cause within a certain selected field. It's a relatively first cause.

RUSSELL: I don't think he'd say so. If there's a world in which most events, but not all, have causes, he will then be able to depict the probabilities and uncertainties by assuming that this particular event you're interested in probably has a cause. And since in any case you won't get more than probability that's good enough.

COPLESTON: It may be that the scientist doesn't hope to obtain more than probability, but in raising the question he assumes that the question of explanation has a meaning. But your general point then, Lord Russell, is that it's illegitimate even to ask the question of the cause of the world?

RUSSELL: Yes, that's my position.

COPLESTON: If it's a question that for you has no meaning, it's of course very difficult to discuss it, isn't it?

RUSSELL: Yes it is very difficult. What do you say—shall we pass on to some other issue?

II. Religious Experience

COPLESTON: Let's. Well, perhaps I might say a word about religious experience, and then we can go on to moral experience. I don't regard religious experience as a strict proof of the existence of God, so the character of the discussion changes somewhat, but I think it's true to say that the best explanation of it is the existence of God. By religious experience I don't mean simply feeling good. I mean a loving, but unclear, awareness of some object which irresistibly seems to the experiencer as something transcending the self, something transcending all the normal objects of experience, something which cannot be pictured or conceptualized, but of the reality of which doubt is impossible—at least during the experience. I should claim that cannot be explained adequately and without residue, simply subjectively. The actual basic experience at any rate is most easily explained on the hypotheses that there is actually some objective cause of that experience.

RUSSELL: I should reply to that line of argument that the whole argument from our own mental states to something outside us, is a very tricky affair. Even where we all admit its validity, we only feel justified in doing so, I think, because of the consensus of mankind. If there's a crowd in a room and there's a clock in a room, they can all see the clock. The fact that they can all see it tends to make them think that it's not an hallucination: whereas these religious experiences do tend to be very private.

COPLESTON: Yes, they do. I'm speaking strictly of mystical experience proper, and I certainly don't include, by the way, what are called visions. I mean simply the experience, and I quite admit it's indefinable, of the transcendent object or of what seems to be a transcendent object. I remember Julian Huxley in some lecture saying that religious experience, or mystical experience, is as much a real experience as falling in love or appreciating poetry and art. Well, I believe that when we appreciate poetry and art we appreciate definite poems or a definite work of art. If we fall in love, well, we fall in love with somebody and not with nobody.

RUSSELL: May I interrupt for a moment here. That is by no means always the case. Japanese novelists never consider that they have achieved a success unless large numbers of real people commit suicide for love of the imaginary heroine.

COPLESTON: Well, I must take your word for these goings on in Japan. I haven't committed suicide, I'm glad to say, but I have been strongly influenced in the taking of two important steps in my life by two biographies. However, I must say I see little resemblance between the real influence of those books on me and the mystic experience proper, so far, that is, as an outsider can obtain an idea of that experience.

RUSSELL: Well, I mean we wouldn't regard God as being on the same level as the characters in a work of fiction. You'll admit there's a distinction here?

COPLESTON: I certainly should. But what I'd say is that the best explanation seems to be the not purely subjectivist explanation. Of course, a subjectivist explanation is possible in the case of certain people in whom there is little relation between the experience and life, in the case of deluded people and hallucinated people, and so on. But when you get what one might call the pure type, say St. Francis of Assisi, when you get an experience that results in an overflow of dynamic and creative love, the best explanation of that it seems to me is the actual existence of an objective cause of the experience.

RUSSELL: Well, I'm not contending in a dogmatic way that there is not a God. What I'm contending is that we don't know that there is. I can only take what is recorded as I should take other records and I do find that a very great many things are reported, and I am sure you would not accept things about demons and devils and what not —and they're reported in exactly the same tone of voice and with exactly the same conviction. And the mystic, if his vision is veridical, may be said to know that there are devils. But I don't know that there are.

COPLESTON: But surely in the case of the devils there have been people speaking mainly of visions, appearances, angels or demons and so on. I should rule out the visual appearances, because I think they can be explained apart from the existence of the object which is supposed to be seen.

RUSSELL: But don't you think there are abundant recorded cases of people who believe that they've heard Satan speaking to them in their hearts, in just the same way as the mystics assert God—and I'm not talking now of an external vision, I'm talking of a purely mental experience. That seems to be an experience of the same sort as mystics' experience of God, and I don't see that from what mystics tell us you can get any argument for God which is not equally an argument for Satan.

COPLESTON: I quite agree, of course, that people have imagined or thought they have heard or seen Satan. And I have no wish in passing to deny the existence of Satan. But I do not think that people have claimed to have experienced Satan in the precise way in which mystics claim to have experienced God. Take the case of a non-Christian, Plotinus. He admits the experience is something inexpressible, the object is an object of love, and therefore, not an object that causes horror and disgust. And the effect of that experience is, I should say, borne out, or I mean the validity of the experience is borne out in the records of the life of Plotinus. At any rate it is more reasonable to suppose that he had that experience if we're willing to accept Porphyry's account of Plotinus's general kindness and benevolence.

RUSSELL: The fact that a belief has a good moral effect upon a man is no evidence whatsoever in favour of its truth.

COPLESTON: No, but if it could actually be proved that the belief was actually responsible for a good effect on a man's life, I should consider it a presumption in favour of some truth, at any rate of the positive part of the belief not of its entire validity. But in any case I am using the character of the life as evidence in favour of the mystic's veracity and sanity rather than as a proof of the truth of his beliefs.

RUSSELL: But even that I don't think is any evidence. I've had experiences myself that have altered my character profoundly. And I thought at the time at any rate that it was altered for the good. Those experiences were important, but they did not involve the existence of something outside me, and I don't think that if I'd thought they did, the fact that they had a wholesome effect would have been any evidence that I was right.

COPLESTON: No, but I think that the good effect would attest your veracity in describing your experience. Please remember that I'm not saying that a mystic's mediation or interpretation of his experience should be immune from discussion or criticism.

RUSSELL: Obviously the character of a young man may be—and often is—immensely affected for good by reading about some great man in history, and it may happen that the great man is a myth and doesn't exist, but the boy is just as much affected for good as if he did. There have been such people. Plutarch's *Lives* take Lycurgus as an example, who certainly did not exist, but you might be very much influenced by reading Lycurgus under the impression that he had previously existed. You would then be influenced by an object that you'd loved, but it wouldn't be an existing object.

COPLESTON: I agree with you on that, of course, that a man may be influenced by a character in fiction. Without going into the question of what it is precisely that influences him (I should say a real value) I think that the situation of that man and of the mystic are different. After all the man who is influenced by Lycurgus hasn't got the irresistible impression that he's experienced in some way the ultimate reality.

RUSSELL: I don't think you've quite got my point about these historical characters—these unhistorical characters in history. I'm not assuming what you call an effect on the reason. I'm assuming that the young man reading about this person and believing him to be real loves him— which is quite easy to happen, and yet he's loving a phantom.

COPLESTON: In one sense he's loving a phantom that's perfectly true, in the sense, I mean, that he's loving X or Y who doesn't exist. But at the same time, it is not, I think, the phantom as such that the young man loves; he perceives a real value, an idea which he recognises as objectively valid, and that's what excites his love.

RUSSELL: Well, in the same sense we had before about the characters in fiction.

COPLESTON: Yes, in one sense the man's loving a phantom—perfectly true. But in another sense he's loving what he perceives to be a value.

III. *The Moral Argument*

RUSSELL: But aren't you now saying in effect, I mean by God whatever is good or the sum total of what is good—the system of what is good, and, therefore, when a young man loves anything that is good he is loving God. Is that what you're saying, because if so, it wants a bit of arguing.

COPLESTON: I don't say, of course, that God is the sum-total or system of what is good in the pantheistic sense; I'm not a pantheist, but I do think that all goodness reflects God in some way and proceeds from Him, so that in a sense the man who loves what is truly good, loves God even if he doesn't advert to God. But still I agree that the validity of such an interpretation of a man's conduct depends on the recognition of God's existence, obviously.

RUSSELL: Yes, but that's a point to be proved.

COPLESTON: Quite so, but I regard the metaphysical argument as probative, but there we differ.

RUSSELL: You see, I feel that some things are good and that other things are bad. I love the things that are good, that I think are good, and I hate the things that I think are bad. I don't say that these things are good because they participate in the Divine goodness.

COPLESTON: Yes, but what's your justification for distinguishing between good and bad or how do you view the distinction between them?

RUSSELL: I don't have any justification any more than I have when I distinguish between blue and yellow. What is my justification for distinguishing between blue and yellow? I can see they are different.

COPLESTON: Well, that is an excellent justification, I agree. You distinguish blue and yellow by seeing them, so you distinguish good and bad by what faculty?

RUSSELL: By my feelings.

COPLESTON: By your feelings. Well, that's what I was asking. You think that good and evil have reference simply to feeling?

RUSSELL: Well, why does one type of object look yellow and another look blue? I can more or less give an answer to that thanks to the physicists, and as to why I think one sort of thing good and another evil, probably there is an answer of the same sort, but it hasn't been gone into in the same way and I couldn't give it you.

COPLESTON: Well, let's take the behaviour of the Commandant of Belsen.[4] That appears to you as undesirable and evil and to me too. To Adolf Hitler we suppose it appeared as something good and desirable. I suppose you'd have to admit that for Hitler it was good and for you its is evil.

RUSSELL: No, I shouldn't quite go so far as that. I mean, I think people can make mistakes in that as they can in other things. If you have jaundice you see things yellow that are not yellow. You're making a mistake.

COPLESTON: Yes, one can make mistakes, but can you make a mistake if it's simply a question of reference to a feeling or emotion? Surely Hitler would be the only possible judge of what appealed to his emotions.

RUSSELL: It would be quite right to say that it appealed to his emotions, but you can say various things about that among others, that if that sort of thing makes that sort of appeal to Hitler's emotions, then Hitler makes quite a different appeal to my emotions.

COPLESTON: Granted. But there's no objective criterion outside feeling then for condemning the conduct of the Commandant of Belsen, in your view?

RUSSELL: No more than there is for the colour-blind person who's in exactly the same state. Why do we intellectually condemn the colour-blind man? Isn't it because he's in the minority?

COPLESTON: I would say because he is lacking in a thing which normally belongs to human nature.

RUSSELL: Yes, but if he were in the majority, we shouldn't say that.

COPLESTON: Then you'd say that there's no criterion outside feeling that will enable one to distinguish between the behaviour of the Commandant of Belsen and the behaviour, say, of Sir Stafford Cripps or the Archbishop of Canterbury.

RUSSELL: The feeling is a little too simplified. You've got to take account of the effects of actions and your feelings towards those effects. You see, you can have an argument about it if you say that certain sorts of occurrences are the sort you like and certain others the sort you don't like. Then you have to take account of the effects of actions. you can very well say that the effects of the actions of the Commandant of Belsen were painful and unpleasant.

COPLESTON: They certainly were, I agree, very painful and unpleasant to all the people in the camp.

RUSSELL: Yes, but not only to the people in the camp, but to outsiders contemplating them also.

COPLESTON: Yes, quite true in imagination. But that's my point. I don't approve of them, and I know you don't approve of them, but I don't see what ground you have for

---

[4] One of Hitler's extermination camps.—E.D.K.

not approving of them, because after all, to the Commandant of Belsen himself, they're pleasant, those actions.

RUSSELL: Yes, but you see I don't need any more ground in that case than I do in the case of colour perception. There are some people who think everything is yellow, there are people suffering from jaundice, and I don't agree with these people. I can't prove that the things are not yellow, there isn't any proof, but most people agree with me that they're not yellow, and most people agree with me that the Commandant of Belsen was making mistakes.

COPLESTON: Well, do you accept any moral obligation?

RUSSELL: Well, I should have to answer at considerable length to answer that. Practically speaking—yes. Theoretically speaking I should have to define moral obligation rather carefully.

COPLESTON: Well, do you think that the word "ought" simply has an emotional connotation?

RUSSELL: No, I don't think that, because you see, as I was saying a moment ago, one has to take account of the effects, and I think right conduct is that which would probably produce the greatest possible balance in intrinsic value of all the acts possible in the circumstances, and you've got to take account of the probable effects of your action in considering what is right.

COPLESTON: Well, I brought in moral obligation because I think that one can approach the question of God's existence in that way. The vast majority of the human race will make, and always have made, some distinction between right and wrong. The vast majority I think has some consciousness of an obligation in the moral sphere. It's my opinion that the perception of values and the consciousness of moral law and obligation are best explained through the hypothesis of a transcendent ground of value and of an author of the moral law. I do mean by "author of the moral law" an arbitrary author of the moral law. I think, in fact, that those modern atheists who have argued in the converse way "there is no God; therefore, there are no absolute values and no absolute law," are quite logical.

RUSSELL: I don't like the word "absolute." I don't think there is anything absolute whatever. The moral law, for example, is always changing. At one period in the development of the human race, almost everybody thought cannibalism was a duty.

COPLESTON: Well, I don't see that differences in particular moral judgments are any conclusive argument against the universality of the moral law. Let's assume for the moment that there are absolute moral values, even on that hypothesis it's only to be expected that different individuals and different groups should enjoy varying degrees of insight into those values.

RUSSELL: I'm inclined to think that "ought," the feeling that one has about "ought" is an echo of what has been told one by one's parents or one's nurses.

COPLESTON: Well, I wonder if you can explain away the idea of the "ought" merely in terms of nurses and parents. I really don't see how it can be conveyed to anybody in other terms than itself. It seems to me that if there is a moral order bearing upon the human conscience, that the moral order is unintelligible apart from the existence of God.

RUSSELL: Then you have to say one or other of two things. Either God only speaks to a very small percentage of mankind—which happens to include yourself—or He deliberately says things that are not true in talking to the consciences of savages.

COPLESTON: Well, you see, I'm not suggesting that God actually dictates moral precepts to the conscience. The human being's ideas of the content of the moral law depends certainly to a large extent on education and environment, and a man has to use his reason in assessing the validity of the actual moral ideas of his social group. But the possibility of criticising the accepted moral code presupposes that there is an objective standard, that there is an ideal moral order, which imposes itself (I meant the obligatory character of which can be recognized). I think that the recognition of this ideal moral order is part of the recognition of contingency. It implies the existence of a real foundation of God.

RUSSELL: But the law-giver has always been, it seems to me, one's parents or someone like. There are plenty of terrestrial law-givers to account for it, and that would explain why people's consciences are so amazingly different in different times and places.

COPLESTON: It helps to explain differences in the perception of particular moral values, which otherwise are inexplicable. It will help to explain changes in the matter of the moral law in the content of the precepts as accepted by this or that nation, or this or that individual. but the form of it, what Kant calls the categorical imperative, the "ought," I really don't see how that can possibly be conveyed to anybody by nurse or parent because there aren't any possible terms, so far as I can see, with which it can be explained. It can't be defined in other terms than itself, because once you've defined it in other terms than itself you've explained it away. It's no longer a moral "ought." It's something else.

RUSSELL: Well, I think the sense of "ought" is the effect of somebody's imagined disapproval, it may be God's imagined disapproval, but it's somebody's imagined disapproval. And I think that is what is meant by "ought."

COPLESTON: It seems to me to be external customs and taboos and things of that sort which can most easily be explained simply through environment and education, but all that seems to me to belong to what I call the matter of the law, the content. The idea of the "ought" as such can never be conveyed to a man by the tribal chief or by anybody else, because there are no other terms in which it could be conveyed. It seems to me entirely—[Russell breaks in].

RUSSELL: But I don't see any reason to say that—I mean we all know about conditioned reflexes. We know that an animal, if punished habitually for a certain sort of act, after a time will refrain. I don't think the animal refrains from arguing within himself, "Master will be angry if I do this." He has a feeling that that's not the thing to do. That's what we can do with ourselves and nothing more.

COPLESTON: I see no reason to suppose that an animal has a consciousness of moral obligation; and we certainly don't regard an animal as morally responsible for his acts of disobedience. But a man has a consciousness of obligation and of moral values. I see no reason to suppose that one could condition all men as one can "condition" an animal, and I don't suppose you'd really want to do so even if one could. If "behaviourism" were true, there would be no objective moral distinction between the emperor Nero and St. Francis of Assisi. I can't help feeling, Lord Russell, you know, that you regard the conduct of the Commandant at Belsen as morally reprehensible, and that you yourself would never under any circumstances act in that way, even if you thought, or had reason to think, that possibly the balance of the happiness of the human race might be increased through some people being treated in that abominable manner.

RUSSELL: No. I wouldn't imitate the conduct of a mad dog. The fact that I wouldn't do it doesn't really bear on this question we're discussing.

COPLESTON: No, but if you were making a utilitarian explanation of right and wrong in terms of consequences, it might be held, and I suppose some of the Nazis of the better type would have held that although it's lamentable to have to act in this way, yet the balance in the long run leads to greater happiness. I don't think you'd say that, would you? I think you'd say that that sort of action is wrong—and in itself, quite apart from whether the general balance of happiness is increased or not. Then, if you're prepared to say that, then I think you must have some criterion of right and wrong, that is outside the criterion of feeling, at any rate. To me, that admission would ultimately result in the admission of an ultimate ground of value in God.

RUSSELL: I think we are perhaps getting into confusion. It is not direct feeling about the act by which I should judge, but rather a feeling as to the effects. And I can't admit many circumstances in which certain kinds of behaviour, such as you have been discussing, would do good. I can't imagine circumstances in which they would have a beneficial effect. I think the persons who think they do are deceiving themselves. But if there were circumstances in which they would have a beneficial effect, then I might be obliged, however reluctantly, to say—"Well, I don't like these things, but I will acquiesce in them," just as I acquiesce in the Criminal Law, although I profoundly dislike punishment.

COPLESTON: Well, perhaps it's time I summed up my position. I've argued two things. First, that the existence of God can be philosophically proved by a metaphysical argument; secondly, that it is only the existence of God that will make sense of man's moral experience and of religious experience. Personally, I think that your way of accounting for man's moral judgments leads inevitably to a contradiction between what your theory demands and your own spontaneous judgments. Moreover, your theory explains moral obligation away, and explaining away is not explanation. As regards the metaphysical argument, we are apparently in agreement that what we call the world consists simply of contingent beings. That is, of beings no one of which can account for its own existence. You say that the series of events needs no explanation: I say that if there were no necessary being , no being which must exist and cannot not-exist, nothing would exist. The infinity of the series of contigent beings, even if proved, would be irrelevant. Something does exist; therefore, there must be something which accounts for this fact, a being which is outside the series of contingent beings. If you had admitted this, we could then have discussed whether that being is personal, good, and so on. On the actual point discussed, whether there is or is not a necessary being, I find myself, I think, in agreement with the great majority of classical philosophers.

You maintain, I think, that existing beings are simply there, and that I have no justification for raising the question of the explanation of their existence. But I would like to point out that this position cannot be substantiated by logical analysis; it expresses a philosophy which itself stands in need of proof. I think we have reached an impasse because our ideas of philosophy are radically different; it seems to me that what I call a part of philosophy, that you call the whole, insofar at least as philosophy is rational. It seems to me, if you will pardon my saying so, that besides your own logical system —which you call "modern" in opposition to antiquated logic, (a tendentious adjective)—you maintain a philosophy which cannot be substantiated by logical analysis. After all, the problem of God's existence is an existential problem whereas logical analysis does not deal directly with problems of existence. So it seems to me, to declare that the terms involved in one set of problems are meaningless because they are not required in dealing with another set of problems, is to settle from the beginning the nature and extent of philosophy, and that is itself a philosophical act which stands in need of justification.

RUSSELL: Well, I should like to say just few words by way of summary on my side. First, as to the metaphysical argument: I don't admit the connotations of such a term as "contingent"or the possibility of explanation in Fr. Copleston's sense. I think the word "contingent" inevitably suggest the possibility of something that wouldn't have this what you might call accidental character of just being there, and I don't think is true except in the purely causal sense. You can sometimes give a causal explanation of one thing as being the effect of something else, but that is merely referring one thing to another thing and there's no—to my mind—explanation in Fr. Copleston's sense of anything at all, nor is there any meaning in calling things "contingent" because there isn't anything else they could be. That's what I should say about that, but I should like to say a few words about Fr. Copleston's accusation that I regard logic as all philosophy—that is by no means the case. I don't by any means regard logic as all philosophy. I think logic is an essential part of philosophy and logic has to be used in philosophy, and in that I think he and I are at one. When the logic that he uses was new—namely, in the time of Aristotle, there had to be a great deal of fuss made about it; Aristotle made a lot of fuss about that logic. Nowadays it's become old and respectable, and you don't have to make so much fuss about it. The logic that I believe in is comparatively new, and therefore I have to imitate Aristotle in making a fuss about it ; but it's not that I think it's all philosophy by any means—I don't think so. I think it's an important part of philosophy, and when I say that, I don't find a meaning for this or that word, that is a position of detail based upon what I've found out about that particular word, from thinking about it. It's not a general position that all words that are used in metaphysics are nonsense, or anything like that which I don't really hold.

As regards the moral argument, I do find that when one studies anthropology or history, there are people who think it their duty to perform acts which I think abominable, and I certainly can't, therefore, attribute Divine origin to the matter of moral obligation, which Fr. Copleston doesn't ask me to; but I think even the form of moral obligation, when it takes the form of enjoining you to eat your father or what not, doesn't seem to me to be such a very beautiful and noble thing; and, therefore, I cannot attribute a Divine origin to this sense of moral obligation, which I think is quite easily accounted for in quite other ways.

CHAPTER FIVE

The Theistic Rejoinders

○ ○ ○ **24**

God: The Cosmological and Design Arguments[1]

Richard Taylor

I. Introduction

AN ACTIVE, LIVING, and religious belief in the gods has probably never arisen and been maintained on purely metaphysical grounds. Such beliefs are found in every civilized land and time, and are often virtually universal in a particular culture, yet relatively few men have much of a conception of metaphysics. There are in fact entire cultures, such as ancient Israel, to whom metaphysics is quite foreign, though these cultures may nevertheless be religious.

Belief in the gods seems to have its roots in human desires and fears, particularly those associated with self-preservation. Like all other creatures, men have a profound will to live, which is what mainly gives one's existence a meaning from one sunrise to the next. Unlike other creatures, however, men are capable of the full and terrible realization of their own inevitable decay. A man can bring before his mind the image of his own grave, and with it the complete certainty of its ultimate reality, and against this his will naturally recoils. It can hardly seem to him less than an absolute catastrophe, the very end, so far as he is concerned, of everything, though he has no difficulty viewing death, as it touches others more or less remote from himself, as a perhaps puzzling, occasionally distressing, but nonetheless, necessary aspect of nature. It is probably partly in response to this fear that he turns to the gods, as those beings of such power that they can overturn this verdict of nature.

The sources of religious belief are doubtless much more complex than this, but they seem to lie in man's will rather than in his speculative intelligence, nevertheless. Men who possess such a belief seldom permit any metaphysical considerations to wrest it from them, while those who lack it are seldom turned toward it by other metaphysical considerations. Still, in every land in which philosophy has flourished, there have been profound thinkers who have sought to discover some metaphysical basis for a rational belief in the existence of some supreme being or beings. Even though religion may properly be a matter of faith rather than reason, still, a philosophical person can hardly help wondering whether, in particular, the existence of God might be something that can

---

[1] Cosmological (First Cause) Argument, sections II–IX; Design (Teleological) Argument, sections X–XII.—E.D.K.

be not merely believed but shown. It is this question that we want now to consider; that is, we want to see whether there are not strong metaphysical considerations from which the existence of some supreme and supranatural being might reasonably be inferred.

PART ONE: THE COSMOLOGICAL ARGUMENT

II. *The Principle of Sufficient Reason*

Suppose you were strolling in the woods and, in addition to the sticks, stones, and other accustomed litter of the forest floor, you one day came upon some quite unaccustomed object, something not quite like what you had ever seen before and would never expect to find in such a place. Suppose, for example, that it is a large ball, about your own height, perfectly smooth and translucent. You would deem this puzzling and mysterious, certainly, but if one considers the matter, it is no more inherently mysterious that such a thing should exist than that anything else should exist. If you were quite accustomed to finding such objects of various sizes around you most of the time, but had never seen an ordinary rock, then upon finding a large rock in the woods one day you would be just as puzzled and mystified. This illustrates the fact that something that is mysterious ceases to seem so simply by its accustomed presence. It is strange indeed, for example, that a world such as ours should exist; yet few men are very often struck by this strangeness, but simply take it for granted.

Suppose, then, that you have found this translucent ball and are mystified by it. Now whatever else you might w· nder about it, there is one thing you would hardly question; namely, that it did not appear there all by itself, that it owes its existence to something. You might not have the remotest idea whence and how it came to be there, but you would hardly doubt that there was an explanation. The idea that it might have come from nothing at all, that it might exist without there being any explanation of its existence, is one that few people would consider worthy of entertaining.

This illustrates a metaphysical belief that seems to be almost a part of reason itself, even though few men ever think upon it; the belief, namely, that there is some explanation for the existence of anything whatever, some reason why it should exist rather than not. The sheer nonexistence of anything, which is not to be confused with the passing out of existence of something, never requires a reason; but existence does. That there should never have been any such ball in the forest does not require any explanation or reason, but that there should ever be such a ball does. If one were to look upon a barren plain and ask why there is not and never has been any large translucent ball there, the natural response would be to ask why there should be; but if one finds such a ball, and wonders why it is there, it is not quite so natural to ask why it should *not* be, as though existence should simply be taken for granted. That anything should not exist, then, and that, for instance, no such ball should exist in the forest, or that there should be no forest for it to occupy, or no continent containing a forest, or no earth, nor any world at all, do not seem to be things for which there needs to be any explanation or reason; but that such things should be, does seem to require a reason.

The principle involved here has been called the principle of sufficient reason. Actually, it is a very general principle, and is best expressed by saying that, in the case of any positive truth, there is some sufficient reason for it, something which, in this sense, makes it true—in short, that there is some sort of explanation, known or unknown, for everything.

Now some truths depend on something else, and are accordingly called *contingent*, while others depend only upon themselves, that is, are true by their very natures and are accordingly called *necessary*. There is, for example, a reason why the stone on my window sill is warm; namely, that the sun is shining upon it. This happens to be true, but not by its very nature. Hence, it is contingent, and depends upon something other than itself. It is also true that all the points of a circle are equidistant from the center, but this truth depends upon nothing but itself. No matter what happens, nothing can make it false. Similarly, it is a truth, and a necessary one, that if the stone on my window sill is a body, as it is, then it has a form, since this fact depends upon nothing but itself for its confirmation. Untruths are also, of course, either contingent or necessary, it being contingently false, for example, that the stone on my window sill is cold, and necessarily false that it is both a body and formless, since this is by its very nature impossible.

The principle of sufficient reason can be illustrated in various ways, as we have done, and if one thinks about it, he is apt to find that he presupposes it in his thinking about reality, but it cannot be proved. It does not appear to be itself a necessary truth, and at the same time it would be most odd to say it is contingent. If one were to try proving it, he would sooner or later have to appeal to considerations that are less plausible than the principle itself. Indeed, it is hard to see how one could even make an argument for it, without already assuming it. For this reason it might properly be called a presupposition of reason itself. One can deny that it is true, without embarrassment or fear of refutation, but one is then apt to find that what he is denying is not really what the principle asserts. We shall, then, treat it here as a datum—not something that is provably true, but as something which all men, whether they ever reflect upon it or not, seem more or less to presuppose.

III. *The Existence of a World*

It happens to be true that something exists, that there is, for example, a world, and while no one ever seriously supposes that this might not be so, that there might exist nothing at all, there still seems to be nothing the least necessary in this, considering it just by itself. That no world should ever exist at all is perfectly comprehensible and seems to express not the slightest absurdity. Considering any particular item in the world it seems not at all necessary in itself that it should ever have existed, nor does it appear any more necessary that the totality of these things, or any totality of things, should ever exist.

From the principle of sufficient reason it follows, of course, that there must be a reason, not only for the existence of everything in the world but for the world itself, meaning by "the world" simply everything that ever does exist, except God, in case there is a god. This principle does not imply that there must be some purpose or goal for everything, or for the totality of all things; for explanations need not, and in fact seldom are, teleological or purposeful. All the principle requires is that there be some sort of reason for everything. And it would certainly be odd to maintain that everything in the world is either purely accidental, or such that it just bestows its own being upon itself, and then to deny this of the world itself. One can indeed *say* that the world exists by its very nature, or is an inherently necessary being. But it is at least very odd and arbitrary to deny of this existing world the need for any sufficient reason, whether independent of itself or not, while presupposing that there is a reason for every other thing that ever exists.

Consider again the strange ball that we imagine has been found in the forest. Now we can hardly doubt that there must be an explanation for the existence of such a thing, though we may have no notion what that explanation is. It is not, moreover, the fact of its having been found in the forest rather than elsewhere that renders an explanation necessary. It matters not in the least where it happens to be, for our question is not how it happens to be *there* but how it happens to exist at all. If we in our imagination annihilate the forest, leaving only this ball in an open field, our conviction that it is a contingent thing and owes its existence to something other than itself is not reduced in the least. If we now imagine the field to be annihilated, and in fact everything else as well to vanish into nothingness, leaving only this ball to constitute the entire physical universe, then we cannot for a moment suppose that its existence has thereby been explained, or the need of any explanation eliminated, or that its existence is suddenly rendered self-explanatory. If we now carry this thought one step further and suppose that no other reality ever has existed or ever will exist, that this ball forever constitutes the entire physical universe, then we must still insist on there being some reason independent of itself why it should exist rather than not. If there must be a reason for the existence of any particular thing, then the necessity of such a reason is not eliminated by the mere supposition that certain other things do *not* exist. And again, it matters not at all what the thing in question is, whether it be large and complex, such as the world we actually find ourselves in, or whether it be something small, simple and insignificant, such as a ball, a bacterium, or the merest grain of sand. We do not avoid the necessity of a reason for the existence of something merely by describing it in this way or that. And it would, in any event, seem quite plainly absurd to say that if the world were comprised entirely of a single ball about six feet in diameter, or of a single grain of sand, then it would be contingent and there would have to be some explanation other than itself why such a thing exists, but that, since the actual world is vastly more complex than this, there is no need for an explanation of its existence, independent of itself.

IV. Beginningless Existence

It should now be noted that it is no answer to the question, why a thing exists, to state *how long* it has existed. A geologist does not suppose that he has explained why there should be rivers and mountains merely by pointing out that they are old. Similarly, if one were to ask, concerning the ball of which we have spoken, for some sufficient reason for its being, he would not receive any answer upon being told that it had been there since yesterday. Nor would it be any better answer to say that it had existed since before anyone could remember, or even that it had always existed; for the question was not one concerning its age but its existence. If, to be sure, one were to ask where a given thing came from, or how it came into being, then upon learning that it had always existed he would learn that it never really *came* into being at all; but he could still reasonably wonder why it should exist at all. If, accordingly, the world—that is, the totality of all things excepting God, in case there is a god—had really no beginning at all, but has always existed in some form or other, then there is clearly no answer to the question, where it came from and when; it did not, on this supposition, *come* from anything at all, at any time. But still, it can be asked why there is a world, why indeed there is a beginningless world, why there should have perhaps always been something rather than nothing. And, if the principle of sufficient reason is a good principle, there must be an answer to that question, an answer that is by no means supplied by giving the world an age, or even an infinite age.

V. Creation

This brings out an important point with respect to the concept of creation that is often misunderstood, particularly by those whose thinking has been influenced by Christian ideas. People tend to think that creation—for example, the creation of the world by God—*means* creation *in time*, from which it of course logically follows that if the world had no beginning in time, then it cannot be the creation of God. This, however, is erroneous, for creation means essentially *dependence*, even in Christian theology. If one thing is the creation of another, then it depends for its existence on that other, and this is perfectly consistent with saying that both are eternal, that neither ever came into being, and hence, that neither was ever created at any point of time. Perhaps an analogy will help convey this point. Consider, then, a flame that is casting beams of light. Now there seems to be a clear sense in which the beams of light are dependent for their existence upon the flame, which is their source, while the flame, on the other hand, is not similarly dependent for its existence upon them. The beams of light arise from the flame, but the flame does not arise from them. In this sense, they are the creation of the flame; they derive their existence from it. And none of this has any reference to time; the relationship of dependence in such a case would not be altered in the slightest if we supposed that the flame, and with it the beams of light, had always existed, that neither had ever *come* into being.

Now if the world is the creation of God, its relationship to God should be thought of in this fashion; namely, that the world depends for its existence upon God, and could not exist independently of God. If God is eternal, as those who believe in God generally assume, then the world may (though it need not) be eternal too, without that altering in the least its dependence upon God for its existence, and hence without altering its being the creation of God. The supposition of God's eternality, on the other hand, does not by itself imply that the world is eternal too; for there is not the least reason why something of finite duration might not depend for its existence upon something of infinite duration —though the reverse is, of course, impossible.

VI. God

If we think of God as "the creator of heaven and earth," and if we consider heaven and earth to include everything that exists except God, then we appear to have, in the foregoing considerations, fairly strong reasons for asserting that God, as so conceived, exists. Now of course most people have much more in mind than this when they think of God, for religions have ascribed to God ever so many attributes that are not all implied by describing him merely as the creator of the world; but that is not relevant here. Most religious persons do, in any case, think of God as being at least the creator, as that being upon which everything ultimately depends, no matter what else they may say about him in addition. It is, in fact, the first item in the creeds of Christianity that God is the "creator of heaven and earth." And, it seems, there are good metaphysical reasons, as distinguished from the persuasions of faith, for thinking that such a creative being exists.

If, as seems clearly implied by the principle of sufficient reason, there must be a reason for the existence of heaven and earth—i.e., for the world—then that reason must be found either in the world itself, or outside it, in something that is literally supranatural, or outside heaven and earth. Now if we suppose that the world—i.e., the totality of all things except God—contains within itself the reason for its existence, we are supposing that it exists by its very nature, that is, that it is a necessary being. In that case there would, of course, be no reason for saying that it must depend upon God or anything else for its existence; for if it exists by its very nature, then it depends upon nothing but itself, much as the sun depends upon nothing but itself for its heat. This, however, is implausible, for we find nothing about the world or anything in it to suggest that it exists by its own nature, and we do find, on the contrary, ever so many things to suggest that it does not. For in the first place, anything which exists by its very nature must necessarily be eternal and indestructible. It would be a self-contradiction to say of anything that it exists by its own nature, or is a necessarily existing thing, and at the same time to say that it comes into being or passes away, or that it ever could come into being or pass away. Nothing about the world seems at all like this, for concerning anything in the world, we can perfectly easily think of it as being annihilated, or as never having existed in the first place, without there being the slightest hint of any absurdity in such a supposition. Some of the things in the universe are, to be sure, very old; the moon, for example, or the stars and the planets. It is even possible to imagine that they have always existed. Yet it seems quite impossible to suppose that they owe their existence to nothing but themselves, that they bestow existence upon themselves by their very natures, or that they are in themselves things of such nature that it would be impossible for them not to exist. Even if we suppose that something, such as the sun, for instance, has existed forever, and will never cease, still we cannot conclude just from this that it exists by its own nature. If, as is of course very doubtful, the sun has existed forever and will never cease, then it is possible that its heat and light have also existed forever and will never cease; but that would not show that the heat and light of the sun exist by their own natures. They are obviously contingent and depend on the sun for their existence, whether they are beginningless and everlasting or not.

There seems to be nothing in the world, then, concerning which it is at all plausible to suppose that it exists by its own nature, or contains within itself the reason for its existence. In fact, everything in the world appears to be quite plainly the opposite, namely, something that not only need not exist, but at some time or other, past or future or both, does not in fact exist. Everything in the world seems to have a finite duration, whether long or short. Most things, such as ourselves, exist only for a short while; they come into being, then soon cease. Other things, like the heavenly bodies, last longer, but they are still corruptible, and from all that we can gather about them, they too seem destined eventually to perish. We arrive at the conclusion, then, that while the world may contain some things which have always existed and are destined never to perish, it is nevertheless doubtful that it contains any such thing and, in any case, everything in the world is capable of perishing, and nothing in it, however long it may already have existed and however long it may yet remain, exists by its own nature, but depends instead upon something else.

While this might be true of everything in the world, is it necessarily true of the world itself? That is, if we grant, as we seem forced to, that nothing in the world exists by its own nature, that everything in the world is contingent and perishable, must we also say that the world itself, or the totality of all these perishable things, is also contingent and perishable? Logically, we are not forced to, for it is logically possible that the totality of all perishable things might itself be imperishable, and hence, that the world might exist by its own nature, even though it is comprised exclusively of things which are contingent. It is not logically necessary that a totality should share the defects of its members. For example, even though every man is mortal, it does not follow from this that the human race, or the totality of all men, is also mortal; for it is possible that there will always be human beings, even though there are no human beings which will always exist. Similarly, it is possible that the world is in itself a necessary thing, even though it is comprised entirely of things that are contingent.

This is logically possible, but it is not plausible. For we find nothing whatever about the world, any more than in its parts, to suggest that it exists by its own nature. Concerning anything in the world, we have not the slightest difficulty in supposing that it should perish, or even, that it should never have existed in the first place. We have almost as little difficulty in supposing this of the world itself. It might be somewhat hard to think of everything as utterly perishing and leaving no trace whatever of its ever having been, but there seems to be not the slightest difficulty in imagining that the world should never have existed in the first place. We can, for instance, perfectly easily suppose that nothing in the world had ever existed except, let us suppose, a single grain of sand, and we can thus suppose that this grain of sand has forever constituted the whole universe. Now if we consider just this grain of sand, it is quite impossible for us to suppose that it exists by its very nature, and could never have failed to exist. It clearly depends for its existence upon something other than itself, if it depends on anything at all. The same will be true if we consider the world to consist, not of one grain of sand, but of two, or a million, or, as we in fact find, of a vast number of stars and planets and all their minuter parts.

It would seem then, that the world, in case it happens to exist at all—and this is quite beyond doubt—is contingent and thus dependent upon something other than itself for its existence, if it depends upon anything at all. And it must depend upon something, for otherwise there could be no reason why it exists in the first place. Now that upon which the world depends must be something that either exists by its own nature or does not. If it does not exist by its own nature, then it, in turn, depends for its existence upon something else, and so on. Now then, we can say either of two things; namely, (1) that the world depends for its existence upon something else, which in turn depends on still another thing, this depending upon still another, *ad infinitum*; or (2) that the world derives its existence from something that exists by its own nature and which is accordingly eternal and imperishable, and is the creator of heaven and earth. The first of these alternatives, however, is impossible, for it does not render a sufficient reason why anything should exist in the first place. Instead of supplying a reason why any world should exist, it repeatedly begs off giving a reason. It explains what is dependent and perishable in terms of what is itself dependent and perishable, leaving us still without a reason why perishable things should exist at all, which is what we are seeking. Ultimately, then, it would seem that the world, or the totality of contingent or perishable things, in case it exists at all, must depend upon something that is necessary and imperishable, and which accordingly exists, not in dependence upon something else, but by its own nature.

VII. "Self-Caused"

What has been said thus far gives some intimation of what meaning should be attached to the concept of a self-caused being, a concept that is quite generally misunderstood, sometimes even by scholars. To say that something—God, for example—is self-caused, or is the cause of its own existence, does not mean that this being brings itself into existence, which is a perfectly absurd idea. Nothing can *bring* itself into existence.

To say that something is self-caused (*causa sui*) means only that it exists, not contingently or in dependence upon something else, but by its own nature, which is only to say that it is a being which is such that it can neither come into being nor perish. Now whether such a being in fact exists or not, there is in any case no absurdity in the idea. We have found, in fact, that the principle of sufficient reason seems to point to the existence of such a being, as that upon which the world, with everything in it, must ultimately depend for its existence.

VIII. "Necessary Being"

A being that depends for its existence upon nothing but itself, and is in this sense self-caused, can equally be described as a necessary being; that is to say, a being that is not contingent, and hence not perishable. For in the case of anything which exists by its own nature, and is dependent upon nothing else, it is impossible that it should not exist, which is equivalent to saying that it is necessary. Many persons have professed to find the gravest difficulties in this concept, too, but that is partly because it has been confused with other notions. If it makes sense to speak of anything as an *impossible* being, or something which by its very nature does not exist, then it is hard to see why the idea of a necessary being, or something which in its very nature exists, should not be just as comprehensible. And of course, we have not the slightest difficulty in speaking of something, such as a square circle or a formless body, as an impossible being. And if it makes sense to speak of something as being perishable, contingent, and dependent upon something other than itself for its existence, as it surely does, then there seems to be no difficulty in thinking of something as imperishable and dependent upon nothing other than itself for its existence.

IX. "First Cause"

From these considerations we can see also what is properly meant by a first cause, an appellative that has often been applied to God by theologians, and which many persons have deemed an absurdity. It is a common criticism of this notion to say that there need not be any first cause, since the series of causes and effects which constitute the history of the universe might be infinite or beginningless and must, in fact, be infinite in case the universe itself had no beginning in time. This criticism, however, reflects a total misconception of what is meant by a first cause. *First* here does not mean first in time, and when God is spoken of as a first cause, he is not being described as a being which, at some time in the remote past, *started* everything. To describe God as a first cause is only to say that he is literally a *primary* rather than a secondary cause, an *ultimate* rather than a derived cause, or a being upon which all other things, heaven and earth, ultimately depend for their existence. It is, in short, only to say that God is the creator, in the sense of creation explained above. Now this, of course, is perfectly consistent with saying that the world is eternal or beginningless. As we have seen, one gives no reason for the existence of a world merely by giving it an age, even if it is supposed to have an infinite age. To use a helpful analogy, we can say that the sun is the first cause of daylight and, for that matter, of the moonlight of the night as well, which means only that daylight and moonlight ultimately depend upon the sun for their existence. The moon, on the other hand, is only a secondary or derivative cause of its light. This light would be no less dependent upon the sun if we affirmed that it had no beginning, for an ageless and beginningless light requires a source no less than an ephemeral one. If we supposed that the sun has always existed, and with it its light, then we would have to say that the sun has always been the first—i.e., the primary or ultimate—cause of its light. Such is precisely the manner in which God should be thought of, and is by theologians often thought of, as the first cause of heaven and earth.

PART TWO: THE DESIGN ARGUMENT

X. *The Nature of the World*

Thus far we have considered nothing about the world except the bare fact of its existence, an existence which, it has seemed, is contingent rather than necessary. It matters not, so far as concerns anything said so far, whether the world is orderly or chaotic, large or small, simple or complex, for the ideas so far elicited would still have whatever force they do have, if any, even if we supposed the world to consist of nothing more than the merest grain of sand.

Many persons, however, have thought that the nature or character of the world and its parts point most clearly to the existence of some supranatural "guiding hand," that is, to some *purposeful* being who, whether he created the world or not, nevertheless fashioned it. What is significant here is not merely that some world or other exists, but rather, that it is the kind of world we find. What we find is not a mere grain of sand, nor a conglomeration of these or similar things, nor a chaos. We find an order and harmony, to say nothing of the mystery and complexity of things that our profoundest science and learning seem only barely to penetrate. Students are sometimes awed by the beautiful machinery and apparently purposeful design of the universe when they receive their initiation to science, whether this is discovered to them in the smallest parts of nature, particularly living things, or in the vastness of the heavens. Of course this orderliness is before our eyes all the time, but we hardly notice it, simply because we are so accustomed to it that we tend to take it for granted. The homeostasis or self-regulation of our own bodies, for instance, whereby the body manages to maintain the most unbelievable internal harmony and to adapt itself to the most diverse and subtle forces acting upon it, represents a wonder which human art cannot really duplicate and our science only dimly comprehends. Yet most men live out their lives without even noticing this seeming miracle that is perpetually before them. The same type of order and seemingly goal-directed change is apparent in the embryological development of living things.

This suggests another feature of the world which, in case it is real and not merely apparent, tends to cast doubt upon the supposition that the world we find ourselves in is the accidental and unintended result of the interacting forces of physical nature; namely, that some things in the world, particularly living organisms, seem purposeful or goal-directed in their very construction. Much modern biology is predicated on the supposition that such seemingly purposeful construction is only apparent and not real; indeed, the main significance of Darwin's work was that he made a convincing case for this. Yet, apart from the requirements of a more or less unconsciously held scientific orthodoxy, it is by no means obvious that this is so. If one considers any living thing whatever, he finds that its powers and construction are perfectly adapted to its mode of life. A hawk, for example, has sharp talons, rapacious beak, keen eyes, strength, and a digestive system all perfectly suited to a predatory mode of life. A lowly spider has likewise precisely what is needed in order to entrap its prey in artfully contrived snares.

So it is with every creature whatever. Its anatomy, powers, and instincts are perfectly suited to its goal or mode of life. One can, of course, insist that it is only *because* such beings are so equipped that they pursue the goals that they do, and deny that they are so equipped *in order* to pursue those goals, just as one can insist that it is only *because* a man is carrying rod and reel that he goes fishing, and deny that he is carrying this equipment *in order* to fish; but this seems artificial, even if one gives the evolutionary theory of the origin of such creatures everything that it claims.

The considerations barely adumbrated here fall into a whole cluster of arguments which are all called, loosely, the argument from design. The common element in them is that they endeavor to establish the existence of some supranatural and creative being or beings from consideration of the apparently artful and purposeful design manifested in the world, particularly in living things. We cannot go into a discussion of these arguments, for they are already embodied in an abundant literature, and are for the most part inconclusive anyway. There is, however, one way of expressing the argument from design which has a peculiarly rational twist and which has, moreover, been hardly more than dimly perceived by most of those who have considered this subject. It rests upon the consideration that our own faculties of sense and cognition are not only remarkable in themselves but are in fact relied upon by us for the discovery of truth. It is this, and its implications, that we want now to consider.

XI. Chance and Evidence

The idea we want to develop here is not easy to grasp without misunderstanding, so it will be best to approach it stepwise by considering first an example or two that should make it quite obvious.

Suppose, then, that you are riding in a railway coach and glancing from the window at one of the stops, you see numerous white stones scattered about on a small hillside near the train in a pattern resembling these letters: THE BRITISH RAILWAYS WELCOMES YOU TO WALES. Now you could scarcely doubt that these stones do not just accidentally happen to exhibit that pattern. You would, in fact, feel quite certain that they were purposefully *arranged* that way to convey an intelligible message. At the same time, however, you could not prove, just from a consideration of their arrangement alone, that they were arranged by a purposeful being. It is possible—at least logically so—that there was no guiding hand at all in back of this pattern, that it is simply the result of the operations of inanimate nature. It is possible that the stones, one by one, rolled down the hill and, over the course of centuries, finally ended up in that interesting arrangement, or that they came in some other accidental way to be so related to each other. For surely the mere fact that something has an interesting or striking shape or pattern, and thus *seems* purposefully arranged, is no proof that it is. There might always be some other explanation. Snowflakes, viewed under magnification, exhibit symmetrical, interesting and often beautiful shapes, and yet we know that these are not designed but can be explained simply in terms of the physics of crystallization. We find *apparently* purposeful arrangements and contrivances around us all the time, but we cannot always conclude that these are in fact the expressions of any purpose. Our own bodies and their organs seem purposeful not only in their individual structures but in their relationships to each other, and yet there are well known theories, resting on such nonpurposeful concepts as chance variation, natural selection, and so on, which are able, at least in the opinion of many learned men, to explain these structures without introducing any ideas of purpose and design at all.

Here, however, is the important point which it is easy to overlook; namely, that *if*, upon seeing from the train window a group of stones arranged as described, you were to conclude that you were entering Wales, and *if* your sole reason for thinking this, whether it was in fact good evidence or not, was that the stones were so arranged, *then* you could not, consistently with that, suppose that the arrangement of the stones was accidental. You would, in fact, be presupposing that they were arranged that way by an intelligent and purposeful being or beings, for the purpose of conveying a certain message having nothing to do with the stones themselves. Another way of expressing the same point is, that it would be *irrational* for you to regard the arrangement of the stones as evidence that you were entering Wales, and at the same time to suppose that they might have come to have that arrangement accidentally, that is, as the result of the ordinary interactions of natural or physical forces. If, for instance, they came to be so arranged over the course of time, simply by rolling down the hill, one by one, and finally just happening to end up that way, or if they were strewn upon the ground that way by the forces of an earthquake or storm or whatnot, then their arrangement would in no sense constitute evidence that you were entering Wales, or for anything whatever unconnected with themselves.

Consider another example. Suppose a stone were dug up and found to be covered with interesting marks, all more or less the same size and more or less in rows. Now there is nothing very remarkable about that. Glaciers and volcanoes have produced stones no less interesting, in abundance. They may at first sight seem purposefully fabricated, but a geologist who knows how they came to be there can usually explain their interesting shapes and properties. Suppose further, however, that the marks on this stone are found to resemble the characters of an ancient alphabet. This, too, does not prove that they were purposefully inscribed, for natural forces can leave such marks as these on stones, and over the course of millions of years it is entirely possible that this should occasionally happen. There are places where one can, at will, pick up stones that are almost perfect rectangles and look exactly as though they were hewn by stonecutters, though in fact they resulted from glaciation. But now suppose that these marks are recognized by a scholar having a knowledge of that alphabet, and that with considerable uncertainty due to the obscurity of some of the marks and the obliteration of others, he renders a translation of them as follows: HERE KIMON FELL LEADING A BAND OF ATHENIANS AGAINST THE FORCES OF XERXES. Now one can, to be sure, still maintain that the marks are accidental, that they are only scratches left by volcanic activity, and that it is only a singular coincidence that they resemble, more or less, some intelligible message. Nature sometimes produces effects hardly less interesting and arresting than this. The point to make again, however, is this: if anyone having a knowledge of this stone concludes, solely on the basis of it, that there was someone named Kimon who died in battle near where this stone was found, then he cannot, rationally, suppose that the marks on the stone are the result of the chance or purposeless operations of the forces of nature. He must, on the contrary, assume that they were inscribed there by someone whose purpose was to record an historical fact. If the marks had a purposeless origin, as from volcanic activity or whatnot, then they cannot reveal any fact whatever except, perhaps, certain facts about themselves or their origin. It would, accordingly, be irrational for anyone to suppose *both* that what is seemingly expressed by the marks is true, and *also* that they appeared as the result of nonpurposeful forces, provided the marks are his *sole* evidence for believing that what they seem to say is true.

XII. Sensation and Evidence

Our own organs of sense, to say nothing of our brains and nervous systems, are things of the most amazing and bewildering complexity and delicacy. No matter how far and minutely psychologists and physiologist press their studies of these organs, they seem hardly any closer to a real understanding of them, and how they enable us to *perceive* the world around us. At best they discover only how they convey stimuli and impress physical changes upon the brain. Theories of perception, drawing upon all the scientific and physiological knowledge accumulated to date, and hardly less crude than the speculations of the Greeks.

Some of these organs, moreover, strikingly resemble things purposefully designed and fabricated by men, though they greatly exceed in their delicacy and versatility anything men have invented. The parts and structure of the eye, for example, closely resemble those of a camera. Yet the comparison of these, however striking, is superficial, for the eye does not take pictures. Unlike a camera, it somehow enables its possessor to perceive and thereby to understand. Things like this can be more or less imitated by men, but they are usually crude and makeshift in comparison. It is sometimes almost irresistible, when considering such a thing as the eye, to suppose that, however it may have originated, it is constructed in that manner *in order* to enable its possessor to see. Many persons quite naturally think in these terms, without at all realizing the implications of such purposeful or teleological conceptions.

It must be noted, however, that just as it is possible for a collection of stones to present a novel and interesting arrangement on the side of a hill, and for marks to appear on a stone in a manner closely resembling some human artifact, and for these things still to be the accidental results of natural, nonpurposeful forces, so also it is possible for such things as our own organs of sense to be the accidental and unintended results, over ages of time, of perfectly impersonal, nonpurposeful forces. In fact, ever so many biologists believe that this is precisely what has happened, that our organs of sense are in no real sense purposeful things, but only appear so because of our failure to consider how they might have arisen through the normal workings of nature. It is supposed, for example, that if we apply the conceptions of chance mutations and variations, natural selection, and so on, then we can see how it is at least possible— perhaps even almost inevitable—that things of this sort should finally emerge, without any purpose behind them at all.

It would be astonishing indeed if a quantity of stones were hurled into the air and fell to earth in a pattern spelling out some intelligible message. Any man would feel, quite irresistibly, that it had been somehow *arranged* that they should fall that way. It would be less astonishing, however, if those stones were thrown a million times, and sooner or later fell to earth in such a pattern. Our astonishment would be still less if we found some perfectly natural, nonpurposeful explanation why they might sooner or later fall in that manner and, having so fallen, be thus preserved. If, for instance, we found that the stones were of slightly different weights, sizes and shapes, that these influenced how they were thrown and how they rolled upon landing, that these slight differences tended to favor the likelihood that certain ones would come to rest in the striking manner in which they do come to rest, and that certain obstructions on the ground would tend to preserve them in this arrangement, and so on, then we might find it entirely plausible how they might fall as they do without the intervention of any purposeful being at all. If our explanation were of this kind, however, then as noted before, their arrangement would constitute no evidence whatever for anything not causally connected with themselves.

The mere complexity, refinement and seemingly purposeful arrangement of our sense organs do not, accordingly, constitute any conclusive reason for supposing that they are the outcome of any purposeful activity. A natural, nonpurposeful explanation of them is possible, and has been attempted—successfully, in the opinion of many.

The important point, however, and one that is rarely considered is that we do not simply *marvel* at these structures, and wonder how they came to be that way. We do not simply view them as amazing and striking things, and speculate upon their origins. We, in fact, whether justifiably or not, *rely* on them for the discovery of things that we suppose to be true and which we suppose to exist quite independently of those organs themselves. We suppose, without even thinking about it, that they reveal to us things that have nothing to do with themselves, their structures, or their origins. Just as we supposed that the stones on the hill told us that we were entering Wales—a fact having nothing to do with the stones themselves—so also we suppose that our senses in some manner "tell us" what is true, at least sometimes. The stones on the hill could, to be sure, have been an accident, in which case we cannot suppose that they really tell us anything at all. So also, our senses and all our faculties could be accidental in their origins, and in that case they do not really tell us anything either. But the fact remains, that we do trust them, without the slightest reflection on the matter. Our seeing something is often thought to be, quite by itself, a good reason for believing that the thing exists, and it would be absurd to suggest that we *infer* this from the structure of our eyes or speculations upon their evolutionary origins. And so it is with our other faculties. Our remembering something is often considered to be, quite by itself, a good reason for believing that the thing remembered did happen. Our hearing a sound is often considered, quite by itself, a good reason for believing that a sound exists; and so on.

We are not here suggesting that our senses are infallible, nor even, that we ought to rely upon their testimony. The point is that we do rely upon them. We do not believe merely that our senses are remarkably interesting things. We do not believe merely that they produce interesting effects within us, nor merely that they produce beliefs in us. We assume, rightly or wrongly, that they are *trustworthy* guides with respect to what is true, and what exists independently of our senses and their origins; and we still assume this, even when they are our only guides.

We saw that it would be irrational for anyone to say *both* that the marks he found on a stone had a natural, nonpurposeful origin and *also* that they reveal some truth with respect to something other than themselves, something that is not merely inferred from them. One cannot rationally believe both of these things. So also, it is now suggested, it would be irrational for one to say *both* that his sensory and cognitive faculties had a natural, nonpurposeful origin and *also* that they reveal some truth with respect to something other than themselves, something that is not merely inferred from them. *If* their origin can be entirely accounted for in terms of chance variations, natural selection, and so on, without supposing that they somehow embody and express the purposes of some creative being, then the most we can say of them is that they exist, that they are complex and wondrous in their construction, and are perhaps in other respects interesting and remarkable. We cannot say that they are, entirely by themselves, reliable guides to any truth whatever save only what can be inferred from their own structure and arrangement. If, on the other hand, we do assume that they are guides to some truths having nothing to do with themselves, then it is difficult to see how we can, consistently with that supposition, believe them to have arisen by accident, or by the ordinary workings of purposeless forces, even over ages of time.

At this point persons who have a deep suspicion of all such arguments as this, and particularly persons who are hostile to any of the claims of religion, are likely to seize upon numberless objections of a sort that it would hardly occur to anyone to apply to our first two examples, involving the stones. Thus, it is apt to be said that our cognitive faculties are not so reliable as some would suppose, which is irrelevant; or that arguments from analogy prove nothing, which is also irrelevant, since none of the foregoing is an argument from analogy. Or it is claimed that we rely on our cognitive faculties only because we have found them reliable in the past, and thus have a sound inductive basis for our trust, which is absurd, if not question-begging. The reason I believe there is a world around me is, quite simply, that I see it, feel it, hear it, and am in fact perpetually in cognitive contact with it, or at least assume myself to be, without even considering the matter. To suggest that I *infer* its existence from the effects that it has within me, and that I find the inference justified on the ground that such inner effects have, in the past, been accompanied by external causes, is not only a ridiculous caricature, but begs the question of how, without relying upon my faculties, I could ever confirm such an idea in the first place. Again, it is sometimes said that the capacity to grasp truths has a decided value to the survival of an organism, and that our cognitive faculties have evolved, quite naturally, through the operation of this principle. This appears farfetched, however, even if for no other reason than that man's capacity to understand what is true, through reliance upon his senses and cognitive faculties, far exceeds what is needed for survival. One might as well say that the sign on the hill welcoming tourists to Wales originated over the course of ages purely by accident, and has been preserved by the utility it was then found to possess. This is of course possible, but also immensely implausible.

XIII. Significance of these Arguments

It would be extravagant indeed to suppose that these reflections amount to any sort of confirmation of religion, or even, that they have much to do with religion. They are purely metaphysical and philosophical considerations having implications of only a purely speculative kind. Even if they are utterly probative, which is of course controversial, it can still be pointed out, correctly, that they are consistent with ever so many views which are radically inconsistent with religion. They imply almost nothing with respect to any divine attributes, such as benevolence, and one could insist with some justification that even the word God, which is supposed to be the proper name of a personal being and not just a label to be attached to metaphysically inferred things, is out of place in them.

No more is claimed for these arguments, however, than that they are good arguments, and that they seem to yield the conclusions derived from them. If they are defective, the defects are not gross or obvious. The reader may suit himself whether they yield those conclusions, and if so, what their human significance might be.

○ ○ ○ *25*

Religious Knowledge
and Mystical Experience
James Bisset Pratt

· I ·

IN SPITE OF innumerable differences between the experience of individual Christians, the general sense of some kind of divine presence . . . is common to a surprisingly large number. For that matter, it is very like the mystical experiences found in some of the non-Christian religions. Naturally it has been differently nurtured and differently expressed in the various religious cultures within which it has arisen. It has had a prominent place in the faith and worship of every Christian generation. In our time it has received, and is receiving, unusual stress. This for two reasons. One is the interest which our time feels in psychology, and the interest which our psychologists have come to feel in religion. The other reason is of a theological sort. . . . Various influences have united, during the last half-century, to diminish the prestige of the historical arguments for the existence of God and to reduce almost to the vanishing point the old confidence in the literal inspiration of the Scriptures. As a result the defenders of the Christian belief have evacuated one position after another, and many of them are today concentrating their strength within the fortifications of what they sometimes call the "inner experience."

At the close of the last century the psychologists awoke to the fact that religion was interesting, and began to take the lead in studying it. The first results of this serious work of psychologists upon religion were heartening in the extreme. The theologians were assured by their technical colleagues of the reality and the depth of the religious life. The next step to be taken by the psychologists was not quite so reassuring, namely, the description and analysis of the experience. The third step was frankly disquieting, though inevitable—the attempt, namely, not only to describe but to explain. Once more it seemed that the Ark of the Lord had fallen into the hands of the Philistines. For if the religious experience could be explained, set within the nexus of scientific laws, it seemed to be in effect explained away; not indeed denied, but put in a position where it could no longer be used as an empirical argument for the existence of God.

In view of this situation the attempt has been made to take back the religious experience from psychology to theology, so to speak, by insisting that theology is an empirical science and that "God" is as objective a fact as are the objects of the physical sciences. Thus it is said that in the experience of moral regeneration and in the mystics' apprehension of the Divine, God is directly presented as a scientific fact and not merely as a hypothesis for the explanation of other facts. In other words, that the religious experience is an experience of God and that this proposition is neither a philosophical hypothesis nor a matter of faith and hope, but a plain fact of science.

In making up our minds as to the tenability of this view we should first ask ourselves what we mean by a fact of science. . . . A little reflection will show that a scientific fact, as distinguished from a private and individual experience, must have the characteristics of being repeatable and verifiable. The experiences of the isolated individual may be as real as you like but they cannot possess the social authority of a scientific fact unless they are describable in terms capable of communication to all rational beings and verifiable by all properly equipped observers. The question now is: Can God, even in the vaguest sense, as a Source of Power not identical with our empirical selves, be truly said to be a directly experienced fact in this scientific sense? Is He a verifiable object in the sense of being directly presented to the experience of all normal or standardized and properly equipped observers? For my part, I cannot honestly answer this question in the affirmative. The experience of moral regeneration through religious influence may give us reasons to infer the influence of a Power not ourselves; but God, if reached in this way, would be an inference (as logical as you like, but still an inference, a hypothesis) and not an empirical fact. The mystical experience is on a different footing from moral regeneration, for it purports to be an immediate apprehension of the Divine as a directly felt object. But while it is conceivable that God for the mystic may be no hypothesis but a fact, can we honestly say He is even here a *scientific* fact? I judge we cannot. For a scientific fact, let me repeat, must be verifiable by all standardized observers with suitable training. And very few would maintain that the God of the mystics is verifiable in this fashion; and certainly He is, at all events, very far from having been thus scientifically verified. The man who doubts the existence of X-rays can be put in a position where he can perceive them; but there is no laboratory in which the mystics' God can be exhibited to the nonmystical. Nor is it an answer to assert that the mystics' God is verifiable by anyone with the proper psychical make-up; for while this is doubtless true, it really is merely a tautologous assertion to the effect that all mystics can perceive what all mystics can perceive. As much could be said of the hallucinatory objects commonly seen under the influence of nitrous oxide. And as a fact, those most eloquent in their assertions that only a few can apprehend God in the mystic fashion are just the mystics themselves. If not all, at any rate a very large portion of them assert that no amount of training, no amount of effort will enable one to attain to the mystic apprehension. It is like the wind which bloweth the where it listeth. What need we any further witness? With mystics and nonmystics agreeing almost universally that God as an object of direct apprehension is not verifiable, it would seem to follow inevitably that God is not a scientific fact and that therefore theology cannot be regarded as an empirical science.

· II ·

Hence we are back again with the religious experience in the hands of the psychologists, and faced with the question: Has the psychological description and explanation of this experience made it valueless in the attempt to give a spiritual interpretation to the universe? Students of the psychology of religion are often tempted to say that it is valueless; and it is, I think, their scientific duty to point out all that can be said to justify this negative interpretation. To put the psychologist's position in summary fashion, one may maintain that since the religious experience is experience, the interpretation of it belongs solely to psychology; and that the question whether the religious experience proves the existence and presence of God is an empirical and scientific question, and one with which, therefore, not the theologian but only the psychologist is qualified to deal. If now the religious experience can be explained in purely naturalistic fashion, it is said, we are not warranted in looking for any divine explanation or in using it as evidence for the existence of God. Can the religious experience be so explained?

With this problem in mind the psychologist proceeds to an elaborate description and analysis of the religious—and especially of the mystical—consciousness; and he come to the conclusion that the religious experience is essentially of the same sort as nonreligious experience, having the same character and the same causation. Thus there would seem to be nothing in it to indicate that the mystic or the religious person has come in touch with God in any peculiar sense. It is in content and character on a par with nonreligious experience. What *appears* to be more is a matter not of actual experience but of interpretation. It may be the philosopher can show that all experience points to God, or somehow implies the Absolute; but the psychologist is very doubtful whether the religious or mystical experience implies God any more directly or obviously or in any other way than the most commonplace experience of sense perception.

The psychologist, moreover, has another argument against what I might call the religious interpretation of the religious experience. Not only does psychological analysis show that the religious experience is like other experience in quality; it also shows that its occurrence, its rise, intensity, and decline may be explained by the same general psychological laws that account for the various changes in the nonreligious consciousness. This, to be sure, is not yet fully proved. The situation is complex; many factors, some of them quite obscure, are involved, and no one could seriously claim that all the factors of the religious experience are known, and it is the necessary hypothesis of psychology that the unknown factors must be of the same general type as the known ones. This position of the psychologist is, in a sense, a matter of faith rather than of demonstration, but it is for him a necessary faith; for unless he make the postulate that psychological laws can explain all the facts of human psychosis, he would have to give up his claim that psychology is a complete science.

· III(A) ·

A good deal has been done to substantiate the first of the two arguments referred to above, by which psychology throws doubt on the significance of mysticism: a large part of religious experience turns out on analysis to be of the same sort as nonreligious experience. Even the more striking phenomena of ecstasy can largely be paralleled by the effects of drugs and of Yoga training. Personally I am not convinced that the peculiar joy of religion, or what Otto calls numinous feeling, is really to be paralleled outside of religion. And so far as I can judge, the central thing in the religious experience—the sense of immediate contact with some being other than, though possibly inclusive of, oneself—is strictly unique. This sense of presence differentiates the religious experience pretty sharply from the various forms of drug ecstasy, and also from the usual results of Yoga. I think it is safe to say that when Yoga brings an intuition of the Absolute as present and directly known, some other factor is at work besides the Yoga methods. In other words, the sort of experience brought about by controllable physical and psychological means lacks the one characteristic that is essential to the religious experience.

It may indeed by argued that what has been added in this experience is easily explained by the rationalizing interpretation of the mystic, on the basis of his already accepted belief in the supernatural. We must distinguish, it is frequently and properly pointed out, between what the mystic actually experiences and his interpretation of it. No one will doubt that he has the sensations which he reports; but interpretation is not the product of psychological introspection but of philosophical theory. It does not grow out of the experience, or at any rate, not out of it alone. As Professor J. M. Moore points out, "our categories and established modes of reaction are present before any particular experience, and condition the form which the experience takes. The relation of experience and interpretation is reciprocal and complex rather than being a simple one way relation of dependence."[1]

There is much truth in this criticism of mystic pronouncements. When the Salvation Army lassie tells us she has seen Christ, when Suzo asserts that he has communed with the Madonna, when the Hindu Vaishnavite[2] recounts his immediate apprehension of Sri Krishna, very few of us will doubt that rationalistic interpretation has been busy, and that what we are given is not a description of actually experienced fact, but an interpretation of some simpler experience, formulated on the plan of some familiar creed. There is a line, however, beyond which this distinction of immediate sense data and interpretation cannot profitably and truthfully be carried. For the simplest elements of actual adult experience are seldom if ever sensations, but what John Laird significantly calls "sign facts."[3] A pure sensation is something that few of us who have passed infancy any longer experience. Our simplest forms of perceptual activity are drenched with meaning. The immediately given is already significant; it is never a mere sense datum, but a sense datum that means more than it is. And this is as true of the religious man's sense of presence as of any other form of experience. What he tells us of the further nature of the being he experiences is doubtless a matter of interpretation, but his immediate awareness that he is in the presence of an Other is hardly to be analyzed further without altering it into something very different from what it really is. This awareness of an Other, stripped of its creedal interpretation, differs, so the mystic asserts, *toto coelo* from a mere belief. It comes with all the immediacy of sense perception. It has, of course, sensuous elements, as every percept has; but to identify it with any collection of mere sense data is to mutilate it beyond recognition. It is, in short, if we may trust the mystics' introspective description (not their interpretation), a sign fact.

In saying this I have not forgotten Professor Leuba's artificial production of the sense of presence in the laboratory.[4] But it is well to remind ourselves in passing that

---

[1] J. M. Moore, *Theories of Religious Experience*, p. 187.—J.B.P.
[2] Persons who claimed to have had religious experiences.—E.D.K.
[3] See John Laird, *A Study of Realism*, chaps. ii, v.—J.B.P.
[4] See Leuba, *The Psychology of Religious Mysticism*, pp. 283–286.—J.B.P.

Professor Leuba did not produce the *religious* sense of presence in his laboratory. His experiments were not dealing with that directly. What his experiments showed was that a sense of presence in general may be induced without anyone actually being present. The subject, that is, may be fooled. In short, like other forms of cognitive experience, the sense of presence may be illusory. But surely we did not need experimental evidence to show us this. Occasionally any of us may be mistaken about the presence of a human fellow. We may suppose ourselves not alone in the room and discover that we are. When in doubt about the matter we put the thing to a test, using various methods to find out. The fact that sometimes we are mistaken does not prove to us that we are always mistaken. Each case must stand on its own merits and be judged by its own evidence. As a fact, the cases of mistake are so small a fraction of the total, and the cases in which we are correct form so large a majority, that in normal human experience this sense of another's presence carries with it a strong a priori probability of its own validity.

Now there is no doubt that the mystic may be mistaken like other people. As Professor James[5] pointed out, his emotion of conviction as to the validity of his experience of presence may be authoritative for him, but it is not for anyone else. It is quite possible that various causes, known or unknown, may have united to delude him. His own certainty is no guarantee of the truth of his assertion. But the fact that he *may be* mistaken does not prove that he *is* mistaken. The fact—if it be a fact—that he is *sometimes* mistaken does not prove that he is *always* mistaken. Here as elsewhere each case must be judged on its merits. Nor can we say that there is so much uncertainty about the cause of this experience that the assertion of the religious man is entirely negligible. The matter is not left as if nothing had happened. Certainly the mystic's evidence is not as good as the ordinary evidence of eye and ear, for we have a means of testing the validity of these instruments of knowledge, and in the vast majority of cases they prove trustworthy. The mystic's assertion does not carry with it the same weight of a priori probability as does the more common conviction that someone we do not see is in the room with us. But the assertion of the mystic is not entirely worthless as evidence. It at least sets us a problem of further investigation; and if such investigation can produce no complete explanation for the mystic's experience, the experience must be set down at least tentatively as having a certain minimal evidential value in favor of the truth of the mystic's assertion. The strength of this evidence will be increased with every demonstration that the religious sense of presence, its joy and its other by-products, are different in quality from the corresponding experiences of the nonreligious life.

The claim to evidential validity on the part of the religious sense of presence is the more difficult wholly to deny because of the immense number of witnesses that might be called upon to give confirmatory testimony. A student of the history of religions can hardly fail to be struck with the ubiquity of this experience. The way it springs up, spontaneously and independently in remotely separated lands, among peoples of unrelated races, in nearly all the ages and in all the religions with which we are acquainted, is at least an impressive fact. Indeed, one might argue that if any evidential value whatever is to be granted the religious experience, one will have to go on and grant it a good deal, because of the cumulative nature of its testimony.

---

[5] William James (in Selection 6).—E.D.K.

· III(B) ·

Whether it has any evidential value is, of course, just the question we are discussing. It will be recalled that there are two principal arguments for the naturalistic interpretation of the religious experience. The one based on the similarity between religious and nonreligious experiences we have discussed. The other argument—which indeed is so closely related to the first as to be hardly separable except for purposes of exposition—consists in pointing out that the same psychological laws obtain among religious facts as those which govern the whole mental life of man. In other words, it is the aim of this argument to show that the various experiences of the religious life follow laws of definite and regular sequence, and are therefore susceptible of purely psychological explanation. Since they can be explained psychologically, the argument continues, they need no other explanation, and hence cannot be used as evidence for anything beyond the human mind with its human contents and its human ways of working.

As I have already pointed out, psychology has not yet been fully successful in making out these laws of regular sequence between religious phenomena and various psychophysical conditions; they represent rather a program and ideal than an actual achievement. Much successful work toward this ideal has been done and more may be expected. The psychologist, I think, is justified in making a working hypothesis of this ideal of complete psychological explanation for all mental facts. In a sense it is a necessary hypothesis, for his claim that psychology is at least potentially a science capable of giving complete explanation and prediction depends upon it. Unfortunately many psychologists often forget that this hypothesis is as yet only a hypothesis and is very far indeed from having been empirically verified. The truth is, we cannot as yet explain all the facts of human experience and of mental activity by psychological laws. To assert in the present state of our ignorance that we can because we must—which means because we want to—is not science but dogma and the will to make believe.

It is, however, perfectly conceivable that some day all the activities of the human mind, including the religious experience, will be explicable in psychological fashion; in other words, that we shall be able to show how, say, the mystical experience follows invariably upon certain definable conditions, and that by going through certain psychophysical processes one may induce it. This possibility opens up a rather interesting logical question. For if this situation should ever be reached, how would it, and how should it be interpreted? The interpretation that would be given it by most psychologists is obvious enough: they would say that the religious experience was thereby shown to be, like any other conscious state, producible by certain definite conditions, and therefore no more significant of objective reality than dreams or hypnosis. But there would be an equally obvious interpretation open to the mystics. It will be recalled that in our discussion of the claims of theology to rank as an empirical science, I argued that this was not admissible because the mystic fact is not a scientific fact; and that it is not a scientific fact because it is not verifiable by all normal or standardized human beings—that is to say, not reproducible at will within the field of awareness. But on the hypothesis we have now set up of the future perfecting of psychology, the mystic experience is to be reproducible at will. We can therefore picture the mystics, or their philosophical defenders, turning the tables on the psychologists by saying: you told us our apprehension of the Divine was not a scientific fact because not verifiable in the sense of being reproducible. Now, thanks to your kind of researches, it is reproducible and verifiable. Is not our apprehension of the Divine, therefore, a fact, and a scientific fact? Is it not a scientific fact in the same sense as your apprehension of brain cells; and immeasurably more scientific than the physicist's apprehension of the invisible electrons? Instead of interpreting it as you do dreams and illusions, should you not rather, on your own showing, interpret it as you do veridical perception?

The situation is sufficiently bewildering. Plainly it will hardly do to argue: mysticism is illusory because its cognitive states are *not* reproducible; and with the next breath to argue, mysticism is illusory because its cognitive states *are* reproducible. To do that would be to blow hot and cold, to play fast and loose with nature. Either the religious experience is reproducible, given certain conditions, or it is not; and from both these opposites we can hardly draw the same conclusion. If it is incumbent upon us to give the devil his due, surely it is only fair to give the Lord a chance!

How, then, should we construe this rather puzzling situation? A good deal, I think, would depend on the actual details of the actual facts which, by hypothesis, psychology shall one day discover. If, for example, it were found that the religious experience, in all its fullness and with its cognizable quality, could be reproduced by a dose of some newly discovered drug, and that it never arose except under psychophysical conditions which were, in the last analysis, identical with those induced by this drug; it would then follow—that the new-found drug was an excellent means for bringing about the psychophysical conditions requisite for the religious experience! It would prove nothing more; and it would still be open to anyone who wished to do so to assert that these identical psychophysical conditions might be produced by the direct action of God. It is unlikely, however, that many would make such an assertion; and probably not only the psychologists but most of us would agree that the religious experience was a symptom of certain physical conditions but without further objective or cosmic significance. We may, however, picture other results from the scientific investigation of the religious consciousness and its "causes." We may well imagine that psychology might discover that the religious experience followed regularly upon a long process of purifying the heart and concentrating the mind, by proper means, upon the thought of the Divine. Now if this were true, if it were a verifiable scientific fact that the experience of the Divine Presence, the immediate and undoubtable sense of the numinous at hand, sufficiently different from every other sort of experience to be distinguishable and recognizable, and having the same compelling objectivity that visual and tactual experiences possess—if this form of cognitive consciousness, I say, were found to follow invariably upon a definable process of heart purification and mind concentration, how should we interpret the logic of the situation?

I think it is perfectly plain that there would be two answers. The conscientious psychologist *as psychologist* would say: The religious consciousness is now fully explained in psychological terms. I leave to the philosopher the explanation of the cosmos, but I have shown that no reference to anything supernatural, to anything outside of human nature, is needed to explain the sense of divine presence and its various by-products. It follows regularly upon definable and predictable psychophysical conditions by laws of regular and invariable sequence. On the other hand, the mystic would say: the direct apprehension of God is now become a verifiable fact. If you doubt my word, put yourself through the long course of mental and spiritual training which the psychologist and I can plan out for you, and you shall see for yourself. If any man will follow the religious life in the light of modern science, he shall know of the doctrine. For it is God who will be working in you, God who will be revealing Himself to you, who can now be *counted on* to reveal Himself to you, through the working of the laws of the human mind which He Himself made. The religious experience is now a scientific fact, and is to be explained by the actual presence of the Divine before the eyes of the soul.

Of these two interpretations which would be correct? By hypothesis all the relevant facts would be in, and further empirical evidence would be unnecessary. The question would be purely a matter of logic. Plainly it would be exceedingly difficult to prove either of the rival interpretations wrong. And I want to suggest that they might *both* be right.

For what, after all, is a psychological explanation? It consists (in logical outline) in tracing laws of regular sequence between the psychosis to be explained and certain definable conditions, either within the psychophysical mechanism of the subject or within so much of the environment as natural science is able to define, understand, and for experimental purposes, control. Psychological explanation is therefore a form of description and generalization. It does not pretend to point out ultimate or original causes. Psychology is not interested in ultimate or original causes. Its explanation is complete if it has constructed a formula of sequence among scientific, i.e., verifiable facts, and on the basis of this sequence is able without failure to predict the psychosis in question one the appearance of the fact with which the formula connects it. Now there is nothing in the actuality of this kind of an explanation inconsistent with the religious interpretation of the situation. The mystic is not interested in denying the validity of the psychologist's explanation, but he is interested in something more. To him explanation means something different from a generalized description of regular sequences. He is interested in ultimate and original causes. And provided we are willing to relieve the concept of the Divine from the attribute of arbitrariness, there is nothing to prevent our supposing that the steady action of the Divine upon the soul is the ultimate cause of the religious experience, and that what the psychologist describes is the regular process by which the soul may be exposed to this Divine influence. The white radiance of eternity, we may suppose, steadily beats upon us, but only in certain conditions of body and mind can we become sensitive to its light. If this were so, it would be quite within the province of psychology to describe exactly and completely what these conditions are, and on the basis of them to predict and "explain" the rise of the religious experience. To do so, and to do it without any reference to the ultimate source of the inflowing Light, would be to give a complete and exhaustive psychological explanation. Yet it would be equally true that religious experience was exactly what the religious man insists that it is—an immediate awareness of a Divine Other.

By making these suggestions I do not mean that God is to be taken as filling the gaps which science leaves, nor that He is to be proved by miraculous interventions. As I have said, it is quite likely that all religious experience will some day be found to have its scientific explanation—in the sense I have indicated. The Unity of the World is not destroyed. God must be conceived as existing in and expressing Himself through all reality. Yet owing to the finiteness of our human nature and our very limited and partial insight, it may be true—and I think it is true—that most of us apprehend the universal Divine more readily and clearly in some parts of our experience than in others. To the angel's vision God may be "as full, as perfect, in a hair as hart." Yet so long as man remains a little lower than the angels it is probable that he will realize God more fully and perfectly in the religious experience than anywhere else. My aim in this chapter has been, not to attack science nor to defend a view of supernatural divine interventions, but to show that something may be said for the faith of the religious man that, in what he knows as his most religious moments, it is God with whom he comes in touch. Later on he may learn that he is in touch with God always and everywhere; but it is in the mystic experience that he first and most fully *recognizes* God.

Possibly we can make a little plainer to ourselves the contribution made by mysticism to the religious view of the world if we put to ourselves one further question. Let us suppose that in all the world's history there had been no mystics, and no suggestion in any mind of an immediate apprehension of the Divine. Would not, I ask, a religious view of the world under those circumstances have been much less probable, much harder to believe, than it is today? Would not many people, would not most people, on hearing a religious philosophy propounded, have asked the question: "Why, if there be a Divine, has it never come in touch with any human mind?" In other words, if there be a God, would you not naturally expect mystics? The facts of mysticism do not indeed prove the existence of God; but the fact of mysticism makes the existence of God considerably more probable.

· *IV* ·

Thus, I believe, a psychological study of the mystical states combined with a philosophical interpretation of the nature of science may make a distinct contribution to the religious view of reality. But if this is to be done, religion, I trust, will make fewer demands of a specific nature than it has been accustomed to make as to the interpretation of the Divine. It will be content to *believe* in God without *defining* Him. More in particular, it will lay less stress than formerly upon the anthropomorphic and excessively personal aspects of the Divine. It will have nothing to say of specific answer to prayer or of Divine interventions. And in place of the dogmatic view of the older theology, it will adopt a more empirical attitude toward the universe, and while less eager to tell who and what God is, it will be more ready to learn.

We come back, then, after our long discussion, to the question: Is the religious experience such as to furnish any relevant empirical evidence on the ultimate religious problems of our time? The answer would seem to be emphatically in the affirmative. A chastened theology may appeal to the fact of the religious life with a certain justifiable confidence. The testimony of the religious consciousness throughout thirty centuries is not without cosmic significance.

o   o   o   *26*

Religious Experience
and Religious Belief
William P. Alston

· *I* ·

CAN RELIGIOUS EXPERIENCE provide any ground or basis for religious belief? Can it serve to justify religious belief, or make it rational? This paper will differ from many others in the literature by virtue of looking at this question in the light of basic epistemological issues. Throughout we will be comparing the epistemology of religious experience with the epistemology of sense experience.

We must distinguish between experience directly, and indirectly, justifying a belief. It indirectly justifies belief B_1 when it justifies some other beliefs, which in turn justify B_1. Thus I have learned indirectly from experience that Beaujolais wine is fruity, because I have learned from experience that this, that, and the other bottle of Beaujolais is fruity, and these propositions support the generalization. Experience will directly justify a belief when the justification does not go through other beliefs in this way. Thus, if I am justified, just by virtue of having the visual experiences I am now having, in taking what I am experiencing to be a typewriter situated directly in front of me, then the belief that there is a typewriter directly in front of me is directly justified by that experience.

We find claims to both direct and indirect justification of religious beliefs by religious experience. Where someone believes that her new way of relating herself to the world after her conversion is to be explained by the Holy Spirit imparting supernatural graces to her, she supposes her belief *that the Holy Spirit imparts graces to her* to be indirectly justified by her experience. What she directly learns from experience is that she sees and reacts to things differently; this is then taken as a reason for supposing that the Holy Spirit is imparting graces to her. When, on the other hand, someone takes himself to be experiencing the presence of God, he thinks that his experience justifies him in supposing that God is *what* he is experiencing. Thus, he supposes himself to be directly justified by his experience in believing God to be present to him.

In this paper I will confine myself to the question of whether religious experience can provide direct justification for religious belief. This has implications for the class of experiences we shall be considering. In the widest sense 'religious experience' ranges over any experiences one has in connection with one's religious life, including any joys, fears, or longings one has in a religious context. But here I am concerned with experiences that could be taken to *directly* justify religious beliefs, i.e. experiences that give rise to a religious belief and that the subject takes to involve a direct awareness of what the religious belief is about. To further focus the discussion, let's confine ourselves to beliefs to the effect that God, as conceived in theistic religions, is doing something that is directed to the subject of the experience—that God is speaking to him, strengthening him, enlightening him, giving him courage, guiding him, sustaining him in being, or just being present to him. Call these "M-beliefs[1] ('M' for manifestation).

Note that our question concerns what might be termed a general "epistemic practice", the accepting of M-beliefs on the basis of experience, rather than some particular belief of that sort. I hold that practices, or habits, of belief formation are the primary subject of justification and that particular beliefs are justified only by issuing from a practice (or the activation of a habit) that is justified. The following discussion of concepts of justification will provide grounds for that judgment.

Whether M-beliefs can be directly justified by experience depends, *inter alia*, on what it is to be justified in a belief. So let us take a look at that.

First, the justification about which we are asking is an "epistemic" rather than a "moral" or "prudential" justification. Suppose one should hold that the practice in question is justified because it makes us feel good. Even if this is true in a sense, it has no bearing on epistemic justification. But why not? What makes a justification *epistemic*? Epistemic justification, as the name implies, has something to do with knowledge, or, more broadly, with the aim at attaining truth and avoiding falsity. At a first approximation, I am justified in believing that p when, from the point of view of that aim, there is something O.K., all right, to be approved, about that fact that I believe that p. But when we come to spell this out further, we find that a fundamental distinction must be drawn between two different ways of being in an epistemically commendable position.

On the one hand there is what we may call a "normative" concept of epistemic justification (J_n), "normative" because it has to do with how we stand *vis-a-vis* norms that specify our intellectual obligations, obligations that attach to one *qua* cognitive subject, *qua* truth-seeker. Stated most generally, J_n consists in one's not having violated one's intellectual obligations. We have to say "not having violated" rather than "having fulfilled" because in all normative spheres, *being justified* is a negative status; it amounts to ones behavior not being in violation of the norms. If belief is under direct voluntary control, we may think of intellectual obligations as attaching directly to believing. Thus one might be obliged to refrain from believing in the absence of adequate evidence. But if, as it seems to me, belief is not, in general, under voluntary control, obligations cannot attach directly to believing. However, I do have voluntary control over moves that can influence a particular belief formation, e.g., looking for more evidence, and moves that can affect my general belief forming habits or tendencies e.g., training myself to be more critical of testimony. If we think of intellectual obligations as attaching to activities that are designed to influence belief formation, we may say that a certain epistemic practice is normatively justified provided it is not the case that the practitioner would not have engaged in it had he satisfied intellectual obligations to engage in activities designed to inhibit it. In other words, the practice is justified if and only if the practitioner did not fail to satisfy an obligation to inhibit it.

However epistemologists also frequently use the term "justified" in such a way that it has to do not with how the subject stands *vis-a-vis* obligations, but rather with the strength of her epistemic position in believing that p, with how likely it is that a belief

---

[1] Pertaining to knowledge.—E.D.K.

of that sort acquired or held in that way is true. To say that a practice is justified in this, as I shall say, "evaluative" sense, (J_e) is to say that beliefs acquired in accordance with that practice, in the sorts of circumstances in which human beings typically find themselves, are generally true. Thus we might say that a practice is J_e if and only if it is reliable.

One further complication in the notion of J_n remains to be canvassed. What is our highest reasonable aspiration for being J_n in accepting a belief on the basis of experience? Being J_n no matter what else is the case? A brief consideration of sense perception would suggest a negative answer. I may be justified in believing that there is a tree in front of me by virtue of the fact that I am currently having a certain kind of sense experience, but this will be true only in "favorable circumstances". If I am confronted with a complicated arrangement of mirrors, I may not be justified in believing that there is an oak tree in front of me, even though it looks for all the world as if there is. Again, it may look for all the world as if water is running uphill, but the general improbability of this greatly diminishes the justification the corresponding belief receives from that experience.

What this shows is that the justification provided by one's experience is only defeasibly so. It is inherently liable to be overriden, diminished, or cancelled by stronger considerations to the contrary. Thus the justification of beliefs about the physical environment that is provided by sense experience is a defeasible or, as we might say, *prima facie*[2] justification. By virtue of having the experience, the subject is in a position such that she will be adequately justified in the belief *unless* there are strong enough reasons to the contrary.

It would seem that direct experiential justification for M-beliefs, is also, at most, *prima facie*. Beliefs about the nature and ways of God are often used to override M-beliefs, particularly beliefs concerning communications from God. If I report that God told me to kill all phenomenologists, fellow Christians will, no doubt, dismiss the report on the grounds that God would not give me any such injunction as that. I shall take it that both sensory experience and religious experience provide, at most, *prima facie* justification.

One implication of this stand is that a particular experiential epistemic practice will have to include some way of identifying defeaters. Different theistic religions, even different branches of the same religion, will differ in this regard, e.g., with respect to what sacred books, what traditions, what doctrines are taken to provide defeaters. We also find difference of this kind in perceptual practice. For example, with the progress of science new defeaters are added to the repertoire. Epistemic practices can, of course, be individuated with varying degrees of detail. To fix our thoughts with regard to the central problem of this paper let's think of a "Christian epistemic practice" (CP) that takes its defeaters from the Bible, the classic creeds, and certain elements of tradition. There will be differences between subsegments of the community of practitioners so defined, but there will be enough commonality to make it a useful construct. My foil to CP, the practice of forming beliefs about the physical environment on the basis of sense-experience, I shall call "perceptual practice" (PP).

Actually it will prove most convenient to think of each of our practices as involving not only the formation of beliefs on the basis of experience, but also the retention of

---

[2] On first glance, on the face of it.—E.D.K.

these beliefs in memory, the formation of rationally self-evident beliefs, and various kinds of reasoning on the basis of all this. *CP* will be the richer complex, since it will include the formation of perceptual beliefs in the usual way, while *PP* will not be thought of as including the distinctive experiential practice of *CP*.

One final preliminary note. J_n is relative to a particular person's situation. If practice P_1 is quite unreliable, I may still be J_n in engaging in it either because I have no way of realizing its unreliability or because I am unable to disengage myself; while you, suffering from neither of these disabilities, are not J_n. When we ask whether a given practice is J_n, we shall be thinking about some normal, reasonably well informed contemporary member of our society.

· II ·

Let's make use of all this in tackling the question as to whether one can be justified in *CP* and in *PP*. Beginning with J_n, we will first have to determine more precisely what one's intellectual obligations are *vis-a-vis* epistemic practices. Since our basic cognitive aim is to come into possession of as much truth as possible and to avoid false beliefs, it would seem that one's basic intellectual obligation *vis-a-vis* practices of belief formation would be to do what one can (or, at least, do as much as could reasonably be expected of one) to see to it that these practices are as *reliable* as possible. But this still leaves us with an option between a stronger and a weaker view as to this obligation. According to the stronger demand one is obliged to refrain (or try to refrain) from engaging in a practice unless one has adequate reasons for supposing it to be reliable. In the absence of sufficient reasons for considering the practice reliable, it is not justified. Practices are guilty until proved innocent. While on the more latitudinarian view one is justified in engaging in a practice provided one does not have sufficient reasons for regarding it to be unreliable. Practices are innocent until proved guilty. Let's take J_{ns} as an abbreviation for 'justified in the normative sense on the stronger requirement', and 'J_{nw}' as an abbreviation for 'justified in the normative sense on the weaker requirement'.

Now consider whether Mr. Everyman is J_{nw} in engaging in *PP*. It would seem so. Except for those who, like Parmenides and Bradley, have argued that there are ineradicable inconsistencies in the conceptual scheme involved in *PP*, philosophers have not supposed that we can show that sense perception is not a reliable guide to our immediate surroundings. Sceptics about *PP* have generally confined themselves to arguing that we can't show that perception is reliable; i.e., they have argued that *PP* is not J_{ns}. I shall assume without further ado that *PP* is J_{nw}.

J_{ns} and J_e can be considered together. Although a practice may actually be reliable without my having adequate reasons for supposing so, and *vice versa*, still in considering whether a given practice is reliable, we will be seeking to determine whether there *are* adequate reasons for supposing it reliable, that is whether Everyman *could* be possessed of such reasons. And if we hold, as we shall, that there are no such reasons, the question of whether they are possessed by one or another subject does not arise.

I believe that there are no adequate non-circular reasons for the reliability of *PP* but I will not be able to argue that point here. If I had a general argument I would unveil it, but, so far as I can see, this thesis is susceptible only of inductive support, by unmasking each pretender in turn. And since this issue has been in the forefront of the

Western philosophical consciousness for several centuries, there have been many pretenders. I do not have time even for criticism of a few representative samples. Instead I will simply assume that PP is not J_{nw}, and then consider what bearing this widely shared view has on the epistemic status of CP.

If J_{nw} is the most we can have for perceptual practice, then if CP is also J_{nw} it will be in at least as strong an epistemic position as the former. (I shall assume without argument that CP can no more be noncircularly shown to be reliable than can PP.) And CP will be J_{nw} for S, provided S has no significant reasons for regarding it as unreliable. Are there any such reasons? What might they be? Well, for one thing, the practice might yield a system that is ineradically internally inconsistent. (I am not speaking of isolated and remediable inconsistencies that continually pop up in every area of thought and experience.) For another, it might yield results that come into ineradicable conflict with the results of other practices to which we are more firmly committed. Perhaps some fundamentalist Christians are engaged in an epistemic practice that can be ruled out on such grounds as these. But I shall take it as obvious that one *can* objectify certain stretches of one's experience, or indeed the whole of one's experience, in Christian terms without running into such difficulties.

· III ·

One may grant everything I have said up to this point and still feel reluctant to allow that CP is J_{nw}. CP does differ from PP in important ways, and it may be thought that some of these differences will affect their relative epistemic status. The following features of PP, which it does not share with CP, have been thought to have this kind of bearing.

1. Within PP there are standard ways of checking the accuracy of any particular perceptual belief.

2. By engaging in PP we can discover regularities in the behavior of the objects putatively observed, and on this basis we can, to a certain extent, effectively predict the course of events.

3. Capacity for PP, and practice of it, is found universally among normal adult human beings.

4. All normal adult human beings, whatever their culture, use basically the same conceptual scheme in objectifying their sense experience.

If CP includes PP as a proper part, as I ruled on above, how can it lack these features? What I mean is that there is no analogue of these features for that distinctive part of CP by virtue of which it goes beyond PP. The extra element of CP does not enable us to discover extra regularities, e.g., in the behavior of God, or increase our predictive powers. M-beliefs are not subject to interpersonal check in the same way as perceptual beliefs. The practice of forming M-beliefs on the basis of experience is not engaged in by all normal adults. And so on.

Before coming to grips with the alleged epistemic bearing of these differences, I want to make two preliminary points. (1) We have to engage in PP to determine that this practice has features 1.-4., and that CP lacks them. Apart from observation, we have no way of knowing that, e.g., while all cultures agree in their way of cognizing the physical environment they differ in their ways of cognizing the divine, or that PP puts us in a position to predict while *CP* doesn't. It might be thought that this is loading the dice in favor of my opponent. If we are to use *PP*, rather than some neutral source, to determine what features it has, shouldn't the same courtesy of self-assessment be accorded *CP*? Why should *it* be judged on the basis of what we learn about it from another practice, while that other practice is allowed to grade itself? To be sure, this is a serious issue only if answers to these questions *are* forthcoming from *CP* that differ from those we arrive at by engaging in *PP*. Fortunately, I can avoid getting involved in these issues by ruling that what I am interested in here is how *CP* looks from the standpoint of *PP*. The person I am primarily concerned to address is one who, like all the rest of us, engages in *PP*, and who, like all of us except for a few outlandish philosophers, regards it as justified. My aim is to show this person that, on his own grounds, *CP* enjoys basically the same epistemic status as *PP*. Hence it is consonant with my purposes to allow *PP* to determine the facts of the matter with respect to both practices. (2) I could quibble over whether the contrast is as sharp as is alleged. Questions can be raised about both sides of the putative divide. On the *PP* side, is it really true that all cultures have objectified sense experience in the same way? Many anthropologists have thought not. And what about the idea that all *normal* adult human beings engage in the same perceptual practice? Aren't we loading the dice by taking participation in what we regard as standard perceptual practice as our basic criterion for normality? On the *CP* side, is it really the case that this practice reveals no regularities to us, or only that they are very different from regularities in the physical world? What about the point that God is faithful to His promises? Or that the pure in heart will see God? However, I believe that when all legitimate quibbles have been duly registered there will still be very significant differences between the two practices in these respects. So rather than contesting the factual allegations, I will concentrate on the *de jure* issue as to what bearing these differences have on epistemic status.

How could the lack of 1.-4. prevent *CP* from being $\mathcal{J}_{nw}$? Only by providing an adequate ground for a judgment of unreliability. And why suppose that? Of course, the lack of these features implies that we lack certain reasons we might conceivably have had for regarding *CP* as reliable. If we could ascertain that *PP* has those features, without using *PP* to do so, that would provide us with strong reasons for judging *PP* to be reliable. And the parallel possibility is lacking for *CP*. This shows that we cannot have *certain* reasons for taking *CP* to be reliable, but it doesn't follow that we have reasons for unreliability. That would follow only if we could also premise that a practice is reliable *only if* (as well as *if*) it has 1.-4. And why suppose that?

My position is that it is a kind of parochialism that makes the lack of 1.-4. appear to betoken untrustworthiness. The reality *CP* claims to put us in touch with is conceived to be vastly different from the physical environment. Why should the sorts of procedures required to put us in effective cognitive touch with this reality not be equally different? Why suppose that the distinctive features of *PP* set an appropriate standard for the cognitive approach to God? I shall sketch out a possible state of affairs in which *CP* is quite trustworthy while lacking 1.-4., and then suggest that we have no reason to suppose that this state of affairs does not obtain.

Suppose, then, that

(A) God is too different from created beings, too "wholly other", for us to be able to grasp any regularities in His behavior.

Suppose further that

(B) for the same reason we can only attain the faintest, sketchiest, and most insecure grasp of what God is like.

Finally, suppose that

(C) God has decreed that a human being will be aware of His presence in any clear and unmistakable fashion only when certain special and difficult conditions are satisfied.

If all this is the case, then it is the reverse of surprising that *CP* should lack 1.-4. even if it does involve a genuine experience of God. It would lack 1.-2. because of (A). It is quite understandable that it should lack 4. because of (B). If our cognitive powers are not fitted to frame an adequate conception of God, it is not at all surprising that there should be wide variation in attempts to do so. This is what typically happens in science when investigators are grappling with a phenomenon no one really understands. A variety of models, analogues, metaphors, hypotheses, hunches are propounded, and it is impossible to secure universal agreement. 3. is missing because of (C). If very difficult conditions are set it is not surprising that few are chosen. Now it is compatible with (A)-(C) that

(D) religious experience should, in general, constitute a genuine awareness of the divine.

and that

(E) although any particular articulation of such an experience might be mistaken to a greater or lesser extent, indeed even though all such articulations might miss the mark to some extent, still such judgments will, for the most part, contain some measure of truth; they, or many of them, will constitute a useful approximation of the truth;

and that

(F) God's designs contain provision for correction and refinement, for increasing the accuracy of the beliefs derived from religious experience. Perhaps as one grows in the spiritual life ones spiritual sight becomes more accurate and more discriminating; perhaps some special revelation is vouchsafed under certain conditions; and there are many other conceivable possibilities.

If something like all this were the case then *CP* would be trustworthy even though it lacks features 1.-4. This is a conceivable way in which *CP* would constitute a road to the truth, while differing from *PP* in respects 1.-4. Therefore unless we have adequate reason for supposing that no such combination of circumstances obtains, we are not warranted in taking the lack of 1.-4. to be an adequate reason for a judgment of untrustworthiness.

Moreover it is not just that A.-C. constitute a bare possibility. In the practice of CP we seem to learn that this is the way things are. As for (A) and (B) it is the common teaching of all the higher religions that God is of a radically different order of being from finite substances and, therefore, that we cannot expect to attain the grasp of His nature and His doings that we have of worldly objects. As for (C), it is a basic theme in Christianity, and in other religions as well, that one finds God within one's experience, to any considerable degree, only as one progresses in the spiritual life. God is not available for *voyeurs*. Awareness of God, and understanding of His nature and His will for us, is not a purely cognitive achievement; it requires the involvement of the whole person; it takes a practical commitment and a practice of the life of the spirit, as well as the exercise of cognitive faculties.

Of course these results that we are using to defend *CP* are derived from that same practice. But in view of the fact that the favorable features of *PP*, 1.-4., are themselves ascertained by engaging in *PP*, our opponent is hardly in a position to fault us on this score. However I have not forgotten that I announced it as my aim to show that even one who engaged only in *PP* should recognize that *CP* is $\mathcal{J}_{nw}$. For this purpose, I ignore what we learn in *CP* and revert to the point that my opponent has no basis for ruling out the conjoint state of affairs A.-F., hence has no basis for taking the lack of 1.-4. to show *CP* to be untrustworthy, and hence has no reason for denying that *CP* is $\mathcal{J}_{nw}$.

I conclude that *CP* has basically the same epistemic status as *PP* and that no one who subscribes to the former is in any position to cavil at the latter.

○ ○ ○   **27**

The Basis of the Moral Law
C. S. Lewis

· I ·

I NOW GO back to what I said . . . that there were two odd things about the human race. First, that they were haunted by the idea of a sort of behaviour they ought to practise, what you might call fair play, or decency, or morality, or the Law of Nature. Second, that they did not in fact do so. Now some of you may wonder why I called this odd. It may seem to you the most natural thing in the world. In particular, you may have thought I was rather hard on the human race. After all, you may say, what I call breaking the Law of Right and Wrong or of Nature, only means that people are not perfect. And why on earth should I expect them to be? That would be a good answer if what I was trying to do was to fix the exact amount of blame which is due to us for not behaving as we expect others to behave. But that is not my job at all. I am not concerned at present with blame; I am trying to find out truth. And from that point of view the very idea of something being imperfect, of its not being what it ought to be, has certain consequences.

If you take a thing like a stone or a tree, it is what it is and there seems no sense in saying it ought to have been otherwise. Of course you may say a stone is "the wrong shape" if you want to use it for a rockery, or that a tree is a bad tree because it does not give you as much shade as you expected. But all you mean is that the stone or tree does not happen to be convenient for some purpose of your own. You are not, except as a joke, blaming them for that. You really know, that, given the weather and the soil, the tree could not have been any different. What we, from our point of view, call a "bad" tree is obeying the laws of its nature just as much as a "good" one.

Now have you noticed what follows? It follows that what we usually call the laws of nature—the way weather works on a tree for example—may not really be *laws* in the strict sense, but only in a manner of speaking. When you say that falling stones always obey the law of gravitation, is not this much the same as saying that the law only means "what stones always do"? You do not really think that when a stone is let go, it suddenly remembers that it is under orders to fall to the ground. You only mean that, in fact, it does fall. In other words, you cannot be sure that there is anything over and above the facts themselves, any law about what ought to happen, as distinct from what does happen. The laws of nature, as applied to stones or trees, may only mean "what Nature, in fact, does." But if you turn to the Law of Human Nature, the Law of Decent Behaviour, it is a different matter. That law certainly does not mean "what human beings, in fact, do"; for as I said before, many of them do not obey this law at all, and none of them obey it completely. The law of gravity tells you what stones do if you drop them; but the Law of Human Nature tells you what human beings ought to do and do not. In other words, when you are dealing with humans, something else comes in above and beyond the actual facts. You have the facts (how men do behave) and you also have something else (how they ought to behave). In the rest of the universe there need not be anything but the facts. Electrons and molecules behave in a certain way, and certain results follow, and that may be the whole story. But men behave in a certain way and that is not the whole story, for all the time you know that they ought to behave differently.

Now this is really so peculiar that one is tempted to try to explain it away. For instance, we might try to make out that when you say a man ought not to act as he does, you only mean the same as when you say that a stone is the wrong shape; namely, that what he is doing happens to be inconvenient to you. But that is simply untrue. A man occupying the corner seat in the train because he got there first, and a man who slipped into it while my back was turned and removed my bag, are both equally inconvenient. But I blame the second man and do not blame the first. I am not angry—except perhaps for a moment before I come to my senses—with a man who trips me up by accident; I am angry with a man who tries to trip me up even if he does not succeed. Yet the first has hurt me and the second has not. Sometimes the behaviour which I call bad is not inconvenient to me at all, but the very opposite. In war, each side may find a traitor on the other side very useful. But though they use him and pay him they regard him as human vermin. So you cannot say that what we call decent behaviour in others is simply the behaviour that happens to be useful to us. And as for decent behaviour in ourselves, I suppose it is pretty obvious that it does not mean the behaviour that pays. It means things like being content with thirty shillings when you might have got three pounds, doing school work honestly when it would be easy to cheat, leaving a girl alone when you would like to make love to her, staying in dangerous places when you could go somewhere safer, keeping promises you would rather not keep, and telling the truth even when it makes you look a fool.

Some people say that though decent conduct does not mean what pays each particular person at a particular moment, still, it means what pays the human race as a whole; and that consequently there is no mystery about it. Human beings, after all, have some sense; they see that you cannot have real safety or happiness except in a society where every one plays fair, and it is because they see this that they try to behave decently. Now, of course, it is perfectly true that safety and happiness can only come from individuals, classes, and nations being honest and fair and kind to each other. It is one of the most important truths in the world. But as an explanation of why we feel as we do about Right and Wrong it just misses the point. If we ask: "Why ought I to be unselfish?" and you reply "Because it is good for society," we may then ask, "Why should I care what's good for society except when it happens to pay *me* personally?" and then you will have to say, "Because you ought to be unselfish"—which simply brings us back to where we started. You are saying what is true, but you are not getting any further. If a man asked what was the point of playing football, it would not be much good saying "in order to score goals," for trying to score goals is the game itself, not the reason for the game, and you would really only be saying that football was football—which is true, but not worth saying. In the same way, if a man asks what is the point of behaving decently, it is no good replying, "in order to benefit society," for trying to benefit society, in other words being unselfish (for "society" after all only means "other people"), is one of the things decent behaviour consists in; all you are really saying is that decent behaviour is decent behaviour. You would have said just as much if you had stopped at the statement, "Men ought to be unselfish."

And that is where I do stop. Men ought to be unselfish, ought to be fair. Not that men are unselfish, nor that they like being unselfish, but that they ought to be. The Moral Law, or Law of Human Nature, is not simply a fact about human behaviour in the same way as the Law of Gravitation is, or may be, simply a fact about how heavy objects behave. On the other hand, it is not a mere fancy, for we cannot get rid of the idea, and most of the things we say and think about men would be reduced to nonsense if we did. And it is not simply a statement about how we should like men to behave for our own convenience; for the behaviour we call bad or unfair is not exactly the same as the behaviour we find inconvenient, and may even be the opposite. Consequently, this Rule of Right and Wrong, or Law of Human Nature, or whatever you call it, must somehow or other be a real thing—a thing that is really there, not made up by ourselves. And yet it is not a fact in the ordinary sense, in the same way as our actual behaviour is a fact. It begins to look as if we shall have to admit that there is more than one kind of reality; that, in this particular case, there is something above and beyond the ordinary facts of men's behaviour, and yet quite definitely real—a real law, which none of us made, but which we find pressing on us.

· II ·

Let us sum up what we have reached so far. In the case of stones and trees and things of that sort, what we call the Laws of Nature may not be anything except a way of speaking. When you say that nature is governed by certain laws, this may only mean that nature does, in fact, behave in a certain way. The so-called laws may not be anything real—anything above and beyond the actual facts which we observe. But in the case of Man, we saw that this will not do. The Law of Human Nature, or of Right and Wrong, must be something above and beyond the actual facts of human behaviour. In this case, besides the actual facts, you have something else—a real law which we did not invent and which we know we ought to obey.

I now want to consider what this tells us about the universe we live in. Ever since men were able to think, they have been wondering what this universe really is and how it came to be there. And, very roughly, two views have been held. First, there is what is called the materialist view. People who take that view think that matter and space just happen to exist, and always have existed, nobody knows why; and that the matter, behaving in certain fixed ways, has just happened, by a sort of fluke, to produce creatures like ourselves who are able to think. By one chance in a thousand something hit our sun and made it produce the planets; and by another thousandth chance the chemicals necessary for life, and the right temperature, occurred on one of these planets, and so some of the matter on this earth came alive; and then, by a very long series of chances, the living creatures developed into things like us. The other view is the religious view. According to it, what is behind the universe is more like a mind than it is like anything else we know. That is to say, it is conscious, and has purposes, and prefers one thing to another. And on this view it made the universe, partly for purposes we do not know, but partly, at any rate, in order to produce creatures like itself—I mean, like itself to the extent of having minds. Please do not think that one of these views was held a long time ago and that the other has gradually taken its place. Wherever there have been thinking men both views turn up. And note this too. You cannot find out which view is the right one by science in the ordinary sense. Science works by experiments. It watches how things behave. Every scientific statement in the long run, however complicated it looks, really means something like, "I pointed the telescope to such and such a part of the sky at 2:20 A.M. on January 15th and saw so-and-so," or, "I put some of this stuff in a pot and heated it to such-and-such a temperature and it did so-and-so." Do not think I am saying anything against science: I am only saying what its job is. And the more scientific a man is, the more (I believe) he would agree with me that this is the job of science—and a very useful and necessary job it is too. But why anything comes to be there at all, and whether there is anything behind the things science observes—something of a different kind—this is not a scientific question. If there is "Something Behind," then either it will have to remain altogether unknown to men or else make itself known in some different way. The statement that there is any such thing, and the statement that there is no such thing, are neither of them statements that science can make. And real scientists do not usually make them. It is usually the journalists and popular novelists who have picked up a few odds and ends of half-baked science from textbooks who go in for them. After all, it is really a matter of common sense. Supposing science ever became complete so that it knew every single thing in the whole universe. Is it not plain that the questions, "Why is there a universe?" "Why does it go on as it does?" "Has it any meanings?" would remain just as they were?

Now the position would be quite hopeless but for this. There is one thing, and only one, in the whole universe which we know more about than we could learn from external observation. That one thing is Man. We do not merely observe men, we *are* men. In this case we have, so to speak, inside information; we are in the know. And because of that, we know that men find themselves under a moral law, which they did not make, and cannot quite forget even when they try, and which they know they ought to obey. Notice the following point. Anyone studying Man from the outside as we study electricity or cabbages, not knowing our language and consequently not able to get any inside knowledge from us, but merely observing what we did, would never get the slightest evidence that we had this moral law. How could he? for his observations would only show what we did, and the moral law is about what we ought to do. In the same way, if there were anything above or behind the observed facts in the case of stones or the weather, we, by studying them from outside, could never hope to discover it.

The position of the question, then, is like this. We want to know whether the universe simply happens to be what it is for no reason or whether there is a power behind it that makes it what it is. Since that power, if it exists, would be not one of the observed facts but a reality which makes them, no mere observation of the facts can find it. There is only one case in which we can know whether there is anything more, namely our own case. And in that one case we find there is. Or put it the other way round. If there was a controlling power outside the universe, it could not show itself to us as one of the facts inside the universe—no more than the architect of a house could actually be a wall or staircase or fireplace in that house. The only way in which we could expect it to show itself would be inside ourselves as an influence or a command trying to get us to behave in a certain way. And that is just what we do find inside ourselves. Surely this ought to arouse our suspicions? In the only case where you can expect to get an answer, the answer turns out to be Yes; and in the other cases, where you do not get an answer, you see why you do not. Suppose someone asked me, when I see a man in a blue uniform going down the street leaving little paper packets at each house, why I suppose that they contain letters? I should reply, "Because whenever he leaves a similar little packet for me I find it does contain a letter." And if he then objected, "But you've never seen all these letters you think the other people are getting," I should say, "Of course not, and I shouldn't expect to, because they're not addressed to me. I'm explaining the packets I'm not allowed to open by the ones I am allowed to open." It is the same about this question. The only packet I am allowed to open is Man. When I do, especially when I open that particular man called Myself, I find that I do not exist on my own, that I am under a law; that somebody or something wants me to behave in a certain way. I do not, of course, think that if I could get inside a stone or tree I should find exactly the same thing, just as I do not think all the other people in the street get the same letters as I do. I should expect, for instance, to find that the stone had to obey the law of gravity—that whereas the sender of the letters merely tells me to obey the law of my human nature, He compels the stone to obey the laws of its stony nature. But I should expect to find that there was, so to speak, a sender of letters in both cases, a Power behind the facts, a Director, a Guide.

Do not think I am going faster than I really am. I am not yet within a hundred miles of the God of Christian theology. All I have got to is a Something which is directing the universe, and which appears in me as a law urging me to do right and making me feel responsible and uncomfortable when I do wrong. I think we have to assume it is more like a mind than it is like anything else we know—because after all the only other thing we know is matter and you can hardly imagine a bit of matter giving instructions. But, of course, it need not be very like a mind, still less like a person. . . .

○ ○ ○ *28*

Anselm's Ontological Arguments
Norman Malcolm

· *I* ·

I BELIEVE THAT in Anselm's *Proslogion* and *Responsio editoris* there are two different pieces of reasoning which he did not distinguish from one another, and that a good deal of light may be shed on the philosophical problem of "the ontological argument" if we do distinguish them. In Chapter 2 of the *Proslogion*[1] Anselm says that we believe that God is *something a greater than which cannot be conceived*. (The Latin is *aliquid quo nihil maius cogitari possit*. Anselm sometimes uses the alternative expressions *aliquid quo maius nihil cogitari potest, id quo maius cogitari nequit, aliquid quo maius cogitari non valet*.) Even the fool of the Psalm who says in his heart there is no God, when he hears this very thing that Anselm says, namely, "something a greater than which cannot be conceived," understands what he hears, and what he understands is in his understanding though he does not understand that it exists.

Apparently Anselm regards it as tautological to say that whatever is understood is in the understanding (*quidquid intelligitur in intellectu est*): he uses *intelligitur* and *in intellectu est* as interchangeable locutions. The same holds for another formula of his: whatever is thought is in thought (*quidquid cogitatur in cogitatione est*).[2]

Of course many things may exist in the understanding that do not exist in reality; for example, elves. Now, says Anselm, something a greater than which cannot be conceived exists in the understanding. But it cannot exist *only* in the understanding, for to exist in reality is greater. Therefore that thing a greater than which cannot be conceived cannot exist only in the understanding, for then a greater thing could be conceived: namely, one that exists both in the understanding and in reality.[3]

Here I have a question. It is not clear to me whether Anselm means that (a) existence in reality by itself is greater than existence in the understanding, or that (b) existence in reality and existence in the understanding together are greater than existence in the understanding alone. Certainly he accepts (b). But he might also accept

---

[1] I have consulted the Latin text of the *Proslogion*, of *Gaunilonis Pro Insipiente*, and of the *Responsio editoris*, in S. Anselmi. *Opera Omnia*, edited by F.C. Schmitt (Secovii, 1938), vol. I. With numerous modifications, I have used the English translation by S. N. Deane: *St. Anselm* (LaSalle, Illinois, 1948).—N.M.

[2] See *Proslogion 1 and Responsio 2*.—N.M.

[3] Anselm's actual words are: "Et certe id quo maius cogitari nequit, non potest esse in solo intellectu. Si enim vel in solo intellectu est, potest cogitari esse et in re, quod maius est. Si ergo id quo maius cogitari non potest, est in solo intellectu: id ipsum quo maius cogitari non potest, est quo maius cogitari potest. Sed certe hoc esse non potest." *Proslogion 2*.—N.M.

(a), as Descartes apparently does in *Meditation III* when he suggests that the mode of being by which a thing is "objectively in the understanding" is *imperfect*.[4] Of course Anselm might accept both (a) and (b). He might hold that in general something is greater if it has both of these "modes of existence" than if it has either one alone, but also that existence in reality is a more perfect mode of existence than existence in the understanding.

In any case, Anselm holds that something is greater if it exists both in the understanding and in reality than if it exists merely in the understanding. An equivalent way of putting this interesting proposition, in a more current terminology, is: something is greater if it is both conceived of and exists than if it is merely conceived of. Anselm's reasoning can be expressed as follows: *id quo maius cogitari nequit* cannot be merely conceived of and not exist, for then it would not be *id quo maius cogitari nequit*. The doctrine that something is greater if it exists in addition to being conceived of, then if it is only conceived of, could be called the doctrine that *existence is a perfection*. Descartes maintained, in so many words, that existence is a perfection,[5] and presumably he was holding Anselm's doctrine, although he does not, in *Meditation V* or elsewhere, argue in the way that Anselm does in *Proslogion 2* .

When Anselm says, "And certainly, that than which nothing greater can be conceived cannot exist merely in the understanding. For suppose it exists merely in the understanding, then it can be conceived to exist in reality, which is greater,"[6] he is claiming that if I conceived of being of great excellence, that being would be *greater* (more excellent, more perfect) if it existed than if it did not exist. His supposition that "it exists merely in the understanding" is the supposition that it is conceived of but does not exist. Anselm repeated this claim in his reply to the criticism of the monk Gaunilo. Speaking of the being a greater than which cannot be conceived, he says:

> I have said that if it exists merely in the understanding it can be conceived to exist in reality, which is greater. Therefore, if it exists merely in the understanding obviously the very being a greater than which cannot be conceived, is one a greater than which can be conceived. What, I ask, can follow better than that? For if it exists merely in the understanding, can it not be conceived to exist in reality? And if it can be so conceived does not he who conceives of this conceive of a thing greater than it, if it does exist merely in the understanding? Can anything follow better than this: that if a being a greater than which cannot be conceived exists merely in the understanding, it is something a greater than which can be conceived? What could be plainer?[7]

He is implying, in the first sentence, that if I conceive of something which does not exist then it is possible for it to exist, and *it will be greater if it exists than if it does not exist*.

The doctrine that existence is a perfection is remarkably queer. It makes sense and is true to say that my future house will be a better one if it is insulated than if it is not insulated; but what could it mean to say that it will be a better house if it exists than if it does not? My future child will be a better man if he is honest than if he is not; but who would understand the saying that he will be a better man if he exists than if he does not? Or who understands the saying that if God exists He is more perfect than if He does not

---

[4] Haldane and Ross, *The Philosophical Works of Descartes*, 2 vols. (Cambridge, 1931), I,163.—N.M.

[5] *Op. cit.*, p.182.—N.M.

[6] *Proslogion 2*; Deane, p. 8.—N.M.

[7] *Responsio 2*; Deane, pp. 157–58.—N.M.

exist? One might say, with some intelligibility, that it would be better (for oneself or for mankind) if God exists than if He does not—but that is a different matter.

A king might desire that his next chancellor should have knowledge, wit, and resolution; but it is ludicrous to add that the king's desire is to have a chancellor who exists. Suppose that two royal councilors, A and B, were asked to draw up separately descriptions of the most perfect chancellor they could conceive, and that the descriptions they produced were identical except that A included existence in his list of attributes of a perfect chancellor and B did not. (I do not mean that B put nonexistence in his list.) One and the same person could satisfy both descriptions. More to the point, any person who satisfied A's description would *necessarily* satisfy B's description and *vice versa*! This is to say that A and B did not produce descriptions that differed in any way but rather one and the same description of necessary and desirable qualities in a chancellor. A only made a show of putting down a desirable quality that B had failed to include.

I believe I am merely restating an observation that Kant made in attacking the notion that "existence" or "being" is a "real predicate." He says:

> By whatever and by however many predicates we any think a thing—even if we completely determine it—we do not make the least addition to the thing when we further declare that this thing *is*. Otherwise, it would not be exactly the same thing that exists, but something more than we had thought in the concept; and we could not, therefore, say that the exact object of my concept exists.[8]

Anselm's ontological proof of *Proslogion* 2 is fallacious because it rests on the false doctrine that existence is a perfection (and therefore that "existence" is a "real predicate"). It would be desirable to have a rigorous refutation of the doctrine but I have not been able to provide one. I am compelled to leave the matter at the more or less intuitive level of Kant's observation. In any case, I believe that the doctrine does not belong to Anselm's other formulation of the ontological argument. It is worth noting that Gassendi anticipated Kant's criticism when he said, against Descartes:

> Existence is a perfection neither in God nor in anything else; it is rather that in the absence of which there is no perfection. . . . Hence neither is existence held to exist in a thing in the way that perfections do, nor if the thing lacks existence is it said to be imperfect (or deprived of a perfection), so much as to be nothing.[9]

· *II* ·

I take up now the consideration of the second ontological proof, which Anselm presents in the very next chapter of the *Proslogion*. (There is no evidence that he thought of himself as offering two different proofs.) Speaking of the being a greater than which cannot be conceived, he says:

> And it so truly exists that it cannot be conceived not to exist. For it is possible to conceive of a being which cannot be conceived not to exist; and this is greater than one which can be conceived not to exist. Hence, if that, than which nothing greater can be conceived,

---

[8] *The Critique of Pure Reason*, tr. by Norman Kemp Smith (London, 1929), p. 505.—N.M.
[9] Haldane and Ross, II, 186.—N.M.

can be conceived not to exist, it is not that than which nothing greater can be conceived. But this is a contradiction. So truly, therefore, is there something than which nothing greater can be conceived, that it cannot even be conceived not to exist. And this being thou are, O Lord, our God.[10]

Anselm is saying two things: first, that a being whose nonexistence is logically impossible is "greater" than a being whose nonexistence is logically possible (and therefore that a being a greater than which cannot be conceived must be one whose nonexistence is logically impossible); second, that *God* is a being than which a greater cannot be conceived.

In regard to the second of these assertions, there certainly is *a* use of the word "God," and I think far the more common use, in accordance with which the statements "God is the greatest of all beings," "God is the most perfect being," "God is the supreme being," are *logically* necessary truths, in the same sense that the statement "A square has four sides" is a logically necessary truth. If there is a man named "Jones" who is the tallest man in the world, the statement "Jones is the tallest man in the world" is merely true and is not a logically necessary truth. It is a virtue of Anselm's unusual phrase, "a being a greater than which cannot be conceived,"[11] to make it explicit that the sentence "God is the greatest of all beings" expresses a logically necessary truth and not a mere matter of fact such as the one we imagined about Jones.

With regard to Anselm's first assertion (namely, that a being whose nonexistence is logically impossible is greater than a being whose nonexistence is logically possible) perhaps the most puzzling thing about it is the use of the word "greater." It appears to mean exactly the same as "superior," "more excellent," "more perfect." This equivalence by itself is of no help to us, however, since the latter expressions would be equally puzzling here. What is required is some explanation of their use.

We do think of *knowledge*, say, as an excellence, a good thing. If A has more knowledge of algebra than B we express this in common language by saying that A has a *better* knowledge of algebra than B, or that A's knowledge of algebra is *superior* to B's, whereas we should not say that B has a better or superior *ignorance* of algebra than A. We do say "greater ignorance," but here the word "greater" is used purely quantitatively.

Previously I rejected *existence* as a perfection. Anselm is maintaining in the remarks last quoted, not that existence is a perfection, but that *the logical impossibility of non-existence is a perfection*. In other words, *necessary existence* is a perfection. His first ontological proof uses the principle that a thing is greater if it exists than if it does not exist. His second proof employs the different principle that a thing is greater if it necessarily exists than if it does not necessarily exist.

Some remarks about the notion of *dependence* may help to make this latter principle intelligible. Many things depend for their existence on other things and events. My house was built by a carpenter: its coming into existence was dependent on a certain creative activity. Its continued existence is dependent on many things: that a tree does

---

[10] *Proslogion* 3; Deane, pp. 8–9.—N.M.

[11] Professor Robert Calhoun has pointed out to me that a similar locution had been used by Augustine. In *De moribus Manichaeorum* (Bk. II, ch. xi, sec. 24), he says that God is a being *quo esse aut cogitari melius nihil possit (Patrologiae Patrum Latinorum*, ed. by J. P. Migne, Paris, 1841–1845, vol. 32: *Augustinus*, vol. 1).—N.M.

not crush it, that it is not consumed by fire, and so on. If we reflect on the common meaning of the word "God" (no matter how vague and confused this is), we realize that it is incompatible with this meaning that God's existence should *depend* on anything. Whether we believe in Him or not we must admit that the "almighty and everlasting God" (as several ancient prayers begin), the "Maker of heaven and earth, and of all things visible and invisible" (as is said in the Nicene Creed), cannot be thought of as being brought into existence by anything or as depending for His continued existence on anything. To conceive of anything as dependent upon something else for its existence is to conceive of it as a lesser being than God.

If a housewife has a set of extremely fragile dishes, then as dishes they are *inferior* to those of another set like them in all respects except that they are *not* fragile. Those of the first set are *dependent* for their continued existence on gentle handling; those of the second set are not. There is a definite connection in common language between the notions of dependency and inferiority, and independence and superiority. To say that something which was dependent on nothing whatever was superior to ("greater than") anything that was dependent in any way upon anything is quite in keeping with the everyday use of the terms "superior" and "greater." Correlative with the notions of dependence and independence are the notions of *limited* and *unlimited*. An engine requires fuel and this is a limitation. It is the same thing to say that an engine's operation is *dependent* on as that it is *limited* by its fuel supply. An engine that could accomplish the same work in the same time and was in other respects satisfactory, but did not require fuel, would be a *superior* engine.

God is usually conceived of as an *unlimited* being. He is conceived of as a being who *could not* be limited, that is, as an absolutely unlimited being. This is no less than to conceive of Him as *something a greater than which cannot be conceived*. If God is conceived to be an absolutely unlimited being He must be conceived to be unlimited in regard to His existence as well as His operation. In this conception it will not make sense to say that He depends on anything for coming into or continuing in existence. Nor, as Spinoza observed, will it make sense to say that something could *prevent* Him from existing.[12] Lack of moisture can prevent trees from existing in a certain region of the earth. But it would be contrary to the concept of God as an unlimited being to suppose that anything other than God Himself could prevent Him from existing, and it would be self-contradictory to suppose that He Himself could do it.

Some may be inclined to object that although nothing could prevent God's existence, still it might just *happen* that He did not exist. And if He did exist that too would be by chance. I think, however, that from the supposition that it could happen that God did not exist it would follow that, if He existed, He would have mere duration and not eternity. It would make sense to ask, "How long has He existed?," "Will He still exist next week?," "He was in existence yesterday but how about today?," and so on. It seems absurd to make God the subject of such questions. According to our ordinary conception of Him, He is an eternal being. And eternity does not mean endless duration, as Spinoza noted. To ascribe eternity to something is to exclude as senseless all sentences that imply that it has duration. If a thing has duration then it would be merely a *contingent* fact, if it was a fact, that its duration was endless. The moon could have endless duration but not eternity. If something has endless duration it will

---

[12] *Ethics*, pt. I, prop. 11.—N.M.

make sense (although it will be false) to say that it will cease to exist, and it will make sense (although it will be false) to say that something will *cause* it to cease to exist. A being with endless duration is not, therefore, an absolutely unlimited being. That God is conceived to be eternal follows from the fact that He is conceived to be an absolutely unlimited being.

I have been trying to expand the argument of *Proslogion* 3. In *Responsio* 1 Anselm adds the following acute point: if you can conceive of a certain thing and this thing does not exist then if it *were* to exist its nonexistence would be *possible*. It follows, I believe, that if the thing were to exist it would depend on other things both for coming into and continuing in existence, and also that it would have duration and not eternity. Therefore it would not be, either in reality or in conception, an unlimited being, *aliquid quo nihil maius cogitari possit*.

Anselm states his argument as follows:

> If it [the thing a greater than which cannot be conceived] can be conceived at all it must exist. For no one who denies or doubts the existence of a being a greater than which is inconceivable, denies or doubts that if it did exist its non-existence, either in reality or in the understanding, would be impossible. For otherwise it would not be a being a greater than which cannot be conceived. But as to whatever can be conceived but does not exist: if it were to exist its non-existence either in reality or in the understanding would be possible. Therefore, if a being a greater than which cannot be conceived, can even be conceived, it must exist.[13]

What Anselm has proved is that the notion of contingent existence or of contingent nonexistence cannot have any application to God. His existence must either be logically necessary or logically impossible. The only intelligible way of rejecting Anselm's claim that God's existence is necessary is to maintain that the concept of God, as a being a greater than which cannot be conceived, is self-contradictory or nonsensical.[14] Supposing that this is false, Anselm is right to deduce God's necessary existence from his characterization of Him as a being a greater than which cannot be conceived.

Let me summarize the proof. If God, a being a greater than which cannot be conceived, does not exist then He cannot *come* into existence. For if He did He would either have been *caused* to come into existence or have *happened* to come into existence, and in either case He would be a limited being, which by our conception of Him He is not. Since He cannot come into existence, if He does not exist His existence is impossible. If He does exist He cannot have come into existence (for the reasons given), nor can He cease to exist, for nothing could cause Him to cease to exist nor could it just happen that He ceased to exist. So if God exists His existence is necessary. Thus God's existence is either impossible or necessary. It can be the former only if the concept of such a being is self-contradictory or in some way logically absurd. Assuming that this is not so, it follows that He necessarily exists.

---

[13] *Responsio* 1; Deane, pp. 154–55.—N.M.

[14] Gaunilo attacked Anselm's argument on this very point. He would not concede that a being a greater than which cannot be conceived existed in his understanding (*Gaunilonis Pro Insipiente*, secs. 4 and 5; Deane, pp. 148–50). Anselm's reply is: "I call on your faith and conscience to attest that this is most false" (*Responsio* 1; Deane, p. 154). Gaunilo's faith and conscience will attest that it is false that "God is not a being a greater than which is inconceivable," and false that "He is not understood (*intelligitur*) or conceived (*cogitatur*)" (*ibid.*). Descartes also remarks that one would go to "strange extremes" who denied that we understand the words "*that thing which is the most perfect that we can conceive*; for that is what all men call God" (Haldane and Ross, II, 129).—N.M.

It may be helpful to express ourselves in the following way: to say, not that *omnipotence* is a property of God, but rather that *necessary omnipotence* is; and to say, not that omniscience is a property of God, but rather that *necessary omniscience* is. We have criteria for determining that a man knows this and that and can do this and that, and for determining that one man has greater knowledge and abilities in a certain subject than another.We could think of various tests to give them. But there is nothing we should wish to describe, seriously and literally, as "testing" God's knowledge and powers. That God is omniscient and omnipotence has not been determined by the application of criteria: rather these are requirements of our conception of Him. They are internal properties of the concept, although they are also rightly said to be properties of God. *Necessary existence* is a property of God in the *same sense* that *necessary omnipotence* and *necessary omniscience* are His properties. And we are not to think that "God necessarily exists" means that it follows necessarily from something that God exists *contingently*. The a priori proposition "God necessarily exists" entails the proposition "God exists," if and only if the latter also is understood as an a priori proposition: in which case the two propositions are equivalent. In this sense Anselm's proof is a proof of God's existence.

Descartes was somewhat hazy on the question of whether existence is a property of things that exist, but at the same time he saw clearly enough that *necessary existence* is a property of God. Both points are illustrated in his reply to Gassendi's remark, which I quoted above:

> I do not see to what class of reality you wish to assign existence, nor do I see why it may not be said to be a property as well as omnipotence, taking the word property as equivalent to any attribute or anything which can be predicted of a thing, as in the present case it should be by all means regarded. Nay, necessary existence in the case of God is also a true property in the strictest sense of the word, because it belongs to Him and forms part of His essence alone.[15]

Elsewhere he speaks of "the necessity of existence" as being "that crown of perfections without which we cannot comprehend God."[16] He is emphatic on the point that necessary existence applies solely to "an absolutely perfect Being."[17]

· III ·

I wish to consider now a part of Kant's criticism of the ontological argument which I believe to be wrong. He says:

> If, in an identical proposition, I reject the predicate while retaining the subject, contradiction results; and I therefore say that the former belongs necessarily to the latter. But if we reject subject and predicate alike, there is no contradiction; for nothing is then left that can be contradicted. To posit a triangle, and yet to reject its three angles, is self-contradictory; but there is no contradiction in rejecting the triangle together with its three angles. The same holds true of the concept of an absolutely necessary being. If its

---

[15] Haldane and Ross, II, 228.—N.M.

[16] *Ibid.*, I, 445.—N.M.

[17] E.g., *ibid.*, Principle 15, p. 225.—N.M.

existence is rejected, we reject the thing itself with all its predicates and no question of contradiction can then arise. There is nothing outside it that would then be contradicted, since the necessity of the thing is not supposed to be derived from anything external; nor is there anything internal that would be contradicted, since in rejecting the thing itself we have at the same time rejected all its internal properties. "God is omnipotent" is a necessary judgment. The omnipotence cannot be rejected if we posit a Deity, that is, and infinite being; for the two concepts are identical. But if we say, "There is no God," neither the omnipotence nor any other of its predicates is given; they are one and all rejected together with the subject, and there is therefore not the least contradiction in such a judgment.[18]

To these remarks the reply is that when the concept of God is correctly understood one sees that one cannot "reject the subject." "There is no God" is seen to be a necessarily false statement. Anselm's demonstration proves that the proposition "God exists" has the same a priori footing as the proposition "God is omnipotent."

Many present-day philosophers, in agreement with Kant, declare that existence is not a property and think that this overthrows the ontological argument. Although it is an error to regard existence as a property of things that have contingent existence, it does not follow that it is an error to regard necessary existence as a property of God. A recent writer says, against Anselm, that a proof of God's existence "based on the necessities of thought" is "universally regarded as fallacious: it is not thought possible to build bridges between mere abstractions and concrete existence."[19] But this way of putting the matter obscures the distinction we need to make. Does "concrete existence" mean contingent existence? Then to build bridges between concrete existence and mere abstractions would be like inferring the existence of an island from the concept of a perfect island, which both Anselm and Descartes regarded as absurd. What Anselm did was to give a demonstration that the proposition "God necessarily exists" is entailed by the proposition "God is a being a greater than which cannot be conceived" (which is equivalent to "God is an absolutely unlimited being"). Kant declares that when "I think a being as the supreme reality, without any defect, the question still remains whether it exists or not."[20] But once one has grasped Anselm's proof of the necessary existence of a being a greater than which cannot be conceived, no question remains as to whether it exists or not, just as Euclid's demonstration of the existence of an infinity of prime numbers leaves no question on that issue.

Kant says that "every reasonable person" must admit that "all existential propositions are synthetic."[21] Part of the perplexity one has about the ontological argument is in deciding whether or not the proposition "God necessarily exists" is or is on an "existential proposition." But let us look around. Is the Euclidean theorem in number theory, "There exists an infinite number of prime numbers," an "existential proposition"? Do we not want to say that *in some sense* it asserts the existence of something? Cannot we say, with equal justification, that the proposition "God necessarily exists" asserts the existence of something, *in some sense*? What we need to understand, in each case, is the particular sense of the assertion. Neither proposition has the same sort of

---

[18] *Op. cit.*, p. 502.—N.M.

[19] J. N. Findlay, "Can God's Existence Be Disproved?," *New Essays in Philosophical Theology*," ed. by A. N. Flew and A. MacIntyre (London, 1955), p. 47.—N.M.

[20] *Op. cit.*, pp. 505–6.—N.M.

[21] *Ibid.*, p. 504.—N.M.

sense as do the propositions, "A low pressure area exists over the Great Lakes," "There still exists some possibility that he will survive," "The pain continues to exist in his abdomen." One good way of seeing the difference in sense of these various propositions is to see the variously different ways in which they are proved or supported. It is wrong to think that all assertions of existence have the same kind of meaning. There are as many kinds of existential propositions as there are kinds of subjects of discourse.

Closely related to Kant's view that all existential propositions are "synthetic" is the contemporary dogma that all existential propositions are contingent. Professor Gilbert Ryle tells us that "Any assertion of the existence of something, like any assertion of the occurrence of something, can be denied without logical absurdity."[22] "All existential statements are contingent," says Mr. I. M. Crombie.[23] Professor J. J. C. Smart remarks that "Existence is not a property" and then goes on to assert that "There can never be any *logical contradiction* in denying that God exists."[24] He declares that "The concept of a logically necessary being is a self-contradictory concept, like the concept of a round square. . . . No existential proposition can be logically necessary," he maintains, for "the truth of a logically necessary proposition depends only on our symbolism, or to put the same thing in another way, on the relationship of concepts" (p. 38). Professor K. E. M. Baier says, "It is no longer seriously in dispute that the notion of a logically necessary being is self-contradictory. Whatever can be conceived of as existing can equally be conceived of as not existing."[25] This is a repetition of Hume's assertion, "Whatever we conceive as existent, we can also conceive as non-existent. There is no being, therefore, whose non-existence implies a contradiction."[26]

Professor J. N. Findlay ingeniously constructs an ontological *dis*proof of God's existence, based on a "modern" view of the nature of "necessity in propositions": the view, namely, that necessity in propositions "merely reflects our use of words, the arbitrary conventions of our language."[27] Findlay undertakes to characterize what he calls "religious attitude," and here there is a striking agreement between his observations and some of the things I have said in expounding Anselm's proof. Religious attitude, he says, presumes *superiority* in its object and superiority so great that the worshiper is in comparison as nothing. Religious attitude finds it "anomalous to worship anything *limited* in any thinkable manner. . . . And hence we are led on irresistibly to demand that our religious object should have an *unsurpassable* supremacy along all avenues, that it should tower *infinitely* above all other objects" (p. 51). We cannot help feeling that "the worthy object of our worship can never be a thing that merely *happens* to exist, nor one on which all other objects merely *happen* to depend. The true object of religious reverence must not be one, merely, to which no *actual* independent realities stand opposed: it must be one to which such opposition is totally *inconceivable*. . . . And not only must the existence of *other* things be unthinkable without him, but his own non-existence must be wholly unthinkable in any circumstances" (p. 52). And now, says Findlay, when we add up these various requirements, what they entail is "not only that there isn't a God, but

[22] *The Nature of Metaphysics*, ed. by D. F. Pears (New York, 1957), p. 150.—N.M.

[23] *New Essays in Philosophical Theology*, p. 114.—N.M.

[24] *Ibid.*, p. 34—N.M.

[25] *The Meaning of Life*, Inaugural Lecture, Canberra University College (Canberra, 1957), p. 8.—N.M.

[26] *Diaglogues Concerning Natural Religion*, pt. IX.—N.M.

[27] Findlay, *op. cit.*, p. 154.—N.M.

that the Divine Existence is either senseless or impossible" (p. 54). For on the one hand, "if God is to satisfy religious claims and needs, He must be a being in every way inescapable, One whose existence and whose possession of certain excellences we cannot possibly conceive away." On the other hand, "modern views make it self-evidently absurd (if they don't make it ungrammatical) to speak of such a Being and attribute existence to Him. It was indeed an ill day for Anselm when he hit upon his famous proof. For on that day he not only laid bare something that is of the essence of an adequate religious object, but also something that entails its necessary non-existence" (p. 55).

Now I am inclined to hold the "modern" view that logically necessary truth "merely reflects our use of words" (although I do not believe that the conventions of language are always *arbitrary*). But I confess that I am unable to see how that view is supposed to lead to the conclusion that "the Divine existence is either senseless or impossible." Findlay does not explain how this result comes about. Surely he cannot mean that this view entails that nothing can have necessary properties: for this would imply that mathematics is "senseless or impossible," which no one wants to hold. Trying to fill in the argument that is missing from his article, the most plausible conjecture I can make is the following: Findlay thinks that the view that logical necessity "reflects the use of words" implies, not that nothing has necessary properties, but that *existence* cannot be a necessary property of anything. That is to say, every proposition of the form "*x* exists," including the proposition "God exists," must be *contingent*.[28] At the same time, our concept of God requires that His existence be *necessary*, that is, that "God exists" be a necessary truth. Therefore, the modern view of necessity proves that what the concept of God requires *cannot* be fulfilled. It proves that God *cannot* exist.

The correct reply is that the view that logical necessity merely reflects the use of words cannot possibly have the implication that every existential proposition must be contingent. That view requires us to *look at* the use of words and not manufacture a priori theses about it. In the Ninetieth Psalm it is said: "Before the mountains were brought forth, or ever thou hadst formed the earth and the world, even from everlasting to everlasting, thou art God." Here is expressed the idea of the necessary existence and eternity of God, an idea that is essential to the Jewish and Christian religions. In those complex systems of thought, those "languages-games," God has the status of a necessary being. Who can doubt that? Here we must say with Wittgenstein, "This language-game is played!"[29] I believe we may rightly take the existence of those religious systems of thought in which God figures as a necessary being to be a disproof of the dogma, affirmed by Hume and others, that no existential proposition can be necessary.

Another way of criticizing the ontological argument is the following. "Granted that the concept of necessary existence follows from the concept of a being a greater than which cannot be conceived, this amounts to no more than granting the *a priori* truth of the *conditional* proposition, 'If such a being exists then it necessarily exists.' This proposition, however, does not entail the *existence* of *anything*, and one can deny its antecedent without contradiction." Kant, for example, compares the proposition (or

---

[28] The other philosophers I have just cited may be led to this opinion by the same thinking. Smart, for example, says that "the truth of the logically necessary proposition depends only on our symbolism, or to put the same thing in another way, on the relationship of concepts" (*supra*). This is very similar to saying that it "reflects our use of words."

[29] *Philosophical Investigations* (New York, 1953), sec. 654.—N.M.

"judgment, as he calls it) "A triangle has three angles" with the proposition "God is a necessary being." He allows that the former is "absolutely necessary" and goes on to say:

> The absolute necessity of the judgment is only a conditional necessity of the thing, or of the predicate in the judgment. The above proposition does not declare that three angles are absolutely necessary, but that, under the condition that there is a triangle (that is, that a triangle is given), three angles will necessarily be found in it.[30]

He is saying, quite correctly, that the proposition about triangles is equivalent to the conditional proposition, "If a triangle exists, it has three angles." He then makes the comment that there is no contradiction "in rejecting the triangle together with its three angles." He proceeds to draw the alleged parallel: "The same holds true of the concept of an absolutely necessary being. If its existence is rejected, we reject the thing itself with all its predicates; and no question of contradiction can then arise."[31] The priest, Caterus, made the same objection to Descartes when he said:

> Though it be conceded that an entity of the highest perfection implies its existence by its very name, yet it does not follow that that very existence is anything actual in the real world, but merely that the concept of existence is inseparably united with the concept of highest being. Hence you cannot infer that the existence of God is anything actual, unless you assume that that highest being actually exists; for then it will actually contain all its perfections, together with this perfection of real existence.[32]

I think that Caterus, Kant, and numerous other philosophers have been mistaken in supposing that the proposition "God is a necessary being" (or "God necessarily exists") is equivalent to the conditional proposition "If God exists then He necessarily exists."[33] For how do they want the antecedent clause, "*If* God exists," to be understood? Clearly they want it to imply that it is *possible* that God does *not* exist.[34] The whole point of

---

[30] *Op. cit.*, pp. 501–2.—N.M.

[31] *Ibid.*, p. 502.—N.M.

[32] Haldane and Ross, II, 7.—N.M.

[33] I have heard it said by more than one person in discussion that Kant's view was that it is really a misuse of language to speak of a "necessary being," on the grounds that necessity is properly predicated only of propositions (judgments) not of *things*. This is not a correct account of Kant. (See his discussion of "The Postulates of Empirical Thought in General," *op. cit.*, pp. 239–56, esp. p. 239 and pp. 247–48.) But if he had held this, as perhaps the above philosophers think he should have, then presumably his view would not have been that the pseudo-proposition "God is a necessary being" is equivalent to the conditional "If God exists then He necessarily exists." Rather his view would have been that the genuine proposition "'God exists' is necessarily true" is equivalent to the conditional "If God exists then He exists" (*not* "If God exists then He *necessarily* exists," which would be an illegitimate formulation, on the view imaginatively attributed to Kant).
"If God exists then He exists" is a foolish tautology which says nothing different from the tautology "If a new earth satellite exists then it exists." If "If God exists then He exists" were a correct analysis of "'God exists' is necessarily true," then "If a new earth satellite exists then it exists" would be a correct analysis of "'A new earth satellite exists' is necessarily true." If the *analysans* is necessarily true then the *analysandum* must be necessarily true, provided the analysis is correct. If this proposed Kantian analysis of "'God exists' is necessarily true" were correct, we should be presented with the consequence that not only is it necessarily true that God exists, but also it is necessarily true that a new earth satellite exists: which is absurd.—N.M.

[34] When summarizing Anselm's proof (in part II, *supra*) I said: "If God exists He necessarily exists." But there I was merely stating an entailment. "If God exists" did not have the implication that it is possible He does not exist. And of course I was not regarding the conditional as *equivalent* to "God necessarily exists."—N.M.

Kant's analysis is to try to show that it is possible to "reject the subject." Let us make this implication explicit in the conditional proposition, so that it reads: "If God exists (and it is possible that He does not) then He necessarily exists." But now it is apparent, I think, that these philosophers have arrived at a self-contradictory position. I do not mean that this conditional proposition, taken alone, is self-contradictory. Their position is self-contradictory in the following way. On the one hand, they agree that the proposition "God necessarily exists" is an a priori truth; Kant implies that it is "absolutely necessary," and Caterus says that God's existence is implied by His very name. On the other hand, they think that it is correct to analyze this proposition in such a way that it will entail the proposition "It is possible that God does not exist." But so far from its being the case that the proposition "God necessarily exists" entails the proposition "It is possible that God does not exist," it is rather the case that they are *incompatible* with one another! Can anything be clearer than that the conjunction "God necessarily exists but it is possible that He does not exist" is self-contradictory? Is it not just as plainly self-contradictory as the conjunction "A square necessarily has four sides but it is possible for a square not to have four sides"? In short, this familiar criticism of the ontological argument is self-contradictory, because it accepts *both* of two incompatible propositions.[35]

One conclusion we may draw from our examination of this criticism is that (contrary to Kant) there is a lack of symmetry, in an important respect, between the proposition "A triangle has three angles" and "God has necessary existence," although both are a priori. The former can be expressed in the conditional assertion "If a triangle exists (and it is possible that none does) it has three angles." The latter cannot be expressed in the corresponding conditional assertion without contradiction.

· IV ·

I turn to the question of whether the idea of a being a greater than which cannot be conceived is self-contradictory. Here Leibniz made a contribution to the discussion of the ontological argument. He remarked that the argument of Anselm and Descartes

> is not a paralogism, but it is an imperfect demonstration, which assumes something that must still be proved in order to render it mathematically evident; that is, it is tacitly assumed that this idea of the all-great or all-perfect being is possible, and implies no contradiction. And it is already something that by this remark it is proved that, assuming that God is possible, he exists, which is the privilege of divinity alone.[36]

Leibniz undertook to give a proof that God is possible. He defined a *perfection* as a simple, positive quality in the highest degree.[37] He argued that since perfections are *simple* qualities they must be compatible with one another. Therefore the concept of a being possessing all perfections is consistent.

---

[35] This fallacious criticism of Anselm is implied in the following remarks by Gilson: "To show that the affirmation of necessary existence is analytically implied in the idea of God, would be . . . to show that God is necessary if He exists, but would not prove that He does exist" (E. Gilson, *The Spirit of Medieval Philosophy*, New York, 1940, p. 62).—N.M.

[36] *New Essays Concerning the Human Understanding*, Bk. IV, ch. 10; ed. by A. G. Langley (LaSalle, Illinois, 1949), p. 504.—N.M.

[37] See *Ibid.*, Appendix X, p. 714.—N.M.

I will not review his argument because I do not find his definition of a perfection intelligible. For one thing, it assumes that certain qualities or attributes are "positive" in their intrinsic nature, and others "negative" or "privative," and I have not been able clearly to understand that. For another thing, it assumes that some qualities are intrinsically simple. I believe that Wittgenstein has shown in the *Investigations* that nothing is *intrinsically* simple, but that whatever has the status of a simple, an indefinable, in one system of concepts, may have the status of a complex thing, a definable thing, in another system of concepts.

I do not know how to demonstrate that the concept of God—that is, of a being a greater than which cannot be conceived—is not self-contradictory. But I do not think that it is legitimate to demand such a demonstration. I also do not know how to demonstrate that either the concept of a material thing or the concept of *seeing* a material thing is not self-contradictory, and philosophers have argued that both of them are. With respect to any particular reasoning that is offered for holding that the concept of seeing a material thing, for example, is self-contradictory, one may try to show the invalidity of the reasoning and thus free the concept from the charge of being self-contradictory *on that ground*. But I do not understand what it would mean to demonstrate *in general*, and not in respect to any particular reasoning, that the concept is not self-contradictory. So it is with the concept of God. I should think there is no more of a presumption that it is self-contradictory than is the concept of seeing a material thing. Both concepts have a place in the thinking and the lives of human beings.

But even if one allows that Anselm's phrase may be free of self-contradiction, one wants to know how it can have any *meaning* for anyone. Why is it that human beings have even *formed* the concept of an infinite being, a being a greater than which cannot be conceived? This is a legitimate and important question. I am sure there cannot be a deep understanding of that concept without an understanding of the phenomena of human life that give rise to it. To give an account of the latter is beyond my ability. I wish, however, to make one suggestion (which should not be understood as autobiographical).

There is the phenomenon of feeling guilt for something that one has done or thought or felt or for a disposition that one has. One wants to be free of guilt. But sometimes the guilt is felt to be so great that one is sure that nothing one could do oneself, nor any forgiveness by another human being, would remove it. One feels a guilt that is beyond all measure, a guilt "a greater than which cannot be conceived." Paradoxically, it would seem, one nevertheless has an intense desire to have this incomparable guilt removed. One requires a forgiveness that is beyond all measure, a forgiveness " a greater than which cannot be conceived." Out of such a storm in the soul, I am suggesting, there arises the conception of a forgiving mercy that is limitless, beyond all measure. This is one important feature of the Jewish and Christian conception of God.

I wish to relate this to a remark made by Kierkegaard, who was speaking about belief in Christianity but whose remark may have a wider application. He says:

> There is only one proof of the truth of Christianity and that, quite rightly, is from the emotions, when the dread of sin and a heavy conscience torture a man into crossing the narrow line between despair bordering upon madness—and Christendom.[38]

---

[38] *The Journals*, tr. by A. Dru (Oxford, 1938), sec. 926.—N.M.

One may think it absurd for a human being to feel a guilt of such magnitude, and even more absurd that, if he feels it, he should *desire* its removal. I have nothing to say about that. It may also be absurd for people to fall in love, but they do it. I wish only to say that there *is* that human phenomenon of an unbearably heavy conscience and that it is importantly connected with the genesis of the concept of God, that is, with the formation of the "grammar" of the word "God." I am sure that this concept is related to human experience in other ways. If one had the acuteness and depth to perceive these connections one could grasp the *sense* of the concept. When we encounter this concept as a problem in philosophy, we do not consider the human phenomena that lie behind it. It is not surprising that many philosophers believe that the idea of a necessary being is an arbitrary and absurd construction.

What is the relation of Anselm's ontological argument to religious belief? This is a difficult question. I can imagine an atheist going through the argument, becoming convinced of its validity, acutely defending it against objections yet remaining an atheist. The only effect it could have on the fool of the Psalm would be that he stopped saying in his heart "There is no God," because he would now realize that this is something he cannot meaningfully say or think. It is hardly to be expected that a demonstrative argument should, in addition, produce in him a living faith. Surely there is a level at which one can view the argument as a piece of logic, following the deductive moves but not being touched religiously? I think so. But even at this level the argument may not be without religious value, for it may help to remove some philosophical scruples that stand in the way of faith. At a deeper level, I suspect that the argument can be thoroughly understood only by one who has a view of that human "form of life" that gives rise to the idea of an infinitely great being, who views it from the *inside* not just from the outside and who has, therefore, at least some inclination to *partake* in that religious form of life. This inclination, in Kierkegaard's words, is "from the emotions." This inclination can hardly be an *effect* of Anselm's argument, but is rather presupposed in the fullest understanding of it. It would be unreasonable to require that the recognition of Anselm's demonstration as valid must produce a conversion.

PART III

A Newer Critique
of Theism

○

I N PART I we examined the classical case for theism, along with critiques of some of the theistic arguments – critiques by writers who rejected classical arguments but who did not reject theism. (The exception may be Hume.) In Part II we examined the two earlier critiques of theism that, for our purposes, began in the eighteenth century and have continued to the present day. These are: the more rational, philosophical critiques that focused on attacking the traditional arguments; and the more cultural ones that focused on such things as the psychological, political, and so on, sources of religious belief and that sought to discredit theism thereby. Now we turn to a third, newer critique of theism that began about 1930 and has continued to the present.

The first two attacks on theism, though different, agree on one point: religious beliefs, the claims of theism, are significant, but false—or at least unsupportable. The third attack differs. It purports to show that the claims of theism are meaningless—in other words, that these claims say nothing about anything.

As I mentioned in the Introduction, the reader is no doubt aware of the first two attacks on theism and can understand why they were made (even if the reader is a theist or sympathetic to religious belief). But the reader may wonder: Just what is the nature of this third attack? Why was it made? And by whom? Because of such questions, it may be helpful for me to elaborate.

First, where did this newer attack on theism originate, and why? It was leveled first in the early 1930s by a group of philosophers and scientists, all of whom were in or near Vienna; hence the group was known as the Vienna Circle. The philosophical position they held was known as logical positivism—later relabeled logical empiricism. This philosophical movement had many main tenets, but the one that theological and religious assertions are meaningless is the one that aroused the most furor.

Second, how did the logical positivists arrive at the view that theological discourse is meaningless? What was their reasoning? Almost all of the positivists were scientists (and a few mathematicians) or philosophers of science. Hence, for them science was a good thing since science progresses and gives us ever increasing knowledge of the world. When there are disputes in science, they get resolved and there is agreement among scientists. But compare science to philosophy—especially the division of philosophy known as metaphysics. For 2500 years philosophers have been disputing whether or not there are universals (abstract entities); whether reality is physical or mental; and what not. They never seem to make any progress. And there is constant disagreement on almost every issue in metaphysics. Hence, the positivists proposed to eliminate metaphysics from philosophy, by showing that all metaphysical assertions are cognitively meaningless.

How did they go about this? By putting forth a criterion of cognitive meaningfulness, one that demarcates meaningful propositions from meaningless ones. Now they held, as many continue to hold, that every statement is either (1) analytic, or (2) synthetic.

(1) Analytic statements are a known priori (and thus necessarily true). Their denials are self-contradictory. They are tautologies—reducible to "*A* is *A*," and so on. Hence, they do not convey any factual information about anything. Examples are: "2 + 2 = 4," "All bachelors are unmarried," "Roses are roses."

(2) Synthetic statements are those that are non-analytic. Hence, they can be true *or* false (not necessarily true). Their truth or falsity is determined a posteriori. They *do* convey factual information about the world. Examples are: "There are four chairs in this room," "Some bachelors are misanthropes," "Roses are fragrant."

Now for the positivists' criterion of meaningfulness. It was (and is) roughly:

Any statement S is cognitively meaningful if and only if either (1) S is a tautology and hence necessarily true (but trivial); or (2) S is empirically verifiable through sense experience.

(1) Applies to all analytic statements; (2) applies to all synthetic statements. All analytic statements must be capable of being shown to be tautologies. All synthetic statements must be capable of being empirically verifiable. You must be able to indicate what *sensory evidence* counts for or against them. Finally, any statement that passes the criterion is meaningful. Any that fails is meaningless.

Thus, take "2 + 2 = 4." Its denial is self-contradictory, so it is analytic—a tautology. It passes condition (1). Or take "There are mountains in Tibet." You can specify what counts for or against this, and you can test it empirically. You can go and look. So it passes condition (2). But not take a metaphysical assertion like this one from Hegelian philosophy: "The absolute enters into, but is itself incapable of, evolution and progress." Or this one from Platonic philosophy: "There exist non-spatial and non-temporal abstract entities." These are not meant to be analytic, otherwise they would be tautologies. So they are intended to be synthetic. But how on earth could you possibly verify them? What test could you run? Or what could you specify, even in principle, as counting for or against them, via sensory evidence? There is no way (said the positivists). Therefore, it follows: All such assertions are meaningless. The same for all metaphysical assertions, said the positivists.

Now let us move to theological assertions. A theologian or religious believer asserts "God exists" (God = a transcendent being). He doesn't mean it to be analytic. If it were, it would say nothing. It would be a mere tautology. So the theologian or believer means it to be synthetic. But what is the sensory evidence by which to verify it? There isn't any. Therefore, since it is neither a tautology, nor empirically verifiable, it is cognitively meaningless! And, of course, the same holds for all theological claims. Like metaphysical assertions, all theological assertions are meaningless. Hence, they say nothing about anything. This was the positivist critique.

At this point, I shall not say anything about whether the positivists' program was correct or not; and hence, I shall not say anything about whether the newer attack on theism succeeded. It therefore follows that I shall not say whether the third answer to our question is correct. All I have tried to do is show how and why the newer attack on theism came about, and how it led to a third possible answer to our main question.

In Chapter Six we shall read some very provocative versions of this third critique by Ayer and Flew. Strictly speaking, the two short essays by Hare and Mitchell do not belong in this chapter but in Chapter Seven. However, since the three pieces by Flew, Hare, and Mitchell (along with a final response by Flew) were all part of one symposium, I have included all of them here rather than breaking up the selection.

Then in Chapter Seven we will look at various responses to the newer critique, responses either by theists or by those who find faults with the critique. These include not only the two short pieces by Hare and Flew, but essays by Wisdom, Braithwaite, Crombie, Hick, Klemke, and some remarks by Wittgenstein.

Finally, in Chapter Eight, we will turn directly to the issue of rationality and justified religious belief.

CHAPTER SIX

The Newer Critique

○

○ ○ ○ **29**

The Elimination of Metaphysics[1]
A. J. Ayer

· I ·

THE TRADITIONAL DISPUTES of philosophers are, for the most part, as unwarranted as they are unfruitful. The surest way to end them is to establish beyond question what should be the purpose and method of a philosophical enquiry. And this is by no means so difficult a task as the history of philosophy would lead one to suppose. For if there are any questions which science leaves it to philosophy to answer, a straightforward process of elimination must lead to their discovery.

We may begin by criticising the metaphysical thesis that philosophy affords us knowledge of a reality transcending the world of science and common sense. Later on, when we come to define metaphysics and account for its existence, we shall find that it is possible to be a metaphysician without believing in a transcendent reality; for we shall see that many metaphysical utterances are due to the commission of logical errors, rather than to a conscious desire on the part of their authors to go beyond the limits of experience. But it is convenient for us to take the case of those who believe that it is possible to have knowledge of a transcendent reality as a starting-point for our discussion. The arguments which we use to refute them will subsequently be found to apply to the whole of metaphysics.

One way of attacking a metaphysician who claimed to have knowledge of a reality which transcended the phenomenal world would be to enquire from what premises his propositions were deduced. Must he not begin, as other men do, with the evidence of his senses? And if so, what valid process of reasoning can possibly lead him to the conception of a transcendent reality? Surely from empirical premises nothing what-soever concerning the properties, or even the existence, of anything super-empirical can legitimately be inferred. But this objection would be met by a denial on the part of the metaphysician that his assertions were ultimately based on the evidence of his senses. He would say that he was endowed with a faculty of intellectual intuition which enabled him to know facts that could not be known through sense-experience. And even if it could be shown that he was relying on empirical premises, and that his venture into a nonempirical world was therefore logically unjustified, it would not follow that the assertions which he made concerning this nonempirical world could not be true. For the fact that a conclusion does not follow from its putative premise is not sufficient to show that it is false. Consequently one cannot overthrow a system of transcendent metaphysics merely by criticising the way in which it comes into being. What is required

---

[1] From *Language, Truth and Logic*, Chapter 1.— E.D.K.

is rather a criticism of the nature of the actual statements which comprise it. And this is the line of argument which we shall, in fact, pursue. For we shall maintain that no statement which refers to a "reality" transcending the limits of all possible sense-experience can possibly have any literal significance; from which it must follow that the labours of those who have striven to describe such a reality have all been devoted to the production of nonsense.

It may be suggested that this is a proposition which has already been proved by Kant. But although Kant also condemned transcendent metaphysics, he did so on different grounds. For he said that the human understanding was so constituted that it lost itself in contradictions when it ventured out beyond the limits of possible experience and attempted to deal with things in themselves. And thus he made the impossibility of a transcendent metaphysic not, as we do, a matter of logic, but a matter of fact. He asserted, not that our minds could not conceivably have had the power of penetrating beyond the phenomenal world, but merely that they were in fact devoid of it. And this leads the critic to ask how, if it is possible to know only what lies within the bounds of sense-experience, the author can be justified in asserting that real things do exist beyond, and how he can tell what are the boundaries beyond which the human understanding may not venture, unless he succeeds in passing them himself. As Wittgenstein says, "in order to draw a limit to thinking, we should have to think both sides of this limit,"[2] a truth to which Bradley gives a special twist in maintaining that the man who is ready to prove that metaphysics is impossible is a brother metaphysician with a rival theory of his own.[3]

Whatever force these objections may have against the Kantian doctrine, they have none whatsoever against the thesis that I am about to set forth. It cannot here be said that the author is himself overstepping the barrier he maintains to be impassable. For the fruitlessness of attempting to transcend the limits of possible sense-experience will be deduced, not from a psychological hypothesis concerning the actual constitution of the human mind, but from the rule which determines the literal significance of language. Our charge against the metaphysician is not that he attempts to employ the understanding in a field where it cannot profitably venture, but that he produces sentences which fail to conform to the conditions under which alone a sentence can be literally significant. Nor are we ourselves obliged to talk nonsense in order to show that all sentences of a certain type are necessarily devoid of literal significance. We need only formulate the criterion which enables us to test whether a sentence expresses a genuine proposition about a matter of fact, and then point out that the sentences under consideration fail to satisfy it. And this we shall now proceed to do. We shall first of all formulate the criterion in somewhat vague terms, and then give the explanations which are necessary to render it precise.

· II ·

The criterion which we use to test the genuineness of apparent statements of fact is the criterion of verifiability. We say that a sentence is factually significant to any given person, if, and only if, he knows how to verify the proposition which it purports to

---

[2] *Tractatus Logico-Philosophicus*, Preface.— A.J.A.
[3] Bradley, *Appearance and Reality*, 2nd ed., p. I.— A.J.A.

express—that is, if he knows what observations would lead him, under certain conditions, to accept the proposition as being true, or reject it as being false. If, on the other hand, the putative proposition is of such a character that the assumption of its truth, or falsehood, is consistent with any assumption whatsoever concerning the nature of his future experience, then, as far as he is concerned, it is, if not a tautology, a mere pseudo-proposition. The sentence expressing it may be emotionally significant to him; but it is not literally significant. And with regard to questions the procedure is the same. We enquire in every case what observations would lead us to answer the question, one way or the other; and, if none can be discovered, we must conclude that the sentence under consideration does not, as far as we are concerned, express a genuine question, however strongly its grammatical appearance may suggest that it does.

As the adoption of this procedure is an essential factor in the argument of this book, it needs to be examined in detail.

In the first place, it is necessary to draw a distinction between practical verifiability, and verifiability in principle. Plainly we all understand, in many cases believe, propositions which we have not in fact taken steps to verify. Many of these are propositions which we could verify if we took enough trouble. But there remain a number of significant propositions, concerning matters of fact, which we could not verify even if we chose; simply because we lack the practical means of placing ourselves in the situation where the relevant observations could be made. A simple and familiar example of such a proposition is the proposition that there are mountains on the farther side of the moon.[4] No rocket has yet been invented which would enable me to go and look at the farther side of the moon,[5] so that I am unable to decide the matter by actual observation. But I do know what observations would decide it for me, if, as is theoretically conceivable, I were once in a position to make them. And therefore I say that the proposition is verifiable in principle, if not in practice, and is accordingly significant. On the other hand, such a metaphysical pseudo-proposition as " the Absolute enters into, but is itself incapable of, evolution and progress,"[6] is not even in principle verifiable. For one cannot conceive of an observation which would enable one to determine whether the Absolute did, or did not, enter into evolution and progress. Of course it is possible that the author of such a remark is using English words in a way in which they are not commonly used by English-speaking people, and that he does, in fact, intend to assert something which could be empirically verified. But until he makes us understand how the proposition that he wishes to express would be verified, he fails to communicate anything to us. And if he admits, as I think the author of the remark in question would have admitted, that his words were not intended to express either a tautology or a proposition which was capable, at least in principle, of being verified, then it follows that he has made an utterance which has no literal significance even for himself.

A further distinction which we must make is the distinction between the "strong" and the "weak" sense of the term "verifiable." A proposition is said to be verifiable, in the strong sense of the term, if, and only if, its truth could be conclusively established in experience. But it is verifiable, in the weak sense, if it is possible for experience to

---

[4] This example has been used by Professor Schlick to illustrate the same point.— A.J.A.

[5] This was written in 1936.—E.D.K.

[6] A remark taken at random from *Appearance and Reality*, by F. H. Bradley.— A.J.A.

render it probable. In which sense are we using the term when we say that a putative proposition is genuine only if it is verifiable?

It seems to me that if we adopt conclusive verifiability as our criterion of significance, as some positivists have proposed,[7] our argument will prove too much. Consider, for example, the case of general propositions of law—such propositions, namely, as "arsenic is poisonous"; "all men are mortal"; "a body tends to expand when it is heated." It is of the very nature of these propositions that their truth cannot be established with certainty by any finite series of observations. But if it is recognised that such general propositions of law are designed to cover an infinite number of cases, then it must be admitted that they cannot, even in principle, be verified conclusively. And then, if we adopt conclusive verifiability as our criterion of significance, we are logically obliged to treat these general propositions of law in the same fashion as we treat the statements of the metaphysician.

In face of this difficulty, some positivists[8] have adopted the heroic course of saying that these general propositions are indeed pieces of nonsense, albeit an essentially important type of nonsense. But here the introduction of the term "important" is simply an attempt to hedge. It serves only to mark the authors' recognition that their view is somewhat too paradoxical, without in any way removing the paradox. Besides, the difficulty is not confined to the case of general propositions of law, though it is there revealed most plainly. It is hardly less obvious in the case of propositions about the remote past. For it must surely be admitted that, however strong the evidence in favour of historical statements may be, their truth can never become more than highly probable. And to maintain that they also constituted an important, or unimportant, type of nonsense would be unplausible, to say the very least. Indeed, it will be our contention that no proposition, other than a tautology, can possibly be anything more than a probable hypothesis. And if this is correct, the principle that a sentence can be factually significant only if it expresses what is conclusively verifiable is self-stultifying as a criterion of significance. For it leads to the conclusion that it is impossible to make a significant statement of fact at all.

Nor can we accept the suggestion that a sentence should be allowed to be factually significant if, and only if, it expresses something which is definitely confutable by experience.[9] Those who adopt this course assume that, although no finite series of observations is ever sufficient to establish the truth of hypothesis beyond all possibility of doubt, there are crucial cases in which a single observation, or series of observations, can definitely confute it. But, as we shall show later on, this assumption is false. A hypothesis cannot be conclusively confuted any more than it can be conclusively verified. For when we take the occurrence of certain observations as proof that a given hypothesis is false, we presuppose the existence of certain conditions. And though, in any given case, it may be extremely improbable that this assumption is false, it is not logically impossible. We shall see that there need be no self-contradiction in holding that some of the relevant circumstances are other than we have taken them to be, and consequently that the hypothesis has not really broken down. And if it is not the case that

---

[7] E.g. M. Schlick, "Positivismus und Realismus," *Erkenntnis*, Vol. I, 1930. F. Waismann, "Logische Analyse des Warscheinlichkeitsbegriffs," *Erkenntnis*, Vol. I, 1930.— A.J.A.

[8] E.g. M. Schlick, "Die Kausalität in der gegenwärtigen Physik," *Naturwissenschaft*, Vol. 19, 1931.—A.J.A.

[9] This has been proposed by Karl Popper in his *Logik der Forschung.*— A.J.A.

any hypothesis can be definitely confuted, we cannot hold that the genuineness of a proposition depends on the possibility of its definite confutation.

Accordingly, we fall back on the weaker sense of verification. We say that the question that must be asked about any putative statement of fact is not, Would any observations make its truth or falsehood logically certain? but simply, Would any observations be relevant to the determination of its truth or falsehood? And it is only if a negative answer is given to this second question that we conclude that the statement under consideration is nonsensical.

· III ·

To make our position clearer, we may formulate it in another way. Let us call a proposition which records an actual or possible observation an experiential proposition. Then we may say that it is the mark of a genuine factual proposition, not that it should be equivalent to an experiential proposition, or any finite number of experiential propositions, but simply that some experiential propositions can be deduced from it in conjunction with certain other premises without being deducible from those other premises alone.[10]

This criterion seems liberal enough. In contrast to the principle of conclusive verifiability, it clearly does not deny significance to general propositions or to propositions about the past. Let us see what kinds of assertion it rules out.

A good example of the kind of utterance that is condemned by our criterion as being not even false but nonsensical would be the assertion that the world of sense-experience was altogether unreal. It must, of course, be admitted that our senses do sometimes deceive us. We may, as the result of having certain sensations, expect certain other sensations to be obtainable which are, in fact, not obtainable. But, in all such cases, it is further sense-experience that informs us of the mistakes that arise out of sense-experience. We say that the senses sometimes deceive us, just because the expectations to which our sense-experiences give rise do not always accord with what we subsequently experience. That is, we rely on our senses to substantiate or confute the judgements which are based on our sensations. And therefore the fact that our perceptual judgements are sometimes found to be erroneous has not the slightest tendency to show that the world of sense-experience is unreal. And, indeed, it is plain that no conceivable observation, or series of observations, could have any tendency to show that the world revealed to us by sense-experience was unreal. Consequently, anyone who condemns the sensible world as a world of mere appearance, as opposed to reality, is saying something which, according to our criterion of significance, is literally nonsensical.

An example of a controversy which the application of our criterion obliges us to condemn as fictitious is provided by those who dispute concerning the number of substances that there are in the world. For it is admitted both by monists, who maintain that reality is one substance, and by pluralists, who maintain that reality is many, that it is impossible to imagine any empirical situation which would be relevant to the solution of their dispute. But if we are told that no possible observation could give any probability either to the assertion that reality was one substance or to the assertion that

---

[10] This is an over-simplified statement, which is not literally correct. I give what I believe to be the correct formulation in the Introduction, p. 13.— A.J.A.—The "Introduction" is actually an addendum, written ten years later.—E.D.K.

it was many, then we must conclude that neither assertion is significant. We shall see later on[11] that there are genuine logical and empirical questions involved in the dispute between monists and pluralists. But the metaphysical question concerning "substance" is ruled out by our criterion as spurious.

A similar treatment must be accorded to the controversy between realists and idealists, in its metaphysical aspect. A simple illustration, which I have made use of in a similar argument elsewhere,[12] will help to demonstrate this. Let us suppose that a picture is discovered and the suggestion made that it was painted by Goya. There is a definite procedure for dealing with such a question. The experts examine the picture to see in what way it resembles the accredited works of Goya, and to see if it bears any marks which are characteristic of a forgery; they look up contemporary records for evidence of the existence of such a picture, and so on. In the end, they may still disagree, but each one knows what empirical evidence would go to confirm or discredit his opinion. Suppose, now, that these men have studied philosophy, and some of them proceed to maintain that this picture is a set of ideas in the perceiver's mind, or in God's mind, others that it is objectively real. What possible experience could any of them have which would be relevant to the solution of this dispute one way or the other? In the ordinary sense of the term "real," in which it is opposed to "illusory," the reality of the picture is not in doubt. The disputants have satisfied themselves that the picture is real, in this sense, by obtaining a correlated series of sensations of sight and sensations of touch. Is there any similar process by which they could discover whether the picture was real, in the sense in which the term "real" is opposed to "ideal"? Clearly there is none. But, if that is so, the problem is fictitious according to our criterion. This does not mean that the realist-idealist controversy may be dismissed without further ado. For it can legitimately be regarded as a dispute concerning the analysis of existential propositions, and so as involving a logical problem which, as we shall see, can be definitively solved.[13] What we have just shown is that the question at issue between idealists and realists becomes fictitious when, as is often the case, it is given a metaphysical interpretation.

There is no need for us to give further examples of the operation of our criterion of significance. For our object is merely to show that philosophy, as a genuine branch of knowledge, must be distinguished from metaphysics. We are not now concerned with the historical question how much of what has traditionally passed for philosophy is actually metaphysical. We shall, however, point out later on that the majority of the "great philosophers" of the past were not essentially metaphysicians, and thus reassure those who would otherwise be prevented from adopting our criterion by considerations of piety.

· *IV* ·

As to the validity of the verification principle, in the form in which we have stated it, a demonstration will be given in the course of this book. For it will be shown that all propositions which have factual content are empirical hypotheses; and that the

---

[11] In Chapter VIII.— A.J.A.

[12] Vide "Demonstration of the Impossibility of Metaphysics," *Mind*, 1934, p. 339.— A.J.A.

[13] Vide Chapter VIII.— A.J.A.

function of an empirical hypothesis is to provide a rule for the anticipation of experience.[14] And this means that every empirical hypothesis must be relevant to some actual, or possible, experience, so that a statement which is not relevant to any experience is not an empirical hypothesis, and accordingly has no factual content. But this is precisely what the principle of verifiability asserts.

It should be mentioned here that the fact that the utterances of the metaphysician are nonsensical does not follow simply from the fact that they are devoid of factual content. It follows from that fact, together with the fact that they are not *a priori* propositions. And in assuming that they are not *a priori* propositions, we are once again anticipating the conclusions of a later chapter in this book.[15] For it will be shown there that *a priori* propositions, which have always been attractive to philosophers on account of their certainty, owe this certainty to the fact that they are tautologies. We may accordingly define a metaphysical sentence as a sentence which purports to express a genuine proposition, but does, in fact, express neither a tautology nor an empirical hypothesis. And as tautologies and empirical hypotheses form the entire class of significant propositions, we are justified in concluding that all metaphysical assertions are nonsensical. . . .

---

[14]   Vide Chapter V.— A.J.A.
[15]   Chapter IV.— A.J.A.

○ ○ ○ *30*

Critique of Religion[1]

A. J. Ayer

THIS MENTION OF God brings us to the question of the possibility of religious knowledge. We shall see that this possibility has already been ruled out by our treatment of metaphysics. But, as this is a point of considerable interest, we may be permitted to discuss it at some length.

It is now generally admitted, at any rate by philosophers, that the existence of a being having the attributes which define the god of any non-animistic religion cannot be demonstratively proved. To see that this is so, we have only to ask ourselves what are the premises from which the existence of such a god could be deduced. If the conclusion that a god exists is to be demonstratively certain, then these premises must be certain; for, as the conclusion of deductive argument is already contained in the premises, any uncertainty there may be about the truth of the premises is necessarily shared by it. But we know that no empirical proposition can ever be anything more than probable. It is only *a priori* propositions that are logically certain. But we cannot deduce the existence of a god from an *a priori* proposition. For we know that the reason why *a priori* propositions are certain is that they are tautologies. And from a set of tautologies nothing but a further tautology can be validly deduced. It follows that there is no possibility of demonstrating the existence of a god.

What is not so generally recognised is that there can be no way of proving that the existence of a god, such as the God of Christianity, is even probable. Yet this also is easily shown. For if the existence of such a god were probable, then the proposition that he existed would be an empirical hypothesis. And in that case it would be possible to deduce from it, and other empirical hypotheses, certain experiential propositions which were not deducible from those other hypotheses alone. But in fact this is not possible. It is sometimes claimed, indeed, that the existence of a certain sort of regularity in nature constitutes sufficient evidence for the existence of a god. But if the sentence "God exists" entails no more than that certain types of phenomena occur in certain sequences, then to assert the existence of a god will be simply equivalent to asserting that there is the requisite regularity in nature; and no religious man would admit that this was all he intended to assert in asserting the existence of a god. He would say that in talking about God, he was talking about a transcendent being who might be known through certain empirical manifestations, but certainly could not be defined in terms of those manifestations. But in that case the term "god" is a metaphysical term. And if "god" is a metaphysical term then it cannot be even probable that a god exists. For to say that "God exists" is to make a metaphysical utterance which cannot be either true

---

[1] More accurately: Critique of theology. From *Language, Truth and Logic*, Chapter. 6.—E.D.K.

or false. And by the same criterion, no sentence which purports to describe the nature of a transcendent god can possess any literal significance.

It is important not to confuse this view of religious assertions with the view that is adopted by atheists, or agnostics.[2] For it is characteristic of an agnostic to hold that the existence of a god is a possibility in which there is no good reason either to believe or disbelieve; and it is characteristic of an atheist to hold that it is at least probable that no god exists. And our view that all utterances about the nature of God are nonsensical, so far from being identical with, or even lending any support to, either of these familiar contentions, is actually incompatible with them. For if the assertion that there is a god is nonsensical, then the atheist's assertion that there is no god is equally nonsensical, since it is only a significant proposition that can be significantly contradicted. As for the agnostic, although he refrains from saying either that there is or that there is not a god, he does not deny that the question whether a transcendent god exists is a genuine question. He does not deny that the two sentences "There is a transcendent god" and "There is no transcendent god" express propositions one of which is actually true and the other false. All he says is that we have no means of telling which of them is true, and therefore ought not to commit ourselves to either. But we have seen that the sentences in question do not express propositions at all. And this means that agnosticism also is ruled out.

Thus we offer the theist the same comfort as we gave to the moralist. His assertions cannot possibly be valid, but they cannot be invalid either. As he says nothing at all about the world, he cannot justly be accused of saying anything false, or anything for which he has insufficient grounds. It is only when the theist claims that in asserting the existence of a transcendent god he is expressing a genuine proposition that we are entitled to disagree with him.

It is to be remarked that in cases where deities are identified with natural objects, assertions concerning them may be allowed to be significant. If, for example, a man tells me that the occurrence of thunder is alone both necessary and sufficient to establish the truth of the proposition that Jehovah is angry, I may conclude that, in his usage of words, the sentence "Jehovah is angry" is equivalent to "It is thundering." But in sophisticated religions, though they may be to some extent based on men's awe of natural process which they cannot sufficiently understand, the "person" who is supposed to control the empirical world is not himself located in it; he is held to be superior to the empirical world, and so outside it; and he is endowed with super-empirical attributes. But the notion of a person whose essential attributes are nonempirical is not an intelligible notion at all. We may have a word which is used as if it named this "person," but, unless the sentences in which it occurs express propositions which are empirically verifiable, it cannot be said to symbolize anything. And this is the case with regard to the word "god," in the usage in which it is intended to refer to a transcendent object. The mere existence of the noun is enough to foster the illusion that there is a real, or at any rate a possible entity corresponding to it. It is only when we enquire what God's attributes are that we discover that "God," in this usage, is not a genuine name.

It is common to find belief in a transcendent god conjoined with belief in an after-life. But, in the form which it usually takes, the content of this belief is not a genuine

[2] This point was suggested to me by Professor H. H. Price.—A.J.A.

hypothesis. To say that men do not ever die, or that the state of death is merely a state of prolonged insensibility, is indeed to express a significant proposition, though all the available evidence goes to show that it is false. But to say that there is something imperceptible inside a man, which is his soul or his real self, and that it goes on living after he is dead, is to make a metaphysical assertion which has no more factual content than the assertion that there is a transcendent god.

It is worth mentioning that, according to the account which we have given of religious assertions, there is no logical ground for antagonism between religion and natural science. As far as the question of truth or falsehood is concerned, there is no opposition between the natural scientist and the theist who believes in a transcendent god. For since the religious utterances of the theist are not genuine propositions at all, they cannot stand in any logical relation to the propositions of science. Such antagonism as there is between religion and science appears to consist in the fact that science takes away one of the motives which make men religious. For it is acknowledged that one of the ultimate sources of religious feeling lies in the inability of men to determine their own destiny; and science tends to destroy the feeling of awe with which men regard an alien world, by making them believe that they can understand and anticipate the course of natural phenomena, and even to some extent control it. The fact that it has recently become fashionable for physicists themselves to be sympathetic towards religion is a point in favour of this hypothesis. For this sympathy towards religion marks the physicists' own lack of confidence in the validity of their hypotheses, which is a reaction on their part from the anti-religious dogmatism of nineteenth-century scientists, and a natural outcome of the crisis through which physics has just passed.

It is not within the scope of this enquiry to enter more deeply into the causes of religious feeling, or to discuss the probability of the continuance of religious belief. We are concerned only to answer those questions which arise out of our discussion of the possibility of religious knowledge. The point which we wish to establish is that there cannot be any transcendent truths of religion. For the sentences which the theist uses to express such "truths" are not literally significant.

An interesting feature of this conclusion is that it accords with what many theists are accustomed to say themselves. For we are often told that the nature of God is a mystery which transcends the human understanding. But to say that something transcends the human understanding is to say that it is unintelligible. And what is unintelligible cannot significantly be described. Again, we are told that God is not an object of reason but an object of faith. This may be nothing more than an admission that the existence of God must be taken on trust, since it cannot be proved. But it may also be an assertion that God is the object of a purely mystical intuition, and cannot therefore be defined in terms which are intelligible to the reason. And I think there are many theists who would assert this. But if one allows that it is impossible to define God in intelligible terms, then one is allowing that it is impossible for a sentence both to be significant and to be about God. If a mystic admits that the object of his vision is something which cannot be described, then he must also admit that he is bound to talk nonsense when he describes it.

For his part, the mystic may protest that his intuition does reveal truths to him, even though he cannot explain to others what these truths are; and that we who do not possess this faculty of intuition can have no ground for denying that it is a cognitive faculty. For we can hardly maintain *a priori* that there are no ways of discovering true propositions except those which we ourselves employ. The answer is that we set no limit to the number of ways in which one may come to formulate a true proposition. We do not in any way deny that a synthetic truth may be discovered by purely intuitive methods as well as by the rational method of induction. But we do say that every synthetic proposition, however it may have been arrived at, must be subject to the test of actual experience. We do not deny *a priori* that the mystic is able to discover truths by his own special methods. We wait to hear what are the propositions which embody his discoveries, in order to see whether they are verified or confuted by our empirical observations. But the mystic, so far from producing propositions which are empirically verified, is unable to produce any intelligible propositions at all. And therefore we say that his intuition has not revealed to him any facts. It is no use his saying that he has apprehended facts but is unable to express them. For we know that if he really had acquired any information, he would be able to express it. He would be able to indicate in some way or other how the genuineness of his discovery might be empirically determined. The fact that he cannot reveal what he "knows," or even himself devise an empirical test to validate his "knowledge," shows that his state of mystical intuition is not a genuinely cognitive state. So that in describing his vision the mystic does not give us any information about the external world; he merely gives us indirect information about the condition of his own mind.

These considerations dispose of the argument from religious experience, which many philosophers still regard as a valid argument in favour of the existence of a god. They say that it is logically possible for men to be immediately acquainted with God, as they are immediately acquainted with a sense-content, and that there is no reason why one should be prepared to believe a man when he says that he is seeing a yellow patch, and refuse to believe him when he is seeing God. The answer to this is that if the man who asserts that he is seeing God is merely asserting that he is experiencing a peculiar kind of sense-content, then we do not for a moment deny that his assertion may be true. But, ordinarily, the man who says that he is seeing God is saying not merely that he is experiencing a religious emotion, but also that there exists a transcendent being who is the object of this emotion; just as the man who says that he sees a yellow patch is ordinarily saying not merely that his visual sense-field contains a yellow sense-content, but also that there exists a yellow object to which the sense-content belongs. And it is not irrational to be prepared to believe a man when he asserts the existence of a yellow object, and to refuse to believe him when he asserts the existence of a transcendent god. For whereas the sentence "There exists here a yellow-coloured material thing" expresses a genuine synthetic proposition which could be empirically verified, the sentence "There exists a transcendent god" has, as we have seen, no literal significance.

We conclude, therefore, that the argument from religious experience is altogether fallacious. The fact that people have religious experiences is interesting from the psychological point of view, but it does not in any way imply that there is such a thing as religious knowledge, any more than our having moral experiences implies that there is such a thing as moral knowledge. The theist, like the moralist, may believe that his experiences are cognitive experiences, but, unless he can formulate his "knowledge" in propositions that are empirically verifiable, we may be sure that he is deceiving himself. It follows that those philosophers who fill their books with assertions that they intuitively "know" this or that moral or religious "truth" are merely providing material for the psycho-analyst. For no act of intuition can be said to reveal a truth about any matter of fact unless it issues in verifiable propositions. And all such propositions are to be incorporated in the system of empirical propositions which constitutes science.

○   ○   ○   *31*

Theology and Falsification
Antony Flew,
R. M. Hare, and
Basil Mitchell

· *I* ·

Antony Flew[1]

LET US BEGIN with a parable. It is a parable developed from a tale told by John Wisdom in his haunting and revelatory article "Gods." Once upon a time two explorers came upon a clearing in the jungle. In the clearing were growing many flowers and many weeds. One explorer says, "Some gardener must tend this plot." The other disagrees, "There is no gardener." So they pitch their tents and set a watch. No gardener is ever seen. "But perhaps he is an invisible gardener." So they set up a barbed-wire fence. They electrify it. They patrol with bloodhounds. (For they remember how H. G. Wells's *The Invisible Man* could be both smelt and touched though he could not be seen.) But no shrieks ever suggest that some intruder has received a shock. No movements of the wire ever betray an invisible climber. The bloodhounds never give cry. Yet still the Believer is not convinced. "But there is a gardener, invisible, intangible, insensible to electric shocks, a gardener who has no scent and makes no sound, a gardener who comes secretly to look after the garden which he loves." At last the Skeptic despairs, "But what remains of your original assertion? Just how does what you call an invisible, intangible, eternally elusive gardener differ from an imaginary gardener or even from no gardener at all?"

In this parable we can see how what starts as an assertion, that something exists or that there is some analogy between certain complexes of phenomena, may be reduced step by step to an altogether different status, to an expression perhaps of a "picture preference."[2] The Skeptic says there is no gardener. The Believer says there is a gardener (but invisible, etc.). One man talks about sexual behaviour. Another man prefers to talk of Aphrodite (but knows that there is not really a superhuman person additional to, and somehow responsible for, all sexual phenomena). The process of qualification may be checked at any point before the original assertion is completely withdrawn and something of that first assertion is completely withdrawn and something of that first assertion will remain (tautology). Mr. Wells's invisible man could

---

[1] Strictly speaking, only this first brief essay belongs in this chapter. The next two parts, by Hare and Mitchell, fit into the next chapter. They are presented here because they were all part of one symposium.—E.D.K.

[2] Cf. J. Wisdom, "Other Minds," *Mind* (1940).—A.F.

not, admittedly, be seen, but in all other respects he was a man like the rest of us. But though the process of qualification may be, and of course usually is, checked in time, it is not always judiciously so halted. Someone may dissipate his assertion completely without noticing that he has done so. A fine brash hypothesis may thus be killed by inches, the death by a thousand qualifications.

And in this, it seems to me, lies the peculiar danger, the endemic evil, of theological utterance. Take such utterances as "God has a plan," "God created the world," "God loves us as a father loves his children." They look at first sight very much like assertions, vast cosmological assertions. Of course, this is no sure sign that they either are, or are intended to be, assertions. But let us confine ourselves to the cases where those who utter such sentences intend them to express assertions. (Merely remarking parenthetically that those who intend or interpret such utterances as crypto-commands, expressions of wishes, disguised ejaculations, concealed ethics, or as anything else but assertions are unlikely to succeed in making them either properly orthodox or practically effective.)

Now to assert that such and such is the case is necessarily equivalent to denying that such and such is not the case. Suppose then that we are in doubt as to what someone who gives vent to an utterance is asserting, or suppose that, more radically, we are skeptical as to whether he is really asserting anything at all, one way of trying to understand (or perhaps it will be to expose) his utterance is to attempt to find what he would regard as counting against, or as being incompatible with, its truth. For if the utterance is indeed an assertion, it will necessarily be equivalent to a denial of the negation of that assertion. And anything which would count against the assertion, or which would induce the speaker to withdraw it and to admit that it had been mistaken, must be part of (or the whole of) the meaning of the negation of that assertion. And to know the meaning of the negation of an assertion is as near as makes no matter to know the meaning of that assertion. And if there is nothing which a putative assertion denies then there is nothing which it asserts either: and so it is not really an assertion. When the Skeptic in the parable asked the Believer, "Just how does what you call an invisible, intangible, eternally elusive gardener differ from an imaginary gardener or even from no gardener at all?" he was suggesting that the Believer's earlier statement had been so eroded by qualification that it was no longer an assertion at all.

Now it often seems to people who are not religious as if there was no conceivable event or series of events the occurrence of which would be admitted by sophisticated religious people to be a sufficient reason for conceding "There wasn't a God after all" or "God does not really love us then." Someone tells us that God loves us as a father loves his children. We are reassured. But then we see a child dying of inoperable cancer of the throat. His earthly father is driven frantic in his efforts to help, but his Heavenly Father reveals no obvious sign of concern. Some qualification is made—God's love is "not a merely human love" or it is "an inscrutable love," perhaps—and we realize that such sufferings are quite compatible with the truth of the assertion that "God loves us as a father (but, of course, . . .)." We are reassured again. But then perhaps we ask: what is this assurance of God's (appropriately qualified) love worth, what is this apparent guarantee really a guarantee against? Just what would have to happen not merely (morally and wrongly) to tempt but also (logically and rightly) to entitle us to say "God does not love us" or even "God does not exist"? I therefore put to the succeeding symposiasts the simple central questions, "What would have to occur or to have occurred to constitute for you a disproof of the love of, or of the existence of, God?"

· *II* ·

R.M. Hare[3]

I wish to make it clear that I shall not try to defend Christianity in particular, but religion in general—not because I do not believe in Christianity, but because you cannot understand what Christianity is, until you have understood what religion is.

I must begin by confessing that, on the ground marked out by Flew, he seems to me to be completely victorious. I therefore shift my ground by relating another parable. A certain lunatic is convinced that all dons want to murder him. His friends introduce him to all the mildest and most respectable dons that they can find, and after each of them has retired, they, "You see, he doesn't really want to murder you; he spoke to you in a most cordial manner; surely you are convinced now?" But the lunatic replies "Yes, but that was only his diabolical cunning; he's really plotting against me the whole time, like the rest of them; I know it I tell you." However many kindly dons are produced, the reaction is still the same.

Now we say that such a person is deluded. But what is he deluded about? About the truth or falsity of an assertion? Let us apply Flew's test to him. There is no behaviour of dons that can be enacted which he will accept as counting against his theory; and therefore his theory, on this test, asserts nothing. But it does not follow that there is no difference between what he thinks about dons and what most of us think about them—otherwise we should not call him a lunatic and ourselves sane, and dons would have no reason to feel uneasy about his presence in Oxford.

Let us call that in which we differ from this lunatic, our respective *bliks*. He has an insane *blik* about dons; we have a sane one. It is important to realize that we save a sane one, not no *blik* at all; for there must be two sides to any argument—if he has a wrong *blik*, then those who are right about dons must have a right one. Flew has shown that a *blik* does not consist in an assertion or system of them; but nevertheless it is very important to have the right *blik*.

Let us try to imagine what it would be like to have different *bliks* about other things than dons. When I am driving my car, it sometimes occurs to me to wonder whether my movements of the steering-wheel will always continue to be followed by corresponding alterations in the direction of the car. I have never had a steering failure, though I have had skids, which must be similar. Moreover, I know enough about how the steering of my car is made to know the sort of thing that would have to go wrong for the steering to fail—steel joints would have to part, or steel rods break, or something—but how do I know that this won't happen? The truth is, I don't know; I just have a *blik* about steel and its properties, so that normally I trust the steering of my car; but I find it not at all difficult to imagine what it would be like to lose this *blik* and acquire the opposite one. People would say I was silly about steel; but there would be no mistaking the reality of the difference between our respective *bliks*—for example, I should never go in a motor-car. Yet I should hesitate to say that the difference between us was the difference between contradictory assertions. No amount of safe arrivals or bench-tests will remove my *blik* and restore the normal one; for my *blik* is compatible with any finite number of such tests.

---

[3] The reader may want to read this section and the next with the selections in the next chapter—E.D.K.

It was Hume who taught us that our whole commerce with the world depends upon our *blik* about the world; and that differences between *bliks* about the world cannot be settled by observation of what happens in the world. That was why, having performed the interesting experiment of doubting the ordinary man's *blik* about the world, and showing that no proof could be given to make us adopt one *blik* rather than another, he turned to backgammon to take his mind off the problem. It seems, indeed, to be impossible even to formulate as an assertion the normal *blik* about the world which makes me put my confidence in the future reliability of steel joints, in the continued ability of the road to support my car, and not gape beneath it revealing nothing below; in the general non-homicidal tendencies of dons; in my own continued well-being (in some sense of that word that I may not now fully understand) if I continue to do what is right according to my lights; in the general likelihood of people like Hitler coming to a bad end. But perhaps a formulation less inadequate than most is to be found in the Psalms: "The earth is weak and all the inhabiters thereof: I bear up the pillars of it."

The mistake of the position which Flew selects for attack is to regard this kind of talk as some sort of *explanation*, as scientists are accustomed to use the word. As such, it would obviously be ludicrous. We no longer believe in God as an Atlas—*nous n'avons pas besoin de cette hypothèse*.[4] But it is nevertheless true to say that, as Hume saw, with a *blik* there can be no explanation; for it is by our *bliks* that we decide what is and what is not an explanation. Suppose we believed that everything that happened, happened by pure chance. This would not of course be an assertion; for it is compatible with anything happening or not happening, and so, incidentally, is its contradictory. But if we had this belief, we should not be able to explain or predict or plan anything. Thus, although we should not be *asserting* anything different from those of a more normal belief, there would be a great difference between us; and this is the sort of difference that there is between those who really believe in God and those who really disbelieve in him.

The word "really" is important, and may excite suspicion. I put it in, because when people have a good Christian upbringing, as have most of those who now profess not to believe in any sort of religion, it is very hard to discover what they really believe. The reason why they find it so easy to think that they are not religious is that they have never got into the frame of mind of one who suffers from the doubts to which religion is the answer. Not for them the terrors of the primitive jungle. Having abandoned some of the more picturesque fringes of religion, they think that they have abandoned the whole thing—whereas in fact they still have got, and could not live without, a religion of a comfortably substantial, albeit highly sophisticated, kind, which differs from that of many "religious people" in little more than this, that "religious people" like to sing Psalms about theirs—a very natural and proper thing to do. But nevertheless there may be a big difference lying behind—the difference between two people who, though side by side, are walking in different directions. I do not know in what direction Flew is walking; perhaps he does not know either. But we have had some examples recently of various ways in which one can walk away from Christianity, and there are any number of possibilities. After all, man has not changed biologically since primitive times; it is

---

[4] "We have no need of that hypothesis."—E.D.K.

his religion that has changed, and it can easily change again. And if you do not think that such changes make a difference, get acquainted with some Sikhs and some Mussulmans of the same Punjabi stock; you will find them quite different sorts of people.

There is an important difference between Flew's parable and my own which we have not yet noticed. The explorers do not *mind* about their garden; they discuss it with interest, but not with concern. But my lunatic, poor fellow, minds about dons; and I mind about the steering of my car; it often has people in it that I care for. It is because I mind very much about what goes on in the garden in which I find myself, that I am unable to share the explorers' detachment.

· III ·
Basil Mitchell [5]

Flew's article is searching and perceptive, but there is, I think, something odd about his conduct of the theologian's case. The theologian surely would not deny that the fact of pain counts against the assertion that God loves men. This very incompatibility generates the most intractable of theological problems—the problem of evil. So the theologian *does* recognize the fact of pain as counting against Christian doctrine. But it is true that he will not allow it—or anything—to count decisively against it; for he is committed by his faith to trust in God. His attitude is not that of the detached observer, but of the believer.

Perhaps this can be brought out by yet another parable. In time of war in an occupied country, a member of the resistance meets one night a stranger who deeply impresses him. They spend that night together in conversation. The Stranger tells the partisan that he himself is on the side of the resistance—indeed that he is in command of it, and urges the partisan to have faith in him no matter what happens. The partisan is utterly convinced at that meeting of the Stranger's sincerity and constancy and undertakes to trust him.

They never meet in conditions of intimacy again. But sometimes the Stranger is seen helping members of the resistance, and the partisan is grateful and says to his friend, "He is on our side."

Sometimes he is seen in the uniform of the police handing over patriots to the occupying power. On these occasions his friends murmur against him: but the partisan still says, "He is on our side." He still believes that, in spite of appearances, the Stranger did not deceive him. Sometimes he asks the Stranger for help and receives it. He is then thankful. Sometimes he asks and does not receive it. Then he says, "The Stranger knows best." Sometimes his friends, in exasperation, say "Well, what *would* he have to do for you to admit that you were wrong and that he is not on our side?" But the partisan refuses to answer. He will not consent to put the Stranger to the test. And sometimes his friends complain, "Well, if *that's* what you mean by his being on our side, the sooner he goes over to the other side the better."

The partisan of the parable does not allow anything to count decisively against the proposition "The Stranger is on our side." This is because he has committed himself to trust the Stranger. But he of course recognizes that the Stranger's ambiguous behaviour *does* count against what he believes about him. It is precisely this situation which constitutes the trial of his faith.

---
[5] See note 3—E.D.K.

When the partisan asks for help and doesn't get it, what can he do? He can (a) conclude that the stranger is not on our side; or (b) maintain that he is on our side, but that he has reasons for withholding help.

The first he will refuse to do. How long can he uphold the second position without its becoming just silly?

I don't think one can say in advance. It will depend on the nature of the impression created by the Stranger in the first place. It will depend, too, on the manner in which he takes the Stranger's behaviour. If he blandly dismisses it as of no consequence, as having no bearing upon his belief, it will be assumed that he is thoughtless or insane. And it quite obviously won't do for him to say easily, "Oh, when used of the Stranger the phrase 'is on our side' *means* ambiguous behaviour of this sort." In that case he would be like the religious man who says blandly of a terrible disaster "It is God's will." No, he will only be regarded as sane and reasonable in his belief, if he experiences in himself the full force of the conflict.

It is here that my parable differs from Hare's. The partisan admits that many things may and do count against his belief: whereas Hare's lunatic who has a *blik* about dons doesn't admit that anything counts against his *blik*. Nothing *can* count against *bliks*. Also the partisan has a reason for having in the first instance committed himself, viz., the character of the Stranger; whereas the lunatic has no reason for his *blik* about dons—because, of course, you can't have reasons for *bliks*.

This means that I agree with Flew that theological utterances must be assertions. The partisan is making an assertion when he says, "The Stranger is on our side."

Do I want to say that the partisan's belief about the Stranger is, in any sense, an explanation? I think I do. It explains and makes sense of the Stranger's behaviour: it helps to explain also the resistance movement in the context of which he appears. In each case it differs from the interpretation which the others put upon the same facts.

"God loves men" resembles "the Stranger is on our side" (and many other significant statements, e.g., historical ones) in not being conclusively falsifiable. They can both be treated in at least three different ways: (1) as provisional hypotheses to be discarded if experience tells against them, (2) as significant articles of faith, (3) as vacuous formulae (expressing, perhaps, a desire for reassurance) to which experience makes no difference and which make no difference to life.

The Christian, once he has committed himself, is precluded by his faith from taking up the first attitude: "Thou shalt not tempt the Lord thy God." He is in constant danger, as Flew has observed, of slipping into the third. But he need not; and, if he does, it is a failure in faith as well as in logic.

· IV ·

Antony Flew

It has been a good discussion; and I am glad to have helped to provoke it. But now . . . it must come to an end: and [I shall] make some concluding remarks. Since it is impossible to deal with all the issues raised or to comment separately upon each contribution, I will concentrate on Mitchell and Hare, as representative of two very different kinds of response to [my] challenge. . . .

The challenge, it will be remembered, ran like this. Some theological utterances seem to, and are intended to, provide explanations or express assertions. Now an assertion, to be an assertion at all, must claim that things stand thus and thus; *and not otherwise*. Similarly an explanation, to be an explanation at all, must explain why this particular thing occurs; *and not something else*. Those last clauses are crucial. And yet sophisticated religious people—or so it seemed to me—are apt to overlook this, and tend to refuse to allow, not merely that anything actually does occur, but that anything conceivably could occur, which would count against their theological assertions and explanations. But insofar as they do this their supposed explanations are actually bogus, and their seeming assertions are really vacuous.

Mitchell's response to this challenge is admirably direct, straightforward, and understanding. He agrees "that theological utterances must be assertions." He agrees that if they are to be assertions, there must be something that would count against their truth. He agrees, too, that believers are in constant danger of transforming their would-be assertions into "vacuous formulae." But he takes me to task for an oddity in my "conduct of the theologian's case. The theologian surely would not deny that the fact of pain counts against the assertion that God loves men. This very incompatibility generates the most intractable of theological problems, the problem of evil." I think he is right. I should have made a distinction between two very different ways of dealing with what looks like evidence against the love of God; the way I stressed was the expedient of qualifying the original assertion; the way the theologian usually takes, at first, is to admit that it looks bad but to insist that there is—there must be—some explanation which will show that, in spite of appearances, there really is a God who loves us. His difficulty, it seems to me, is that he has given God attributes which rule out all possible saving explanations. In Mitchell's parable of the Stranger it is easy for the believer to find plausible excuses for ambiguous behaviour; for the Stranger is a man. But suppose the Stranger is God. We cannot say that he would like to help but cannot; God is omnipotent. We cannot say that he would help if he only knew; God is omniscient. We cannot say that he is not responsible for the wickedness of others; God creates those others. Indeed and omnipotent, omniscient God must be an accessory before (and during) the fact to every human misdeed; as well as being responsible for every non-moral defect in the universe. So, though I entirely concede that Mitchell was absolutely right to insist against me that the theologian's first move is to look for an *explanation*, I still think that in the end, if relentlessly pursued, he will have to resort to the avoiding action of *qualification*. And there lies the danger of the death by a thousand qualifications, which would, I agree, constitute "a failure in faith as well as in logic."

Hare's approach is fresh and bold. He confesses that "on the ground marked out by Flew, he seems to me to be completely victorious." He therefore introduces the concept of *blik*. But while I think that there is room for some such concept in philosophy, and that philosophers should be grateful to Hare for his invention, I nevertheless want to insist that any attempt to analyze Christian religious utterance as expressions or affirmations of a *blik* rather than as (at least would-be) assertions about the cosmos is fundamentally misguided. First, because thus interpreted they would be entirely unorthodox. If Hare's religion really is a *blik*, involving no cosmological assertions about the nature and activities of a supposed personal creator, then surely he is not a Christian at all? Second, because thus interpreted, they could scarcely do the job they do. If they were not even intended as assertions, then many religious activities would become fraudulent, or merely silly. If "You ought *because* it is God's will" asserts no more than "You ought," then the person who prefers the former phraseology is not really giving a reason, but a fraudulent substitute for one, a dialectical dud check. If "My soul must be immortal *because* God loves his children, etc." asserts no more than "My soul must be immortal," then the man who reassures himself with theological arguments for immortality is being as silly as the man who tries to clear his overdraft by writing his bank a check on the same account. (Of course neither of these utterances would be distinctively Christian; but this discussion never pretended to be so confined.) Religious utterances may indeed express false or even bogus assertions: but I simply do not believe that they are not both intended and interpreted to be or at any rate to presuppose assertions, at least in the context or religious practice, whatever shifts may be demanded, in another context, by the exigencies of theological apologetic.

One final suggestion. The philosophers of religion might well draw upon George Orwell's last appalling nightmare, *1984*, for the concept of *doublethink*. "*Doublethink* means the power of holding two contradictory beliefs simultaneously, and accepting both of them. The party intellectual knows that he is playing tricks with reality, but by the exercise of *doublethink* he also satisfies himself that reality is not violated." Perhaps religious intellectuals too are sometimes driven to doublethink in order to retain their faith in a loving God in face of the reality of a heartless and indifferent world. But of this more another time, perhaps.

CHAPTER SEVEN

The Theistic and Other Responses

○ ○ ○ *32*

Gods
John Wisdom

1. *THE EXISTENCE OF God is not an experimental issue in the way it was.* An atheist or ag-nostic might say to a theist "You still think there are spirits in the trees, nymphs in the streams, a God of the world." He might say this because he noticed the theist in time of drought pray for rain and make a sacrifice and in the morning look for rain. But disagreement about whether there are gods is now less of this experimental or betting sort than it used to be. This is due in part, if not wholly, to our better knowledge of why things happen as they do.

It is true that even in these days it is seldom that one who believes in God has no hopes or fears which an atheist has not. Few believers now expect prayer to still the waves, but some think it makes a difference to people and not merely in ways the atheist would admit. Of course with people, as opposed to waves and machines, one never knows what they won't do next, so that expecting prayer to make a difference to them is not so definite a thing as believing in its mechanical efficacy. Still, just as primitive people pray in a business-like way for rain, so some people still pray for others with a real feeling of doing something to help. However, in spite of this persistence of an experimental element in some theistic belief, it remains true that Elijah's method[1] on Mount Carmel of settling the matter of what god or gods exist would be far less appropriate today than it was then.

2. *Belief in gods is not merely a matter of expectation of a world to come.* Someone may say "The fact that a theist no more than an atheist expects prayer to bring down fire from heaven or cure the sick does not mean that there is no difference between them as to the facts, it does not mean that the theist has no expectations different from the atheist's. For very often those who believe in God believe in another world and believe that God is there and that we shall go to that world when we die."

This is true, but I do not want to consider here expectations as to what one will see and feel after death nor what sort of reasons these logically unique expectations could have. So I want to consider those theists who do not believe in a future life, or rather, I want to consider the differences between atheists and theists insofar as these differences are not a matter of belief in a future life.

3. *What are these differences? And is it that theists are superstitious or that atheists are blind?* A child may wish to sit awhile with his father and he may, when he has done what his father dislikes, fear punishment and feel distress at causing vexation, and while his father is alive he may feel sure of help when danger threatens and feel that there is sympathy for him when disaster has come. When his father is dead he will no longer

---

[1] See 1 Kings 17–18.—E.D.K.

expect punishment or help. Maybe for a moment an old fear will come or a cry for help escape him, but he will at once remember that this is no good now. He may feel that his father is no more until perhaps someone says to him that his father is still alive though he lives now in another world and one so far away that there is no hope of seeing him or hearing his voice again. The child may be told that nevertheless his father can see him and hear all he says. When he has been told this the child will still fear no punishment nor expect any sign of his father, but now, even more than he did when his father was alive, he will feel that his father sees him all the time and will dread distressing him and when he has done something wrong he will feel separated from his father until he has felt sorry for what he has done. Maybe when he himself comes to die he will be like a man who expects to find a friend in the strange country where he is going, but even when this is so, it is by no means all of what makes the difference between a child who believes that his father lives still in another world and one who does not.

Likewise one who believes in God may face death differently from one who does not, but there is another difference between them besides this. This other difference may still be described as belief in another world, only this belief is not a matter of expecting one thing rather than another here or hereafter, it is not a matter of a world to come but of a world that now is, though beyond our senses.

We are at once reminded of those other unseen worlds which some philosophers "believe in" and others "deny," while non-philosophers unconsciously "accept" them by using them as models with which to "get the hang of" the patterns in the flux of experience. We recall the timeless entities whose changeless connections we seek to represent in symbols, and the values which stand firm amidst our flickering satisfaction and remorse, and the physical things which, though not beyond the corruption of moth and rust, are yet more permanent than the shadows they throw upon the screen before our minds. We recall, too, our talk of souls and of what lies in their depths and is manifested to us partially and intermittently in our own feelings and the behaviour of others. The hypothesis of mind, of other human minds and of animal minds, is reasonable because it explains for each of us why certain things behave so cunningly all by themselves unlike even the most ingenious machines. Is the hypothesis of minds in flowers and trees reasonable for like reasons? Is the hypothesis of a world mind reasonable for like reasons—someone who adjusts the blossom to the bees, someone whose presence may at times be felt—in a garden in high summer, in the hills when clouds are gathering, but not, perhaps, in a cholera epidemic?

4. *The question "Is belief in gods reasonable?" has more than one source.* It is clear now that in order to grasp fully the logic of belief in divine minds we need to examine the logic of belief in animal and human minds. But we cannot do that here and so for the purposes of this discussion about divine minds let us acknowledge the reasonableness of our belief in human minds without troubling ourselves about its logic. The question of the reasonableness of belief in divine minds then becomes a matter of whether there are facts in nature which support claims about divine minds in the way facts in nature support our claims about human minds.

In this way we resolve the force behind the problem of the existence of gods into two components, one metaphysical and the same which prompts the question "Is there *ever any* behaviour which gives reason to believe in *any* sort of mind?" and one which finds expression in "Are there other mind-patterns in nature beside the human and animal patterns which we can all easily detect, and are these other mind-patterns superhuman?"

Such overdetermination of a question syndrome is common. Thus, the puzzling questions "Do dogs think?" "Do animals feel?" are partly metaphysical puzzles and partly scientific questions. They are not purely metaphysical; for the reports of scientists about the poor performances of cats in cages and old ladies' stories about the remarkable performances of their pets are not irrelevant. But nor are these questions purely scientific; for the stories never settle them and therefore they have other sources. One other source is the metaphysical source we have already noticed, namely, the difficulty about getting behind an animal's behaviour to its mind, whether it is a non-human animal or a human one.

But there's a third component in the force behind these questions, these disputes have a third source, and it is one which is important in the dispute which finds expression in the words "I believe in God," "I do not." This source comes out well if we consider the question "Do flowers feel?" Like the questions about dogs and animals this question about flowers comes partly from the difficulty we sometimes feel over inference from *any* behaviour to thought or feeling and partly from ignorance as to what behaviour is to be found. But these questions, as opposed to a like question about human beings, come also from hesitation as to whether the behaviour in question is *enough* mind-like, that is, is it enough similar to or superior to human behaviour to be called "mind-proving"? Likewise, even when we are satisfied that human behaviour shows mind and even when we have learned whatever mind-suggesting things there are in nature which are not explained by human and animal minds, we may still ask "But are these things sufficiently striking to be called a mind-pattern? Can we fairly call them manifestations of a divine being?"

"The question," someone may say, "has then become merely a matter of the application of a name. And 'What's in a name?' "

5. *But the line between a question of fact and a question or decision as to the application of a name is not so simple as this way of putting things suggests.* The question "What's in a name?" is engaging because we are inclined to answer both "Nothing" and "Very much." And this "Very much" has more than one source. We might have tried to comfort Heloïse by saying "It isn't that Abelard no longer loves you, for this man isn't Abelard"; we might have said to poor Mr. Tebrick in Mr. Garnet's *Lady into Fox* "But this is no longer Silvia." But if Mr. Tebrick replied "Ah, but it is!" this might come not at all from observing facts about the fox which we have not observed, but from noticing facts about the fox which we had missed, although we had in a sense observed all that Mr. Tebrick had observed. It is possible to have before one's eyes all the items of a pattern and still to miss the pattern. Consider the following conversation:

"And I think Kay and I are pretty happy. We've always been happy."
Bill lifted up his glass and put it down without drinking.
"Would you mind saying that again?" he asked.
"I don't see what's so queer about it. Taken all in all, Kay and I have really been happy."
"All right," Bill said gently, "Just tell me how you and Kay have been happy."
Bill had a way of being amused by things which I could not understand.
"It's a little hard to explain," I said. "It's like taking a lot of numbers that don't look alike and that don't mean anything until you add them all together."
I stopped, because I hadn't meant to talk to him about Kay and me.
"Go ahead," Bill said. "What about the numbers." And he began to smile.
"I don't know why you think it's so funny," I said. "All the things that two people do together, two people like Kay and me, add up to something. There are the kids and the

house and the dog and all the people we have known and all the times we've been out to dinner. Of course, Kay and I do quarrel sometimes but when you add it all together, all of it isn't as bad as the parts of it seem. I mean, maybe that's all there is to anybody's life."

Bill poured himself another drink. He seemed about to say something and checked himself. He kept looking a me.[2]

Or again, suppose two people are speaking of two characters in a story which both have read[3] or of two friends which both have known, and one says "Really she hated him," and the other says "She didn't, she loved him." Then the first may have noticed what the other has not although he knows no incident in the lives of the people they are talking about which the other doesn't know too, and the second speaker may say "She didn't, she loved him" because he hasn't noticed what the first noticed, although he can remember every incident the first can remember. But then again he may say "She didn't, she loved him" not because he hasn't noticed the patterns in time which the first has noticed but because though he has noticed them he doesn't feel he still needs to emphasize them with "Really she hated him." The line between using a name because of how we feel and because of what we have noticed isn't sharp. "A difference as to the facts," "a discovery," "a revelation," these phrases cover many things. Discoveries have been made not only by Christopher Columbus and Pasteur, but also by Tolstoy and Dostoievsky[4] and Freud. Things are revealed to us not only by the scientists with microscopes, but also by the poets, the prophets, and the painters. What is so isn't merely a matter of "the facts." For sometimes when there is agreement as to the facts there is still argument as to whether defendant did or did not "exercise reasonable care," was or was not "negligent."

And though we shall need to emphasize how much "There is a God" evinces an attitude to the familiar,[5] we shall find in the end that it also evinces some recognition of patterns in time easily missed and that, therefore, difference as to there being any gods is in part a difference as to what is so and therefore as to the facts, though not in the simple ways which first occurred to us.

6. *Let us now approach these same points by a different road.*

6.1. *How it is that an explanatory hypothesis, such as the existence of God, may start by being experimental and gradually become something quite different can be seen from the following story*:

Two people return to their long neglected garden and find among the weeds a few of the old plants surprisingly vigorous. One says to the other "It must be that a gardener has been coming and doing something about these plants." Upon inquiry they find that no neighbour has ever seen anyone at work in their garden. The first man says to the other "He must have worked while people slept." The other says "No, someone would have heard him and besides, anybody who cared about the plants would have kept down these weeds." The first man says "Look at the way these are arranged. There is purpose and a feeling for beauty here. I believe that someone comes, someone invisible to mortal eyes. I believe that the more carefully we look the more we shall find

---

[2] J. P. Marquand, *H. M. Pulham, Esq.* (New York: Little, Brown & Co., 1941), p. 320.—J.W.

[3] E.g., Havelock Ellis's autobiography.—J.W.

[4] Russian novelists.—E.D.K.

[5] "Persuasive Definitions," *Mind* (July, 1938), by Charles Leslie Stevenson, should be read here. [Also his *Ethics and Language* (New Haven, Conn.: Yale University Press), 1945.]—J.W.

confirmation of this." They examine the garden ever so carefully and sometimes they come on new things suggesting that a gardener comes and sometimes they come on new things suggesting the contrary and even that a malicious person has been at work. Besides examining the garden carefully they also study what happens to gardens left without attention. Each learns all the other learns about this and about the garden. Consequently, when after all this, one says "I still believe a gardener comes" while the other says "I don't," their different words now reflect no difference as to what they have found in the garden, no difference as to what they would find in the garden if they looked further and no difference about how fast untended gardens fall into disorder. At this stage, in this context, the gardener hypothesis has ceased to be experimental, the difference between one who accepts and one who rejects it is now not a matter of the one expecting something the other does not expect. What is the difference between them? The one says "A gardener comes unseen and unheard. He is manifested only in his works with which we are all familiar," the other says "There is no gardener" and with this difference in what they say about the gardener goes a difference in how they feel towards the garden, in spite of the fact that neither expects anything of it which the other does not expect.

But is this the whole difference between them—that the one calls the garden by one name and feels one way towards it, while the other calls it by another name and feels in another way towards it? And if this is what the difference has become then is it any longer appropriate to ask "Which is right?" or "Which is reasonable?"

And yet surely such questions *are* appropriate when one person says to another "You still think the world's a garden and not a wilderness, and that the gardener has not forsaken it" or "You still think there are nymphs of the streams, a presence in the hills, a spirit of the world." Perhaps when a man sings "God's in His heaven" we need not take this as more than an expression of how he feels. But when Bishop Gore or Dr. Joad[6] write about belief in God and young men read them in order to settle their religious doubts the impression is not simply that of persons choosing exclamations with which to face nature and the "changes and chances of this mortal life." The disputants speak as if they are concerned with a matter of scientific fact, or of trans-sensual, trans-scientific and metaphysical fact, but still of fact and still a matter about which reasons for and against may be offered, although no scientific reasons in the sense of field surveys for fossils or experiments on delinquents are to the point.

6.2. *Now can an interjection have a logic?* Can the manifestation of an attitude in the utterance of a word, in the application of a name have a logic? When all the facts are known how can there still be a question of fact? How can there still be a question? Surely as Hume says " . . . after every circumstance, every relation is known, the understanding has no further room to operate."[7]

6.3. When the madness of these questions leaves us for a moment *we can all easily recollect disputes which though they cannot be settled by experiment are yet disputes in which one party may be right and the other wrong* and in which both parties may offer reasons and the one better reasons that the other. *This may happen in pure and applied mathematics and logic.* Two accountants or two engineers provided with the same data may reach different results and this difference is resolved not by collecting further data but

6 A philosopher who wrote some popular books.—E.D.K.
7 Hume, *An Enquiry Concerning the Principles of Morals*, Appendix I.—J.W.

by going over the calculations again. Such differences indeed share with differences as to what will win a race, the honour of being among the most "settlable" disputes in the language.

6.4. *But it won't do to describe the theistic issue as one settlable by such calculation*, or as one about what can be deduced in this *vertical* fashion from the facts we know. No doubt dispute about God has sometimes, perhaps especially in mediaeval times, been carried on in this fashion. But nowadays it is not and we must look for some other analogy, some other case in which a dispute is settled, but not by experiment.

6.5. *In courts of law* it sometimes happens that opposing counsel are agreed as to the facts and are not trying to settle a question of further fact, are not trying to settle whether the man who admittedly had quarrelled with the deceased did or did not murder him, but are concerned with whether Mr. *A* who admittedly handed his long-trusted clerk signed blank checks did or did not exercise reasonable care, whether a ledger is or is not a document,[8] whether a certain body was or was not a public authority.

In such cases we notice that the process of argument is not a *chain* of demonstrative reasoning. It is a presenting and re-presenting of those features of the case which *severally cooperate* in favour of the conclusion, in favour of saying what the reasoner wishes said, in favour of calling the situation by the name by which he wishes to call it. The reasons are like the legs of a chair, not the links of a chain. Consequently although the discussion is a priori and the steps are not a matter of experience, the procedure resembles scientific argument in that the reasoning is not *vertically* extensive but *horizontally* extensive—it is a matter of the cumulative effect of several independent premises, not of the repeated transformation of one or two. And because the premises are severally inconclusive the process of deciding the issue becomes a matter of weighing the cumulative effect of one group of severally inconclusive items against the cumulative effect of another group of severally inconclusive items, and thus lends itself to description in terms of conflicting "probabilities." This encourages the feeling that the issue is one of fact—that it is a matter of guessing from the premises at a further fact, at what is to come. But this is a muddle. *The dispute does not cease to be a priori because it is a matter of the cumulative effect of severally inconclusive premises.* The logic of the dispute is not that of a chain of deductive reasoning as in a mathematic calculation. But nor is it a matter of collecting from several inconclusive items of information an expectation as to something further, as when a doctor from a patient's symptoms guesses at what is wrong, or a detective from many clues guesses the criminal. It has its own sort of logic and its own sort of end—the solution of the question at issue is a decision, a ruling by the judge. But it is not an arbitrary decision, though the rational connections are neither quite like those in vertical deductions nor like those in inductions in which from many signs we guess at what is to come; and though the decision manifests itself in the application of a name it is no more merely the application of a name than is the pinning on of a medal merely the pinning on of a bit of metal. Whether a lion with stripes is a tiger or a lion is, if you like, merely a matter

---

8 *The Times*, March 2, 1945. Also in *The Times* of June 13, 1945, contrast the case of Hannah v. Peel with that of the cruiser cut in two by a liner. In the latter case there is not agreement as to the facts. See also the excellent articles by Dr. Glanville L. Williams in the *Law Quarterly Review*, "Language and the Law" (January and April 1945) and "The Doctrine of Repugnancy" (October 1943, January 1944, and April 1944). The author, having set out how arbitrary are many legal decisions, needs now to set out how far from arbitrary they are—if his readers are ready for the next phase in the dialectic process.—J.W.

of the application of a name. Whether Mr. So-and-So of whose conduct we have so complete a record did or did not exercise reasonable care is not merely a matter of the application of a name or, if we choose to say it is, then we must remember that with this name a game is lost and won and a game with very heavy stakes. With the judges' choice of a name for the facts goes an attitude, and the declaration, the ruling, is an exclamation evincing that attitude. But *it is an exclamation which not only has a purpose but also has a logic,* a logic surprisingly like that of "futile," "deplorable," "graceful," "grand," "divine."

6.6. *Suppose two people are looking at a picture or natural scene.* One says "Excellent" or "Beautiful" or "Divine"; the other says "I don't see it." He means he doesn't see the beauty. And this reminds us of how we felt the theist accuse the atheist of blindness and the atheist accuse the theist of seeing what isn't there. And yet surely each sees what the other sees. It isn't that one can see part of the picture which the other can't see. So the difference is in a sense not as to the facts. And so it cannot be removed by one disputant discovering to the other what so far he hasn't seen. It isn't that the one sees the picture in a different light and so, as we might say, sees a different picture. Consequently the difference between them cannot be resolved by putting the picture in a different light. And yet surely this is just what can be done in such a case—not by moving the picture but by talk perhaps. To settle a dispute as to whether a piece of music is good or better than another we listen again, with a picture we look again. Someone perhaps points to emphasize certain features and we see it in a different light. Shall we call this "field work" and "the last of observation" or shall we call it "reviewing the premises" and "the beginning of deduction (horizontal)"?

If in spite of all this we choose to say that a difference as to whether a thing is beautiful is not a factual difference, we must be careful to remember that there is a procedure for settling these differences and that this consists not only in reasoning and redescription as in the legal case, but also in a more literal re-setting-before with re-looking or re-listening.

6.7. *And if we say, as we did at the beginning, that when a difference as to the existence of a God is not one as to future happenings then it is not experimental and therefore not as to the facts, we must not forthwith assume that there is not right and wrong about it,* no rationality or irrationality, no appropriateness or inappropriateness, no procedure which tends to settle it, *nor even that this procedure is in no sense a discovery of new facts.* After all even in science this is not so. Our two gardeners, even when they had reached the stage when neither expected any experimental result which the other did not, might yet have continued the dispute, each presenting and re-presenting the features of the garden favouring his hypothesis, that is, fitting his model for describing the accepted fact; each emphasizing the pattern he wishes to emphasize. True, in science, there is seldom or never a pure instance of this sort of dispute, for nearly always with difference of hypothesis goes some difference of expectation as to the facts. But scientists argue about rival hypotheses with a vigour which is not exactly proportioned to difference in expectations of experimental results.

The difference as to whether a God exists involves our feelings more than most scientific disputes and in this respect is more like a difference as to whether there is beauty in a thing.

7. *The Connecting Technique.* Let us consider again the technique used in revealing or proving beauty, in removing a blindness, in inducing an attitude which is lacking, in reducing a reaction that is inappropriate. Besides running over in a special way the

features of the picture, tracing the rhythms, making sure that this and that are not only seen but noticed, and their relation to each other—besides all this—there are other things we can do to justify our attitude and alter that of the man who cannot see. For features of the picture may be brought out by setting beside it other pictures; just as the merits of an argument may be brought out, proved, by setting beside it other arguments, in which striking but irrelevant features of the original are changed and relevant features emphasized; just as the merits and demerits of a line of action may be brought out by setting beside it other actions. To use Susan Stebbing's example: Nathan brought out for David certain features of what David had done in the matter of Uriah the Hittite by telling him a story about two sheep-owners.[9] This is the kind of thing we very often do when someone is "inconsistent" or "unreasonable." This is what we do in referring to other cases in law. The paths we need to trace from other cases to the case in question are often numerous and difficult to detect and the person with whom we are discussing the matter may well draw attention to connections which, while not incompatible with those we have tried to emphasize, are of an opposite inclination. A may have noticed in *B* subtle and hidden likenesses to an angel and reveal these to *C*, while *C* has noticed in *B* subtle and hidden likenesses to a devil which he reveals to *A*.

Imagine that a man picks up some flowers that lie half withered on a table and gently puts them in water. Another man says to him "You believe flowers feel." He says this although he knows that the man who helps the flowers doesn't expect anything of them which he himself doesn't expect; for he himself expects the flowers to be "refreshed" and to be easily hurt, injured, I mean, by rough handling, while the man who puts them in water does not expect them to whisper "Thank you." The skeptic says "You believe flowers feel" because something about the way the other man lifts the flowers and puts them in water suggests an attitude to the flowers which he feels inappropriate although perhaps he would not feel it inappropriate to butterflies. He feels that this attitude to flowers is somewhat crazy *just as it is sometimes felt that a lover's attitude is somewhat crazy even when this is not a matter of his having false hopes about how the person he is in love with will act.* It is often said in such cases that reasoning is useless. But the very person who says this feels that the lover's attitude is crazy, is inappropriate like some dreads and hatreds, such as some horrors of enclosed places. And often one who says "It is useless to reason" proceeds at once to reason with the lover, nor is this reasoning always quite without effect. We may draw the lover's attention to certain things done by her he is in love with and trace for him a path to these from things done by others at other times[10] which have disgusted and infuriated him. And by this means we may weaken his admiration and confidence, make him feel it unjustified and arouse his suspicion and contempt and make him feel our suspicion and contempt reasonable. It is possible, of course, that he has already noticed the analogies, the connections, we point out and that he has accepted them—that is, he has not denied them nor passed them off. He has recognized them and they have altered his attitude, altered his love, but he still loves. We then feel that perhaps it is we who are blind and cannot see what he can see.

8. *Connecting and Disconnecting.* But before we confess ourselves thus inadequate there are other fires his admiration must pass through. For when a man has an attitude

---

[9] See 2 Samuel 11–12.—E.D.K.

[10] Thus, like the scientist, the critic is concerned to show up the irrelevance of time and space.—J.W.

which it seems to us he should not have or lacks one which it seems to us he should have, then not only do we suspect that he is not influenced by connections which we feel should influence him and draw his attention to these, but also we suspect he is influenced by connections which should not influence him and draw his attention to these. It may, for a moment, seem strange that we should draw his attention to connections which we feel should not influence him, and which, since they do influence him, he has in a sense already noticed. But we do—such is our confidence in "the light of reason."

Sometimes the power of these connections comes mainly from a man's mismanagement of the language he is using. This is what happens in the Monte Carlo fallacy, where by mismanaging the laws of chance a man passes from noticing that a certain colour or number has not turned up for a long while to an improper confidence that now it soon will turn up. In such cases our showing up the false connections is a process we call "explaining a fallacy in reasoning." To remove fallacies in reasoning we urge a man to call a spade a spade, ask him what he means by "the State" and having pointed out ambiguities and vaguenesses ask him to reconsider the steps in his argument.

9. Unspoken Connections. Usually, however, wrongheadedness or wrongheartedness in a situation, blindness to what is there or seeing what is not, does not arise merely from mismanagement of language but is more due to connections which are not mishandled in language, for the reason that they are not put into language at all. And often these misconnections too, weaken in the light of reason, if only we can guess where they lie and turn it on them. Insofar as these connections are not presented in language the process of removing their power is not a process of correcting the mismanagement of language. But it is still akin to such a process; for though it is not a process of setting out fairly what has been set out unfairly, it is a process of setting out fairly what has not been set out at all. And we must remember that the line between connections ill-presented or half-presented in language and connections operative but not presented in language, or only hinted at, is not a sharp one.

Whether or not we call the process of showing up these connections "reasoning to remove bad unconscious reasoning" or not, it is certain that in order to settle in ourselves what weight we shall attach to someone's confidence or attitude we not only ask him for his reasons but also look for unconscious reasons both good and bad; that is, for reasons which he can't put into words, isn't explicitly aware of, is hardly aware of, isn't aware of at all—perhaps it's long experience which he *doesn't* recall which lets him know a squall is coming, perhaps it's old experience which he *can't* recall which makes the cake in the tea mean so much and makes Odette so fascinating.[11]

I am well aware of the distinction between the question "What reasons are there for the belief that S is P?" and the question "What are the sources of beliefs that S is P?" There are cases where investigation of the rationality of a claim which certain persons make is done with very little inquiry into why they say what they do, into the causes of their beliefs. This is so when we have very definite ideas about what is really logically relevant to their claim and what is not. Offered a mathematical theorem we ask for the proof; offered the generalization that parental discord causes crime we ask for the correlation coefficients. But even in this last case, if we fancy that only the figures are reasons, we underestimate the complexity of the logic of our conclusion; and yet it is difficult to describe the other features of the evidence which have weight and there is apt to be disagreement about the weight they should have. In criticizing other

---

[11] Proust, *Swann's Way*, Vol. I, 58, Vol. II. Phoenix Edition.—J.W.

conclusions, and especially conclusions which are largely the expression of an attitude, we have not only to ascertain what reasons there are for them but also to decide what things are reasons and how much. This latter process of sifting reasons from causes is part of the critical process for every belief, but in some spheres it has been done pretty fully already. In these spheres we don't need to examine the actual processes to belief and distil from them a logic. But in other spheres this remains to be done. Even in science or on the stock exchange or in ordinary life we sometimes hesitate to condemn a belief or a hunch[12] merely because those who believe it cannot offer the sort of reasons we had hoped for. And now suppose Miss Gertrude Stein[13] finds excellent the work of a new artist while we see nothing in it. We nervously recall, perhaps, how pictures by Picasso,[14] which Miss Stein admired and others rejected, later came to be admired by many who gave attention to them, and we wonder whether the case is not a new instance of her perspicacity and our blindness. But if, upon giving all our attention to the work in question, we still do not respond to it, and we notice that the subject matter of the new pictures is perhaps birds in wild places and learn that Miss Stein is a bird-watcher, then we begin to trouble ourselves less about her admiration.

It must not be forgotten that our attempt to show up misconnections in Miss Stein may have an opposite result and reveal to us connections we had missed. Thinking to remove the spell exercised upon his patient by the old stories of the Greeks, the psychoanalyst may himself fall under that spell and find in them what his patient has found and, incidentally, what made the Greeks tell those tales.

10. *Now what happens, what should happen, when we inquire in this way into the reasonableness, the propriety of belief in gods?* The answer is: A double and opposite-phased change. Wordsworth writes:

> . . . And I have felt
> A presence that disturbs me with the joy
> Of elevated thoughts; a sense sublime
> Of something far more deeply interfused,
> Whose dwelling is the light of setting suns,
> And the round ocean and the living air,
> And the blue sky, and in the mind of man:
> A motion and a spirit, that impels
> All thinking things, all objects of all thought,
> And rolls through all things. . . .[15]

We most of us know this feeling. But is it well placed like the feeling that here is first-rate work, which we sometimes rightly have even before we have fully grasped the picture we are looking at or the book we are reading? Or is it misplaced like the feeling in a house that has long been empty that someone secretly lives there still. Wordsworth's feeling *is* the feeling that the world is haunted, that something watches in the hills and manages the stars. The child feels that the stone tripped him when he stumbled, that the bough struck him when it flew back in his face. He has to learn that the wind isn't

---

[12] Here I think of Mr. Stace's interesting reflections in *Mind* (January 1945), "The Problem of Unreasoned Beliefs."—J.W.

[13] A twentieth-century avant-garde novelist.—E.D.K.

[14] The famous twentieth-century painter.—E.D.K.

[15] Tintern Abbey.—J.W.

buffeting him, that there is not a devil in it, that he was wrong, that his attitude was inappropriate. And as he learns that the wind wasn't hindering him so he also learns it wasn't helping him. But we know how, though he learns, his attitude lingers. It is plain that Wordsworth's feeling is of this family.

Belief in gods, it is true, is often very different from belief that stones are spiteful, the sun kindly. For the gods appear in human form and from the waves and control these things and by so doing reward and punish us. But varied as are the stories of the gods, they have a family likeness and we have only to recall them to feel sure of the other main sources which cooperate with animism to produce them.

What are the stories of the gods? What are our feelings when we believe in God? They are feelings of awe before power, dread of the thunderbolts of Zeus, confidence in the everlasting arms, unease beneath the all-seeing eye. They are feelings of guilt and inescapable vengeance, of smothered hate and of a security we can hardly do without. We have only to remind ourselves of these feelings and the stories of the gods and goddesses and heroes in which these feelings find expression to be reminded of how we felt as children to our parents and the big people of our childhood. Writing of a first telephone call from his grandmother, Proust says:

> . . . it was rather that this isolation of the voice was like a symbol, a presentation, a direct consequence of another isolation, that of my grandmother, separated for the first time in my life, from myself. The orders or prohibitions which she addressed to me at every moment in the ordinary course of my life, the tedium of obedience or the fire of rebellion which neutralized the affection that I felt for her were at this moment eliminated. . . . "Granny!" I cried to her . . . but I had beside me only that voice, a phantom, as unpalpable as that which would come to revisit me when my grandmother was dead. "Speak to me!" but then it happened that, left more solitary still, I ceased to catch the sound of her voice. My grandmother could no longer hear me . . . I continued to call her, sounding the empty night, in which I felt that her appeals also must be straying. I was shaken by the same anguish which, in the distant past, I had felt once before, one day when, a little child, in a crowd, I had lost her.

Giorgio de Chirico, writing of Courbet, says:

> The word yesterday envelops us with its yearning echo, just as, on waking, when the sense of time and the logic of things remain a while confused, the memory of a happy hour we spent the day before may sometimes linger reverberating within us. At times we think of Courbet and his work as we do of our own father's youth.

When a man's father fails him by death or weakness how much he needs another father, one in the heavens with whom is "no variableness nor shadow of turning."

We understood Mr. Kenneth Graham when he wrote of the Golden Age we feel we have lived in under the Olympians. Freud says: "The ordinary man cannot imagine this Providence in any other form but that of a greatly exalted father, for only such a one could understand the needs of the sons of men, or be softened by their prayers and be placated by the signs of their remorse. The whole thing is so patently infantile, so incongruous with reality. . . ." "So incongruous with reality"! It cannot be denied.

But here a new aspect of the matter may strike us.[16] For the very facts which make us feel that now we can recognize systems of superhuman, subhuman, elusive beings for

---

[16] I owe to the late Dr. Susan Isaacs the thought of this different aspect of the matter, of this connection between the heavenly Father and "the good father" spoken of in psychoanalysis.—J.W.

what they are—the persistent projections of infantile phantasies—include facts which make these systems less fantastic. What are these facts? They are patterns in human reactions which are well described by saying that we are as if there were hidden within us powers, persons, not ourselves and stronger than ourselves. That this is so may perhaps be said to have been common knowledge yielded by ordinary observation of people,[17] but we did not know the degree in which this is so until recent study of extraordinary cases in extraordinary conditions had revealed it. I refer, of course, to the study of multiple personalities and the wider studies of psychoanalysts. Even when the results of this work are reported to us, that is not the same as tracing the patterns in the details of the cases on which the results are based; and even that is not the same as taking part in the studies oneself. One thing not sufficiently realized is that some of the things shut within us are not bad but good.

Now the gods, good and evil and mixed, have always been mysterious powers outside us rather than within. But they have also been within. It is not a modern theory but an old saying that in each of us a devil sleeps. Eve said: "The serpent beguiled me." Helen says to Menelaus:

> . . . And yet how strange it is!
> I ask not thee; I ask my own sad thought,
> What was there in my heart, that I forgot
> My home and land and all I loved, to fly
> With a strange man? Surely it was not I,
> But Cypris there![18]

Elijah found that God was not in the wind, nor in the thunder, but in a still small voice. The kingdom of Heaven is within us, Christ insisted, though usually about the size of a grain of mustard seed, and he prayed that we should become one with the Father in Heaven.

New knowledge made it necessary either to give up saying "The sun is sinking" or to give the words a new meaning. In many contexts we preferred to stick to the old words and give them a new meaning which was not entirely new but, on the contrary, *practically* the same as the old. The Greeks did not speak of the dangers of repressing instincts but they did speak of the dangers of thwarting Dionysos, of neglecting Cypris for Diana, of forgetting Poseidon for Athena. We have eaten of the fruit of a garden we can't forget though we were never there, a garden we still look for though we can never find it. Maybe we look for too simple a likeness to what we dreamed. Maybe we are not as free as we fancy from the old idea that Heaven is a happy hunting ground,

---

[17] Consider Tolstoy and Dostoievsky—I do not mean, of course, that their observation was ordinary.—J.W.

[18] Euripides, *The Trojan Woman*, Gilbert Murray's translation. Roger Hinks in *Myth and Allegory in Ancient Art* writes (p. 108): "Personifications made their appearance very early in Greek poetry. . . . It is out of the question to call these terrible beings 'abstractions'. . . . They are real demons to be worshipped and propitiated. . . . These beings we observe correspond to states of mind. The experience of man teaches him that from time to time his composure is invaded and overturned by some power from outside, panic, intoxication, sexual desire."

> What use to shoot off guns at unicorns?
> Where one horn's hit another fierce horn grows.
> These beasts are fabulous, and none were born
> Of woman who could lay a fable low.
>   *The Glass Tower*, Nicholas Moore, p. 100.—J.W.

or a city with streets of gold. Lately Mr. Aldous Huxley[19] has recommended our seeking not somewhere beyond the sky or late in time but a timeless state not made of the stuff of this world, which he rejects, picking it into worthless pieces. But this sounds to me still too much a looking for another place, not indeed one filled with sweets but instead so empty that some of us would rather remain in the Lamb or the Elephant,[20] where, as we know, they stop whimpering with another bitter and, so far from sneering at all things, hang pictures of winners at Kempton[21] and stars of the 'nineties. Something good we have for each other is freed there, and in some degree and for awhile the miasma of time is rolled back without obliging us to deny the present.

The artists who do most for us don't tell us only of fairylands. Proust, Manet, Breughel, even Botticelli and Vermeer[22] show us reality. And yet they give us for a moment exhilaration without anxiety, peace without boredom. And those who, like Freud, work in a different way against that which too often comes over us and forces us into deadness or despair,[23] also deserve critical, patient, and courageous attention. For they, too, work to release us from human bondage into human freedom.

Many have tried to find ways of salvation. The reports they bring back are always incomplete and apt to mislead even when they are not in words but in music or paint. But they are by no means useless; and not the worst of them are those which speak of oneness with God. But insofar as we become one with Him He becomes one with us. St. John says He is in us as we love one another.

This love, I suppose, is not benevolence but something that comes of the oneness with one another of which Christ spoke.[24] Sometimes it momentarily gains strength.[25] Hate and the Devil do too. And what is oneness without otherness?

---

[19] A novelist.—E.D.K.

[20] Famous British pubs.—E.D.K.

[21] A race track.—E.D.K.

[22] Painters.—E.D.K.

[23] Matthew Arnold, *Summer Night*—J.W.

[24] John 16:21.—J.W.

[25] "The Harvesters" in *The Golden Age*, Kenneth Graham.—J.W.

○   ○   ○   **33**

Theology and Falsification
I. M. Crombie[1]

· I ·

THERE ARE SOME who hold that religious statements cannot be fully meaningful, on the ground that those who use them allow nothing to count decisively against them, that is, as incapable of falsification. This paper is an attempted answer to this view; and in composing it I have had particularly in mind [the preceding] article by Antony Flew. I shall offer only a very short, and doubtless tendentious, summary of my opponent's views.

Briefly, then, it is contended that there are utterances made from time to time by Christians and others, which are said by those who make them to be statements, but which are thought by our opponents to lack some of the properties which anything must have before it deserves to be called a statement. "There is a God," "God loves us as a father loves his children," "He shall come again with glory . . . " are examples of such utterances. *Prima facie*[2] such utterances are neither exhortations, nor questions, nor expressions of wishes; *prima facie* they appear to assert the actuality of some state of affairs; and yet (and this is the objection) they are allowed to be compatible with any and every state of affairs. If they are compatible with any and every state of affairs, they cannot mark out some one state of affairs (or group of states of affairs); and if they do not mark out some one state of affairs, how can they be statements? In the case of any ordinary statement, such as "It is raining," there is at least one situation (the absence of falling water) which is held to be incompatible with the statement, and it is the incompatibility of the situation with the statement which gives the statement its meaning. If, then, religious "statements" are compatible with anything and everything, how can they be statements? How can the honest inquirer find out what they mean, if nobody will tell him what they are incompatible with? Are they not much more like such exhortations as "Keep smiling," whose confessed purpose is to go on being in point whatever occurs? Furthermore, is it not true that they only appear to be statements to those of us who use them, because we deceive ourselves by a sort of conjuring trick, oscillating backwards and forwards between a literal interpretation of what we say when we say it, and a scornful rejection of such anthropomorphism when anybody challenges us? When we *say*: "He shall come again with glory . . . ," do we not picture real angels sitting on real clouds; when asked whether we really mean the clouds, we hedge; offer perhaps another picture, which again we refuse to take literally;

---

[1] This paper was composed to be read to a non-philosophical audience. In composing it I have also filched shamelessly (and shamefully no doubt distorted) some unpublished utterances of Dr. A. M. Farrer's.—I.M.C.

[2] On first appearance.—E.D.K.

and so on indefinitely. Whatever symbolism we offer, we always insist that only a crude man would take it literally, and yet we never offer him anything but symbolism; deceived by our imagery into supposing that we have something in mind, in fact there is nothing on which we are prepared to take our stand.

· *II* ·

This is the position I am to try to criticize. It is, I think, less novel than its clothes; but nonetheless it is important. I turn to criticism.

A. Let us begin by dismissing from our inquiry the troublesome statement "There is a God" or "God exists." As every student of logic knows, all statements asserting the existence of something offer difficulties of their own, with which we need not complicate our embarrassment.

That being dismissed, I shall want to say of statements about God that they consist of two parts. Call them, if you like, subject and predicate. Whatever you call them, there is that which is said, and that which it is said about—namely God. It is important to make this distinction, for different problems arise about the different parts. As a first approximation towards isolating the difference, we may notice that the predicate is normally composed of ordinary words, put to unordinary uses, whereas the subject-word is "God," which has no other use. In the expression "God loves us," the word "God" is playing, so to speak, on its home ground, the phrase "loves us" is playing away. Now there is one set of questions which deal with the problem of why we say, and what we mean by saying, that God loves us, rather than hates us, and there is another set of questions concerned with the problem of what it is that this statement is being made about.

B. To approach the matter from an angle which seems to me to afford a good view of it, I shall make a few observations about the epistemological nature of religious belief. Let me caution the reader that, in doing so, I am not attempting to describe how religious belief in fact arises.

Theoretically, then, not in how it arises, but in its logical structure, religious belief has two parents; and it also has a nurse. Its logical mother is what one might call *undifferentiated theism*, its logical father is particular events or occasions interpreted as theophanic,[3] and the extraparental nurture is provided by religious activity.

A word, first, about the logical mother. It is in fact the case that there are elements in our experience which lead people to a certain sort of belief, which we call a belief in God. (We could, if we wished, call it rather an attitude than a belief, so long as we were careful not to call it an attitude to life; for it is of the essence of the attitude to hold that nothing whatever in life may be identified with that towards which it is taken up.) Among the elements in experience which provoke this belief or attitude, perhaps the most powerful is what I shall call a sense of contingency. Others are moral experience, and the beauty and order of nature. Others may be actual abnormal experience of the type called religious or mystical. There are those to whom conscience appears in the form of an unconditional demand; to whom the obligation to one's neighbour seems to be something imposed on him and on me by a third party who is set over us both. There are those to whom the beauty and order of nature appears as the intrusion into nature

---

[3] From "theophany": the appearance of God to man.—E.D.K.

of a realm of beauty and order beyond it. There are those who believe themselves or others to be enriched by moments of direct access to the divine. Now there are two things that must be said about these various theistic interpretations of our experience. The first is that those who so interpret need not be so inexpert in logic as to suppose that there is anything of the nature of a deductive or inductive argument which leads from a premise asserting the existence of the area of experience in question to a conclusion expressing belief in God. Nobody who takes seriously the so-called moral argument need suppose that the *prima facie* authority of conscience cannot be naturalistically explained. He can quite well acknowledge that the imperativeness which so impresses him could be a mere reflection of his jealousy of his father, or a vestigial survival of tribal taboo. The mystic can quite well acknowledge that there is nothing which logically forbids the interpretation of the experience which he enjoys in terms of the condition of his liver or the rate of his respiration. If, being acquainted with the alternative explanations, he persists in rejecting them, it need not be, though of course it sometimes is, because he is seized with a fallacious refutation of their validity. All that is necessary is that he should be honestly convinced that, in interpreting them, as he does, theistically, he is in some sense facing them more honestly, bringing out more of what they contain or involve that could be done by interpreting them in any other way. The one interpretation is preferred to the other, not because the latter is thought to be refutable on paper, but because it is judged to be unconvincing in the light of familiarity with the facts. There is a partial parallel to this in historical judgment. Where you and I differ in our interpretation of a series of events, there is nothing outside the events in question which can overrule either of us, so that each man must accept the interpretation which seems, on fair and critical scrutiny, the most convincing to him. The parallel is only partial, however, for in historical (and literary) interpretation there is something which to some extent controls one's interpretation, and that is one's general knowledge of human nature; and in metaphysical interpretation there is nothing analogous to this. That, then, is my first comment on theistic interpretations; for all that these journeys of the mind are often recorded in quasi-argumentative form, they are not in any ordinary sense arguments, and their validity cannot be assessed by asking whether they conform to the laws either of logic or of scientific method. My second comment upon them is that, in stating them, we find ourselves saying things which we cannot literally mean. Thus the man of conscience uses some such concept as the juridical concept of authority, and locates his authority outside nature; the man of beauty and order speaks of an intrusion from another realm; the mystic speaks of experiencing God. In every case such language lays the user open to devastating criticism, to which he can only retort by pleading that such language, while it is not to be taken strictly, seems to him to be the natural language to use.

To bring these points into a somewhat stronger light, let me say something about the sense of contingency, the conviction which people have, it may be in blinding moments, or it may be in a permanent disposition of a man's mind, that we, and the whole world in which we live, derive our being from something outside us. The first thing I want to say about this is that such a conviction is to no extent like the conclusion of an argument; the sense of dependence feels not at all like being persuaded by arguments, but like seeing, as it were, through a gap in the rolling mists of argument, which alone, one feels, could conceal the obvious truth. One is not *persuaded* to believe that one is contingent; rather one feels that it is only by persuasion that one could ever believe anything else. The second thing I want to say about this conviction of contingency is that in expressing it, . . . we turn the word "contingent" to work which is not its normal employment, and which it cannot properly do.

For the distinction between necessity and contingency is not a distinction between different sorts of entities, but between different sorts of statement. A necessary statement is one whose denial involves a breach of the laws of logic, and a contingent statement is one in which this is not the case. (I do not, of course, assert that this is the only way in which these terms have been used in the history of philosophy; but I do assert that this is the only use of them which does not give rise to impossible difficulties. I have no space to demonstrate this here; and indeed I do not think that it is any longer in need of demonstration.) But in this, the only coherent, sense of "contingent," the existence of the world may be contingent fact, but so unfortunately is that of God. For *all* existential statements are contingent; that is to say, it is never true that we can involve ourselves in a breach of the laws of logic by merely denying of something that it exists. We cannot therefore in this sense contrast the contingent existence of the world with the necessary existence of God.

It follows that if a man persists in speaking of the contingency of the world, he must be using the term in a new or transferred sense. It must be that he is borrowing[4] a word from the logician and putting it to work which it cannot properly do. Why does he do this, and how can he make clear what precisely this new use is? For it is no good saying that when we are talking about God we do not use words in their ordinary senses unless we are prepared to say in what senses it is that we do use them. And yet how can we explain to the honest inquirer what is the new sense in which the word "contingent" is being used when we use it of the world? For if it is proper to use it, in this sense, of everything with which we are acquainted, and improper to use it only of God, with whom we are not acquainted, how can the new use be learnt? For we normally learn the correct use of a word by noticing the differences between the situations in which it may be applied and those in which it may not; but the word "contingent" is applicable in all the situations in which we ever find ourselves. If I said that everything but God was flexible, not of course in the ordinary sense, but in some other, how could you discover what the new sense was?

The answer must be that when we speak of the world as contingent, dependent, an effect or product, and so contrast it with a necessary, self-existent being, a first cause or a creator, we say something which on analysis will not do at all (for devastating criticisms can be brought against all these formulations), but which seems to us to be the fittest sort of language for our purpose. Why we find such language appropriate, and how, therefore, it is to be interpreted, is not at all an easy question; that it does in some way, it may be in some logically anomalous way, convey the meaning of those who use it, seems however to be an evident fact. How it is that the trick is worked, how it is that this sort of distortion of language enables believers to give expression to their beliefs, this it is the true business of the natural theologian to discuss. Farrer, for example, in *Finite and Infinite*, has done much to elucidate what it is that one is striving

---

[4] It might be argued that, historically, the borrowing was the other way round. To decide that we should have to decide where the frontier between logic and metaphysics really comes in the work of those whose doctrine on the relationship between these disciplines is unsatisfactory.—I.M.C.

to express when one speaks of the contingency of the world, and so to enlighten the honest inquirer who wishes to know how the word "contingent" is here being used.

What I have said about contingency and necessity applies also to obligation and its transcendent ground (or goodness and its transcendent goal), to design and its transcendent designer, to religious experience and its transcendent object. In all these cases we use language which on analysis will not do, but which seems to us to be appropriate for the expression of our beliefs; and in all these cases the question can be, and is, discussed, why such language is chosen, and how it is to be understood.

That then is the logical mother of religious belief; call her natural theism, or what you will, she is a response, not precisely logical, and yet in no sense emotional or evaluative, to certain elements in our experience, whose characteristic is that they induce us, not to make straightforward statements about the world, but to strain and distort our media of communication in order to express what we make of them. In herself she is an honest woman; and if she is sometimes bedizened in logical trappings, and put out on the streets as an inductive argument, the fault is hardly hers. Her function is not to prove to us that God exists, but to provide us with a "meaning" for the word "God." Without her we should not know whither statements concerning the word were to be referred; the subject in theological utterances would be unattached. All that we should know of them is that they were not to be referred to anything with which we are or could hope to be acquainted; that, and also that they were to be understood in terms of whatever it is that people suppose themselves to be doing when they build churches and kneel down in them. And that is not entirely satisfactory; for while there is much to be said in practice for advising the honest inquirer into the reference of the word "God" to pursue his inquiry by familiarizing himself with the concrete activity of religion, it remains true that the range and variety of possible delusions which could induce such behaviour is theoretically boundless, and, as visitors to the Pacific coast of the United States can testify, in practice very large.

The logical father of religious belief, that which might bring us on from the condition of merely possessing the category of the divine, into the condition of active belief in God, this consists, in Christianity (and if there is nothing analogous in other religions, so much the worse for them), in the interpretation of certain objects or events as a manifestation of the divine. It is, in other words, because we find that, in thinking of certain events in terms of the category of the divine, we can give what seems to us the most convincing account of them, that we can assure ourselves that the notion of God is not just an empty aspiration. Without the notion of God we could interpret nothing as divine, and without concrete events which we felt impelled to interpret as divine we could not know that the notion of divinity had any application to reality. Why it is that as Christians we find ourselves impelled to interpret the history of Israel, the life and death of Christ, and the experience of his Church as revelatory of God, I shall not here attempt to say; it is an oft-told tale, and I shall content myself with saying that we can hardly expect to feel such an impulsion so long as our knowledge of these matters is superficial and altogether from without. Whyever we feel such an impulsion, it is not, of course, a logical impulsion; that is, we may resist it (or fail to feel it) without thereby contravening the laws of logic, or the rules of any pragmatically accredited inductive procedure. On the anthropological level the history of Israel, Old and New, is certainly the history of a religious development from its tribal origins. We may decide, or we may not, that it is something more, something beyond the wit of man to invent, something which seems to us to be a real and coherent communication from a real and coherent, though superhuman, mind. We may decide, or we may not; neither decision breaks the rules, for in such a unique matter there are no rules to conform to or to break. The judgment is our own; and in the language of the New Testament it judges us; that is, it reveals what, up to the moment of our decision, the Spirit of God has done in us—but that, of course, is to argue in a circle.

Belief, thus begotten, is nurtured by the practice of the Christian life—by the conviction so aroused (or, of course, not aroused; but then it is starvation and not nurture) that the Christian warfare is a real warfare. Something will have to be said about this later on, but for the moment I propose to dismiss it, and to return to the consideration of the significance of religious utterances in the light of the dual parentage of religious belief.

C. I have argued that unless certain things seem to us to be signs of divine activity, then we may hope that there is a God, but we cannot properly believe that there is. It follows from this that religious belief must properly involve treating something as revelatory of God; and that is to say that it must involve an element of authority (for to treat something as divine revelation is to invest it with authority). That what we say about God is said on authority (and, in particular, on the authority of Christ) is of the first importance in considering the significance of these statements. In what way this is so, I shall hope to make clear as we go along.

If we remember that our statements about God rest on the authority of Christ, whom we call His Word, we can see what seems to me the essential clue to the interpretation of the logical nature of such utterances, and that is, in a word, the notion of parable. To elucidate what I mean by "parable" (for I am using the word in an extended sense) let us consider Christ's action on Palm Sunday, when he rode into Jerusalem on an ass. This action was an act of teaching. For it had been said to Jerusalem that her king would come to her riding upon an ass. Whoever, therefore, deliberately chose this method of entry, was saying in effect: "What you are about to witness (namely my Passion, Death and Resurrection) is the coming of the Messianic King to claim his kingdom." The prophecy of Messiah's kingdom was to be interpreted, not in the ordinary sense, but in the sense of the royal kingship of the Crucified. To interpret in this way is to teach by violent paradox, indeed, but nonetheless it is to teach. Part of the lesson is that it is only the kings of the Gentiles that lord it over their subjects; if any man will be a king in Israel (God's chosen people), he must humble himself as a servant; part of it is that the Crucifixion is to be seen as Messianic, that is as God's salvation of His chosen people. Now the logical structure which is involved here is something like this: You are told a story (Behold, thy king cometh, meek and lowly, and riding upon an ass). You will not know just what the reality to which the story refers will be like until it happens. If you take the story at its face value (an ordinary, though humble, king, bringing an ordinary political salvation), you will get it all wrong. If you bring to bear upon its interpretation all that the Law and the Prophets have taught you about God's purposes for His people, though you will still not know just what it will be like until it happens, nonetheless you will not go wrong by believing it; for then you will know that Christ ought to have suffered these things, and to enter into his glory, and so you will learn what the story has to tell you of God's purposes for man, and something therefore, indirectly, of God. If you remember what Isaiah says about humility and sacrifice, you will see that what is being forecast is that God's purposes will be accomplished by a man who fulfils the Law and the Prophets in humble obedience.

This story is . . . one that can be fairly fully interpreted. There are others that cannot. There is, for example, Hosea's parable in which he likens himself to God, and Israel to his unfaithful wife, and expresses his grief at his wife's unfaithfulness. If, now, you ask for this to be fully interpreted, if you ask Hosea to tell you what he supposes it is like for the Holy One of Israel, of whom no similitude may be made, to be grieved, demanding to know, not what would happen in such a case to the unfaithful sinner who had provoked the divine wrath, but what was the condition of the divine mind in itself, then no doubt he would have regarded the very question as blasphemous. As an inspired prophet, he felt himself entitled to say that God was grieved, without presuming to imagine what such a situation was like, other than in its effects. What he said was said on authority; it was not his own invention, and therefore he could rely on its truth, without supposing himself to understand its full meaning. Insofar as Hosea's parable is "interpreted," the interpretation is confined to identifying the *dramatis personae*[5] (Hosea = God; his wife = Israel).[6] It is noteworthy that the interpretation which is sometimes given to the parables of the New Testament is usually of the same sketchy kind (the reapers are the angels). In Plato's famous parable of prisoners in a cave, it is quite possible to describe the situation which the parable seeks to illuminate. One can describe how a man can begin by being content to establish rough laws concerning what follows what in nature, how he may proceed from such a condition to desire explanation of the regularities which are forced on his attention, rising thus to more abstract and mathematical generalizations, and then, through the study of mathematics, to completely abstract speculation. One cannot similarly describe the situation which the parable of the Prodigal Son is intended to illustrate (or rather one can only describe the human end of it); and no attempt is ever made to do so.

I make no apology for these paragraphs about the Bible; after all the Bible is the source of Christian belief, and it cannot but illuminate the logical nature of the latter to consider the communicational methods of the former. But we must turn back to more general considerations. It is, then, characteristic of a parable that the words which are used in it are used in their ordinary senses. Elsewhere this is not always so. If you speak of the virtues of a certain sort of car, the word "virtue," being applied to a car, comes to mean something different from what it means in application to human beings. If you speak of hot temper, the word "hot" does not mean what it means in the ordinary way. Now many people suppose that something of the latter sort is happening in religious utterances. When God is said to be jealous, or active in history, it is felt that the word "jealous" or "active" must be being used here in a transferred sense. But if it is being used in a transferred sense, some means or other must be supplied whereby the new sense can be taken. The activity of God is presumably not like the activity of men (it does not make Him hot or tired); to say then that God is active must involve modifying the meaning of the word. But, if the word is undergoing modification, it is essential that we should know in what direction. In the case of ordinary transfers, how do we know what sort of modification is involved? This is a large question, but roughly,

[5] Persons of the drama.—E.D.K.
[6] See the first several chapters of *Hosea*, one of the books in the Old Testament.—E.D.K.

I think, the answer is in two ways. Firstly there is normally a certain appropriateness, like the appropriateness of "hot" in "hot temper"; and secondly we can notice the circumstances in which the word gets used and withheld in its transferred sense. If I hear the phrase "Baroque music," the meaning of the word "Baroque" in its normal architectural employment may set me looking in a certain direction; and I can clinch the matter by asking for examples, "Bach? Buxtehude? Beethoven?" But for either of these ways to be of any use to me, I must know something about *both* ends of the transfer. I must know something about Baroque architecture, *and* I must be able to run through musical styles in my head, to look for the musical analogue of Baroque features. If I cannot stumble on your meaning without assistance, I can still do so by eliciting from you that Bach and Buxtehude are, Handel and Mozart are not, examples of the sort of music you have in mind. This is informative to me if and only if I know something of Buxtehude and Bach, Handel and Mozart.

Now we all know what it is like for a man to be active. We can quote examples, decide correctly, and so forth. But what about divine activity? Surely we cannot have it both ways. Either God can be moderately like a man, so that the word "active," used of Him, can set us looking in the right direction; or He can be quite unlike a man, in which case it cannot. Nor can we be helped by the giving of examples, unless it is legitimate to point to examples of divine activity—to say, "Now here God is being active, but not there." This constitutes the force of Flew's demand that we should tell him how statements about God can be falsified. In essence Flew is saying: "When you speak about God, the words which occur in the predicate part of your statements are not being used in the ordinary sense; you make so great a difference between God and man that I cannot even find that the words you use set me looking in anything that might perhaps be the right direction. You speak of God as being outside time; and when I think what I mean by 'activity,' I find that that word, as used about a timeless being, suggests to me nothing whatsoever. There is only one resort left; give me examples of when one of your statements is, and is not, applicable. If, as no doubt you will say, that is an unfair demand, since they are always applicable (e.g., God is always active, so that there are no cases of his inactivity to be pointed to), I will not insist on actual examples; make them up if you like. But do not point to *everything* and say, '*That* is what I mean'; for *everything* is not *that*, but this and this and this and many other mutual incompatibles; and black and white and red and green and kind and cruel and coal and ink and everything else together cannot possibly elucidate to me the meaning of a word."

As I have said, the answer must be that when we speak about God, the words we use are intended in their ordinary sense (for we cannot make a transfer, failing familiarity with both ends of it), although we do not suppose that in their ordinary interpretation they can be strictly true of Him. We do not even know how much of them applies. To some extent it may be possible to take a word like "activity" and whittle away that in it which most obviously does not apply. It is, however, an exaggeration, at the least, to suppose that this process of whittling away leaves us in the end with a kernel about which we can say that we know that it does apply. A traditional procedure is to compose a scale on which inanimate matter is at the bottom, the characteristically human activities, such as thinking and personal relationship, at the top, and to suppose that the scale is pointing towards God; and so on this assumption the first thing to do is to pare away from the notion of human activity whatever in it is common to what stands below it on the scale—for example actual physical moving about. Taking the human residue, we try to decide what in it is positive, and what is negative, mere limitation. The tenuous ghost of a concept remaining we suppose to be the essential structure of activity (that structure which is common to running and thinking) and so to be realized also in divine activity. Perhaps this is how we imagine our language to be related to the divine realities about which we use it; but such ghostly and evacuated concepts are clearly too tenuous and elusive to be called the meanings of the words we use. To think of God thus is to think of Him not in our own image, but in the rarefied ghost of our own image; and so we think of Him in our own image, but do not suppose that in so thinking of Him we begin to do Him justice. What we do, then, is in essence to think of God in parables. The things we say about God are said on the authority of the words and acts of Christ, who spoke in human language, using parable; and so we too speak of God in parable—authoritative parable, authorized parable; knowing that the truth is not literally that which our parables represent, knowing therefore that now we see in a glass darkly, but trusting, because we trust the source of the parables, that in believing them and interpreting them in the light of each other, we shall not be misled, that we shall have such knowledge as we need to possess for the foundation of the religious life.

So far so good. But it is only the predicates of theological utterances which are parabolic; it is only in what is *said about* God that words are put to other than customary employment. When we say "God is merciful," it is "merciful" that is in strange company—deprived of its usual escort of human sentiments. But the word "God" only occurs in statements about God. Our grasp of this word, therefore, cannot be derived from our grasp of it in ordinary human contexts, for it is not used in such contexts. How then is our grasp of it to be accounted for? In other words, if I have given some account of how, and in what sense, we understand the meaning of the things we say about God, I have still to give some account of how, and in what sense, we know what it is that we are saying them about.

In thus turning back from the predicate to the subject of religious utterances, we are turning from revealed theology to natural theology, from the logical father to the logical mother of religious belief. And the answer to the question: "What grasp have we of the meaning of the word 'God'?" must be dealt with along the following lines. Revelation is important to the believer not for what it is in itself (the biography of a Jew, and the history of his forerunners and followers), nor because it is revelation of nothing in particular, but because it is revelation of God. In treating it as something important, something commanding our allegiance, we are bringing to bear upon it the category of the transcendent, of the divine. Of the nature of that category I have already spoken. In other words, there must exist within a man's mind the contrast between the contingent and the necessary, the derivative and the underivative, the finite and infinite, the perfect and the imperfect, if anything is to be for him a revelation of God. Given that contrast, we are given also that to which the parables or stories are referred. What is thus given is certainly not knowledge of the object to which they apply; it is something much more like a direction. We do not, that is, know to what to refer our parables; we know merely that we are to refer them out of experience, and out of it *in which direction*. The expression "God" is to refer to that object, whatever it is, and if there be one, which is such that the knowledge of it would be to us knowledge of the unfamiliar term in the contrast between finite and infinite.

Statements about God, then, are in effect parables, which are referred, by means of the proper name "God," out of our experience in a certain direction. We may, if we like, by the process of whittling away, which I have mentioned, try to tell ourselves what part of the meaning of our statements applies reasonably well, what part outrageously badly; but the fact remains that, in one important sense, when we speak about God, we do not know what we mean (that is, we do not know what that which we are talking about is like), and do not need to know, because we accept the images, which we employ, on authority. Because our concern with God is religious and not speculative (it is contemplative in part, but that is another matter), because our need is not to know what God is like, but to enter into relation with him, the authorized images serve our purpose. They belong to a type of discourse—parable—with which we are familiar, and therefore they have communication value, although in a sense they lack descriptive value.

· *III* ·

If this is so, how do we stand with regard to verification and falsification? Must we, to preserve our claim to be making assertions, be prepared to say what would count against them? Let us see how far we can do so. Does anything count against the assertion that God is merciful? Yes, suffering. Does anything count decisively against it? No, we reply, because it is true. Could anything count decisively against it? Yes, suffering which was utterly, eternally, and irredeemably pointless. Can we then design a crucial experiment? No, because we can never see all of the picture. Two things at least are hidden from us; what goes on in the recesses of the personality of the sufferer, and what shall happen hereafter.·

Well, then, the statement that God is merciful is not testable; it is compatible with any and every tract of experience which we are in fact capable of witnessing. It cannot be verified; does this matter?

To answer this, we must make up our mind why the demand for verification or falsification is legitimate. On this large matter I shall be summary and dogmatic, as follows. (1) The demand that a statement of fact should be verifiable is a conflation of two demands. (2) The *first* point is that all statements of fact must be verifiable in the sense that there must not exist a *rule of language* which precludes testing the statement. That is to say, the way the statement is to be taken must not be such that to try to test it is to show that you do not understand it. If I say that it is wrong to kill, and you challenge my statement and adduce as evidence against it that thugs and headhunters do so out of religious duty, then you have not understood my statement. My statement was not a statement of fact, but a moral judgment, and your statement that it should be tested by anthropological investigations shows that you did not understand it. But so long as there exists no *logical* (or we might say *interpretational*) ban on looking around for verification, the existence of a *factual* ban on verification does not matter. "Caesar had mutton before he crossed the Rubicon" cannot in fact be tested, but by trying to devise ways of testing it you do not show that you have not understood it; you are merely wasting your time. (3) The *second* point is that, *for me fully* to understand a statement, *I* must know what a test of it would be like. If I have no idea how to test whether somebody had mutton, then I do not know what "having mutton" means. This stipulation is concerned not with the logical nature of the expression, but with its communication value for me. (4) There are then two stipulations, and they are different. The first is a logical stipulation, and it is to the effect that nothing can be a statement of fact if it is untestable in the sense that the notion of testing it is precluded by correctly interpreting it. The second is a communicational stipulation, and it is to the effect that nobody can fully understand a statement, unless he has a fair idea how a situation about which it was true would differ from a situation about which it was false.

Now with regard to these two stipulations, how do religious utterances fare? With regard to the first, there is no language rule implicit in a correct understanding of them which precludes putting them to the test (there may be a rule of faith, but that is another matter). If a man says, "How can God be loving, and allow pain?" he does *not* show that he has misunderstood the statement that God is loving. There *is* a *prima facie* incompatibility between the love of God, and pain and suffering. The Christian maintains that it is *prima facie* only; others maintain that it is not. They may argue about it, and the issue cannot be decided; but it cannot be decided, not because (as in the case of, e.g., moral or mathematical judgments) the appeal to facts is *logically* the wrong way of trying to decide the issue, and shows that you have not understood the judgment; *but* because, since our experience is limited in the way it is, we cannot get into position to decide it, any more than we can get into position to decide what Julius Caesar had for breakfast before he crossed the Rubicon. For the Christian the operation of getting into position to decide it is called dying; and, though we can all do that, we cannot return to report what we find. By this test, then, religious utterances can be called statements of fact; that is their *logical* classification.

With regard to the second stipulation, the case is a little complicated, for here we are concerned with communication value, and there are two levels, the one on which we remain within the parable, and the other on which we try to step outside it. Now, on the first level we know well enough how to test a statement like "God loves us"; it is, for example, like testing "My father loves me." In fact, of course, since with parents and schoolmasters severity is notoriously a way of displaying affection, the decisive testing of such a statement is not easy; but there is a point beyond which it is foolish to continue to have doubts. Now, within the parable, we are supposing "God loves us" to be a statement like "My father loves me," "God" to be a subject similar to "My father," "God loves us" being thus related to "My father loves me" as the latter is related to "Aristotle's father loved him." We do not suppose that we can actually test "God loves us," for reasons already given (any more than we can test the one about Aristotle); but the communication value of the statement whose subject is "God" is derived from the communication value of the statement with a different proper name as subject. If we try to step outside the parable, then we must admit that we do not know what the situation about which our parable is being told is like; we should only know if we could know God, and know even as we have also been known; see, that is, the unfolding of the divine purposes in their entirety. Such ignorance is what we ought to expect. We do not know how what we call the divine wrath differs from the divine mercy (because we do not know how they respectively resemble human wrath and mercy); but we do know how what *we mean* when we talk about the wrath of God differs from what *we mean* when we talk about His mercy, because then we are within the parable, talking within the framework of admitted ignorance, in language which we accept because we trust its source. We know what is meant *in* the parable, when the father of the Prodigal sees him coming a great way off and runs to meet him, and we can therefore think in terms of this image. We know that we are here promised that whenever we come to ourselves and return to God, He will come to meet us. This is enough to encourage us to return, and to make us alert to catch the signs of the divine response; but it does not lead us to presume to an understanding of the mind and heart of God. In talking we remain within the parable, and so our statements communicate; we do not know how the parable applies, but we believe that it does apply, and that we shall one day see how. (Some even believe, perhaps rightly, that in our earthly condition we may by direct illumination of our minds be enabled to know progressively more about the realities to which our parables apply, and in consequence about the manner of their application.)

Much of what I have said agrees very closely with what the atheist says about religious belief, except that I have tried to make it sound better. The atheist alleges that the religious man supposes himself to know what he means by his statements only because, until challenged, be interprets them anthropomorphically; when challenged, however, he retreats rapidly backwards towards complete agnosticism. I agree with this, with two provisos. The first is that the religious man does not suppose himself to know what he means by his statements (for what religious man supposes himself to be the Holy Ghost?); he knows what his statements mean within the parable, and believes that they are the right statements to use. (Theology is not a science; it is a sort of art of enlightened ignorance.) The second proviso is that the agnosticism is not complete; for the Christian, under attack, falls back not in any direction, but in one direction; he falls back upon the person of Christ, and the concrete realities of the Christian life.

Let us consider this for a moment with regard to the divine love. I could be attacked in this sort of way: "You have contended," my opponent might argue, "that when we say that God loves us the communication value of the statement is determined by the communication value of a similar statement about a human subject; and that we know the statement to be the right statement, but cannot know *how* it is the right statement, that is, what the divine love is like. But this will not do. Loving is an activity with two poles, the lover and the loved. We may not know the lover, in the case of God, but we *are*, and therefore *must know*, the loved. Now, to say that the image or parable of human love is the right image to use about God must imply that there is some similarity or analogy between human and divine love. Father's love may be superficially very unlike mother's, but unless there is some similarity of structure between them, we cannot use the same word of both. But we cannot believe that there is any similarity between the love of God and human love, unless we can detect some similarity between being loved by God and being loved by man. But if being loved by God is what we experience all the time, then it is not like being loved by man; it is like being let down right and left. And in the face of so great a discrepancy, we cannot believe that God loves us, if that is supposed to be in any sense a statement of sober fact."

I cannot attempt to answer this objection; it involves the whole problem of religion. But there is something I want to say about it, which is that the Christian does not attempt to evade it either by helter-skelter flight, or by impudent bluff. He has his prepared positions onto which he retreats; and he knows that if these positions are taken, then he must surrender. He does not believe that they can be taken, but that is another matter. There are three main fortresses behind which he goes. For, first, he looks for the resurrection of the dead, and the life of the world to come; he believes, that is, that we do not see all of the picture, and that the parts which we do not see are precisely the parts which determine the design of the whole. He admits that if this hope be vain then we are of all men the most miserable. Second, he claims that he sees in Christ the verification, and to some extent also the specification, of the divine love.

That is to say, he finds in Christ not only convincing evidence of God's concern for us, but also what sort of love the divine love is, what sort of benefits God is concerned to give us. He sees that, on the New Testament scale of values, it is better for a man to lose the whole world if he can thereby save his soul (which means his relationship to God); and that for that hope it is reasonable to sacrifice all that he has, and to undergo the death of the body and the mortification of the spirit. Third, he claims that in the religious life, of others, if not as yet in his own, the divine love may be encountered, that the promise "I will not fail thee nor forsake thee" is, if rightly understood, confirmed there. If, of course, this promise is interpreted as involving immunity from bodily suffering, it will be refuted; but no reader of the New Testament has any right so to interpret it. It is less glaringly, but as decisively, wrong to interpret it as involving immunity from spiritual suffering; for in the New Testament only the undergoing of death (which means the abdication of control over one's destiny) can be the beginning of life. What then does it promise? It promises that to the man who begins on the way of the Christian life, on the way that is of seeking life through death, of seeking relationship with God through the abdication of the self-sovereignty claimed by Adam, that to him the fight will be hard but not impossible, progress often indiscernible, but real, progress which is towards the paring away of self-hood, and which is therefore often given through defeat and humiliation, but a defeat and humiliation which are not final, which leave it possible to continue. This is the extra-parental nurture of religious belief of which I spoke earlier, and it is the third of the prepared positions onto which the Christian retreats, claiming that the image and reflection of the love of God may be seen not only hereafter, not only in Christ, but also, if dimly, in the concrete process of living the Christian life.

One final word. Religion has indeed its problems; but it is useless to consider them outside their religious context. Seen as a whole religion makes rough sense, though it does not make limpidity.

○ ○ ○ ***34***

An Empiricist's View of the Nature of Religious Belief
R. B. Braithwaite

· *I* ·

THE MEANING OF any statement . . . will be taken as being given by the way it is used. The kernel for an empiricist of the problem of the nature of religious belief is to explain, in empirical terms, how a religious statement is used by a man who asserts it in order to express his religious conviction.

Since I shall argue that the primary element in this use is that the religious assertion is used as a moral assertion, I must first consider how moral assertions are used. According to the view developed by various moral philosophers since the impossibility of regarding moral statements as verifiable propositions was recognized, a moral assertion is used to express an *attitude* of the man making the assertion. It is not used to assert the proposition that he has the attitude—a verifiable psychological proposition; it is used to show forth or evince his attitude. The attitude is concerned with the action which he asserts to be good; it is a highly complex state, and contains elements to which various degrees of importance have been attached by moral philosophers who have tried to work out an "ethics without propositions." One element in the attitude is a feeling of approval towards the action; this element was taken as the fundamental one in the first attempts, and views of ethics without propositions are frequently lumped together as "emotive" theories of ethics. But discussion of the subject during the last twenty years has made it clear, I think, that no emotion or feeling of approval is fundamental to the use of moral assertions; it may be the case that the moral asserter has some specific feeling directed on to the course of action said to be right, but this is not the most important element in his "pro-attitude" towards the course of action: what is primary is his intention to perform the action when the occasion for it arises.

The form of ethics without propositions which I shall adopt is therefore a conative rather than an emotive theory: it makes the primary use of a moral assertion that of expressing the intention of the asserter to act in a particular sort of way specified in the assertion. A utilitarian, for example, in asserting that he ought to act so as to maximize happiness, is thereby declaring his intention to act, to the best of his ability, in accordance with the policy of utilitarianism: he is not asserting any proposition, or necessarily evincing any feeling of approval; he is subscribing to a policy of action. There will doubtless be empirical propositions which he may give as reasons for his adherence to the policy (e.g., that happiness is what all, or what most people, desire), and his having the intention will include his understanding what is meant by pursuing

the policy, another empirically verifiable proposition. But there will be no specifically moral proposition which he will be asserting when he declares his intention to pursue the policy. This account is fully in accord with the spirit of empiricism, for whether or not a man has the intention of pursuing a particular behaviour policy can be empirically tested, both by observing what he does and by hearing what he replies when he is questioned about his intentions.

Not all expressions of intentions will be moral assertions: for the notion of morality to be applicable it is necessary either that the policy of action intended by the asserter should be a general policy (e.g., the policy of utilitarianism) or that it should be subsumable under a general policy which the asserter intends to follow and which he would give as the reason for his more specific intention. There are difficulties and vaguenesses in the notion of a general policy of action, but these need not concern us here. All that we require is that, when a man asserts that he ought to do so-and-so, he is using the assertion to declare that he resolves, to the best of his ability, to do so-and-so. And he will not necessarily be insincere in his assertion if he suspects, at the time of making it, that he will not have the strength of character to carry out his resolution.

The advantage this account of moral assertions has over all others, emotive non-propositional ones as well as cognitive propositional ones, is that it alone enables a satisfactory answer to be given to the question: What is the reason for my doing what I think I ought to do? The answer it gives is that, since my thinking that I ought to do the action is my intention to do it if possible, the reason why I do the action is simply that I intend to do it, if possible. On every other ethical view there will be a mysterious gap to be filled somehow between the moral judgment and the intention to act in accordance with it: there is no such gap if the primary use of a moral assertion is to declare such an intention.

· II ·

Let us now consider what light this way of regarding moral assertions throws upon assertions of religious conviction. The idealist philosopher McTaggart described religion as "an emotion resting on a conviction of a harmony between ourselves and the universe at large"[1] and many educated people at the present time would agree with him. If religion is essentially concerned with emotion, it is natural to explain the use of religious assertions on the lines of the original emotive theory of ethics and to regard them as primarily evincing religious feelings or emotions. The assertion, for example, that God is our Heavenly Father will be taken to express the asserter's feeling secure in the same way as he would feel secure in his father's presence. But explanations of religion in terms of feeling, and of religious assertions as expressions of such feelings, are usually propounded by people who stand outside any religious system; they rarely satisfy those who speak from inside. Few religious men would be prepared to admit that their religion was a matter merely of feeling: feelings—of joy, of consolation, of being at one with the universe—may enter into their religion, but to evince such feelings is certainly not the primary use of their religious assertions.

This objection, however, does not seem to me to apply to treating religious assertions in the conative way in which recent moral philosophers have treated moral

---

[1] J. M. E. McTaggart, *Some Dogmas of Religion* (London, 1906), p. 3.—R.B.B.

statements—as being primarily declarations of adherence to a policy of action, declarations of commitment to a way of life. That the way of life led by the believer is highly relevant to the sincerity of his religious conviction has been insisted upon by all the moral religions, above all, perhaps, by Christianity. "By their fruits ye shall know them." The view which I put forward for your consideration is that the intention of a Christian to follow a Christian way of life is not only the criterion for the sincerity of his belief in the assertions of Christianity; it is the criterion for the meaningfulness of his assertions. Just as the meaning of a moral assertion is given by its use in expressing the asserter's intention to act, so far as in him lies, in accordance with the moral principle involved, so the meaning of a religious assertion is given by its use in expressing the asserter's intention to follow a specified policy of behaviour. To say that it is belief in the dogmas of religion which is the cause of the believer's intending to behave as he does is to put the cart before the horse: it is the intention to behave which constitutes what is known as religious conviction.

But this assimilation of religious to moral assertions lays itself open to an immediate objection. When a moral assertion is taken as declaring the intention of following a policy, the form of the assertion itself makes it clear what the policy is with which the assertion is concerned. For a man to assert that a certain policy ought to be pursued, which on this view is for him to declare his intention of pursuing the policy, presupposes his understanding what it would be like for him to pursue the policy in question. I cannot resolve not to tell a lie without knowing what a lie is. But if a religious assertion is the declaration of an intention to carry out a certain policy, what policy does it specify? The religious statement itself will not explicitly refer to a policy, as does a moral statement; how then can the asserter of the statement know what is the policy concerned, and how can he intend to carry out a policy if he does not know what the policy is? I cannot intend to do something I know not what.

The reply to this criticism is that, if a religious assertion is regarded as representative of a large number of assertions of the same religious system, the body of assertions of which the particular one is a representative specimen is taken by the asserter as implicitly specifying a particular way of life. It is not more necessary for an empiricist philosopher to explain the use of a religious statement taken in isolation from other religious statements than it is for him to give a meaning to a scientific hypothesis in isolation from other scientific hypotheses. We understand scientific hypotheses, and the terms that occur in them, by virtue of the relation of the whole system of hypotheses to empirically observable facts; and it is the whole system of hypotheses, not one hypothesis in isolation, that is tested for its truth-value against experience. So there are good precedents, in the empiricist way of thinking, for considering a system of religious assertions as a whole, and for examining the way in which the whole system is used.

If we do this, the fact that a system of religious assertions has a moral function can hardly be denied. For to deny it would require any passage from the assertion of a religious system to a policy of action to be mediated by a moral assertion. I cannot pass from asserting a fact, of whatever sort, to intending to perform an action, without having the hypothetical intention to intend to do the action if I assert the fact. This holds however widely fact is understood—whether as an empirical fact or as a non-empirical fact about goodness or reality. Just as the intention-to-act view of moral assertions is the only view that requires no reason for my doing what I assert to be my duty, so the similar view of religious assertions is the only one which connects them to ways of life without requiring an additional premise. Unless a Christian's assertion that God is love (*agape*)—which I take to epitomize the assertions of the Christian religion—be taken to declare his intention to follow an agapeistic way of life, he could be asked what is the connection between the assertion and the intention, between Christian belief and Christian practice. And this question can always be asked if religious assertions are separated from conduct. Unless religious principles are moral principles, it makes no sense to speak of putting them into practice.

The way to find out what are the intentions embodied in a set of religious assertions, and hence what is the meaning of the assertions, is by discovering what principles of conduct the asserter takes the assertions to involve. These may be ascertained both by asking him questions and by seeing how he behaves, each test being supplemental to the other. If what is wanted is not the meaning of the religious assertions made by a particular man but what the set of assertions would mean were they to be made by anyone of the same religion (which I will call their *typical* meaning), all that can be done is to specify the form of behaviour which is in accordance with what one takes to be the fundamental moral principles of the religion in question. Since different people will take different views as to what these fundamental moral principles are, the typical meaning of religious assertions will be different for different people. I myself take the typical meaning of the body of Christian assertions as being given by their proclaiming intentions to follow an agapeistic way of life, and for a description of this way of life—a description in general and metaphorical terms, but an empirical description nevertheless—I should quote most of the Thirteenth Chapter of I Corinthians. Others may think that the Christian way of life should be described somewhat differently, and will therefore take the typical meaning of the assertions of Christianity to correspond to their different view of its fundamental moral teaching.

My contention then is that the primary use of religious assertions is to announce allegiance to a set of moral principles: without such allegiance there is no "true religion." This is borne out by all the accounts of what happens when an unbeliever becomes converted to a religion. The conversion is not only a change in the propositions believed—indeed there may be no specifically intellectual change at all; it is a change in the state of will. An excellent instance is C. S. Lewis's . . . account of his conversion from an idealist metaphysic—"a religion (as he says) that cost nothing"— to a theism where he faced (and he quotes George MacDonald's phrase) "something to be neither more nor less nor other than *done*." There was no intellectual change, for (as he says) "there had long been an ethic (theoretically) attached to my Idealism": it was the recognition that he had to do something about it, that "an attempt at complete virtue must be made."[2] His conversion was a reorientation of the will.

· III ·

In assimilating religious assertions to moral assertions I do not wish to deny that there are any important differences. One is the fact already noticed that usually the behaviour policy intended is not specified by one religious assertion in isolation. Another difference is that the fundamental moral teaching of the religion is frequently given, not in abstract terms, but by means of concrete examples—of how to behave, for instance, if one meets a man set upon by thieves on the road to Jericho. A resolution

---

[2] C. S. Lewis, *Surprised by Joy* (London, 1955), pp. 198, 212–13.—R.B.B.

to behave like the good Samaritan does not, in itself, specify the behaviour to be resolved upon in quite different circumstances. However, absence of explicitly recognized general principles does not prevent a man from acting in accordance with such principles; it only makes it more difficult for a questioner to discover upon what principles he is acting. And the difficulty is not only one way round. If moral principles are stated in the most general form, as most moral philosophers have wished to state them, they tend to become so far removed from particular courses of conduct that it is difficult, if not impossible, to give them any precise content. It may be hard to find out what exactly is involved in the imitation of Christ; but it is not very easy to discover what exactly is meant by the pursuit of Aristotle's *eudaemonia*[3] or of Mill's *happiness*. The tests for what it is to live agapeistically are as empirical as are those for living in quest of happiness; but in each case the tests can best be expounded in terms of examples of particular situations.

A more important difference between religious and purely moral principles is that, in the higher religions at least, the conduct preached by the religion concerns not only external but also internal behaviour. The conversion involved in accepting a religion is a conversion, not only of the will, but of the heart. Christianity requires not only that you should behave towards your neighbour as if you loved him as yourself: it requires that you should love him as yourself. And though I have no doubt that the Christian concept of *agape*[4] refers partly to external behaviour—the agapeistic behaviour for which there are external criteria—yet being filled with *agape* includes more than behaving agapeistically[5] externally: it also includes an agapeistic frame of mind. I have said that I cannot regard the expression of a feeling of any sort as the primary element in religious assertion; but this does not imply that intention to feel in a certain way is not a primary element, nor that it cannot be used to discriminate religious declarations of policy from declarations which are merely moral. Those who say that Confucianism is a code of morals and not, properly speaking, a religion are, I think, making this discrimination.

The resolution proclaimed by a religious assertion may then be taken as referring to inner life as well as to outward conduct. And the superiority of religious conviction over the mere adoption of a moral code in securing conformity to the code arises from a religious conviction changing what the religious man wants. It may be hard enough to love your enemy, but once you have succeeded in doing so it is easy to behave lovingly towards him. But if you continue to hate him, it requires a heroic perseverance continually to behave as if you loved him. Resolutions to feel, even if they are only partly fulfilled, are powerful reinforcements of resolutions to act.

But though these qualifications may be adequate for distinguishing religious assertions from purely moral ones, they are not sufficient to discriminate between assertions belonging to one religious system and those belonging to another system in the case in which the behaviour policies, both of inner life and of outward conduct, inculcated by the two systems are identical. For instance, I have said that I take the fundamental moral teaching of Christianity to be the preaching of an agapeistic way of life. But a Jew or a Buddhist may, with considerable plausibility, maintain that the fundamental moral teaching of his religion is to recommend exactly the same way of

---

[3] Well-being; happiness.—E.D.K.

[4] (Christian) love.—E.D.K.

[5] Lovingly.—E.D.K.

life. How then can religious assertions be distinguished into those which are Christian, those which are Jewish, those which are Buddhist, by the policies of life which they respectively recommend if, on examination, these policies turn out to be the same?

Many Christians will, no doubt, behave in a specifically Christian manner in that they will follow ritual practices which are Christian and neither Jewish nor Buddhist. But though following certain practices may well be the proper test for membership of a particular religious society, a church, not even the most ecclesiastically minded Christian will regard participation in a ritual as the fundamental characteristic of a Christian way of life. There must be some more important difference between an agapeistically policied Christian and an agapeistically policied Jew than that the former attends a church and the latter a synagogue.

The really important difference, I think, is to be found in the fact that the intentions to pursue the behaviour policies, which may be the same for different religions, are associated with thinking of different *stories* (or sets of stories). By a story I shall here mean a proposition or set of propositions which are straightforwardly empirical propositions capable of empirical test and which are thought of by the religious man in connection with his resolution to follow the way of life advocated by his religion. On the assumption that the ways of life advocated by Christianity and by Buddhism are essentially the same, it will be the fact that the intention to follow this way of life is associated in the mind of a Christian with thinking of one set of stories (the Christian stories) while it is associated in the mind of a Buddhist with thinking of another set of stories (the Buddhist stories) which enables a Christian assertion to be distinguished from a Buddhist one.

· *IV* ·

A religious assertion will, therefore, have a propositional element which is lacking in a purely moral assertion, in that it will refer to a story as well as to an intention. The reference to the story is not an assertion of the story taken as a matter of empirical fact: it is a telling of the story, or an alluding to the story, in the way in which one can tell, or allude to, the story of a novel with which one is acquainted. To assert the whole set of assertions of the Christian religion is both to tell the Christian doctrinal story and to confess allegiance to the Christian way of life.

The story, I have said, is a set of empirical propositions, and the language expressing the story is given a meaning by the standard method of understanding how the story-statements can be verified. The empirical story-statements will vary from Christian to Christian; the doctrines of Christianity are capable of different empirical interpretations, and Christians will differ in the interpretations they put upon the doctrines. But the interpretations will all be in terms of empirical propositions. Take, for example, the doctrine of Justification by means of the Atonement. Matthew Arnold[6] imagined it in terms of

> . . . a sort of infinitely magnified and improved Lord Shaftesbury, with a race of vile offenders to deal with, whom his natural goodness would incline him to let off, only his sense of justice will not allow it; then a younger Lord Shaftesbury, on the scale of his father and very dear to him, who might live in grandeur and splendour if he liked, but

---

[6] A nineteenth-century poet and essayist.—E.D.K.

who prefers to leave his home, to go and live among the race of offenders, and to be put to an ignominious death, on condition that his merits shall be counted against their demerits, and that his father's goodness shall be restrained no longer from taking effect, but any offender shall be admitted to the benefit of it on simply pleading the satisfaction made by the son—and then, finally, a third Lord Shaftesbury, still on the same high scale, who keeps very much in the background, and works in a very occult manner, but very efficaciously nevertheless, and who is busy in applying everywhere the benefits of the son's satisfaction and the father's goodness.[7]

Arnold's "parable of the three Lord Shaftesburys" got him into a lot of trouble: he was "indignantly censured" (as he says) for wounding "the feelings of the religious community by turning into ridicule an august doctrine, the object of their solemn faith."[8] But there is no other account of the Anselmian doctrine of the Atonement that I have read which puts it in so morally favourable a light. Be that as it may, the only way in which the doctrine can be understood verificationally is in terms of human beings—mythological beings, it may be, who never existed, but who nevertheless would have been empirically observable had they existed.

For it is not necessary, on my view, for the asserter of a religious assertion to believe in the truth of the story involved in the assertions: what is necessary is that the story should be entertained in thought, i.e., that the statement of the story should be understood as having a meaning. I have secured this by requiring that the story should consist of empirical propositions. Educated Christians of the present day who attach importance to the doctrine of the Atonement certainly do not believe an empirically testable story in Matthew Arnold's or any other form. But it is the fact that entertainment in thought of this and other Christian stories forms the context in which Christian resolutions are made which serves to distinguish Christian assertions from those made by adherents of another religion, or of no religion.

What I am calling a *story* Matthew Arnold called a *parable* and a *fairytale*. Other terms which might be used are *allegory, fable, tale, myth*. I have chosen the word "story" as being the most neutral term, implying neither that the story is believed nor that it is disbelieved. The Christian stories include straightforward historical statements about the life and death of Jesus of Nazareth; a Christian (unless he accepts the unplausible Christ-myth theory) will naturally believe some or all of these. Stories about the beginning of the world and of the Last Judgment as facts of past or of future history are believed by many unsophisticated Christians. But my contention is that belief in the truth of the Christian stories is not the proper criterion for deciding whether or not an assertion is a Christian one. A man is not, I think, a professing Christian unless he both proposes to live according to Christian moral principles and associates his intention with thinking of Christian stories; but he need not believe that the empirical propositions presented by the stories correspond to empirical fact.

But if the religious stories need not be believed, what function do they fulfill in the complex state of mind and behaviour known as having a religious belief? How is entertaining the story related to resolving to pursue a certain way of life? My answer is that the relation is a psychological and causal one. It is an empirical psychological fact that many people find it easier to resolve upon and to carry through a course of action

---

[7] Matthew Arnold, *Literature and Dogma* (1873), pp. 306–7.—R.B.B.

[8] Matthew Arnold, *God and the Bible* (1875), pp. 18–19.—R.B.B.

which is contrary to their natural inclinations if this policy is associated in their minds with certain stories. And in many people the psychological link is not appreciably weakened by the fact that the story associated with the behaviour policy is not believed. Next to the Bible and the Prayer Book the most influential work in English Christian religious life has been a book whose stories are frankly recognized as fictitious— Bunyan's *Pilgrim's Progress*; and some of the most influential works in setting the moral tone of my generation were the novels of Dostoievsky. It is completely untrue, as a matter of psychological fact, to think that the only intellectual considerations which affect action are belief: it is *all* the thoughts of a man that determine his behaviour; and these include his phantasies, imaginations, ideas of what he would wish to be and do, as well as the propositions which he believes to be true. . . .

There is one story common to all the moral theistic religions which has proved of great psychological value in enabling religious men to preserve in carrying out their religious behaviour policies—the story that in so doing they are doing the will of God. And here it may look as if there is an intrinsic connection between the story and the policy of conduct. But even when the story is literally believed, when it is believed that there is a magnified Lord Shaftesbury who commands or desires the carrying out of the behaviour policy, that in itself is no reason for carrying out the policy: it is necessary also to have the intention of doing what the magnified Lord Shaftesbury commands or desires. But the intention to do what a person commands or desires, irrespective of what this command or desire may be, is no part of a higher religion; it is when the religious man finds that what the magnified Lord Shaftesbury commands or desires accords with his own moral judgement that he decides to obey or to accede to it. But this is no new decision, for his own moral judgement is a decision to carry out a behaviour policy; all that is happening is that he is describing his old decision in a new way. In religious conviction the resolution to follow a way of life is primary; it is not derived from believing, still less from thinking of, any empirical story. The story may psychologically support the resolution, but it does not logically justify it.

. *V* .

In this lecture I have been sparing in my use of the term "religious belief" (although it occurs in the title), preferring instead to speak of religious assertions and of religious conviction. This was because for me the fundamental problem is that of the meaning of statements used to make religious assertions, and I have accordingly taken my task to be that of explaining the use of such assertions, in accordance with the principle that meaning is to be found by ascertaining use. In disentangling the elements of this use I have discovered nothing which can be called "belief" in the sense of this word applicable either to an empirical or to a logically necessary proposition. A religious assertion, for me, is the assertion of an intention to carry out a certain behaviour policy, subsumable under a sufficiently general principle to be a moral one, together with the implicit or explicit statement, but not the assertion, of certain stories. Neither the assertion of the intention nor the reference to the stories includes belief in its ordinary senses. But in avoiding the term "belief" I have had to widen the term "assertion," since I do not pretend that either the behaviour policy intended or the stories entertained are adequately specified by the sentences used in making isolated religious assertions. So assertion has been extended to include elements not explicitly expressed in the verbal form of the assertion. If we drop the linguistic expression of the assertion altogether the remainder is what may be called religious belief. Like moral belief, it is not a species of ordinary belief, of belief in a proposition. A moral belief is an intention to behave in a certain way: a religious belief is an intention to behave in a certain way (a moral belief) together with the entertainment of certain stories associated with the intention in the mind of the believer. This solution of the problem of religious belief seems to me to do justice both to the empiricist's demand that meaning must be tied to empirical use and to the religious man's claim for his religious beliefs to be taken seriously.

Seriously, it will be retorted, but not objectively. If a man's religion is all a matter of following the way of life he sets before himself and of strengthening his determination to follow it by imagining exemplary fairytales, it is purely subjective: his religion is all in terms of his own private ideals and of his own private imaginations. How can he even try to convert others to his religion if there is nothing objective to convert them to? How can he argue in its defence if there is no religious proposition which he believes, nothing which he takes to be the fundamental truth about the universe? And is it of any public interest what mental techniques he uses to bolster up his will? Discussion about religion must be more than the exchange of autobiographies.

But we are all social animals; we are all members one of another. What is profitable to one man in helping him to persevere in the way of life he has decided upon may well be profitable to another man who is trying to follow a similar way of life; and to pass on information that might prove useful would be approved by almost every morality. The autobiography of one man may well have an influence upon the life of another, if their basic wants are similar.

But suppose that these are dissimilar, and that the two men propose to conduct their lives on quite different fundamental principles. Can there be any reasonable discussion between them? This is the problem that has faced the many moral philosophers recently who have been forced, by their examination of the nature of thinking, into holding nonpropositional theories of ethics. All I will here say is that to hold that the adoption of a set of moral principles is a matter of the personal decision to live according to these principles does not imply that beliefs as to what are the practical consequences of following such principles are not relevant to the decision. An intention, it is true, cannot be logically based upon anything except another intention. But in considering what conduct to intend to practice, it is highly relevant whether or not the consequences of practicing that conduct are such as one would intend to secure. As R. M. Hare has well said, an ultimate decision to accept a way of life, "far from being arbitrary, . . . would be the most well-founded of decisions, because it would be based upon a consideration of everything upon which it could possibly be founded."[9] And in this consideration there is a place for every kind of rational argument.

Whatever may be the case with other religions, Christianity has always been a personal religion demanding personal commitment to a personal way of life. In the words of another Oxford philosopher, "the questions 'What shall I do?' and 'What moral principles should I adopt?' must be answered by each man for himself."[10] Nowell-Smith takes this as part of the meaning of morality: whether or not this is so, I am certain that it is of the very essence of the Christian religion.

[9] R. M. Hare, *The Language of Morals* (Oxford, 1952), p. 69.—R.B.B.
[10] P. H. Nowell-Smith, *Ethics* (1954), p. 320.—R.B.B.

○ ○ ○ *35*

Theology and Verification
John Hick

To ASK 'Is the existence of God verifiable?' is to pose a question which is too imprecise to be capable of being answered.[1] There are many different concepts of God, and it may be that statements employing some of them are open to verification or falsification while statements employing others of them are not. Again, the notion of verifying is itself by no means perfectly clear and fixed; and it may be that on some views of the nature of verification the existence of God is verifiable, whereas on other views it is not.

Instead of seeking to compile a list of various different concepts of God and the various possible senses of 'verify,' I wish to argue with regard to one particular concept of deity, namely the Christian concept, that divine existence is in principle verifiable; and as the first stage of this argument I must indicate what I mean by 'verifiable.'

· I ·

The central core of the concept of verification, I suggest, is the removal of ignorance or uncertainty concerning the truth of some proposition. That p is verified (whether p embodies a theory, hypothesis, prediction, or straightforward assertion) means that something happens which makes it clear that p is true. A question is settled so that there is no longer room for rational doubt concerning it. The way in which grounds for rational doubt are excluded varies, of course, with the subject-matter. But the general feature common to all cases of verification is the ascertaining of truth by the removal of grounds for rational doubt. Where such grounds are removed, we rightly speak of verification having taken place.

To characterize verification in this way is to raise the question whether the notion of verification is purely logical or is both logical and psychological. Is the statement that p is verified simply the statement that a certain state of affairs exists (or has existed), or is it the statement also that someone is aware that this state of affairs exists (or has existed) and notes that its existence establishes the truth of p? A geologist predicts that the earth's

---

[1] In this article I assume that an indicative sentence expresses a factual assertion if and only if the state in which the universe would be if the putative assertion could correctly be said to be true differs in some experienceable way from the state in which the universe would be if the putative assertion could correctly be said to be false, all aspects of the universe other than that referred to in the putative assertion being the same in either case. This criterion acknowledges the important core of truth in the logical positivist verification principle. 'Experienceable' in the above formulation means, in the case of alleged subjective or private facts (e.g. pains, dreams, after-images, etc.), 'experienceable by the subject in question' and, in the case of alleged objective or public facts, 'capable in principle of being experienced by anyone'. My contention is going to be that 'God exists' asserts a matter of objective fact.—J.H.

surface will be covered with ice in 15 million years time. Suppose that in 15 million years time the earth's surface *is* covered with ice, but that in the meantime the human race has perished, so that no one is left to observe the event or to draw any conclusion concerning the accuracy of the geologist's prediction. Do we now wish to say that his prediction has been verified, or shall we deny that it has been verified, on the ground that there is no one left to do the verifying?

The range of 'verify' and its cognates is sufficiently wide to permit us to speak in either way. But the only sort of verification of theological propositions which is likely to interest us is one in which human beings participate. We may therefore, for our present purposes, treat verification as a logico-psychological rather than as a purely logical concept. I suggest, then, that 'verify' be construed as a verb which has its primary uses in the active voice: I verify, you verify, we verify, they verify, or have verified. The impersonal passive, it is verified, now becomes logically secondary. To say that p has been verified is to say that (at least) someone has verified it, often with the implication that his or their report to this effect is generally accepted. But it is impossible, on this usage, for p to have been verified without someone having verified it. 'Verification' is thus primarily the name for an event which takes place in human consciousness.[2] It refers to an experience, the experience of ascertaining that a given proposition or set of propositions is true. To this extent verification is a psychological notion. But of course it is also a logical notion. For needless to say, not *any* experience is rightly called an experience of verifying p. Both logical and psychological conditions must be fulfilled in order for verification to have taken place. In this respect, 'verify' is like 'know.' Knowing is an experience which someone has or undergoes, or perhaps a dispositional state in which someone is, and it cannot take place without someone having or undergoing it or being in it; but not by any means every experience which people have, or every dispositional state in which they are, is rightly called knowing.

With regard to this logico-psychological concept of verification, such questions as the following arise. When A, but nobody else, has ascertained that p is true, can p be said to have been verified; or is it required that others also have undergone the same ascertainment? How public, in other words, must verification be? Is it necessary that p could in principle be verified by anyone, without restriction, even though perhaps only A has in fact verified it? If so, what is meant here by 'in principle'; does it signify, for example, that p must be verifiable by anyone who performs a certain operation; and does it imply that to do this is within everyone's power?

These questions cannot, I believe, be given any general answer applicable to all instances of the exclusion of rational doubt. The answers must be derived in each case from an investigation of the particular subject-matter. It will be the object of subsequent sections of this article to undertake such an investigation concerning the Christian concept of God.

Verification is often construed as the verification of a prediction. However, verification, as the exclusion of grounds for rational doubt, does not necessarily consist

---

[2] This suggestion is closely related to Carnap's insistence that, in contrast to 'true', 'confirmed' is time-dependent. To say that a statement is confirmed, or verified, is to say that it has been confirmed at a particular time—and, I would add, by a particular person. See Rudolf Carnap, 'Truth and Confirmation', *Readings in Philosophical Analysis*, ed. H. Feigl and W. Sellars (New York: Appleton-Century-Crofts, 1949), pp. 119f.—J.H.

in the proving correct of a prediction; a verifying experience does not always need to have been predicted in order to have the effect of excluding rational doubt. But when we are interested in the verifiability of propositions as the criterion for their having factual meaning, the notion of prediction becomes central. If a proposition contains or entails predictions which can be verified or falsified, its character as an assertion (though not of course its character as a true assertion) is thereby guaranteed.

Such predictions may be and often are conditional. For example, statements about the features on the dark side of the moon are rendered meaningful by the conditional predictions which they entail to the effect that if an observer comes to be in such a position in space, he will make such-and-such observations. It would in fact be more accurate to say that the prediction is always conditional, but that sometimes the conditions are so obvious and so likely to be fulfilled in any case that they require no special mention, while sometimes they require for their fulfilment some unusual expedition or operation. A prediction, for example, that the sun will rise within twenty-four hours is intended unconditionally, at least as concerns conditions to be fulfilled by the observer; he is not required by the terms of the prediction to perform any special operation. Even in this case, however, there is an implied negative condition that he shall not put himself in a situation (such as immuring himself in the depths of a coal mine) from which a sunrise would not be perceptible. Other predictions, however, are explicitly conditional. In these cases it is true for any particular individual that in order to verify the statement in question he must go through some specified course of action. The prediction is to the effect that if you conduct such an experiment you will obtain such a result; for example, if you go into the next room you will have such-and-such visual experiences, and if you then touch the table which you see you will have such-and-such tactual experiences, and so on. The content of the 'if' clause is of course always determined by the particular subject-matter. The logic of 'table' determines what you must do to verify statements about tables; the logic of 'molecule' determines what you must do to verify statements about molecules; and the logic of 'God' determines what you must do to verify statements about God.

In those cases in which the individual who is to verify a proposition must himself first perform some operation, it clearly cannot follow from the circumstance that the proposition is true that everybody has in fact verified it, or that everybody will at some future time verify it. For whether or not any particular person performs the requisite operation is a contingent matter.

· II ·

What is the relation between verification and falsification? We are all familiar today with the phrase, 'theology and falsification.' A. G. N. Flew and others,[3] taking their cue from John Wisdom,[4] have raised instead of the question, 'What possible experiences would

---

[3] *New Essays in Philosophical Theology*, ed. Antony Flew and Alasdair MacIntyre (London: S.C.M., 1955), ch. VI.—J.H.

[4] 'Gods', *Proceedings of the Aristotelian Society*, Vol. 45 (1944–5). Reprinted in *Logic and Language*, First Series, ed. Antony Flew (Oxford: Blackwell, 1955), and in John Wisdom, *Philosophy and Psycho-Analysis* (Oxford: Blackwell, 1952).—J.H.

verify "God exists"?' the matching question, 'What possible experiences would falsify "God exists"? What conceivable state of affairs would be incompatible with the existence of God?' In posing the question in this way it was apparently assumed that verification and falsification are symmetrically related, and that the latter is apt to be the more accessible of the two.

In the most common cases, certainly, verification and falsification are symmetrically related. The logically simplest case of verification is provided by the crucial instance. Here it is integral to a given hypothesis that if, in specified circumstances, A occurs, the hypothesis is thereby shown to be true, whereas if B occurs the hypothesis is thereby shown to be false. Verification and falsification are also symmetrically related in the testing of such a proposition as 'There is a table in the next room.' The verifying experiences in this case are experiences of seeing and touching, predictions of which are entailed by the proposition in question, under the proviso that one goes into the next room; and the absence of such experiences in those circumstances serves to falsify the proposition.

But it would be rash to assume, on this basis, that verification and falsification must always be related in this symmetrical fashion. They do not necessarily stand to one another as do the two sides of a coin, so that once the coin is spun it must fall on one side or the other. There are cases in which verification and falsification each correspond to a side on a different coin, so that one can fail to verify without this failure constituting falsification.

Consider, for example, the proposition that 'there are three successive sevens in the decimal determination of π.' So far as the value of π has been worked out, it does not contain a series of three sevens, but it will always be true that such a series may occur at a point not yet reached in anyone's calculations. Accordingly, the proposition may one day be verified, if it is true, but can never be falsified, if it is false.

The hypothesis of continued conscious existence after bodily death provides an instance of a different kind of such asymmetry, and one which has a direct bearing upon the theistic problem. This hypothesis has built into it a prediction that one will after the date of one's bodily death have conscious experiences, including the experience of remembering that death. This is a prediction which will be verified in one's own experience if it is true, but which cannot be falsified if it is false. That is to say, it can be false, but *that* it is false can never be a fact which anyone has experimentally verified. But this circumstance does not undermine the meaningfulness of the hypothesis, since it is also such that if it be true, it will be known to be true.

It is important to remember that we do not speak of verifying logically necessary truths, but only propositions concerning matters of fact. Accordingly verification is not to be identified with the concept of logical certification or proof. The exclusion of rational doubt concerning some matter of fact is not equivalent to the exclusion of the logical possibility or error or illusion. For truths concerning fact are not logically necessary. Their contrary is never self-contradictory. But at the same time the bare logical possibility of error does not constitute ground for rational doubt as to the veracity of our experience. If it did, no empirical proposition could ever be verified, and indeed the notion of empirical verification would be without use and therefore without sense. What we rightly seek, when we desire the verification of a factual proposition, is not a demonstration of the logical impossibility of the proposition's being false (for this would be a self-contradictory demand), but such weight of evidence as suffices, in the type of case in question, to exclude rational doubt.

· III ·

These features of the concept of verification—that verification consists in the exclusion of grounds for rational doubt concerning the truth of some proposition; that this means its exclusion from particular minds; that the nature of the experience which serves to exclude grounds for rational doubt depends upon the particular subject matter; that verification is often related to predictions and that such predictions are often conditional; that verification and falsification may be asymmetrically related; and finally, that the verification of a factual proposition is not equivalent to logical certification—are all relevant to the verification of the central religious claim, 'God exists.' I wish now to apply these discriminations to the notion of eschatological[5] verification, which has been briefly employed by Ian Crombie in his contribution to *New Essays in Philosophical Theology*,[6] and by myself in *Faith and Knowledge*.[7] This suggestion has on each occasion been greeted with disapproval by both philosophers and theologians. I am, however, still of the opinion that the notion of eschatological verification is sound; and further, that no viable alternative to it has been offered to establish the factual character of theism.

The strength of the notion of eschatological verification is that it is not an *ad hoc* invention but is based upon an actually operative religious concept of God. In the language of the Christian faith, the word 'God' stands at the centre of a system of terms, such as Spirit, grace, Logos, incarnation, Kingdom of God, and many more; and the distinctly Christian conception of God can only be fully grasped in its connection with these related terms.[8] It belongs to a complex of notions which together constitute a picture of the universe in which we live, of man's place therein, of a comprehensive divine purpose interacting with human purposes, and of the general nature of the eventual fulfilment of that divine purpose. This Christian picture of the universe, entailing as it does certain distinctive expectations concerning the future, is a very different picture from any that can be accepted by one who does not believe that the God of the New Testament exists. Further, these differences are such as to show themselves in human experience. The possibility of experiential confirmation is thus built into the Christian concept of God; and the notion of eschatological verification seeks to relate this fact to the logical problem of meaning.

Let me first give a general indication of this suggestion, by repeating a parable which I have related elsewhere,[9] and then try to make it more precise and eligible for discussion. Here, first, is the parable.

Two men are travelling together along a road. One of them believes that it leads to a Celestial City, the other that it leads nowhere; but since this is the only road there is, both must travel it. Neither has been this way before, and therefore neither is able to

---

[5] Eschatology is a system of doctrines concerning last, final states—death, judgment, life in the hereafter.—E.D.K.

[6] p. 126.—J.H.

[7] (New York: Cornell, 1957), pp. 150–62.—J.H.

[8] Its clear recognition of this fact, with regard not only to Christianity but to any religion is one of the valuable features of Ninian Smart's *Reasons and Faiths* (London: Routledge and Kegan Paul, 1958). He remarks, for example, that 'the claim that God exists can only be understood by reference to many, if not all, other propositions in the doctrinal scheme from which it is extrapolated' (p. 12).—J.H.

[9] *Faith and Knowledge*, pp. 150f.—J.H.

say what they will find around each next corner. During their journey they meet both
with moments of refreshment and delight, and with moments of hardship and danger.
All the time one of them thinks of his journey as a pilgrimage to the Celestial City and
interprets the pleasant parts as encouragements and the obstacles as trials of his purpose
and lessons in endurance, prepared by the king of that city and designed to make of him
a worthy citizen of the place when at last he arrives there. The other, however, believes
none of this and sees their journey as an unavoidable and aimless ramble. Since he has
no choice in the matter, he enjoys the good and endures the bad. But for him there is
no Celestial City to be reached, no all-encompassing purpose ordaining their journey;
only the road itself and the luck of the road in good weather and in bad.

During the course of the journey the issue between them is not an experimental
one. They do not entertain different expectations about the coming details of the road,
but only about its ultimate destination. And yet when they do turn the last corner it will
be apparent that one of them has been right all the time and the other wrong. Thus
although the issue between them has not been experimental, it has nevertheless from
the start been a real issue. They have not merely felt differently about the road; for one
was feeling appropriately and the other inappropriately in relation to the actual state
of affairs. Their opposed interpretations of the road constituted genuinely rival assertions, though assertions whose assertion-status has the peculiar characteristic of
being guaranteed retrospectively by a future crux.

This parable has of course (like all parables) strict limitations. It is designed to
make only one point: that Christian doctrine postulates an ultimate unambiguous state
of existence *in patria* as well as our present ambiguous existence *in via*.[10] There is a state
of having arrived as well as a state of journeying, an eternal heavenly life as well as an
earthly pilgrimage. The alleged future experience of this state cannot, of course, be
appealed to as evidence for theism as a present interpretation of our experience; but it
does suffice to render the choice between theism and atheism a real and not a merely
empty or verbal choice. And although this does not affect the logic of the situation, it
should be added that the alternative interpretations are more than theoretical, for they
render different practical plans and policies appropriate now.

The universe as envisaged by the theist, then, differs as a totality from the universe
as envisaged by the atheist. This difference does not, however, from our present
standpoint within the universe, involve a difference in the objective content of each or
even any of its passing moments. The theist and the atheist do not (or need not) expect
different events to occur in the successive details of the temporal process. They do not
(or need not) entertain divergent expectations of the course of history viewed from
within. But the theist does and the atheist does not expect that when history is
completed it will be seen to have led to a particular end-state and to have fulfilled a
specific purpose, namely that of creating 'children of God.'

· IV ·

The idea of an eschatological verification of theism can make sense, however, only if the
logically prior idea of continued personal existence after death is intelligible. A desultory
debate on this topic has been going on for several years in some of the philosophical

---

[10] "*In patria*": at the destination; "*in via*": on route.—E.D.K.

periodicals. C. I. Lewis has contended that the hypothesis of immortality 'is an hypothesis about our own future experience. And our understanding of what would verify it has no lack of clarity.'[11] And Moritz Schlick agreed, adding, 'We must conclude that immortality, in the sense defined [i.e. "survival after death", rather than "never-ending life"], should not be regarded as a "metaphysical problem," but is an empirical hypothesis, because it possesses logical verifiability. It could be verified by following the prescription: "Wait until you die!"'[12] However, others have challenged this conclusion, either on the ground that the phrase 'surviving death' is self-contradictory in ordinary language or, more substantially, on the ground that the traditional distinction between soul and body cannot be sustained.[13] I should like to address myself to this latter view. The only self of which we know, it is said, is the empirical self, the walking, talking, acting, sleeping individual who lives, it may be, for some sixty to eighty years and then dies. Mental events and mental characteristics are analysed into the modes of behaviour and behavioural dispositions of this empirical self. The human being is described as an organism capable of acting in the 'high-level' ways which we characterize as intelligent, thoughtful, humorous, calculating, and the like. The concept of mind or soul is thus not the concept of a 'ghost in the machine' (to use Gilbert Ryle's loaded phrase[14]), but of the more flexible and sophisticated ways in which human beings behave and have it in them to behave. On this view there is no room for the notion of soul in distinction from body; and if there is no soul in distinction from body, there can be no question of the soul surviving the death of the body. Against this philosophical background the specifically Christian (and also Jewish) belief in the resurrection of the flesh, or body, in contrast to the Hellenic notion of the survival of a disembodied soul, might be expected to have attracted more attention than it has. For it is consonant with the conception of man as an indissoluble psycho-physical unity, and yet it also offers the possibility of an empirical meaning for the idea of 'life after death.'

Paul is the chief Biblical expositor of the idea of the resurrection of the body.[15] His view, as I understand it, is this. When someone has died he is, apart from any special divine action, extinct. A human being is by nature mortal and subject to annihilation by death. But in fact God, by an act of sovereign power, either sometimes or always resurrects or (better) reconstitutes or recreates him—not, however, as the identical physical organism that he was before death, but as a *soma pneumatikon* ('spiritual body') embodying the dispositional characteristics and memory traces of the deceased physical organism, and inhabiting an environment with which the *soma pneumatikon* is continuous as the *ante-mortem* body was continuous with our present world. In discussing this notion we may well abandon the word 'spiritual,' as lacking today any precise established usage, and speak of 'resurrection bodies' and of 'the resurrection

---

[11] 'Experience and Meaning,' *Philosophical Review*, Vol. 43 (1934), reprinted in Feigl and Sellars, op. cit., p. 142.—J.H.

[12] 'Meaning and Verification,' *Philosophical Review*, Vol. 45 (1936), reprinted in Feigl and Sellars, op. cit., p. 160.—J.H.

[13] E.g. Antony Flew, 'Death,' *New Essays in Philosophical Theology*, ed. Flew; 'Can a Man Witness his own Funeral?,' *Hibbert Journal*, Vol. 54 (1956).—J.H.

[14] *The Concept of Mind* (London: Hutchinson, 1949), which contains an important exposition of the interpretation of 'mental' qualities as characteristics of behaviour.—J.H.

[15] 1 Cor. 15.—J.H.

world.' The principal questions to be asked concern the relation between the physical world and the resurrection world, and the criteria of personal identity which are operating when it is alleged that a certain inhabitant of the resurrection world is the same person as an individual who once inhabited this world. The first of these questions turns out on investigation to be the more difficult of the two, and I shall take the easier one first.

Let me sketch a very odd possibility (concerning which, however, I wish to emphasize not so much its oddness as its possibility!), and then see how far it can be stretched in the direction of the notion of the resurrection body. In the process of stretching it will become even more odd than it was before; but my aim will be to show that, however odd, it remains within the bounds of the logically possible. This progression will be presented in three pictures, arranged in a self-explanatory order.

First picture: Suppose that at some learned gathering in this country one of the company were suddenly and inexplicably to disappear, and that at the same moment an exact replica of him were suddenly and inexplicably to appear at some comparable meeting in Australia. The person who appears in Australia is exactly similar, as to both bodily and mental characteristics, with the person who disappears in America. There is continuity of memory, complete similarity of bodily features, including even fingerprints, hair and eye colouration and stomach contents, and also of beliefs, habits, and mental propensities. In fact there is everything that would lead us to identify the one who appeared with the one who disappeared, except continuity of occupancy of space. We may suppose, for example, that a deputation of the colleagues of the man who disappeared fly to Australia to interview the replica of him which is reported there, and find that he is in all respects but one exactly as though he had travelled from, say, Princeton to Melbourne by conventional means. The only difference is that he describes how, as he was sitting listening to Dr. Z reading a paper, on blinking his eyes he suddenly found himself sitting in a different room listening to a different paper by an Australian scholar. He asks his colleagues how the meeting had gone after he ceased to be there, and what they had made of his disappearance, and so on. He clearly thinks of himself as the one who was present with them at their meeting in the United States. I suggest that faced with all these circumstances his colleagues would soon, if not immediately, find themselves thinking of him and treating him as the individual who had so inexplicably disappeared from their midst. We should be extending our normal use of 'same person' in a way which the postulated facts would both demand and justify if we said that the one who appears in Australia is the same person as the one who disappears in America. The factors inclining us to identify them would far outweigh the factors disinclining us to do this. We should have no reasonable alternative but to extend our usage of 'the same person' to cover the strange new case.

Second picture: Now let us suppose that the event in America is not a sudden and inexplicable disappearance, indeed not a disappearance at all, but a sudden death. Only, at the moment when the individual dies, a replica of him as he was at the moment before his death, complete with memory up to that instant, appears in Australia. Even with the corpse on our hands, it would still, I suggest, be an extension of 'same person' required and warranted by the postulated facts, to say that the same person who died has been miraculously recreated in Australia. The case would be considerably odder than in the previous picture, because of the existence of the corpse in America contemporaneously with the existence of the living person in Australia. But I submit that, although the oddness of this circumstance may be stated as strongly as you please, and can indeed hardly be overstated, yet it does not exceed the bounds of the logically possible. Once again we must imagine some of the deceased's colleagues going to Australia to interview the person who has suddenly appeared there. He would perfectly remember them and their meeting, be interested in what had happened, and be as amazed and dumbfounded about it as anyone else; and he would perhaps be worried about the possible legal complications if he should return to America to claim his property; and so on. Once again, I believe, they would soon find themselves thinking of him and treating him as the same person as the dead Princetonian. Once again the factors inclining us to say that the one who died and the one who appeared are the same person would outweigh the factors inclining us to say that they are different people. Once again we should have to extend our usage of 'the same person' to cover this new case.

Third picture: My third supposal is that the replica, complete with memory, etc. appears, not in Australia, but as a resurrection replica in a different world altogether, a resurrection world inhabited by resurrected persons. This world occupies its own space, distinct from the space with which we are now familiar. That is to say, an object in the resurrection world is not situated at any distance or in any direction from an object in our present world, although each object is either world is spatially related to each other object in the same world.

Mr. *X*, then, dies. A Mr. *X* replica, complete with the set of memory traces which Mr. *X* had at the last moment before his death, comes into existence. It is composed of other material than physical matter, and is located in a resurrection world which does not stand in any spatial relationship with the physical world. Let us leave out of consideration St. Paul's hint that the resurrection body may be as unlike the physical body as is a full grain of wheat from the wheat seed, and consider the simpler picture in which the resurrection body has the same shape as the physical body.[16]

In these circumstances, how does Mr. *X* know that he has been resurrected or re-created? He remembers dying; or rather he remembers being on what he took to be his death-bed, and becoming progressively weaker until, presumably, he lost consciousness. But how does he know that (to put it Irishly) his 'dying' proved fatal; and that he did not, after losing consciousness, begin to recover strength, and has now simply waked up?

The picture is readily enough elaborated to answer this question. Mr. *X* meets and recognizes a number of relatives and friends and historical personages whom he knows to have died; and from the fact of their presence, and also from their testimony that he has only just now appeared in their world, he is convinced that he has died. Evidences of this kind could mount up to the point at which they are quite as strong as the evidence which, in pictures one and two, convince the individual in question that he has been miraculously translated to Australia. Resurrected persons would be individually no more in doubt about their own identity than we are now, and would be able to identify one another in the same kind of ways, and with a like degree of assurance, as we do now.

If it be granted that resurrected persons might be able to arrive at a rationally founded conviction that their existence is *post-mortem*,[17] how could they know that the world in which they find themselves is in a different space from that in which their

---

[16] As would seem to be assumed, for example, by Irenaeus (*Adversus Haereses*, Bk. II, ch. 34, s. 1).—J.H.

[17] After death.—E.D.K.

physical bodies were? How could such a one know that he is not in a like situation with the person in picture number two, who dies in America and appears as a full-blooded replica in Australia, leaving his corpse in the U.S.A.—except that now the replica is situated, not in Australia, but on a planet of some other star?

It is of course conceivable that the space of the resurrection world should have properties which are manifestly incompatible with its being a region of physical space. But on the other hand, it is not of the essence of the notion of a resurrection world that its space should have properties different from those of physical space. And supposing it not to have different properties, it is not evident that a resurrected individual could learn from any direct observations that he was not on a planet of some sun which is at so great a distance from our own sun that the stellar scenery visible from it is quite unlike that which we can now see. The grounds that a resurrected person would have for believing that he is in a different space from physical space (supposing there to be no discernible difference in spatial properties) would be the same as the grounds that any of us may have now for believing this concerning resurrected individuals. These grounds are indirect and consist in all those considerations (e.g. Luke 16:26) which lead most of those who consider the question to reject as absurd the possibility of, for example, radio communication or rocket travel between earth and heaven.

· V ·

In the present context my only concern is to claim that this doctrine of the divine creation of bodies, composed of a material other than that of physical matter, which bodies are endowed with sufficient correspondence of characteristics with our present bodies, and sufficient continuity of memory with our present consciousness, for us to speak of the same person being raised up again to life in a new environment, is not self-contradictory. If, then, it cannot be ruled out *ab initio*[18] as meaningless, we may go on to consider whether and how it is related to the possible verification of Christian theism.

So far I have argued that a survival prediction such as is contained in the *corpus* of Christian belief is in principle subject to future verification. But this does not take the argument by any means as far as it must go if it is to succeed. For survival, simply as such, would not serve to verify theism. It would not necessarily be a state of affairs which is manifestly incompatible with the non-existence of God. It might be taken just as a surprising natural fact. The atheist, in his resurrection body, and able to remember his life on earth, might say that the universe has turned out to be more complex, and perhaps more to be approved of, than he had realized. But the mere fact of survival, with a new body in a new environment, would not demonstrate to him that there is a God. It is fully compatible with the notion of survival that the life to come be, so far as the theistic problem is concerned, essentially a continuation of the present life, and religiously no less ambiguous. And in this event, survival after bodily death would not in the least constitute a final verification of theistic faith.

I shall not spend time in trying to draw a picture of a resurrection existence which would merely prolong the religious ambiguity of our present life. The important question, for our purpose, is not whether one can conceive of after-life experiences

---

[18] From the beginning.—E.D.K.

which would *not* verify theism (and in point of fact one can fairly easily conceive them), but whether one can conceive of after-life experiences which *would* serve to verify theism.

I think that we can. In trying to do so I shall not appeal to the traditional doctrine, which figures especially in Catholic and mystical theology, of the Beatific Vision of God. The difficulty presented by this doctrine is not so much that of deciding whether there are grounds for believing it, as of deciding what it means. I shall not, however, elaborate this difficulty, but pass directly to the investigation of a different and, as it seems to me, more intelligible possibility. This is the possibility not of a direct vision of God, whatever that might mean, but of a *situation* which points unambiguously to the existence of a loving god. This would be a situation which, so far as its religious significance is concerned, contrasts in a certain important respect with our present situation. Our present situation is one which in some ways seems to confirm and in other ways to contradict the truth of theism. Some events around us suggest the presence of an unseen benevolent intelligence and others suggest that no such intelligence is at work. Our situation is religiously ambiguous. But in order for us to be aware of this fact we must already have some idea, however vague, of what it would be for our situation to be not ambiguous, but on the contrary wholly evidential of God. I therefore want to try to make clearer this presupposed concept of a religiously unambiguous situation.

There are, I suggest, two possible developments of our experience such that, if they occurred in conjunction with one another (whether in this life or in another life to come), they would assure us beyond rational doubt of the reality of God, as conceived in the Christian faith. These are, *first*, an experience of the fulfilment of God's purpose for ourselves, as this has been disclosed in the Christian revelation; in conjunction, *second*, with an experience of communion with God as he has revealed himself in the person of Christ.

The divine purpose for human life, as this is depicted in the New Testament documents, is the bringing of the human person, in society with his fellows, to enjoy a certain valuable quality of personal life, the content of which is given in the character of Christ—which quality of life (i.e. life in relationship with God, described in the Fourth Gospel as eternal life) is said to be the proper destiny of human nature and the source of man's final self-fulfilment and happiness. The verification situation with regard to such a fulfilment is asymmetrical. On the one hand, so long as the divine purpose remains unfulfilled, we cannot know that it never will be fulfilled in the future; hence no final falsification is possible of the claim that this fulfilment will occur—unless, of course, the prediction contains a specific time clause which, in Christian teaching, it does not. But on the other hand, if and when the divine purpose *is* fulfilled in our own experience, we must be able to recognize and rejoice in that fulfilment. For the fulfilment would not be for us the promised fulfilment without our own conscious participation in it.

It is important to note that one can say this much without being cognizant in advance of the concrete form which such fulfilment will take. The before-and-after situation is analogous to that of a small child looking forward to adult life and then, having grown to adulthood, looking back upon childhood. The child possesses and can use correctly in various contexts the concept of 'being grown up,' although he does not know, concretely, what it is like to be grown-up. But when he reaches adulthood he is nevertheless able to know that he has reached it; he is able to recognize the experience of living a grown-up life even though he did not know in advance just what to expect. For his understanding of adult maturity grows as he himself matures. Something similar may be supposed to happen in the case of the fulfilment of the divine purpose for human life. That fulfilment may be as far removed from our present condition as is mature adulthood from the mind of a little child; nevertheless, we possess already a comparatively vague notion of this final fulfilment, and as we move towards it our concept will itself become more adequate; and if and when we finally reach that fulfilment, the problem of recognizing it will have disappeared in the process.

The other feature that must, I suggest, be present in a state of affairs that would verify theism, is that the fulfilment of God's purpose be apprehended *as* the fulfilment of God's purpose and not simply as a natural state of affairs. To this end it must be accompanied by an experience of communion with God as he has made himself known to men in Christ.

The specifically Christian clause, 'as he has made himself known to men in Christ,' is essential, for it provides a solution to the problem of recognition in the awareness of God. Several writers have pointed out the logical difficulty involved in any claim to have encountered God.[19] How could one know it was *God* whom one had encountered? God is described in Christian theology in terms of various absolute qualities, such as omnipotence, omnipresence, perfect goodness, infinite love, etc., which cannot as such be observed by us, as can their finite analogues, limited power, local presence, finite goodness, and human love. One can recognize that a being whom one 'encounters' has a given finite degree of power, but how does one recognize that he has *un*limited power? How does one observe that an encountered being is *omni*present? How does one perceive that his goodness and love, which one can perhaps see to exceed any human goodness and love, are actually infinite? Such qualities cannot be given in human experience. One might claim, then, to have encountered a Being whom one presumes, or trusts, or hopes to be God; but one cannot claim to have encountered a Being whom one recognized to be the infinite, almighty, eternal Creator.

This difficulty is met in Christianity by the doctrine of the Incarnation—although this was not among the considerations which led to the formulation of that doctrine. The idea of incarnation provides answers to the two related questions: 'How do we know that God has certain absolute qualities which, by their very nature, transcend human experience?' and 'How can there be an eschatological verification of theism which is based upon a recognition of the presence of God in his Kingdom?'

In Christianity God is known as 'the God and Father of our Lord Jesus Christ.'[20] God is the Being about whom Jesus taught; the Being in relation to whom Jesus lived, and into a relationship with whom he brought his disciples; the Being whose *agape* towards men was seen on earth in the life of Jesus. In short, God is the transcendent Creator who has revealed himself in Christ. Now Jesus's teaching about the Father is a part of that self-disclosure, and it is from this teaching (together with that of the prophets who preceded him) that the Christian knowledge of God's transcendent being is derived. Only God himself knows his own infinite nature; and our human belief about that nature is based upon his self-revelation to men in Christ. As Karl

---

[19] For example, R. W. Hepburn, *Christianity and Paradox* (London: C. A. Watts, 1958), pp. 56f.—J.H.

[20] 2 Cor. 11:31.—J.H.

Barth expresses it, 'Jesus Christ is the knowability of God.'[21] Our beliefs about God's infinite being are not capable of observational verification, being beyond the scope of human experience, but they are susceptible of indirect verification by the removal of rational doubt concerning the authority of Christ. An experience of the reign of the Son in the Kingdom of the Father would confirm that authority, and therewith, indirectly, the validity of Jesus's teaching concerning the character of God in his infinite transcendent nature.

The further question as to how an eschatological experience of the Kingdom of God could be known to be such has already been answered by implication. It is God's union with man in Christ that makes possible man's recognition of the fulfilment of God's purpose for man as being indeed the fulfilment of *God's* purpose for him. The presence of Christ in his Kingdom marks this as being beyond doubt the Kingdom of the God and Father of the Lord Jesus Christ.

It is true that even the experience of the realization of the promised Kingdom of God, with Christ reigning as Lord of the New Aeon, would not constitute a logical certification of his claims nor, accordingly, of the reality of God. But this will not seem remarkable to any philosopher in the empiricist tradition, who knows that it is only a confusion to demand that a factual proposition be an analytic truth. A set of expectations based upon faith in the historic Jesus as the incarnation of God, and in his teaching as being divinely authoritative, could be so fully confirmed in *post-mortem* experience as to leave no grounds for rational doubt as to the validity of that faith.

· *VI* ·

There remains of course the problem (which falls to the New Testament scholar rather than to the philosopher) whether Christian tradition, and in particular the New Testament, provides a sufficiently authentic 'picture' of the mind and character of Christ to make such recognition possible. I cannot here attempt to enter into the vast field of Biblical criticism, and shall confine myself to the logical point, which only emphasizes the importance of the historical question, that a verification of theism made possible by the Incarnation is dependent upon the Christian's having a genuine contact with the person of Christ, even though this is mediated through the life and tradition of the Church.

One further point remains to be considered. When we ask the question, '*To whom* is theism verified?' one is initially inclined to assume that the answer must be, 'To everyone.' We are inclined to assume that, as in my parable of the journey, the believer must be confirmed in his belief, and the unbeliever converted from his unbelief. But this assumption is neither demanded by the nature of verification nor by any means unequivocally supported by our Christian sources.

We have already noted that a verifiable prediction may be conditional. 'There is a table in the next room' entails conditional predictions of the form: if someone goes into the next room he will see, etc. But no one is compelled to go into the next room. Now it may be that the predictions concerning human experience which are entailed by the proposition that God exists are conditional predictions and that no one is compelled to fulfil those conditions. Indeed we stress in much of our theology that the

---

[21] *Church Dogmatics*, Vol. II, Pt. I, p. 150.—J.H.

manner of the divine self-disclosure to men is such that our human status as free and responsible beings is respected, and an awareness of God never is forced upon us. It may then be a condition of *post-mortem* verification that we be already in some degree conscious of God by an uncompelled response to his modes of revelation in this world. It may be that such a voluntary consciousness of God is an essential element in the fulfilment of the divine purpose for human nature, so that the verification of theism which consists in an experience of the final fulfilment of that purpose can only be experienced by those who have already entered upon an awareness of God by the religious mode of apperception which we call faith.

If this be so, it has the consequence that only the theistic believer can find the vindication of his belief. This circumstance would not of course set any restriction upon who can become a believer, but it would involve that while theistic faith can be verified—found by one who holds it to be beyond rational doubt—yet it cannot be proved to the non-believer. Such an asymmetry would connect with that strain of New Testament teaching which speaks of a division of mankind even in the world to come.

Having noted this possibility I will only express my personal opinion that the logic of the New Testament as a whole, though admittedly not always its explicit content, leads to a belief in ultimate universal salvation. However, my concern here is not to seek to establish the religious facts, but rather to establish that there are such things as religious facts, and in particular that the existence or non-existence of the God of the New Testament is a matter of fact, and claims as such eventual experiential verification.

○ ○ ○ **36**

The Logic of God
The Modes of Thought and the Logic of God
John Wisdom

· *I* ·

I SHOULD LIKE to say what I aim to do in these lectures and then do it. But there are difficulties about this. I have nothing to say—nothing except what everybody knows. People sometimes ask me what I do. Philosophy I say and I watch their faces very closely. 'Ah—they say—that's a very deep subject isn't it?' I don't like this at all. I don't like their tone. I don't like the change in their faces. Either they are frightfully solemn. Or they have to manage not to smile. And I don't like either. Now scientists don't have to feel like this. They tell us what we don't know until they tell us—how very fast germs in the blood breed and that this stuff will stop them, what will or at least what won't take the stain out of the carpet. Even if I were a historian it would be better. Maybe you don't want to know just how the Abbey at Bury St. Edmunds was run in the time of Abbot Samson, but at least you probably don't know and if only I did I could tell you. But as it is I haven't anything to say except what everybody knows already. And this instantly puts into my head a thought which I try not to but can't help but think namely 'Have I anything to say at all worth saying'—a question which I fear is by now in your mind even if it wasn't before I started. Fortunately this brings me to what I want to do. For I want to urge that one who has nothing to say except what everybody knows already may yet say something worth saying and I want to bring out a little how this happens. This is itself something which everybody knows so if I succeed I succeed twice over rather like one who proves that someone in this room is whispering by pointing to someone who is whispering and saying, in a whisper, 'He is whispering.' On the other hand even if I fail to demonstrate that what I claim is true it may still be true. Of course—for as everybody knows, one who says 'Someone is whispering' may be right although in attempting to support this statement he points to the wrong person. And everybody knows that a child *may* get the right answer to a sum although he has made at least one mistake in his calculations. Everybody knows this. But don't we sometimes become unduly confident that what a man says is false because his argument is invalid or his premisses false? And if we do then there are occasions on which it is worth saying to us 'A man may be right in what he says although his argument is invalid and/or his premisses false'—a thing which everybody knows.

Perhaps you now hope that satisfied with these antics I will say no more. But no. I am not content to show that it is sometimes worth saying what everybody knows— that seems to me hardly worth saying. I want if I can to bring out a little of how, when, and why it is sometimes worth saying what everybody knows. I want to bring out the several ways of doing this and also how it is connected with informing people of what they do not know—Unlike philosophers, scientists need feel no embarrassment about accepting the salaries they are paid. Motor vans hurry with the late editions. And very properly. For we want to know what won. But how does anyone ever say to another anything worth saying when he doesn't know anything the other doesn't know?

And yet of course there are those who manage this. They say 'You look *lovely* in that hat' to people who know this already. But this instance isn't a very clear one. For those to whom such things are said sometimes know not merely that what is said is so but are also very well aware of how what is said is so. Imagine something different. Imagine someone is trying on a hat. She is studying the reflection in a mirror like a judge considering a case. There's a pause and then a friend says in tones too clear, 'My dear, it's the Taj Mahal.' Instantly the look of indecision leaves the face in the mirror. All along she has felt there was about the hat something that wouldn't quite do. Now she sees what it is. And all this happens in spite of the fact that the hat could be seen perfectly clearly and completely before the words 'The Taj Mahal' were uttered. And the words were not effective because they referred to something hidden like a mouse in a cupboard, like germs in the blood, like a wolf in sheep's clothing. To one about to buy false diamonds the expert friend murmurs 'Glass,' to one terrified by what he takes to be a snake the good host whispers 'Stuffed.' But that's different, that *is* to tell somebody something he doesn't know—that that snake won't bite, that cock won't fight. But to call a hat the Taj Mahal is not to inform someone that it has mice in it or will cost a fortune. It is more like saying to someone 'Snakes' of snakes in the grass but *not* concealed by the grass but still so well camouflaged that one can't see what's before one's eyes. Even this case is different from that of the hat and the woman. For in the case of the snakes the element of warning, the element of predictive warning, is still there mixed, intimately mixed, with the element of revealing what is already visible. This last element is there unmixed when someone says of a hat which is plainly and completely visible 'It's the Taj Mahal .' And there is another difference. There's nothing preposterous about calling a snake a snake, but to call a hat the Taj Mahal— well, it involves poetic licence.

At this point someone protests. In philosophy there's always someone who protests. And here he says, 'I don't know what you're making all this fuss about. In the first place a woman who says of a hat "It's the Taj Mahal" just means "It is like the Taj Mahal" or "It is in some respects like the Taj Mahal." By saying this she makes her friend feel that the hat is impossible. Well what of it? What has all this got to do with what you say is your main point, namely, that one person may show something to another without telling him anything he doesn't know? In this case nobody shows anybody anything—all that happens is that somebody is persuaded not to buy a hat. The hat you say was seen perfectly clearly from the first. Now it isn't seen any more clearly at the finish. The change is a change in feeling. It may be expressed in the words "I see now" or "It's impossible" but that is just an expression of a different attitude to the hat.

'And by the way may I ask what all this has got to do with philosophy? Here is mankind bewildered in a bewildering world. And what do you offer? Talk about talk about a hat.'

My answer is this: In the first place it isn't true that the words about the hat only influence the hearer's feelings to the hat. They alter her apprehension of the hat just as the word 'A hare' makes what did look like a clump of earth *look* like an animal, a hare in fact; just as the word 'A cobra' may change the look of something in the corner by the bed. It is just because in these instances words change the apprehension of what is already before one that I refer to them.

Again it isn't true that the words 'It's the Taj Mahal' meant 'It is like the Taj Mahal.' This more sober phrase is an inadequate substitute. This reformulation is a failure. It's feebler than the original and yet it's still too strong. For the hat isn't like the Taj Mahal, it's much smaller and the shape is very different. And the still more sober substitute 'It is in some respects like the Taj Mahal' is still more inadequate. It's *much* too feeble. Everything is like everything in some respects—a man like a monkey, a monkey like a mongoose, a mongoose like a mouse, a mouse like a micro-organism, and a man after all is an organism too. Heaven forbid that we should say there are no contexts in which it is worth while to remark this sort of thing. But it is not what the woman in the hat shop remarked. What she said wasn't the literal truth like 'It's a cobra' said of what is, unfortunately, a cobra. But what she said revealed the truth. Speaking soberly what she said was false but then thank heaven we don't always speak soberly. Someone has said 'The best of life is but intoxication' and that goes for conversation. People sometimes speak wildly but if we tame their words what we get are words which are tame and very often words which don't do anything near what the wild ones did. If for 'It's the Taj Mahal' we put 'It is in some respects like the Taj Mahal' we get the sort of negligible stuff that so often results from trying to put poetry into prose, from submission to the muddled metaphysics which pretends that a metaphor is no more than an emotive flourish unless and until we happen to have the words and the wits to translate it into a set of similes.

'But,' says the protesting voice, 'what she said about the hat wasn't poetry.'

'All right, all right it wasn't poetry. And the bread in the upper room wasn't the body of Christ that later hung upon the Cross. Nor of course are there three incorruptibles and yet but one incorruptible, three persons yet one God. But sometimes one is less concerned with whether what one says is true, literally true, than one is to press past illusion to the apprehension of reality, its unity and its diversity.'

'Well let that pass,' says the sober voice, 'since it agitates you so much, let it pass. It all seems rather vague to me and I don't know what you mean about the judge and his judgements. Could anything be further from poetry, more sober? However let it pass, let it pass and come to my second point. What has this conversation about a hat got to do with philosophy, this rather bizarre conversation about a hat?

My answer is this: Is conversation about the nature and reality of goodness and beauty philosophical, metaphysical conversation? Is conversation about the reality and ultimate nature of the soul philosophical, metaphysical conversation? Is conversation about the reality and ultimate nature of matter philosophical, metaphysical conversation? Is conversation about the reality and ultimate nature of philosophical, metaphysical discussion philosophical, metaphysical conversation? It is. Well, the conversation about the hat throws light on all that—and more immediately conversation about conversation about the hat is a bit of metaphysics and bears on other bits. It *is* a member of the family of metaphysical conversations and its character throws a light on the other members of that family; and the conversation about the hat itself is a member of the family of *Attempts to come at the truth* and its character throws light on the character of the other members of that vast family. The character of any one human being throws light on the characters of all the rest and they on it. For what is the character of a woman, of a man, of anything at all but the way she, he, it is like and unlike men, monkeys, microbes, the dust, the angels high in heaven, God on his throne—all that is and all that might have been.

'Hold on, hold on,' says the voice. 'This sounds rather like church. It's so obscure.'

This makes me want to mutter 'Thank heaven for the church.' It is often obscurantist. But sometimes in those lecture halls we endeavour to substitute for it the light seems a thought too bright and on the brilliant plains of intellectual orthodoxy we half remember something lost in Lyonesse or something that was never found. Still—I must answer that voice of protest, that voice which somehow in spite of its anticlerical bias is also the voice of honesty, order, law, conscience saying 'Let's get this clear. How can consideration of a conversation about a hat make metaphysics more manageable? Even if the conversation about the hat does a little illuminate the hat, isn't it a far cry to philosophy which professes to illuminate reality?'

· *II* ·

At the end of the last discussion I was left facing the question: Why all this about a hat and the Taj Mahal? If you want to bring out the fact that we sometimes use words neither to give information as when we say 'That will be fifteen guineas' nor to express and evoke feeling as when we exclaim '*Fifteen* guineas!' but to give a greater apprehension of what is already before us then why don't you choose a better example? For instance why not take the case of an accountant who has before him the assets and liabilities of a firm and asks 'Are they solvent?' or a statistician who has before him the records of births and deaths for the last 50 years and asks 'Has the average man today a greater expectation of life than he had 20 years ago?' Here are questions which can be settled on the basis of facts already ascertained and which are yet definite questions which can be settled by an agreed, definite, mathematical, deductive procedure. Why choose as an example a statement so preposterous and loosely worded that the question 'Is it true?' is hardly a question at all. . . . It not only cannot be answered by collecting new data by observation but also cannot be answered by any definite deductive procedure.

My answer is: That is why I chose it. We all know and, what is more, we all recognize that there are questions which though they don't call for further investigation but only for reflection are yet perfectly respectable because the reflection they call for may be carried out in a definite demonstrative procedure which gives results Yes or No. My point is that this isn't the only sort of reflection and that the other sorts are not poor relations. Maybe they tend to have deplorable associates but they themselves we cannot afford to ignore. For they too take us toward a better apprehension of reality and also help us to understand better the character of all reflection including the more normal members of the family.

We do not deny that vague and queer things are said and that people make some show of considering them. We do not say that drama, novels, poetry, never show us anything of the truth. But we are apt to half-feel that what is said in poetry is always more a matter of fancy than of fact, that it is not within the scope of reason. I am urging that there is more of poetry in science and more of science in poetry than our philosophy permits us readily to grasp. 'There is within the flame of love a sort of wick or snuff that doth abate it' is not so far from 'There is within the central rail on the Inner Circle a sort of current that, etc.' 'There is between a rising tide and the rising moon a sort of bond that, etc.' Newton with his doctrine of gravitation gave us a so much greater apprehension of nature not so much because he told us what we would or would not see, like Pasteur or one who predicts what will be first past the post, but because he enabled us to see anew a thousand familiar incidents. To hint that when we are concerned with questions which are still unanswered even when we have left no stone unturned, no skid mark unmeasured, then thinking is no use, is to forget that when the facts are agreed upon we still must hear argument before we give judgement. To hint that, when argument cannot show that in the usual usage of language the correct answer is Yes or No it shows us nothing, is to forget that such argument is in such a case just as necessary and just as valuable for an apprehension of the case before us as it is in those cases when it happens that we can express that greater apprehension in a word—Guilty, Not Guilty, Mad, Not Mad, Negligent, Not Negligent, Cruel, Not Cruel. To hint that whenever, in our efforts to portray nature, we break the bonds of linguistic convention and say what is preposterous then counsel must throw up the case because we are no longer at the bar of reason—to say this is to denigrate the very modes of thought that we need most when most we need to think.

And yet, in one's efforts to think clearly it is easy to speak as if it were a waste of time to try to answer a question which hasn't an answer Yes or No, Right or Wrong, True or False. And when lately some people had the courage to say, 'A statement hasn't really a meaning unless it can be settled either by observation or by the sort of definite procedure by which questions of mathematics or logic are settled, otherwise it isn't a real, meaningful, worthwhile question but verbal, emotive, or nonsensical' then we welcomed this bold pronouncement because it seemed to say what we had long felt but not had the courage to say.

It is easy to see that this principle as it stands won't do. Consider the question 'Here are the records for births and deaths for the last fifty years. Does the average man live longer today than he did twenty years ago?' This is not itself a hypothetical, mathematical question. It is not the question '*If* the figures were as follows what *would* the answer be?' It is the question 'These being the figures what *is* the answer?' This is a question about what has actually happened.

However it is settled by a definite deductive procedure. So such a case leaves it open to us to reformulate our tempting principle as follows: A question is a real, meaningful question only if either it can be answered by observation or it can be answered by demonstration from premises which are either self-evident or obtained by describing what we have observed.

This unspoken formula frames I submit a prevalent, though often unspoken, habit of thought. We know the man who when we are vigorously discussing some point interposes with 'Look—we must define our terms, mustn't we?' He has been educated; he has been taught. His intentions are of the best. He is an ally against fluffy and futile talk. And yet so often by the time he has finished it seems somehow as if the questions he has answered aren't the ones we were interested in and worse still we seem to be unable to say what we were interested in. For example, suppose a man says to his wife, 'The children ought to clean their shoes before going to school.' 'Oh, don't be so fussy,' she says. 'I am not being fussy,' he says, 'I'm merely concerned that the children should learn the ordinary politeness of taking some care of their appearance and not arrive at school in a slovenly state.' '*Slovenly*,' she says but at this point the good friend intervenes. He addresses himself to the wife. 'Look,' he says with his pleasant smile, 'we must define our terms, mustn't we? One can't begin to answer a question until one has defined one's terms.' 'In that case one can't begin,' she says, 'for when one defines a word one puts another in its place.' 'Yes,' he says, 'but you know I don't mean that we ought to define *every* word we use. I mean we need to define the *vague* ones.' 'By equally vague ones I suppose,' she says. 'No, no,' he says, 'by more precise ones.' 'But,' she says, 'if what you put in place of the vague is something not vague then the new words can't have the same meaning as the old ones had.' 'I see what you mean,' he says, 'but still, what is the use of arguing about a question which hasn't a definite answer? One must know what one means.' 'Certainly one must know or come to know what one means,' she says, 'but that doesn't mean that there is no use in arguing about questions which haven't definite answers. They are just the ones which are most interesting— those and the ones which can't mean what they seem to mean, because they are so preposterous. For instance I said just now that Jack was fussy. We both knew what I meant—I meant like an old hen. I daresay there is something to be said for saying he is not fussy. But if so I want to have it said and I want to have my say too. Now you say that we can't discuss this question until we have defined our terms. I suppose you mean the terms "fussy" or "slovenly." But we were discussing it until you interposed. 'Well,' he says, 'I interposed because it seemed to me that you were discussing a question which couldn't be answered. You said Jack was fussy, he said he wasn't. But this wasn't a real dispute, it was a question of words.'

She: It *wasn't* a question of words, it was a real question, a very real question.

He: Well of course it was a question you and he had strong feelings about. Or rather the word 'fussy' is an *emotive* word because it expresses our feelings and when you said that Jack was fussy because he said the children ought to clean their shoes before going to school, you expressed how you felt about their doing this and about Jack—and when he said he was not fussy he expressed his feelings about this and about you. But there wasn't any real question between you.

She: What d'you mean, no *real* question?

He: Well, I mean 'Is Jack fussy?' isn't a question like 'Has Jack diphtheria?' which can be settled by taking a swab from his throat. Nor is it like 'Has he the money for the tickets? They cost 15/- and he has 10/-, one shilling, three sixpences and half a crown. Now is that 15/-?" There is a procedure for settling such a question.

She: You are not now saying that we can't answer a question unless we can define our terms. But what are you saying? Is it that questions which can't be settled by observation nor by deduction aren't really questions? But what do you mean 'aren't really questions'? Do you mean that there is no definite procedure for answering them? But what d' you call a definite procedure? Is legal procedure when cases are quoted in order to show for example that in the case before the court there was negligence or that there was not—is this a definite procedure? And does it always lead to an answer? Whenever I get a glimpse of what you mean it seems preposterous and it only doesn't seem preposterous when I don't know what you mean. But I want to *come* to know what you mean. I want to know what's at the back of your saying that questions which seem to be real questions aren't really; I want to know what makes you say it, what reasons you have, whether you are right or wrong or neither. Or is this not a real question because it hasn't a definite answer so that it is futile to discuss it?

'Well,' he says, 'I think you know what I mean. I mean that there are lots of questions which seem as if they could be answered by observation or deduction when they can't be really because they are matters of words or matters of feeling.'

She: We all know that this sometimes happens. For instance one person might say that a certain food is in short supply and another that it is not because the one means that people can't get as much of it as they want to buy and the other means that there is no less of this food on the market than usual. Or to take a more trivial but simpler instance: I remember I once said of two horses which had the same father that they were half-brothers and someone else said that they were not and it turned out that this was because he didn't call *horses* half-brothers unless they had the same *mother*.

He: I don't mean just trivial instances like that. I mean that there are questions which seem important to us and seem to call for much thought because they seem difficult to answer when really they are difficult to answer only because there is no way of answering them, so that they have no answers. For instance take an old question which has very much concerned people—the question 'Did someone make the world?' 'Is there Someone behind it all?' This seems as if it could be answered like 'Who made this watch?' 'Who laid out this garden?' 'Is there a master mind behind all these seemingly disconnected crimes?' But it can't be answered in that way. It couldn't be. What I mean is this: when you are told that there is someone, God, who brings the young lions their prey and feeds the cattle upon a thousand hills, it is natural to think that if you watch, perhaps in the hush at dawn or at sunset, you will see something to confirm this statement. You watch. What d'you see? Antelopes feeding perhaps, or zebras come down to drink. A lion springs—with wonderful acceleration it is true— but still his own acceleration. And if anything saves that zebra it's the way he comes round on his hocks and gets going. There are the stars and the flowers and the animals. But there's no one to be seen. And no one to be heard. There's the wind and there's the thunder but if you call there's no answer except the echo of your own voice. It is natural to infer that those who told us that there is someone who looks after it all are wrong. But that is a mistake we are told. No such inference is legitimate they say, because God is invisible.

She: God is a spirit and cannot be seen nor heard. But the evidences of his existence lie in order and arrangement of nature.

He: That is what is so often said. But it suggests that in nature there are evidences of God as there are in a watch the evidences of a maker, in a cathedral, the evidences of an architect, in a garden, the evidences of a gardener. And this is to suggest that God *could* be seen. It then turns out that this is a mistake. A gardener may be elusive, an architect retiring, a watch-maker hard to find, but we know what it would be to see them and so confirm the guesses that it is they who are responsible for what we see before us. Now what would it be like to see God? Suppose some seer were to see, imagine we all saw, move upwards from the ocean to the sky some prodigious figure which declared in dreadful tones the moral law or prophesied most truly—our fate. Would this be to see God?

Wouldn't it just be a phenomenon which later we were able to explain or not able to explain but in neither case the proof of a living God. The logic of God if there is such a logic isn't like that.

She: Indeed, indeed. The way to knowledge of God is not as simple as we might confusedly hope. An evil and adulterous generation seeketh after a sign and there shall no sign be given it save the sign of the prophet Jonah. And that is not an arbitrary decree but one by which God Himself is bound. What you call 'the logic of God' couldn't be simpler than it is without His being less than He is, for the simpler the possible proofs that something is so the simpler it is for it to be so.

He: What d'you mean?

She: Well, if we mean by 'a rainbow' only a certain appearance in the sky then it is easy to know at a glance whether today there is a rainbow or not. But in that case a rainbow is only an appearance in the sky. The moment it is more, that moment it's harder to know. If one who says 'There's a rainbow' means not merely that there is a certain appearance in the sky but that that appearance is linked with water and the sun, then the appearance is no longer by itself a proof that what he says is so. It may be a sign but it is not one from which he can read off the answer to the question 'Is there a rainbow?' as he could when by 'a rainbow' was meant no more than a certain appearance in the sky. When a rainbow is more than the appearance of a rainbow then that appearance is not a sign which makes it beside the point to look for the rest of what makes a rainbow a rainbow. The simplest people are sometimes very good at telling whether a storm is coming but the full proof, the full confirmation of what they reckon is so, cannot be less complex than all that makes a storm. Horses are quick to know whether one is angry, babies to know whether one loves them, but the full proof of what they feel is so cannot be less complex than is anger or love itself—as you say it is not merely that there *is* not some fool-proof proof of God. There *couldn't* be. But that doesn't mean that there are no evidences of God's existence; it doesn't mean that there are no proofs of his existence; nor that these are not to be found in experience; not even that they are not to be found in what we see and hear. One cannot see power but it's from what we see that we know that power is present when we watch the tube-train mysteriously move towards the Marble Arch, and the more we watch, the more explicable the mystery becomes, the more, without limit, the proof approaches a demonstration. Each day a thousand incidents confirm the doctrine that energy is indestructible: and if the present proof is not a demonstration that is not because the conclusion calls for reasons of a kind we never get. It is because the doctrine is infinite in its implications so that beyond any conceivable evidence at any time there is still evidence beyond that time—evidence for or evidence against—until no wheels are turning and time stops. In the same way, as the scroll of nature unrolls the proof of an eternal God prevails—or fails—until on the day of judgement doctrine, like theory, must become a verdict and all be lost or won.

· III ·

He: I understand that you are now saying that the order and arrangement of nature proves the existence of God, not as the moving machinery of a mill indicates the flow of water beneath it, but as the behaviour of an electrical machine proves the presence of electricity because electricity just is such behaviour. The average man is invisible but we may know whether he is orderly or disorderly because his existence and nature are deducible from that of individual men. He is orderly if they are orderly because his being orderly just is their being orderly. But now if the existence of God is deducible from the fact that nature is orderly then one who says that God exists merely puts in theological words what others express in the words, 'In nature nothing is inexplicable, there is always a reason why.' And those who speak of God would not allow that this is all they mean. This is why I say that the question, 'Does God exist?' cannot be answered by observation and also cannot be answered by deduction. And this is why I say that though it seems to be a question it is not. The statement 'God's in his heaven' may express a feeling but it is not something that could be true or false, because nothing would make it false and therefore nothing would make it true.

She: You make too little of a move in thought which from a mass of data extracts and assembles what builds up into the proof of something which, though it doesn't go beyond the data, gives us an apprehension of reality which before we lacked. The move from the myriad transactions of the market to the conclusion that sterling is stronger isn't negligible. The move from the bewildering and apparently disorderly flux of nature to the doctrine that all that happens happens in order is one which called for our best efforts and gave us a very different apprehension of nature. Perhaps it took Spinoza a long way towards God.

Still it *is* very true that those who speak of God don't mean merely that nature is orderly. Nature would be orderly if it were nothing but an enormous clock slowly but inevitably running down. But then I am not saying that if there is order in Nature that proves that God exists. The fact that a machine is electrical is not deducible from the fact that its behaviour is orderly. If there were no order in its behaviour it couldn't be electrical but there could be order in its behaviour without its being electrical. It might run by falling weights. It is the fact that the order in its behaviour is of a certain character which make the machine electrical. It doesn't need winding but from time to time it stops or goes more slowly just when the fire goes out—that's what makes it electrical. The mere fact that Nature is orderly would never prove that Energy is indestructible. What makes this true is the fact that the order in nature is of a certain character. It might have been of a different character but, as it is, each day confirms the doctrine of the conservation of energy.

The order of nature might have been of a character which would make it fair to say, 'It is all in the hands of someone who made it and then fell asleep' or, 'It's all in the hands of someone who arranges the little ironies of fate.' For all I have said to the contrary it may be of this character. For I am not trying to prove that God does exist but only to prove that it is wrong to say that there could be no proof that he does or that he does not.

He: But surely this comparison of the logic of God with the logic of Energy isn't a legitimate comparison.

She: I don't know whether it's legitimate or not. I am making it.

He: Yes but—well, it's like this: I understand you when you say that just as those who speak of the existence and properties of Energy don't deduce all they say from the fact that the procession of events in nature is orderly but from the particular character of that procession of events, so those who speak of God don't deduce his existence and properties merely from the fact that the procession of events is orderly but from the particular character of that procession. But surely the question 'Does God exist?' is very different from the question 'Does Energy exist?' I don't mean merely that the questions are different like the question 'Is there any milk?' is different from 'Is there any wine?' Those questions are very unlike because milk is very unlike wine. But they are very like in the sort of procedure which settles them; that is, the logic of milk is like the logic of wine. But surely the way we know of the existence of energy is very different from the way, if any, in which we know of the existence of God. For one thing, people have spoken of knowing the presence of God not from looking around them but from their own hearts. The logic of God may be more like the logic of Energy or of Life than at first appears but surely it is very different.

She: It *is* different. One can't expect to bring out the idiosyncrasies in what you call 'the logic of God' by a single comparison. The way in which we know God Who has been called 'the Soul of the World,' 'the Mind of the Universe,' might also be compared with the way one knows the soul or mind of another creature. It is clear that one couldn't find the soul behind the face of one's neighbor or one's cat as one could find at last the elusive and even ghostly inhabitant of the house next door. Because of this people have said that when we speak of the consciousness of another this is a way of speaking of those sequences of bodily events which are the manifestations of consciousness, just as when we speak of energy that is a way of speaking of the manifestations of energy and when we speak of a procession that is just a way of speaking of what makes up the procession. Here again this comparison is dangerous unless it is accompanied by a warning. For it neglects the fact that though one who has never tasted what is bitter or sweet and has never felt pain may know very well the behaviour characteristic of, for instance, pain, he yet cannot know pain nor even that another is in pain—not in the way he could had he himself felt pain. It is from looking round him that a man knows of the pain, of the love and of the hate in the world, but it is also from his own heart.

He: Yes, but what I mean is this. Even though we couldn't see energy because it isn't the sort of thing which could be seen we know very well what to look for in order to know of its existence and where it flows, we can measure it and deduce the laws of its transmission and conservation. Even when we ask of someone, 'Is he really pleased to see us?' we know what to look for to prove that the answer is 'Yes,' and what to look for to prove that the answer is 'No.' We may ask him and beg him to tell us the truth, and if we are not satisfied we may await developments, watch for further signs, and these may, in your words, approach more and more a demonstration. But with the questions 'Does God exist?' 'Is this what He approves or that?' there is no agreement as to what to look for, no agreement as to what the character of the order of events must be to count in favour of the answer 'Yes' or in favour of the answer 'No.'

She: Not *no* agreement. If there were *no* agreement that *would* make the question meaningless. But it is not true that there is no agreement. One could describe a future for the world which were it to come would prove the triumph of the Devil. Hells, it is true, are more easily described than Heavens, and Paradise lost than Paradise regained. Descriptions of heaven are apt to be either extremely hazy or to involve too much music or too much hunting. And this isn't a joke, it may spell a contradiction in perfection. But it's not true that we haven't a clue about the kingdom of heaven. Every description of what appears to be heaven and turns out to be hell makes plainer the boundaries of heaven. We don't know what would be heaven and this shows itself in the fluctuating logic of heaven, that is to say in our feeble grasp of what it is we do want to do with the words, 'Will the kingdom of heaven come?' 'Does God exist?' But this doesn't prove that there isn't anything we want to do with them. An artist may not know what he wants to do, and only come to know by doing first one thing which isn't what he wanted to do and then another which also isn't what he wanted to do. But this doesn't prove that there wasn't anything he wanted to do. On the contrary in finding what he didn't want to do he may find at last what he did. In the same way with words, finding out what one didn't mean, one may find out at last what one did mean.

Now with regard to God and the Devil and whether there is any meaning in asking whether they exist: Freud so far from thinking these questions meaningless says in the last of the New Introductory Lectures: 'It seems not to be true that there is a power in the universe which watches over the well-being of every individual with parental care and brings all his concerns to a happy ending. On the contrary, the destinies of man are incompatible with a universal principle of benevolence or with—what is to some degree contradictory—a universal principle of justice. Earthquakes, floods and fires do not differentiate between the good and devout man and the sinner and unbeliever. And, even if we leave inanimate nature out of the account and consider the destinies of individual men in so far as they depend on their relations with others of their own kind, it is by no means the rule that virtue is rewarded and wickedness punished, but it happens often enough that the violent, the crafty and the unprincipled seize the desirable goods of the earth for themselves, while the pious go empty away. Dark, unfeeling and unloving powers determine human destiny . . . ' Something about the facts, Freud feels, is brought out by saying not merely that often men do evil things but by saying too that 'dark, unfeeling and unloving powers determine human destiny.' It's preposterous but we know what he means—not clearly, but obscurely. Others have spoken in the same way. St. Paul says, 'that which I do I allow not: for what I would that I do not; but what I hate, that do I.' Euripides makes Helen say to Menelaus:

> . . . And yet how strange it is!
> I ask not thee; I ask my own sad thought,
> What was there in my heart, that I forgot
> My home and land and all I loved, to fly
> With a strange man? Surely it was not I,
> But Cypris there!

He: It's all very well for her to say, 'It was not I.' The fact is she did it.

She: There is evasion in such words as there has been ever since Eve said, 'The serpent beguiled me,' ever since Adam said, 'The woman that thou gavest me she gave me of the tree.' There is an evasion and confusion and inappropriate humility perhaps in one who says, 'Yet not I but the grace of God that dwelleth in me.' And yet is it all evasion and confusion? Is it for nothing that we speak of someone as not having been himself, as never having been able to be himself. We speak of compulsive acts, compulsive thought, of having been possessed. Possessed by what? A demon evil or good or both good and evil. And why do we speak so? Because we come on something done by Dr. Jekyll which is out of order, out of character, inexplicable, if it was Dr. Jekyll who was in control. It is in an effort to understand, to bring order into the apparently chaotic, that we find ourselves saying preposterously, 'It wasn't really Dr. Jekyll, it was Mr. Hyde—or the Devil himself.'

He: But there is no need to speak of the Devil here. It is just that there was more in Dr. Jekyll than appeared.

She: Not just that. There was more than there appeared in the man who called about the gas meter and left with the pearls. But that's different. *We* were taken aback when we found he'd gone with the pearls, but *he* wasn't. It was all in order as far as he was concerned. But in those cases of multiple personality, for example in that case Dr. Morton Prince studied, the one personality, Miss Beauchamp, was horrified to learn of the lies which Sally, the other personality, told. Miss Beauchamp couldn't have told such lies and still be Miss Beauchamp.

He: Yes, but Sally was just a part of Miss Beauchamp's unconscious. There were in her desires and thought which she didn't allow, as St. Paul says, which she didn't know, to translate St. Paul's Greek still more literally.

She: I am not denying that we can explain the seemingly inexplicable and grasp the order in what seems like chaos with the help of the conceptions of the unconscious, of the Super-ego, of the id, of internal objects, of ghosts that are gone whenever we turn to see them, of currents hidden in the depths of the soul. But if the logic of God and of the Devil is more eccentric than it seems so also is the logic of the Super-Ego and the Id and the Unconscious. Indeed what makes us speak of the unconscious and the good and the evil in it, the wine of life and the poison of death so mixed, is closely connected with what makes us speak of a hidden power for good—God—and a hidden power for evil—the Devil. For when we speak of the thoughts and acts of Mr. So-and-So as 'coming out of his unconscious' we are often inclined to say that they are not altogether his, that he is compelled, driven, helped, possessed by something not himself. When we recognize the unconscious in the soul we no longer find adequate the model of objects with definite shapes, and we begin to think of the soul as the energy continually flowing and transformed. For example Natasha in *War and Peace* though she loves Prince André Bolkonsky is fascinated by Prince Kouragine. His fast horses stand at the gate and it is nothing in her that prevents her flying with him. It was after Bolkonsky had heard of all this that his friend Peter Bezukov visited him and told him that Natasha was very ill. Bolkonsky replied that he was sorry to hear of her illness and—Tolstoy says—an evil smile like his father's curled his pinched lips. He said, 'Then Prince Kouragine did not after all consent to give her his hand.' Peter replied, 'He could not—he is already married.' Prince André laughed evilly—again reminding one of his father.

Here I feel the presence of evil, evil that has flowed from the father to the son. Anger against Natasha was justified if you like. But that's not what I am now thinking about. Whether anger was or was not justified—in that laugh we feel evil, an evil that we can't place altogether in Prince André. We feel inclined to trace it also to his father. But then when we come to the father it doesn't seem to lie altogether in him either. He was the man who a little before he died accused the daughter who loved him of 'endless imaginary crimes, loaded her with the bitterest reproaches, accused her of having poisoned his existence . . . dismissed her from his presence, saying she might do whatever she pleased, that he should have nothing more to say to her, and that he never would set eyes on her again.' And this was only the climax of what had gone on for years. This wasn't out of character. Or *was* it? For later he is dying. He makes a desperate effort to speak. 'I'm always thinking of you' he says, and as she bows her head to hide her tears he strokes her hair and says, 'I called you all night.' 'If I had but known,' she says. Dark, unfeeling, and unloving powers determine human destiny.

Or is this going too far? Is it evil and unloving power only that determines human destiny and directs the course of nature? Or is there also at work a good and loving power? It has been said that once at least a higher gift than grace did flesh and blood refine, God's essence and his very self—in the body of Jesus. Whether this statement is true or false is not now the point but whether it's so obscure as to be senseless. Obscure undoubtedly it is but senseless it is not, beyond the scope of reason it is not. For to say that in Nero God was incarnate is not to utter a senseless string of words nor merely to express a surprising sentiment; it is to make a statement which is absurd because it is against all reason. If I say of a cat, 'This cat is an abracadabra' I utter a senseless string of words, I don't make a statement at all and therefore don't make an absurd statement. But if I say of a cat which is plainly dead, 'In this cat there is life' I make a statement which is absurd because it is against all reason. The cat is not hunting, eating, sleeping, breathing; it is stiff and cold. In the same way the words, 'In Nero God was incarnate' are not without any meaning; one who utters them makes a statement, he makes a statement which is absurd and *against* all reason and therefore *not* beyond the scope of reason. Now if a statement is not beyond the scope of reason then any logically parallel statement is also not beyond the scope of reason. For example, the statement, 'Your house is well designed' is not beyond the scope of reason. It may be obviously true or absurdly false or obviously neither true nor false, but it's not beyond the scope of reason. The statement, 'My house is well designed' is logically parallel to the statement, 'Your house is well designed.' The statement, 'My house is well designed' may be absurdly false or neither true nor false or obviously true. But like the parallel statement about your house it is not beyond the scope of reason. The statement 'In Jesus God was incarnate' is logically parallel to 'In Nero God was incarnate.' The latter we noticed is not beyond the scope of reason. Therefore the statement 'In Jesus God was incarnate' is not beyond the scope of reason.

And we may come at the same result more directly. Consider the words 'Was there someone, Jesus, in whom God was incarnate?' These words call first for investigation. Was there such a person as Jesus is alleged to have been? Was there someone born of a virgin? Was there someone who rose from the dead? Was there someone who said all or some or most of the things Jesus is alleged to have said? Did someone speak as this man is said to have spoken? These things settled, we have only started. How far does the rest of experience show that what this man said was true? Did what Jesus said reveal what we hadn't known or what we had known but hadn't recognized? Was there someone, Jesus, who was God incarnate? The question calls for investigation but it also calls like every other question for thought, reflection, reason. He made himself the Son of God. 'Preposterous presumption' the priests said, but was it the truth? The facts agreed upon, still a question is before the bar of reason as when, the facts agreed upon, still a question comes before a court. 'Was there negligence or was there not?' To such a question maybe the answer is 'Yes,' maybe the answer is 'No,' maybe the answer is neither 'Yes' nor 'No.' But the question is not beyond the scope of reason. On the contrary it calls for very careful consideration and not the less when what's relevant is conflicting and not the less because what's relevant is not enumerable because there's not a separate name for every relevant feature of the case and an index to measure its weight. In a cat crouched to spring burns the flame of life. There are signs we can mention—nothing moves but, very slightly, the tail and there's something about the eyes but what? She springs. Still the proof of life eludes language but it's there, was there, and will be there, in the moving picture before us. Was Jesus God incarnate? The law in this matter is not as simple nor as definite nor as fully written out in statutes as we might wish it could be. The question is large, slippery, subtle. But it is not true that nothing is more relevant to it than another, so that nothing supports one answer more than it supports the other. On the contrary every incident in the life of Christ is relevant to this question as every incident in the life of Nero is relevant to the same question about him. To both much more is relevant. For an affirmative answer to either implies the existence of God. And to this question every incident in the history of the world is relevant—whether it is the fall of a sparrow or the coming to harvest, the passing of an empire or the fading of a smile.

Here ends this talk about how in the end questions about God and the Devil are to be answered.

The statement 'There is someone who feeds the cattle upon a thousand hills, who can match the powers of evil and lift up the everlasting doors' is not one to which what is still hidden from us in space and time is all irrelevant. But it seems to me it is not only this that makes the question, 'Is the statement true?' a hard one. It is also the fact that this question calls upon us to consider all that is already before us, in case it should happen that having eyes we see not, and having ears we hear not.

The consideration this question calls for cannot be conducted by a definite step by step procedure like that of one who calculates the height or weight or prospects of life of the average man or the Bengal tiger. Nor is it a question which though it has no answer 'Yes' or 'No' may yet be considered on perfectly conventional lines like the question before the court 'Was there or was there not neglect of duty?' For the statement 'There is one above who gives order and life amongst disorder and death' when taken on perfectly conventional lines is as preposterous as the statement that the sun doesn't move though we see it climb the sky. Nor are the new lines on which the statement is to be taken firmly fixed as they are with 'We are turning to the sun at n m.p.h.' And yet in spite of all this and whatever the answer may be the old questions 'Does God exist?' 'Does the Devil exist? aren't senseless, aren't beyond the scope of thought and reason. On the contrary they call for new awareness of what has so long been about us, in case knowing nature so well we never know her.

Nothing in all this makes less of the call for critical attention, whatever sort of statement we are considering. Nothing in all this makes less of the need to get clear about what we mean by a statement, to get clear as to what we are comparing with what. Just this is called for, just this done, in that statement so obvious yet so preposterous, 'My dear, it's the Taj Mahal.'

○ ○ ○ *37*

Are Religious Statements Meaningful?
E. D. Klemke

DURING THE PAST twenty or so years, there has taken place, in philosophical circles, a severe questioning of the meaningfulness of religious statements. The philosophical position known as logical positivism, or as some now prefer, logical empiricism, achieved notorious fame by its thesis: Religious statements (along with metaphysical, ethical, and aesthetic propositions) are meaningless.[1] It has been profoundly shocking to me to note that theologians (with few exceptions, primarily in England) have almost completely ignored this discussion. And, I truly believe, at their peril. For, whether or not the discussion has yielded an adequate solution of the problems, it has not been irrelevant. On the contrary, it has extreme relevance for the theologian or the philosopher of religion. And I do not see how a serious attempt at theology, or philosophy of religion, can fail to take cognizance of the philosophical controversy. I say this even though I am fully aware that the movement is not quite as vigorous as it once was[2] and that it has been somewhat superseded (in England, at least) by what is loosely referred to as Oxford analysis.[3] The latter, in my opinion, often obscures many issues, instead of clarifying them. I shall not, however, attempt to demonstrate that here.[4]

My topic, then, is the status of religious statements. Are they meaningful or not? Why? Or, since there is not merely one kind, which of them are meaningful and which (if any) meaningless? My "program" is as follows: In Section I, I shall schematically classify the various types of religious statements, or sentences which purport to be statements, in contrast with sentences which, clearly, are not statements. As we shall see, of

---

[1] The reader who is unacquainted with this philosophical "movement" will find an especially vivid (though not necessarily the most capable) summary in A. J. Ayer, *Language, Truth, and Logic* (2d ed.; New York: Dover, 1946). See also Feigl and Sellars, *Readings in Philosophical Analysis* (New York: Appleton-Century-Crofts, 1949); or Richard von Mises, *Positivism* (Cambridge: Harvard University Press, 1951.) [See my last footnote.]—E.D.K.

[2] It is, nevertheless, still alive, in spite of the protests of its adversaries. For a more popular presentation, with excellent bibliographies at the end of each chapter, see John Hospers, *An Introduction to Philosophical Analysis* (New York: Prentice-Hall, Inc., 1953). —E.D.K.

[3] See, e.g., John Urmson, *Philosophical Analysis* (London: Oxford University Press, 1956), Part III. A more popular treatment is given in Ryle *et al.*, *The Revolution in Philosophy* (London: Macmillan & Co., Ltd., 1957). See also A. G. N. Flew (ed.), *Logic and Language* ("First and Second Series" [Oxford: Basil Blackwell, 1955]); Flew (ed.), *Essays in Conceptual Analysis* (London: Macmillan & Co., Ltd., 1956). The "sacred book" of the movement is Ludwig Wittgenstein, *Philosophical Investigations* (Oxford: Basil Blackwell, 1953).—E.D.K.

[4] An excellent critique may be found in Gustav Bergmann, "The Revolt against Logical Atomism," *Philosophical Quarterly*, Vol. VII, No. 29; Vol. VIII, No. 30. An even better one may be found in Arthur Pap, *Semantics and Necessary Truth* (New Haven: Yale University Press, 1958), Part Two.—E.D.K.

those sentences which purport to be statements, some among them are problematical and peculiar. The problem of meaningfulness arises in connection with these. In Section II, I shall state the views of philosophical analysts who have maintained that these problematical sentences are meaningless, and I shall attempt to show why the conclusion was reached. (I shall here ignore the refinements which individual philosophers have made on this doctrine, as they are not important for our purposes.) Before turning to an attempted resolution of the problem (or, if you will, an "answer" to the analysts), I shall, in Section III, present R. G. Collingwood's doctrine of absolute presuppositions. Finally, in Section IV, I shall use Collingwood's doctrine, though not his specific views concerning it, to suggest a possible answer as to the status of religious assertions of the problematical type.

First, some definitions are needed. By "religious sentences" I mean: (*a*) sentences which are found within the Christian faith (omitting from consideration here other religions); (*b*) *all kinds* of such sentences, not merely those which refer to the deity or those which are creedal utterances, etc. By "statement" I mean an indicative sentence which expresses an assertion, which is intended to be literally interpreted, and which may be appropriately labeled either "true" or "false." By "apparent statement" I mean an indicative sentence which obviously has poetical, rather than literal, intent. By "non-statement" I mean a sentence or phrase which expresses an ejaculation, exhortation, etc. I add to these, in a tenuous position, another category, "pseudo-statement," which I shall define in the sequel. In my initial discussion pseudo-statements will be included within the class of statements. But, as we shall see, I believe that they must form a separate class, since they lack the characteristics which actual statements possess.

By a "literal" statement I mean one which is either: (*a*) a logical truth (and, thus, analytic or tautological) or (*b*) an empirical assertion which is capable of verification in the broad sense. By "verification in the broad sense" I mean the finding of some actual or possible state of affairs which will confirm or disconfirm the statement. I shall elaborate these points in later parts of the paper.

So much for preliminaries. I turn now to a rough schematic classification of the various kinds of religious sentences. Whether or not my specific classification is complete is beside the point. For whatever scheme is used, certain sentences will still be peculiar. And here is where the problem of meaningfulness arises.

· I ·

1. There are, of course, many kinds of religious sentences which are *nonstatements*. Some of these are: (*A*) Commands or exhortations: "Thou shalt not take the name of the Lord thy God in vain" or "Love one another." (*B*) Prayers: "Lord, have mercy unto me." (*C*) Blessings: "Grace to you and peace from God our Father and the Lord Jesus Christ." (*D*) Questions: "Whence cometh my help?" (*E*) Ejaculations: "Woe is me, wretched man that I am!" etc.

Since none of the above utterances (and others like them) are statements, as no assertions are made in them, it would be inappropriate to apply tests for truth or falsity, or to attempt verification of them. We may, therefore, pass by them.

2. Many religious sentences *seem* to be statements but are only *apparent statements*. Some examples are: "The Lord is my shepherd" or "Faith moves mountains." I presume that I do not have to argue the case. I believe that most religious persons would

deny that these sentences are to be literally interpreted. Sentences of this type seem to assert something, yet not in the same sense in which "Jones is my auto mechanic" or "The Smith Company moves houses" do. In seeking to understand sentences of the above sort, we realize that we must not be too literal, that these are figurative expressions, etc. For example, faith has never been known to move structures such as Mount Everest, but "genuine" faith has been known (it is often said) to perform wonders somewhat similar. Perhaps, indeed, it moves psychical or "spiritual" mountains. And so on, with respect to other apparent statements.

3. I turn now to the class of (actual) *statements.* I distinguish at least five types of religious sentences which *have been held* to be actual statements. As I have already indicated, sentences of the fifth type are problematic.

(1) Many religious statements are *descriptions.* There are, e.g., statements which describe the actions, character, or beliefs of certain religious individuals or groups. Some instances are: "Many Christians pray," or "X believes the assertions of the Apostles' Creed," etc. As no particular problems arise in connection which such statements, I move on to the next.

(2) Certain religious statements may be called *explanations.* Some examples are: "The lack of rain in X is due to the people's sinfulness" (where X is a specified region or country); or "Britain's military failure of 1916 occurred because farmers planted potatoes on Sunday,"[5] etc. Undoubtedly, assertions of this crude kind are seldom made today by sophisticated Christians. However, statements of this *sort* are often encountered. It is possible to test these explanatory hypotheses for validity. Sufficient tests might lead one to believe that there is or is not a connection between, say, the people's sinfulness and rainfall, or between Sunday planting and military failures. To be sure, we may not obtain certainty. This, however, is not the point. As Hume (and others) have emphasized, matter-of-fact statements are never certain.

(3) Some religious statements are *historical statements.* We might (roughly) divide them into two (or more) groups. (*a*) Some historical statements cause no further problems with respect to verification than those which are found in the case of non-religious historical assertions. Instances of these might be: "Jesus was born in Bethlehem," "The apostle Paul was imprisoned," etc. Admittedly, the evidence is scanty. But so is it, in a sense, with respect to judgments about, say, Socrates. And, of course, statements of this kind are also only probable. But, at least, one would know what to look for as evidence by which to assess some "degree" of probability. (*b*) Other historical statements (within Christianity) are more difficult to confirm. Examples are: "Jesus healed paralytics instantaneously," or "Jesus arose from the dead," etc. Perhaps, *in practice,* such sentences cannot be verified. But they are certainly not unverifiable *in principle.* Again, one would know what to look for if one had been there at the time of the supposed resurrection, or the healings. (I pass over the spiritual interpretation of the resurrection.)

(4) Certain religious statements might be called "*autobiographical statements,*" or, perhaps, "testimonies." Examples of these are: "I am persuaded that nothing can separate us from the love of Christ," or "I am convinced that Christ died for me," etc. Sentences of this kind are somewhat similar to both historical statements and

---

[5] Bertrand Russell, *Unpopular Essays* (New York: Simon & Schuster, 1950), p. 75.—E.D.K.

descriptions. But they are more limited than either of those kinds of statements are. They characterize certain attitudes, passions, concerns, and convictions of various individuals. They are not "emotive" utterances, however, since it is possible to confirm the statements. One could find some state of affairs in the world, e.g., the asserter's beliefs or actions, which provides confirmation of the statements.

(5) I turn, finally, to the last type of religious sentences which have, traditionally, been held to be statements. Our main problem arises in connection with these. Perhaps some examples will reveal the difficulty: "God exists," "God created the world," "God is triune," "Jesus is the Son of God" (or "Jesus is divine"), "God loves us," "God has given men free will," "The Holy Spirit descended upon them," "There is a life after the death of the body," etc.

Sentences such as these purport to be statements. Most religious people who utter such sentences would believe them not to be disguised exhortations, ejaculations, etc. Nor would they be content to say that they are only apparent statements. (Some religious people, of course, would.) And, since they are not descriptive, explanatory, historical, or autobiographical statements, they must form a separate class by themselves. What should they be called? Let us withhold a label for the time being.

More important than a name is the status which such sentences possess. Surely sentences of type (5) are not statements, according to the criteria to which all other statements are subjected. Consider: Actual statements, remember, are those which are confirmable (or disconfirmable) by some state of affairs which warrants the truth (or falsity) of the statements. Sentences of type (5) are not so confirmable—or, even, disconfirmable (as will be shown in Section II). Thus, if they are held to be actual statements, then "statement" will mean something different, in this case, from what it normally does. Hence one is faced with a decision. Either: (*a*) the sentences in (5) are not statements; or (*b*) our usual definition of "statement" is not correct. The religious man hesitates to assert (*a*). Yet, if (*b*) is espoused, then "statement" will now have two meanings: (i) a normal one which has been given clarity, consistency, and adequacy by the tools of logical and philosophical analysis; and (ii) a peculiar religious meaning which denies the characterizations possessed by the usual one. But if one must resort to this maneuver, then some sentences will be statements by the religious criterion but (at the same time) nonstatements by the normal criterion. But, now, what sense does it make to still use the word "statement" for such sentences? Are we not "trying to have our cake and eat it too"?

· II ·

A view which has gained rather wide acceptance in recent years among philosophical analysts runs as follows:

(*A*) Sentences of type (5) are not confirmable.

    (1) Rational demonstration does not prove them.

    (2) Religious experience does not confirm them.

    (3) They are unverifiable in principle.

(*B*) Sentences of type (5) are not falsifiable.

(*C*) The resort to revelation, faith, etc., fails to provide a third alternative.

Hence: Since only verifiable (or falsifiable) sentences are meaningful, sentences of
type (5) are cognitively meaningless.[6]

The view deserves a fair run for its money. I shall act as its advocate, by giving content
to the above structure. The philosophical analyst argues as follows:

(*A*) Sentences of type (5) are not confirmable. Take the sentence "God exists."
(That is, he exists actually, and not merely for thought.) Obviously, as far as grammar
is concerned, this is a proper statement. However, grammar is not the only criterion
by which to judge whether or not a sentence is meaningful. "Happiness travels at the
speed of 60 miles per hour," is grammatically proper. Yet it has no clear meaning. In
a similar way, it is appropriate to ask whether "God exists" has any meaning. And, of
course, if it is the case that "God exists" is meaningless, then "God does not exist" is
equally meaningless—as Ayer has shown.[7] One cannot, therefore, escape the problem
by professing atheism, for, if the affirmation of a sentence is absurd, then the denial is
equally absurd.

(1) Rational demonstration does not prove sentences of type (5) to be true.
Sufficient labors have been spent upon the traditional arguments for the existence of
God to show that they are not valid. Even theologians and philosophers of religion
have admitted this.[8] A few fallacies in reasoning might be mentioned. The sentence
"God exists" is held, in the ontological argument and in variants of the cosmological
argument, to be logically necessary; but no existential proposition can be logically
necessary. And the argument from analogy, which occurs in the teleological argument,
is shaky, since arguments from analogy never bridge the leap from the finite evidence
to the infinite existent.

One might object that although these particular arguments, and all variants of
them, are invalid, the conclusion may, nevertheless, be true. Very well, what other
means shall we attempt in order to discover whether or not "God exists" is true?

(2) Let us try the religious experience claim. Some religious people profess to
have knowledge of the existence of God upon the basis of direct experience of God.
They say that our knowledge of God rests upon the revelation of his personal presence,
or that our knowledge of God comes through a direct, personal encounter or confrontation with him. It must be noticed that people who talk this way do not simply
assert that they had an unusual experience. They claim to have had an experience of *God*.

But this procedure is incapable of establishing what it hopes to establish. Just as
the assertion that God exists cannot be shown to be warrantable by means of rational
demonstration, so it cannot be shown to be warrantable by the religious experience
claim. For all that the sentence "I have had an experience of God" can certify is that
I have had certain feelings, sensations, etc. It cannot confirm the further assertion that
God exists. The method of religious experience can, thus, give one a feeling or "inner
assurance" that God exists or may exist, but it cannot confirm that God does, in fact,

---

[6] This position is discussed in Ayer's book (see footnote 1). Many contributors to a recent volume of
essays also argue for it. See A. Flew and A. Macintyre (eds.), *New Essays in Philosophical Theology* (New
York: Macmillan Co., 1955).—E.D.K.

[7] Ayer, *op. cit.*, chap. vi. —E.D.K.

[8] I shall not rehash old arguments. If the reader is unconvinced, I refer him to H. J. Paton, *The Modern
Predicament* (New York: Macmillan Co., 1955), chaps. xii-xiv.—E.D.K.

exist. In order for the assertion "God exists" to be warrantable, it would have to be intersubjectively testable. Yet the possibility of such testability is precisely what proponents of the religious experience claim deny. They maintain that the way of knowing God through religious experience is unique. They say that one cannot know what the experience of God is until one has had it. And apparently only a few are privileged to have it.

Thus, the religious experience method never answers the question: "How can you know when anyone has had an experience of God?" There are certain tests by which I can know, with a high degree of probability, as to whether or not I have had, say, an experience of flying in an airplane. But what tests can be devised by which I can know whether or not I have had an experience of God? The proponents of the religious-experience claim are silent here. In place of tests they posit the notion of an "immediacy" of knowledge which is supposed to carry its own guaranty of confirmation. But, surely, many people who claim to have had genuine experiences of something or other have been wrong! Therefore, the religious-experience method cannot confirm the assertion, "I have had direct experiences of God, and God exists." The most which it can confirm is the assertion, "I have had some kind of peculiar experience, by which it seems to me that God exists," and this is something very different from the first sentence.

Other methods which have been used in the attempt to confirm the sentence "God exists" (the moral arguments, etc.) bring us no nearer to a satisfactory conclusion. Our purpose here is not to give an exhaustive treatment of the alternatives with respect to the single sentence "God exists" but to indicate the kinds of problems which one encounters with sentences of type (5). It may be objected that we have unfairly selected the most difficult sentence of this group. However, the other sentences of this type presuppose the sentence "God exists" and would be meaningless if this one were no statement at all. In fact, many of the others include the assertion of God's existence when attributing qualities or actions to God. Thus, in actual practice, religious people think of the sentence "God loves us" as expressing both "God exists" and "He loves us." Hence the problems reappear.

(3) The primary difficulty with sentences of type (5) arises not merely because such assertions are unverifiable *in practice*; rather, it lies in the fact that such sentences are not even verifiable *in principle*. There is no conceivable way by which one could test such sentences. If a sentence refers to God, e.g., we not only face the problem that we cannot find some actual state of affairs by which to confirm it. We are further handicapped by the fact that we could not conceive of any possible method of verification. To take an example now famous in philosophical literature, the sentence "There are mountains on the other side of the moon" is, at present, unverifiable in practice. *Yet, if we could some day reach the moon and survive*, we would, at least, know what to look for in order to confirm the sentence. It is, thus, verifiable in principle, though not in practice. The theological sentences which we have been considering are not only unverifiable in practice but also in principle. One cannot imagine any conceivable state of affairs by which to confirm such sentences.

(B) Thus far, we have primarily dealt with the question: What state of affairs would one have to find in order to *confirm* such sentences as "God exists," etc.? We found that such sentences are incapable of verification (or confirmation). Let us, now, ask the question with respect to *falsification*. That is: What state of affairs would one have to find which would constitute a falsification of such sentences as "God exists"?

In other words, what events would have to occur in order to be a sufficient reason for stating "There is no God" or "God does not love us," etc.?

Antony Flew has discussed this problem with respect to the sentence, "God loves us as a father loves his children."[9] Many religious people hold this sentence to be true. But suppose that we see a child dying of cancer. His earthly father is greatly concerned and expresses his love for the child by attempting every possible method of providing help for him. But God, the "heavenly Father," shows no apparent sign of concern. At this point, religious people often qualify the assertion by adding, "Well, God's love is not a merely human love," or "God's ways, including his way of loving, are inscrutable." Thus, the severe sufferings of the child are held to be compatible with the assertion that "God loves us as a father loves his children"—plus the qualifications. But if the sentence must be qualified—"God's love is different; he has reasons we know not of," etc.—why maintain it? What is this affirmation of God's love worth if it must be so qualified as to mean something different from the original sentence? What would have to happen in order to persuade and entitle us to say "God does *not* love us?" What state of affairs would have to occur in order to constitute a falsification of the assertion that God loves us? Religious people maintain that no conceivable experience could falsify sentences of this sort.

Thus we are left with the peculiar situation whereby *all* states of affairs are held to be commensurate with an assertion such as "God loves us as a father loves his children," and similar assertions. To a neutral observer, certain states of affairs would seem to show that God loves us, while others would indicate that he does not love us. To the religious person, however, there is no conceivable state of affairs which would be a demonstration that God does not love us. Even innocent children, dying in agony, are held to be no falsification of the sentence "God loves us." But if *every* state of affairs is compatible with the sentence "God loves us," then no falsification is possible. And if no falsification is possible, then the sentence seems to have no straightforward meaning, and is, hence, cognitively meaningless.

Thus, whether we attempt to verify or falsify a sentence of type (5), we note that there are no criteria which are acceptable. It would seem therefore, that such sentences are cognitively meaningless. One need not thereby deny that such assertions may possess some other status. They may, for example, be expressive of certain emotions, feelings, and attitudes which are felt by the one who utters them, and which, perhaps, evoke similar emotions and attitudes in others.

(*C*) There have been various attempts to completely escape the predicament in which we find ourselves. These, too, have failed. Some, e.g., have said that sentences of type (5) are known to be true by revelation. They are "revealed truths," rather than natural truths, and, therefore, not subject to verification. But this is a fruitless effort. For sophisticated religious people deny that any propositions are presented in revelation, and naïve religious people must posit the notion of inspiration by which to give the revealed propositions the status of truth, forgetting that the notion of inspiration itself is impossible of verification.

Other religious people suggest still another alternative. They maintain that there are "truths of faith" as over against "truths of reason." In this view it is appropriate to seek verification of sentences which fall into the "reason" category, but it is

---

[9] Flew and Macintyre, *op.cit.*, pp. 98-99.—E.D.K.

inappropriate to seek verification of those which are in the "faith" group. The meaning of faith, they tell us, is to believe where no proof is possible. Yet beliefs are often notoriously incredible, as well as incompatible at times. Apparently some religious people once believed that Joshua commanded the moon to stand still, or that the bodies of the saints were raised after Jesus' death and appeared to many people. Where is one to draw the line as to what may or may not be believed? How can one know that the belief that God created the world is any more true than the belief that Jesus spoke to demons, and was answered? Furthermore, various religions seem to hold incompatible views with respect to the nature or activity of the deity. What certifies the Christian view, or particular opinions within the Christian view?

In conclusion, it may be affirmed that religious statements of the first four types are meaningful. But religious sentences of type (5) are meaningless.

Thus runs the argument against permitting the status of statements to religious sentences of the fifth type. Can we "save" such sentences from the onslaught? Before answering the question, I would like to turn, briefly, to some interesting insights of R. G. Collingwood, which may reveal a possible path toward an "answer." In Section III, I shall merely state Collingwood's views. In Section IV, I shall apply one of these doctrines toward a possible solution of our problem.

· III ·

The particular views of Collingwood which are of relevance for the issue at hand are found in *An Essay on Metaphysics*.[10] The opening pages of the work are devoted to a consideration of Aristotle's metaphysics, in which Collingwood finds three definitions of metaphysics: (i) Metaphysics is the science of pure being. (ii) Metaphysics is the science of the highest being. (iii) Metaphysics is the science which deals with the presuppositions underlying ordinary science. Collingwood argues that the first of these definitions cannot be true, as a science of pure being is a contradiction in terms. He dismisses the second definition. He affirms the third as being the proper one, and his book is an effort to explain its meaning.[11] As distinct from metaphysics, the science of pure being—or attempts at it—may be called ontology. It does not designate any actual science. It merely refers to the mistakes which people have made. Thus, by rejecting ontology, Collingwood develops a doctrine of "metaphysics without ontology."[12]

Metaphysics, then, is the science which deals with the presuppositions underlying ordinary science, that is, any science other than metaphysics (and in the broad sense of science, i.e., any organized body of knowledge). However, certain presuppositions are of greater interest to the metaphysician than others. These are *absolute*, as distinct from *relative*, presuppositions.

A relative presupposition is one which may stand relatively to one question as its presupposition and relatively to another question as its answer. Collingwood's homely example is that of a man measuring the distance between two points with an old tape. In asking the question, "What is the distance between these two points?" he is making

[10] R. G. Collingwood, *An Essay on Metaphysics* (London: Oxford University Press, 1940).—E.D.K.

[11] *Ibid.*, pp. 11–16—E.D.K.

[12] *Ibid.*, p. 17.—E.D.K.

a presupposition, namely, "My tape is accurate (to a certain degree)." This presupposition is also an answer to another question: "Is my tape accurate?" The answer that the tape is accurate was obtained by checking it with some more reliable measure. Thus relative presuppositions may be verified. Since they are answers to questions, they are also propositions, or statements, as well as presuppositions. Therefore, with respect to them it is appropriate to ask: "Are they true (or false)?"[13]

An absolute presupposition, however, is "one which stands, relatively to all questions to which it is related, as a presupposition, never as an answer."[14] Collingwood's illustration (again a commonsensical one) is as follows. Suppose that one were to talk to a pathologist about a certain disease and were to ask him what is the cause of the event, E, which occurs in this disease. He would answer that the cause of E is C, and he would perhaps recommend some authority on the matter. One finds in the course of the discussion that the pathologist, as well as his authority, assumed that E has a cause before it was known what the cause is. If you then asked him: "Why did you assume that it has a cause?" you would probably be told: "Because everything that happens has a cause." If you then asked how, in turn, *this* is known, you would here encounter one of the pathologist's absolute presuppositions, and you would be told that this is not something which we can prove or verify. We simply have to take it for granted. Thus absolute presuppositions are unverifiable, that is to say, *they are not propositions, or statements.* The distinction between truth and falsity, or verifiability and unverifiability, does not apply to them at all.[15]

Metaphysics, then, is the attempt to find out what *absolute presuppositions* have been held by certain persons or groups of persons on certain occasions and in the course of certain "pieces" of thinking. To ask whether or not absolute presuppositions are true, or upon what evidence they may be accepted, is to engage in pseudo-metaphysics.[16]

Metaphysical questions and presuppositions are, thus, historical questions and presuppositions. The metaphysician merely attempts to state what presuppositions were made by various scientists in various periods of history. And he may attempt to compare presuppositions and inquire as to how certain ones grew out of others as the result of internal strain.[17]

In a section entitled "Examples," Collingwood discusses the absolute presupposition "God exists" as an instance (among others) of the kind of presuppositions which have been held in history. He considers the question with reference to the Christian patristic writers, to whom, Collingwood believes, the existence of God was an absolute presupposition of all the thinking done by reflective Christians, especially that which was done in natural science.[18] Since their affirmation, "God exists," is an absolute presupposition, it follows that it is not a proposition or statement. It is, therefore, neither true nor false. And it can neither be proved nor disproved. It can only be presupposed or believed in.[19]

---

[13] *Ibid.*, pp. 29–30.—E.D.K.

[14] *Ibid.*, p. 31.—E.D.K.

[15] *Ibid.*, pp. 31–32.—E.D.K.

[16] *Ibid.*, p. 47.—E.D.K.

[17] *Ibid.*, pp. 70 ff.—E.D.K.

[18] *Ibid.*, p. 186.—E.D.K.

[19] *Ibid.*, p.188.—E.D.K.

Collingwood then traces the history of this absolute presupposition back to the pre-Christian Greek era and shows how it, along with certain subordinate presuppositions, was held, knowingly or unknowingly, by natural scientists throughout the course of their work.[20] This is an extremely interesting discussion. However, I shall not summarize it because it is, for various reasons, somewhat beside the point for the topic at hand, which is not the relationship of the presupposition of the existence of God to natural science but the significance of this presupposition, and others like it, for theology or philosophy of religion.

So much, then, for Collingwood. I turn, next, to an application of the doctrine of absolute presuppositions to our problem concerning the status of religious sentences of type (5). In so doing, I must make it clear that I am departing from Collingwood's views. This application of the doctrine was apparently never noted by Collingwood. At least he never discussed the matter. Perhaps this is a result of his belief that absolute presuppositions are peculiar to certain historical eras. Thus, he seems to have thought that "God exists" was an absolute presupposition for the few centuries before and after Christ, but not for the present day. My application will also depart from this feature of Collingwood's theory.

· IV ·

At the end of Section II, we were left with the view of the philosophical analyst, according to which sentences of type (5) are meaningless and, hence, not genuine statements. Nor are they apparent statements or non-statements. Rather, they are, in his opinion, nonsense. Our task was to see whether religious sentences of type (5) could be "saved" from this fate.

The solution of the problem which I should like to suggest may now be stated. I must make it clear that I put it forth only as a possible solution. I do not even imply that I agree with it. It runs as follows:

The philosophical analyst is right in one respect. Sentences of type (5) are not statements. Let us, therefore, remove them from their position as a type under group 3 (statements) and give them a separate classification which above I have called pseudo-statements. I believe that the theologian must "yield" at this point. Why? Because I, for one, find the arguments of the analyst (presented in Section II) to be sound. It was there shown that sentences of type (5) cannot be statements by all the ordinary criteria for statements. Why, then, continue the pretense that they, nevertheless, somehow are statements? Intellectual honesty ought to be the rule in theology as well as in other disciplines.

However, the analyst is wrong in another respect. Pseudo-statements are not meaningless. They merely have different criteria for meaningfulness from those of statements. Let me explain. It is true that sentences such as "God exists," "God loves us," etc., are not statements (or propositions). It is, therefore, inappropriate to ask whether they are true or false. It is also inappropriate to seek verification, or falsification, of them. This, as I said, does not destroy their meaningfulness. Such sentences *are* meaningful. But they are meaningful (to use Collingwood's term) as *absolute presuppositions*, and not as statements. This is the important point.

---

[20] *Ibid.*, pp. 213–27.—E.D.K.

In other words, the existence of God, God's love for man, God's activity in Christ, etc., might be construed as presuppositions (and absolute ones) of all the thinking that is done by Christians not only in natural science but in ethics, theology, and other areas of thought. They are also presuppositions (if one may extend the term) of a certain mode of existence, one which can be characterized and structured by thought. This mode of existence, or way of life, has been called "salvation" or "the new birth."

Now, if we agree with Collingwood that the task of the metaphysician is to discover what absolute presuppositions are, or have been, held and to state them, what is the theologian's task—to explain them, to prove them to be true, to give reasons for them? Obviously not, if it is held that such assertions are absolute presuppositions and not statements. The theologian must, therefore, not yield to the temptation to become apologetic for the absolute presuppositions. He will accept them as sentences which are not to be proved but merely to be supposed or believed in.

Well, then, what is left for the theologian to do? Have we disenfranchised him? On the contrary, he has an important task but from a somewhat different focus. He will expound, not a theology, but an "anthropology."

Perhaps an illustration is in order. Take the sentence, "Jesus is God and man" (or "Jesus is the Son of God," "Jesus is divine," etc.). Even theologians who have denied that this sentence (or some variant) could be "proved" (whatever that would be) have, nevertheless, thought that one could give rational grounds for the belief that Jesus is divine. They did this by the categories of ontology and with the notion of second person of the Trinity, e.g. Thus the language of *Logos, homoousios*, etc. the categories were not only ontological but supernatural. Thus the two natures doctrine of the creedal formulation.

This attempt served a purpose. To continue it in our day is, in my opinion, utterly fruitless. Hence the theologian (or philosopher of religion) who wishes to preserve the meaningfulness of the sentence "Jesus is God" (or some variant) must take another approach. One of the alternatives is: to consider such sentences as being absolute presuppositions, not statements or propositions. But if this path is followed, then the theologian will not ask: Is it *true* that Jesus is God? How may we find some rational grounds for asserting that sentence to be true? etc. Rather, he will ask: What results from our presupposing that Jesus is God? And have we any means of affirming him as such without the use of supernatural or ontological categories?

It is conceivable that an affirmative answer can be given to the latter question. The task may be achieved if the theologian is content to describe and discuss that which is within experience, rather than beyond it; that which is "natural" rather than "supernatural"; that which is commonsensical rather than ontological; that which may be formulated in statements rather than uttered in perplexing pseudo-statements. He will refrain from asserting problematic sentences of type (5), which, nevertheless, continue to be *held* by him as absolute presuppositions. But his own assertions are not presuppositions. They are, rather, statements. And statements deal with very ordinary and commonsensical matters, such as the mode of existence in which one lives and the concerns and interests of men. Hence no ontological categories are found in the theologian's language. And he will not expound *doctrines* of the Trinity, Incarnation, etc.

This might be put in another way. The theologian will describe the order of possibility and the order of historical being but not the order of ontological objects.

Let me elucidate. I find Kierkegaard to be of help at this point.[21] A *possible* (or possibility), according to Kierkegaard, is that about which one can have meaningful discourse. Such discourse will be in the form of statements which describe or explicate the possible. A possible, hence, is anything which can be reflected about, anything concerning which one can utter significant propositions. Some possibles elicit interest, concern, and passion. These may be called ethical or behavioral possibles. Now behavioral possibles are never exclusive for one's *thought*. They form a plurality. And one can think and elucidate many possible modes of existence, and all with equal rational plausibility. In thought, one can never reduce the multiplicity to a unity. One can never find only one to be true or right and the others false or wrong. Rather, the greater one's intelligence is, the more possibles one can find, or the more plausibility can be given to those which one has already conceived. However, when one seeks to actualize a possible in one's *existence*, he finds that they are exclusive. One can maximally actualize only one at a time.[22]

How does this apply to such sentences as "Jesus is God" and to the task of the theologian? Christ can be (and was, by Kierkegaard) construed as a kind of possibility. He can be conceived as one who presents a challenge (an existential challenge, if you please) to all men. Because of his life, death, teaching, etc., he commands attention. And having heard of him, many men are influenced to re-examine their lives and some to shift their interests, concerns, and enthusiasms from themselves to him. Christ, himself, actualized a certain mode of existence. The mode which he realized is present to all men as a possibility. For those who choose to actualize it, Christ "becomes" God. I use quotes around "becomes" intentionally. What I mean is: those who actualize the possibility believe him to be God, i.e., believe him to be that which can fully control and captivate one's interests. For those who actualize the possibility, the divinity of Christ is their absolute presupposition. Is he God independently of their supposing him to be so? Who knows? Not only can one not answer the question, but the asking of it is inappropriate. All one can say is that one's supposing him to be God makes him God for one's self. Whether or not he *is* God ("from all eternity") one cannot know, and does not ask.

Hence the discourse of the theologian will include historical statements. These will be, for example, about a man, Jesus, who lived, taught, etc., nearly 2,000 years ago. These are neutral statements which can be believed by religious and non-religious men alike. And, of course, they are only probable, as are *all* historical statements. As I already mentioned, the theologian's discourse will not include ontological assertions, such as sentences of type (5). These are merely supposed or believed in. The theologian's discourse will also include testimonies. He will discuss the transformation of personality which resulted when he and/or others exchanged one passionate interest (in his own existence) for another (an interest in Christ's existence). He will elucidate

---

[21] S. Kierkegaard, *Concluding Unscientific Postscript*, trans. D. F. Swenson and W. Lowrie (Princeton, N.J.: Princeton University Press, 1944), pp. 267 ff. See also Paul L. Holmer, "Philosophical Criticism and Christology," *Journal of Religion*, XXXIV (1954), 88–100. Professor Holmer arrives at conclusions similar to those presented here. However, he leaves the status of sentences such as "Jesus is divine," etc., in a somewhat vague position. I believe that they can, and ought to, be more adequately characterized, and I *suggest* that they might be held to be absolute presuppositions.—E.D.K.

[22] This paragraph expresses the "heart" of Kierkegaard's doctrine of the Stages.—E.D.K.

how such transfer of interests has made men into "new creatures," how it resynthesized the factors of men's personalities. And the theologian's discourse may include exhortations. He will, perhaps, invite others to accept the mode of existence which Christ presented, not because of a "proof" that Christ is God, but simply because others have found Christ capable of maintaining their maximum enthusiasm and passion and because such interest has brought about a new synthesis of personality, a revitalized mode of existence.

The theologian, then, has a more limited task than he has heretofore had. It is to delineate Christ as a possible—a conceivable mode of existence, one alternative among others. The task of the religious man is to transform the possible from a possibility to an actuality in his own existence. With respect to both the theologian and the "ordinary" man, the question "Is Jesus *really* divine?" etc., does not arise. For both of them, it is an absolute presupposition which stands at the basis of their thinking and their mode of existence. It is significant both for thought and for life.

I have briefly portrayed what might be considered as an alternative way of dealing with religious sentences of type (5)—sentences which I referred to as "pseudo-statements." To those who insist upon the verification of such sentences as a requirement for their meaningfulness, such sentences will remain pseudo-statements, and no more. But to those who adopt the approach which I have suggested, and which comes largely from some insights of Collingwood, with a few hints from Kierkegaard, these sentences might be considered to be absolute presuppositions. Those who find the latter approach attractive will, I think, see that the notion of absolute presuppositions has significant implications with respect to theological assertions. I cannot expand the point any further at this time. I have tried to indicate how the implications of the doctrine might be construed with respect to one absolute presupposition, namely, the divinity of Christ. A similar treatment might be given to other religious presuppositions.

I repeat: In describing the form in which such a view might be developed, I do not imply that I agree with the position. I merely suggest it as a possible alternative.

Lectures on Religious Belief [1]
Ludwig Wittgenstein

· *I* ·

AN AUSTRIAN GENERAL said to someone: "I shall think of you after my death, if that should be possible." We can imagine one group who would find this ludicrous, another who wouldn't.

(During the war, Wittgenstein saw consecrated bread being carried in chromium steel. This struck him as ludicrous.)

Suppose that someone believed in the Last Judgement, and I don't, does this mean that I believe the opposite to him, just that there won't be such a thing? I would say: "not at all, or not always."

Suppose I say that the body will rot, and another says "No. Particles will rejoin in a thousand years, and there will be a Resurrection of you."

If someone said: "Wittgenstein, do you believe in this?" I'd say: "No." "Do you contradict the man?" I'd say: "No."

If you say this, the contradiction already lies in this.

Would you say: "I believe the opposite", or "There is no reason to suppose such a thing"? I'd say neither.

Suppose someone were a believer and said: "I believe in a Last Judgement," and I said: "Well, I'm not so sure. Possibly." You would say that there is an enormous gulf between us. If he said "There is a German aeroplane overhead," and I said "Possibly I'm not so sure," you'd say we were fairly near.

It isn't a question of my being anywhere near him, but on an entirely different plane, which you could express by saying: "You mean something altogether different, Wittgenstein."

The difference might not show up at all in any explanation of the meaning.

Why is it that in this case I seem to be missing the entire point?

Suppose somebody made this guidance for this life: believing in the Last Judgement. Whenever he does anything, this is before his mind. In a way, how are we to know whether to say he believes this will happen or not?

Asking him is not enough. He will probably say he has proof. But he has what you might call an unshakeable belief. It will show, not by reasoning or by appeal to ordinary grounds for belief, but rather by regulating for in all his life.

This is a very much stronger fact—foregoing pleasures, always appealing to this picture. This in one sense must be called the firmest of all beliefs, because the man risks

---

[1] This selection consists of some notes that were taken by some students and University colleagues at Wittgenstein's lectures.—E.D.K.

things on account of it which he would not do on things which are by far better established for him. Although he distinguishes between things well-established and not well-established.

Lewy[2]: Surely, he would say it is extremely well-established.

First, he may use "well-established" or not use it at all. He will treat this belief as extremely well-established, and in another way as not well-established at all.

If we have a belief, in certain cases we appeal again and again to certain grounds, and at the same time we risk pretty little—if it came to risking our lives on the ground of this belief.

There are instances where you have a faith—where you say "I believe"—and on the other hand this belief does not rest on the fact on which our ordinary everyday beliefs normally do rest.

How should we compare beliefs with each other? What would it mean to compare them?

You might say: "We compare the states of mind."

How do we compare states of mind? This obviously won't do for all occasions. First, what you say won't be taken as the measure for the firmness of a belief? But, for instance, what risks you would take?

The strength of a belief is not comparable with the intensity of a pain.

An entirely different way of comparing beliefs is seeing what sorts of grounds he will give.

A belief isn't like a momentary state of mind. "At 5 o'clock he had very bad toothache."

Suppose you had two people, and one of them, when he had to decide which course to take, thought of retribution, and the other did not. One person might, for instance, be inclined to take everything that happened to him as a reward or punishment, and another person doesn't think of this at all.

If he is ill, he may think: "What have I done to deserve this?" This is one way of thinking of retribution. Another way is, he thinks in a general way whenever he is ashamed of himself: "This will be punished."

Take two people, one of whom talks of his behaviour and of what happens to him in terms of retribution, the other one does not. These people think entirely differently. Yet, so far, you can't say they believe different things.

Suppose someone is ill and he says: "This is a punishment," and I say: "If I'm ill, I don't think of punishment at all." If you say: "Do you believe the opposite?"—you can call it believing the opposite, but it is entirely different from what we would normally call believing the opposite.

I think differently, in a different way. I say different things to myself. I have different pictures.

It is this way: if someone said: "Wittgenstein, you don't take illness as punishment, so what do you believe?"—I'd say: "I don't have any thoughts of punishment."

There are, for instance, these entirely different ways of thinking first of all—which needn't be expressed by one person saying one thing, another person another thing.

What we call believing in a Judgement Day or not believing in a Judgement Day— The expression of belief may play an absolutely minor role.

---

2 A philosopher present at the lectures.—E.D.K.

If you ask me whether or not I believe in a Judgement Day, in the sense in which religious people have belief in it, I wouldn't say: "No. I don't believe there will be such a thing." It would seem to me utterly crazy to say this.

And then I give an explanation: "I don't believe in . . . ", but then the religious person never believes what I describe.

I can't say. I can't contradict that person.

In one sense, I understand all he says—the English words "God," "separate," etc. I understand. I could say: "I don't believe in this," and this would be true, meaning I haven't got these thoughts or anything that hangs together with them. But not that I could contradict the thing.

You might say: "Well, if you can't contradict him, that means you don't understand him. If you did understand him, then you might." That again is Greek to me. My normal technique of language leaves me. I don't know whether to say they understand one another or not.

These controversies look quite different from any normal controversies. Reasons look entirely different from normal reasons.

They are, in a way, quite inconclusive.

The point is that if there were evidence, this would in fact destroy the whole business.

Anything that I normally call evidence wouldn't in the slightest influence me.

Suppose, for instance, we knew people who foresaw the future; make forecasts for years and years ahead; and they described some sort of a Judgement Day. Queerly enough, even if there were such a thing, and even if it were more convincing than I have described but, belief in this happening wouldn't be at all a religious belief.

Suppose that I would have to forego all pleasures because of such a forecast. If I do so and so, someone will put me in fires in a thousand years, etc. I wouldn't budge. The best scientific evidence is just nothing.

A religious belief might in fact fly in the face of such a forecast, and say "No. There it will break down."

As it were, the belief as formulated on the evidence can only be the last result— in which a number of ways of thinking and acting crystallize and come together.

A man would fight for his life not to be dragged into the fire. No induction. Terror. That is, as it were, part of the substance of the belief.

That is partly why you don't get in religious controversies, the form of controversy where one person is *sure* of the thing, and the other says: 'Well, possibly.'

You might be surprised that there hasn't been opposed to those who believe in Resurrection those who say "Well, possibly."

Here believing obviously plays much more this role: suppose we said that a certain picture might play the role of constantly admonishing me, or I always think of it. Here, an enormous difference would be between those people for whom the picture is constantly in the foreground, and the others who just didn't use it at all.

Those who said: "Well, possibly it may happen and possibly not" would be on an entirely different plane.

This is partly why one would be reluctant to say: "These people rigorously hold the opinion (or view) that there is a Last Judgement." "Opinion" sounds queer.

It is for this reason that different words are used: 'dogma,' 'faith.'

We don't talk about hypothesis, or about high probability. Nor about knowing.

In a religious discourse we use such expressions as: "I believe that so and so will happen," and use them differently to the way in which we use them in science.

Although, there is a great temptation to think we do. Because we do talk of evidence, and do talk of evidence by experience.

We could even talk of historic events.

It has been said that Christianity rests on an historic basis.

It has been said a thousand times by intelligent people that indubitability is not enough in this case. Even if there is as much evidence as for Napoleon. Because the indubitability wouldn't be enough to make me change my whole life.

It doesn't rest on an historic basis in the sense that the ordinary belief in historic facts could serve as a foundation.

Here we have a belief in historic facts different from a belief in ordinary historic facts. Even, they are not treated as historical, empirical, propositions.

Those people who had faith didn't apply the doubt which would ordinarily apply to *any* historical propositions. Especially propositions of a time long past, etc.

What is the criterion of reliability, dependability? Suppose you give a general description as to when you say a proposition has a reasonable weight of probability. When you call it reasonable, is this *only* to say that for it you have such and such evidence, and for others you haven't?

For instance, we don't trust the account given of an event by a drunk man.

Father O'Hara[3] is one of those people who make it a question of science.

Here we have people who treat this evidence in a different way. They base things on evidence which taken in one way would seem exceedingly flimsy. They base enormous things on this evidence. Am I to say they are unreasonable? I wouldn't call them unreasonable.

I would say, they are certainly not *reasonable*, that's obvious.

'Unreasonable' implies, with everyone, rebuke.

I want to say: they don't treat this as a matter of reasonability.

Anyone who reads the Epistles will find it said: not only that it is not reasonable, but that it is folly.

Not only is it not reasonable, but it doesn't pretend to be.

What seems to me ludicrous about O'Hara is his making it appear to be *reasonable*.

Why shouldn't one form of life culminate in an utterance of belief in a Last Judgement? But I couldn't either say "Yes" or "No" to the statement that there will be such a thing. Nor "Perhaps," nor "I'm not sure."

It is a statement which may not allow of any such answer.

If Mr. Lewy is religious and says he believes in a Judgement Day, I won't even know whether to say I understand him or not. I've read the same things as he's read. In a most important sense, I know what he means.

If an atheist says: "There won't be a Judgement Day, and another person says there will," do they mean the same?—Not clear what criterion of meaning the same is. They might describe the same things. You might say, this already shows that they mean the same.

---

[3] Contribution to a Symposium on *Science and Religion* (Long: Gerald Howe, 1931, pp. 107–116).—E.D.K.

We come to an island and we find beliefs there, and certain beliefs we are inclined to call religious. What I'm driving at is, that religious beliefs will not . . . They have sentences, and there are also religious statements.

These statements would not just differ in respect to what they are about. Entirely different connections would make them into religious beliefs, and there can easily be imagined transitions where we wouldn't know for our life whether to call them religious beliefs or scientific beliefs.

You may say they reason wrongly.

In certain cases you would say they reason wrongly, meaning they contradict us. In other cases you would say they don't reason at all, or "It is an entirely different kind of reasoning." The first, you would say in the case in which they reason in a similar way to us, and make something corresponding to our blunders.

Whether a thing is a blunder or not—it is a blunder in a particular system. Just as something is a blunder in a particular game and not in another.

You could also say that where we are reasonable, they are not reasonable— meaning they don't use *reason* here.

If they do something very like one of our blunders, I would say, I don't know. It depends on further surroundings of it.

It is difficult to see, in cases in which it has all the appearances of trying to be reasonable.

I would definitely call O'Hara unreasonable. I would say, if this is religious belief, then it's all superstition.

But I would ridicule it, not by saying it is based on insufficient evidence. I would say: here is a man who is cheating himself. You can say: this man is ridiculous because he believes, and bases it on weak reasons.

· II ·

The word 'God' is amongst the earliest learnt—pictures and catechisms, etc. But not the same consequences as with pictures of aunts. I wasn't shown [that which the picture pictured].

The word is used like a word representing a person. God sees, rewards, etc.

"Being shown all these things, did you understand what this word meant?" I'd say: "Yes and no. I did learn what it didn't mean. I made myself understand. I could answer questions, understand questions when they were put in different ways—and in that sense could be said to understand."

If the question arises as to the existence of a god of God, it plays an entirely different role to that of the existence of any person or any object I ever heard of. One said, had to say, that one *believed* in the existence, and if one did not believe, this was regarded as something bad. Normally if I did not believe in the existence of something no one would think there was anything wrong in this.

Also, there is this extraordinary use of the word 'believe.' One talks of believing and at the same time one doesn't use 'believe' as one does ordinarily. You might say (in the normal use): "You only believe—oh well. . . . " Here it is used entirely differently; on the other hand it is not used as we generally use the word 'know.'

If I even vaguely remember what I was taught about God, I might say: "Whatever believing in God may be, it can't be believing in something we can test, or find means of testing." You might say: "This is nonsense, because people say they believe on *evidence* or say they believe on religious experiences." I would say: "The mere fact that someone says they believe on evidence doesn't tell me enough for me to be able to say now whether I can say of a sentence 'God exists' that your evidence is unsatisfactory or insufficient."

Suppose I know someone, Smith. I've heard that he has been killed in a battle in this war. One day you come to me and say: "Smith is in Cambridge." I inquire, and find you stood at Guildhall and saw at the other end a man and said: "That was Smith." I'd say: "Listen. This isn't sufficient evidence." If we had a fair amount of evidence he was killed I would try to make you say that you're being credulous. Suppose he was never heard of again. Needless to say, it is quite impossible to make inquiries: "Who at 12.05 passed Market Place into Rose Crescent?" Suppose you say: "He was there." I would be extremely puzzled.

Suppose there is a feast on Mid-Summer Common. A lot of people stand in a ring. Suppose this is done every year and then everyone says he has seen one of his dead relatives on the other side of the ring. In this case, we could ask everyone in the ring. "Who did you hold by the hand?" Nevertheless, we'd all say that on that day we see our dead relatives. You could in this case say: "I had an extraordinary experience. I had the experience I can express by saying: 'I say my dead cousin.'" Would we say you are saying this on insufficient evidence? Under certain circumstances I would say this, under other circumstances I wouldn't. Where what is said sounds a bit absurd I would say: "Yes, in this case insufficient evidence." If altogether absurd, then I wouldn't.

Suppose I went to somewhere like Lourdes in France. Suppose I went with a very credulous person. There we see blood coming out of something. He says: "There you are, Wittgenstein, how can you doubt?" I'd say: "Can it only be explained one way? Can't it be this or that?" I'd try to convince him that he'd seen nothing of any consequence. I wonder whether I would do that under all circumstances. I certainly know that I would under normal circumstances.

"Oughtn't one after all to consider this?" I'd say: "Come on. Come on." I would treat the phenomenon in this case just as I would treat an experiment in a laboratory which I thought badly executed.

"The balance moves when I will it to move." I point out it is not covered up, a draught can move it, etc.

I could imagine that someone showed an extremely passionate belief in such a phenomenon, and I couldn't approach his belief at all by saying: "This could just as well have been brought about by so and so" because he could think this blasphemy on my side. Or he might say: "It is possible that these priests cheat, but nevertheless in a different sense a miraculous phenomenon takes place there."

I have a statue which bleeds on such and such a day in the year. I have red ink, etc. "You are a cheat, but nevertheless the Deity uses you. Red ink in a sense, but not red ink in a sense."

Cf. Flowers at seance with label. People said: "Yes, flowers are materialized with label." What kind of circumstances must there be to make this kind of story not ridiculous?

I have a moderate education, as all of you have, and therefore know what is meant by insufficient evidence for a forecast. Suppose someone dreamt of the Last Judgement, and said he now knew what it would be like. Suppose someone said: "This is poor evidence." I would say: "If you want to compare it with the evidence for it's raining to-morrow it is no evidence at all." He may make it sound as if by stretching the point you may call it evidence. But it may be more than ridiculous as evidence. But now, would I be prepared to say: "You are basing your belief on extremely slender evidence, to put it mildly." Why should I regard this dream as evidence—measuring its validity as though I were measuring the validity of the evidence for meteorological events?

If you compare it with anything in Science which we call evidence, you can't credit that anyone could soberly argue: "Well, I had this dream . . . therefore . . . Last Judgement." You might say: "For a blunder, that's too big." If you suddenly wrote numbers down on the blackboard, and then said: "Now, I'm going to add," and then said: "2 and 21 is 13," etc. I'd say: "This is no blunder."

There are cases where I'd say he's mad, or he's making fun. Then there might be cases where I look for an entirely different interpretation altogether. In order to see what the explanation is I should have to see the sum, to see in what way it is done, what he makes follow from it, what are the different circumstances under which he does it, etc.

I mean, if a man said to me after a dream that he believed in the Last Judgement, I'd try to find what sort of impression it gave him. One attitude: "It will be in about 2,000 years. It will be bad for so and so and so, etc." Or it may be one of terror. In the case where there is hope, terror, etc., would I say there is insufficient evidence if he says: "I believe . . . "? I can't treat these words as I normally treat 'I believe so and so.' It would be entirely beside the point, and also if he said his friend so and so and his grandfather had had the dream and believed, it would be entirely beside the point.

I would not say: "If a man said he dreamt it would happen to-morrow," would he take his coat?, etc.

Case where Lewy has visions of his dead friend. Cases where you don't try to locate him. And case where you try to locate him in a business-like way. Another case where I'd say: "We can pre-suppose we have a broad basis on which we agree."

In general, if you say: "He is dead" and I say: "He is not dead" no-one would say: "Do they mean the same thing by 'dead'?" In the case where a man has visions I wouldn't offhand say: "He means something different."

Cf. A person having persecution mania.

What is the criterion for meaning something different? Not only what he takes as evidence for it, but also how he reacts, that he is in terror, etc.

How am I to find out whether this proposition is to be regarded as an empirical proposition—'You'll see your dead friend again?' Would I say: "He is a bit superstitious?" Not a bit.

He might have been apologetic. (The man who stated it categorically was more intelligent than the man who was apologetic about it.)

'Seeing a dead friend,' again means nothing much to me at all. I don't think in these terms. I don't say to myself: "I shall see so and so again" ever.

He always says it, but he doesn't make any search. He puts on a queer smile. "His story had that dreamlike quality." My answer would be in this case "Yes," and a particular explanation.

Take "God created man." Pictures of Michelangelo showing the creation of the world. In general, there is nothing which explains the meanings of words as well as a picture, and I take it that Michelangelo was as good as anyone can be and did his best, and here is the picture of the Deity creating Adam.

If we ever say this, we certainly wouldn't think this the Deity. The picture has to be used in an entirely different way if we are to call the man in that queer blanket 'God,' and so on. You could imagine that religion was taught by means of these pictures. "Of course, we can only express ourselves by means of picture." This is rather queer . . . I could show Moore the pictures of a tropical plant. There is a technique of comparison between picture and plant. If I showed him the picture of Michelangelo and said: "Of course, I can't show you the real thing, only the picture" . . . The absurdity is, I've never taught him the technique of using this picture.

It is quite clear that the role of pictures of Biblical subjects and role of the picture of God creating Adam are totally different ones. You might ask this question: "Did Michelangelo think that Noah in the ark looked like this, and that God creating Adam looked like this?" He wouldn't have said that God or Adam looked as they look in this picture.

It might seem as though, if we asked such a question as: "Does Lewy *really* mean what so and so means when he says so and so is alive?"—it might seem as though there were two sharply divided cases, one in which he would say he didn't mean it literally. I want to say this is not so. There will be cases where we will differ, and where it won't be a question at all of more or less knowledge, so that we can come together. Sometimes it will be a question of experience, so you can say: "Wait another 10 years." And I would say: "I would disencourage this kind of reasoning" and Moore would say: "I wouldn't disencourage it." That is, one would *do* something. We would take sides, and that goes so far that there would really be great differences between us, which might come out in Mr. Lewy saying: "Wittgenstein is trying to undermine reason," and this wouldn't be false. This is actually where such questions rise.

CHAPTER EIGHT

Rationality and Justified Religious Belief

○

○ ○ ○ *39*

Rational Theistic Belief without Proof
John Hick

· *I* ·

THE RELIGIOUS REJECTION OF THE THEISTIC ARGUMENTS

WE HAVE SEEN that the major theistic arguments are all open to serious philosophical objections. Indeed we have in each case concluded, in agreement with the majority of contemporary philosophers, that these arguments fail to do what they profess to do. Neither those which undertake strictly to demonstrate the existence of an absolute Being, nor those which profess to show divine existence to be probable, are able to fulfil their promise. We have seen that it is impossible to demonstrate the reality of God by *a priori* reasoning, since such reasoning is confined to the realm of concepts; impossible to demonstrate it by *a posteriori* reasoning, since this would have to include a premise begging the very question at issue; and impossible to establish it as in a greater or lesser degree probable, since the notion of probability lacks any clear meaning in this context. A philosopher unacquainted with modern developments in theology might well assume that theologians would, *ex officio*,[1] be supporters of the theistic proofs and would regard as a fatal blow this conclusion that there can be neither a strict demonstration of God's existence nor a valid probability argument for it. In fact however such an assumption would be true only of certain theological schools. It is true of the more traditional Roman Catholic theology, of sections of conservative Protestantism, and of most of those Protestant apologists who continue to work within the tradition of nineteenth-century idealism. It has never been true, on the other hand, of Jewish religious thought; and it is not true of that central stream of contemporary Protestant theology which has been influenced by the 'neo-orthodox' movement, the revival of Reformation studies and the 'existentialism' of Kierkegaard and his successors; or of the most significant contemporary Roman Catholic thinkers, who are on this issue (as on so many others) in advance of the official teaching of the magisterium. Accordingly we have now to take note of the theological rejection of the theistic proofs, ranging from a complete lack of concern for them to a positive repudiation of them as being religiously irrelevant or even harmful. There are several different considerations to be evaluated.

1. It has often been pointed out that for the man of faith, as he is depicted in the Bible, no theistic proofs are necessary. Philosophers in the rationalist tradition,

---

[1] By virtue of an office held.—E.D.K.

holding that to know means to be able to prove, have been shocked to find that in the Bible, which is supposed to be the basis of Western religion, no attempt whatever is made to demonstrate the existence of God. Instead of professing to establish the divine reality by philosophical reasoning the Bible throughout takes this for granted. Indeed to the biblical writers it would have seemed absurd to try to establish by logical argumentation that God exists. For they were convinced that they were already having to do with him and he with them in all the affairs of their lives. They did not think of God as an inferred entity but as an experienced reality. Many of the biblical writers were (sometimes, though doubtless not at all times) as vividly conscious of being in God's presence as they were of living in a material world. It is impossible to read their pages without realizing that to them God was not a proposition completing a syllogism, or an idea adopted by the mind, but the supreme experiential reality. It would be as sensible for a husband to desire a philosophical proof of the existence of the wife and family who contribute so much of the meaning and value of his life as for the man of faith to seek for a proof of the existence of the God within whose purpose he believes that he lives and moves and has his being.

As Cook Wilson wrote:

> If we think of the existence of our friends; it is the 'direct knowledge' which we want: merely inferential knowledge seems a poor affair. To most men it would be as surprising as unwelcome to hear it could not be directly known whether there were such existences as their friends, and that it was only a matter of (probable) empirical argument and inference from facts which are directly known. And even if we convince ourselves on reflection that this is really the case, our actions prove that we have a confidence in the existence of our friends which can't be derived from an empirical argument (which can never be certain) for a man will risk his life for his friend. We don't want merely inferred friends. Could we possibly be satisfied with an inferred God?

In other words the man of faith has no need of theistic proofs; for he has something which for him is much better. However it does not follow from this that there may not be others who do need a theistic proof, nor does it follow that there are in fact no such proofs. All that has been said about the irrelevance of proofs to the life of faith may well be true, and yet it might still be the case that there are valid arguments capable of establishing the existence of God to those who stand outside the life of faith.

2. It has also often been pointed out that the God whose existence each of the traditional theistic proofs professes to establish is only an abstraction from and a pale shadow of the living God who is the putative object of biblical faith. A First Cause of the Universe might or might not be a deity to whom an unqualified devotion, love and trust would be appropriate; Aquinas's *Et hoc omnes intelligunt Deum* ('and this all understand to be God') is not the last step in a logical argument but merely an exercise of the custom of overlooking a gap in the argument at this point. A Necessary Being, and indeed a being who is metaphysically absolute in every respect—omnipotent, omniscient, eternal, uncreated—might be morally good or evil. As H. D. Aitken has remarked, "Logically there is no reason why an almighty and omniscient being might not be a perfect stinker.' A divine Designer of the world whose nature is read off from the appearances of nature might, as Hume showed, be finite or infinite, perfect or imperfect, omniscient or fallible, and might indeed be not one being but a veritable pantheon. It is only be going beyond what is proved, or claimed to have been proved, and identifying the First Cause, Necessary Being, or Mind behind Nature with the

God of biblical faith that these proofs could ever properly impel to worship. By themselves and without supplementation of content and infusion of emotional life from religious traditions and experiences transcending the proofs themselves they would never lead to the life of faith.

The ontological argument on the other hand is in this respect in a different category. If it succeeds it establishes the reality of a being so perfect in every way that no more perfect can be conceived. Clearly if such a being is not worthy of worship none ever could be. It would therefore seem that unlike the other proofs, the ontological argument, if it were logically sound, would present the relatively few persons who are capable of appreciating such abstract reasoning with a rational ground for worship. On the other hand, however, whilst this is the argument that would accomplish most if it succeeded it is also the argument which is most absolutely incapable of succeeding; for it is, as we have seen, inextricably involved in the fallacy of professing to deduce existence from a concept.

3. It is argued by some religious writers that a logical demonstration of the existence of God would be a form of coercion and would as such be incompatible with God's evident intention to treat his human creatures as free and responsible persons. A great deal of twentieth-century theology emphasises that God as the infinite personal reality, having made man as person in his own image, always treats men as persons, respecting their relative freedom and autonomy. He does not override the human mind by revealing himself in overwhelming majesty and power, but always approaches us in ways that leave room for an uncompelled response of human faith. Even God's own entry into our earthly history, it is said, was in an 'incognito' that could be penetrated only by the eyes of faith. As Pascal put it, 'willing to appear openly to those who seek him with all their heart, and to be hidden from those who flee from him with all their heart, he so regulates the knowledge of himself that he has given indications of himself which are visible to those who seek him and not to those who do not seek him. There is enough light for those to see who only desire to see, and enough obscurity for those who have a contrary disposition.' God's self-revealing actions are accordingly always so mediated through the events of our temporal experience that men only become aware of the divine presence by interpreting and responding to these events in the way which we call religious faith. For if God were to disclose himself to us in the coercive manner in which our physical environment obtrudes itself we should be dwarfed to nothingness by the infinite power thus irresistibly breaking open the privacy of our souls. Further, we should be spiritually blinded by God's perfect holiness and paralysed by his infinite energy; 'for human kind cannot bear very much reality.' Such a direct, unmediated confrontation breaking in upon us and shattering the frail autonomy of our finite nature would leave no ground for a free human response of trust, self-commitment and obedience. There could be no call for a man to venture upon a dawning consciousness of God's reality and thus to receive this consciousness as an authentic part of his own personal existence precisely because it has not been injected into him or clamped upon him by magisterial exercise of divine omnipotence.

The basic principle invoked here is that for the sake of creating a personal relationship of love and trust with his human creatures God does not force an awareness of himself upon them. And (according to the view which we are considering) it is only a further application of the same principle to add that a logically compelling demonstration of God's existence would likewise frustrate this purpose. For men—or at least those of them who are capable of following the proof—could then be forced to know that God is real. Thus Alasdair MacIntyre, when a Christian apologist, wrote: 'For if we could produce logically cogent arguments we should produce the kind of certitude that leaves no room for decision; where proof is in place,decision is not. We do not decide to accept Euclid's conclusions; we merely look to the rigour of his arguments. If the existence of God were demonstrable we should be as bereft of the possibility of making a free decision to love God as we should be if every utterance of doubt or unbelief was answered by thunderbolts from heaven.' This is the 'religious coercion' objection to the theistic proofs.

To what extent is it a sound objection? We may accept the theological doctrine that for God to force men to know him by the coercion of logic would be incompatible with his purpose of winning the voluntary response and worship of free moral beings. But the question still remains whether the theistic proofs could ever do this. Could a verbal proof of divine existence compel a consciousness of god comparable in coerciveness with a direct manifestation of his divine majesty and power? Cold anyone be moved and shaken in their whole being by the demonstration of a proposition, as men have been by a numinous experience of overpowering impressiveness? Would the things that have just been said about an overwhelming display of divine glory really apply to verbal demonstrations—that infinite power would be irresistibly breaking in upon the privacy of our souls and that we should be blinded by God's perfect holiness and paralyzed by his infinite energy? Indeed could a form of words, culminating in the proposition that 'God exists', ever have power by itself to produce more than what Newman calls a notional assent in our minds?

It is of course true that the effect of purely rational considerations such as those which are brought to bear in the theistic proofs are much greater in some minds than in others. The more rational the mind the more considerable is the effect to be expected. In many persons—indeed taking mankind as a whole, in the great majority—the effect of a theistic proof, even when no logical flaw is found in it, would be virtually nil! But in more sophisticated minds the effect must be greater, and it is at least theoretically possible that there are minds so rational that purely logical considerations can move them as effectively as the evidence of their senses. It is therefore conceivable that someone who is initially agnostic might be presented with a philosophical proof of divine existence—say the ontological argument, with its definition of God as that than which no more perfect can be conceived—and might as a result be led to worship the being whose reality has thus been demonstrated to him. This seems to be possible; but I believe that even in such a case there must, in addition to an intelligent appreciation of the argument, be a distinctively religious response to the idea of God which the argument presents. Some propensity to respond to unlimited perfection as holy and as rightly claiming a response of unqualified worship and devotion must operate, over and above the purely intellectual capacity for logical calculation. For we can conceive of a purely or merely logical mind, a kind of human calculating machine, which is at the same time devoid of the capacity for numinous feeling and worshipping response. Such a being might infer that God exists but be no more existentially interested in this conclusion than many people are in, say, the fact that the Shasta Dam is 602 feet high. It therefore seems that when the acceptance of a theistic proof leads to worship, a religious reaction occurs which turns what would otherwise be a purely abstract conclusion into an immensely significant and moving fact. In Newman's terminology, when a notional assent to the proposition that God exists becomes a real assent, equivalent to an actual living belief and faith in God, there has been a free human response to an idea which could instead have been rejected by being held at the notional level. In other words, a verbal proof of God's existence cannot by itself break down our human freedom; it can only lead to a notional assent which has little or no positive religious value or substance.

I conclude, then, that the theological objections to the theistic proofs are considerably less strong than the philosophical ones; and that theologians who reject natural theology would therefore do well to do so primarily on philosophical rather than on theological grounds. These philosophical reasons are, as we have seen, very strong; and we therefore now have to consider whether, in the absence of any theistic proofs, it can nevertheless be rational to believe in the existence of God.

· *II* ·

CAN THERE BE RATIONAL THEISTIC BELIEF WITHOUT PROOFS?

During the period dominated by the traditional theistic arguments the existence of God was often treated by philosophers as something to be discovered through reasoning. It was seen as the conclusion of an inference; and the question of the rationality of the belief was equated with that of the soundness of the inference. But from a religious point of view, as we have already seen, there has always been something very odd about this approach. The situation which it envisages is that of people standing outside the realm of faith, for whom the apologist is trying to build a bridge of rational inference to carry them over the frontier into that realm. But of course this is not the way in which religious faith has originally or typically or normally come about. When the cosmological, ontological, teleological and moral arguments were developed, theistic belief was already a functioning part of an immemorially established and developing form of human life. The claims of religion are claims made by individuals and communities on the basis of their experience—and experience which is none the less their own for occurring within an inherited framework of ideas. We are not dealing with a merely conceivable metaphysical hypothesis which someone has speculatively invented but which hardly anyone seriously believes. We are concerned, rather, with convictions born out of experience and reflection and living within actual communities of faith and practice. Historically, then, the philosophical 'proofs' of God have normally entered in to support and confirm but not to create belief. Accordingly the proper philosophical approach would seem to be a probing of the actual foundations and structure of a living and operative belief rather than of theoretical and non-operative arguments subsequently formulated for holding those beliefs. The question is not whether it is possible to prove, starting from zero, that God exists; the question is whether the religious man, given the distinctively religious form of human existence in which he participates, is properly entitled as a rational person to believe what he does believe?

At this point we must consider what we mean by a rational belief. If by a belief we mean a proposition believed, then what we are to be concerned with here are not rational beliefs but rational *believings*. Propositions can be well-formed or ill-formed, and they can be true or false, but they cannot be rational or irrational. It is *people* who are rational or irrational, and derivatively their states and their actions, including their acts and states of believing. Further, apart from the believing of analytic propositions, which are true by definition and are therefore rationally believed by anyone who understands them, the rationality of acts (or states) of believing has to be assessed separately in each case. For it is a function of the relation between the proposition believed and the evidence on the basis of which the believer believes it. It might conceivably be rational for Mr X to believe p but not rational for Mr Y to believe p, because in relation to the data available to Mr. X p is worthy of belief but not in relation to the data available to Mr Y. Thus the question of the rationality of belief in the reality of God is the question of the rationality of a particular person's believing, given the data that he is using; or that of the believing of a class of people who share the same body of data. Or putting the same point the other way round, any assessing of the belief-worthiness of the proposition that God exists must be an assessing of it in relation to particular ranges of data.

Now there is one area of data or evidence which is normally available to those who believe in God, and that provides a very important part of the ground of their believing, but which is normally not available to and therefore not taken into account by those who do not so believe; and this is religious experience. It seems that the religious man is in part basing his believing upon certain data of religious experience which the non-religious man is not using because he does not have them. Thus our question resolves itself into one about the theist's right, given his distinctively religious experience, to be certain that God exists. It is the question of the rationality or irrationality, the well-groundedness or ill-groundedness, of the religious man's claim to know God. The theist cannot hope to prove that God exists; but despite this it may nevertheless be possible for him to show it to be wholly reasonable for him to believe that God exists.

What is at issue here is not whether it is rational for someone else, who does not participate in the distinctively religious mode of experience, to believe in God on the basis of the religious man's reports. I am not proposing any kind of 'argument from religious experience' by which God is inferred as the cause of the special experiences described by mystics and other religious persons. It is not the non-religious man's theoretical use of someone else's reported religious experience that is to be considered, but the religious man's own practical use of it. The question is whether he is acting rationally in trusting his own experience and in proceeding to live on the basis of it.

In order to investigate this question we must consider what counts as rational belief in an analogous case. The analogy that I propose is that between the religious person's claim to be conscious of God and any man's claim to be conscious of the physical world as an environment, existing independently of himself, of which he must take account.

In each instance a realm of putatively cognitive experience is taken to be veridical and is acted upon as such, even though its veridical character cannot be logically demonstrated. So far as sense experience is concerned this has emerged both from the failure of Descartes' attempt to provide a theoretical guarantee that our senses relate us to a real material environment, and from the success of Hume's attempt to show that our normal non-solipsist belief in an objective world of enduring objects around us in space is neither a product of, nor justifiable by, philosophical reasoning but is what has been called in some expositions of Hume's thought (though the term does not seem to have been used by Hume himself) a natural belief. It is a belief which naturally and indeed inevitably arises in the normal human mind in response to normal human perceptual experience. It is a belief on the basis of which we live and the rejection of which, in favour of a serious adoption of the solipsist alternative, would so disorient our relationship to other persons within a common material environment that we should be accounted insane. Our insanity would consist in the fact that we should no longer regard other people as independent centres of consciousness, with their own purposes and wills, with whom interpersonal relationships are possible. We should instead be living in a one-person world.

It is thus a basic truth in, or a presupposition of, our language that it is rational or sane to believe in the reality of the external world that we inhabit in common with other people, and irrational or insane not to do so.

What are the features of our sense experience in virtue of which we all take this view? They would seem to be twofold: the givenness or the involuntary character of this form of cognitive experience, and the fact that we can and do act successfully in terms of our belief in an external world. That is to say, being built and circumstanced as we are we cannot help initially believing as we do, and our belief is not contradicted, but on the contrary continuously confirmed, by our continuing experience. These characteristics jointly constitute a sufficient reason to trust and live on the basis of our perceptual experience in the absence of any positive reason to distrust it; and our inability to exclude the theoretical possibility of our experience as a whole being purely subjective does not constitute such a reason. This seems to be the principle on which, implicitly, we proceed. And it is, by definition, rational to proceed in this way. That is to say, this is the way in which all human beings do proceed and have proceeded, apart from a very small minority who have for that very reason been labelled by the majority as insane. This habitual acceptance of our perceptual experience is thus, we may say, part of our operative concept of human rationality.

We can therefore now ask whether a like principle may be invoked on behalf of a parallel response to religious experience. 'Religious experience' is of course a highly elastic concept. Let us restrict attention, for our present purpose, to the theistic 'sense of the presence of God', the putative awareness of a transcendent divine Mind within whose field of consciousness we exist and with whom therefore we stand in a relationship of mutual awareness. This sense of 'living in the divine presence' does not take the form of a direct vision of God, but of experiencing events in history and in our own personal life as the medium of God's dealing with us. Thus religious differs from non-religious experience, not as the awareness of a different world, but as a different way of experiencing the same world. Events which can be experienced as having a purely natural significance are experienced by the religious mind as having also and at the same time religious significance and as mediating the presence and activity of God.

It is possible to study this type of religious experience either in its strongest instances, in the primary and seminal religious figures, or in its much weaker instances in ordinary adherents of the traditions originated by the great exemplars of faith. Since we are interested in the question of the claims which religious experience justifies it is appropriate to look at that experience in its strongest and purest forms. A description of this will accordingly apply only very partially to the ordinary rank-and-file believer either of today or in the past.

If then we consider the sense of living in the divine presence as this was expressed by, for example, Jesus of Nazareth, or by St Paul, St Francis, St Anselm or the great prophets of the Old Testament, we find that their 'awareness of God' was so vivid that he was as indubitable a factor in their experience as was their physical environment. They could no more help believing in the reality of God than in the reality of the material world and of their human neighbours. Many of the pages of the Bible resound with the sense of God's presence as a building might reverberate from the tread of some gigantic being walking through it. God was known to the prophets and apostles as a dynamic will interacting with their own wills; a sheerly given personal reality, as inescapably to be reckoned with as destructive storm and life-giving sunshine, the fixed contours of the land, or the hatred of their enemies and the friendship of their neighbours.

Our question concerns, then, one whose 'experience of God' has this compelling quality, so that he is no more inclined to doubt its veridical character than to doubt the evidence of his senses. Is it rational for him to take the former, as it is certainly rational for him to take the latter, as reliably cognitive of an aspect of his total environment and thus as knowledge in terms of which to act? Are the two features noted above in our sense experience—its givenness, or involuntary character, and the fact that we can successfully act in terms of it—also found here? It seems that they are. The sense of the presence of God reported by the great religious figures has a similar involuntary and compelling quality; and as they proceed to live on the basis of it they are sustained and confirmed by their further experiences in the conviction that they are living in relation, not to illusion, but to reality. It therefore seems prima facie, that the religious man *is* entitled to trust his religious experience and to proceed to conduct his life in terms of it.

The analogy operating within this argument is between our normal acceptance of our sense experience as perception of an objective external world, and a corresponding acceptance of the religious experience of 'living in God's presence' as the awareness of a divine reality external to our own minds. In each case there is a solipsist alternative in which one can affirm *solus ipse* to the exclusion of the transcendent—in the one case denying a physical environment transcending our own private consciousness and in the other case denying a divine Mind transcending our own private consciousness. It should be noted that this analogy is not grounded in the perception of particular material objects and does not turn upon the contrast between veridical and illusory sense perceptions, but is grounded in our awareness of an objective external world as such and turns upon the contrast between this and a theoretically possible solipsist interpretation of the same stream of conscious experience.

· III ·

RELIGIOUS AND PERCEPTUAL BELIEF

Having thus set forth the analogy fairly boldly and starkly I now want to qualify it by exploring various differences between religious and sensory experience. The resulting picture will be more complex than the first rough outline presented so far; and yet its force as supporting the rationality of theistic faith will not, I think, in the end have been undermined.

The most obvious difference is that everyone has and cannot help having sense experiences, whereas not everyone has religious experiences, at any rate of the very vivid and distinct kind to which we have been referring. As bodily beings existing in a material environment, we cannot help interacting consciously with that environment. That is to say, we cannot help 'having' a stream of sense experiences; and we cannot help accepting this as the perception of a material world around us in space. When we open our eyes in daylight we cannot but receive the visual experiences that come to us; and likewise with the other senses. And the world which we thus perceive is not plastic to our wishes but presents itself to us as it is, whether we like it or not. Needless to say, our senses do not coerce us in any sense of the word 'coerce' that implies unwillingness on our part, as when a policeman coerces an unwilling suspect to accompany him to the police station. Sense experience is coercive in the sense that we cannot when sane believe that our material environment is not broadly as we perceive it to be, and that if we did momentarily persuade ourselves that what we experience is not there we should quickly be penalized by the environment and indeed, if we persisted, destroyed by it.

In contrast to this we are not obliged to interact consciously with a spiritual environment. Indeed it is a commonplace of much contemporary theology that God does not force an awareness of himself upon mankind but leaves us free to know him by an uncompelled response of faith. And yet once a man has allowed himself freely to become conscious of God—it is important to note—that experience is, at its top levels of intensity, coercive. It creates the situation of the person who *cannot help* believing in the reality of God. The apostle, prophet or saint may be so vividly aware of God that he can no more doubt the veracity of his religious awareness than of his sense experience. During the periods when he is living consciously in the presence of God, when God is to him the divine Thou, the question whether God exists simply does not arise. Our cognitive freedom in relation to God is not to be found at this point but at the prior stage of our coming to be aware of him. The individual's own free receptivity and responsiveness plays an essential part in his dawning consciousness of God; but once he *has* become conscious of God that consciousness can possess a coercive and indubitable quality.

It is a consequence of this situation that whereas everyone perceives and cannot help perceiving the physical world, by no means everyone experiences the presence of God. Indeed only rather few people experience religiously in the vivid and coercive way reported by the great biblical figures. And this fact immediately suggests a skeptical question. Since those who enjoy a compelling religious experience form such a small minority of mankind, ought we not to suspect that they are suffering from a delusion comparable with that of the paranoiac who hears threatening voices from the walls or the alcoholic who sees green snakes?

This is of course a possible judgement to make. But this judgement should not be made *a priori*, in the absence of specific grounds such as we have in the other cases mentioned. And it would in fact be difficult to point to adequate evidence to support this hypothesis. On the contrary the general intelligence and exceptionally high moral quality of the great religious figures clashes with any analysis of their experience in terms of abnormal psychology. Such analyses are not indicated, as is the parallel view of paranoiacs and alcoholics, by evidence of general disorientation to reality or of incapacity to live a productive and satisfying life. One the contrary, Jesus of Nazareth, for example, has been regarded by hundreds of millions of people as the fulfillment of the ideal possibilities of human nature. A more reasonable negative position would therefore seem to be the agnostic one that whilst it is proper for the religious man himself, given his distinctive mode of experience, to believe firmly in the reality of God, one does not oneself share that experience and therefore has no ground upon which to hold that belief. Theism is then not positively denied, but is on the other hand consciously and deliberately not affirmed. This agnostic position must be accepted by the theist as a proper one. For if it is reasonable for one man, on the basis of his distinctively religious experience, to affirm the reality of God it must also be reasonable for another man, in the absence of any such experience, not to affirm the reality of God.

The next question that must be raised is the closely connected one of the relation between rational belief and truth. I suggested earlier that, strictly, one should speak of rational believings rather than of rational beliefs. But nevertheless it is sometimes convenient to use the latter phrase, which we may then understand as follows. By a rational belief we shall mean a belief which it is rational for the one who holds it to hold, given the data available to him. Clearly such beliefs are not necessarily or always true. It is sometimes rational for an individual to have, on the basis of incomplete data, a belief which is in fact false. For example, it was once rational for people to believe that the sun revolves round the earth; for it was apparently perceived to do so, and the additional theoretical and observational data were not yet available from which it has since been inferred that it is the earth which revolves round the sun. If, then, a belief may be rational and yet false, may not the religious man's belief be of this kind? May it not be that when the data of religious experience are supplemented in the believer's mind by further data provided by the sciences of psychology or sociology, it ceases to be rational for him to believe in God? Might it not then be rational for him instead to believe that his 'experience of the presence of God' is to be understood as an effect of a buried infancy memory of his father as a benevolent higher power; or of the pressure upon him of the human social organism of which he is a cell; or in accordance with some other naturalistic theory of the nature of religion?

Certainly this is possible. Indeed we must say, more generally, that all our beliefs, other than our acceptance of logically self-certifying propositions, are in principle open to revision or retraction in the light of new data. It is always conceivable that something which it is now rational for us to believe, it may one day not be rational for us to believe. But the difference which this general principle properly makes to our present believing varies from a maximum in relation to beliefs involving a considerable theoretical element, such as the higher-level hypotheses of the sciences, to a minimum in relation to perceptual beliefs, such as the belief that I now see a sheet of paper before me. And I have argued that so far as the great primary religious figures are concerned, belief in the reality of God is closer to the latter in that it is analogous to belief in the reality of the perceived material world. It is not an explanatory hypothesis, logically comparable with those developed in the sciences, but a perceptual belief. God was not, for Amos or Jeremiah or Jesus of Nazareth, an inferred entity but an experienced personal presence. If this is so, it is appropriate that the religious man's belief in the reality of God should be no more provisional than his belief in the reality of the physical world. The situation is in each case that, given the experience which he has and which is part of him, he cannot help accepting as 'there' such aspects of his environment as he experiences. He cannot help believing either in the reality of the material world which he is conscious of inhabiting, or of the personal divine presence which is overwhelmingly evident to him and to which his mode of living is a free response. And I have been suggesting that it is as reasonable for him to hold and to act upon the one belief as the other.

· *IV* ·

THE PROBLEM OF CONFLICTING RELIGIOUS BELIEFS

We must now take note of another circumstance which qualifies and threatens to erode our analogy. What are we to make of the immense variety of the forms of religious experience, giving rise as they do to apparently incompatible beliefs? In contrast to this, human sense experience reveals a world which is public in that normally the perceptions of any two individuals can readily be correlated in terms of the hypothesis of a common world which they jointly inhabit.

The variety commonly brought under the name of religion is indeed as wide as the range of man's cultural and psychological diversities. By no means all religious experience is theistic; ultimate reality is apprehended as non-personal and as multi-personal as well as unipersonal. And if we choose to extend the notion of religious experience, as Abraham Maslow has recently done by his concept of peak-experiences, the variety is multiplied again. But even apart from this last expansion of the field it is clearly true that religious experience is bewilderingly varied in content and that the different reports to which it gives rise cannot easily be correlated as alternative accounts of the same reality. And therefore since one could restate the argument of the earlier part of this chapter from the point of view of many different religions, with their different forms of religious experience and belief, the question arises whether the argument does not prove too much. In establishing the rationality of the Judaic-Christian theist's belief in the reality of God, must it not also and equally establish the rationality of the Buddhist's belief, arising out of *his* own coercive religious experience, and likewise of Hindu belief and of Islamic belief, and so on?

We need, I think, have no hesitation in accepting this implication. The principle which I have used to justify as rational the faith of a Christian who on the basis of his own religious experience cannot help believing in the reality of 'the God and Father of our Lord Jesus Christ', also operates to justify as rational the faith of a Muslim who on the basis of *his* religious experience cannot help believing in the reality of Allah and his providence; and the faith of the Buddhist who on the basis of *his* religious experience cannot help accepting the Buddhist picture of the universe; and so on.

But this is not the end of the matter. Various possibilities now open before us. I can only in conclusion attempt a small-scale map of the different paths that may be taken, showing in what direction they each lead and forecasting to some extent the kind of difficulties that are to be expected if one chooses to travel along them.

The first fork in the road is constituted by the alternative possibilities that the truth concerning the nature of the universe will, and that it will not, ultimately be a matter of public knowledge. The question is whether there will eventually be a situation in which all rational persons will find themselves obliged to agree, on the basis of a common body of experience, that the universe has this or that specific character. The issue, in other words, is that of the ultimate public verifiability and falsifiability of religious faiths.

On the one hand, in one conceivable picture of the universe it is possible for adherents of different and incompatible faiths to remain, so long as they continue to exist and to hold beliefs, under the impression that their own understanding of the universe is true; for they never meet an experiential crux which either verifies or falsifies their faith. This is a not always acknowledged feature of the pictures adopted both by the non-eschatological religions and by most atheistic and naturalistic theories. On the other hand, in another possible picture of the universe, or rather family of pictures painted by the different eschatological religions, the future development of human experience will narrow down the options until eventually only one faith is compatible with the facts and it becomes irrational to hold any contrary view. Thus it is affirmed in Christianity, in Islam, in one type of Judaism and perhaps in one type of Buddhism that the universe has a certain definite structure and is moving towards a certain definite fulfilment such that in the light of that fulfilment it will be beyond rational doubt that the universe has the particular character that it has.

Both types of universe are logically possible. If Christianity is true we are living in a universe of the latter type, in which religious faith is ultimately verified; and since we are now investigating the rationality of the Christian belief in God we shall want at this first fork to take the verifiability-of-faiths option in order to explore it further and to see where it leads.

Travelling along this path, then, we now meet a second fork in the road, offering two rival conceptions of the relations between the different religions. Along one path we affirm the ultimate compatibility of the plurality of religious faiths, whilst along the other path we deny this. The latter, incompatibility thesis leads us to the following picture: it is at the moment rational for adherents of different religions, whose experience is such that they cannot help believing as they do, to hold their respective beliefs. But—still assuming the verifiability-of-faiths thesis—it will eventually cease to be possible for rational persons to adhere to rival and incompatible understandings of the universe. For according to this option in its strongest form, there is one true faith and many false ones—this view corresponding of course to the traditional dogmatic stances of the eschatological religions, such as Christianity and Islam. There is however a specifically Christian reason for abandoning this stance. This is that belief in the redeeming love of God for all his human creatures makes it incredible that the divine activity in relation to mankind should have been confined to those within the reach of the influence of the Christian revelation. The majority of the human beings who have existed since man began have lived either before or outside the historical influence of Jesus of Nazareth. Thus the doctrine that there is no salvation outside historic Christianity would in effect deny the universal love and redeeming activity of God.

Any modification of that traditional claim soon leads us over onto the alternative path, at the end of which lies the conclusion that the different forms of religious experience, giving rise to the different religions of the world, are properly to be understood as experiences of different aspects of one immensely complex and rich divine reality. If this is so, the beliefs of the different religions will be related to a larger truth as the experiences which gave rise to those beliefs are related to larger reality.

The further exploration of this possibility would take us beyond our present necessarily limited inquiry. I have argued that when on the basis of his own compelling religious experience someone believes in the reality of God, he is believing rationally; and I have added the rider that when we set alongside this argument the fact of the plurality of religions and their forms of religious experience, we are led to postulate a divine reality of which the different religions of the world represent different partial experiences and partial knowledge. This latter possibility remains, however, to be adequately developed and examined.

○ ○ ○ *40*

Religious Belief without Evidence
Alvin Plantinga

· *I* ·

WHAT I MEAN to discuss, in this paper, is the question, Is belief in God rational? That is to say, I which to discuss the question "Is it rational, or reasonable, or rationally acceptable, to believe in God?" I mean to *discuss* this question, not answer it. My initial aim is not to argue that religious belief *is* rational (although I think it is) but to try to understand this question.

The first thing to note is that I have stated the question misleadingly. What I really want to discuss is whether it is rational to believe that God exists—that there is such a person as God. Of course there is an important difference between believing that God exists and believing *in* God. To believe that God exists is just to accept a certain proposition—the proposition that there really is such a person as God—as true. According to the book of James (2:19) the devils believe this proposition, and they tremble. To believe *in* God, however, is to trust him, to commit your life to him, to make his purposes your own. The devils do not do that. So there is a difference between believing in God and believing that he exists; for purposes of economy, however, I shall use the phrase 'belief in God' as a synonym for 'belief that God exists.'

Our question, therefore, is whether belief in god is rational. This question is widely asked and widely answered. Many philosophers—most prominently, those in the great tradition of natural theology—have argued that belief in God *is* rational; they have typically done so by providing what they took to be *demonstrations* or *proofs* of God's existence. Many others have argued that belief in God is *ir*rational. If we call those of the first group 'natural theologians', perhaps we should call those of the second 'natural atheologians.' (That would at any rate be kinder than calling them 'unnatural theologians.') J. L. Mackie, for example, opens his statement of the problem of evil as follows: "I think, however, that a more telling criticism can be made by way of the traditional problem of evil. Here it can be shown, not merely that religious beliefs lack rational support, but that they are positively irrational. . . ." And a very large number of philosophers take it that a central question—perhaps *the* central question—of philosophy of religion is the question whether religious belief in general and belief in God in particular is rationally acceptable.

Now an apparently straightforward and promising way to approach this question would be to take a definition of rationality and see whether belief in God conforms to it. The chief difficulty with this appealing course, however, is that no such definition of rationality seems to be available. If there *were* such a definition, it would set out some conditions for a belief's being rationally acceptable—conditions that are severally necessary and jointly sufficient. That is, each of the conditions would have to be met by a belief that is rationally acceptable; and if a belief met all the conditions, then it would follow that it is rationally acceptable. But it is monumentally difficult to find any non-trivial necessary conditions at all. Surely, for example, we cannot insist that S's belief that p is rational only if it is *true*. For consider Newton's belief that if x, y and z are moving colinearly, then the motion of z with respect to x is the sum of the motions of y with respect to x and z with respect to y. No doubt Newton was rational in accepting this belief; yet it was false, at least if contemporary physicists are to be trusted. And if they aren't—that is, if they are wrong in contradicting Newton—then *they* exemplify what I'm speaking of; they rationally believe a proposition which, as it turns out, is false.

Nor can we say that a belief is rationally acceptable only if it is possibly true, not necessarily false in the broadly logical sense. For example, I might do the sum $735 + 421 + 9,216$ several times and get the same answer: $10,362$. I am then rational in believing that $735 + 421 + 9,216 = 10,362$, even though the fact is I've made the same error each time—failed to carry a '1' from the first column—and thus believe what is necessarily false. Or I might be a mathematical neophyte who hears from his teacher that every continuous function is differentiable. I need not be irrational in believing this, despite the fact that it is necessarily false. Examples of this sort can be multiplied.

So this question presents something of an initial enigma in that it is by no means easy to say what it is for a belief to be rational. And the fact is those philosophers who ask this question about belief in God do not typically try to answer it by giving necessary and sufficient conditions for rational belief. Instead, they typically ask whether the believer has *evidence* or *sufficient evidence* for his belief; or they may try to argue that in fact there is sufficient evidence for the proposition that there is *no* God; but in any case they try to answer this question by finding evidence for or against theistic belief. Philosophers who think there are sound arguments for the existence of God—the natural theologians—claim there is good evidence *for* this proposition; philosophers who believe that there are sound arguments for the non-existence of God naturally claim that there is evidence *against* this proposition. But they concur in holding that belief in God is rational only if there is, on balance, a preponderance of evidence for it—or less radically, only if there is not, on balance, a preponderance of evidence against it.

The nineteenth-century philosopher W. K. Clifford provides a splendid if somewhat strident example of the view that the believer in God must have evidence if he is not to be irrational. Here he does not discriminate against religious belief; he apparently holds that a belief of any sort at all is rationally acceptable only if there is sufficient evidence for it. And he goes on to insist that it is wicked, immoral, monstrous, and perhaps even impolite to accept a belief for which one does not have sufficient evidence:

> Whoso would deserve well of his fellows in this matter will guard the purity of his belief with a very fanaticism of jealous care, lest at any time it should rest on an unworthy object, and catch a stain which can never be wiped away.

He adds that if a

> belief has been accepted on insufficient evidence, the pleasure is a stolen one. Not only does it deceive ourselves by giving us a sense of power which we do not really possess,

but it is sinful, because it is stolen in defiance of our duty to mankind. That duty is to guard ourselves from such beliefs as from a pestilence which may shortly master our body and spread to the rest of the town.

And finally:

To sum up: it is wrong always, everywhere, and for anyone to believe anything upon insufficient evidence.

(It is not hard to detect, in these quotations, the "tone of robustious pathos" with which William James credits him.) Clifford finds it utterly obvious, furthermore, that those who believe in God do indeed so believe on insufficient evidence and thus deserve the above abuse. A believer in God is, on his view, at best a harmless pest and at worst a menace to society; in either case he should be discouraged.

Now there are some initial problems with Clifford's claim. For example, he doesn't tell us how *much* evidence is sufficient. More important, the notion of evidence is about as difficult as that of rationality: What is evidence? How do you know when you have some? How do you know when you have sufficient or enough? Suppose, furthermore, that a person thinks he has sufficient evidence for a proposition *p* when in fact he does not—would he then be irrational in believing *p*? Presumably a person can have sufficient evidence for what is false—else either Newton did not have sufficient evidence for his physical beliefs or contemporary physicists don't have enough for *theirs*. Suppose, then, that a person has sufficient evidence for the false proposition that he has sufficient evidence for *p*. Is he then irrational in believing *p*? Presumably not; but if not, having sufficient evidence is not, contrary to Clifford's claim, a necessary condition for believing *p* rationally.

But suppose we temporarily concede that these initial difficulties can be resolved and take a deeper look at Clifford's position. What is essential to it is the claim that we must evaluate the rationality of belief in God by examining its relation to *other* propositions. We are directed to estimate its rationality by determining whether we have *evidence* for it—whether we know, or at any rate rationally believe, some other propositions which stand in the appropriate relation to the proposition in question. And belief in God is rational, or reasonable, or rationally acceptable, on this view, only if there are other propositions with respect to which it is thus evident.

According to the Cliffordian position, then, there is a set of propositions *E* such that my belief in God is rational if and only if it is evident with respect to *E*—if and only if *E* constitutes, on balance, evidence for it. But what propositions are to be found in *E*? Do we know that belief in God is not itself in *E*? If it *is*, of course, then it is certainly evident with respect to *E*. How does a proposition get into *E* anyway? How do we decide which propositions are the ones such that my belief in God is rational if and only if it is evident with respect to them? Should we say that *E* contains the propositions that I *know*? But then, for our question to be interesting, we should first have to argue or agree that I don't know that God exists—that I only *believe* it, whether rationally or irrationally. This position is widely taken for granted, and indeed taken for granted by theists as well as others. But why should the latter concede that he doesn't know that God exists—that at best he rationally believes it? The Bible regularly speaks of *knowledge* in this context—not just rational or well-founded belief. Of course it is true that the believer has *faith*—faith in God, faith in what He reveals, faith that God exists—but this by no means settles the issue. The question is whether he doesn't also *know* that God exists. Indeed, according to the Heidelberg Catechism, knowledge is an essential element of faith, so that one has true faith that *p* only if he knows that *p*:

> True faith is not only a certain (i.e., sure) knowledge whereby I hold for truth all that God has revealed in His word, but also a deep-rooted assurance created in me by the Holy Spirit through the gospel that not only others but I too have had my sins forgiven, have been made forever right with God and have been granted salvation. (Q21)

So from this point of view a man has true faith that *p* only if he knows that *p* and also meets a certain further condition: roughly (where *p* is a universal proposition) that of accepting the universal instantiation of *p* with respect to himself. Now of course the theist may be unwilling to concede that he does not have true faith that God exists; accordingly he may be unwilling to concede—initially, at any rate—that he does not know, but only believes that God exists. . . .

· *II* [1] ·

[Both] Aquinas and the evidentialist objector [to theism] concur in holding that belief in God is rationally acceptable only if there is evidence for it—if, that is, it is probable with respect to some body of propositions that constitutes the evidence. And here we can get a better understanding of Aquinas and the evidentialist objector if we see them as accepting some version of *classical foundationalism*. This is a *picture* or total way of looking at faith, knowledge, justified belief, rationality, and allied topics. This picture has been enormously popular in Western thought; and despite a substantial opposing groundswell, I think it remains the dominant way of thinking about these topics. According to the foundationalist some propositions are properly basic and some are not; those that are not are rationally accepted only on the basis of *evidence*, where the evidence must trace back, ultimately, to what *is* properly basic. The existence of God, furthermore, is not among the propositions that are properly basic; hence a person is rational in accepting theistic belief only if he has evidence for it. The vast majority of those in the western world who have thought about our topic have accepted some form of classical foundationalism. The evidentialist objection to belief in God, furthermore, is obviously rooted in this way of looking at things. So suppose we try to achieve a deeper understanding of it.

Earlier I said the first thing to see about the evidentialist objection is that it is a *normative* contention or claim. The same thing must be said about foundationalism: this thesis is a normative thesis, a thesis about how a system of beliefs *ought* to be structured, a thesis about the properties of a correct, or acceptable, or rightly structured system of beliefs. According to the foundationalist there are norms, or duties, or obligations with respect to belief just as there are with respect to actions. To conform to these duties and obligations is to be rational; to fail to measure up to them is to be irrational. To be rational, then, is to exercise one's epistemic powers *properly*—

---

[1] In the paragraphs omitted here, the author discusses attacks on theism from an evidentialist perspective. He then turns to the foundationalist view of knowledge—beginning with the classical version held by Aquinas, Descartes, and so on.—E.D.K.

to exercise them in such a way as to go contrary to none of the norms for such exercise. . . .

I think we can understand foundationalism more fully if we introduce the idea of a *noetic structure*. A person's noetic structure is the set of propositions he believes, together with certain epistemic relations that hold among him and these propositions. As we have seen, some of my beliefs may be based upon others; it may be that there are a pair of propositions *A* and *B* such that I believe *B*, and believe *A* on the *basis* of *B*. An account of a person's noetic structure, then, would specify which of his beliefs are basic and which nonbasic. Of course it is abstractly possible that *none* of his beliefs is basic; perhaps he holds just three beliefs, *A, B,* and *C,* and believes each of them on the basis of the other two. We might think this improper or irrational, but that is not to say it could not be done. And it is also possible that *all* of his beliefs are basic; perhaps he believes a lot of propositions but does not believe any of them on the basis of any others. In the typical case, however, a noetic structure will include both basic and nonbasic beliefs. It may be useful to give some examples of beliefs that are often basic for a person. Suppose I seem to see a tree; I have that characteristic sort of experience that goes with perceiving a tree. I may then believe the proposition that I see a tree. It is *possible* that I believe that proposition *on the basis* of the proposition that I seem to see a tree; in the typical case, however, I will not believe the former on the basis of the latter because in the typical case I will not believe the latter at all. I will not be paying any attention to my experience but will be concentrating on the tree. Of course I *can* turn my attention to my experience, notice how things look to me, and acquire the belief that I seem to see something that looks like *that*; and if you challenge my claim that I see a tree, perhaps I *will* thus turn my attention to my experience. But in the typical case I will not believe that I see a tree on the basis of a proposition about my experience; for I believe *A* on the basis of *B* only if I believe *B*, and in the typical case where I perceive a tree I do not believe (or entertain) any propositions about my experience. Typically I take such a proposition as basic. Similarly, I believe I had breakfast this morning; this too is basic for me. I do not believe this proposition on the basis of some proposition about my experience—for example, that I seem to remember having had breakfast. In the typical case I will not have even considered *that* question—the question whether I *seem* to remember having had breakfast; instead I simply believe that I had breakfast; I take it as basic.

Second, an account of a noetic structure will include what we might call an index of degree of belief. I hold some of my beliefs much more firmly than others. I believe both that $2 + 1 = 3$ and that London, England, is north of Saskatoon, Saskatchewan; but I believe the former more resolutely than the latter. Some beliefs I hold with maximum firmness; others I do in fact accept, but in a much more tentative way. . . .

Third, a somewhat vaguer notion: an account of *S*'s noetic structure would include something like an index of *depth of ingression*. Some of my beliefs are, we might say, on the periphery of my noetic structure. I accept them, and may even accept them firmly, but I could give them up without much change elsewhere in my noetic structure. I believe there are some large boulders on the top of the Grand Teton. If I come to give up this belief (say by climbing it and not finding any), that change need not have extensive reverberations throughout the rest of my noetic structure; it could be accommodated with minimal alteration elsewhere. So its depth of ingression into my noetic structure is not great. On the other hand, if I were to come to believe that there simply is no such thing as the Grand Teton, or no mountains at all, or no such thing as the state of Wyoming, that would have much greater reverberations. And suppose I were to come to think there had not been much of a past (that the world was created just five minutes ago, complete with all its apparent memories and traces of the past) or that there were not any other persons: these changes would have even greater reverberations; these beliefs of mine have great depth of ingression into my noetic structure. . . .

Now foundationalism is best construed, I think, as a thesis about *rational* noetic structures. A noetic structure is rational if it could be the noetic structure of a person who was completely rational. To be completely rational, as I am here using the term, is not to believe only what is true, or to believe all the logical consequences of what one believes, or to believe all necessary truths with equal firmness, or to be uninfluenced by emotion in forming belief; it is, instead, to do the right thing with respect to one's believings. It is to violate no epistemic duties. From this point of view, a rational person is one whose believings meet the appropriate standards; to criticize a person as irrational is to criticize her for failing to fulfill these duties or responsibilities, for failing to conform to the relevant norms or standards. To draw the ethical analogy, the irrational is the impermissible; the rational is the permissible. . . .

A rational noetic structure, then, is one that could be the noetic structure of a wholly rational person; and foundationalism, as I say, is a thesis about such noetic structures. We may think of the foundationalist as beginning with the observation that some of our beliefs are based upon others. According to the foundationalist a rational noetic structure will *have a foundation*—a set of beliefs not accepted on the basis of others; in a rational noetic structure some beliefs will be basic. Nonbasic beliefs, of course, will be accepted on the basis of other beliefs, which may be accepted on the basis of still other beliefs, and so on until the foundations are reached. In a rational noetic structure, therefore, every nonbasic belief is ultimately accepted on the basis of basic beliefs. . . .

According to the foundationalist, therefore, every rational noetic structure has a foundation, and all nonbasic beliefs are ultimately accepted on the basis of beliefs in the foundations. But a belief cannot properly be accepted on the basis of just *any* other belief; in a rational noetic structure, A will be accepted on the basis of B only if B *supports* A or is a member of a set of beliefs that together support A. It is not clear just what this relation—call it the "supports" relation—is; and different foundationalists propose different candidates. Presumably, however, it lies in the neighborhood of *evidence*; if A supports B, then A is evidence for B, or makes B evident; or perhaps B is likely or probable with respect to B. This relation admits of degrees. My belief that Feike can swim is supported by my knowledge that nine out of ten Frisians can swim and Feike is a Frisian; it is supported more strongly by my knowledge that the evening paper contains a picture of Feike triumphantly finishing first in the fifteen-hundred meter freestyle in the 1980 summer Olympics. And the foundationalist holds, sensibly enough, that in a rational noetic structure the strength of a nonbasic belief will depend upon the degree of support from foundational beliefs. . . .

By way of summary, then, let us say that according to foundationalism: (1) in a rational noetic structure the believed-on-the-basis-of relation is asymmetric and irreflexive, (2) a rational noetic structure has a foundation, and (3) in a rational noetic structure nonbasic belief is proportional in strength to support from the foundations.

· *III* ·

Next we note a further and fundamental feature of classic varieties of foundationalism: they all lay down certain conditions of proper basicality. From the foundationalist point of view not just any kind of belief can be found in the foundations of a rational noetic structure; a belief to be properly basic (that is, basic in a rational noetic structure) must meet certain conditions. It must be capable of functioning foundationally, capable of bearing its share of the weight of the whole noetic structure. Thus Thomas Aquinas, as we have seen, holds that a proposition is properly basic for a person only if it is self-evident to him or "evident to the senses."

Suppose we take a brief look at self-evidence. Under what conditions does a proposition have it? What kinds of propositions are self-evident? Examples would include very simple arithmetical truths such as

(1) $2 + 1 = 3$;

simple truths of logic such as

(2) No man is both married and unmarried;

perhaps the generalizations of simple truths of logic, such as

(3) For any proposition p the conjunction of p with its denial is false;

and certain propositions expressing identity and diversity; for example,

(4) Redness is distinct from greenness,

(5) The property of being prime is distinct from the property of being composite,

and

(6) The proposition *all men are mortal* is distinct from the proposition *all mortals are men*.

· ·

Still other candidates—candidates which may be less than entirely uncontroversial—come from many other areas; for example,

(7) If p is necessarily true and p entails q, then q is necessarily true,

(8) If e^1 occurs before e^2 and e^2 occurs before e^3, then e^1 occurs before e^3,

and

(9) It is wrong to cause unnecessary (and unwanted) pain just for the fun of it.

What is it that characterizes these propositions? According to the tradition the outstanding characteristic of a self-evident proposition is that one simply sees it to be true upon grasping or understanding it. Understanding a self-evident proposition is sufficient for apprehending its truth. Of course this notion must be relativized to *persons*; what is self-evident to you might not be to me. Very simple arithmetical truths will be self-evident to nearly all of us, but a truth like $17 + 18 = 35$ may be self-evident only to some. And of course a proposition is self-evident to a person only if he does in fact grasp it, so a proposition will not be self-evident to those who do not apprehend the concepts it involves. As Aquinas says, some propositions are self-evident only to the learned; his example is the truth that immaterial substances do not occupy space. Among those propositions whose concepts not everyone grasps, some are such that anyone who *did* grasp them would see their truth; for example,

(10) A model of a first-order theory T assigns truth to the axioms of T.

Others —17 + 13 = 30, for example—may be such that some but not all of those who apprehend them also see that they are true.

But how shall we understand this "seeing that they are true"? Those who speak of self-evidence explicitly turn to this visual metaphor and expressly explain self-evidence by reference to vision. There are two important aspects to the metaphor and two corresponding components to the idea of self-evidence. First, there is the *epistemic* component: a proposition p is self-evident to a person S only if S has *immediate* knowledge of p—that is, knows p, and does not know p on the basis of his knowledge of other propositions. Consider a simple arithmetic truth such as $2 + 1 = 3$ and compare it with one like $24 \times 24 = 576$. I know each of these propositions, and I know the second but not the first on the basis of computation, which is a kind of inference. So I have immediate knowledge of the first but not the second.

But there is also a phenomenological component. Consider again our two propositions; the first but not the second has about it a kind of luminous aura or glow when you bring it to mind or consider it. Locke speaks, in this connection, of an "evident luster"; a self-evident proposition, he says, displays a kind of "clarity and brightness to the attentive mind." Descartes speaks instead of "clarity and distinctness"; each, I think, is referring to the same phenomenological feature. And this feature is connected with another: upon understanding a proposition of this sort one feels a strong inclination to accept it; this luminous obviousness seems to compel or at least impel assent. Aquinas and Locke, indeed, held that a person, or at any rate a normal, well-formed human being, finds it impossible to withhold assent when considering a self-evident proposition. The phenomenological component of the idea of self-evidence, then, seems to have a double aspect: there is the luminous aura that $2 + 1 = 3$ displays, and there is also an experienced tendency to accept or believe it. Perhaps, indeed, the luminous aura *just is* the experienced impulsion toward acceptance; perhaps these are the very same thing. In that case the phenomenological component would not have the double aspect I suggested it did have; in either case, however, we must recognize this phenomenological aspect of self-evidence.

Aquinas therefore holds that self-evident propositions are properly basic. I think he means to add that propositions "evident to the senses" are also properly basic. By this latter term I think he means to refer to *perceptual* propositions—propositions whose truth or falsehood we can determine by looking or employing some other sense. He has in mind, I think, such propositions as

(11) There is a tree before me,
(12) I am wearing shoes,

and

(13) That tree's leaves are yellow.

So Aquinas holds that a proposition is properly basic if and only if it is either self-evident or evident to the senses. Other foundationalists have insisted that propositions basic in a rational noetic structure must be *certain* in some important sense. Thus it is plausible to see Descartes as holding that the foundations of a rational noetic structure include, not such propositions as (11)–(13), but more cautious claims—claims about one's own mental life; for example,

(14) It seems to me that I see a tree,
(15) I seem to see something green,

or, as Professor Chisholm puts it,

(16) I am appeared greenly to.

Propositions of this latter sort seem to enjoy a kind of immunity from error not enjoyed by those of the former. I could be mistaken in thinking I see a pink rat; perhaps I am hallucinating or the victim of an illusion. But it is at the least very much harder to see that I could be mistaken in believing that I *seem* to see pink rat, in believing that I am appeared pinkly (or pink ratly) to. Suppose we say that a proposition with respect to which I enjoy this sort of immunity from error is incorrigible for me; then perhaps Descartes means to hold that a proposition is properly basic for *S* only if it is either self-evident or incorrigible for *S*.

By way of explicit definition:

(17) p is incorrigible for S if and only if (a) it is not possible that S believe p and p be false, and (b) it is not possible that S believe ~p and p be true.

. . . .

Here we have a further characteristic of foundationalism: the claim that not just any proposition is properly basic. Ancient and medieval foundationalists tended to hold that a proposition is properly basic for a person only if it is either self-evident or evident to the senses: modern foundationalists—Descartes, Locke, Leibniz, and the like—tended to hold that a proposition is properly basic for *S* only if either self-evident or incorrigible for *S*. Of course this is a historical generalization and is thus perilous; but perhaps it is worth the risk. And now let us say that a *classical foundationalist* is any one who is either an ancient and medieval or a modern foundationalist.

· IV ·

Now suppose we return to the main question: Why should not belief in God be among the foundations of my noetic structure? The answer, on the part of the classical foundationalist, was that even if this belief is *true*, it does not have the characteristics a proposition must have to deserve a place in the foundations. There is no room in the foundations for a proposition that can be rationally accepted only on the basis of other propositions. The only properly basic propositions are those that are self-evident or incorrigible or evident to the senses. Since the proposition that God exists is none of the above, it is not properly basic for anyone; that is, no well-formed, rational noetic structure contains this proposition in its foundations. But now we must take a closer look at this fundamental principle of classical foundationalism:

(18)   A proposition p is properly basic for a person S if and only if p is either self-evident to S or incorrigible for S or evident to the senses for S.

(18) contains two claims: first, a proposition is properly basic *if* it is self-evident, incorrigible, or evident to the senses, and, second, a proposition is properly basic *only if* it meets this condition. The first seems true enough; suppose we concede it. But what is to be said for the second? Is there any reason to accept it? Why does the foundationalist accept it? Why does he think the theist ought to?

We should note first that if this thesis, and the correlative foundationalist thesis that a proposition is rationally acceptable only if it follows from or is probable with respect to what is properly basic—if these claims are true, then enormous quantities of what we all in fact believe are irrational. One crucial lesson to be learned from the development of modern philosophy—Descartes through Hume, roughly—is just this: relative to propositions that are self-evident and incorrigible, most of the beliefs that form the stock in trade of ordinary everyday life are not probable—at any rate there is no reason to think they are probable. Consider all those propositions that entail, say, that there are enduring physical objects, or that there are persons distinct from myself, or that the world has existed for more than five minutes: none of these propositions, I think, is more probable than not with respect to what is self-evident or incorrigible for me; at any rate no one has given good reason to think any of them is. And now suppose we add to the foundations propositions that are evident to the senses, thereby moving from modern to ancient and medieval foundationalism. Then propositions entailing the existence of material objects will of course be probable with respect to the foundations, because included therein. But the same cannot be said either for propositions about the past or for propositions entailing the existence of persons distinct from myself; as before, these will not be probable with respect to what is properly basic.

And does not this show that the thesis in question is false? The contention is that

(19) A is properly basic for me only if A is self-evident or incorrigible or evident to the senses for me.

But many propositions that do not meet these conditions *are* properly basic for me. I believe, for example, that I had lunch this noon. I do not believe this proposition on the basis of other propositions; I take it as basic; it is in the foundations of my noetic structure. Furthermore, I am entirely rational in so taking it, even though this proposition is neither self-evident nor evident to the senses nor incorrigible for me. Of course this may not convince the foundationalist; he may think that in fact I do *not* take that proposition as basic, or perhaps he will bite the bullet and maintain that if I really do take it as basic, then the fact is I *am*, so far forth, irrational.

Perhaps the following will be more convincing. According to the classical foundationalist (call him F) a person S is rational in accepting (19) only if either (19) is properly basic (self-evident or incorrigible or evident to the senses) for him, or he believes (19) on the basis of propositions that are properly basic for him and support (19). Now presumably if F knows of some support for (19) from propositions that are self-evident or evident to the senses or incorrigible, he will be able to provide a good argument—deductive, inductive, probabilistic or whatever—whose premises are self-evident or evident to the senses or incorrigible and whose conclusion is (19). So far as I know, no foundationalist has provided such an argument. It therefore appears that the foundationalist does not know of any support for (19) from propositions that are (on his account) properly basic. So if he is to be rational in accepting (19), he must (on his own account) accept it as basic. But according to (19) itself, (19) is properly basic for *F* only if (19) is self-evident or incorrigible or evident to the senses for him. Clearly (19) meets none of these conditions. Hence it is not properly basic for *F*. But then *F* is self-referentially inconsistent in accepting (19); he accepts (19) as basic, despite the fact that (19) does not meet the condition for proper basicality that (19) itself lays down.

Furthermore, (19) is either false or such that in accepting it the foundationalist is violating his epistemic responsibilities. For *F* does not know of any argument or evidence for (19). Hence if it is true, he will be violating his epistemic responsibilities in accepting it. So (19) is either false or such that *F* cannot rationally accept it. Still further, if the theist were to accept (19) at the foundationalist's urging but without argument, he would be adding to his noetic structure a proposition that is either false or such that in accepting it he violates his noetic responsibilities. But if there is such a thing as the ethics of belief, surely it will proscribe believing a proposition one knows to be either false or such that one ought not to believe it. Accordingly, I ought not to accept (19) in the absence of argument from premises that meet the condition it lays down. The same goes for the foundationalist: if he cannot find such an argument for (19), he ought to give it up. Furthermore, he ought not to urge and I ought not to accept any objection to theistic belief that crucially depends upon a proposition that is true only if I ought not believe it. . . .

Now we could canvass revisions of (19), and later I shall look into the proper procedure for discovering and justifying such criteria for proper basicality. It is evident, however, that classical foundationalism is bankrupt, and insofar as the evidentialist objection is rooted in classical foundationalism, it is poorly rooted indeed.

Of course the evidentialist objection *need* not presuppose classical foundationalism; someone who accepted quite a different version of foundationalism could no doubt urge this objection. But in order to evaluate it, we should have to see what criterion of proper basicality was being invoked. In the absence of such specification the objection remains at best a promissory note. So far as the present discussion goes, then, the next move is up to the evidentialist objector. He must specify a criterion for proper basicality that is free from self-referential difficulties, rules out belief in God as properly basic, and is such that there is some reason to think it is true. . . .

· V ·

Suppose we think of natural theology as the attempt to prove or demonstrate the existence of God. This enterprise has a long and impressive history—a history stretching back to the dawn of Christendom and boasting among its adherents many of the truly great thinkers of the Western world. One thinks, for example, of Anselm, Aquinas, Scotus, and Ockham, of Descartes, Spinoza, and Leibniz. Recently—since the time of Kant, perhaps—the tradition of natural theology has not been as overwhelming as it once was; yet it continues to have able defenders both within and without officially Catholic philosophy.

Many Christians, however, have been less than totally impressed. In particular Reformed or Calvinist theologians have for the most part taken a dim view of this enterprise. A few Reformed thinkers—B. B. Warfield, for example—endorse the theistic proofs, but for the most part the Reformed attitude has ranged from tepid endorsement, through indifference, to suspicion, hostility, and outright accusations of blasphemy. And this stance is initially puzzling. It looks a little like the attitude some Christians adopt toward faith healing: it can't be done, but even if it could it shouldn't be. What exactly, or even approximately, do these sons and daughters of the Reformation have against proving the existence of God? What *could* they have against it? What could be less objectionable to any but the most obdurate atheist?

· *VI* ·

By way of answering this question, I want to consider three representative Reformed thinkers. Let us begin with the nineteenth-century Dutch theologian Herman Bavinck;

> A distinct natural theology, obtained apart from any revelation, merely through observation and study of the universe in which man lives, does not exist. . . .
> Scripture urges us to behold heaven and earth, birds and ants, flowers and lilies, in order that we may see and recognize God in them. "Lift up your eyes on high, and see who hath created these." Is. 40:26. Scripture does not reason in the abstract. It does not make God the conclusion of a syllogism, leaving it to us whether we think the argument holds or not. But it speaks with authority. Both theologically and religiously it proceeds from God as the starting point.
> We receive the impression that belief in the existence of God is based entirely upon these proofs. But indeed that would be "a wretched faith, which, before it invokes God, must first prove his existence." The contrary, however, is the truth. There is not a single object the existence of which we hesitate to accept until definite proofs are furnished. Of the existence of self, of the world round about us, of logical and moral laws, etc., we are so deeply convinced because of the indelible impressions which all these things make upon our consciousness that we need no arguments or demonstration. Spontaneously, altogether involuntarily: without any constraint or coercion, we accept that existence. Now the same is true in regard to the existence of God. The so-called proofs are by no means the final grounds of our most certain conviction that God exists. This certainty is established only by faith; that is, by the spontaneous testimony which forces itself upon us from every side.

According to Bavinck, then, belief in the existence of God is not based upon proofs or arguments. By "argument" here I think he means arguments in the style of natural theology—the sort given by Aquinas and Scotus and later by Descartes, Leibniz, Clarke, and others. And what he means to say, I think, is that Christians do not *need* such arguments. Do not need them for what?

Here I think Bavinck means to hold two things. First, arguments or proofs are not, in general, the source of the believer's confidence in God. Typically the believer does not believe in God on the basis of arguments; nor does he believe such truths as that God has created the world on the basis of arguments. Second, argument is not needed for *rational justification*; the believer is entirely within his epistemic right in believing, for example, that God has created the world, even if he has no argument at all for that conclusion. The believer does not need natural theology in order to achieve rationality or epistemic propriety in believing; his belief in God can be perfectly rational even if he knows of no cogent argument, deductive or inductive, for the existence of God— indeed, even if there is no such argument.

Bavinck has three further points. First he means to add, I think, that we cannot come to knowledge of God on the basis of argument; the arguments of natural theology just do not work. (And he follows this passage with a more or less traditional attempt to refute the theistic proofs, including an endorsement of some of Kant's fashionable confusions about the ontological argument.) Second, Scripture "proceeds from God as the starting point," and so should the believer. There is nothing by way of proofs or arguments for God's existence in the Bible; that is simply presupposed. The same should be true of the Christian believer then; he should *start* from belief in God rather than from the premises of some argument whose conclusion is that God exists. What is it that makes those premises a better starting point anyway? And third, Bavinck points out that belief in God relevantly resembles belief in the existence of the self and of the external world—and, we might add, belief in our minds and the past. In none of these areas do we typically *have* proof or arguments, or *need* proofs or arguments.

Suppose we turn next to John Calvin, who is as good a Calvinist as any, According to Calvin God has implanted in us all an innate tendency, or nisus, or disposition to believe in him:

> 'There is within the human mind, and indeed by natural instinct, an awareness of divinity.' This we take to be beyond controversy. To prevent anyone from taking refuge in the pretense of ignorance, God himself has implanted in all men a certain understanding of his divine majesty. Ever renewing its memory, he repeatedly sheds fresh drops. Since, therefore, men one and all perceive that there is a God and that he is their Maker, they are condemned by their own testimony because they have failed to honor him and to consecrate their lives to his will. If ignorance of God is to be looked for anywhere, surely one is most likely to find an example of it among the more backward folk and those more remote from civilization. Yet there is, as the eminent pagan says, no nation so barbarous, no people so savage, that they have not a deep-seated conviction that there is a God. So deeply does the common conception occupy the minds of all, so tenaciously does it inhere in the hearts of all! Therefore, since from the beginning of the world there has been no region, no city, in short, no household, that could do without religion, there lies in this a tacit confession of a sense of deity inscribed in the hearts of all.
>
> Indeed, the perversity of the impious, who though they struggle furiously are unable to extricate themselves from the fear of God, is abundant testimony that this conviction, namely, that t*here is some God*, is naturally inborn in all, and is fixed deep within, as it were in the very marrow. . . . From this we conclude *that it is not a doctrine that must first be learned in school*, but one of which each of us is master from his mother's womb and which nature itself permits no one to forget.

Calvin's claim, then, is that God has created us in such a way that we have a strong tendency or inclination toward belief in him. This tendency has been in part overlaid or suppressed by sin. Were it not for the existence of sin in the world, human beings would believe in God to the same degree and with the same natural spontaneity that we believe in the existence of other persons, an external world, or the past. This is the natural human condition; it is because of our presently unnatural sinful condition that many of us find belief in God difficult or absurd. The fact is, Calvin thinks, one who does not believe in God is in an epistemically substandard position—rather like a man who does not believe that his wife exists, or thinks she is like a cleverly constructed robot and has no thoughts, feelings, or consciousness.

Although this disposition to believe in God is partially suppressed, it is nonetheless universally present. And it is triggered or actuated by a widely realized condition:

> Lest anyone, then, be excluded from access to happiness, he not only sowed in men's minds that seed of religion of which we have spoken, but revealed himself and daily

discloses himself in the whole workmanship of the universe. As a consequence, men cannot open their eyes without being compelled to see him.

Like Kant, Calvin is especially impressed in this connection, by the marvelous compages of the starry heavens above:

> Even the common folk and the most untutored, who have been taught only by the aid of the eyes, cannot be unaware of the excellence of divine art, for it reveals itself in this innumerable and yet distinct and well-ordered variety of the heavenly host.

And Calvin's claim is that one who accedes to this tendency and in these circumstances accepts the belief that God has created the world—perhaps upon beholding the starry heavens or the splendid majesty of the mountains, or the intricate, articulate beauty of a tiny flower—is entirely within his epistemic rights in so doing. It is not that such a person is justified or rational in so believing by virtue of having an implicit argument—some version of the teleological argument, say. No; he does not need any argument for justification or rationality. His belief need not be based on any other propositions at all; under these conditions he is perfectly rational in accepting belief in God in the utter absence of any argument, deductive or inductive. Indeed, a person in these conditions, says Calvin, *knows* that God exists.

Elsewhere Calvin speaks of "arguments from reason" or rational arguments:

> The prophets and apostles do not boast either of their keenness or of anything that obtains credit for them as they speak; nor do they dwell upon rational proofs. Rather, they bring forward God's holy name, that by it the whole world may be brought into obedience to him. Now we ought to see how apparent it is not only by plausible opinion but by clear truth that they do not call upon God's name heedlessly or falsely. If we desire to provide in the best way for our consciences—that they may not be perpetually beset by the instability of doubt or vacillation, and that they may not also boggle at the smallest quibbles—we ought to seek our conviction in a higher place than human reasons, judgments, or conjectures, that is, in the secret testimony of the Spirit. (book 1, chapter 7, p.78)

Here the subject for discussion is not belief in the existence of God, but belief that God is the author of the Scriptures; I think it is clear, however, that Calvin would say the same thing about belief in God's existence. The Christian does not *need* natural theology, either as the source of his confidence or to justify his belief. Furthermore, the Christian *ought* not to believe on the basis of argument; if he does, his faith is likely to be "unstable and wavering," the "subject of perpetual doubt." If my belief in God is based on argument, then if I am to be properly rational, epistemically responsible, I shall have to keep checking the philosophical journals to see whether, say, Antony Flew has finally come up with a good objection to my favorite argument. This could be bothersome and time-consuming; and what do I do if someone does find a flaw in my argument? Stop going to church? From Calvin's point of view believing in the existence of God on the basis of rational argument is like believing in the existence of your spouse on the basis of the analogical argument for other minds—whimsical at best and unlikely to delight the person concerned. . . .

Karl Barth joins Calvin and Bavinck in holding that the believer in God is entirely within his epistemic rights in believing as he does even if he does not know of any good theistic argument. They all hold that belief in God is *properly basic*—that is, such that it is rational to accept it without accepting it on the basis of any other proposition or beliefs at all. In fact, they think the Christian ought not to accept belief in God on the basis of argument; to do so is to run the risk of a faith that is unstable and wavering, subject to all the wayward whim and fancy of the latest academic fashion. What the Reformers held was that a believer is entirely rational, entirely within his epistemic rights, in *starting with* belief in God, in accepting it as basic, and in taking it as premise for argument to other conclusions.

In rejecting natural theology, therefore, these Reformed thinkers mean to say first of all that the propriety or rightness of belief in God in no way depends upon the success or availability of the sort of theistic arguments that form the natural theologian's stock in trade. I think this is their central claim here, and their central insight. As these Reformed thinkers see things, one who takes belief in God as basic is not thereby violating any epistemic duties or revealing a defect in his noetic structure; quite the reverse. The correct or proper way to believe in God, they thought, was not on the basis of arguments from natural theology or anywhere else; the correct way is to take belief in God as basic.

I spoke earlier of classical foundationalism, a view that incorporates the following three theses:

(1) In every rational noetic structure there is a set of beliefs taken as basic—that is, not accepted on the basis of any other beliefs,

(2) In a rational noetic structure nonbasic belief is proportional to support from the foundations,

and

(3) In a rational noetic structure basic beliefs will be self-evident or incorrigible or evident to the senses.

Now I think these three Reformed thinkers should be understood as rejecting classical foundationalism. They may have been inclined to accept (1); they show no objection to (2); but they were utterly at odds with the idea that the foundations of a rational noetic structure can at most include propositions that are self-evident or evident to senses or incorrigible. In particular, they were prepared to insist that a rational noetic structure can include belief in God as basic. As Bavinck put it, "Scripture . . . does not make God the conclusion of a syllogism, leaving it to us whether we think the argument holds or not. But it speaks with authority. Both theologically and religiously it proceeds from God as the starting point." And of course Bavinck means to say that we must emulate Scripture here.

In the passages I quoted earlier, Calvin claims the believer does not need argument—does not need it, among other things, for epistemic respectability. We may understand him as holding, I think, that a rational noetic structure may very well contain belief in God among its foundations. Indeed, he means to go further, and in two separate directions. In the first place he thinks a Christian *ought* not believe in God on the basis of other propositions; a proper and well-formed Christian noetic structure will *in fact* have belief in God among its foundations. And in the second place Calvin claims that one who takes belief in God as basic can *know* that God exists. Calvin holds that one can *rationally accept* belief in God as basic; he also claims that one can *know* that

God exists even if he has no argument, even if he does not believe on the basis of other propositions. A foundationalist is likely to hold that some properly basic beliefs are such that anyone who accepts them *knows* them. More exactly, he is likely to hold that among the beliefs properly basic for a person S, some are such that if S accepts them, S knows them. He could go on to say that *other* properly basic beliefs cannot be known if taken as basic, but only rationally believed; and he might think of the existence of God as a case in point. Calvin will have none of this; as he sees it, one needs no arguments to know that God exists. . . .

· *VII* ·

It is tempting to raise the following sort of question. If belief in God is properly basic, why cannot *just any* belief be properly basic? Could we not say the same for any bizarre aberration we can think of? What about voodoo or astrology? What about the belief that the Great Pumpkin returns every Halloween? Could I properly take *that* as basic? Suppose I believe that if I flap my arms with sufficient vigor, I can take off and fly about the room; could I defend myself against the charge of irrationality by claiming this belief is basic? If we say that belief in God is properly basic, will we not be committed to holding that just anything, or nearly anything, can properly be taken as basic, thus throwing wide the gates to irrationalism and superstition?

Certainly not. According to the Reformed epistemologist certain beliefs are properly basic in certain circumstances; those same beliefs may *not* be properly basic in other circumstances. Consider the belief that I see a tree: this belief is properly basic in circumstances that are hard to describe in detail, but include my being appeared to in a certain characteristic way; that same belief is not properly basic in circumstances including, say, my knowledge that I am sitting in the living room listening to music with my eyes closed. What the Reformed epistemologist holds is that there are widely realized circumstances in which belief in God is properly basic; but why should that be thought to commit him to the idea that just about *any* belief is properly basic in any circumstances, or even to the vastly weaker claim that for any belief there are circumstances in which it is properly basic? Is it just that he rejects the criteria for proper basicality purveyed by classical foundationalism? But why should *that* be thought to commit him to such tolerance of irrationality? Consider an analogy. In the palmy days of positivism the positivists went about confidently wielding their verifiability criterion and declaring meaningless much that was clearly meaningful. Now suppose someone rejected a formulation of that criterion—the one to be found in the second edition of A. J. Ayer's *Language, Truth and Logic* for example. Would that mean she was committed to holding that

(1) T' was brillig; and the slithy toves did gyre and gymble in the wabe,

contrary to appearances, makes good sense? Of course not. But then the same goes for the Reformed epistemologist: the fact that he rejects the criterion of proper basicality purveyed by classical foundationalism does not mean that he is committed to supposing just anything is properly basic.

But what then is the problem? Is it that the Reformed epistemologist not only rejects those criteria for proper basicality but seems in no hurry to produce what he takes to be a better substitute? If he has no such criterion, how can he fairly reject belief in the Great Pumpkin as properly basic?

This objection betrays an important misconception. How *do* we rightly arrive at or develop criteria for meaningfulness, or justified belief, or proper basicality? Where do they come from? Must one have such a criterion before one can sensibly make any judgments—positive or negative—about proper basicality? Surely not. Suppose I do not know of a satisfactory substitute for the criteria proposed by classical foundationalism; I am nevertheless entirely within my epistemic rights in holding that certain propositions in certain conditions are not properly basic.

Some propositions seem self-evident when in fact they are not; that is the lesson of some of the Russell paradoxes. Nevertheless it would be irrational to take as basic the denial of a proposition that seems self-evident to you. Similar, suppose it seems to you that you see a tree; you would then be irrational in taking as basic the proposition that you do not see a tree or that there are no trees. In the same way, even if I do not know of some illuminating criterion of meaning, I can quite properly declare (1) (above) meaningless.

And this raises an important question—one Roderick Chisholm has taught us to ask. What is the status of criteria for knowledge, or proper basicality, or justified belief? Typically these are universal statements. The modern foundationalist's criterion for proper basicality, for example, is doubly universal:

(2)   For any proposition A and person S, A is properly basic for S if and only if A is incorrigible for S or self-evident to S.

But how could one know a thing like that? What are its credentials? Clearly enough, (2) is not self-evident or just obviously true. But if it is not, how does one arrive at it? What sorts of arguments would be appropriate? Of course a foundationalist might find (2) so appealing he simply takes it to be true, neither offering argument for it nor accepting it on the basis of other things he believes. If he does so, however, his noetic structure will be self-referentially incoherent. (2) itself is neither self-evident nor incorrigible; hence if he accepts (2) as basic, the modern foundationalist violates in accepting it the condition of proper basicality he himself lays down. On the other had, perhaps the foundationalist will try to produce some argument for it from premises that are self-evident or incorrigible: it is exceedingly hard to see, however, what such an argument might be like. And until he has produced such arguments, what shall the rest of us do—we who do not find (2) at all obvious or compelling? How could he use (2) to show us that belief in God, for example, is not properly basic? Why should we believe (2) or pay it any attention?

The fact is, I think, that neither (2) nor any other revealing necessary and sufficient condition for proper basicality follows from clearly self-evident premises by clearly acceptable arguments. And hence the proper way to arrive at such a criterion is, broadly speaking, *inductive*. We must assemble examples of beliefs and conditions such that the former are obviously properly basic in the latter, and examples of beliefs and conditions such that the former are obviously *not* properly basic in the latter. We must then frame hypotheses as to the necessary and sufficient conditions of proper basicality and test these hypotheses by reference to those examples. Under the right conditions, for example, it is clearly rational to believe that you see a human person before you: a being who has thoughts and feelings, who knows and believes things, who makes decisions and acts. It is clear, furthermore, that you are under no obligation to reason to this belief from others you hold; under those conditions that belief is properly basic for you. But then (2) must be mistaken; the belief in question, under those circumstances, is properly basic, though neither self-evident nor incorrigible for you. Similarly, you may seem to remember that you had breakfast this morning, and perhaps you know of no reason to suppose your memory is playing you tricks. If so, you are entirely justified in taking that belief as basic. Of course it is not properly basic on the criteria offered by classical foundationalists, but that fact counts not against you but against those criteria. . . .

Accordingly, criteria for proper basicality must be reached from below rather than above; they should not be presented *ex cathedra* but argued to and tested by a relevant set of examples. But there is no reason to assume, in advance, that everyone will agree on the examples. The Christian will of course suppose that belief in God is entirely proper and rational; if he does not accept this belief on the basis of other propositions, he will conclude that it is basic for him and quite properly so. Followers of Bertrand Russell and Madelyn Murray O'Hare may disagree; but how is that relevant? Must my criteria, or those of the Christian community, conform to their examples? Surely not. The Christian community is responsible to *its* set of examples, not to theirs. . . .

So, the Reformed epistemologist can properly hold that belief in the Great Pumpkin is not properly basic, even though he holds that belief in God is properly basic and even if he has no full-fledged criterion of proper basicality. Of course he is committed to supposing that there is a relevant *difference* between belief in God and belief in the Great Pumpkin if he holds that the former but not the latter is properly basic. But this should prove no great embarrassment; there are plenty of candidates. These candidates are to be found in the neighborhood of the conditions that justify and ground belief in God—conditions I shall discuss in the next section. Thus, for example, the Reformed epistemologist may concur with Calvin in holding that God has implanted in us a natural tendency to see his hand in the world around us; the same cannot be said for the Great Pumpkin, there being no Great Pumpkin and no natural tendency to accept beliefs about the Great Pumpkin.

o   o   o   *41*

In Search of the
Foundations of Theism

Philip Quinn

· *I* ·

FOUNDATIONALISM COMES IN two varieties. Descriptive foundationalism is a thesis about the structure of a body of beliefs, and normative foundationalism is a thesis about the structure of epistemic justification for a body of beliefs. Both varieties partition a body of beliefs into two subclasses, a foundational class and a founded class. For descriptive foundationalism, the foundational class is the class of basic beliefs. A belief is basic for a person at a time provided it is accepted by that person at that time but is not accepted by that person at that time on the basis of any of his or her other beliefs at that time. For normative foundationalism, the foundational class is the class of properly basic beliefs. A belief is properly basic for a person at a time just in case it is basic for the person at the time and its being basic for the person at the time is contrary to no correct canon of epistemic propriety and results from no epistemic deficiency on his or her part at that time. For descriptive foundationalism, the founded class is the class of beliefs based on basic beliefs, and for normative foundationalism, the founded class is the class of beliefs properly based on properly basic beliefs.

It surely is possible that, for some human persons at some times, certain propositions that self-evidently entail that God exists are basic. But is it also possible that, for some human persons at some times, certain propositions that self-evidently entail that God exists are *properly* basic? In other words, could such propositions *be*, or at least *be among*, the normative foundations of theism, at least for some people at some times? The answers to these questions depend, of course, on what the correct criteria for proper basicality turn out to be.

Recently Alvin Plantinga has been arguing that it is in order for a religious epistemologist to return affirmative answers to these questions.[1] There are two prongs

---

[1] Alvin Plantinga, "Is Belief in God Properly Basic?" *Nous* 15 (1981). Additional discussion related to the charge that modern foundationalism is self-referentially incoherent may be found in Alvin Plantinga, "Is Belief in God Rational?" *Rationality and Religious Belief*, edited by C. F. Delaney (Notre Dame: Univ. of Notre Dame Press, 1979). Material from both these papers has subsequently been incorporated into Alvin Plantinga, "Rationality and Religious Belief," *Contemporary Philosophy of Religion*, edited by Steven M. Cahn and David Shatz (New York: Oxford Univ. Press, 1982). And some of the same themes are further amplified in Alvin Plantinga, "Reason and Belief in God," *Faith and Rationality*, edited by Alvin Plantinga and Nicholas Wolterstorff (Notre Dame: Univ. of Notre Dame Press, 1983).—P.Q.

to Plantinga's argument. The first is destructive: It is an attempt to show that certain criteria for proper basicality, according to which propositions that self-evidently entail the existence of God could not be properly basic, are seriously defective and must be rejected. The second is constructive: It is an attempt to elaborate a procedure for justifying criteria for proper basicality that will allow that some propositions self-evidently entailing that God exists could turn out to be properly basic.

This paper has two aims. The first is to criticize Plantinga's argument. In the first section of the paper, I argue for two claims: (1) that Plantinga has failed to show that the criteria for proper basicality he proposes to reject are in any way defective; and (2) that Plantinga's procedure for justifying criteria for proper basicality provides no better reason for adopting criteria according to which some propositions that self-evidently entail the existence of God can be properly basic than for adopting a criterion according to which no such propositions can be properly basic. The paper's second aim is exploratory. Although Plantinga's argument is unsuccessful, it may nevertheless be true that some propositions that self-evidently entail that God exists could be properly basic. And so, in the second section of the paper, I go on to argue, on the hypothesis that this is true, for two additional claims: (1) that actually being properly basic would be a relatively unimportant feature of such propositions because they would be at least as well justified if properly based on other properly basic propositions and could always be so based; and (2) that such propositions would seldom, if ever, be properly basic for intellectually sophisticated adult theists in our culture.

· *II* ·

CRITIQUE OF PLANTINGA

The criteria for proper basicality Plantinga proposes to reject are those of classical foundationalism. Classical foundationalism is the disjunction of ancient or medieval foundationalism and modern foundationalism. The criterion for proper basicality of ancient or medieval foundationalism is the triply universal claim:

(1) For any proposition p, person S, and time t, p is properly basic for S at t if and only if p is self-evident to S at t or is evident to the sense of S at t.

And the criterion for proper basicality of modern foundationalism is this triply universal claim:

(2) For any proposition p, person S, and time t, p is properly basic for S at t if and only if p is incorrigible for S at t or is self-evident to S at t.

Although Plantinga thinks the propositions expressed by both (1) and (2) should be rejected on grounds of self-referential incoherence, he actually discusses only the latter proposition at any length. However, it is clear that if his argument for self-referential incoherence succeeds against the proposition expressed by (2), a similar argument will, *mutatis mutandis*, work equally well against the proposition expressed by (1). But what exactly is the argument? And how much does it really prove?

Consider the proposition expressed by (2). What place does it have in the modern foundationalist's own structure of epistemic justification? Is it in the foundational class? Does the modern foundationalist suppose that it is ever properly basic for anyone? If he or she does, then he or she must hold that for someone at some time it is either incorrigible or self-evident. Plantinga believes it to be "neither self-evident nor incorrigible."[2] I agree. I think the proposition expressed by (2) is never incorrigible for or self-evident to me. Are Plantinga and I idiosyncratic in this respect? Could the modern foundationalist with any plausibility claim that we are just plain mistaken on this point? I think the answer to these questions has to be negative. It seems to me perfectly clear that the proposition expressed by (2) is never incorrigible for or self-evident to anyone. Hence, no one, not even a modern foundationalist, is entitled to suppose that the proposition expressed by (2) is ever properly basic for anyone.

Does this suffice to show that modern foundationalism is self-referentially incoherent? Obviously it does not. What would be self-referentially incoherent would be to affirm the proposition expressed by (2), to assert that it is itself never incorrigible for or self-evident to anyone, and also to claim that it is itself properly basic for someone at some time. But this leaves the modern foundationalist with the option of continuing to affirm the proposition expressed by (2) while conceding that it is itself never properly basic for anyone. For all that has been said so far, proposition expressed by (2), though never properly basic for anyone, is for some people at some times properly based on propositions that, by its own lights, are properly basic for those people at those times. In discussion, Plantinga has claimed that no modern foundationalist has ever given a good argument for the view that the proposition expressed by (2) is, for some people at some times, properly based on propositions that by its own lights, are properly basic for them then. Maybe this is so. But, even if it is, this does not show that modern foundationalism is self-referentially incoherent. All it shows is that the modern foundationalist has so far not completed the task of justifying the proposition expressed by (2) in the only way that remains open to him or her, namely, by showing how it can, for some people at some times, be properly based on propositions that are, by its own lights, properly basic for them at those times. Can this be done, and, if so, how? More generally, how could any criterion for proper basicality be justified?

Plantinga offers us an explicit answer to the more general question. He says:

> . . . the proper way to arrive at such a criterion is, broadly speaking, *inductive*. We must assemble examples of beliefs and conditions such that the former are obviously properly basic in the latter, and examples of beliefs and conditions such that the former are obviously *not* properly basic in the latter. We must then frame hypotheses as to the necessary and sufficient conditions of proper basicality and test these hypotheses by reference to those examples.[3]

As I understand the proposed procedure, it requires that we do two things. First, we are to assemble the data upon which the induction will be based. A datum may be represented as an ordered pair whose first member is a belief and whose second member is a condition. Positive data are data such that the beliefs that are their first members are obviously properly basic in the conditions that are their second members; negative data are data such that the beliefs that are their first members are obviously not properly

---

[2] Plantinga, "Is Belief in God Properly Basic?" 49.—P.Q.
[3] Ibid., 50.—P.Q.

basic in the conditions that are their second members. Call the set of data, presumably finite, so assembled 'the initial set'. Second, we are to frame hypotheses stating necessary and sufficient conditions for proper basicality and test them against the data in the initial set. A hypothesis will pass the test posed by the data in the initial set if and only if all of the positive data in the initial set and none of the negative data in that set satisfy its necessary and sufficient conditions for proper basicality. So far, so good.

However, two questions about this procedure quickly arise. First, how do we know that there will be *any* hypothesis at all stating nontrivial necessary and sufficient conditions for proper basicality that will pass the test posed by the data in the initial set? Maybe the initial set will itself be inconsistent or in some other way subtly incoherent. So perhaps we should be allowed to throw data out of the initial set should we discover that it is in some fashion incoherent. But, second, how do we know that there will be *only one* hypothesis stating nontrivial necessary and sufficient conditions for proper basicality that will pass the test posed by the data in the initial set? If the initial set is finite and our hypotheses are universally quantified, as the classical foundationalist's criteria are, then the data in the initial set will underdetermine the truth of hypotheses. In that case, there may very well be several interesting hypotheses that all pass the test posed by the data in the initial set and yet disagree radically about the proper basicality of examples outside the initial set. So perhaps we should also be allowed to add data to the initial set if this will help us to eliminate at least some of those hypotheses that have passed the test posed by the data in the initial set. These considerations make one thing very clear. Plantinga has so far given us only the rough outlines of the first stage of a broadly inductive procedure for arriving at a uniquely justified criterion of proper basicality. Many more details would need to be filled in before we could have any rational assurance that correct application of the procedure would yield exactly one hypothesis about conditions necessary and sufficient for proper basicality inductively best supported by, or most firmly based upon, the data in the initial set in some suitable revision of the initial set.

But, rough though it be, Plantinga's sketch of the first stage of a procedure for justifying criteria of proper basicality is nonetheless well enough developed to permit us to see that it confronts at the outset at least one important difficulty. This is because, as Plantinga himself acknowledges, there is no reason to assume in advance that everyone will agree on what is to go into the initial set. Plantinga says:

> The Christian will of course suppose that belief in God is entirely proper and rational; if he doesn't accept this belief on the basis of other propositions, he will conclude that it is basic for him and quite properly so. Followers of Bertrand Russell and Madelyn Murray O'Hare (*sic!*) may disagree, but how is that relevant! Must my criteria, or those of the Christian community, conform to their examples? Surely not. The Christian community is responsible to *its* set of examples, not to theirs.[4]

The difficulty is, of course, that this is a game any number can play. Followers of Muhammed, followers of Buddha, and even followers of the Reverend Moon can join in the fun. Even the modern foundationalist can play. When a modern foundationalist, under optimal conditions for visual perception, seems to see a green beach ball in front of her, she can claim that one thing that is obviously properly basic for her then is this:

---

4 Idem.—P.Q.

(3) I am being appeared to greenly.

And one thing that is obviously not properly basic for her then, she can say, is this:

(4) I am seeing a green beachball.

After all, as she sees it, the propositions expressed by the latter sentence is for her then properly based, at least in part, on the proposition expressed by the former. And she can then mimic Plantinga's own argument in this fashion: "Followers of G. E. Moore and Alvin Plantinga may disagree, but how is that relevant? Must my criteria, or those of the community of modern foundationalists, conform to their examples? Surely not. The community of modern foundationalists is responsible to *its* set of examples, not to theirs." It would seem that what is sauce for Russell's goose should also be sauce for Plantinga's gander. Turn about *is*, in this case, fair play.

Ad hominem arguments to one side, the problem is that fidelity to the data in an initial set constructed from intuitions about what is obvious is a very weak constraint on the justification of a criterion for proper basicality. The modern foundationalist can easily choose the data in his or her initial set so that his or her criterion for proper basicality passes the test they pose by making sure (1) that the only beliefs that nearly everyone would admit are, in the associated conditions, incorrigible or self-evident are the first members of positive data, and (2) that all beliefs that nearly everyone would, in the associated conditions, not consider incorrigible or self-evident are either the first members of negative data or outside the initial set altogether. How is this to be accomplished?

Suppose a modern foundationalist is contemplating believing that she is being appeared to redly in conditions optimal for visual experience in which she is being appeared to redly. Surely she can plausibly say that it is self-evident to her that that belief would be properly basic for her in those conditions, and clearly she can also reasonably claim that it is self-evident to her that that belief would be self-evident to her in those conditions. Now suppose the same modern foundationalist in contemplating believing that Jove is expressing disapproval in conditions optimal for auditory experience in which she is being appeared to thunderously. Surely she can plausibly say that it is self-evident to her that that belief would not be properly basic for her in those conditions, and clearly she can also reasonably claim that it is self-evident to her that that belief would be neither incorrigible nor self-evident to her in those conditions. After having assembled a rich initial set of positive and negative data by ringing the changes on these two thought experiments, the modern foundationalist is then in a position to claim and properly so, that his or her criterion, though not itself properly basic, is properly based, in accord with what Plantinga has told us about proper procedures for justifying criteria for proper basicality, on beliefs that are properly basic by its own lights.

It is important to understand that the data I am supposing the modern foundationalist might use to justify his or her criterion of proper basicality derive from thought experiments about hypothetical situations. My claim is not that when, for instance, a person in fact believes that Jove is expressing disapproval in conditions optimal for auditory experience in which she is being appeared to thunderously, it will then in fact be self-evident to her that that belief is not properly basic for her in those conditions. After all, she may not even wonder whether that belief is properly basic for her in those conditions when she happens to have the belief in the conditions. Rather my claim is that when a modern foundationalist contemplates the hypothetical situation of believing that Jove is expressing disapproval in conditions optimal for auditory experience in which she is being appeared to thunderously, then she can will plausibility maintain that it is self-evident to her that that belief would not in those conditions be properly basic for her. Because I hold that our intuitions about such hypothetical situations often provide the ultimate and decisive test of philosophical generalizations, I think the role of such beliefs about hypothetical situations in confirming or disconfirming philosophical generalizations is best explained on the supposition that they can be, in the right circumstances, self-evident.

In discussion, Plantinga has objected to this line of argument. If I understand his objection, it goes as follows. To say that a belief is properly basic in a set of circumstances is to say, among other things, that in those circumstances a person could accept the belief without displaying some kind of noetic defect. But what constitutes a noetic defect depends upon what constitutes the proper working of one's noetic equipment. So a proposition to the effect that a certain person on a certain occasion is displaying no such defect cannot possibly be self-evident because it cannot be self-evident to one that all one's noetic equipment is in proper working order. Hence, a proposition to the effect that a certain belief is properly basic on a certain occasion cannot possibly be self-evident either.

I concede, of course, that it is not usually self-evident to one that all one's noetic equipment is in proper working order. But if Plantinga's objection is to have any force against my argument, it must apply to the particular hypothetical case I have described above. I believe it does not. Our modern foundationalist is supposed to be contemplating believing that she is being appeared to redly in conditions optimal for visual experience in which she is being appeared to redly. It seems quite clear to me that it could be self-evident to her that she would display no noetic defect in accepting that belief in those conditions. To be sure, her noetic equipment might then have some defects of which she was unaware. She might then, for example, not be able to recognize the taste of ordinary table salt. But that is irrelevant provided she would display none of these defects in accepting the belief that she is being appeared to redly in the specified circumstances. For all that is required is that it could be self-evident to her that she would display no such defect in accepting that belief in those circumstances. Because I believe this requirement can be met, I conclude that Plantinga's objection fails. In short, it can be self-evident to one that one is displaying no noetic defect in accepting a certain belief on a certain occasion without it also being self-evident to one then that all one's noetic equipment is in proper working order.

I do not expect that this reply will bring Plantinga's objections to an end. I suspect Plantinga will continue to think the modern foundationalist has made some mistake if he or she proceeds in this fashion to justify his or her criterion for proper basicality. But it is not obvious that this is so; nor is it obvious what precisely the mistake might be. After all, one of the rules of the game specifies that the community of modern foundationalists is permitted to be responsible to *its* set of examples. Hence, absent a good argument by Plantinga that establishes that a mistake must occur in such a procedure, I think we are entitled to hold that Plantinga's own procedure for justifying criteria for proper basicality provides no better reason for adopting criteria according to which some propositions that self-evidently entail the existence of God can be properly basic than for adopting a criterion, namely, the one proposed by the modern foundationalist, according to which no such propositions can be properly basic.

Of course, nothing I have said rules out the possibility that Plantinga could use the inductive procedure he advocates to justify a criterion of proper basicality according to which some propositions that self-evidently entail that God exists can be properly basic. Indeed, if, as his talk about being responsible to the examples of the Christian community suggests, he would take some such propositions to be the first members of positive data in his initial set and thereafter not delete all such positive data in revising his initial set, it is pretty obvious that Plantinga can succeed in this task, though success at so cheap a price may be thought by some to come uncomfortably close to question begging. But if Plantinga does succeed in performing this exercise, then I think the conclusion we should draw is that his fight with classical foundationalism has resulted in a standoff.

· III ·

WHAT IF BELIEF IN GOD COULD BE PROPERLY BASIC?

If my critique of Plantinga has been successful, I have shown that he fails to prove that belief in propositions that self-evidently entail God's existence could ever be properly basic for anyone. But it might be true that belief in such propositions could be properly basic, even if Plantinga has not proved it. And if it were, what would be the consequences for religious epistemology? I now turn to an exploration of this issue.

Plantinga's examples of beliefs that could be properly basic in the right conditions include the following items:

(5) God is speaking to me.
(6) God disapproves of what I have done.

and

(7) God forgives me for what I have done.

And according to Plantinga, the right conditions include a component that is, broadly speaking, experiential. He says,

> Upon reading the Bible, one may be impressed with a deep sense that God is speaking to him. Upon having done what I know is cheap, or wrong, or wicked I may feel guilty in God's sight and form the belief that *God disapproves of what I've done*. Upon confession and repentance, I may feel forgiven, forming the belief *God forgives me for what I've done*.[5]

It strikes me that part of what makes the suggestion that beliefs like those expressed by (5)–(7) could be properly basic in conditions like those partially described in the quoted passage seem attractive is an analogy with an extremely plausible view about how certain Moorean commonsense beliefs are often justified. When I have the experience of seeming to see a hand in front of me in the right conditions, I may be justified in believing that

(8) I see a hand in front of me.

---

[5] Ibid., 46.—P.Q.

This justification may be direct in the sense of being grounded directly in the experience itself without passing through the intermediary of a belief about the way I am being appeared to such as

(9) It seems to me that I see a hand in front of me.

For I may not in the circumstances have entertained, much less accepted, the proposition expressed by (9), but, on the view under consideration, my justification for believing the proposition expressed by (8) is in no way defective on that account. Hence, the proposition expressed by (8) may be basic, and quite properly so, in the right conditions. And if this is, as I believe it to be, an attractive view about how believing the proposition expressed by (8) can be, and sometimes is, justified, then there is an argument from analogy for supposing that propositions like those expressed by (5)–(7) may also be properly basic in conditions that include an experiential component of the right sort for grounding such beliefs. To be sure, there are significant disanalogies. The direct justification of the belief expressed by (8) is grounded in a mode of sensory experience that is now generally believed by nonskeptical epistemologists to be reliable in the right conditions. By contrast, the direct justification of the beliefs expressed by (5)–(7) is grounded in a mode of experience that, though it may be reliable in the right conditions, is not now generally believed by nonskeptical epistemologists to be so. But, although such considerations might be taken to show that the analogical argument is not very strong, it does not deprive the positive analogy of heuristic and explanatory capabilities. I am going to make use of these capabilities in the remainder of the discussion.

When I have the experience of seeming to see a hand in front of me in the right conditions, though the proposition expressed by (8) could then be properly basic for me, it could instead be the case that the proposition expressed by (9) is then properly basic for me and the proposition expressed by (8) is then properly based, at least in part, on the proposition expressed by (9). For when I have that experience in those conditions, I might well be attending mainly to the qualitative aspects of my visual experience with the result that the proposition expressed by (9) is then basic for me. If this happens, the proposition expressed by (9) would clearly be properly basic for me. I might well also then base the proposition expressed by (8) in part, on the proposition expressed by (9). And, if this too happens, then the proposition expressed by (8) would be properly based, in part, on the proposition expressed by (9) because the latter proposition does nothing more than serve to articulate that part of the content of my visual experience that is relevant to justifying the former. If the proposition expressed by (8) were indirectly justified by being properly based on the proposition expressed by (9), it would be no less well justified than if it were directly justified by being directly grounded in visual experience. Since, by hypothesis, my visual experience in those conditions suffices to confer a certain degree of justification on the proposition expressed by (8), the amount of justification that reaches the proposition expressed by (8) from that experience will not be less in those conditions if it passes by way of the proposition expressed by (9) than if it is transmitted directly without intermediary. But neither would its justification be any better if indirect in this way. Moreover, it could happen that at a certain time the proposition expressed by (8) is properly basic for me and at a later time it is no longer properly basic, though still justified, for me because in the interval it has come to be properly based on the proposition expressed by (9). For in the interval I might, for example, have come to wonder whether I was justified in believing the proposition expressed by (8) and as a result come to believe the proposition expressed by (9) and to base properly on this belief my belief in the proposition expressed by (8). And if such a process did occur, I think the degree to which the proposition expressed by (8) was justified for me would, other things remaining unaltered, stay constant through it.

By analogy, similar things seem true of the examples that are Plantinga's prime candidates for religious beliefs that could be properly basic. When I am impressed with a deep sense that God is speaking to me, if the proposition expressed by (5) could then be properly basic for me, then it could instead be the case that some other proposition is among those then properly basic for me and the proposition expressed by (5) is then properly based in part on it. Such a proposition is:

(10)   It seems to me that God is speaking to me.

If the proposition expressed by (5) were indirectly justified for me by being properly based on the proposition expressed by (10), its justification would be no better, and no worse, than if it were properly basic and directly justified for me by being directly grounded in my experiential sense that God is speaking to me, other things remaining the same. And it could happen that in the course of time the proposition expressed by (5) changes from being properly basic for me to being properly based in part for me on the proposition expressed by (10) without gain or loss of degree of justification.

So, oddly enough, if certain propositions that self-evidently entail the existence of God can be properly basic for a person at a time, it is epistemically unimportant whether such propositions actually are properly basic for that person at that time. Without loss of degree of justification, such theistic propositions can just as well be properly based, at least in part, on others that are descriptive of the person's experience at the time and are then properly basic for the person. Although such theistic propositions would not need to be based on the evidence of other propositions, they always could be so based. So the cautious philosopher who did so base them would be every bit as justified in believing in the existence of God as the reckless mystic who did not.

There is another salient feature of directly justified Moorean beliefs like the one expressed by (8) which would have an analogue in the case of religious beliefs like those expressed by (5)–(7) if they could be properly basic in the right conditions. This is that the kind of justification conferred on such Moorean beliefs by direct grounding in experience of the right sort is defeasible. So, for example, a potential defeater for the proposition expressed by (8) is this:

(11)   I am not hallucinating a hand.

If propositions such as (8) are taken to be properly basic in the right conditions, then a full specification of those conditions must include reference to the status of potential defeaters such as (11). What would it be reasonable to say about potential defeaters when specifying in fuller detail the right conditions for proper basicality of the proposition expressed by (8)? Several possibilities come to mind.

It might be suggested that conditions are right for the proposition expressed by (8) to be properly basic for me only if none of its potential defeaters is true. This suggestion clearly misses the mark. When I have the experience of seeming to see a hand in front of me, it may be that the proposition expressed by (8) is true and the proposition expressed by (11) is false, and yet I am justified in rejecting the former and accepting the latter because, for instance, I remember taking a large dose of some hallucinogen only an hour ago and hallucinating wildly in the interval. Merely to insist that potential defeaters be false in order for conditions to be right for proper basicality is to require much too little.

Alternatively, it might be suggested that conditions are right for the proposition expressed by (8) to be properly basic for me only if each of its potential defeaters is such that I have some reason to think it is false. Clearly this suggestion errs in the direction of demanding too much. I have never exhaustively enumerated the potential defeaters of the proposition expressed by (8), and I am inclined to doubt that I would ever complete such a task if I began it. I have certainly never mobilized or acquired a reason against each of them. No one I know has ever tried to do such a thing in defense of all of his or her Moorean commonsense beliefs. So if such beliefs frequently are properly basic in virtue of being directly grounded in sensory experience, as I think they are, conditions are often right for proper basicality without such an elaborate structure of reasons for the falsity of potential defeaters having been mobilized.

It does, however, seem initially plausible to suppose that conditions are right for the proposition expressed by (8) to be properly basic for me only if I have no sufficiently substantial reasons to think that any of its potential defeaters is true and this is not due to epistemic negligence on my part. Two features of this claim require a bit of explanation. First, if the only reason I think that some potential defeater of the proposition expressed by (8) is true is, for instance, that I remember once, long ago, having mistaken a tree's branches for a hand, then that will not usually suffice to undermine the *prima facie* justification the proposition expressed by (8) has in the right experiential conditions to such an extent that that proposition is not properly basic. More generally, since *prima facie* justification comes in degrees, although any good reason one has for thinking one of a proposition's potential defeaters is true will undermine that proposition's *prima facie* justification to some degree, slight reasons will usually not singly undermine it to the extent that it is no longer *prima facie* justified. Instead, it will usually remain *prima facie* justified in the presence of one or a few such reasons but to a lesser degree than it would be in their absence. It takes a sufficiently substantial reason for thinking one of its potential defeaters is true to rob a proposition of proper basicality in conditions in which it would otherwise be properly basic.[6] Second, if I happen to lack sufficiently substantial reasons to think that any potential defeater of the proposition expressed by (8) is true merely because, for example, I have negligently failed to recall that I ingested some hallucinogenic substance only an hour ago and have been hallucinating wildly in the interval, then clearly conditions are not right for the proposition expressed by (8) to be properly basic for me, even though it may in fact be basic for me. More generally, a proposition is not *prima facie* justified if one negligently ignores good reasons for thinking one of its potential defeaters is true that would be sufficiently substantial to undermine the proposition's *prima facie*

---

[6] I came to appreciate this point as a result of reflecting on comments by Jonathan Malino and William P. Alston.—P.Q.

justification to such an extent that it would not be *prima facie* justified. Such epistemic negligence would constitute an epistemic deficiency.

By analogy, it also seems initially plausible to say that conditions are right for the propositions expressed by (5)–(7) to be properly basic for me only if I have no sufficiently substantial reason to think that any of their potential defeaters is true and this is not due to epistemic negligence on my part. But there is the rub. A potential defeater of the propositions expressed by (5)–(7) is this:

(12)   God does not exist.

And, unfortunately, I do have very substantial reasons for thinking that the proposition expressed by (12) is true. My reasons derive mainly from one of the traditional problems of evil. What I know, partly from experience and partly from testimony, about the amount and variety of nonmoral evil in the universe confirms highly for me the proposition expressed by (12). Of course, this is not indefeasible confirmation of the proposition expressed by (12). It could be defeated by other things I do not know. Perhaps it is not even undefeated confirmation. Maybe it even is defeated by other things I do know. Nevertheless, it does furnish me with a very substantial reason for thinking that the proposition expressed by (12) is true. Moreover, I dare say that many, perhaps most, intellectually sophisticated adults in our culture are in an epistemic predicament similar to mine. As I see it, an intellectually sophisticated adult in our culture would have to be epistemically negligent not to have very substantial reasons for thinking that what (12) expresses is true. After all, nontrivial atheological reasons, ranging from various problems of evil to naturalistic theories according to which theistic belief is illusory or merely projective, are a pervasive, if not obtrusive, component of the rational portion of our cultural heritage.

But, even if such reasons are very substantial, are they sufficiently substantial to make it the case that the propositions expressed by (5)–(7) would no longer be properly basic in conditions of the sort described by Plantinga in which, we are supposing, they could have been properly basic but for the presence of such substantial reasons? On reflection, I am convinced that such reasons are, taken collectively, sufficiently substantial, though I confess with regret that I cannot at present back up my intuitive conviction with solid arguments. But I conjecture that many, perhaps most, intellectually sophisticated adults in our culture will share my intuitive conviction of this point. And so I conclude that many, perhaps most, intellectually sophisticated adult theists in our culture are seldom, if ever, in conditions that are right for propositions like those expressed by (5)–(7) to be properly basic for them.

It does not follow from this conclusion that intellectually sophisticated adult theists in our culture cannot be justified in believing propositions like those expressed by (5)–(7). For all that I have said, some such propositions are such that, for every single one of their potential defeaters that is such that there is some very substantial reason to think it is true, there is an even better reason to think it is false. And so, for all I know, some intellectually sophisticated adult theists in our culture could be, or perhaps even are, in the fortunate position, with respect to some such propositions and their potential defeaters, of having, for each potential defeater that some epistemically nonnegligent, intellectually sophisticated adult in our culture has a very substantial reason to think is true, an even better reason to think it is false. But if there are such fortunate theists in our culture, they are people who have already accomplished at least one of the main tasks traditionally assigned to natural theology. Although they may know of no proof of the existence of God, they possess reasons good enough to defend some proposition that self-evidently entails the existence of God against all of its potential defeaters that epistemically nonnegligent, intellectually sophisticated adults in our culture have very substantial reasons to believe. I tend to doubt that many intellectually sophisticated adult theists in our culture are in this fortunate position for any appreciable portion of their lives.

But suppose someone were in this fortunate position. Such a person would have reasons good enough to defend theistic belief against all of its potential defeaters that epistemically nonnegligent, intellectually sophisticated adults in our culture have very substantial reasons to believe, and such reasons would be parts of such a person's total case for the rationality of theistic belief. But would such a person's theistic belief have to be based on such reasons? That depends, of course, on exactly what is involved in basing one belief on others. Plantinga is prudently reticent about describing the basing relation; he says only that, "although this relation isn't easy to characterize in a revealing and nontrivial fashion, it is nonetheless familiar."[7] On the basis of the examples Plantinga gives, I once conjectured in discussion that he thinks the relation is characterized by something like the following principle:

(13)   For any person S and distinct propositions p and q, S believes q on the basis of p only if S entertains p, S accepts p, S infers q from p, and S accepts q.[8]

If Plantinga does have in mind some such narrow conception of the basing relation, then our hypothetical fortunate person's theistic belief clearly need not be based on all the reasons, including defenses against potential defeaters that have very substantial support, in the person's total case for the rationality of theistic belief. After all, some such defenses may consist only of considerations that show that certain atheological arguments are unsound or otherwise defective, and our fortunate person's belief need not be based, in this narrow sense, on such considerations. Indeed, for all I know, it is possible that all our fortunate person's successful defenses against potential defeaters that have substantial support are of this sort. Hence, for all I know, our fortunate person could have a successful total case for the rationality of theistic belief made up entirely of reasons such that belief in some proposition that self-evidently entails the existence of God needs none of them for a basis. Thus, for all I know, on this narrow conception of the basing relation, our fortunate person's theistic belief might be properly basic in the right conditions.

If I were to endorse some such narrow conception of the basing relation, I would have to revise my earlier proposal about when it is plausible to suppose conditions are right for propositions to be properly basic for me. I am inclined to believe that the appropriate thing to say, in light of the line of reasoning developed in the previous

---

[7]   Plantinga, "Is Belief in God Properly Basic?" 41.—P.Q.

[8]   In a more thorough treatment, it would be important to worry about the temporal references in this principle. If I have just looked up the spelling of *umbrageous* in my dictionary, then my belief about how that word is spelled may now be based on my belief about what *my* dictionary says. But if I last looked up its spelling many months ago, then my belief about how *umbrageous* is spelled may now only be based on my belief that I seem to remember seeing it spelled that way in *some dictionary or other*. Presumably bases of the sort specified by this principle can and sometimes do shift with time.—P.Q.

paragraph, is that it seems plausible to suppose that conditions are right for propositions like those expressed by (5)–(7) to be, in the narrow sense, properly basic for me only if (i) either I have no sufficiently substantial reason to think that any of their potential defeaters is true, or I do have some such reasons but, for each such reason I have, I have an even better reason for thinking the potential defeater in question is false, and (ii), in either case, my situation involves no epistemic negligence on my part. I could then put the point I am intent on pressing by saying that, depending on which of the two disjuncts in the first clause of this principle one imagines my satisfying, I would have to be nonnegligently either rather naive and innocent or quite fortunate and sophisticated in order for conditions to be right for propositions like those expressed by (5)–(7) to be, in the narrow sense, properly basic for me. When I examine my epistemic predicament, I find myself forced to conclude that I am in neither of those extreme situations. Since I have very substantial reasons for thinking the proposition expressed by (12) is true, innocence has been lost. But, because I have not yet done enough to defend theistic belief against potential defeaters that have substantial support, I have not reached the position of our hypothetical fortunate person. Innocence has not, so to speak, been regained. Hence, conditions are not now right for propositions like those expressed by (5)–(7) to be, in the narrow sense, properly basic for me. My conjecture is that many, perhaps most, intellectually sophisticated persons in our culture are in an epistemic predicament similar to mine in this respect for most of their adult lives.

There is, of course, nothing wrong with construing the basing relation in some such narrow fashion provided one is tolerably clear about what one is doing. Surely there is such a relation, and Plantinga is free to use it in his theories if he wishes. But I think it may be more perspicuous, or at least equally illuminating, to look at matters in a slightly different way. Consider again our hypothetical fortunate person who has reasons good enough to defend theistic belief against all of its potential defeaters that epistemically nonnegligent, intellectually sophisticated adults in our culture have very substantial reasons to believe. I would say that, for such a person, theistic belief would be based, in a broad sense, on all the reasons that are parts of the person's total case for the rationality of theistic belief. In employing this broad conception of the basing relation, I am aiming to draw attention to the fact that, if the person did not have all those reasons and were like many, perhaps most, intellectually sophisticated adults in our culture, theistic belief would not be rational for the person, or at least its rationality would be diminished to an appreciable extent if some of those reasons were absent. On this broad conception of the basing relation, I would not need to revise the principle concerning the right conditions for certain propositions to be, in the broad sense, properly basic for me, to which I had ascribed initial plausibility, in order to accommodate the hypothetical fortunate person, for the fortunate person's theistic belief would be, in the broad sense, properly based on all the reasons that comprise his or her total case for the rationality of theistic belief. Reasons that are, in the broad sense, part of a basis for theistic belief need not be related to a proposition that self-evidently entails the existence of God in the same way that the premises of an inference are related to its conclusion. They may instead provide part of a basis for theistic belief roughly in the same way a physicist's demonstration that the so-called "clock paradox" does not reveal an inconsistency in special relativity provides part of a basis for special relativity. Or, to cite what may be a more helpful analogy in the present context, they may provide part of a basis for theistic belief in much the same way Richard Swinburne's argument in *The Coherence of Theism* that the claim that God exists is not demonstrably incoherent provides part of the basis for Swinburne's claim in *The Existence of God* that God's existence is more probable than not.[9] And if I am right about the epistemic predicament of many, perhaps most, intellectually sophisticated adult theists in our culture, for them theistic belief stands in need of at least some basis of this kind if it is to be rational. This may, in the end, be a point on which Plantinga and I have a disagreement that is not merely verbal. I would insist, and Plantinga, for all I know, might not, that many, perhaps most, intellectually sophisticated adult theists in our culture must, if their belief in God is to be rational, have a total case for the rationality of theistic belief that includes defenses against defeaters that have very substantial support.

· *IV* ·

CONCLUSION

If theistic belief can be *prima facie* justified by experience at all, then there may be less difference between Plantinga and his opponents than one might at first have thought.[10] Plantinga locates a proper doxastic foundation for theistic belief at the level of propositions like that expressed by (5); a modern foundationalist would wish to claim that there is a subbasement in the truly proper doxastic structure at the level of propositions like that expressed by (10).

Plantinga's view has the advantage of psychological realism. I doubt that most theists generate their doxastic structures by first entertaining and accepting propositions like that expressed by (10) and then inferring from them, together perhaps with some epistemic principles, propositions like that expressed by (5). Nonetheless, I think there is something to be said on behalf of what I take to be an important insight captured by the modern foundationalist's position, though perhaps not perfectly articulated there. Although it may be a mistake to suppose that a phenomenological belief like the one expressed by (10) must always mediate between experience and a belief like the one expressed by (5) in a properly constructed structure of *prima facie* justification for a belief like the one expressed by (5), experience of the sort that could serve to ground a belief like the one expressed by (5) is itself so thoroughly shaped and penetrated by conceptual elements that, if it grounds a belief like the one expressed by (5) directly, then the belief is based on a cognitive state of the believer, even if that state is not an explicit belief with a phenomenological proposition for its object. Perhaps it is at the level of such cognitive states that we may hope to discover the real evidential foundations in experience for theistic belief.[11]

---

[9] See Richard Swinburne, *The Coherence of Theism* (Oxford: Clarendon Press, 1977) and Richard Swinburne, *The Existence of God* (Oxford: Clarendon Press, 1979).—P.Q.

[10] A recent defense of the view that theistic belief can be *prima facie* justified by experience of certain kinds may be found in William P. Alston, "Religious Experience and Religious Belief," *Nous* 16 (1982).—P.Q.

[11] Some of the material in this paper was included in comments on Plantinga's "Is Belief in God Properly Basic?" I read at the 1981 meeting of the Western Division of the American Philosophical Association. Robert Audi was the other commentator on Plantinga's paper. Earlier versions of the present paper were read in 1984 at the Greensboro Symposium on the Logic of Religious Concepts, where Jonathan Malino was my commentator, and at the University of Notre Dame, where Alvin Plantinga was my commentator. In making various revisions, I have profited by the comments of Audi, Malino, and Plantinga and also by written criticism from William P. Alston, Roderick M. Chisholm, George I. Mavrodes, and Ernest Sosa.—P.Q.

○ ○ ○ *42*

Can Religious Belief Be Rational?
Louis Pojman

· *I* ·

INTRODUCTION

IN THIS ESSAY I argue for a thoroughly rationalistic faith. I argue that religious faith has a moral dimension underlying it, so that any faith that is not rational for a person to hold may also be immoral. I outline a notion of an ethics of belief that makes rational believing a *prima facie* moral duty and casts moral censure at leaps of faith beyond the evidence. Then I outline a coherentist strategy for justifying religious belief within the bounds of reason.

Nearly every Christian theologian has demurred from the idea of a wholly rational faith. The Catholic tradition, stemming from Thomas Aquinas, avers that the subset of doctrines, the preambles, are in accordance with reason but that such doctrines as the incarnation and the trinity are beyond its pale. On the other side of the spectrum we have the antirationalists, who believe that the key to religious belief is a miracle of faith "which subverts all the principles of understanding," as Hume skeptically but Hamann and Kierkegaard approvingly put it. (It's a fascinating intellectual anecdote in the history of philosophy that Hamann discovered Hume's dictum and set it forth in his writings as the essence of faith, where it was read by Kierkegaard, who thought Hamann had originated it and applauded him for his brilliant insight.) For Tertullian, Hamann, Kierkegaard, and Shestov the very irrationality of Christianity is reason for embracing it. If God is wholly other, we should expect his truth to seem contradictory to sinful human minds. Modern fideists, following some remarks by Wittgenstein, claim that religious belief is groundless and not subject to rational scrutiny. Somewhere in between these opposing positions is the reformed view (that of Calvin, Warfield, and Bavinck) of natural theology as somehow an irreverent activity. As Barth puts it, to reason about faith is to assume the standpoint of unbelief; it "makes reason a judge over Christ." Most recently, a well-argued version of this position has been developed by Alvin Plantinga, which claims that belief in God may be properly basic to the foundations of one's noetic structure, as justified as our belief that there are other minds or as any of our immediate empirical or memory beliefs (e.g., the memory belief that I had breakfast this morning).[1]

Although I have learned much from Plantinga and have sympathy for a great deal in his position, especially since he has modified it lately to include the notion that reason could infirm faith's stance, I find two problems with his position, which I have tried to remedy:

---

[1] The most complete version of Plantinga's views is his essay "Reason and Belief in God," in *Faith and Rationality*, edited by Alvin Plantinga and Nicholas Wolterstorff (Notre Dame: Univ. of Notre Dame Press, 1983).—L.P.

(1) The criteria of proper basicality for Plantinga seem so open-ended that virtually any world view, no matter how implausible to thoughtful people, could be justified. Although honest people will certainly differ about what is properly basic, one should suspect or even not fully accept one's own beliefs as basic if they fail to win support from the consensus of rationally informed people or epistemologists as basic or evidential. There are limits to what can count as properly basic, and although exact criteria are hard to come by, not everything can properly be part of the foundations of a noetic structure. As far as I understand the logic of Plantinga's position, there are no epistemically neutral criteria that would eliminate anyone's favorite insane belief. Here his position reminds one of Hare's famous paranoid student who had a *blik* (read "properly basic belief") that all dons were out to harm him.

(2) Secondly, I doubt that theoretical beliefs such as the existence of a divine creator of the universe fit as well into a foundationalist view of epistemology as they do into a coherentist framework. Would we believe in God if the concept had no support at all from our beliefs about the world's having a cause, a design or order, if we didn't have testimony of various encounters with the divine, if there were no claims to miraculous events confirming divine authority? Theistic belief does not stand unsupported, alone and in isolation, but as part and parcel of many other considerations that together helps us make sense of the world. Although a great many of our core beliefs cannot easily be traced back to their origins or justificatory basis, we can still offer considerations for them, showing that they are supported by other beliefs in an all-encompassing network of beliefs. Our noetic structure may well be more in the metaphorical shape of a web than in the shape of a house with a foundation. It is the very foundational metaphor that makes Plantinga's views so implausible to some of us.

· II ·

THE ETHICS OF BELIEF

First let me state why there are ethical duties to believe according to the best evidence available. Often the beliefs that we have affect the well-being of others. Suppose that you are a physician who is consulted about certain symptoms. You prescribe a drug that you have a hunch will help the patient, but your diagnosis is wrong and the patient dies. When examiners inquire into the situation, they discover that you hadn't kept up on your medicine and that your mistake would have been easily prevented had you been aware of side effects of the drug in question (and had you not misdiagnosed the symptoms). Since you could have had correct beliefs about these matters had you read the latest literature in the area, which was abundantly available, you are rightly judged to be culpably ignorant. You had an obligation to keep up with the literature. At bottom, an ethic of belief may reduce to an ethic of investigation and openness to criticism, but the point is that we are responsible for many of the beliefs that we have and that, as guides to actions, eventually result in action that may harm or help our fellow humans.

Of course, the duty to believe according to the best evidence is not our only moral duty, and perhaps there are times when another duty overrides it, but it is a duty that ought to be taken with the utmost seriousness, more than most thinkers have afforded it. Besides, how confident can we be of our beliefs if we know deep down that they are not backed up by good evidence?

If we apply this to religious belief, we can see that it is also important that we follow the best reasons in forming our belief states. Since the best justified beliefs have the best chance of being true and hence reliable, we should seek to justify even our most personal religious beliefs or doubt them. It would seem that a morally good God who created us as rational would honor doxastic honesty even if it led to unbelief.[2]

· *III* ·

RATIONALITY AND CONCEPTUAL FRAMEWORKS

Sometimes it is claimed that we use a clear-cut decision-making process, similar to the one used in mathematics and empirical science, when we arrive at justified belief or truth. A person has a duty to believe exactly according to the available evidence. Hence there is no excuse for anyone to believe anything on insufficient evidence. Such is the case of Descartes and logical positivism, which is echoed in Clifford's classical formula, "It is wrong always, everywhere, and for anyone to believe anything on insufficient evidence." Laying aside the criticism that the statement itself is self-referentially incoherent (it doesn't give us sufficient evidence for believing itself), the problem is that different data will count as evidence to different degrees according to the background beliefs a person has. The contribution of Polanyi, Popper, and Wittgenstein has been to demonstrate the power of perspectivism, the thesis that the way we evaluate or even pick out evidence is determined by our prior picture of the world, which itself is made up of a loosely connected and mutually supporting network of propositions. Do the farmer, the real estate dealer, and the landscape artist on looking at a field see the same field?

The nonperspectivist position, seen in Plato, Aquinas, Descartes, Locke, Clifford, and Chisholm, seems damaged beyond repair. However, the reaction has been to claim that since what is basic is the conceptual (fiduciary) framework, no interchange between world views is possible. As Karl Barth says, "Belief can only preach to unbelief." No argument is possible. We may call this reaction to the postcritical critique of rationalism "hard-perspectivism."

The nonperspectivist writes as though arriving at the truth were a matter of impartial evaluation of the evidence, and the hard-perspectivist writes as though no meaningful communication were possible. The world views (*Weltanschauugen*) are discontinuous. As fideists often say, "The believer and unbeliever live in different worlds."[3] There is an infinite qualitative distinction existing between various forms of life that no amount of argument or discussion can bridge. For hard-perspectivists, including Wittgensteinian fideists, reason can only have intramural significance. There are no bridges between world views.

However, hard-perspectivism is not the only possible reaction to the postcritical revolution. One may accept the insight that our manner of evaluating evidence is strongly affected by our conceptual frameworks without opting for a view that precludes communication across world views. One may recognize the depth of a conceptual

---

[2] See my book, *Religious Belief and the Will* (London: Routledge & Kegan Paul, forthcoming), part 2, chap. 2.—L.P.

[3] Alvin Plantinga suggests that the believer and the unbeliever have different conceptions of reason. Op. cit., 91.—L.P.

framework and still maintain that communication between frameworks is possible and that reason may have an intermural as well as intramural significance in the process. Such a view has been called soft-perspectivist. The soft-perspectivist is under no illusion regarding the difficulty of effecting a massive shift in the total evaluation of an immense range of data, of producing new patterns of feeling and acting in persons, but he or she is confident that the program is viable. One of the reasons given in support of this is that there is something like a core rationality common to every human culture, especially with regard to practical life. Certain rules of inference (deductive and inductive) have virtually universal application. Certain assumptions (basic beliefs) seem common to every culture (e.g., that there are other minds, that there is time, that things move, that perceptions are generally to be trusted, and so on). Through sympathetic imagination one can attain some understanding of another's conceptual system; through disappointment one can begin to suspect weakness in one's own world view and thus seek for a more adequate explanation. It is not my purpose here to produce a full defense of a soft-perspective position, but only to indicate its plausibility. The assumption on which this essay is written is that the case for soft-perspectivism can be made. And if it is true, then it is possible for reason to play a significant role in the examination, revision, and rejection of one's current beliefs and in the acquisition of new beliefs.

· IV ·

DOES RATIONALITY IMPLY A NEUTRALITY
THAT IS INCOMPATIBLE WITH RELIGIOUS FAITH?

We may say that postcritical rationalists of the soft-perspectivist variety are individuals who seek to support all their beliefs (especially their convictions)[4] with good reasons. They attempt to evaluate the evidence as impartially as possible, to accept the challenge of answering criticisms, and to remain open to the possibility that they might be wrong and may need to revise, reexamine, or reject any one of their beliefs (at least those not involving broadly logical necessity). This character description of the rationalist is often interpreted to mean that rationalists must be neutral and detached with regard to their beliefs.[5] This is a mistake. It is a confusion between *impartiality* and *neutrality*. Both concepts imply conflict situations (e.g., war, a competitive sport, a legal trial, an argument), but to be neutral signifies not taking sides, doing nothing to influence the outcome, remaining passive in the fray; whereas impartiality *involves* one in the conflict in that it calls for a judgment in favor of the party that is right. To the extent that one party is right or wrong (measured by objective criteria) neutrality and impartiality are incompatible concepts. To be neutral is to detach oneself from the struggle; to be impartial (rational) is to commit oneself to a position—though not partially (i.e., unfairly or arbitrarily) but in accordance with an objective standard. The model of the neutral person is an atheist who is indifferent about football watching a game between Notre Dame and Southern Methodist. The model of the partial or prejudiced person is

---

[4] I follow McClendon and Smith's definition of *conviction* here as "a persistent belief such that if X has a conviction, it will not be easily relinquished without making X a significantly different person than before." James McClendon and James Smith, *Understanding Religious Convictions* (Notre Dame: Univ. of Notre Dame Press, 1975), 7.—L.P.

[5] Even McClendon and Smith make this mistake in their usually reliable work. Ibid., 108.—L.P.

the coach who, on any given dispute, predictably judges his team to be in the right and the other to be in the wrong and for whom it is an axiom that any judgment by a referee against his team is, at best, of dubious merit. The model of the impartial person is the referee in the game, who, knowing that his wife has just bet their life savings on the underdog, Southern Methodist, still manages to call what any reasonable spectator would judge to be a fair game. He does not let his wants or self-interest enter into the judgment he makes.

To be rational does not lessen the passion involved in religious beliefs. Rational believers, who believe that they have good grounds for believing that a perfect being exists, are not less likely to trust that being absolutely than believers who do not think that they have reasons. Likewise, persons who live in hope of God's existence may be as passionate about their commitment as persons who entertain no doubts. In fact the rational hoper or believer will probably judge it to be irrational not to be absolutely committed to such a being. Hence the charge leveled against the rationalist by Kierkegaard and others that rational inquiry cools the passions seems unfounded.

However, nonrationalists have a slightly different but related argument at hand. They may argue that if there were sufficient evidence available, it might be the case that one might be both religious and rational. But there is not sufficient evidence; hence the very search for evidence simply detracts believers from worship and passionate service, leading them on a wild-goose chase for evidence that does not exist. The believer is involved in cool calculation instead of passionate commitment, questioning instead of obeying.

There are at least two responses to this charge. First of all, how does the nonrationalist know that there is not sufficient evidence for a religious claim? How does the nonrationalist know that not merely a demonstrative proof but even a cumulative case with some force is impossible? It would seem reasonable to expect that a good God would not leave his creatures wholly in the dark about so important a matter. The nonrationalist's answer (that of Calvin and Kierkegaard, and suggested by Plantinga) that sin has destroyed the use of reason or our ability to see God seem unduly ad hoc and inadequate. It would seem that little children in nontheistic cultures should manifest some theistic tendencies on this view, for which there is no evidence. Second, why cannot the search for truth itself be a way of worshipping God? A passionate act of service? Again one would expect the possession of well-founded beliefs to be God's will for us. Is the person who in doubt prays, "God, if you exist, please show me better evidence," any less passionate a worshipper than the person who worships without doubts?

A word is in order about the relation of the emotions and passions to religious belief. The claims of a religion cannot but move a person. Anyone who does not see the importance of its claims either does not have a sense of selfhood or does not understand what is being said, for a religion claims to explain who and why one is and what one can expect to become. It claims to make sense out of the world. For example, to entertain the proposition that a personal, loving Creator exists is to entertain a proposition whose implications affect every part of a person's understanding of self and world. If the proposition is true, the world is personal rather than mechanistic, friendly rather than strange, purposeful rather than simply a vortex of chance and necessity. If it is not true, a different set of entailments follow that are likely to lead to different patterns of feeling and action. If Judeo-Christian theism is accepted, the believer has an additional reason for being a moral person, for treating fellow humans with equal respect. It is because God has created all persons in his image, as infinitely precious, destined to enjoy his fellowship forever. Theism can provide a more adequate metaphysical basis for morality. Hence it can be both descriptively and prescriptively significant.

· V ·

TOWARDS A THEORY OF RATIONALITY

It is often said that rational persons tailor the strength of their beliefs to the strength of the evidence. The trouble with this remark is that it is notoriously difficult to give sense to any discussion of discovering objective criteria for what is to count as evidence and to what extent it is to count. One of my criticisms of Swinburne's usually perceptive work is that he tries to apply the concept of probabilities to world views, as though we somehow could identify evidential wholes without comparing them to other outcomes.

Deciding *what* is to count as evidence for something else in part depends on a whole network of other considerations, and deciding *to what extent* something is to count as evidence involves weighing procedures that are subjective. Two judges may have the same evidence before them and come to different verdicts. Two equally rational persons may have the same evidence about the claims of a religion and still arrive at different conclusions in the matter. It would seem that the prescription to tailor one's beliefs according to the evidence is either empty or a shorthand for something more complex. I think that it is the latter. Let me illustrate what I think it signifies.

Consider any situation in which our self-interest may conflict with the truth. Take the case of three German wives who are suddenly confronted with evidence that their husbands have been unfaithful. Their surnames are Uberglaubig, Misstrauisch, and Wahrnehmen. Each is disturbed about the evidence and makes further inquiries. Mrs. Uberglaubig is soon finished and finds herself rejecting all the evidence, maintaining resolutely her husband's fidelity. Others, even relatives of Mr. Uberglaubig, are surprised by her credulity, for the evidence against Mr. Uberglaubig is the sort that would lead most people to conclude that he was unfaithful. No matter how much evidence is adduced, Mrs. Uberglaubig is unchanged in her judgment. She seems to have a fixation about her husband's fidelity. Mrs. Misstrauisch seems to suffer from an opposite weakness. If Mrs. Uberglaubig overbelieves, she seems to underbelieve. She suspects the worst and even though others who know Mr. Misstrauisch deem the evidence against him weak (especially in comparison to the evidence presented against Mr. Uberglaubig), she is convinced that her husband is unfaithful. No evidence seems to be sufficient to reassure her. It is as thought the very suggestion of infidelity were enough to stir up doubts and disbelief. Mrs. Wahrnehmen also considers the evidence, which is considerable, and comes to a judgment, though with some reservations. Suppose she finds herself believing that her husband is faithful. Others may differ in their assessment of the situation, but Mrs. Wahrnehmen is willing and able to discuss the matter, gives her grounds, and considers the objections of others. Perhaps we can say that she is more self-aware, more self-controlled, and more self-secure than the other women. She seems to have the capacity to separate her judgment from her hopes, wants, and fears in a way that the other two women do not.

This should provide some clue to what it means to be rational. It does not necessarily mean having true beliefs (though we would say that rationality tends toward truth), for it might just turn out that by luck Mr. Wahrnehmen is indeed an adulterer and Mr. Uberglaubig innocent. Still, we would want to say that Mrs. Wahrnehmen was justified in her beliefs but Mrs. Uberglaubig was not.

What does characterize rational judgment are two properties, one being *intentional* and the other being *capacity-behavioral*. First, rationality involves an intention to seek the truth or the possession of a high regard for the truth, especially when there may be a conflict between it and one's wishes. It involves a healthy abhorrence of being deceived combined with a parallel desire to have knowledge in matters vital to one's life. Mrs. Wahrnehmen and Mrs. Misstrauisch care about the truth in a way that Mrs. Uberglaubig does not. But secondly, it involves a skill or behavioral capacity to judge impartially, to examine the evidence objectively, to know what sort of things count in coming to a considered judgment. It is as though Mrs. Wahrnehmen alone were able to see clearly through the fog of emotion and self-interest, focusing on some ideal standard of evidence. Of course, there is no such simple standard of evidence, any more than there is for the art critic in making a judgment on the authenticity of a work of art. Still, the metaphor of the ideal standard may be useful. It draws attention to the objective feature in rational judgment, a feature that is internalized in the person of the expert. Like learning to discriminate between works of art of with regard to criminal evidence, rationality is a learned trait that calls for a long apprenticeship (a lifetime?) under the cooperative tutelage of other rational persons. Some people with little formal education seem to learn this better than some "well-educated" people, but despite this uncomfortable observation, I would like to believe that it is the job of education to train people to judge impartially over a broad range of human experience.

As a skill combined with an intention, rationality may seem to be in a shaky situation. How do we decide who has the skill or who has the right combination of traits? There is no certain way, but judge we must in this life, and the basis of our judgment will be manifestations of behavior that we classify as truth directed, noticing that persons with this skill seek out evidence and pay attention to criticism and counterclaims, that they usually support their judgment with recognizable good reasons, that they revise and reject their beliefs in the light of new information. These criteria are not foolproof, and it seems impossible to give an exact account of the process involved in rational decisions or belief, but this seems to be the case with any skill. In the end rationality seems more like a set of trained intuitions than anything else.

Let us carry our story a little further. Suppose now Mrs. Wahrnehmen receives some new information to the effect that her husband has been unfaithful. Suppose it becomes known to others who were previously convinced by her arguments acquitting her husband, and suppose that the new evidence infirms many of those arguments, so that the third parties now come to believe that Mr. Wahrnehmen is an adulterer. Should Mrs. Wahrnehmen give up her belief? Perhaps not. At least, it may not be a good thing to give it up at once. If she has worked out a theory to account for a great many of her husband's actions, she might better cling to her theory and work out some ad hoc hypotheses to account for this evidence. This principle of clinging to one's theory in spite of adverse evidence is what Peirce debunkingly and Lakatos approvingly call the principle of tenacity.[6] It receives special attention in Lakatos's treatment of a progressive research program. In science, theoretical change often comes as a result of

---

[6] Basil Mitchell, "Faith and Reason: A False Antithesis?" *Religious Studies* 16 (June 1980); I. Lakatos, "Falsification and Methodology of Scientific Research Programs," in *Criticism and the Growth of Knowledge*, edited by I. Lakatos and A. Musgrave (Cambridge: Cambridge Univ. Press, 1970) 91–196.—L.P.

persevering with a rather vaguely formulated hypothesis (a core hypothesis), which the researcher will hold on to in spite of a good many setbacks. Scientists must be ready to persevere (at least for a time) even in the face of their own doubts and their recognition of the validity of their opponents' objections. If maximum fruitfulness of the experiment is to be attained, it must endure through many modifications as new evidence comes in. As Basil Mitchell has pointed out, a scientific thesis is like a growing infant, which "could be killed by premature antisepsis." The biographies of eminent scientists and scholars are replete with instances of going it alone in the face of massive intellectual opposition and finally overturning a general verdict. Hence researchers cushion the core hypothesis against the blows and shocks that might otherwise force them to give it up. They invent ad hoc explanations in the hope of saving the core hypothesis. They surround the core hypothesis with a battery of such hypotheses, and as the ad hoc hypotheses fall, they invent new ones. Mitchell compares this process to a criminal network, in which the mastermind (core hypothesis) always manages to escape detection and punishment "by sacrificing some of his less essential underlings, unless or until the final day of reckoning comes and his entire empire collapses."[7]

Admittedly, each ad hoc hypothesis weakens the system, but the core hypothesis may nevertheless turn out to approximate a true or adequate theory. But the more ad hoc hypotheses it becomes necessary to invent, the less plausibility attaches to the core hypothesis, until the time comes when the researcher is forced to give up the core hypothesis and conclude that the whole project has outlived its usefulness. In Lakatos's words, it has become a "degenerative research project."[8] No one can say exactly when that time comes in a particular project, but every experimental scientist fears it and, meanwhile, lives in hope that the current project will bear fruit.

Let us apply this paradigm to rational religious believers. Once they find themselves with a deep conviction, they have a precedent or model in science for clinging to it tenaciously, experimenting with it, drawing out all its implications, and surrounding it with tentative ad hoc or auxiliary explanations in order to cushion it from premature antisepsis. Nevertheless, if the analogy with the scientist holds, they must recognize that the time may come when they are forced to abandon their conviction because of the enormous accumulation of counterevidence. Such rational persons probably cannot say exactly when and how this might happen, and they do not expect it to happen, but they acknowledge the possibility of its happening. There is no clear decision procedure that tells us when we have crossed over the fine line between plausibility and implausibility, but suddenly the realization hits us that we now disbelieve theory *A* and believe theory *B*, whereas up to this point the reverse was true. Conversions or paradigm switches occur every day in the minds of both the highly rational and the less rational. There is also a middle zone where a person considering two seemingly incompatible explanatory theories can find something plausible in each of them, so that the person cannot be said to believe either one. Still, such individuals may place their hope in one theory and live by it in an experimental faith, keeping themselves open to new evidence and maintaining the dialogue with those who differ so as not to slip into a state of self-deception. The

---

[7] Mitchell, op. cit.—L.P.

[8] Lakatos, op. cit., 118.—L.P.

whole matter of double vision and experimental faith is quite complicated, but often we can see the world in more than one way and yet find our moral bearings. What I want to emphasize is the Kierkegaardian point (used in an unKierkegaardian manner) that more important than *what* one believes is the manner in which one believes, the *how* of believing, the openness of mind, the willingness to discuss the reasons for one's belief, the carefulness of one's examination of new and conflicting evidence, one's commitment to follow the argument and not simply one's emotions, one's training as a rational person that enables one to recognize what is to count as a good argument.

This leads me to say a few things about the role and mode of argument in rationality. One of the problems that has plagued discussion in philosophy of religion through the ages is that the way philosophers have written has implied that unless one had a deductive proof for a religious thesis, one had no justification for it. The result of this narrow view of argument in religious matters has pushed those who believe in religion to the point of conceding too much, that is, that religion is not rational. This is one of the main reasons for the incommensurabilist position. I think that this is a mistake. Our concept of argument must be broadened from mere deductive and strict inductive argument to include non-rule-governed judgments. What I have in mind is the sort of intuitive judgment illustrated by the art critic in assessing an authentic work of art, the chicken sexer in identifying the sex of the baby chicks without knowing or being able to tell us how he knows the chicks's sexual identity, or the water diviner in discovering underground springs without knowing how he does so. Another example of non-rule-governed reasoning is a child's invention of new sentences. The child follows rules, which seem to be programmed into her, but she does not do it consciously and cannot tell us what the rules are. Later, however, she may be able to do so.

Perhaps even more typical of everyday non-rule-governed reasoning is the process whereby judges or juries make judgments when the evidence is ambiguous or there is considerable evidence on both sides of an issue. In weighing pros and cons and assessing conflicting evidence, the judge or jury does not normally go through standard logical procedures to arrive at a verdict. They rely on intangible and intuitive weighing procedures. It is hard to see how the deductive and strict inductive schemes or argument can account for our judgments when we have good reasons for and against a conclusion. Nor is it easy to see how deductive and strict inductive reasoning account for the decisions experts make in distinguishing the valuable from the mediocre. They cannot formalize their judgment, and we may not be able to offer an account of it, but we would still recognize it as valid and importantly rational. Perhaps we ought generally to aim at formalizing our judgments as carefully as possible, using the traditional forms of reasoning, but it is not always necessary or possible to do this. We can be said to be rational because we typically arrive at decisions and judgments that other rational creatures would regard as a fair estimation of the evidence (this excuses the occasional idiosyncratic judgment); because we attempt to face the challenge of our opponent with the grounds of our beliefs; and because we are honest about the deficiencies of our positions. It is a whole family of considerations that leads us to an overall conclusion about whether another person is rational and not simply whether or not the person is able to provide sound deductive or inductive arguments. Of course, induction plays a strong role in our relying on another's judgments. It is because we have generally found that people of this sort usually make reliable judgments in cases of such-and-such a type that we are ready to take their intuitions as credible.

A great deal more needs to be said about non-rule-governed judgments, but this discussion at least shows that something broader than the standard moves is needed in an account of rational argument. There is a need to recognize the important role that intuition plays in reasoning itself or, at least, in the reasoning of the trained person. This is what the Greeks called *phronesis* ("wise insight") and *ortho logos* ("correct thinking"), and it should be given greater emphasis in modern philosophy.

· VI ·

IS A RATIONAL ACCOUNT OF RELIGION
COMPATIBLE WITH THE BIBLICAL PICTURE OF FAITH?

Let me turn finally to the important objection that the position that I have outlined distorts the biblical notion of faith. Biblical faith is, the critic affirms, believing against or without sufficient evidence. As Hick points out, there is little deductive reasoning in the Scriptures, but the Holy of Holies is taken as the starting point of all thinking.[9]

But the claim that this is the sole meaning of faith in the Bible seems an unwarranted generalization. Actually, several different but related concepts of faith are found in the Bible, including loyalty, trust, fear, and obedience, as well as propositional belief. What we have called rational faith seems duly accounted for in the miracles and prophecy of the Bible, especially the Old Testament, which in part serve as evidence for the Hebrew faith. When Elijah, in 1 Kings 18, competes with the priests of Baal on Mr. Carmel to determine which god is more powerful, we are given a concrete scientific testing of competing hypotheses. When John the Baptist's disciples come to ask Jesus if he is the Messiah, Jesus does not rebuke them for seeking ground for their beliefs but immediately "cures many diseases and plagues and evil spirits" and opens the eyes of the blind; only after this does he answer them, "Go and tell John what you have seen and heard: the blind receive their sight, the lame walk, lepers are cleansed, and the deaf here, the dead are raised up, the poor have the good news preached to them" (Luke 7:20–22). When Jesus does chide his disciples for unbelief it seems to be for good reasons. "Don't you remember what the Scriptures demand? Don't you trust me in spite of my being with you so long and having proved my reliability over and over?" What the Scriptures deny is *sight*. We cannot see God directly and live, for there is another dimension to his reality, but we can see him *indirectly* through his works (Rom. 1:20f). When Thomas doubts good evidence (viz., the witness of his fellow disciples and the words of Jesus' prophecy), he is given evidence, the point being not that evidence is contrary to faith but that dependence on too much outward evidence may get in the way of inward discernment. There is just enough evidence to satisfy a person passionately concerned but not enough to produce a comfortable proof.

Usually, nonrationalists make their point about the antipathy between faith and reason in the Bible by pointing to Abraham's reliance on God even to the point of being willing to kill his son, Isaac. Abraham, the father of faith, is put forth as the paradigm of believing against all evidence. As Kierkegaard puts it, "Abraham believed by virtue of the absurd," despite the impossibility of the promise to give him a son when he was old or to bring him back after he was sacrificed. He believed God would somehow bring it

---

[9] John Hick, *Arguments for the Existence of God* (New York: Macmillan, 1971), chap. 7.—L.P.

about that Isaac would live in spite of the fact that he was going to kill him. The reader will recall the story. God tells Abraham to go to Mr. Moriah and sacrifice Isaac in order to prove his love for God. Abraham proceeds to carry out the command, but at the last moment an angel stops him, showing him a lamb in the thicket to be used for the offering. The story of Abraham and Isaac has usually been taken as the height of religious faith: believing God when it really affects one's deepest earthly commitments. It is taken to prove that faith is irrational, that faith involves believing against all standards of rationality.

Of course, many Old Testament scholars dismiss the literalness of the story and interpret it within the context of Middle Eastern child sacrifice. The story, according to these scholars, provides the pictorial grounds for breaking with the custom. But even leaving aside this plausible explanation, we might contend that Abraham's action can be seen as rational given his noetic framework. One can imagine him replying to a friendly skeptic years after the incident in the following manner:

> I heard a voice. It was the same voice (or so I believed) that commanded me years before to leave my country, my kindred, and my father's house to venture forth into the unknown. It was the same voice that promised me that I would prosper. I hearkened, and though the evidence seemed weak, the promise was fulfilled. It was the same voice that promised me a son in my old age and Sarah's old age, when childbearing was thought to be impossible. Yet it happened. My trust was vindicated. My whole existence has been predicated on the reality of that voice. I already became an exception by hearkening unto it the first time. I have never regretted it. This last call was in a tone similar to the other calls. The voice was unmistakable. To deny its authenticity would be to deny the authenticity of the others. In doing so, I should be admitting that my whole life has been founded on an illusion. But I don't believe that it has, and I prefer to take the risk of obeying what I take to be the voice of God and disobey certain norms than to obey the norms and miss the possibility of any absolute relation to the Absolute. And what's more, I'm ready to recommend that all people who feel so called by a higher power do exactly as I have done.

It seems to me that even if we accept the story of Abraham's offering his son as a sacrifice at face value, we can give it an interpretation not inconsistent with the commensurabilist's position. Abraham has had inductive evidence that following the voice is the best way to live. We can generalize the principle on which Abraham acted to be as follows:

> If one acts on a type of intuition I in an area of experience E, over a period of time t and with remarkable success, and no other information is relevant or overriding, one can be said to have good reason for following that intuition (I_n an instance of type I) the next time it presents itself in an E-type situation.

Given the cultural context of Abraham's life, his actions seem amenable to a rationalist account. Of course, what this shows is that given enough background data, almost any proposition could be considered *rational* for an individual believer. Irrationality would occur if Abraham neglected counterevidence at his disposal.

My point in all this has not been to prove that the Bible contains a fully developed philosophy of faith and reason but simply to indicate that it seems far closer to the commensurabilist's position than the fideist might imagine. My impression is that the Scriptures pay a great deal of attention to evidence, acts of deliverance, and the testimony of the saints and prophets who hear God's voice and sometimes even get a vision of his splendor.

Let me end this article on a conciliatory note. I can appreciate the criticism of someone who feels that my approach overemphasizes the rational and intellectual aspects of believing at the expense of the emotional and volitional aspects, the feelings of divine presence and inner certainty and devotion. I do not want to deny the importance of these feelings. My point has been simply that they are compatible with a rationalist perspective. Further thought on the matter may reveal that my approach to religion as an experimental faith in a viable hypothesis fails to get at the heart of religious commitment. But even so, the general quest for justification may not be inappropriate. Complex as religious phenomena are, profound as the feelings are, at some point religious experience needs to be scrutinized honestly and carefully by the believer him- or herself. When Barth and Bultmann protest that God does not need to justify himself before man, the proper response is to echo Karl Jasper's reply to Bultmann: "I do not say that God has to justify himself, but that everything that appears in the world and claims to be God's word, God's act, God's revelation, has to justify itself."[10] This outline of a commensurabilist position with regard to religious belief is intended as a small step in doing just that.

---

[10] Quoted in John Macquarrie, *Twentieth Century Religious Thought* (New York: Harper & Row, 1966), 334.—L.P.

PART IV

Related Issues in the Philosophy of Religion

○

W E HAVE NOW examined the main question in the philosophy of religion: Is religious belief a viable option for our time? We did this by: looking at the classical case for theism via the traditional arguments for the existence of God; examining the two earlier critiques of theism, both cultural and philosophical, and the responses by twentieth-century theists to the latter; examining the newer critique of theism and responses by theists (traditional and nontraditional) and by others to that critique; and considering the issue of the rationality and justification of religious belief.

Hence, in answer to our main question, we have examined these answers and the cases made for them. The three possible answers to our main questions are (again):

1. Yes, religious belief is a viable option because theological assertions, including "God exists," are both meaningful and true.

2. No, religious belief is not a viable option because theological assertions are false, or at least unsupportable.

There are two forms of this answer:

2a. Theological assertions must be rejected because the arguments on behalf of them are fallacious.

2b. Theological assertions must be rejected because historical and scientific evidence shows that they stem from such things as primitive mythology and so on.

3. No, religious belief is not a viable option for our time because theological assertions are all cognitively and factually meaningless.

As I mentioned in the Introduction, there are many other closely related issues in the philosophy of religion. Many would hold these to be just as important as our main question. Others hold that the main question cannot be answered without giving consideration to some or all of these.

In this part we shall examine six of these related issues.

1. The Problem of Evil (Chapter Nine)

One of the greatest difficulties that confronts those who believe in traditional theism is the problem of evil. The problem was succinctly stated in ancient times by Epicurus: "Is [God] willing to prevent evil, but not able? Then he is impotent [rather than omnipotent]. Is he able but not willing? Then he is malevolent [rather than omnibenevolent]. Is he both willing and able? Whence then is evil?"

More recently, J. L. Mackie has formulated the problem clearly and concisely. Consider these three statements:

A. God is omnipotent (all-powerful).

B. God is wholly good (supremely benevolent).

C. Evil exists.

There seems to be a contradiction in holding all three of these statements to be true at once. Most any two could be true, but not all three. Thus, one must be false. Why is there a contradiction? If (A) were true, God *could* have created a world with no evil (suffering), or less evil, or no unmerited suffering. If (B) were true, God *would* have wished to create such a world. Now (C) is clearly true. There is much evil—including severe and unmerited suffering in the world. Therefore, it seems that (A) or (B) *must* be false.

Thus the problem of evil may be stated thus: Can the fact of evil in the world (including suffering that is undeserved and unmerited) be reconciled with the existence of an all-powerful and supremely benevolent God?

It is widely recognized that there are two forms of evil commonly known as moral evil and natural or physical evil. Moral evil is the evil caused by humans. For example, deceit, cruelty, murder, and so forth. Natural evil is the evil caused by natural phenomena such as earthquakes, tornadoes, and so forth. It should be noted that it is not the mere occurrence of such phenomena that the word "evil" denotes. It is rather the *pain* and *suffering* to humans (and perhaps other animals) that is evil, especially when that suffering seems excessive or unmerited. For example, innocent children and newborn babies suffer and/or die from natural disasters, birth defects, and the like. Therefore, it would be better to call this problem the problem of suffering. These issues are discussed in Chapter Nine.

2. Belief and Faith (Chapter Ten)

There are some who hold that the main (and other) issue(s) in the philosophy of religion cannot be dealt with or solved via reason and arguments. Instead, there are some questions that can be answered only through faith. We must, it is said, distinguish the "eyes of reason" from the "eyes of faith." Sometimes it is said that even in science we must at certain points have faith. We may come to a point where we believe, but we don't have knowledge.

Such talk leads to a host of questions. Among them: Is there a distinction between faith (as used in religion) and belief (as used in science or elsewhere)? Is there a domain of issues that is inaccessible to reason and must therefore be approached via faith and/or passion? Is faith really unreasonable or could it be that faith is one mode of cognition? These are some of the problems that are explored in Chapter Ten.

3. Miracles (Chapter Eleven)

In most of the major religions of the world, reports of miracles having been performed are common. This has been especially true of the main religious leaders (for example, Christ) but also of some followers of those leaders. These reports, along with reports of religious experiences, have often been taken as providing evidence for the particular truth of those religions and their doctrines.

It is important here to be clear as to just what has been meant by miracles. We often use the word "miracle" to refer to some surprising, unexpected event, but one that has a natural explanation and that does not violate any law of nature. But in religious contexts, a miracle is regarded as something very different, namely, a violation or suspension of natural laws by special action and intervention by God. To believers in miracles, these are events in which God, often through a mediator, suspends or breaches certain natural laws by intervening in the world in order to achieve some end or prove some point.

It is important to examine this and related claims, and we shall do so briefly in Chapter Eleven.

4. Life after Death (Chapter Twelve)

Along with the belief in a divine being, the belief in and yearning for immortality has been one of the central beliefs in many though not all religions and has been held even by those who have no theistic commitments.

Is there any good reason (or are there any arguments) to support the claim that we survive the death of our bodies—either for some period of time or forever? This is the main question that will be briefly explored in Chapter Twelve.

5. Religion and Ethics (Chapter Thirteen)

There are many who hold that there can be no ethics without religion. Unless there is some transcendent ground for our ethical beliefs, then they are mere opinions. Without God, "everything is possible."

A more specific form of this view is: There can be no objective basis for our distinguishing right from wrong (good from bad) except in terms of what God commands (or forbids). Thus, according to this view:

X is right if and only if X is what God commands or wills.
X is wrong if and only if X is what God forbids.

Some hold even stronger formulations:

> X is right = X is what God commands.
> X is right = X is what God forbids.

This issue will be explored in some detail in Chapter Thirteen.

6. Religion and the Meaning of Life (Chapter Fourteen)

At some point in his/her life, almost every reflective and sensitive person has asked: What is the meaning of life? What is the point of it all? Is life worth living? And one tends to believe that if life has no meaning or purpose it is not worth living. Thus, many have concluded (and I am among them): The problem of the meaning of life is one of the most important of all philosophical problems.

Some have maintained that there is only one basis for providing a meaning to life: the existence of God, or at least faith in the existence of God. Without God, or faith in his existence, life would have no meaning or purpose and hence would not be worth living. Others have disputed this claim.

This leads to some very important problems: Does human life have any meaning or purpose? If so, how? And what sort of meaning is it? If life has no meaning, why doesn't it?

The two main answers that have been given to these questions are: the theistic answer, that is, the meaning of life can be found only in the existence of God and God's plan or through faith in God's existence. Without God, or faith in God, life has no meaning or purpose and, hence, is not worth living; and the non-theistic answer: Even if life has no preconceived meaning or purpose, on a cosmic scale, this does not imply that it has no meaning or purpose. Rather, by denying such objective outer-imposed meaning, this leaves humans free to forge their own meaning and purpose—and to do so in terms of activities and goals that lie within the natural universe. Hence, meaning and purpose can be found even if there is no God. And it can be found without faith in God. This issue will be examined in some detail in Chapter Fourteen.

There are other closely related issues in the philosophy of religion. However, we can't hope to cover all of them within the scope of a single volume. I have selected those that most students and readers find to be most interesting and most important.

CHAPTER NINE

The Problem of Evil

○

○ ○ ○ *43*

God and Evil
H. J. McCloskey

I. The Problem Stated

EVIL IS A problem for the theist in that a contradiction is involved in the fact of evil on the one hand, and the belief in the omnipotence and perfection of God on the other. God cannot be both all-powerful and perfectly good if evil is real. This contradiction is well set out in its detail by Mackie in his discussion of the problem.[1] In his discussion Mackie seeks to show that this contradiction cannot be resolved in terms of man's free will. In arguing in this way Mackie neglects a large number of important points, and concedes far too much to the theist. He implicitly allows that while physical evil creates a problem, this problem is reducible to the problem of moral evil, and that therefore the satisfactoriness of solutions of the problem of evil turns on the compatibility of free will and absolute goodness. In fact physical evils create a number of distinct problems which are not reducible to the problem of moral evil. Further, the proposed solution of the problem of moral evil in terms of free will renders the attempt to account for physical evil in terms of moral good, and the attempt thereby to reduce the problem of evil to the problem of moral evil, completely untenable. Moreover, the account of moral evil in terms of free will breaks down on more obvious and less disputable grounds than those indicated by Mackie. Moral evil can be shown to remain a problem whether or not free will is compatible with absolute goodness. I therefore propose in this paper to reopen the discussion of "the problem of evil" by approaching it from a more general standpoint, examining a wider variety of solutions than those considered by Mackie and his critics.

The fact of evil creates a problem for the theist; but there are a number of simple solutions available to a theist who is content seriously to modify his theism. He can either admit a limit to God's power, or he can deny God's moral perfection. He can assert either (1) that God is not powerful enough to make a world that does not contain evil, or (2) that God created only the good in the universe and that some other power created the evil, or (3) that God is all-powerful but morally imperfect, and chose to create an imperfect universe. Few Christians accept these solutions, and this is no doubt partly because such "solutions" ignore the real inspiration of religious beliefs, and partly because they introduce embarrassing complications for the theist in his attempts to deal

---

[1] "Evil and Omnipotence," *Mind*, 1955. [In the opening paragraphs of his essay Mackie writes, "The problem of evil, in the sense in which I shall be using the phrase, is a problem only for someone who believes that there is a God who is both omnipotent and wholly good. . . . In its simplest form the problem is this: (A) God is omnipotent; (B) God is wholly good; and yet (C) evil exists. There seems to be some contradiction between these three propositions, so that if any two of them were true, the third would be false. But at the same time all three are essential parts of most theological positions: The theologian, it seems, at once *must* adhere and cannot consistently adhere to all three."—H.J.M.

with other serious problems. However, if any one of these "solutions" is accepted, then the problem of evil is avoided, and a weakened version of theism is made secure from attacks based upon the fact of the occurrence of evil.

For more orthodox theism, according to which God is both omnipotent and perfectly good, evil creates a real problem; and this problem is well stated by the Jesuit Father G. H. Joyce. Joyce writes:

> The existence of evil in the world must at all times be the greatest of all problems which the mind encounters when it reflects on God and His relation to the world. If He is, indeed, all-good and all-powerful, how has evil any place in the world which He has made? Whence came it? Why is it here? If He is all-good why did He allow it to arise? If all-powerful why does He not deliver us from the burden? Alike in the physical and moral order creation seems so grievously marred that we find it hard to understand how it can derive in its entirety from God.[2]

The facts which give rise to the problem are of two general kinds, and give rise to two distinct types of problem. These two general kinds of evil are usually referred to as "physical" and as "moral" evil. These terms are by no means apt—suffering for instance is not strictly physical evil—and they conceal significant differences. However, this terminology is too widely accepted and too convenient to be dispensed with here, the more especially as the various kinds of evil, while important as distinct kinds, need not for our purposes be designated by separate names.

Physical evil and moral evil then are the two general forms of evil which independently and jointly constitute conclusive grounds for denying the existence of God in the sense defined, namely as an all-powerful, perfect Being. The acuteness of these two general problems is evident when we consider the nature and extent of the evils of which account must be given. To take physical evils, looking first at the less important of these.

(A) PHYSICAL EVILS

Physical evils are involved in the very constitution of the earth and animal kingdom. There are deserts and icebound areas; there are dangerous animals of prey, as well as creatures such as scorpions and snakes. There are also pests such as flies and fleas and the hosts of other insect pests, as well as the multitude of lower parasites such as tapeworms, hookworms, and the like. Secondly, there are the various natural calamities and the immense human suffering that follows in their wake—fires, floods, tempests, tidal-waves, volcanoes, earthquakes, droughts, and famines. Thirdly, there are the vast numbers of diseases that torment and ravage man. Diseases such as leprosy, cancer, poliomyelitis, appear *prima facie*[3] not to be creations which are to be expected of a benevolent Creator. Fourthly, there are the evils with which so many are born—the various physical deformities and defects such as misshapen limbs, blindness, deafness, dumbness, mental deficiency, and insanity. Most of these evils contribute toward increasing human pain and suffering; but not all physical evils are reducible simply to pain. Many of these evils are evils whether or not they result in pain. This is important,

---

[2] Joyce: *Principles of Natural Theology*, chap. 17. All subsequent quotations from Joyce in this paper are from this chapter of this work.—H.J.M.

[3] On first appearance.—E.D.K.

for it means that, unless there is one solution to such diverse evils, it is both inaccurate and positively misleading to speak of the problem of physical evil. Shortly I shall be arguing that no one "solution" covers all these evils, so we shall have to conclude that physical evils create not one problem but a number of distinct problems for the theist.

The nature of the various difficulties referred to by the theist as the problem of physical evil is indicated by Joyce in a way not untypical among the more honest, philosophical theists, as follows:

> The actual amount of suffering which the human race endures is immense. Disease has store and to spare of torments for the body: and disease and death are the lot to which we must all look forward. At all times, too, great numbers of the race are pinched by want. Nor is the world ever free for very long from the terrible sufferings which follow in the track of war. If we concentrate our attention on human woes, to the exclusion of the joys of life, we gain an appalling picture of the ills to which the flesh is heir. So too if we fasten our attention on the sterner side of nature, on the pains which men endure from natural forces—on the storms which wreck their ships, the cold which freezes them to death, the fire which consumes them—if we contemplate this aspect of nature alone we may be led to wonder how God came to deal so harshly with His Creatures as to provide them with such a home.

Many such statements of the problem proceed by suggesting, if not by stating, that the problem arises at least in part by concentrating one's attention too exclusively on one aspect of the world. This is quite contrary to the facts. The problem is not one that results from looking at only one aspect of the universe. It may be the case that over-all pleasure predominates over pain, and that physical goods in general predominate over physical evils, but the opposite may equally well be the case. It is both practically impossible and logically impossible for this question to be resolved. However, it is not an unreasonable presumption, with the large bulk of mankind inadequately fed and housed and without adequate medical and health services, to suppose that physical evils at present predominate over physical goods. In the light of the facts at our disposal, this would seem to be a much more reasonable conclusion than the conclusion hinted at by Joyce and openly advanced by less cautious theists, namely that physical goods in fact outweigh physical evils in the world.

However, the question is not, Which predominates, physical good or physical evil? The problem of physical evil remains a problem whether the balance in the universe is on the side of physical good or not, because the problem is that of accounting for the fact that physical evil occurs at all.

(B) MORAL EVIL

Physical evils create one of the groups of problems referred to by the theist as "the problem of evil." Moral evil creates quite a distinct problem. Moral evil is simply immorality—evils such as selfishness, envy, greed, deceit, cruelty, callousness, coward-ice, and the larger scale evils such as wars and the atrocities they involve.

Moral evil is commonly regarded as constituting an even more serious problem than physical evil. Joyce so regards it, observing:

> The man who sins thereby offends God. . . . We are called on to explain how God came to create an order of things in which rebellion and even final rejection have such a place. Since a choice from among an infinite number of possible worlds lay open to

God, how came He to choose one in which these occur? Is not such a choice in flagrant opposition to the Divine Goodness?

Some theists seek a solution by denying the reality of evil or by describing it as a "privation" or absence of good. They hope thereby to explain it away as not needing a solution. This, in the case of most of the evils which require explanation, seems to amount to little more than an attempt to sidestep the problem simply by changing the name of that which has to be explained. It can be exposed for what it is simply by describing some of the evils which have to be explained. That is why a survey of the data to be accounted for is a most important part of the discussion of the problem of evil.

In *The Brothers Karamazov*, Dostoyevski introduces a discussion of the problem of evil by reference to some then recently committed atrocities. Ivan states the problem:

> "By the way, a Bulgarian I met lately in Moscow," Ivan went on . . . "told me about the crimes committed by Turks in all parts of Bulgaria through fear of a general rising of the Slavs. They burn villages, murder, outrage women and children, and nail their prisoners by the ears to the fences, leave them till morning, and in the morning hang them—all sorts of things you can't imagine. People talk sometimes of bestial cruelty, but that's a great injustice and insult to the beasts; a beast can never be so cruel as a man, so artistically cruel. The tiger only tears and gnaws and that's all he can do. He would never think of nailing people by the ears, even if he were able to do it. These Turks took a pleasure in torturing children too; cutting the unborn child from the mother's womb, and tossing babies up in the air and catching them on the points of their bayonets before their mothers' eyes. Doing it before the mother's eyes was what gave zest to the amusement. Here is another scene that I thought very interesting. Imagine a trembling mother with her baby in her arms, a circle of invading Turks around her. They've planned a diversion: They pet the baby to make it laugh. They succeed; the baby laughs with glee, holds out its little hands to the pistol, and he pulls the trigger in the baby's face and blows out its brains. Artistic, wasn't it?"[4]

Ivan's statement of the problem was based on historical events. Such happenings did not cease in the nineteenth century. *The Scourge of the Swastika* by Lord Russell of Liverpool contains little else than descriptions of such atrocities; and it is simply one of a host of writings giving documented lists of instances of evils, both physical and moral.

Thus the problem of evil is both real and acute. There is a clear *prima facie* case that evil and God are incompatible—both cannot exist. Most theists admit this, and that the onus is on them to show that the conflict is not fatal to theism; but a consequence is that a host of proposed solutions are advanced.

The mere fact of such a multiplicity of proposed solutions, and the widespread repudiation of each other's solutions by theists, in itself suggests that the fact of evil is an insuperable obstacle to theism as defined here. It also makes it impossible to treat of all proposed solutions, and all that can be attempted here is an examination of those proposed solutions which are most commonly invoked and most generally thought to be important by theists.

Some theists admit the reality of the problem of evil, and then seek to sidestep it, declaring it to be a great mystery which we poor humans cannot hope to comprehend. Other theists adopt a rational approach and advance rational arguments to show that

---

[4] P. 244, Garnett translation, Heinemann.—H.J.M.

evil, properly understood, is compatible with, and even a consequence of, God's goodness. The arguments to be advanced in this paper are directed against the arguments of the latter theists; but insofar as these arguments are successful against the rational theists, to that extent they are also effective in showing that the nonrational approach in terms of great mysteries is positively irrational.

II. Proposed Solutions to the Problem of Physical Evil

Of the large variety of arguments advanced by theists as solutions to the problem of physical evil, five popularly used and philosophically significant solutions will be examined. They are, in brief: (i) Physical good (pleasure) requires physical evil (pain) to exist at all. (ii) Physical evil is God's punishment of sinners. (iii) Physical evil is God's warning and reminder to man. (iv) Physical evil is the result of the natural laws, the operations of which are on the whole good. (v) Physical evil increases the total good.

(I) PHYSICAL GOOD IS IMPOSSIBLE WITHOUT PHYSICAL EVIL

Pleasure is possible only by way of contrast with pain. Here the analogy of color is used. If everything were blue we should, it is argued, understand neither what color is nor what blue is. So with pleasure and pain.

The most obvious defect of such an argument is that it does not cover all physical goods and evils. It is an argument commonly invoked by those who think of physical evil as creating only one problem, namely the problem of human pain. However, the problems of physical evils are not reducible to the one problem, the problem of pain; hence the argument is simply irrelevant to much physical evil. Disease and insanity are evils, but health and sanity are possible in the total absence of disease and insanity. Further if the argument were in any way valid even in respect of pain, it would imply the existence of only a speck of pain, and not the immense amount of pain in the universe. A speck of yellow is all that is needed for an appreciation of blueness and of color generally. The argument is therefore seen to be seriously defective on two counts even if its underlying principle is left unquestioned. If its underlying principle is questioned, the argument is seen to be essentially invalid. Can it seriously be maintained that if an individual were born crippled and deformed and never in his life experienced pleasure, that he could not experience pain, not even if he were severely injured? It is clear that pain is possible in the absence of pleasure. It is true that it might not be distinguished by a special name and called pain, but the state we now describe as a painful state would nonetheless be possible in the total absence of pleasure. So too the converse would seem to apply. Plato brings this out very clearly in Book 9 of the *Republic* in respect of the pleasures of taste and smell. These pleasures seem not to depend for their existence on any prior experience of pain. Thus the argument is unsound in respect of its main contention; and in being unsound in this respect, it is at the same time ascribing a serious limitation to God's power. It maintains that God cannot create pleasure without creating pain, although as we have seen, pleasure and pain are not correlatives.

(II) PHYSICAL EVIL IS GOD'S PUNISHMENT FOR SIN

This kind of explanation was advanced to explain the terrible Lisbon earthquake in the 18th century, in which 40,000 people were killed. There are many replies to this argument, for instance Voltaire's. Voltaire asked: "Did God in this earthquake select the 40,000 least virtuous of the Portugese citizens?" The distribution of disease and pain is in no obvious way related to the virtue of the persons afflicted, and popular saying has it that the distribution is slanted in the opposite direction. The only way of meeting the fact that evils are not distributed proportionately to the evil of the sufferer is by suggesting that all human beings, including children, are such miserable sinners, that our offences are of such enormity, that God would be justified in punishing all of us as severely as it is possible for humans to be punished; but even then, God's apparent caprice in the selection of His victims requires explanation. In any case it is by no means clear that young children, who very often suffer severely, are guilty of sin of such an enormity as would be necessary to justify their sufferings as punishment.

Further, many physical evils are simultaneous with birth—insanity, mental defectiveness, blindness, deformities, as well as much disease. No crime or sin of *the child* can explain and justify these physical evils as punishment; and for a parent's sin to be punished in the child is injustice or evil of another kind.

Similarly, the sufferings of animals cannot be accounted for as punishment. For these various reasons, therefore, this argument must be rejected. In fact it has dropped out of favor in philosophical and theological circles, but it continues to be invoked at the popular level.

(III) PHYSICAL EVIL IS GOD'S WARNING TO MEN

It is argued, for instance of physical calamities, that "they serve a moral end which compensates the physical evil which they cause. The awful nature of these phenomena, the overwhelming power of the forces at work, and man's utter helplessness before them rouse him from the religious indifference to which he is so prone. They inspire a reverential awe of the Creator who made them, and controls them, and a salutary fear of violating the laws which He has imposed" (Joyce). This is where immortality is often alluded to as justifying evil.

This argument proceeds from a proposition that is plainly false; and that the proposition from which it proceeds is false is conceded implicitly by most theologians. Natural calamities do not necessarily turn people to God, but rather present the problem of evil in an acute form; and the problem of evil is said to account for more defections from religion than any other cause. Thus if God's object in bringing about natural calamities is to inspire reverence and awe, He is a bungler. There are many more reliable methods of achieving this end. Equally important, the use of physical evil to achieve this object is hardly the course one would expect a benevolent God to adopt when other, more effective, less evil methods are available to Him, for example, miracles, special revelation, etc.

(IV) EVILS ARE THE RESULTS OF THE OPERATION OF LAWS OF NATURE

This fourth argument relates to most physical evil, but it is more usually used to account for animal suffering and physical calamities. These evils are said to result from the operation of the natural laws which govern these objects, the relevant natural laws being the various causal laws, the law of pleasure-pain as a law governing sentient beings, etc. The theist argues that the nonoccurrence of these evils would involve either the constant intervention by God in a miraculous way, and contrary to his own natural laws, or else the construction of a universe with different components subject to different laws of nature; for God, in creating a certain kind of being, must create it subject to its appropriate law: He cannot create it and subject it to any law of his own choosing. Hence He creates a world which has components and laws good in their total effect, although calamitous in some particular effects.

Against this argument three objections are to be urged. First, it does not cover all physical evil. Clearly not all disease can be accounted for along these lines. Secondly, it is not to give a reason against God's miraculous intervention simply to assert that it would be unreasonable for Him constantly to intervene in the operation of His own laws. Yet this is the only reason that theists seem to offer here. If, by intervening in respect to the operation of His laws, God could thereby eliminate an evil, it would seem to be unreasonable and evil of Him not to do so. Some theists seek a way out of this difficulty by denying that God has the power miraculously to intervene; but this is to ascribe a severe limitation to His power. It amounts to asserting that when His Creation has been effected, God can do nothing else except contemplate it. The third objection is related to this, and is to the effect that it is already to ascribe a serious limitation to God's omnipotence to suggest that He could not make sentient beings which did not experience pain, nor sentient beings without deformities and deficiencies, nor natural phenomena with different laws of nature governing them. There is no reason why better laws of nature governing the existing objects are not possible on the divine hypothesis. Surely, if God is all-powerful, He could have made a better universe in the first place, or one with better laws of nature governing it, so that the operation of its laws did not produce calamities and pain. To maintain this is not to suggest that an omnipotent God should be capable of achieving what is logically impossible. All that has been indicated here is logically possible, and therefore not beyond the powers of a being Who is really omnipotent.

This fourth argument seeks to exonerate God by explaining that He created a universe sound on the whole, but such that He had no direct control over the laws governing His creations, and had control only in His selection of His creations. The previous two arguments attribute the detailed results of the operations of these laws directly to God's will. Theists commonly use all three arguments. It is not without significance that they betray such uncertainty as to whether God is to be *commended* or *exonerated*.

(V) THE UNIVERSE IS BETTER WITH EVIL IN IT

This is the important argument. One version of it runs:

> Just as the human artist has in view the beauty of his composition as a whole, not making it his aim to give to each several part the highest degree of brilliancy, but that measure of adornment which most contributes to the combined effect, so it is with God [Joyce].

Another version of this general type of argument explains evil not so much as a *component* of a good whole, seen out of its context as a mere component, but rather as a *means* to a greater good. Different as these versions are, they may be treated here as one general type of argument, for the same criticisms are fatal to both versions.

This kind of argument if valid simply shows that some evil may enrich the universe; it tells us nothing about *how much* evil will enrich this particular universe, and how much will be too much. So, even if valid in principle—and shortly I shall argue that it is not valid—such an argument does not in itself provide a justification for the evil in the universe. It shows simply that the evil which occurs might have a justification. In view of the immense amount of evil the probabilities are against it.

This is the main point made by Wisdom in his discussion of this argument. Wisdom sums up his criticism as follows:

> It remains to add that, unless there are independent arguments in favor of this world's being the best logically possible world, it is probable that some of the evils in it are not logically necessary to a compensating good; it is probable because there are so many evils.[5]

Wisdom's reply brings out that the person who relies upon this argument as a conclusive and complete argument is seriously mistaken. The argument, if valid, justifies only some evil. A belief that it justifies all the evil that occurs in the world is mistaken, for a second argument, by way of a supplement to it, is needed. This supplementary argument would take the form of a proof that all the evil that occurs is *in fact* valuable and necessary as a means to greater good. Such a supplementary proof is in principle impossible; so, at best, this fifth argument can be taken to show only that some evil *may be* necessary for the production of good, and that the evil in the world may perhaps have a justification on this account. This is not to justify a physical evil, but simply to suggest that physical evil might nonetheless have a justification, although we may never come to know this justification.

Thus the argument even if it is valid as a general form of reasoning is unsatisfactory because inconclusive. It is, however, also unsatisfactory in that it follows on the principle of the argument that, just as it is possible that evil in the total context contributes to increasing the total ultimate good, so equally, it will hold that good in the total context may increase the ultimate evil. Thus if the principle of the argument were sound, we could never know whether evil is really evil, or good really good. (Esthetic analogies may be used to illustrate this point.) By implication it follows that it would be dangerous to eliminate evil because we may thereby introduce a discordant element into the divine symphony of the universe; and, conversely, it may be wrong to condemn the elimination of what is good, because the latter may result in the production of more, higher goods.

So it follows that, even if the general principle of the argument is not questioned, it is still seen to be a defective argument. On the one hand, it proves too little—it justifies only some evil and not necessarily all the evil in the universe; on the other hand, it proves too much because it creates doubts about the goodness of apparent goods. These criticisms in themselves are fatal to the argument as a solution to the problem of physical evil.

However, because this is one of the most popular and plausible accounts of physical evil, it is worthwhile considering whether it can properly be claimed to establish even the very weak conclusion indicated above.

---

[5] *Mind*, 1931.—H.J.M.

Why, and in what way, is it supposed that physical evils such as pain and misery, disease and deformity, will heighten the total effect and add to the value of the moral whole? The answer given is that physical evil enriches the whole by giving rise to moral goodness. Disease, insanity, physical suffering, and the like are said to bring into being the noble moral virtues—courage, endurance, benevolence, sympathy, and the like. This is what the talk about the enriched whole comes to. W. D. Niven makes this explicit in his version of the argument:

> Physical evil has been the goad which has impelled men to most of those achievements which made the history of man so wonderful. Hardship is a stern but fecund parent of invention. Where life is easy because physical ills are at a minimum we find man degenerating in body, mind, and character.

And Niven concludes by asking:

> Which is preferable—a grim fight with the possibility of splendid triumph; or no battle at all?[6]

The argument is: Physical evil brings moral good into being, and in fact is an essential precondition for the existence of some moral goods. Further, it is sometimes argued in this context that those moral goods which are possible in the total absence of physical evils are more valuable in themselves if they are achieved as a result of a struggle. Hence physical evil is said to be justified on the grounds that moral good plus physical evil is better than the absence of physical evil.

A common reply, and an obvious one, is that urged by Mackie.[7] Mackie argues that while it is true that moral good plus physical evil together are better than physical good alone, the issue is not as simple as that, for physical evil also gives rise to and makes

---

[6] W. D. Niven, *Encyclopedia of Religion and Ethics*. Joyce's corresponding argument runs:
   Pain is the great stimulant to action. Man no less than animals is impelled to work by the sense of hunger. Experience shows that were it not for this motive the majority of men would be content to live in indolent ease. Man must earn his bread.
   One reason plainly why God permits suffering is that man may rise to a height of heroism which would otherwise have been beyond his scope. Nor are these the only benefits which it confers. That sympathy for others which is one of the most precious parts of our experience, and one of the most fruitful sources of well-doing, has its origin in the fellow-feeling engendered by endurance of similar trials. Furthermore, were it not for these trials, man would think little enough of a future existence, and of the need of striving after his last end. He would be perfectly content with his existence, and would reck little of any higher good. These considerations here briefly advanced suffice at least to show how important is the office filled by pain in human life, and with what little reason it is asserted that the existence of so much suffering is irreconcilable with the wisdom of the Creator.
   And:
   It may be asked whether the Creator could not have brought man to perfection without the use of suffering. Most certainly He could have conferred upon him a similar degree of virtue without requiring any effort on his part. Yet it is easy to see that there is a special value attaching to a conquest of difficulties such as man's actual demands, and that in God's eyes this may well be an adequate reason for assigning this life to us in preference to another. . . . Pain has value in respect to the next life, but also in respect to this. The advance of scientific discovery, the gradual improvement of the organization of the community, the growth of material civilization are due in no small degree to the stimulus afforded by pain.—H.J.M.

[7] Mackie, "Evil and Omnipotence," *Mind*, 1955.—H.J.M.

possible many moral evils that would not or could not occur in the absence of physical evil. It is then urged that it is not clear that physical evils (for example, disease and pain) plus some moral goods (for example, courage) plus some moral evil (for example, brutality) are better than physical good and those moral goods which are possible and which would occur in the absence of physical evil.

This sort of reply, however, is not completely satisfactory. The objection it raises is a sound one, but it proceeds by conceding too much to the theist, and by overlooking two more basic defects of the argument. It allows implicitly that the problem of physical evil may be reduced to the problem of moral evil; and it neglects the two objections which show that the problem of physical evil cannot be so reduced.

The theist therefore happily accepts this kind of reply, and argues that if he can give a satisfactory account of moral evil he will then have accounted for both physical and moral evil. He then goes on to account for moral evil in terms of the value of free will and/or its goods. This general argument is deceptively plausible. It breaks down for the two reasons indicated here, but it breaks down at another point as well. If free will alone is used to justify moral evil, then even if no moral good occurred, moral evil would still be said to be justified; but physical evil would have no justification. Physical evil is not essential to free will; it is only justified if moral good actually occurs, and if the moral good which results from physical evils outweighs the moral evils. This means that the argument from free will cannot alone justify physical evil along these lines; and it means that the argument from free will and its goods does not justify physical evil, because such an argument is incomplete, and necessarily incomplete. It needs to be supplemented by factual evidence that it is logically and practically impossible to obtain.

The correct reply, therefore, is first that the argument is irrelevant to many instances of physical evil, and secondly that it is not true that physical evil plus the moral good it produces is better than physical good and its moral goods. Much pain and suffering, in fact much physical evil generally, for example in children who die in infancy, animals, and the insane passes unnoticed; it therefore has no morally uplifting effects upon others, and cannot by virtue of the examples chosen have such effects on the sufferers. Further, there are physical evils such as insanity and much disease to which the argument is inapplicable. So there is a large group of significant cases not covered by the argument. And where the argument is relevant, its premise is plainly false. It can be shown to be false by exposing its implications in the following way.

We either have obligations to lessen physical evil or we have not. If we have obligations to lessen physical evil, then we are thereby reducing the total good in the universe. If, on the other hand, our obligation is to increase the total good in the universe, it is our duty to prevent the reduction of physical evil and possibly even to increase the total amount of physical evil. Theists usually hold that we are obliged to reduce the physical evil in the universe; but in maintaining this, the theist is, in terms of this account of physical evil, maintaining that it is his duty to reduce the total amount of real good in the universe, and thereby to make the universe worse. Conversely, if by eliminating the physical evil he is not making the universe worse, then that amount of evil which he eliminates was unnecessary and in need of justification. It is relevant to notice here that evil is not always eliminated for morally praiseworthy reasons. Some discoveries have been due to positively unworthy motives, and many other discoveries which have resulted in a lessening of the sufferings of mankind have been due to no higher a motive than a scientist's desire to earn a reasonable living wage.

This reply to the theist's argument brings out its untenability. The theist's argument is seen to imply that war plus courage plus the many other moral virtues war brings into play are better than peace and its virtues; that famine and its moral virtues are better than plenty; that disease and its moral virtues are better than health. Some Christians in the past, in consistency with this mode of reasoning, opposed the use of anesthetics to leave scope for the virtues of endurance and courage, and they opposed state aid to the sick and needy to leave scope for the virtues of charity and sympathy. Some have even contended that war is a good in disguise, again in consistency with this argument. Similarly, the theist should, in terms of this fifth argument, in his heart if not aloud regret the discovery of the Salk polio vaccine because Dr. Salk has in one blow destroyed infinite possibilities of moral good.

There are three important points that need to be made concerning this kind of account of physical evil. (*a*) We are told, as by Niven, Joyce, and others, that pain is a goad to action and that part of its justification lies in this fact. This claim is empirically false as a generalization about all people and all pain. Much pain frustrates action and wrecks people and personalities. On the other hand, many men work and work well without being goaded by pain or discomfort. Further, to assert that men need goading is to ascribe another evil to God, for it is to claim that God made men naturally lazy. There is no reason why God should not have made men naturally industrious; the one is no more incompatible with free will than the other. Thus the argument from physical evil being a goad to man breaks down on three distinct counts. Pain often frustrates human endeavor, pain is not essential as a goad with many men, and where pain is a goad to higher endeavors, it is clear that less evil means to this same end are available to an omnipotent God. (*b*) The real fallacy in the argument is in the assumption that all or the highest moral excellence results from physical evil. As we have already seen, this assumption is completely false. Neither all moral goodness nor the highest moral goodness is triumph in the face of adversity or benevolence toward others in suffering. Christ Himself stressed this when He observed that the two great commandments were commandments to love. Love does not depend for its possibility on the existence and conquest of evil. (*c*) The "negative" moral virtues which are brought into play by the various evils—courage, endurance, charity, sympathy, and the like—besides not representing the highest forms of moral virtue, are in fact commonly supposed by the theist and atheist alike not to have the value this fifth argument ascribes to them. We—theists and atheists alike—reveal our comparative valuations of these virtues and of physical evil when we insist on state aid for the needy; when we strive for peace, for plenty, and for harmony within the state.

In brief, the good man, the morally admirable man, is he who loves what is good knowing that it is good and preferring it because it is good. He does not need to be torn by suffering or by the spectacle of another's sufferings to be morally admirable. Fortitude in his own sufferings and sympathetic kindness in others' may reveal to us his goodness; but his goodness is not necessarily increased by such things.

Five arguments concerning physical evil have now been examined. We have seen that the problem of physical evil is a problem in its own right, and one that cannot be reduced to the problem of moral evil; and further, we have seen that physical evil creates not one but a number of problems to which no one nor any combination of the arguments examined offers a solution.

III. Proposed Solutions to the Problem of Moral Evil

The problem of moral evil is commonly regarded as being the greater of the problems concerning evil. As we shall see, it does create what appears to be insuperable difficulties for the theist; but so too, apparently, do physical evils.

For the theist moral evil must be interpreted as a breach of God's law and as a rejection of God Himself. It may involve the eternal damnation of the sinner, and in many of its forms it involves the infliction of suffering on other persons. Thus it aggravates the problem of physical evil, but its own peculiar character consists in the fact of sin. How could a morally perfect, all-powerful God create universe in which occur such moral evils as cruelty, cowardice, and hatred, the more especially as these evils constitute a rejection of God Himself by His creations, and as such involve them in eternal damnation?

The two main solutions advanced relate to free will and to the fact that moral evil is a consequence of free will. There is a third kind of solution, more often invoked implicitly than as an explicit and serious argument, which need not be examined here as its weaknesses are plainly evident. This third solution is to the effect that moral evils and even the most brutal atrocities have their justification in the moral goodness they make possible or bring into being.

(I) FREE WILL ALONE PROVIDES A JUSTIFICATION FOR MORAL EVIL

This is perhaps the more popular of the serious attempts to explain moral evil. The argument in brief runs: Men have free will; moral evil is a consequence of free will; a universe in which men exercise free will even with lapses into moral evil is better than a universe in which men become *automata* doing good always because predestined to do so. Thus on this argument it is the mere fact of the supreme value of free will itself that is taken to provide a justification for its corollary moral evil.

(II) THE GOODS MADE POSSIBLE BY FREE WILL PROVIDE A BASIS FOR ACCOUNTING FOR MORAL EVIL

According to this second argument, it is not the mere fact of free will that is claimed to be of such value as to provide a justification of moral evil, but the fact that free will makes certain goods possible. Some indicate the various moral virtues as the goods that free will makes possible, while others point to beatitude, and others again to beatitude achieved by man's own efforts or the virtues achieved as a result of one's own efforts. What all these have in common is the claim that the good consequences of free will provide a justification of the bad consequences of free will, namely moral evil.

Each of these two proposed solutions encounters two specific criticisms, which are fatal to their claims to be real solutions.

(I) [FREE WILL ALONE PROVIDES A JUSTIFICATION FOR MORAL EVIL]

To consider first the difficulties to which the former proposed solution is exposed. (*a*) A difficulty for the first argument—that it is free will alone that provides a justification for moral evil—lies in the fact that the theist who argues in this way has to allow that it is logically possible on the free will hypothesis that all men should always will what is evil, and that even so, a universe of completely evil men possessing free will is better than one in which men are predestined to virtuous living. It has to be contended that the value of free will itself is so immense that it more than outweighs the total moral evil, the eternal punishment of the wicked, and the sufferings inflicted on others by the sinners in their evilness. It is this paradox that leads to the formulation of the second argument; and it is to be noted that the explanation of moral evil switches to the second argument or to a combination of the first and second arguments, immediately the theist refuses to face the logical possibility of complete wickedness, and insists instead that in fact men do not always choose what is evil.

(*b*) The second difficulty encountered by the first argument relates to the possibility that free will is compatible with less evil, and even with no evil, that is, with absolute goodness. If it could be shown that free will is compatible with absolute goodness, or even with less moral evil than actually occurs, then all or at least some evil will be left unexplained by free will alone.

Mackie, in his recent paper, and Joyce, in his discussion of this argument, both contend that free will is compatible with absolute goodness. Mackie argues that if it is not possible for God to confer free will on men and at the same time ensure that no moral evil is committed, He cannot really be omnipotent. Joyce directs his argument rather to fellow-theists, and it is more of an *ad hominem* argument[8] addressed to them. He writes:

> Free will need not (as is often assumed) involve the power to choose wrong. Our ability to misuse the gift is due to the conditions under which it is exercised here. In our present state we are able to reject what is truly good, and exercise our power of preference in favor of some baser attraction. Yet it is not necessary that it should be so. And all who accept Christian revelation admit that those who attain their final beatitude exercise freedom of will, and yet cannot choose aught but what is truly good. They possess the knowledge of Essential Goodness; and to it, not simply to good in general, they refer every choice. Moreover, even in our present condition it is open to omnipotence so to order our circumstances and to confer on the will such instinctive impulses that we should in every election adopt the right course and not the wrong one.

To this objection, that free will is compatible with absolute goodness and that therefore a benevolent, omnipotent God would have given man free will and ensured his absolute virtue, it is replied that God is being required to perform what is logically impossible. It is logically impossible, so it is argued, for free will and absolute goodness to be combined, and hence, if God lacks omnipotence only in this respect, He cannot be claimed to lack omnipotence in any sense in which serious theists have ascribed it to Him.

Quite clearly, if free will and absolute goodness are logically incompatible, then God, in not being able to confer both on man, does not lack omnipotence in any

---

[8] Literally, argument directed to or against the man.—E.D.K.

important sense of the term. However, it is not clear that free will and absolute goodness are logically opposed; and Joyce does point to considerations which suggest that they are not logical incompatibles. For my own part I am uncertain on this point; but my uncertainty is not a factual one but one concerning a point of usage. It is clear that an omnipotent God could create rational agents predestined always to make virtuous "decisions"; what is not clear is whether we should describe such agents as having free will. The considerations to which Joyce points have something of the status of test cases, and they would suggest that we should describe such agents as having free will. However, no matter how we resolve the linguistic point, the question remains—Which is more desirable, free will and moral evil and the physical evil to which free will gives rise, or this special free will or pseudo-free will which goes with absolute goodness? I suggest that the latter is clearly preferable. Later I shall endeavor to defend this conclusion; for the moment I am content to indicate the nature of the value judgment on which the question turns at this point.

The second objection to the proposed solution of the problem of moral evil in terms of free will alone, is related to the contention that free will is compatible with less moral evil than occurs, and possibly with no moral evil. We have seen what is involved in the latter contention. We may now consider what is involved in the former. It may be argued that free will is compatible with less moral evil than in fact occurs on various grounds. (1) God, if He were all-powerful, could miraculously intervene to prevent some or perhaps all moral evil; and He is said to do so on occasions in answer to prayers (for example, to prevent wars) or of His own initiative (for instance, by producing calamities which serve as warnings or by working miracles, etc.).

(2) God has made man with a certain nature. This nature is often interpreted by theologians as having a bias to evil. Clearly God could have created man with a strong bias to good, while still leaving scope for a decision to act evilly. Such a bias to good would be compatible with freedom of the will. (3) An omnipotent God could so have ordered the world that it was less conducive to the practice of evil.

These are all considerations advanced by Joyce, and separately and jointly, they establish that God could have conferred free will upon us, and at least very considerably *reduced* the amount of moral evil that would have resulted from the exercise of free will. This is sufficient to show that *not all* the moral evil that exists can be justified by reference to free will alone. This conclusion is fatal to the account of moral evil in terms of free will alone. The more extreme conclusion that Mackie seeks to establish— that absolute goodness is compatible with free will—is not essential as a basis for refuting the free will argument. The difficulty is as fatal to the claims of theism whether all moral evil or only some moral evil is unaccountable. However, whether Mackie's contentions are sound is still a matter of logical interest, although not of any real moment in the context of the case against theism once the fact that less moral evil is compatible with free will has been established.

(II) [THE GOODS MADE POSSIBLE BY FREE WILL PROVIDE A BASIS FOR ACCOUNTING FOR MORAL EVIL]

The second free will argument arises out of an attempt to circumvent these objections. It is not free will but the value of the goods achieved through free will that is said to be so great as to provide a justification for moral evil.

(*a*) This second argument meets a difficulty in that it is now necessary for it to be supplemented by a proof that the number of people who practice moral virtue or who attain beatitude and/or virtue after a struggle is sufficient to outweigh the evilness of moral evil, the evilness of their eternal damnation, and the physical evil they cause to others. This is a serious defect in the argument, because it means that the argument can at best show that moral evil *may have* a justification, and not that it has a justification. It is both logically and practically impossible to supplement and complete the argument. It is necessarily incomplete and inconclusive even if its general principle is sound.

(*b*) This second argument is designed also to avoid the other difficulty of the first argument—that free will may be compatible with no evil and certainly with absolute goodness it is still better that virtue and beatitude be attained after a genuine personal struggle; and this, it is said, would not occur if God in conferring free will nonetheless prevented moral evil or reduced the risk of it. Joyce argues in this way:

> To receive our final beatitude as the fruit of our labors, and as the recompense of a hard-won victory, is an incomparably higher destiny than to receive it without any effort on our part. And since God in His wisdom has seen fit to give us such a lot as this, it was inevitable that man should have the power to choose wrong. We could not be called to merit the reward due to victory without being exposed to the possibility of defeat.

There are various objections which may be urged here. First, this argument implies that the more intense the struggle, the greater is the triumph and resultant good, and the better the world; hence we should apparently, on this argument, court temptation and moral struggles to attain greater virtue and to be more worthy of our reward. Secondly, it may be urged that God is being said to be demanding too high a price for the goods produced. He is omniscient. He knows that many will sin and not attain the goods or the Good free will is said to make possible. He creates men with free will, with the natures men have, in the world as it is constituted, knowing that in His doing so He is committing many to moral evil and eternal damnation. He could avoid all this evil by creating men with rational wills predestined to virtue, or He could eliminate much of it by making men's natures and the conditions in the world more conducive to the practice of virtue. He is said not to choose to do this. Instead, at the cost of the sacrifice of the many, He is said to have ordered things so as to allow fewer men to attain this higher virtue and higher beatitude that result from the more intense struggle.

In attributing such behavior to God, and in attempting to account for moral evil along these lines, theists are, I suggest, attributing to God immoral behavior of a serious kind—of a kind we should all unhesitatingly condemn in a fellow human being.

We do not commend people for putting temptation in the way of others. On the contrary, anyone who today advocated, or even allowed where he could prevent it, the occurrence of evil and the sacrifice of the many—even as a result of their own freely chosen actions—for the sake of the higher virtue of the few would be condemned as an immoralist. To put severe temptation in the way of the many, knowing that many and perhaps even most will succumb to the temptation, for the sake of the higher virtue of the few would be blatant immorality; and it would be immoral whether or not those who yielded to the temptation possessed free will. This point can be brought out by considering how a conscientious moral agent would answer the question: Which should I choose for other people, a world in which there are intense moral struggles and the possibility of magnificent triumphs and the certainty of many defeats, or a world in which there are less intense struggles, less magnificent triumphs, but more triumphs and fewer defeats, or a world in which there are no struggles, no triumphs, and no defeats? We are constantly answering less easy questions than this in a way that conflicts with the theist's contentions. If by modifying our own behavior we can save someone else from an intense moral struggle and almost certain moral evil, for example if by refraining from gambling or excessive drinking ourselves we can help a weaker person not to become a confirmed gambler or an alcoholic, or if by locking our car and not leaving it unlocked and with the key in it we can prevent people yielding to the temptation to become car thieves, we feel obliged to act accordingly, even though the persons concerned would freely choose the evil course of conduct. How much clearer is the decision with which God is said to be faced—the choice between the higher virtue of some and the evil of others, or the higher but less high virtue of many more, and the evil of many fewer. Neither alternative denies free will to men.

These various difficulties dispose of each of the main arguments relating to moral evil. There are in addition to these difficulties two other objections that might be urged.

If it could be shown that man has not free will, both arguments collapse; and even if it could be shown that God's omniscience is incompatible with free will, they would still break down. The issues raised here are too great to be pursued in this paper; and they can simply be noted as possible additional grounds from which criticisms of the main proposed solutions of the problem of moral evil may be advanced.

The other general objection is by way of a follow-up to points made in objections (b) to both arguments (i) and (ii). It concerns the relative value of free will and its goods and evils, and the value of the best of the alternatives to free will and its goods. Are free will and its goods so much more valuable than the next best alternatives that their superior value can really justify the immense amount of evil that is introduced into the world by free will?

Theologians who discuss this issue ask: Which is better—men with free will striving to work out their own destinies, or automata-machine-like creatures, who never make mistakes because they never make decisions? When put in this form we naturally doubt whether free will plus moral evil plus the possibility of the eternal damnation of the many and the physical evil of untold billions are quite so unjustified after all; but the fact of the matter is that the question has not been fairly put. The real alternative is, on the one hand, rational agents with free wills making many bad and some good decisions on rational and nonrational grounds, and "rational" agents predestined always "to choose" the right things for the right reasons—that is, if the language of automata must be used, rational automata. Predestination does not imply the absence of rationality in all senses of that term. God, were He omnipotent, could preordain the decisions and the reasons upon which they were based; and such a mode of existence would seem to be in itself a worthy mode of existence, and one preferable to an existence with free will, irrationality, and evil.

IV. Conclusion

In this paper it has been maintained that God, were He all-powerful and perfectly good, would have created a world in which there was no unnecessary evil. It has not been argued that God ought to have created a perfect world, nor that He should have made one that is in any way logically impossible. It has simply been argued that a benevolent God could, and would, have created a world devoid of superfluous evil. It has been contended that there is evil in this world—unnecessary evil—and that the more popular and philosophically more significant of the many attempts to explain this evil are completely unsatisfactory. Hence we must conclude from the existence of evil that there cannot be an omnipotent, benevolent God.

○ ○ ○ *44*

The Irenaean Theodicy[1]
John Hick

I. The Negative Task of Theodicy

AT THE OUTSET of an attempt to present a Christian theodicy—a defence of goodness of God in face of the evil in His world—we should recognize that, whether or not we can succeed in formulating its basis, an implicit theodicy is at work in the Bible, at least in the sense of an effective reconciliation of profound faith in God with a deep involvement in the realities of sin and suffering. The Scriptures reflect the character-istic mixture of good and evil in human experience. They record every kind of sorrow and suffering from the terrors of childhood to the "stony griefs of age": cruelty, torture, violence, and agony; poverty, hunger, calamitous accident; disease, insanity, folly; every mode of man's inhumanity to man and of his painfully insecure existence in the world. In these writings there is no attempt to evade the clear verdict of human experience that evil is dark, menacingly ugly, heart-rending, crushing. And the climax of this biblical history of evil was the execution of Jesus of Nazareth. Here were pain and violent destruction, gross injustice, the apparent defeat of the righteous, and the premature death of a still-young man. But further, for Christian faith, this death was the slaying of God's Messiah, the one in whom mankind was to see the mind and heart of God made flesh. Here, then, the problem of evil rises to its ultimate maximum; for in its quality this was an evil than which no greater can be conceived. And yet throughout the biblical history of evil, including even this darkest point, God's purpose of good was moving visibly or invisibly towards its far-distant fulfilment. In this faith the prophets saw both personal and national tragedy as God's austere but gracious disciplining of His people. And even the greatest evil of all, the murder of the son of God, has been found by subsequent Christian faith to be also, in an astounding paradox, the greatest good of all, so that through the centuries the Church could dare to sing on the eve of its triumphant Easter celebrations, "O felix culpa, quae talem ac tantum meruit habere redemptorem."[2] For this reason there is no room within the

---

[1] For a characterization of Irenaeus, see the beginning of Part III.—E.D.K.

[2] "O certe necessarium Adae peccatum, quod Christi morte deletum est! O felix culpa, quae talem ac tantum meruit habere redemptorem!" (O truly necessary sin of Adam, which is cancelled by Christ's death! O fortunate crime (*or*, O happy fault), which merited [to have] such and so great a redeemer!) These famous phrases occur in the Roman Missal in the *Exultet* for the evening before Easter Day. The date and authorship of this *Exultet* are uncertain. It has been attributed, but without adequate evidence, to St. Augustine, to St. Ambrose, and to Gregory the Great. As part of the Easter liturgy it goes back at least to the seventh century and possibly to the beginnings of the fifth century. On its history see Arthur O. Lovejoy, *Essays in the History of Ideas*, 1948 (New York: Capricorn Books, 1960), pp. 286 – 7.—J.H.

Christian thought-world for the idea of tragedy in any sense that includes the idea of finally *wasted* suffering and goodness.[3]

In all this a Christian theodicy is latent; and our aim must be to try to draw it out explicitly. The task, like that of theology in general, is one of "faith seeking understanding," seeking in this case an understanding of the grounds of its own practical victory in the face of the harsh facts of evil. Accordingly, from the point of view of apologetics, theodicy has a negative rather than a positive function. It cannot profess to create faith, but only to preserve an already existing faith from being overcome by this dark mystery. For we cannot share the hope of the older schools of natural theology of inferring the existence of God from the evidences of nature; and one main reason for this, as David Hume made clear in his *Dialogues*, is precisely the fact of evil in its many forms. For us today the live question is whether this renders impossible a rational belief in God: meaning by this, not a belief in God that has been arrived at by rational argument (for it is doubtful whether a religious faith is ever attained in this way), but one that has arisen in a rational individual in response to some compelling element in his experience, and decisively illuminates and is illuminated by his experience as a whole. The aim of Christian theodicy must thus be the relatively modest and defensive one of showing that the mystery of evil, largely incomprehensible though it remains, does not render irrational a faith that has arisen, not from the inferences of natural theology, but from participation in a stream of religious experience which is continuous with that recorded in the Bible.

2. *The Traditional Theodicy Based upon Christian Myth*

We can distinguish, though we cannot always separate, three relevant facets of the Christian religion: Christian experience, Christian mythology, and Christian theology.

Religious experience is "the whole experience of religious persons,"[4] constituting an awareness of God acting towards them in and through the events of their lives and of world history, the interpretative element within which awareness is the cognitive aspect of faith. And distinctively *Christian experience*, as a form of this, is the Christian's seeing of Christ as his "Lord and Saviour," together with the pervasive recreative effects of this throughout his life, transforming the quality of his experience and determining his responses to other people. Christian faith is thus a distinctive consciousness of the world and of one's existence within it, radiating from and illuminated by a consciousness of God in Christ. It is because there are often a successful facing and overcoming of the challenge of evil at this level that there can, in principle at least, be an honest and serious—even though tentative and incomplete—Christian theodicy.

By *Christian mythology* I mean the great persisting imaginative pictures by means of which the corporate mind of the Church has expressed to itself the significance of the historical events upon which its faith is based, above all the life, death, and resurrection of Jesus who was the Christ. The function of these myths is to convey in universally understandable ways the special importance and meaning of certain items of mundane experience.

---

[3] Cf. D. D. Raphael, *The Paradox of Tragedy* (London: George Allen & Unwin Ltd., 1960), pp. 43 f.—J.H.
[4] William Temple, *Nature, Man and God* (London: Macmillan & Co. Ltd., 1934), p. 334.—J.H.

By *Christian theology* I mean the attempts by Christian thinkers to speak systematically about God on the basis of the data provided by Christian experience. Thus it is a fact of the Christian faith-experience that "God was in Christ";[5] and the various Christological theories are attempts to understand this by seeing it in the context of other facts both of faith and of nature. Again, it is another facet of this basic fact of faith that in Christ God was "reconciling the world unto Himself";[6] and the various atonement theories are accordingly attempts to understand this further aspect of the experience. The other departments of Christian doctrine stand in a similar relationship to the primary data of Christian experience.

In the past, theology and myth have been closely twined together. For the less men knew about the character of the physical universe the harder it was for them to identify myth as myth, as distinct from history or science. This fact has profoundly affected the development of the dominant tradition of Christian theodicy. Until comparatively recent times the ancient myth of the origin of evil in the fall of man was quite reasonably assumed to be history. The theologian accordingly accepted it as providing "hard" data, and proceeded to build his theodicy upon it. This mythological theodicy was first comprehensively developed by Augustine, and has continued substantially unchanged within the Roman Catholic Church to the present day. It was likewise adopted by the Reformers of the sixteenth century and has been virtually unquestioned as Protestant doctrine until within approximately the last hundred years. Only during this latest period has it been possible to identify as such its mythological basis, to apply a theological criticism to it, and then to go back to the data of Christian experience and build afresh, seeking a theodicy that can hope to make sense to Christians in our own and succeeding centuries.

But first, in order to see how the hitherto dominant theodicy has arisen, and why it is now utterly unacceptable, we must trace the outline of the mythology that underlies it. The story of the fall of man is part of a more comprehensive cosmic story. In this great amalgam of Jewish and Christian themes, God created spiritual beings, the angels and archangels, to be His subjects and to love and serve Him in the heavenly spheres. But a minority of them revolted against God in envy of His supremacy, and were defeated and cast into an abode suited to their now irreconcilably evil natures. Either to replenish the citizenry of heaven thus depleted by the expulsion of Satan and his followers, or as an independent venture of creation, God made our world, and mankind within it consisting initially of a single human pair. This first man and woman, living in the direct knowledge of God, were good, happy, and immortal, and would in due course have populated the earth with descendants like themselves. But Satan, in wicked spite, successfully tempted them to disobey their Creator, who then expelled them from this paradisal existence into a new situation of hardship, danger, disease, and inevitable death. This was the fall of man, and as a result of it the succeeding members of the human race have been born as fallen creatures in a fallen world, participating in the effects of their parents' rebellion against their Maker. But God in Christ has made the atonement for man's sin that His own eternal justice required and has offered free forgiveness to as many as will

---

[5] II Corinthians v. 19.—J.H.

[6] *Ibid.*—J.H.

commit themselves to Christ as their Saviour. At the last judgement, when faith and life alike will be tested, many will enter into eternal life whilst others, preferring their own darkness to God's light, will linger in a perpetual living death.

This great cosmic drama is the official Christian myth. With only minor variations it has constituted the accepted framework of thought of the great majority of Christians in the past, and still fulfils this role for the great majority today. By means of it Christian faith, which began as a crucial response of trust towards one in whom the disciples had experienced God directly at work on earth, broadened out into a comprehensive vision of the universe. The great creation-fall-redemption myth has thus brought within the scope of the simplest human soul a pictorial grasp of the universal significance of the life and death of Jesus. Jesus himself was not a mythological figure; he lived in Palestine and his life and death and resurrection made their impact upon living people, and through them upon others in a long succession of faith down to ourselves today. But the cosmic picture, sketched by St. Paul and completed by St. Augustine, of the beginning of our present human situation in the fall of humanity from a condition of paradisal perfection into one of sin and pain and death, and of its end in the separation of mankind into those destined for the eternal bliss or torment of heaven or hell, is a product of the religious imagination. It expresses the significance of the present reality of sin and sorrow by seeing them as flowing from a first dramatic act of rebellion; and the significance of the experience of reconciliation with God by means of the picture of a juridical arrangement taking place within the councils of the Trinity and being transacted in time on the cross of Christ; and the significance of man's inalienable personal responsibility by the picture of a divine administration directing souls to their appropriate final destinations.

This great cosmic drama in three acts has constituted a valid myth in the sense that it has successfully fulfilled the conserving and communicating function of a myth in the minds of countless people. By means of natural images it has vividly brought home to the simplest understandings the claim that Christ stands at the center of the universe and is of crucial importance for all men. And when religious myths thus work effectively it is as absurd to criticize them for being myths rather than science or history as it would be for us today to insist that they *are* science or history and to proceed to draw scientific or historical conclusions from them.

Because we can no longer share the assumption, upon which traditional Christian theodicy has been built, that the creation-fall myth is basically authentic history,[7] we inevitably look at that theodicy critically and see in it inadequacies to which in the past piety has tended to blind the eyes of faith.

For, in general, religious myths are not adapted to the solving of problems. Their function is to illumine by means of unforgettable imagery the religious significance of some present or remembered fact of experience. But the experience which myth thus emphasizes and illumines is itself the locus of mystery. Hence it is not surprising that Christian mythology mirrors Christian experience in presenting but not resolving the profound mystery of evil. Nor is it surprising that when this pictorial presentation of

---

[7] One of the most eloquent recent presentations of the traditional conception of a temporal fall of man is that of C. S. Lewis in *The Problem of Pain* (London: The Centenary Press, 1940), pp. 65 f.—J.H.

the problem has mistakenly been treated as a solution to it, the "solution" has suffered from profound incoherences and contradiction.

This traditional solution (representing the theological, in distinction from the philosophical, side of Augustine's thought on the theodicy problem) finds the origin of evil, as we have seen, in the fall, which was the beginning both of sin and, as its punishment, of man's sorrows and sufferings. But this theory, so simple and mythologically satisfying, is open to insuperable scientific, moral, and logical objections. To begin with less fundamental aspects of the traditional solution, we know today that the conditions that were to cause human disease and mortality and the necessity for man to undertake the perils of hunting and the labours of agriculture and building, were already part of the natural order prior to the emergence of man and prior therefore to any first human sin, as were also the conditions causing such further "evils" as earthquake, storm, flood, drought, and pest. And, second, the policy of punishing the whole succeeding human race for the sin of the first pair is, by the best human moral standards, unjust and does not provide anything that can be recognized by these standards as a theodicy. Third, there is a basic and fatal incoherence at the heart of the mythically based "solution." The Creator is preserved from any responsibility for the existence of evil by the claim that He made men (or angels) as free and finitely perfect creatures, happy in the knowledge of Himself, and subject to no strains or temptations, but that they themselves inexplicably and inexcusably rebelled against Him. But this suggestion amounts to a sheer self-contradiction. It is impossible to conceive of wholly good beings in a wholly good world becoming sinful. To say that they do is to postulate the self-creation of evil *ex nihilo!* There must have been some moral flaw in the creature or in his situation to set up the tension of temptation; for creaturely freedom in itself and in the absence of any temptation cannot lead to sin. Thus the very fact that the creature sins refutes the suggestion that until that moment he was a finitely perfect being living in an ideal creaturely relationship to God. And indeed (as we have already seen) the two greatest upholders of this solution implicitly admit the contradiction. Augustine,[8] who treats of evil at its first occurrence in the fall of Satan and his followers, has to explain the eruption of sin in supposedly perfect angels by holding that God had in effect predestined their revolt by withholding from them the assurance of eternal bliss with which, in contrast, He had furnished the angels who remained steadfast.[9] And Calvin, who treats the subject primarily at the point of the fall of man, holds that "all are not created in equal condition; rather, eternal life is foreordained for some, eternal damnation for others."[10] Thus the myth, when mistakenly pressed to serve as a theodicy, can be saved only by adding to it the new and questionable doctrine of an absolute divine predestination. And this in turn leads the theodicy to contradict itself. For its original intention was to blame evil upon the misuse of creaturely free will. But now this misuse is itself said to fall under the divine predestinating decrees. Thus the theodicy collapses into radical incoherence, and its more persistent defenders have become involved in ever more desperate and implau-

---

[8] Fifth-century Christian theologian.—E.D.K.

[9] *City of God*, bk. xi, chaps. 11 and 13; bk. xii, chap. 9.—J.H.

[10] *Institutes*, bk. III, chap. xxi, para. 5—J.H.

sible epicycles of theory to save it. For example, to salvage the view of the fall of man as a temporal event that took place on this earth some definite (if unknown) number of years ago, it has been suggested that after emerging from his subhuman precursors man lived in the paradisal state for only a very brief period, lasting perhaps no more than a matter of hours. Again, attempts have been made to protect the fall doctrine from the encroachments of scientific research by locating the primal calamity in a pre-mundane sphere. In the third century Origen[11] had taught that some of the spirits whom God created rebelled against the divine majesty and were cast down into the material world to constitute our human race;[12] and in the nineteenth century the German Protestant theologian Julius Müller, impressed by the overwhelming difficulties of affirming an historical fall, in effect revived Origen's theory as an explanation of the apparently universal evil propensities of man. All men are sinful, he suggested, because in another existence prior to the present life they have individually turned away from God.[13]

The difficulties and disadvantages of such a view are, I think, not far to seek. The theory is without grounds in Scripture or in science, and it would have claim to consideration only if it could provide a solution, even if a speculative one, to the question of the origin of moral evil. But in fact it is not able to do this. It merely pushes back into an unknown and unknowable realm the wanton paradox of finitely perfect creatures, dwelling happily and untempted in the presence of God, turning to sin. Whether on earth or in heaven, this still amounts to the impossible self-creation of evil *ex nihilo*.[14] If evil could thus create itself out of nothing in the midst of a wholly good universe, it could do so in a mundane Garden of Eden as easily as, or perhaps more easily than, in the highest heaven. Nothing, then, is gained for theodicy by postulating a premundane fall of human souls.

As a variation which he regarded as superior to the notion of a premundane fall of individuals, N. P. Williams proposed the idea of "a collective fall of the race-soul of humanity at an indefinitely remote past."[15] This collective fall occurred, according to Williams, during the long period between the first emergence of man as a biological species and his subsequent development to the point at which there were primitive societies, and therefore moral laws which could be transgressed. "We must," he says, "postulate some unknown factor or agency which interfered to arrest the development of corporate feeling, just when man was becoming man, some mysterious and maleficent influence which cut into the stream of the genetic evolution of our race at some point during the twilit age which separates pre-human from human history."[16] This evil influence which attacked and corrupted mankind is also "the mysterious

---

[11] A (Christian) "church father" and theologian.—E.D.K.

[12] *De Principiis*, bk. II, chap. I, para. 1. Cf. ibid., chap. ix, para. 6.—J.H.

[13] *The Christian Doctrine of Sin*, bk. IV, chap. 4. Cf. bk. III, pt. i, chap. 3, sect. 1, and chap. 4, sect. 3.—J.H.

[14] Out of nothing.—E.D.K.

[15] N. P. Williams, *The Ideas of the Fall and of Original Sin* (London Longmans, Green & Co. Ltd., 1927), p. 513.—J.H.

[16] N. P. Williams, *op. cit.*, pp. 518–19.—J.H.

power which vitiates the whole of sub-human life with cruelty and selfishness,"[17] and thus accounts not only for moral evil but also for the disorder, waste, and pain in nature. Accordingly the original calamity was not merely a fall of man but of the Life-Force itself, which we must conceive "as having been at the beginning, when it first sprang forth from the creative fecundity of the Divine Being, free, personal, and self-conscious."[18] This World-Soul was created good, but "at the beginning of Time, and in some transcendental and incomprehensible manner, it turned away from God and in the direction of Self, thus shattering its own interior being, which depended upon God for its stability and coherence, and thereby forfeiting its unitary self-consciousness, which it has only regained, after aeons of myopic striving, in sporadic fragments which are the separate minds of men and perhaps of superhuman spirits."[19]

Williams is, I think, justified in claiming that such a speculation cannot be excluded *ab initio*[20] as impermissible to a responsible Christian theologian. As he points out,

> Such a substitution of the idea of a corruption of the whole cosmic energy at some enormously remote date for the idea of a voluntary moral suicide of Man in comparatively recent times would be no greater a revolution than that which was effected by St Anselm, when he substituted a satisfactional theory of the Atonement for the view which regarded the death of Christ as a ransom paid to the Devil—a view which had behind it the venerable authority of a thousand years of Christian history.[21]

Williams' suggestion preserves the central thought of the Augustinian fall doctrine that the ultimate source of evil lies in an original conscious turning away from God on the part of created personal life. But precisely because of its faithfulness to that tradition his theory fails to throw any new light upon the problem of evil. Whether the self-creation of evil *ex nihilo* be located in an historical Adam and Eve, or in a multitude of souls in a pre-mundane realm, or in a single world-soul at the beginning of time, it is equally valueless from the point of view of theodicy. In order for a soul or souls to fall there must be, either in them or in their environment, some flaw which produces temptation and leads to sin; and this flaw in the creation cannot be traced back to any other ultimate source than the Creator of all that is. Thus Williams' theory is open to the same objection as Müller's: namely, that it is a speculation whose only point would be to solve or lighten the problem of evil, but that it fails to do this.[22]

3. The "Vale of Soul-Making" Theodicy

Fortunately there is another and better way. As well as the "majority report" of the Augustinian tradition, which has dominated Western Christendom, both Catholic and Protestant, since the time of Augustine himself, there is the "minority report" of

---

[17] *Ibid.*, p. 520.—J.H.

[18] *Ibid.*, p. 525.—J.H.

[19] *Ibid.*, p. 526.—J.H.

[20] From the beginning.—E.D.K.

[21] *Ibid.*, p. 524.—J.H.

[22] A pre-mundane fall has been propounded by Canon Peter Green in *The Problem of Evil* (London: Longmans, Green & Co., 1920), chap. 7, and in *The Pre-Mundane Fall* (London: A. R. Mowbray & Co., 1944); and by C. W. Formby in *The Unveiling of the Fall* (London: Williams & Norgate, 1923).—J.H.

the Irenaean tradition. This latter is both older and newer than the other, for it goes back to St. Irenaeus[23] and others of the early Hellenistic Fathers of the Church in the two centuries prior to St. Augustine, and it has flourished again in more developed forms during the last hundred years.

Instead of regarding man as having been created by God in a finished state, as a finitely perfect being fulfilling the divine intention for our human level of existence, and then falling disastrously away from this, the minority report sees man as still in process of creation. Irenaeus himself expressed the point in terms of the (exegetically dubious) distinction between the "image" and the "likeness" of God referred to in Genesis i. 26: "Then God said, Let us make man in our image, after our likeness."[24] His view was that man as a personal and moral being already exists in the image, but has not yet been formed into the finite likeness of God. By this "likeness" Irenaeus means something more than personal existence as such; he means a certain valuable quality of personal life which reflects finitely the divine life. This represents the perfecting of man, the fulfilment of God's purpose for humanity, the "bringing of many sons of glory,"[25] the creating of "children of God" who are "fellow heirs with Christ" of his glory.[26]

And so man, created as a personal being in the image of God, is only the raw material for a further and more difficult stage of God's creative work. This is the leading of men as relatively free and autonomous persons, through their own dealings with life in the world in which He has placed them, towards that quality of personal existence that is the finite likeness of God. The features of the likeness are revealed in the person of Christ, and the process of man's creation into it is the work of the Holy Spirit. In St. Paul's words, "And we all, with unveiled faces, beholding the glory of the Lord, are being changed into his likeness (εἰκών) from one degree of glory to another; for this comes from the Lord who is the Spirit";[27] or again, "For God knew his own before ever they were, and also ordained that they should be shaped to the likeness (εἰκών) of his Son."[28] In Johannine terms, the movement from the image to the likeness is a transition from one level of existence, that of animal life (*Bios*), to another and higher level, that of eternal life (*Zoe*), which includes but transcends the first. And the fall of man was seen by Irenaeus as a failure within the second phase of this creative process, a failure that has multiplied the perils and complicated the route of the journey in which God is seeking to lead mankind.

In the light of modern anthropological knowledge some form of two-stage conception of the creation of man has become an almost unavoidable Christian tenet. At the very least we must acknowledge as two distinguishable stages the fashioning of *homo sapiens* as a product of the long evolutionary process, and his sudden or gradual

---

[23] Also a church father.—E.D.K.

[24] *Against Heresies*, v. vi. 1.—J.H.

[25] Hebrews ii. 10.—J.H.

[26] Romans viii. 17.—J.H.

[27] II Corinthians iii. 18.—J.H.

[28] Romans viii. 29. Other New Testament passages expressing a view of man as undergoing a process of spiritual growth within God's purpose, are: Ephesians ii. 21; iii. 16; Colossians ii. 19; I John iii. 2; II Corinthians iv. 16.—J.H.

spiritualization as a child of God. But we may well extend the first stage to include the development of man as a rational and responsible person capable of personal relationship with the personal Infinite who has created him. This first stage of the creative process was, to our anthropomorphic imaginations, easy for divine omnipotence. By an exercise of creative power God caused the physical universe to exist, and in the course of countless ages to bring forth within it organic life, and finally to produce out of organic life personal life; and when man had thus emerged out of the evolution of the forms of organic life, a creature had been made who has the possibility of existing in conscious fellowship with God. But the second stage of the creative process is of a different kind altogether. It cannot be perfected by omnipotent power as such. For personal life is essentially free and self-directing. It cannot be perfected by divine fiat, but only through the uncompelled responses and willing co-operation of human individuals in their actions and reactions in the world in which God has placed them. Men may eventually become the perfected persons whom the New Testament calls "children of God," but they cannot be created ready-made as this.

The value-judgement that is implicitly being invoked here is that one who has attained to goodness by meeting and eventually mastering temptations, and thus by rightly making responsible choices in concrete situations, is good in a richer and more valuable sense than would be one created *ab initio* in a state either of innocence or of virtue. In the former case, which is that of the actual moral achievements of mankind, the individual's goodness has within it the strength of temptations overcome, a stability based upon an accumulation of right choices, and a positive and responsible character that comes from the investment of costly personal effort. I suggest, then, that it is an ethically reasonable judgement, even though in the nature of the case not one that is capable of demonstrative proof, that human goodness slowly built up through personal histories of moral effort has a value in the eyes of the Creator which justifies even the long travail of the soul-making process.

The picture with which we are working is thus developmental and teleological. Man is in process of becoming the perfected being whom God is seeking to create. However, this is not taking place—it is important to add—by a natural and inevitable evolution, but through a hazardous adventure in individual freedom. Because this is a pilgrimage within the life of each individual, rather than a racial evolution, the progressive fulfilment of God's purpose does not entail any corresponding progressive improvement in the moral state of the world. There is no doubt a development in man's ethical situation from generation to generation through the building of individual choices into public institutions, but this involves an accumulation of evil as well as of good.[29] It is thus probable that human life was lived on much the same moral plane two thousand years ago or four thousand years ago as it is today. But nevertheless during this period uncounted millions of souls have been through the experience of earthly life, and God's purpose has gradually moved towards its fulfilment within each one of them, rather than within a human aggregate composed of different units in different generations.

---

[29] This fact is symbolized in early Christian literature both by the figure of the Antichrist, who continually opposes God's purposes in history, and by the expectation of cataclysmic calamity and strife in the last days before the end of the present world order.—J.H.

If, then, God's aim in making the world is "the bringing of many sons to glory,"[30] that aim will naturally determine the kind of world that He has created. Antitheistic writers almost invariably assume a conception of the divine purpose which is contrary to the Christian conception. They assume that the purpose of a loving God must be to create a hedonistic paradise; and therefore to the extent that the world is other than this, it proves to them that God is either not loving enough or not powerful enough to create such a world. They think of God's relation to the earth on the model of a human being building a cage for a pet animal to dwell in. If he is humane he will naturally make his pet's quarters as pleasant and healthful as he can. Any respect in which the cage falls short of the veterinarian's ideal, and contains possibilities of accident or disease, is evidence of either limited benevolence or limited means, or both. Those who use the problem of evil as an argument against belief in God almost invariably think of the world in this kind of way. David Hume, for example, speaks of an architect who is trying to plan a house that is to be as comfortable and convenient as possible. If we find that "the windows, doors, fires, passages, stairs, and the whole economy of the building were the source of noise, confusion, fatigue, darkness, and the extremes of heat and cold" we should have no hesitation in blaming the architect. It would be in vain for him to prove that if this or that defect were corrected greater ills would result: "still you would assert in general, that, if the architect had had skill and good intentions, he might have formed such a plan of the whole, and might have adjusted the parts in such a manner, as would have remedied all or most of these inconveniences."[31]

But if we are right in supposing that God's purpose for man is to lead him from human *Bios*, or the biological life of man, to that quality of *Zoe*, or the personal life of eternal worth, which we see in Christ, then the question that we have to ask is not, Is this the kind of world that an all-powerful and infinitely loving being would create as an environment for his human pets? or, Is the architecture of the world the most pleasant and convenient possible? The question that we have to ask is rather, Is this the kind of world that God might make as an environment in which moral beings may be fashioned, through their own free insights and responses, into "children of God"?

Such critics as Hume are confusing what heaven ought to be, as an environment for perfected finite beings, with what this world ought to be, as an environment for beings who are in process of becoming perfected. For if our general conception of God's purpose is correct the world is not intended to be a paradise, but rather the scene of a history in which human personality may be formed towards the pattern of Christ. Men are not to be thought of on the analogy of animal pets, whose life is to be made as agreeable as possible, but rather on the analogy of human children, who are to grow to adulthood in an environment whose primary and overriding purpose is not immediate pleasure but the realizing of the most valuable potentialities of human personality.

Needless to say, this characterization of God as the heavenly Father is not a merely random illustration but an analogy that lies at the heart of the Christian faith.

---

[30] Hebrews ii. 10.—J.H.

[31] *Dialogues Concerning Natural Religion*, pt. xi. Kemp-Smith's ed. (Oxford: Clarendon Press, 1935), p. 251.—J.H.

Jesus treated the likeness between the attitude of God to man, and the attitude of human parents at their best towards their children, as providing the most adequate way for us to think about God. And so it is altogether relevant to a Christian understanding of this world to ask, How does the best parental love express itself in its influence upon the environment in which children are to grow up? I think it is clear that a parent who loves his children, and wants them to become the best human beings that they are capable of becoming, does not treat pleasure as the sole and supreme value. Certainly we seek pleasure for our children, and take great delight in obtaining it for them; but we do not desire for them unalloyed pleasure at the expense of their growth in such even greater values as moral integrity, unselfishness, compassion, courage, humour, reverence for the truth, and perhaps above all the capacity for love. We do not act on the premise that pleasure is the supreme end of life; and if the development of these other values sometimes clashes with the provision of pleasure, then we are willing to have our children miss a certain amount of this, rather than fail to come to possess and to be possessed by the finer and more precious qualities that are possible to the human personality. A child brought up on the principle that the only or the supreme value is pleasure would not be likely to become an ethically mature adult or an attractive or happy personality. And to most parents it seems more important to try to foster quality and strength of character in their children than to fill their lives at all times with the utmost possible degree of pleasure. If, then, there is any true analogy between God's purpose for his human creatures, and the purpose of loving and wise parents for their children, we have to recognize that the presence of pleasure and the absence of pain cannot be the supreme and overriding end for which the world exists. Rather, this world must be a place of soul-making. And its value is to be judged, not primarily by the quantity of pleasure and pain occurring in it at any particular moment, but by its fitness for its primary purpose, the purpose of soul-making.[32]

In all this we have been speaking about the nature of the world considered simply as the God-given environment of man's life. For it is mainly in this connection that the world has been regarded in Irenaean and in Protestant thought.[33] But such a way of thinking involves a danger of anthropocentrism from which the Augustinian and Catholic tradition has generally been protected by its sense of the relative insignificance of man within the totality of the created universe. Man was dwarfed within the

---

[32] The phrase "the vale of Soul-making" was coined by the poet John Keats in a letter written to his brother and sister in April 1819. He says, "The common cognomen of this world among the misguided and superstitious is 'a vale of tears' from which we are to be redeemed by a certain arbitrary interposition of God and taken to Heaven—What a little circumscribed straightened notion! Call the world if you Please 'The vale of Soul-making.'" In this letter he sketches a teleological theodicy. "Do you not see," he asks, "how necessary a World of Pains and troubles is to school an Intelligence and make it a Soul?" (*The Letters of John Keats*, ed. by M. B. Forman. London: Oxford University Press, 4th ed., 1952, pp. 334–35.)

[33] Thus Irenaeus said that "the creation is suited to [the wants of] man; for man was not made for its sake, but creation for the sake of man" (*Against Heresies*, v. xxix. 1), and Calvin said that "because we know that the universe was established especially for the sake of mankind, we ought to look for this purpose in his governance also." (*Inst.* I. xvi. 6.)—J.H.

medieval world-view by the innumerable hosts of angels and archangels above him—unfallen rational natures which rejoice in the immediate presence of God, reflecting His glory in the untarnished mirror of their worship. However, this higher creation has in our modern world lost its hold upon the imagination. Its place has been taken, as the minimizer of men, by the immensities of outer space and by the material universe's unlimited complexity transcending our present knowledge. As the spiritual environment envisaged by Western man has shrunk, his physical horizons have correspondingly expanded. Where the human creature was formerly seen as an insignificant appendage to the angelic world, he is now seen as an equally insignificant organic excrescence, enjoying a fleeting moment of consciousness on the surface of one of the planets of a minor star. Thus the truth that was symbolized for former ages by the existence of the angelic hosts is today impressed upon us by the vastness of the physical universe, countering the egoism of our species by making us feel that this immense prodigality of existence can hardly all exist for the sake of man—though, on the other hand, the very realization that it is not all for the sake of man may itself be salutary and beneficial to man!

However, instead of opposing man and nature as rival objects of God's interest, we should perhaps rather stress man's solidarity as an embodied being with the whole natural order in which he is embedded. For man is organic to the world; all his acts and thoughts and imaginations are conditioned by space and time; and in abstraction from nature he would cease to be human. We may, then, say that the beauties and sublimities and powers, the microscopic intricacies and macroscopic vastnesses, the wonders and the terrors of the natural world and of the life that pulses through it, are willed and valued by their Maker in a creative act that embraces man together with nature. By means of matter and living flesh God both builds a path and weaves a veil between Himself and the creature made in His image. Nature thus has permanent significance; for God has set man in a creaturely environment, and the final fulfillment of our nature in relation to God will accordingly take the form of an embodied life within "a new heaven and a new earth."[34] And as in the present age man moves slowly towards that fulfilment through the pilgrimage of his earthly life, so also "the whole creation" is "groaning in travail," waiting for the time when it will be "set free from its bondage to decay."[35]

And yet however fully we thus acknowledge the permanent significance and value of the natural order, we must still insist upon man's special character as a personal creature made in the image of God; and our theodicy must still centre upon the soul-making process that we believe to be taking place within human life.

This, then, is the starting-point from which we propose to try to relate the realities of sin and suffering to the perfect love of an omnipotent Creator. And as will become increasingly apparent, a theodicy that starts in this way must be eschatological in its ultimate bearings. That is to say, instead of looking to the past for its clue to the mystery of evil, it looks to the future, and indeed to that ultimate future to which only

---

[34] Revelation xxi. 1.—J.H.
[35] Romans viii. 21 – 22.—J.H.

faith can look. Given the conception of a divine intention working in and through human time towards a fulfilment that lies in its completeness beyond human time, our theodicy must find the meaning of evil in the part that it is made to play in the eventual outworking of that purpose; and must find the justification of the whole process in the magnitude of the good to which it leads. The good that outshines all ill is not a paradise long since lost but a kingdom which is yet to come in its full glory and permanence. . . .

CHAPTER TEN

Belief and Faith

○

○ ○ ○ *45*

The Ethics of Belief
W. K. Clifford

A SHIP-OWNER WAS about to send to sea an emigrant-ship. He knew that she was old, and not over-well built at the first; that she had seen many seas and climes, and often had needed repairs. Doubts had been suggested to him that possibly she was not seaworthy. These doubts preyed upon his mind and made him unhappy; he thought that perhaps he ought to have her thoroughly overhauled and refitted, even though this should put him to great expense. Before the ship sailed, however, he succeeded in overcoming these melancholy reflections. He said to himself that she had gone safely through so many voyages and weathered so many storms that it was idle to suppose she would not come safely home from this trip also. He would put his trust in Providence, which could hardly fail to protect all these unhappy families that were leaving their father-land to seek for better times elsewhere. He would dismiss from his mind all ungenerous suspicions about the honesty of builders and contractors. In such ways he acquired a sincere and comfortable conviction that his vessel was thoroughly safe and seaworthy; he watched her departure with a light heart, and benevolent wishes for the success of the exiles in their strange new home that was to be; and he got his insurance money when she went down in midocean and told no tales.

[1.] What shall we say of him? Surely this, that he was verily guilty of the death of those men. It is admitted that he did sincerely believe in the soundness of his ship; but the sincerity of his conviction can in no wise help him, because *he had no right to believe on such evidence as was before him.* He had acquired his belief not by honestly earning it in patient investigation, but by stifling his doubts. And although in the end he may have felt so sure about it that he could not think otherwise, yet inasmuch as he had knowingly and willingly worked himself into that frame of mind, he must be held responsible for it.

[2.] Let us alter the case a little, and suppose that the ship was not unsound after all; that she made her voyage safely, and many others after it. Will that diminish the guilt of her owner? Not one jot. When an action is once done, it is right or wrong forever; no accidental failure of its good or evil fruits can possibly alter that. The man would not have been innocent, he would only have been not found out. The question of right or wrong has to do with the origin of his belief, not the matter of it; not what it was, but how he got it; not whether it turned out to be true or false, but whether he had a right to believe on such evidence as was before him.

[1, 2 cont.] There was once an island in which some of the inhabitants professed a religion teaching neither the doctrine of original sin nor that of eternal punishment. A suspicion got abroad that the professors of this religion had made use of unfair means to get their doctrines taught to children. They were accused of wresting the laws of their country in such a way as to remove children from the care of their natural and legal guardians; and even of stealing them away and keeping them concealed from their friends and relations. A certain number of men formed themselves into a society for the purpose of agitating the public about this matter. They published grave accusations against individual citizens of the highest position and character, and did all in their power to injure those citizens in the exercise of their profession. So great was the noise they made, that a Commission was appointed to investigate the facts; but after the Commission had carefully inquired into all the evidence that could be got, it appeared that the accused were innocent. Not only had they been accused on insufficient evidence, but the evidence of their innocence was such as the agitators might easily have obtained, if they had attempted a fair inquiry. After these disclosures the inhabitants of that country looked upon the members of the agitating society, not only as persons whose judgment was to be distrusted, but also as no longer to be counted honorable men. For although they had sincerely and conscientiously believed in the charges they had made, *yet they had no right to believe on such evidence as was before them*. Their sincere convictions, instead of being honestly earned by patient inquiring, were stolen by listening to the voice of prejudice and passion.

Let us vary this case also, and suppose, other things remaining as before, that a still more accurate investigation proved the accused to have been really guilty. Would this make any difference in the guilt of the accusers? Clearly not; the question is not whether their belief was true or false, but whether they entertained it on wrong grounds. They would no doubt say, "Now you see that we were right after all; next time perhaps you will believe us." And they might be believed, but they would not thereby become honorable men. They would not be innocent, they would only be not found out. Every one of them, if he chose to examine himself *in foro conscientiae*,[1] would know that he had acquired and nourished a belief, when he had no right to believe on such evidence as was before him; and therein he would know that he had done a wrong thing.

It may be said, however, that in both of these supposed cases it is not the belief which is judged to be wrong, but the action following upon it. The shipowner might say, "I am perfectly certain that my ship is sound, but still I feel it my duty to have her examined, before trusting the lives of so many people to her." And it might be said to the agitator, "However convinced you were of the justice of your cause and the truth of your convictions, you ought not to have made a public attack upon any man's character until you had examined the evidence on both sides with the utmost patience and care."

In the first place, let us admit that, so far as it goes, this view of the case is right and necessary; right, because even when a man's belief is so fixed that he cannot think otherwise, he still has a choice in regard to the action suggested by it, and so cannot escape the duty of investigating on the ground of the strength of his convictions; and necessary, because those who are not yet capable of controlling their feelings and thoughts must have a plain rule dealing with overt acts.

But this being premised as necessary, it becomes clear that it is not sufficient, and that our previous judgment is required to supplement it. For it is not possible so to sever the belief from the action it suggests as to condemn the one without condemning

---

[1] In the forum of his conscience.—E.D.K.

the other. No man holding a strong belief on one side of a question, or even wishing to hold a belief on one side, can investigate it with such fairness and completeness as if he were really in doubt and unbiased; so that the existence of a belief not founded on fair inquiry unfits a man for the performance of this necessary duty.

[3.] Nor is that truly a belief at all which has not some influence upon the actions of him who holds it. He who truly believes that which prompts him to an action has looked upon the action to lust after it, he has committed it already in his heart. If a belief is not realized immediately in open deeds, it is stored up for the guidance of the future. It goes to make a part of that aggregate of beliefs which is the link between sensation and action at every moment of all our lives, and which is so organized and compacted together that no part of it can be isolated from the rest, but every new addition modifies the structure of the whole. No real belief, however trifling and fragmentary it may seem, is ever truly insignificant; it prepares us to receive more of its like, confirms those which resembled it before, and weakens others; and so gradually it lays a stealthy train in our inmost thoughts, which may some day explode into overt action, and leave its stamp upon our character forever.

[4.] And no one man's belief is in any case a private matter which concerns himself alone. Our lives are guided by that general conception of the course of things which has been created by society for social purposes. Our words, our phrases, our forms and processes and modes of thought, are common property, fashioned and perfected from age to age; an heirloom which every succeeding generation inherits as a precious deposit and a sacred trust to be handed on to the next one, not unchanged but enlarged and purified, with some clear marks of its proper handiwork. Into this, for good or ill, is woven every belief of every man who has speech of his fellows. An awful privilege, and an awful responsibility, that we should help to create the world in which posterity will live.

In the two supposed cases which have been considered, it has been judged wrong to believe on insufficient evidence, or to nourish belief by suppressing doubts and avoiding investigation. The reason of this judgment is not far to seek: It is that in both these cases the belief held by one man was of great importance to other men. But for as much as no belief held by one man, however seemingly trivial the belief, and however obscure the believer, is ever actually insignificant or without its effect on the fate of mankind, we have no choice but to extend our judgment to all cases of belief whatever. Belief, that sacred faculty which prompts the decisions of our will, and knits into harmonious working all the compacted energies of our being, is ours not for ourselves, but for humanity. It is rightly used on truths which have been established by long experience and waiting toil, and which have stood in the fierce light of free and fearless questioning. Then it helps to bind men together, and to strengthen and direct their common action. It is desecrated when given to unproved and unquestioned statements, for the solace and private pleasure of the believer; to add a tinsel splendor to the plain straight road of our life and display a bright mirage beyond it; or even to drown the common sorrows of our kind by a self-deception which allows them not only to cast down but also to degrade us. Whoso would deserve well of his fellows in this matter will guard the purity of his belief with a very fanaticism of jealous care, lest at any time it should rest on an unworthy object and catch a stain which can never be wiped away.

It is not only the leader of men, statesman, philosopher, or poet, that owes this bounden duty to mankind. Every rustic who delivers in the village alehouse his slow, infrequent sentences may help to kill or keep alive the fatal superstitions which clog his race. Every hard-worked wife of an artisan may transmit to her children beliefs which shall knit society together, or rend it in pieces. No simplicity of mind, no obscurity of station can escape the duty of questioning all that we believe.

It is true that this duty is a hard one, and the doubt which comes out of it is often a very bitter thing. It leaves us bare and powerless where we thought that we were safe and strong. To know all about anything is to know how to deal with it under all circumstances. We feel much happier and more secure when we think we know precisely what to do, no matter what happens, than when we have lost our way and do not know where to turn. And if we have supposed ourselves to know all about anything, and to be capable of doing what is fit in regard to it, we naturally do not like to find that we are really ignorant and powerless, that we have to begin again at the beginning, and try to learn what the thing is and how it is to be dealt with—if indeed anything can be learned about it. It is the sense of power attached to a sense of knowledge that makes men desirous of believing, and afraid of doubting.

This sense of power is the highest and best of pleasures when the belief on which it is founded is a true belief, and has been fairly earned by investigation. For then we may justly feel that it is common property, and holds good for others as well as for ourselves. Then we may be glad, not that I have learned secrets by which I am safer and stronger, but that *we men* have got mastery over more of the world; and we shall be strong, not for ourselves, but in the name of Man and in his strength. But if the belief has been accepted on insufficient evidence, the pleasure is a stolen one. Not only does it deceive ourselves by giving us a sense of power which we do not really possess, but it is sinful, because it is stolen in defiance of our duty to mankind. That duty is to guard ourselves from such beliefs as from a pestilence, which may shortly master our own body and then spread to the rest of the town. What would be thought of one who, for the sake of a sweet fruit, should deliberately run the risk of bringing a plague upon his family and his neighbors?

[5.] And, as in other such cases, it is not the risk only which has to be considered; for a bad action is always bad at the time when it is done, no matter what happens afterwards. Every time we let ourselves believe for unworthy reasons, we weaken our powers of self-control, of doubting, of judicially and fairly weighing evidence. We all suffer severely enough from the maintenance and support of false beliefs and the fatally wrong actions which they lead to, and the evil born when one such belief is entertained is great and wide. But a greater and wider evil arises when the credulous character is maintained and supported, when a habit of believing for unworthy reasons is fostered and made permanent. If I steal money from any person, there may be no harm done by the mere transfer of possession; he may not feel the loss, or it may prevent him from using the money badly. But I cannot help doing this great wrong toward Man, that I make myself dishonest. What hurts society is not that it should lose its property, but that it should become a den of thieves; for then it must cease to be society. This is why we ought not to do evil that good may come; for at any rate this great evil has come, that we have done evil and are made wicked thereby. In like manner, if I let myself believe anything on insufficient evidence, there may be no great harm done by the mere belief; it may be true after all, or I may never have occasion to exhibit it in outward acts. But I cannot help doing this great wrong toward Man, that I make myself credulous. The danger to society is not merely that it should believe wrong things, though that is great enough, but that it should become credulous, and lose the habit of testing things and inquiring into them; for then it must sink back into savagery.

The harm which is done by credulity in a man is not confined to the fostering of a credulous character in others, and consequent support of false beliefs. Habitual want of care about what I believe leads to habitual want of care in others about the truth of what is told to me. Men speak the truth to one another when each reveres the truth in his own mind and in the other's mind; but how shall my friend revere the truth in my mind when I myself am careless about it, when I believe things because I want to believe them, and because they are comforting and pleasant? Will he not learn to cry "Peace" to me, when there is no peace? By such a course I shall surround myself with a thick atmosphere of falsehood and fraud, and in that I must live. It may matter little to me, in my cloud-castle of sweet illusions and darling lies; but it matters much to Man that I have made my neighbors ready to deceive. The credulous man is father to the liar and the cheat; he lives in the bosom of this his family, and it is no marvel if he should become even as they are. So closely are our duties knit together, that whoso shall keep the whole law, and yet offend in one point, he is guilty of all.

To sum up: It is wrong always, everywhere, and for any one to believe anything upon insufficient evidence. . . .

"But," says one, "I am a busy man; I have no time for the long course of study which would be necessary to make me in any degree a competent judge of certain questions, or even able to understand the nature of the arguments." Then he should have no time to believe.

○ ○ ○ **46**

The Will to Believe
William James

· I ·

IN THE RECENTLY published Life by Leslie Stephen of his brother, Fitz-James, there is an account of a school to which the latter went when he was a boy. The teacher, a certain Mr. Guest, used to converse with his pupils in this wise: "Gurney, what is the difference between justification and sanctification? Stephen, prove the omnipotence of God!" etc. In the midst of our Harvard freethinking and indifference we are prone to imagine that here at your good old orthodox College conversation continues to be somewhat upon this order; and to show you that we at Harvard have not lost all interest in these vital subjects, I have brought with me tonight something like a sermon on justification by faith to read to you—I mean an essay in justification of faith, a defense of our right to adopt a believing attitude in religious matters, in spite of the fact that our merely logical intellect may not have been coerced. "The Will to Believe," accordingly, is the title of my paper.

I have long defended to my own students the lawfulness of voluntarily adopted faith; but as soon as they have got well imbued with the logical spirit, they have as a rule refused to admit my contention to be lawful philosophically, even though in point of fact they were personally all the time chock-full of some faith or other themselves. I am all the while, however, so profoundly convinced that my own position is correct, that your invitation has seemed to me a good occasion to make my statements more clear. Perhaps your minds will be more open than those with which I have hitherto had to deal. I will be as little technical as I can, though I must begin by setting up some technical distinctions that will help us in the end.

· II ·

Let us give the name of *hypothesis* to anything that may be proposed to our belief; and just as the electrician speak of live and dead wires, let us speak of any hypothesis as either *live* or *dead*. A live hypothesis is one which appeals as a real possibility to him to who it is proposed. If I as you to believe in the Mahdi, the notion makes no electric connection with your nature—it refuses to scintillate with any credibility at all. As an hypothesis it is completely dead. To an Arab, however (even if he be not one of the Mahdi's followers), the hypothesis is among the mind's possibilities: it is alive. This shows that deadness and liveness in an hypothesis are not intrinsic properties, but relations to the individual thinker. They are measured by his willingness to act irrevocably. Practically, that means belief; but there is some believing tendency wherever there is willingness to act at all.

Next, let us call the decision between two hypotheses an *option*. Options may be of several kinds. They may be (1) *living* or *dead*, (2) *forced* or *avoidable*, (3) *momentous* or *trivial*; and for our purposes we may call an option a *genuine* option when it is of the forced, living, and momentous kind.

1. A living option is one in which both hypotheses are live ones. If I say to you: "Be a theosophist or be a Mohammedan," it is probably a dead option, because for you neither hypothesis is likely to be alive. But if I say: "Be an agnostic or be a Christian," it is otherwise: trained as you are, each hypothesis makes some appeal, however small, to your belief.

2. Next, if I say to you: "Choose between going out with your umbrella or without it," I do not offer you a genuine option, for it is not forced. You can easily avoid it by not going out at all. Similarly, if I say, "Either love me or hate me," "Either call my theory true or call it false," your option is avoidable. You may remain indifferent to me, neither loving nor hating, and you may decline to offer any judgment as to my theory. But if I say, "Either accept this truth or go without it," I put on you a forced option, for there is no standing place outside of the alternative. Every dilemma based on a complete logical disjunction, with no possibility of not choosing, is an option of this forced kind.

3. Finally, if I were Dr. Nansen and proposed to you to join my North Pole expedition, your option would be momentous; for this would probably be your only similar opportunity, and your choice now would either exclude you from the North Pole sort of immortality altogether or put at least the chance of it into your hands. He who refuses to embrace a unique opportunity loses the prize as surely as if he tried and failed. *Per contra*, the option is trivial when the opportunity is not unique, when the stake is insignificant, or when the decision is reversible if it later prove unwise. Such trivial options abound in the scientific life. A chemist finds an hypothesis live enough to spend a year in its verification: he believes in it to that extent. But if his experiments prove inconclusive either way, he is quit for his loss of time, no vital harm being done.

It will facilitate our discussion if we keep all these distinctions well in mind.

· III ·

The next matter to consider is the actual psychology of human opinion. When we look at certain facts, it seems as if our passional and volitional nature lay at the root of all our convictions. When we look at others, it seems as if they could do nothing when the intellect had once said its say. Let us take the latter facts up first.

Does it not seem preposterous on the very face of it to talk of our opinions being modifiable at will? Can our will either help or hinder our intellect in its perceptions of truth? Can we, by just willing it, believe that Abraham Lincoln's existence is a myth, and that the portraits of him in *McClure's Magazine* are all of someone else? Can we, by any effort of our will, or by any strength of wish that it were true, believe ourselves well and about when we are roaring with rheumatism in bed, or feel certain that the sum of the two one-dollar bills in our pocket must be a hundred dollars? We can *say* any of these things, but we are absolutely impotent to believe them; and of just such things is the whole fabric of the truths that we do believe in made up—matters of fact, immediate or remote, as Hume said, and relations between ideas, which are either there or not there for us if we see them so, and which if not there cannot be put there by any action of our own.

In Pascal's *Thoughts* there is a celebrated passage known in literature as Pascal's wager.[1] In it he tries to force us into Christianity by reasoning as if our concern with truth resembled our concern with the stakes in a game of chance. Translated freely his words are these: You must either believe or not believe that God is—which will you do? Your human reason cannot say. A game is going on between you and the nature of things which at the day of judgment will bring out either heads or tails. Weigh what your gains and your losses would be if you should stake all you have on heads, or God's existence: if you win in such case, you gain eternal beatitude; if you lose, you lose nothing at all. If there were an infinity of chances, and only one for God in this wager, still you ought to stake your all on God; for though you surely risk a finite loss by this procedure, any finite loss is reasonable, even a certain one is reasonable, if there is but the possibility of infinite gain. Go, then, and take holy water, and have masses said; belief will come and stupefy your scruples—*Cela vous fera croire et vous abêtira*. Why should you not? At bottom, what have you to lose?

You probably feel that when religious faith expresses itself thus, in the language of the gaming-table, it is put to its last trumps. Surely Pascal's own personal belief in masses and holy water had far other springs; and this celebrated page of his is but an argument for others, a last desperate snatch as a weapon against the hardness of the unbelieving heart. We feel that a faith in masses and holy water adopted wilfully after such a mechanical calculation would lack the inner soul of faith's reality; and if we were ourselves in the place of the Deity, we should probably take particular pleasure in cutting off believers of this pattern from their infinite reward. It is evident that unless there be some preexisting tendency to believe in masses and holy water, the option offered to the will by Pascal is not a living option. Certainly no Turk ever took to masses and holy water on its account; and even to us Protestants these means of salvation seem such foregone impossibilities that Pascal's logic, invoked for them specifically, leaves us unmoved. As well might the Mahdi write to us, saying, "I am the Expected One whom God has created in his effulgence. You shall be infinitely happy if you confess me; otherwise you shall be cut off from the light of the sun. Weigh, then, your infinite gain if I am genuine against your finite sacrifice if I am not!" His logic would be that of Pascal; but he would vainly use it on us, for the hypothesis he offers us is dead. No tendency to act on it exists in us to any degree.

The talk of believing by our volition seems, then, from one point of view, simply silly. From another point of view it is worse than silly, it is vile. When one turns to the magnificent edifice of the physical sciences, and sees how it was reared; what thousands of disinterested moral lives of men lie buried in its mere foundations; what patience and postponement, what choking down of preference, what submission to the icy laws of outer fact are wrought into its very stones and mortar, how absolutely impersonal it stands in its vast augustness—then how besotted and contemptible seems every little sentimentalist who comes blowing his voluntary smoke-wreaths, and pretending to decide things from out of his private dream! Can we wonder if those bred in the rugged and manly school of science should feel like spewing such subjectivism out of their mouths? The whole system of loyalties which grow up in the schools of science go dead against its toleration; so that it is only natural that those who

---

[1] Blaise Pascal, *Pensées*, J. Chevalier, ed. (Paris, 1954) No. 451. In English translation by F. W. Trotter (New York: E. P. Dutton & Co., 1932), No. 233.—w.j.

have caught the scientific fever should pass over to the opposite extreme, and write sometimes as if the incorruptibly truthful intellect ought positively to prefer bitterness and unacceptableness to the heart in its cup.

> It fortifies my soul to know
> That, though I perish, Truth is so—

sings Clough, while Huxley exclaims:

> My only consolation lies in the reflection that, however bad our posterity may become, so far as they hold by the plain rule of not pretending to believe what they have no reason to believe, because it may be to their advantage so to pretend [the word "pretend" is surely here redundant], they will not have reached the lowest depth of immorality.

And that delicious *enfant terrible*, Clifford, writes:

> Belief is desecrated when given to unproved and unquestioned statements for the solace and private pleasure of the believer. . . . Whoso would deserve well of his fellows in this matter will guard the purity of his belief with a very fanaticism of jealous care, lest at any time it should rest on an unworthy object, and catch a stain which can never be wiped away. . . . If [a] belief has been accepted on insufficient evidence [even though the belief be true, as Clifford on the same page explains] the pleasure is a stolen one. . . . It is sinful because it is stolen in defiance of our duty to mankind. That duty is to guard ourselves from such beliefs as from a pestilence which may shortly master our own body and then spread to the rest of the town. . . . It is wrong always, everywhere, and for everyone, to believe anything upon insufficient evidence.

All this strikes one as healthy, even when expressed, as by Clifford, with somewhat too much of robustious pathos in the voice. Free-will and simple wishing do seem, in the matter of our credences, to be only fifth wheels to the coach. Yet if anyone should thereupon assume that intellectual insight is what remains after wish and will and sentimental preference have taken wing, or that pure reason is what then settles our opinions, he would fly quite as directly in the teeth of the facts.

It is only our already dead hypotheses that our willing nature is unable to bring to life again. But what has made them dead for us is for the most part a previous action of our willing nature of an antagonistic kind. When I say "willing nature," I do not mean only such deliberate volitions as may have set up habits of belief that we cannot now escape from—I mean all such factors of belief as fear and hope, prejudice and passion, imitation and partisanship, the circumpressure of our caste and set. As a matter of fact we find ourselves believing, we hardly know how or why. Mr. Balfour gives the name of "authority" to all those influences, born of the intellectual climate, that make hypotheses possible or impossible for us, alive or dead. Here in this room, we all of us believe in molecules and the conservation of energy, in democracy and necessary progress, in Protestant Christianity and the duty of fighting for "the doctrine of the immortal Monroe," all for no reasons worthy of the name. We see into these matters with no more inner clearness, and probably with much less, than any disbeliever in them might possess. His unconventionality would probably have some grounds to show for its conclusions; but for us, not insight, but the *prestige* of the opinions, is what makes the spark shoot from them and light up our sleeping magazines of faith. Our reason is quite satisfied, in nine hundred and ninety-nine cases out of every thousand of us, if it can find a few arguments that will do to recite in case our credulity is criticized by someone else. Our faith is faith in someone else's faith, and in the greatest matters this is most the case. Our belief in truth itself, for instance, that there is a truth, and that our minds and it are made for each other—what is it but a passionate affirmation of desire, in which our social system backs us up? We want to have a truth; we want to believe that our experiment and studies and discussions must put us in a continually better and better position towards it; and on this line we agree to fight out our thinking lives. But if a pyrrhonistic skeptic asks us *how we know* all this, can our logic find a reply? No! certainly it cannot. It is just one volition against another—we willing to go in for life upon a trust or assumption which he, for his part, does not care to make.

As a rule we disbelieve all facts and theories for which we have no use. Clifford's cosmic emotions find no use for Christian feelings. Huxley belabors the bishops because there is no use for sacerdotalism in his scheme of life. Newman, on the contrary, goes over to Romanism, and finds all sorts of reasons good for staying there, because a priestly system is for him an organic need and delight. Why do so few "scientists" even look at the evidence for telepathy, so called? Because they think, as a leading biologist, now dead, once said to me, that even if such a thing were true, scientists ought to band together to keep it suppressed and concealed. It would undo the uniformity of Nature and all sorts of other things without which scientists cannot carry on their pursuits. But if this very man had been shown something which as a scientist he might *do* with telepathy, he might not only have examined the evidence, but even have found it good enough. This very law which the logicians would impose upon us—if I may give the name of logicians to those who would rule out our willing nature here—is based on nothing but their own natural wish to exclude all elements for which they, in their professional quality of logicians, can find no use.

Evidently, then, our non-intellectual nature does influence our convictions. There are passional tendencies and volitions which run before and others which come after belief, and it is only the latter that are too late for the fair; and they are not too late when the previous passional work has been already in their own direction. Pascal's argument, instead of being powerless, then seems a regular clincher, and is the last stroke needed to make our faith in masses and holy water complete. The state of things is evidently far from simple; and pure insight and logic, whatever they might do ideally, are not the only things that really do produce our creeds.

· IV ·

Our next duty, having recognized this mixed-up state of affairs, is to ask whether it be simply reprehensible and pathological, or whether, on the contrary, we must treat it as a normal element in making up our minds. The thesis I defend is, briefly stated, this: *Our passional nature not only lawfully may, but must, decide an option between propositions, whenever it is a genuine option that cannot by its nature be decided on intellectual grounds; for to say, under such circumstances, "Do not decide, but leave the question open" is itself a passional decision—just like deciding yes or no—and is attended with the same risk of losing the truth.* The thesis thus abstractly expressed will, I trust, soon become quite clear. But I must first indulge in a bit more of preliminary work.

. V .

It will be observed that for the purposes of this discussion we are on "dogmatic" ground—ground, I mean, which leaves systematic philosophical skepticism altogether out of account. The postulate that there is truth, and that it is the destiny of our minds to attain it, we are deliberately resolving to make, though the skeptic will not make it. We part company with him, therefore, absolutely, at this point. But the faith that truth exists, and that our minds can find it, may be held in two ways. We may talk of the *empiricist* way and of the *absolutist* way of believing in truth. The absolutists in this matter say that we cannot only attain to knowing truth, but we can *know when* we have attained to knowing it; while the empiricists think that although we may attain it, we cannot infallibly know when. To *know* is one thing, and to know for certain *that* we know is another. One may hold to the first being possible without the second; hence the empiricists and the absolutists, although neither of them is a skeptic in the usual philosophic sense of the term, show very different degrees of dogmatism in their lives.

If we look at the history of opinions, we see that empiricist tendency has largely prevailed in science, while in philosophy the absolutist tendency has had everything its own way. The characteristic sort of happiness, indeed, which philosophies yield has mainly consisted in the conviction felt by each successive school or system that by it bottom-certitude had been attained. "Other philosophies are collections of opinions, mostly false; *my* philosophy gives standing-ground forever"—who does not recognize in this the keynote of every system worthy of the name? A system, to be a system at all, must come as a *closed* system, reversible in this or that detail, perchance, but in its essential features never!

Scholastic orthodoxy, to which one must always go when one wishes to find perfectly clear statement, has beautifully elaborated this absolutist conviction in a doctrine which it calls that of "objective evidence." If, for example, I am unable to doubt that I now exist before you, that two is less than three, or that if all men are mortal then I am mortal too, it is because these things illumine my intellect irresistibly. The final ground of this objective evidence possessed by certain propositions is the *adaequatio intellectûs nostri cum re* [conformity of our minds to fact]. The certitude it brings involves an *aptitudinem ad extorquendum certum assensum* [a power to compel sure assent] on the part of the truth envisaged, and on the side of the subject a *quietem in cognitione* [assurance in knowing], when once the object is mentally received, that leaves no possibility of doubt behind; and in the whole transaction nothing operates but the *entitas ipsa* [reality] of the object and the *entitas ipsa* [reality] of the mind. We slouchy modern thinkers dislike to talk in Latin—indeed, we dislike to talk in set terms at all; but at bottom our own state of mind is very much like this whenever we uncritically abandon ourselves: You believe in objective evidence, and I do. Of some things we feel that we are certain: we know, and we know that we do know. There is something that gives a click inside of us, a bell that strikes twelve, when the hands of our mental clock have swept the dial and meet over the meridian hour. The greatest empiricists among us are only empiricists on reflection: when left to their instincts, they dogmatize like infallible popes. When the Cliffords tell us how sinful it is to be Christian on such "insufficient evidence," insufficiency is really the last thing they have in mind. For them the evidence is absolutely sufficient, only it makes the other way. They believe so completely in an anti-Christian order of the universe that there is no living option: Christianity is a dead hypothesis from the start.

. *VI* .

But now, since we are all such absolutists by instinct, what in our quality of students of philosophy ought we to do about the fact? Shall we espouse and indorse it? Or shall we treat it as a weakness of our nature from which we must free ourselves, if we can?

I sincerely believe that the latter course is the only one we can follow as reflective men. Objective evidence and certitude are doubtless very fine ideals to play with, but where on this moonlit and dream-visited planet are they found? I am, therefore, myself a complete empiricist so far as my theory of human knowledge goes. I live, to be sure, by the practical faith that we must go on experiencing and thinking over our experience, for only thus can our opinions grow more true; but to hold any one of them—I absolutely do not care which—as if it never could be reinterpretable or corrigible, I believe to be a tremendously mistaken attitude, and I think that the whole history of philosophy will bear me out. There is but one indefectibly certain truth, and that is the truth that pyrrhonistic skepticism itself leaves standing—the truth that the present phenomenon of consciousness exists. That, however, is the bare starting-point of knowledge, the mere admission of a stuff to be philosophized about. The various philosophies are but so many attempts at expressing what this stuff really is. And if we repair to our libraries what disagreement do we discover! Where is a certainly true answer found? Apart from abstract propositions of comparison (such as two and two are the same as four), propositions which tell us nothing by themselves about concrete reality, we find no proposition ever regarded by anyone as evidently certain that has not either been called a falsehood, or at least had its truth sincerely questioned by someone else. The transcending of the axioms of geometry, not in play but in earnest, by certain of our contemporaries (as Zöllner and Charles H. Hinton), and his rejection of the whole Aristotelian logic by the Hegelians, are striking instances in point.

No concrete test of what is really true has ever been agreed upon. Some make the criterion external to the moment of perception, putting it either in revelation, the *consensus gentium,*[2] the instincts of the heart, or the systematized experience of the race. Others make the perceptive moment its own test—Descartes, for instances, with his clear and distinct ideas guaranteed by the veracity of God; Reid with his "common-sense"; and Kant with his forms of synthetic judgment a priori. The inconceivability of the opposite; the capacity to be verified by sense; the possession of complete organic unity of self-relation, realized when a thing is its own other—are standards which, in turn, have been used. The much lauded objective evidence is never triumphantly there; it is a mere aspiration or *Grenzbegriff,*[3] marking the infinitely remote ideal of our thinking life. To claim that certain truths now possess it, is simply to say that when you think them true and they *are* true, then their evidence is objective, otherwise it is not. But practically one's conviction that the evidence one goes by is of the real objective brand, is only one more subjective opinion added to the lot. For what a contradictory

---

[2] Consensus of the people or masses.—E.D.K.

[3] Limiting concept.—E.D.K.

array of opinions have objective evidence and absolute certitude been claimed! The world is rational through and through—its existence is an ultimate brute fact; there is a personal God—a personal God is inconceivable; there is an extra-mental physical world immediately known—the mind can only know its own ideas; a moral imperative exists—obligation is only the resultant of desires; a permanent spiritual principle is in everyone—there are only shifting states of mind; there is an endless chain of causes— there is an absolute first cause; an eternal necessity—a freedom; a purpose—no purpose; a primal One—a primal Many; a universal continuity—an essential discontinuity in things; an infinity—no infinity. There is this—there is that; there is indeed nothing which someone has not thought absolutely true, while his neighbor deemed it absolutely false; and not an absolutist among them seems ever to have considered that the trouble may all the time be essential, and that the intellect, even with truth directly in its grasp, may have no infallible signal for knowing whether it be truth or no. When, indeed, one remembers that the most striking practical application to life of the doctrine of objective certitude has been the conscientious labors of the Holy Office of the Inquisition, one feels less tempted than ever to lend the doctrine a respectful ear.

But please observe, now, that when as empiricists we give up the doctrine of objective certitude, we do not thereby given up the quest or hope of truth itself. We still pin our faith on its existence, and still believe that we gain an ever better position towards it by systematically continuing to roll up experiences and think. Our great difference from the scholastic lies in the way we face. The strength of his system lies in the principles, the origin, the *terminus a quo* of his thought; for us the strength is in the outcome, the upshot, the *terminus ad quem*. Not where it comes from but what it leads to is to decide. It matters not to an empiricist from what quarter an hypothesis may come to him: he may have acquired it by fair means or by foul; passion may have whispered or accident suggested it; but if the total drift of thinking continues to confirm it, that is what he means by its being true.

· VII ·

One more point, small but important, and our preliminaries are done. There are two ways of looking at our duty in the matter of opinion—ways entirely different, and yet ways about whose difference the theory of knowledge seems hitherto to have shown very little concern. *We must know the truth*; and *we must avoid error*—these are our first and great commandments as would-be knowers; but they are not two ways of stating an identical commandment, they are two separable laws. Although it may indeed happen that when we believe the truth *A*, we escape as an incidental consequence from believing the falsehood *B*, it hardly ever happens that by merely disbelieving *B* we necessarily believe *A*. We may in escaping *B* fall into believing other falsehoods, *C* or *D*, just as bad as *B*; or we may escape *B* by not believing anything at all, not even *A*.

Believe truth! Shun error!—these, we see, are two materially different laws; and by choosing between them we may end by coloring differently our whole intellectual life. We may regard the chase for truth as paramount, and the avoidance of error as secondary; or we may, on the other hand, treat the avoidance of error as more imperative, and let truth take its chance. Clifford, in the instructive passage which I have quoted, exhorts us to the latter course. Believe nothing, he tells us, keep your mind in suspense forever, rather than by closing it on insufficient evidence incur the awful risk of believing lies. You, on the other hand, may think that the risk of being in error is a very small matter when compared with the blessings of real knowledge, and be ready to be duped many times in your investigation rather than postpone indefinitely the chance of guessing true. I myself find it impossible to go with Clifford. We must remember that these feelings of our duty about either truth or error are in any case only expressions of our passional life. Biologically considered, our minds are as ready to grind out falsehood as veracity, and he who says, "Better go without belief forever than believe a lie!" merely shows his own preponderant private horror of becoming a dupe. He may be critical of many of his desires and fears, but this fear he slavishly obeys. He cannot imagine anyone questioning its binding force. For my own part, I have also a horror of being duped; but I can believe that worse things than being duped may happen to a man in this world: so Clifford's exhortation has to my ears a thoroughly fantastic sound. It is like a general informing his soldiers that it is better to keep out of battle forever than to risk a single wound. Not so are victories either over enemies or over nature gained. Our errors are surely not such awfully solemn things. In a world where we are so certain to incur them in spite of all our caution, a certain lightness of heart seems healthier than this excessive nervousness on their behalf. At any rate, it seems the fittest thing for the empiricist philosopher.

· VIII ·

And now, after all this introduction, let us go straight at our question. I have said, and now repeat it, that not only as a matter of fact do we find our passional nature influencing us in our opinions, but that there are some options between opinions in which this influence must be regarded both as an inevitable and as a lawful determinant of our choice.

I fear here that some of you my hearers will begin to scent danger, and lend an inhospitable ear. Two first steps of passion you have indeed had to admit as necessary— we must think so as to avoid dupery, and we must think so as to gain truth; but the surest path to those ideal consummations, you will probably consider, is from now onwards to take no further passional step.

Well, of course, I agree as far as the facts will allow. Wherever the option between losing truth and gaining it is not momentous, we can throw the chance of *gaining truth* away, and at any rate save ourselves from any chance of *believing falsehood*, by not making up our minds at all till objective evidence has come. In scientific questions, this is almost always the case; and even in human affairs in general, the need of acting is seldom so urgent that a false belief to act on is better than no belief at all. Law courts, indeed, have to decide on the best evidence attainable for the moment, because a judge's duty is to make law as well as to ascertain it, and (as a learned judge once said to me) few cases are worth spending much time over: the great thing is to have them decided on *any* acceptable principle, and got out of the way. But in our dealing with objective nature we obviously are recorders, not makers, of the truth; and decisions for the mere sake of deciding promptly and getting on to the next business would be wholly out of place. Throughout the breadth of physical nature facts are what they are quite independently of us, and seldom is there any such hurry about them that the risks of being duped by believing a premature theory need be faced. The questions here are always trivial options, the hypotheses are hardly living (at any rate not living for us spectators), the choice between believing truth or falsehood is seldom forced. The attitude of skeptical balance is therefore the absolutely wise one if we would escape mistakes. What difference, indeed, does it make to most of us whether we have or have not a theory of the Röntgen rays, whether we believe or not in mind-stuff, or have a conviction about the causality of conscious states? It makes no difference. Such options are not forced on us. On every account it is better not to make them, but still keep weighing reasons *pro et contra* with an indifferent hand.

I speak, of course, here of the purely judging mind. For purposes of discovery such indifference is to be less highly recommended, and science would be far less advanced than she is if the passionate desires of individuals to get their own faiths confirmed had been kept out of the game. See, for example, the sagacity which Spencer and Weismann now display. On the other hand, if you want an absolute duffer in an investigation, you must, after all, take the man who has no interest whatever in its results: he is the warranted incapable, the positive fool The most useful investigator, because the most sensitive observer, is always he whose eager interest in one side of the question is balanced by an equally keen nervousness lest he become deceived. Science has organized this nervousness into a regular *technique*, her so-called method of verification; and she has fallen so deeply in love with the method that one may even say she has ceased to care for truth by itself at all. It is only truth as technically verified that interests her. The truth of truths might come in merely affirmative form, and she would decline to touch it. Such truth as that, she might repeat with Clifford, would be stolen in defiance of her duty to mankind. Human passions, however, are stronger than technical rules. *"Le coeur a ses raisons,"* as Pascal says, *"que la raison ne connaît pas"*;[4] and however indifferent to all but the bare rules of the game the umpire, the abstract intellect, may be, the concrete players who furnish him the materials to judge of are usually, each one of them, in love with some pet "live hypothesis" of his own. Let us agree, however, that wherever there is no forced option, the dispassionately judicial intellect with no pet hypothesis, saving us, as it does, from dupery at any rate, ought to be our ideal.

The question next arises: Are there not somewhere forced options in our speculative questions, and can we (as men who may be interested at least as much in positively gaining truth as in merely escaping dupery) always wait with impunity till the coercive evidence shall have arrived? It seems a priori improbable that the truth should be so nicely adjusted to our needs and powers as that. In the great boarding-house of nature, the cakes and the butter and the syrup seldom come out so even and leave the plates so clean. Indeed, we should view them with scientific suspicion if they did.

· IX ·

Moral questions immediately present themselves as questions whose solution cannot wait for sensible proof. A moral question is a question not of what sensibly exists, but of what is good, or would be good if it did exist. Science can tell us what exists; but to compare the *worths*, both of what exists and of what does not exist, we must consult not science, but what Pascal calls our heart. Science herself consults her heart when she lays it down that the infinite ascertainment of fact and correction of false belief are the supreme goods for man. Challenge the statement, and science can only repeat it

---

4 The heart has its reasons of which reason knows not.—E.D.K.

oracularly, or else prove it by showing that such ascertainment and correction bring man all sorts of other goods which man's heart in turn declares. The question of having moral beliefs at all or not having them is decided by our will. Are our moral preferences true or false, or are they only odd biological phenomena, making things good or bad for *us*, but in themselves indifferent? How can your pure intellect decide? If your heart does not *want* a world of moral reality, your head will assuredly never make you believe in one. Mephistophelian skepticism, indeed, will satisfy the head's play-instincts much better than any rigourous idealism can. Some men (even at the student age) are so naturally cool-hearted that the moralistic hypothesis never has for them any pungent life, and in their supercilious presence the hot young moralist always feels strangely ill at ease. The appearance of knowingness is on their side, of naïveté and gullibility on his. Yet, in the inarticulate heart of him, he clings to it that he is not a dupe, and that there is a realm in which (as Emerson says) all their wit and intellectual superiority is no better than the cunning of a fox. Moral skepticism can no more be refuted or proved by logic than intellectual skepticism can. When we stick to it that there *is* truth (be it of either kind), we do so with our whole nature, and resolve to stand or fall by the results. The skeptic with his whole nature adopts the doubting attitude; but which of us is the wiser, Omniscience only knows.

Turn now from these wide questions of good to a certain class of questions of fact, *questions concerning personal relations*, states of mind between one man and another. *Do you like me or not?*—for example. Whether you do or not depends, in countless instances, on whether I meet you half-way, am willing to assume that you must like me, and show you trust and expectation. The previous faith on my part in your liking's existence is in such cases what makes your liking come. But if I stand aloof, and refuse to budge an inch until I have objective evidence, until you shall have done something apt, as the absolutists say, *ad extorquendum assensum meum* [to compel my assent], ten to one your liking never comes. How many women's hearts are vanquished by the mere sanguine insistence of some man that they *must* love him! he will not consent to the hypothesis that they cannot. The desire for a certain kind of truth here brings about that special truth's existence; and so it is in innumerable cases of other sorts. Who gains promotions, boons, appointments, but the man in whose life they are seen to play the part of live hypotheses, who discounts them, sacrifices other things for their sake before they have come, and takes risks for them in advance? His faith acts on the powers above him as a claim, and creates its own verification.

A social organism of any sort whatever, large or small, is what it is because each member proceeds to his own duty with a trust that the other members will simultaneously do theirs. Wherever a desired result is achieved by the cooperation of many independent persons, its existence as a fact is a pure consequence of the precursive faith in one another of those immediately concerned. A government, an army, a commercial system, a ship, a college, an athletic team, all exist on this condition, without which not only is nothing achieved, but nothing is even attempted. A whole train of passengers (individually brave enough) will be looted by a few highwaymen, simply because the latter can count on one another, while each passenger fears that if he makes a movement of resistance, he will be shot before anyone else backs him up. If we believed that the whole car-full would rise at once with us, we should each severally rise, and train-robbing would never even be attempted. There are, then, cases where a fact cannot come at all unless a preliminary faith exists in its coming. *And where faith in a fact can help create the fact*, that would be an insane logic which should say that faith running ahead of scientific evidence is the "lowest kind of immorality" into which a thinking being can fall. Yet such is the logic by which our scientific absolutists pretend to regulate our lives!

· X ·

In truths dependent on our personal action, then, faith based on desire is certainly a lawful and possibly an indispensable thing.

But now, it will be said, these are all childish human cases, and have nothing to do with great cosmical matters, like the question of religious faith. Let us then pass on to that. Religions differ so much in their accidents that in discussing the religious question we must make it very generic and broad. What then do we now mean by the religious hypothesis? Science says things are; morality says some things are better than other things; and religion says essentially two things.

First, she says that the best things are the more eternal things, the overlapping things, the things in the universe that throw the last stone, so to speak, and say the final word. "Perfection is eternal"—this phrase of Charles Secrétan seems a good way of putting this first affirmation of religion, and affirmation which obviously cannot yet be verified scientifically at all.

The second affirmation of religion is that we are better off even now if we believe her first affirmation to be true.

Now, let us consider what the logical elements of this situation are *in case the religious hypothesis in both its branches be really true*. (Of course, we must admit that possibility at the outset. If we are to discuss the question at all, it must involve a living option. If for any of you religion be a hypothesis that cannot, by any living possibility, be true, then you need go no further. I speak to the "saving remnant" alone.) So proceeding, we see, first, that religion offers itself as a *momentous* option. We are supposed to gain, even now, by our belief, and to lose by our non-belief, a certain vital good. Secondly, religion is a *forced* option, so far as that good goes. We cannot escape the issue by remaining skeptical and waiting for more light, because, although we do avoid error in that way *if religion be untrue*, we lose the good, *if it be true*, just as certainly as if we positively chose to disbelieve. It is as if a man should hesitate indefinitely to ask a certain woman to marry him because he was not perfectly sure that she would prove an angel after he brought her home. Would he not cut himself off from that particular angel-possibility as decisively as if he went and married someone else? Skepticism, then, is not avoidance of option; it is option of a certain particular kind of risk. *Better risk loss of truth than chance of error*—that is your faith-vetoer's exact position. He is actively playing his stake as much as the believer is; he is backing the field against the religious hypothesis, just as the believer is backing the religious hypothesis against the field. To preach skepticism to us as a duty until "sufficient evidence" for religion be found, is tantamount therefore to telling us, when in presence of the religious hypothesis, that to yield to our fear of its being error is wiser and better than to yield to our hope that it may be true. It is not intellect against all passions, then; it is only intellect with one passion laying down its law. And by what, forsooth, is the supreme wisdom of this passion warranted? Dupery for dupery, what proof is there that dupery through hope is so much worse than dupery through fear? I, for one, can see no proof; and I simply refuse obedience to the scientist's command to imitate his kind of option, in a case where my own stake is important enough to give me the right to choose my own form of risk. If religion be true and the evidence for it be still insufficient, I do not wish, by putting your extinguisher upon my nature (which feels to me as if it had after all some business in this matter), to forfeit my sole chance in life of getting upon the winning side—that chance depending, of course, on my willingness to run the risk of acting as if my passional need of taking the world religiously might be prophetic and right.

All this is on the supposition that it really may be prophetic and right, and that, even to us who are discussing the matter, religion is a live hypothesis which may be true. Now, to most of us religion comes in a still further way that makes a veto on our active faith even more illogical. The more perfect and more eternal aspect of the universe is represented in our religions as having personal form. The universe is no longer a mere *It* to us, but a *Thou*, if we are religious; and any relation that may be possible from person to person might be possible here. For instance, although in one sense we are passive portions of the universe, in another we show a curious autonomy, as if we were small, active centres on our own account. We feel, too, as if the appeal of religion to us were made to our own active goodwill, as if evidence might be forever withheld from us unless we met the hypothesis half-way. To take a trivial illustration: just as a man who in a company of gentlemen made no advances, asked a warrant for every concession, and believed no one's word without proof, would cut himself off by such churlishness from all the social rewards that a more trusting spirit would earn— so here, one who should shut himself up in snarling logicality and try to make the gods extort his recognition willy-nilly, or not get it at all, might, cut himself off forever from his only opportunity of making the gods' acquaintance. This feeling, forced on us we know not whence, that by obstinately believing that there are gods (although not to do so would be so easy both for our logic and our life) we are doing the universe the deepest service we can, seems part of the living essence of the religious hypothesis. If the hypothesis *were* true in all its parts, including this one, then pure intellectualism, with its veto on our making willing advances, would be an absurdity; and some participation of our sympathetic nature would be logically required. I, therefore, for one, cannot see my way to accepting the agnostic rules for truth-seeking, or wilfully agree to keep my willing nature out of the game. I cannot do so for this plain reason, that *a rule of thinking which would absolutely prevent me from acknowledging certain kinds of truth if those kinds of truth were really there, would be an irrational rule.* That for me is the long and short of the formal logic of the situation, no matter what the kinds of truth might materially be.

I confess I do not see how this logic can be escaped. But sad experience makes me fear that some of you may still shrink from radically saying with me, *in abstracto*, that we have the right to believe at our own risk any hypothesis that is live enough to tempt our will. I suspect, however, that if this is so, it is because you have got away from the abstract logical point of view altogether, and are thinking (perhaps without realizing it) of some particular religious hypothesis which for you is dead. The freedom to "believe what we will" you apply to the case of some patent superstition; and the faith you think of is the faith defined by the schoolboy when he said, "Faith is when you believe something that you know ain't true." I can only repeat that this is misapprehension. *In concreto*, the freedom to believe can only cover living options which the intellect of the individual cannot by itself resolve; and living options never seem absurdities to him who has them to consider. When I look at the religious question as it really puts itself to concrete men, and when I think of all the possibilities which both practically and theoretically it involves, then this command that we shall put a stopper on our heart, instincts, and courage, and *wait*—acting of course meanwhile more or less as if religion were *not* true—till doomsday, or till such time as our intellect and senses working together may have raked in evidence enough—this command, I say, seems to me the queerest idol ever manufactured in the philosophic cave. Were we scholastic absolutists, there might be more excuse. If we had an infallible intellect with its objective certitudes, we might feel ourselves disloyal to such a perfect organ of knowledge in not trusting to it exclusively, in not waiting for its releasing word. But if we are empiricists, if we believe that no bell in us tolls to let us know for certain when truth is in our grasp, then it seems a piece of idle fantasticality to preach so solemnly our duty of waiting for the bell. Indeed we *may* wait if we will—I hope you do not think that I am denying that—but if we do so, we do so at our peril as much as if we believed. In either case we *act*, taking our life in our hands. No one of us ought to issue vetoes to the other, nor should we bandy words of abuse. We ought, on the contrary, delicately and profoundly to respect one another's mental freedom: then only shall we bring about the intellectual republic; then only shall we have that spirit of inner tolerance without which all our outer tolerance is soulless, and which is empiricism's glory; then only shall we live and let live, in speculative as well as in practical things.

I began by a reference to Fitz-James Stephen; let me end by a quotation from him.

> What do you think of yourself? What do you think of the world?... These are questions with which all must deal as it seems good to them. They are riddles of the Sphinx, and in some way or other we must deal with them.... In all important transactions of life we have to take a leap in the dark.... If we decide to leave the riddles unanswered, that is a choice; if we waver in our answer, that, too, is a choice: but whatever choice we make, we make it at our peril. If a man chooses to turn his back altogether on God and the future, no one can prevent him; no one can show beyond reasonable doubt that he is mistaken. If a man thinks otherwise and acts as he thinks, I do not see that anyone can prove that *he* is mistaken. Each must act as he thinks best; and if he is wrong, so much the worse for him. We stand on a mountain pass in the midst of whirling snow and blinding mist, through which we get glimpses now and then of paths which may be deceptive. If we stand still we shall be frozen to death. If we take the wrong road we shall be dashed to pieces. We do not certainly know whether there is any right one. What must we do? "Be strong and of good courage." Act for the best, hope for the best, and take what comes.... If death ends all, we cannot meet death better.[5]

---

[5] *Liberty, Equality, Fraternity*, 2nd ed. (London, 1874), p. 353.—W.J.

∘ ∘ ∘ **47**

Religious Faith as Interpretation
John Hick

· I ·

WE COME NOW to our main problem. What manner of cognition is the religious man's awareness of God, and how is it related to his other cognitions?

We become conscious of the existence of other objects in the universe, whether things or persons, either by experiencing them for ourselves or by inferring their existence from evidences within our experience. The awareness of God reported by the ordinary religious believer is of the former kind. He professes, not to have inferred that there is a God, but that God as a living being has entered into his own experience. He claims to enjoy something which he describes as an experience of God. The ordinary believer does not, however, report an awareness of God as existing in isolation from all other objects of experience. His consciousness of the divine does not involve a cessation of his consciousness of a material and social environment. It is not a vision of God in solitary glory, filling the believer's entire mind and blotting out his normal field of perception. Whether such phrases correctly describe the mystic's goal, the ultimate Beatific Vision which figures in Christian doctrine, is a question for a later chapter. But at any rate the ordinary person's religious awareness here on earth is not of that kind. He claims instead an apprehension of God meeting him in and through his material and social environments. He finds that in his dealings with the world of men and things he is somehow having to do with God, and God with him. The moments of ordinary life possess, or may possess, for him in varying degrees a religious significance. As has been well said, religious experience is "the whole experience of religious persons."[1] The believer meets God not only in moments of worship, but also when through the urgings of conscience he feels the pressure of the divine demand upon his life; when through the gracious actions of his friends he apprehends the divine grace; when through the marvels and beauties of nature he traces the hand of the Creator; and he has increasing knowledge of the divine purpose as he responds to its behests in his own life. In short, it is not apart from the course of mundane life, but in it and through it, that the ordinary religious believer claims to experience, however imperfectly and fragmentarily, the divine presence and activity.

This at any rate, among the variety of claims to religious awareness which have been and might be made, is the claim whose epistemological credentials we are to examine. Can God be known through his dealings with us in the world which he has

---

[1] William Temple, *Nature, Man and God* (London, 1934), p. 334.—J.H.

made? The question concerns human experience, and the possibility of an awareness of the divine being mediated through awareness of the world, the supernatural through the natural.

In answer to this query I shall try to show, in various fields, that "mediated" knowledge, such as is postulated by this religious claim, is already a common and accepted feature of our cognitive experience. To this end we must study a basic characteristic of human experience, which I shall call "significance," together with the correlative mental activity by which it is apprehended, which I shall call "interpretation." We shall find that interpretation takes place in relation to each of the three main types of existence, or orders of significance, recognized by human thought—the natural, the human, and the divine; and that in order to relate ourselves appropriately to each, a primary and unevidenceable act of interpretation is required which, when directed toward God, has traditionally been termed "faith." Thus I shall try to show that while the object of religious knowledge is unique, its basic epistemological pattern is that of all our knowing.

This is not to say that the logic of theistic belief has no peculiarities. It does indeed display certain unique features; and these (I shall try to show) are such as follow from the unique nature of its object, and are precisely the peculiarities which we should expect if that object is real. In the present chapter, then, we shall take note of the common epistemological pattern in which religious knowledge partakes, and in the following chapter we shall examine some special peculiarities of religious knowing, and especially its noncompulsory character.

· II ·

"Significance" seems to be the least misleading word available to name the fundamental characteristic of experience which I wish to discuss. Other possible terms are "form" and "meaning." But "form," as the word is used in the traditional matter-form distinction, would require careful editing and commentary to purge it of unwanted Aristotelian associations. "Meaning," on the other hand, has been so overworked and misused in the past, not only by plain men and poets, but also by theologians and philosophers,[2] as to be almost useless today, except in its restricted technical use as referring to the equivalence of symbols. We may perhaps hope that after a period of exile the wider concept of "meaning" will be readmitted into the philosophical comity of notions. Indeed Brand Blanshard has long braved the post —Ogden and Richards ban by his use of the phrase "perceptual meaning."[3] I propose here, however, to use the less prejudged term "significance."

By significance I mean that fundamental and all pervasive characteristic of our conscious experience which *de facto*[4] constitutes it for us the experience of a "world" and not of a mere empty void or churning chaos. We find ourselves in a relatively stable and ordered environment in which we have come to feel, so to say, "at home." The world has become intelligible to us, in the sense that it is a familiar place in which

---

[2] Cf. Ogden and Richards, *The Meaning of Meaning* (7th ed.; London, 1945), ch. 8.—J.H.

[3] *The Nature of Thought* (London, 1939), I, chs. 4–6.—J.H.

[4] In fact.—E.D.K.

we have learned to act and react in appropriate ways. Our experience is not just an unpredictable kaleidoscope of which we are bewildered spectators, but reveals to us a familiar, settled cosmos in which we live and act, a world in which we can adopt purposes and adapt means to ends. It is in virtue of this homely, familiar, intelligible character of experience—its possession of significance—that we are able to inhabit and cope with our environment.

If this use of "significance" be allowed it will, I think, readily be granted that our consciousness is essentially consciousness of significance. Mind could neither emerge nor persist in an environment which was totally nonsignificant to it. For this reason it is not possible to define "significance" ostensively by pointing to contrasting examples of significant and nonsignificant experience. In its most general form at least, we must accept the Kantian thesis that we can be aware only of that which enters into a certain framework of basic relations which is correlated with the structure of our own consciousness. These basic relations represent the minimal conditions of significance for the human mind. The totally nonsignificant is thus debarred from entering into our experience. A completely undifferentiated field, or a sheer "buzzing, booming confusion," would be incapable of sustaining consciousness. For our consciousness is (to repeat) essentially consciousness of significance. Except perhaps in very early infancy or in states of radical breakdown, the human mind is always aware of its environment as having this quality of fundamental familiarity or intelligibility. Significance, then, is simply the most general characteristic of our experience.

Significance, so defined, has an essential reference to action. Consciousness of a particular kind of environmental significance involves a judgment, implicit or explicit, as to the appropriateness of a particular kind, or range of kinds, of action in relation to that environment. The distinction between types of significance is a distinction between the reactions, occurrent and dispositional, which they render appropriate. For the human psychophysical organism has evolved under the pressure of a continual struggle to survive, and our system of significance-attributions has as a result an essentially pragmatic orientation. Our outlook is instinctively empirical and practical. Physiologically we are so constituted as to be sensitive only to a minute selection of the vast quantity and complexity of the events taking place around us—that precise selection which is practically relevant to us. Our ears, for example, are attuned to a fragment only of the full range of sound waves, and our eyes to but a fraction of the multitudinous variations of light. Our sense organs automatically select from nature those aspects in relation to which we must act. We apprehend the world only at the macroscopic level at which we have practical dealings with it. As Norman Kemp Smith has said, "The function of sense-perception, as of instinct, is not knowledge but power, not insight but adaptation."[5] For an animal to apprehend more of its environment than is practically relevant to it would prove a fatal complication; it would be bemused and bewildered, and unable to react selectively to the stimuli indicating danger, food, and so on. And it is equally true at the human level that the significance of a given object or situation for a given individual consists in the practical *difference* which the existence of that object makes to that individual. It is indeed one of the

---

[5] *Prolegomena to an Idealist Theory of Knowledge* (London, 1924), pp. 32–33.—J.H.

marks of our status as dependent beings that we live by continual adaptation to our environment; and from this follows the essentially practical bearing of that which constitutes significance for us.

Although the locus of significance is primarily our environment as a whole, we can in thought divide this into smaller units of significance. We may accordingly draw a provisional distinction between two species of significance, object-significance and situational significance, and note the characteristics of significance first in terms of the former.

Every general name, such as "hat," "book," "fire," "house," names a type of object-significance. For these are isolable aspects of our experience which (in suitable contexts) render appropriate distinctive patterns of behavior. The word "hat," for example, does not name a rigidly delimited class of objects but a particular use to which things can be put, namely, as a covering for the head. Objects are specially manufactured for this use; but if necessary many other items can be made to fulfill the function of a hat. This particular way of treating things, as headgear, is the behavioral correlate of the type of object-significance which we call "being a hat." Indeed the boundaries of each distinguishable class of objects are defined by the two *foci* [6] of (1) physical structure and (2) function in relation to human interests. Our names are always in part names for functions or uses or kinds of significance as apprehended from the standpoint of the agent.

Significance, then, is a relational concept. A universe devoid of consciousness would be neither significant nor nonsignificant. An object or a sense-field is significant *for* or *to* a mind. We are only concerned here with significance for the human mind, but it is well to remember that the lower animals also are aware of their environment as being significant, this awareness being expressed not in words or concepts but in actions and readinesses for action.

There is, I hope, no suggestion of anything occult about this fundamental feature of our experience which I am calling "significance." The difficulty in discussing it is not novelty but, on the contrary, overfamiliarity. It is so completely obvious that we can easily overlook its importance, or even its existence. There is also the related difficulty that we do not apprehend significance as such, but only each distinguishable aspect of our experience as having its own particular type of significance. For significance is a genus which exists only in its species. Just as we perceive the various colors, but never color in general, so we perceive this and that kind of significance, but never significance *simpliciter*.[7]

· III ·

After this preliminary characterization of the nature of significance, we may take note of the mental activity of interpretation which is its subjective correlate. The word "interpretation" suggests the possibility of differing judgments; we tend to call a conclusion an interpretation when we recognize that there may be other and variant

---

[6] Plural of "focus."—E.D.K.

[7] Wholly and absolutely; in every respect.—E.D.K.

accounts of the same subject matter. It is precisely because of this suggestion of ambiguity in the given, and of alternative modes of construing data, that "interpretation" is a suitable correlate term for "significance."

Two uses of "interpretation" are to be distinguished. In one of its senses, an interpretation is a (true or false) *explanation*, answering the question, Why? We speak, for example, of a metaphysician's interpretation of the universe. In its other sense, an interpretation is a (correct or incorrect) *recognition*,[8] or attribution of significance, answering the question, What? ("What is that, a dog or a fox?") These two meanings are closely connected. For all explanation operates ultimately in terms of recognition. We explain a puzzling phenomenon by disclosing its context, revealing it as part of a wider whole which does not, for us, stand in need of explanation. We render the unfamiliar intellectually acceptable by relating it to the already recognizable, indicating a connection or continuity between the old and the new. But in the unique case of the universe as a whole the distinction between explanation and recognition fails to arise. For the universe has no wider context in terms of which it might be explained; an explanation of it can therefore only consist in a perception of its significance. In this case, therefore, interpretation is both recognition and explanation. Hence the theistic recognition, or significance-attribution, is also a metaphysical explanation or theory. However, although the explanatory and the recognition aspects of theistic faith are inseparable, they may usefully be distinguished for purposes of exposition. In the present chapter we shall be examining interpretation, including the religious interpretation, as a recognition, or perception of significance.

An act of recognition, or of significance-attribution, is a complex occurrence dealing with two different types of ambiguity in the given. There are, on the one hand, interpretations which are mutually exclusive (e.g., "That is a fox" and "That is a dog," referring to the same object), and on the other hand interpretations which are mutually compatible (e.g., "That is an animal" and "That is a dog"; or "He died by asphyxiation" and "He was murdered"). Of two logically alternative interpretations only one (at most) can be the correct interpretation. But two compatible interpretations may both be correct. We shall be concerned henceforth with this latter kind of difference, in which several levels or layers or orders of significance are found in the same field of data.

The following are some simple examples of different levels or orders of object-significance.

(a) I see a rectangular red object on the floor in the corner. So far I have interpreted it as a "thing" (or "substance"), as something occupying space and time. On looking more closely, however, I see that it is a red-covered book. I have now made a new interpretation which includes my previous one, but goes beyond it.

(b) There is a piece of paper covered with writing. An illiterate savage can perhaps interpret it as something made by man. A literate person, who does not know the particular language in which it is written, can interpret it as being a document. But

---

[8] This is a slightly off-dictionary sense of "recognition," equating it, not with the identification of the appearances of an object at different times as appearances of the same object, but with the apprehension of what has been discussed above as the "significance" of objects.—J.H.

someone who understands the language can find in it the expression of specific thoughts. Each is answering the question, "What is it?" correctly, but answering it at different levels. And each more adequate attribution of significance presupposes the less adequate ones.

This relationship between types of significance, one type being superimposed upon and interpenetrating another, is a pattern which we shall find again in larger and more important spheres.

We have already noted that significance is essentially related to action. The significance of an object to an individual consists in the practical difference which that object makes to him, the ways in which it affects either his immediate reactions or his more long-term plans and policies. There is also a reciprocal influence of action upon our interpretations. For it is only when we have begun to act upon our interpretations, and have thereby verified that our environment is capable of being successfully inhabited in terms of them, that they become fully "real" modes of experience. Interpretations which take the dispositional form of readiness for action, instead of immediate overt activity, borrow this feeling of "reality" from cognate interpretations which are being or have already been confirmed in action. (For example, when I see an apple on the sideboard, but do not immediately eat it, I nevertheless perceive it as entirely "real" because I have in the past verified similar interpretations of similar apple-like appearances.) It is by acting upon our interpretations that we build up an apprehension of the world around us; and in this process interpretations, once confirmed, suggest and support further interpretations. The necessity of acting-in-terms-of to "clinch" or confirm an interpretation has its importance, as we shall note later, in relation to the specifically religious recognition which we call theistic faith.

We have been speaking so far only of object-significance. But, as already indicated, object-significance as contrasted with situational significance is an expository fiction. An object absolutely per se and devoid of context would have no significance for us. It can be intelligible only as part of our familiar world. What significance would remain, for example, to a book without the physical circumstance of sight, the conventions of language and writing, the acquired art of reading, and even the literature of which the book is a part and the civilization within which it occurs? An object owes its significance as much to its context as to itself; it is what it is largely because of its place in a wider scheme of things. We are indeed hardly ever conscious of anything in complete isolation. Our normal consciousness is of groups of objects standing in recognizable patterns of relations to one another. And it is the resulting situation taken as a whole that carries significance for us, rendering some ranges of action and reaction appropriate and others inappropriate. We live and plan and act all the time in terms of the situational significance of our environment; although of course our interest may focus at any given moment upon a particular component object within the current situation.

We do not, it is true, as plain men generally think of the familiar situations which constitute our experience from moment to moment as having "significance" and of our actions as being guided thereby. But in the fundamental sense in which we are using the term, our ordinary consciousness of the world is undoubtedly a continuous consciousness of significance. It is normally consciousness of a routine or humdrum significance which is so familiar that we take it entirely for granted. The significance for me, for example, of my situation at the present moment is such that I go on quietly working; this is the response rendered appropriate by my interpretation of my contemporary experience. No fresh response is required, for my routine reactions are already adjusted to the prevailing context of significance. But this significance is none the less real for being undramatic.

The component elements of situational significance are not only physical objects—tables, mountains, stars, houses, hats, and so on—but also such nonmaterial entities as sounds and lights and odors and, no less important, such psychological events and circumstances as other people's thoughts, emotions, and attitudes. Thus the kinds of situational significance in terms of which we act and react are enormously complex. Indeed the philosopher who would trace the morphology of situational significance must be a dramatist and poet as well as analyst. Attempts at significance-mapping have been undertaken by some of the existentialist writers: what they refer to as the existential character of experience is the fact that we are ourselves by definition *within* any relational system which constitutes a situation for us. However, these writers have usually been concerned to bring out the more strained and hectic aspects of human experience, presenting it often as a vivid nightmare of metaphysical anxieties and perils. They are undoubtedly painting from real life, particularly in this anguished age, but I venture to think that they are depicting it in a partial and one-sided manner.

A "situation" may be defined, then, as a state of affairs which, when selected for attention by an act of interpretation, carries its own distinctive practical significance for us. We may be involved in many different situations at the same time and may move by swift or slow transitions of interpretation from one to another. There may thus occur an indefinitely complex interpenetration of situations. For example I am, let us say, sitting in a room playing a game of chess with a friend. The game, isolated by the brackets of imagination, is a situation in itself in which I have a part to play as one of the two competing intelligences presiding over the chess board. Here is an artificial situation with its conventional boundaries, structure, and rules of procedure. But from time to time my attention moves from the board to the friend with whom I am playing, and I exchange some conversation with him. Now I am living in another situation which contains the game of chess as a sub-situation. Then suddenly a fire breaks out in the building, and the attention of both of us shifts at once to our wider physical situation; and so on. There are the wider and wider spatial situations of the street, the city, the state, continent, globe, Milky Way, and finally, as the massive permanent background situation inclusive of all else, the physical universe. And there are also the widening circles of family, class, nation, civilization, and all the other groupings within the inclusive group of the human species as a whole. The complex web of interplays within and between these two expanding series gives rise to the infinite variety of situations of which our human life is composed.

Finally, enfolding and interpenetrating this interlocking mass of finite situations there is also, according to the insistent witness of theistic religion, the all-encompassing situation of being in the presence of God and within the sphere of an on-going divine purpose. Our main concern, after these prolonged but unavoidable preliminaries, is to be with this alleged ultimate and inclusive significance and its relation to the more limited and temporary significances through which it is mediated.

Our inventory, then, shows three main orders of situational significance, corresponding to the threefold division of the universe, long entertained by human thought, into nature, man, and God. The significance for us of the physical world, nature, is that of an objective environment whose character and "laws" we must learn, and toward which we have continually to relate ourselves aright if we are to survive. The significance for us of the human world, man, is that of a realm of relationships in which we are responsible agents, subject to moral obligation. This world of moral significance is, so to speak, superimposed upon the natural world, so that relating ourselves to the moral world is not distinct from the business of relating ourselves to the natural world but is rather a particular manner of so doing. And likewise the more ultimately fateful and momentous matter of relating ourselves to the divine, to God, is not distinct from the task of directing ourselves within the natural and ethical spheres; on the contrary, it entails (without being reducible to) a way of so directing ourselves.

· IV ·

In the case of each of these three realms, the natural, the human, and the divine, a basic act of interpretation is required which discloses to us the existence of the sphere in question, thus providing the ground for our multifarious detailed interpretations within that sphere.

Consider first the level of natural significance. This is the significance which our environment has for us as animal organisms seeking survival and pleasure and shunning pain and death. In building houses, cooking food, avoiding dangerous precipices, whirlpools, and volcanoes, and generally conducting ourselves prudently in relation to the material world, we are all the time taking account of what I am calling (for want of a better name) the *natural* significance of our environment.

We have already noted some instances of natural significance when discussing the recognition of objects and situations. It is a familiar philosophical tenet, and one which may perhaps today be taken as granted, that all conscious experience of the physical world contains an element of interpretation. There are combined in each moment of experience a presented field of data and an interpretative activity of the subject. The perceiving mind is thus always in some degree of a selecting, relating and synthesizing agent, and experiencing our environment involves a continuous activity of interpretation. "Interpretation" here is of course an unconscious and habitual process, the process by which a sense-field is perceived, for example, as a three-dimensional room, or a particular configuration of colored patches within that field as a book lying upon a table. Interpretation in this sense is generally recognized as a factor in the genesis of sense perception. We have now to note, however, the further and more basic act of interpretation which reveals to us the very existence of a material world, a world which we explore and inhabit as our given environment. In attending to this primary interpretative act we are noting the judgment which carries us beyond the solipsist predicament into an objective world of enduring, causally interacting objects, which we share with other people. Given the initial rejection of solipsism[9] (or rather given the interpretative bias of human nature which has prevented all but the most enthusiastic of philosophers from falling into solipsism) we can, I

---

[9] A solipsist holds that nothing exists (or can be known to exist) except himself or herself (as a mind) and the contents of his or her mind.—E.D.K.

think, find corroborations of an analogical kind to support our belief in the unob-
served continuance of physical objects and the reality of other minds. But the all-
important first step, or assumption, is unevidenced and unevidenceable—except for
permissive evidence, in that one's phenomenal experience is "there" to be interpreted
either solipsistically or otherwise. But there is no event within our phenomenal
experience the occurrence or nonoccurrence of which is relevant to the truth or falsity
of the solipsist hypothesis. That hypothesis represents one possible interpretation of
our experience as a whole, and the contrary belief in a plurality of minds existing in a
common world represents an alternative and rival interpretation.

It may perhaps be objected that it does not make any practical difference whether
solipsism be true or not, and that these are not therefore two *different* interpretations
of our experience. For if our experience, phenomenally considered, would be identical
on either hypothesis, then the alternative (it will be said) is a purely verbal one; the
choice is merely a choice of synonyms. I do not think, however, that this is the case.
Phenomenally, there is no difference between a dream in which we know that we are
dreaming and one in which we do not. But, nevertheless, there is a total difference
between the two experiences—total not in the sense that every, or indeed any, isolable
aspects of them differ, but in the sense that the two experiences taken as wholes are of
different kinds. We are aware of precisely the same course of events, but in the one
case this occurs within mental brackets, labeled as a dream, while in the other case we
are ourselves immersed within the events and live through them as participants. The
phenomena are apprehended in the one case as dream constituents and in the other
case as "real." And the difference caused by a genuine assent to solipsism would be
akin to the sudden realization during an absorbing dream that it IS only a dream. If
the solipsist interpretation were to be seriously adopted and whole-heartedly believed,
experience would take on an unreal character in contrast with one's former nonsolipsist
mode of experience. Our personal relationships in particular, our loves and friend-
ships, our hates and enmities, rivalries and co-operations, would have to be treated
not as transsubjective meetings with other personalities, but as dialogues and dramas
with oneself. There would be only one person in existence, and other "people,"
instead of being apprehended as independent centers of intelligence and purpose,
would be but humanlike appearances. They could not be the objects of affection or
enmity, nor could their actions be subjected to moral judgment in our normal
nonsolipsist sense. In short, although it must be very difficult, if not impossible, for
the sanely functioning mind seriously to assent to solipsism and to apperceive in terms
of it, yet this does represent at least a logically possible interpretation of experience,
and constitutes a *different* interpretation from our ordinary belief in an independently
existing world of things and persons. It follows that our normal mode of experience is
itself properly described as an interpretation, an interpretation which we are unable to
justify by argument but which we have nevertheless no inclination or reason to doubt.
Indeed as Hume noted, nature has not left this to our choice, "and has doubtless
esteem'd it an affair of too great importance to be trusted to our uncertain reasonings
and speculations. We may well ask, What causes induce us to believe in the existence of
body [i.e., matter]? but 'tis vain to ask, Whether there be body or not? That is a point,
which we must take for granted in all our reasonings."[10]

---

[10] *Treatise*, bk. 1, pt, IV, SEC. 2 (Selby-Bigge's ed., pp. 187–88).—J.H.

But the ordering of our lives in relation to an objective material environment thus revealed to us by a basic act of interpretation is not the most distinctively human level of experience. It is characteristic of mankind to live not only in terms of the natural significance of his world but also in the dimension of personality and responsibility. And so we find that presupposing consciousness of the physical world, and supervening upon it, is the kind of situational significance which we call "being responsible" or "being under obligation." The sense of moral obligation, or of "oughtness," is the basic datum of ethics. It is manifested whenever someone, in circumstances requiring practical decision, feels "obligated" to act, or to refrain from acting, in some particular way. When this occurs, the natural significance of his environment is interpenetrated by another, ethical significance. A traveler on an unfrequented road, for example, comes upon a stranger who has met with an accident and who is lying injured and in need of help. At the level of natural significance this is just an empirical state of affairs, a particular configuration of stone and earth and flesh. But an act or reflex of interpretation at the moral level reveals to the traveler a situation in which he is under obligation to render aid. He feels a categorical imperative laid upon him, demanding that he help the injured man. The situation takes on for him a peremptory ethical significance, and he finds himself in a situation of inescapable personal responsibility.

As has often been remarked, it is characteristic of situations exhibiting moral significance that they involve, directly or indirectly, more than one person. The other or others may stand either in an immediate personal relationship to the moral agent or, as in large-scale social issues, in a more remote causal relationship. (The sphere of politics has been defined as that of the *im*personal relationships between persons.) Ethical significance, as the distinctive significance of situations in which persons are components, includes both of these realms. To feel moral obligation is to perceive (or misperceive) the practical significance for oneself of a situation in which one stands in a responsible relationship to another person or to other people. That the perception of significance in personal situations sets up (in Kant's terms) a categorical imperative, while natural situations give rise only to hypothetical imperatives, conditional upon our own desires, is a defining characteristic of the personal world.

Clearly, moral significance presupposes natural significance. For in order that we may be conscious of moral obligations, and exercise moral intelligence, we must first be aware of a stable environment in which actions have foreseeable results, and in which we can learn the likely consequences of our deeds. It is thus a precondition of ethical situations that there should be a stable medium, the world, with its own causal laws, in which people meet and in terms of which they act. The two spheres of significance, the moral and the physical, interpenetrate in the sense that all occasions of obligation have reference, either immediately or ultimately, to overt action. Relating oneself to the ethical sphere is thus a particular manner of relating oneself to the natural sphere: ethical significance is mediated to us in and through the natural world.

As in the case of natural situational significance, we can enter the sphere of ethical significance only by our own act of interpretation. But at this level the interpretation is a more truly voluntary one. That is to say, it is not forced upon us from outside, but depends upon an inner capacity and tendency to interpret in this way, a tendency which we are free to oppose and even to overrule. If a man chooses to be a moral solipsist, or absolute egoist, recognizing no responsibility toward other people, no one can prove to him that he has any such responsibilities. The man who, when confronted with some standard situation having ethical significance, such as a bully wantonly injuring a child, fails to see it as morally significant, could only be classified as suffering from a defect of his nature analogous to physical blindness. He can of course be compelled by threats of punishment to conform to a stated code of behavior; but he cannot be compelled to feel moral obligation. He must see and accept for himself his own situation as a responsible being and its corollary of ethical accountability.

Has this epistemological paradigm—of one order of significance superimposed upon and mediated through another—any further application? The contention of this chapter is that it has. As ethical significance interpenetrates natural significance, so religious significance interpenetrates both ethical and natural. The divine is the highest and ultimate order of significance, mediating neither of the others and yet being mediated through both of them.

But what do we mean by religious significance? What is it that, for the ethical monotheist, possesses this significance, and in what does the significance consist?

The primary locus of religious significance is the believer's experience as a whole. The basic act of interpretation which reveals to him the religious significance of life is a uniquely "total interpretation". . . . But we must at this point indicate what is intended by the phrase "total interpretation," and offer some preliminary character- ization of its specifically theistic form.

Consider the following imagined situation. I enter a room in a strange building and find that a militant secret society appears to be meeting there. Most of the members are armed, and as they take me for a fellow member I judge it expedient to acquiesce in the role. Subtle and blood-thirsty plans are discussed for a violent overthrow of the constitution. The whole situation is alarming in the extreme. Then I suddenly notice behind me a gallery in which there are batteries of arc lights and silently whirring cameras, and I realize that I have walked by accident onto the set of a film. This realization consists in a change of interpretation of my immediate environment. Until now I had automatically interpreted it as being "real life," as a dangerous situation demanding considerable circumspection on my part. Now I interpret it as having practical significance of a quite different kind. But there is no corresponding change in the observable course of events. The meeting of the "secret society" proceeds as before, although now I believe the state of affairs to be quite other than I had previously supposed it to be. The same phenomena are interpreted as constituting an entirely different practical situation. And yet not quite the same phenomena, for I have noticed important new items, namely, the cameras and arc lights. But let us now in imagination expand the room into the world, and indeed expand it to include the entire physical universe. This is the strange room into which we walk at birth. There is no space left for a photographers' gallery, no direction in which we can turn in search of new clues which might reveal the significance of our situation. Our interpretation must be a *total* interpretation, in which we assert that the world as a whole (as experienced by ourselves) is of this or that kind, that is to say, affects our plans and our policies in such and such ways.

The monotheist's faith-apprehension of God as the unseen Person dealing with him in and through his experience of the world is from the point of view of epistemology an interpretation of this kind, an interpretation of the world as a whole as mediating a divine presence and purpose. He sees in his situation as a human being a significance to which the appropriate response is a religious trust and obedience. His interpretative leap carries him into a world which exists through the will of a holy, righteous, and loving Being who is the creator and sustainer of all that is. Behind the world—to use an almost inevitable spatial metaphor—there is apprehended to be an omnipotent, personal Will whose purpose toward mankind guarantees men's highest good and blessedness. The believer finds that he is at all times in the presence of this holy Will. Again and again he realizes, either at the time or in retrospect, that in his dealings with the circumstances of his own life he is also having to do with a transcendent Creator who is the determiner of his destiny and the source of all good.

Thus the primary religious perception, or basic act of religious interpretation, is not to be described as either a reasoned conclusion or an unreasoned hunch that there is a God. It is, putatively, an apprehension of the divine presence within the believer's human experience. It is not an inference to a general truth, but a "divine-human encounter," a mediated meeting with the living God.

As ethical significance presupposes natural, so religious significance presupposes both ethical and natural. Entering into conscious relation with God consists in large part in adopting a particular style and manner of acting towards our natural and social environments. For God summons men to serve him *in* the world, and in terms of the life of the world. Religion is not only a way of cognizing but also, and no less vitally, a way of living. To see the world as being ruled by a divine love which sets infinite value upon each individual and includes all men in its scope, and yet to live as though the world were a realm of chance in which each must fight for his own interests against the rest, argues a very dim and wavering vision of God's rule. So far as that vision is clear it issues naturally in a trust in the divine purpose and obedience to the divine will. We shall be able to say more about this practical and dispositional response, in which the apprehension of the religious significance of life so largely consists, when we come to examine a particular form of theistic faith. At present we are concerned only with the general nature of the awareness of God.

Rudolf Otto has a somewhat obscure doctrine of the schematization of the Holy in terms of ethics.[11] Without being committed to Otto's use of the Kantian notion, or to his general philosophy of religion, we have been led to a parallel conception of the religious significance of life as schematized in, mediated through, or expressed in terms of, its natural and moral significance. As John Oman says of the Hebrew prophets,

> What determines their faith is not a theory of the Supernatural, but an attitude towards the Natural, as a sphere in which a victory of deeper meaning than the visible and of more abiding purpose than the fleeting can be won. . . . The revelation of the Supernatural was by reconciliation to the Natural: and this was made possible by realising in the Natural the meaning and purpose of the Supernatural.[12]

In one respect this theistic interpretation is more akin to the natural than to the ethical interpretation. For while only *some* situations have moral significance, *all* situations have for embodied beings a continuous natural significance. In like manner

---

[11] *The Idea of the Holy*, trans. by J. W. Harvey (London, 1923), ch. 7.—J.H.
[12] *The Natural and the Supernatural* (Cambridge, 1931), p. 448.—J.H.

the sphere of the basic religious interpretation is not merely this or that isolable situation, but the uniquely total situation constituted by our experience as a whole and in all its aspects, up to the present moment.

But on the other hand the theistic interpretation is more akin to the ethical than to the natural significance-attribution in that it is clearly focused in some situations and imperceptible in others. Not all the moments of life mediate equally the presence of God to the ordinary believer. He is not continuously conscious of God's presence (although possibly the saint is), but conscious rather of the divine Will as a reality in the background of his life, a reality which may at any time emerge to confront him in absolute and inescapable demand. We have already observed how one situation may interpenetrate another, and how some sudden pressure or intrusion can cause a shift of interpretation and attention so that the mind moves from one interlocking context to another. Often a more important kind of significance will summon us from a relatively trivial kind. A woman may be playing a game of cards when she hears her child crying in pain in another room; and at once her consciousness moves from the artificial world of the game to the real world in which she is the mother of the child. Or an officer in the army reserve may be living heedless of the international situation until sudden mobilization recalls him to his military responsibility. The interrupting call of duty may summon us from trivial or relatively unimportant occupations to take part in momentous events. Greater and more ultimate purposes may without warning supervene upon lesser ones and direct our lives into a new channel. But the final significance, which takes precedence over all others as supremely important and overriding, is (according to theism) that of our situation as being in the presence of God. At any time a man may be confronted by some momentous decision, some far-reaching moral choice either of means or of ends, in which his responsibility as a servant of God intrudes upon and conflicts with the requirements of his earthly "station and its duties," so that the latter pales into unimportance and he acts in relation to a more ultimate environment whose significance magisterially overrules his customary way of life. When the call of God is clearly heard other calls become inaudible, and the prophet or saint, martyr or missionary, the man of conscience or of illumined mind may ignore all considerations of worldly prudence in responding to a claim with which nothing else whatever may be put in the balance.

$\cdot$ V $\cdot$

To recapitulate and conclude this stage of the discussion, the epistemological point which I have sought to make is this. There is in cognition of every kind an unresolved mystery. The knower-known relationship is in the last analysis *sui generis*:[13] the mystery of cognition persists at the end of every inquiry—though its persistence does not prevent us from cognizing. We cannot explain, for example, how we are conscious of sensory phenomena as constituting an objective physical environment; we just find ourselves interpreting the data of our experience in this way. We are aware that we live in a real world, though we cannot prove by any logical formula that it *is* a real world. Likewise we cannot explain how we know ourselves to be responsible beings subject

---

[13] Unique; a class by itself.—E.D.K.

to moral obligations; we just find ourselves interpreting our social experience in this way. We find ourselves inhabiting an ethically significant universe, though we cannot prove that it *is* ethically significant by any process of logic. In each case we discover and live in terms of a particular aspect of our environment through an appropriate act of interpretation; and having come to live in terms of it we neither require nor can conceive any further validation of its reality. The same is true of the apprehension of God. The theistic believer cannot explain *how* he knows the divine presence to be mediated through his human experience. He just finds himself interpreting his experience in this way. He lives in the presence of God, though he is unable to prove by any dialectical process that God exists.

To say this is not of course to demonstrate that God *does* exist. The outcome of the discussion thus far is rather to bring out the similarity of epistemological structure and status between men's basic convictions in relation to the world, moral responsibility, and divine existence. The aim of the present chapter has thus been to show how, if there be a God, he is known to mankind, and how such knowledge is related to other kinds of human knowing. I hope that at least the outline of a possible answer to these questions has now been offered.

CHAPTER ELEVEN

Miracles

○

○ ○ ○ *48*

Against Miracles
David Hume

· I ·

THERE IS, IN Dr. Tillotson's writings, an argument against the *real presence*, which is as concise, and elegant, and strong as any argument can possibly be supposed against a doctrine so little worthy of a serious refutation. It is acknowledged on all hands, says that learned prelate, that the authority, either of the scripture or of tradition, is founded merely in the testimony of the apostles, who were eye-witnesses to those miracles of our Saviour, by which he proved his divine mission. Our evidence, then, for the truth of the *Christian* religion is less than the evidence for the truth of our senses; because, even in the first authors of our religion, it was no greater; and it is evident it must diminish in passing from them to their disciples; nor can anyone rest such confidence in their testimony, as in the immediate object of his senses. But a weaker evidence can never destroy a stronger; and therefore, were the doctrine of the real presence ever so clearly revealed in scripture, it were directly contrary to the rules of just reasoning to give our assent to it. It contradicts sense, though both the scripture and tradition, on which it is supposed to be built, carry not such evidence with them as sense; when they are considered merely as external evidences, and are not brought home to everyone's breast, by the immediate operation of the Holy Spirit.

Nothing is so convenient as a decisive argument of this kind, which must at least *silence* the most arrogant bigotry and superstition, and free us from their impertinent solicitations. I flatter myself, that I have discovered an argument of a like nature, which, if just, will, with the wise and learned, be an everlasting check to all kinds of superstitious delusion, and consequently, will be useful as long as the world endures. For so long, I presume, will the accounts of miracles and prodigies be found in all history, sacred and profane.

Though experience be our only guide in reasoning concerning matters of fact; it must be acknowledged, that this guide is not altogether infallible, but in some cases is apt to lead us into errors. One, who in our climate, should expect better weather in any week of June than in one of December, would reason justly, and conformably to experience; but it is certain that he may happen, in the event, to find himself mistaken. However, we may observe, that, in such a case, he would have no cause to complain of experience; because it commonly informs us beforehand of the uncertainty, by that contrariety of events, which we may learn from a diligent observation. All effects follow not with like certainty from their supposed causes. Some events are found, in all countries and all ages, to have been constantly conjoined together: Others are found to have been more variable, and sometimes to disappoint our expectations; so that, in our reasonings concerning matter of fact, there are all imaginable degrees of assurance, from the highest certainty to the lowest species of moral evidence.

A wise man, therefore, proportions his belief to the evidence. In such conclusions as are founded on an infallible experience, he expects the event with the last degree of assurance, and regards his past experience as a full *proof* of the future existence of that event. In other cases, he proceeds with more caution: he weighs the opposite experiments: he considers which side is supported by the greater number of experiments: to that side he inclines, with doubt and hesitation; and when at last he fixes his judgement, the evidence exceeds not what we properly call *probability*. All probability, then, supposes an opposition of experiments and observations, where the one side is found to overbalance the other, and to produce a degree of evidence, proportioned to the superiority. A hundred instances or experiments on one side, and fifty on another, afford a doubtful expectation of any event; though a hundred uniform experiments, with only one that is contradictory, reasonably beget a pretty strong degree of assurance. In all cases, we must balance the opposite experiments, where they are opposite, and deduct the smaller number from the greater, in order to know the exact force of the superior evidence.

To apply these principles to a particular instance; we may observe, that there is no species of reasoning more common, more useful, and even necessary to human life, than that which is derived from the testimony of men, and the reports of eye-witnesses and spectators. This species of reasoning, perhaps, one may deny to be founded on the relation of cause and effect. I shall not dispute about a word. It will be sufficient to observe that our assurance in any argument of this kind is derived from no other principle than our observation of the veracity of human testimony, and of the usual conformity of facts to the reports of witnesses. It being a general maxim that no objects have any discoverable connection together, and all the inferences, which we can draw from one to another, are founded merely on our experience of their constant and regular conjunction; it is evident, that we ought not to make an exception to this maxim in favour of human testimony, whose connection with any event seems, in itself, as little necessary as any other. Were not the memory tenacious to a certain degree; had not men commonly an inclination to truth and a principle of probity; were they not sensible to shame, when detected in a falsehood: were not these, I say, discovered by *experience* to be qualities inherent in human nature, we should never repose the least confidence in human testimony. A man delirious, or noted for falsehood and villainy, has no manner of authority with us.

And as the evidence, derived from witnesses and human testimony, is founded on past experience, so it varies with the experience, and is regarded either as a *proof* or a *probability*, according as the conjunction between any particular kind of report and any kind of object has been found to be constant or variable. There are a number of circumstances to be taken into consideration in all judgements of this kind; and the ultimate standard, by which we determine all disputes that may arise concerning them, is always derived from experience and observation. Where this experience is not entirely uniform on any side, it is attended with an unavoidable contrariety in our judgements, and with the same opposition and mutual destruction of argument as in every other kind of evidence. We frequently hesitate concerning the reports of others. We balance the opposite circumstances, which cause any doubt or uncertainty; and when we discover a superiority on any side, we incline to it; but still with a diminution of assurance, in proportion to the force of its antagonist.

This contrariety of evidence, in the present case, may be derived from several different causes from the opposition of contrary testimony; from the character or number of the witnesses; from the manner of their delivering their testimony; or from the union of all these circumstances. We entertain a suspicion concerning any matter of fact, when the witnesses contradict each other; when they are but few, or of a doubtful character; when they have an interest in what they affirm; when they deliver their testimony with hesitation, or on the contrary, with too violent asseverations. There are many other particulars of the same kind, which may diminish or destroy the force of any argument, derived from human testimony.

Suppose, for instance, that the fact, which the testimony endeavours to establish, partakes of the extraordinary and the marvellous; in that case, the evidence, resulting from the testimony, admits of a diminution, greater or less, in proportion as the fact is more or less unusual. The reason why we place any credit in witnesses and historians, is not derived from any *connection*, which we perceive a priori, between testimony and reality, but because we are accustomed to find a conformity between them. But when the fact attested is such a one as has seldom fallen under our observation, here is a contest of two opposite experiences; of which the one destroys the other, as far as its force goes, and the superior can only operate on the mind by the force, which remains. The very same principle of experience, which gives us a certain degree of assurance in the testimony of witnesses, gives us also, in this case, another degree of assurance against the fact, which they endeavour to establish; from which contradiction there necessarily arises a counterpoise, and mutual destruction of belief and authority.

"I should not believe such a story were it told me by Cato" was a proverbial saying in Rome, even during the lifetime of that philosophical patriot. The incredibility of a fact, it was allowed, might invalidate so great an authority.

The Indian prince, who refused to believe the first relations concerning the effects of frost, reasoned justly; and it naturally required very strong testimony to engage his assent to facts that arose from a state of nature, with which he was unacquainted, and which bore so little analogy to those events, of which he had had constant and uniform experience. Though they were not contrary to his experience, they were not conformable to it.[1]

---

[1] No Indian, it is evident, could have experience that water did not freeze in cold climates. This is placing nature in a situation quite unknown to him; and it is impossible for him to tell a priori what will result from it. It is making a new experiment, the consequence of which is always uncertain. One may sometimes conjecture from analogy what will follow; but still this is but conjecture. And it must be confessed that, in the present case of freezing, the event follows contrary to the rules of analogy, and is such as a rational Indian would not look for. The operations of cold upon water are not gradual, according to the degrees of cold; but whenever it comes to the freezing point, the water passes in a moment from the utmost liquidity to perfect hardness. Such an event, therefore, may be denominated *extraordinary*, and requires a pretty strong testimony to render it credible to people in a warm climate. But still it is not *miraculous*, nor contrary to uniform experience of the course of nature in cases where all the circumstances are the same. The inhabitants of Sumatra have always seen water fluid in their own climate, and the freezing of their rivers ought to be deemed a prodigy. But they never saw water in Muscovy during the winter; and therefore they cannot reasonably be positive what would there by the consequence.—D.H.

But in order to increase the probability against the testimony of witnesses, let us suppose that the fact, which they affirm, instead of being only marvellous, is really miraculous; and suppose also, that the testimony considered apart and in itself, amounts to an entire proof; in that case, there is proof against proof, of which the strongest must prevail, but still with a diminution of its force, in proportion to that of its antagonist.

A miracle is a violation of the laws of nature; and as a firm and unalterable experience has established these laws, the proof against a miracle, from the very nature of the fact, is as entire as any argument from experience can possibly be imagined. Why is it more than probable that all men must die; that lead cannot, of itself, remain suspended in the air; that fire consumes wood, and is extinguished by water; unless it be that these events are found agreeable to the laws of nature, and there is required a violation of these laws, or in other words, a miracle to prevent them? Nothing is esteemed a miracle, if it ever happen in the common course of nature. It is no miracle that a man, seemingly in good health, should die on a sudden: because such a kind of death, though more unusual than any other, has yet been frequently observed to happen. But it is a miracle that a dead man should come to life; because that has never been observed in any age or country. There must, therefore, be a uniform experience against every miraculous event, otherwise the event would not merit that appellation. And as a uniform experience amounts to a proof, there is here a direct and full *proof*, from the nature of the fact, against the existence of any miracle; nor can such a proof be destroyed, or the miracle rendered credible, but by an opposite proof, which is superior.[2]

The plain consequence is (and it is a general maxim worthy of our attention) "that no testimony is sufficient to establish a miracle, unless the testimony be of such a kind that its falsehood would be more miraculous than the fact which it endeavours to establish; and even in that case there is a mutual destruction of arguments, and the superior only gives us an assurance suitable to that degree of force, which remains, after deducting the inferior." When anyone tells me that he saw a dead man restored to life, I immediately consider with myself whether it be more probable that this person should either deceive or be deceived, or that the fact, which he relates, should really have happened. I weigh the one miracle against the other; and according to the superiority which I discover, I pronounce my decision, and always reject the greater

---

[2] Sometimes an event may not, *in itself, seem* to be contrary to the laws of nature, and yet, if it were real, it might, by reason of some circumstances, be denominated a miracle; because, in *fact*, it is contrary to these laws. Thus if a person, claiming a divine authority, should command a sick person to be well, a healthful man to fall down dead, the clouds to pour rain, the winds to blow, in short, should order many natural events, which immediately follow upon his command; these might justly be esteemed miracles, because they are really, in this case, contrary to the laws of nature. For if any suspicion remain that the event and command concurred by accident, there is on miracle and no transgression of the laws of nature. If this suspicion be removed, there is evidently a miracle, and a transgression of these laws; because nothing can be more contrary to nature than that the voice or command of a man should have such an influence. A miracle may be accurately defined, *a transgression of a law of nature by a particular volition of the Deity, or by the interposition of some invisible agent*. A miracle may either by discoverable by men or not. This alters not its nature and essence. The raising of a house or ship into the air is a visible miracle. The raising of a feather, when the wind wants ever so little of a force requisite for that purpose, is as real a miracle, though not so sensible with regard to us.—D.H.

miracle. If the falsehood of his testimony would be more miraculous than the event which he relates; then, and not till then, can he pretend to command my belief or opinion.

· II ·

In the foregoing reasoning we have supposed that the testimony, upon which a miracle is founded, may possibly amount to an entire proof, and that the falsehood of that testimony would be a real prodigy. But it is easy to show that we have been a great deal too liberal in our concession, and that there never was a miraculous event established on so full an evidence.

For *first*, there is not to be found, in all history, any miracle attested by a sufficient number of men, of such unquestioned good sense, education, and learning, as to secure us against all delusion in themselves; of such undoubted integrity, as to place them beyond all suspicion of any design to deceive others; of such credit and reputation in the eyes of mankind, as to have a great deal to lose in case of their being detected in any falsehood; and at the same time, attesting facts performed in such a public manner and in so celebrated a part of the world, as to render the detection unavoidable. All which circumstances are requisite to give us a full assurance in the testimony of men.

Secondly. We may observe in human nature a principle which, if strictly examined, will be found to diminish extremely the assurance, which we might, from human testimony, have, in any kind of prodigy. The maxim, by which we commonly conduct ourselves in our reasonings, is that the objects of which we have no experience resemble those of which we have; that what we have found to be most usual is always most probable; and that where there is an opposition of arguments, we ought to give the preference to such as are founded on the greatest number of past observations. But though, in proceeding by this rule, we readily reject any fact which is unusual and incredible in an ordinary degree; yet in advancing farther, the mind observes not always the same rule; but when anything is affirmed utterly absurd and miraculous, it rather the more readily admits of such a fact, upon account of that very circumstance, which ought to destroy all its authority. The passion of *surprise* and *wonder*, arising from miracles, being an agreeable emotion, gives a sensible tendency towards the belief of those events, from which it is derived. And this goes so far, that even those who cannot enjoy this pleasure immediately, nor can believe those miraculous events, of which they are informed, yet love to partake of the satisfaction at second-hand or by rebound, and place a pride and delight in exciting the admiration of others.

With what greediness are the miraculous accounts of travellers received, their descriptions of sea and land monsters, their relations of wonderful adventures, strange men, and uncouth manners? But if the spirit of religion join itself to the love of wonder, there is an end of common sense; and human testimony, in these circumstances, loses all pretensions to authority. A religionist may be an enthusiast, and imagine he sees what has no reality: he may know his narrative to be false, and yet persevere in it, with the best intentions in the world, for the sake of promoting so holy a cause: or even where this delusion has not place, vanity, excited by so strong a temptation, operates on him more powerfully than on the rest of mankind in any other circumstances; and self-interest with equal force. His auditors may not have, and commonly have not, sufficient judgement to canvass his evidence: what judgement they have, they renounce by principle, in these sublime and mysterious subjects: or if they were ever so willing to employ it, passion and a heated imagination disturb the regularity of its operations. Their credulity increases his impudence: and his impudence overpowers their credulity.

Eloquence, when at its highest pitch, leaves little room for reason or reflection; but addressing itself entirely to the fancy or the affections, captivates the willing hearers, and subdues their understanding. Happily, this pitch it seldom attains. But what a Tully or a Demosthenes could scarcely effect over a Roman or Athenian audience, every *Capuchin*, every itinerant or stationary teacher can perform over the generality of mankind, and in a higher degree, by touching such gross and vulgar passions.

The many instances of forged miracles, and prophecies, and supernatural events, which, in all ages, have either been detected by contrary evidence, or which detect themselves by their absurdity, prove sufficiently the strong propensity of mankind to the extraordinary and the marvellous, and ought reasonably to beget a suspicion against all relations of this kind. This is our natural way of thinking, even with regard to the most common and most credible events. For instance: There is no kind of report which rises so easily, and spreads so quickly, especially in country places and provincial towns, as those concerning marriages; insomuch that two young persons of equal condition never see each other twice, but the whole neighborhood immediately join them together. The pleasure of telling a piece of news so interesting, of propagating it, and of being the first reporters of it, spreads the intelligence. And this is so well known, that no man of sense gives attention to these reports, till he find them confirmed by some greater evidence. Do not the same passions, and others still stronger, incline the generality of mankind to believe and report, with the greatest vehemence and assurance, all religious miracles?

Thirdly. It forms a strong presumption against all supernatural and miraculous relations, that they are observed chiefly to abound among ignorant and barbarous nations; or if a civilized people has ever given admission to any of them, that people will be found to have received them from ignorant and barbarous ancestors, who transmitted them with that inviolable sanction and authority, which always attend received opinions. When we peruse the first histories of all nations, we are apt to imagine ourselves transported into some new world; where the whole frame of nature is disjointed, and every element performs its operations in a different manner from what it does at present. Battles, revolutions, pestilence, famine, and death are never the effect of those natural causes, which we experience. Prodigies, omens, oracles, judgements, quite obscure the few natural events that are intermingled with them. But as the former grow thinner every page, in proportion as we advance nearer the enlightened ages, we soon learn that there is nothing mysterious or supernatural in the case, but that all proceeds from the usual propensity of mankind towards the marvellous, and that, though this inclination may at intervals receive a check from sense and learning, it can never be thoroughly extirpated from human nature.

"It is strange," a judicious reader is apt to say, upon the perusal of these wonderful historians, "that such prodigious events never happen in our days." But it is nothing strange, I hope, that men should lie in all ages. You must surely have seen instances enough of that frailty. You have yourself heard many such marvellous relations started, which, being treated with scorn by all the wise and judicious, have at last been abandoned even by the vulgar. Be assured that those renowned lies, which have spread and flourished to such a monstrous height, arose from like beginnings but being sown in a more proper soil, shot up at last into prodigies almost equal to those which they relate.

It was a wise policy in that false prophet, Alexander, who though now forgotten, was once so famous, to lay the first scene of his impostures in Paphlagonia, where, as Lucian tells us, the people were extremely ignorant and stupid, and ready to swallow even the grossest delusion. People at a distance, who are weak enough to think the matter at all worth inquiry, have no opportunity of receiving better information. The stories come magnified to them by a hundred circumstances. Fools are industrious in propagating the imposture; while the wise and learned are contented, in general, to deride its absurdity, without informing themselves of the particular facts, by which it may be distinctly refuted. And thus the impostor above mentioned was enabled to proceed, from his ignorant Paphlagonians, to the enlisting of votaries, even among the Grecian philosophers, and men of the most eminent rank and distinction in Rome: nay, could engage the attention of that sage emperor Marcus Aurelius; so far as to make him trust the success of a military expedition to his delusive prophecies.

The advantages are so great, of starting an imposture among an ignorant people, that, even though the delusion should be too gross to impose on the generality of them (*which, though seldom, is sometimes the case*) it has a much better chance for succeeding in remote countries than if the first scene had been laid in a city renowned for arts and knowledge. The most ignorant and barbarous of these barbarians carry the report abroad. None of their countrymen have a large correspondence, or sufficient credit and authority to contradict and beat down the delusion. Men's inclination to the marvellous has full opportunity to display itself. And thus a story, which is universally exploded in the place where it was first started, shall pass for certain at a thousand miles distance. But had Alexander fixed his residence at Athens, the philosophers of that renowned mart of learning had immediately spread, throughout the whole Roman empire, their sense of the matter; which, being supported by so great authority, and displayed by all the force of reason and eloquence, had entirely opened the eyes of mankind. It is true; Lucian, passing by chance through Paphlagonia, had an opportunity of performing this good office. But, though much to be wished, it does not always happen that every Alexander meets with a Lucian, ready to expose and detect his impostures.

I may add as a *fourth* reason, which diminishes the authority of prodigies, that there is no testimony for any, even those which have not been expressly detected, that is not opposed by an infinite number of witnesses; so that not only the miracle destroys the credit of testimony, but the testimony destroys itself. To make this the better understood, let us consider that, in matters of religion, whatever is different is contrary; and that it is impossible the religions of ancient Rome, of Turkey, of Siam, and of China should, all of them, be established on any solid foundation. Every miracle, therefore, pretended to have been wrought in any of these religions (and all of them abound in miracles), as its direct scope is to establish the particular system to which it is attributed; so has it the same force, though more indirectly, to overthrow every other system. In destroying a rival system, it likewise destroys the credit of those miracles, on which that system was established; so that all the prodigies of different religions are to be regarded as contrary facts, and the evidences of these prodigies, whether weak or strong, as opposite to each other. According to this method of reasoning, when we believe any miracle of Mahomet or his successors, we have for our warrant the testimony of a few barbarous Arabians: and on the other hand, we are to regard the authority of Titus Livius, Plutarch, Tacitus, and, in short, of all the authors and witnesses, Grecian, Chinese, and Roman Catholic, who have related any miracle in their particular religion; I say, we are to regard their testimony in the same light as if they had mentioned that Mahometan miracle, and had in express terms contradicted it, with the same certainty as they have for the miracle they relate. This argument may appear over subtle and refined; but is not in reality different from the reasoning of a judge, who supposes that the credit of two witnesses, maintaining a crime against anyone, is destroyed by the testimony of two others, who affirm him to have been two hundred leagues distant, at the same instant when the crime is said to have been committed.

One of the best attested miracles in all profane history, is that which Tacitus reports of Vespasian, who cured a blind man in Alexandria, by means of his spittle, and a lame man by the mere touch of his foot; in obedience to a vision of the god Serapis, who had enjoined them to have recourse to the emperor, for these miraculous cures. The story may be seen in that fine historian; where every circumstance seems to add weight to the testimony, and might be displayed at large with all the force of argument and eloquence, if anyone were now concerned to enforce the evidence of that exploded and idolatrous superstition. The gravity, solidity, age, and probity of so great an emperor, who, through the whole course of his life, conversed in a familiar manner with his friends and courtiers, and never affected those extraordinary airs of divinity assumed by Alexander and Demetrius. The historian, a contemporary writer, noted for candour and veracity, and withal, the greatest and most penetrating genius, perhaps, of all antiquity; and so free from any tendency to credulity, that he even lies under the contrary imputation, of atheism and profaneness: the persons, from whose authority he related the miracle, of established character for judgement and veracity, as we may well presume; eye-witnesses of the fact, and confirming their testimony, after the Flavian family was despoiled of the empire, and could no longer give any reward, as the price of a lie. *Utrumque, qui interfuere, nunc quoque memorant, postquam nullum mendacio pretium.* [Now those who were present remember afterwards, when there is no reward for lying.] To which if we add the public nature of the facts, as related, it will appear that no evidence can well be supposed stronger for so gross and so palpable a falsehood.

There is also a memorable story related by Cardinal de Retz, which may well deserve our consideration. When that intriguing politician fled into Spain, to avoid the persecution of his enemies, he passed through Saragossa, the capital of Arragon, where he was shown, in the cathedral, a man, who had served seven years as a doorkeeper, and was well known to everybody in town, that had ever paid his devotions at that church. He had been seen, for so long a time, wanting a leg; but recovered that limb by the rubbing of holy oil upon the stump; and the cardinal assures us that he saw him with two legs. This miracle was vouched by all the canons of the church; and the whole company in town were appealed to for a confirmation of the fact; whom the cardinal found, by their zealous devotion, to be thorough believers of the miracle. Here the relater was also contemporary to the supposed prodigy, of an incredulous and libertine character, as well as of great genius; the miracle of so *singular* a nature as could scarcely admit of a counterfeit, and the witnesses very numerous, and all of them, in a manner, spectators of the fact, to which they gave their testimony. And what adds mightily to the force of the evidence, and may double our surprise on this occasion, is that the cardinal himself, who relates the story, seems not to give any credit to it, and consequently cannot be suspected of any concurrence in the holy fraud. He considered justly that it was not requisite, in order to reject a fact of this nature, to be able accurately to disprove the testimony, and to trace its falsehood, through all the circumstances of knavery and credulity which produced it. He knew that, as this was commonly altogether impossible at any small distance of time and place; so was it extremely difficult, even where one was immediately present, by reason of the bigotry, ignorance, cunning, and roguery of a great part of mankind. He therefore concluded, like a just reasoner, that such an evidence carried falsehood upon the very face of it, and that a miracle, supported by any human testimony, was more properly a subject of derision than of argument.

There surely never was a greater number of miracles ascribed to one person than those which were lately said to have been wrought in France upon the tomb of Abbé Paris, the famous Jansenist, with whose sanctity the people were so long deluded. The curing of the sick, giving hearing to the deaf, and sight to the blind, were everywhere talked of as the usual effects of that holy sepulchre. But what is more extraordinary; many of the miracles were immediately proved upon the spot, before judges of unquestioned integrity, attested by witnesses of credit and distinction, in a learned age, and on the most eminent theatre that is now in the world. Nor is this all: a relation of them was published and dispersed everywhere; nor were the *Jesuits*, though a learned body, supported by the civil magistrate, and determined enemies to those opinions, in whose favour the miracles were said to have been wrought, ever able distinctly to refute or detect them. Where shall we find such a number of circumstances, agreeing to the corroboration of one fact? And what have we to oppose to such a cloud of witnesses, but the absolute impossibility or miraculous nature of the events which they relate? And this surely, in the eyes of all reasonable people, will alone be regarded as a sufficient refutation.

Is the consequence just, because some human testimony has the utmost force and authority in some cases, when it relates the battle of Philippi or Pharsalia for instance; that therefore all kinds of testimony must, in all cases, have equal force and authority? Suppose that the Caesarean and Pompeian factions had, each of them, claimed the victory in these battles, and that the historians of each party had uniformly ascribed the advantage to their own side; how could mankind, at this distance, have been able to determine between them? The contrariety is equally strong between the miracles related by Herodotus or Plutarch, and those delivered by Mariana, Bede, or any monkish historian.

The wise lend a very academic faith to every report which favours the passion of the reporter; whether it magnifies his country, his family, or himself, or in any other way strikes in with his natural inclinations and propensities. But what greater temptation than to appear a missionary, a prophet, an ambassador from heaven? Who would not encounter many dangers and difficulties, in order to attain so sublime a character? Or if, by the help of vanity and a heated imagination, a man has first made a convert of himself, and entered seriously into the delusion; who ever scruples to make use of pious frauds, in support of so holy and meritorious a cause?

The smallest spark may here kindle into the greatest flame; because the materials are always prepared for it. The *avidum genus auricularum*, the gazing populace, receive greedily, without examination, whatever sooths superstition, and promotes wonder.

How many stories of this nature have, in all ages, been detected and exploded in their infancy? How many more have been celebrated for a time, and have afterwards sunk into neglect and oblivion? Where such reports, therefore, fly about, the solution of the phenomenon is obvious; and we judge in conformity to regular experience and observation, when we account for it by the known and natural principles of credulity and delusion. And shall we, rather than have a recourse to so natural a solution, allow of a miraculous violation of the most established laws of nature?

I need not mention the difficulty of detecting a falsehood in any private or even public history, at the place, where it is said to happen; much more when the scene is removed to ever so small a distance. Even a court of judicature, with all the authority, accuracy, and judgement, which they can employ, find themselves often at a loss to distinguish between truth and falsehood in the most recent actions. But the matter never comes to any issue, if trusted to the common method of altercations and debate and flying rumours; especially when men's passions have taken part on either side.

In the infancy of new religions, the wise and learned commonly esteem the matter too inconsiderable to deserve their attention or regard. And when afterwards they would willingly detect the cheat, in order to undeceive the deluded multitude, the season is now past, and the records and witnesses, which might clear up the matter, have perished beyond recovery.

No means of detection remain, but those which must be drawn from the very testimony itself of the reporters: and these, though always sufficient with the judicious and knowing, are commonly too fine to fall under the comprehension of the vulgar.

Upon the whole, then, it appears that no testimony for any kind of miracle has ever amounted to a probability, much less to a proof; and that, even supposing it amounted to a proof, it would be opposed by another proof; derived from the very nature of the fact, which it would endeavour to establish. It is experience only which gives authority to human testimony; and it is the same experience which assures us of the laws of nature. When, therefore, these two kinds of experience are contrary, we have nothing to do but subtract the one from the other, and embrace an opinion, either on one side or the other, with that assurance which arises from the remainder. But according to the principle here explained, this subtraction, with regard to all popular religions, amounts to an entire annihilation; and therefore we may establish it as a maxim that no human testimony can have such force as to prove a miracle, and make it a just foundation for any such system of religion.

I beg the limitations here made may be remarked, when I say that a miracle can never be proved; so as to be the foundation of a system of religion. For I own that otherwise there may possibly be miracles, or violations of the usual course of nature, of such a kind as to admit of proof from human testimony; though, perhaps, it will be impossible to find any such in all the records of history. Thus, suppose all authors, in all languages, agree that, from the first of January 1600, there was a total darkness over the whole earth for eight days: suppose that the tradition of this extraordinary event is still strong and lively among the people: that all travellers, who return from foreign countries, bring us accounts of the same tradition, without the least variation or contradiction: it is evident that our present philosophers, instead of doubting the fact, ought to receive it as certain, and ought to search for the causes whence it might be derived. The decay, corruption, and dissolution of nature is an event rendered probable by so many analogies, that any phenomenon, which seems to have a tendency towards that catastrophe, comes within the reach of human testimony, if that testimony be very extensive and uniform.

But suppose that all the historians who treat of England should agree that, on the first of January 1600, Queen Elizabeth died; that both before and after her death she was seen by her physicians and the whole court, as is usual with persons of her rank; that her successor was acknowledged and proclaimed by the parliament; and that, after being interred a month, she again appeared, resumed the throne, and governed England for three years: I must confess that I should be surprised at the concurrence of so many odd circumstances, but should not have the least inclination to believe so miraculous an event. I should not doubt of her pretended death, and of those other public circumstances that followed it: I should only assert it to have been pretended, and that it neither was, nor possibly could be real. You would in vain object to me the difficulty, and almost impossibility of deceiving the world in an affair of such consequence; the wisdom and solid judgement of that renowned queen; with the little or no advantage which she could reap from so poor an artifice. All this might astonish me; but I would still reply that the knavery and folly of men are such common phenomena, that I should rather believe the most extraordinary events to arise from their concurrence than admit of so signal a violation of the laws of nature.

But should this miracle be ascribed to any new system of religion; men, in all ages, have been so much imposed on by ridiculous stories of that kind, that this very circumstance would be a full proof of a cheat, and sufficient, with all men of sense, not only to make them reject the fact, but even reject it without further examination. Though the Being to whom the miracle is ascribed, be, in this case, Almighty, it does not, upon that account, become a whit more probable; since it is impossible for us to know the attributes or actions of such a Being, otherwise than from the experience which we have of His productions, in the usual course of nature. This still reduces us to past observation, and obliges us to compare the instances of the violation of truth in the testimony of men, with those of the violation of the laws of nature by miracles, in order to judge which of them is most likely and probable. As the violations of truth are more common in the testimony concerning religious miracles than in that concerning any other matter of fact; this must diminish very much the authority of the former testimony, and make us form a general resolution, never to lend any attention to it, with whatever specious pretence it may be covered.

Lord Bacon seems to have embraced the same principles of reasoning. "We ought," says he, "to make a collection or particular history of all monsters and prodigious births or productions, and in a word of everything new, rare, and extraordinary in nature. But this must be done with the most severe scrutiny, lest we depart from truth. Above all, every relation must be considered as suspicious, which depends in any degree upon religion, as the prodigies of Livy: and no less so, everything that is to be found in the writers of natural magic or alchimy, or such authors, who seem, all of them, to have an unconquerable appetite for falsehood and fable."[3]

---

[3] *Novum Organum*, Bk. II, Aphorism 19.—D.H.

I am the better pleased with the method of reasoning here delivered, as I think it may serve to confound those dangerous friends or disguised enemies to the *Christian religion*, who have undertaken to defend it by the principles of human reason. Our most holy religion is founded on *faith*, not on reason; and it is a sure method of exposing it to put it to such a trial as it is, by no means, fitted to endure. To make this more evident, let us examine those miracles related in scripture; and not to lose ourselves in too wide a field, let us confine ourselves to such as we find in the *Pentateuch*, which we shall examine, according to the principles of these pretended Christians, not as the word or testimony of God Himself, but as the production of a mere human writer and historian. Here then we are first to consider a book, presented to us by a barbarous and ignorant people, written in an age when they were still more barbarous, and in all probability long after the facts which it relates, corroborated by no concurring testimony, and resembling those fabulous accounts, which every nation gives of its origin. Upon reading this book, we find it full of prodigies and miracles. It gives an account of a state of the world and of human nature entirely different from the present: of our fall from that state: of the age of man, extended to near a thousand years: of the destruction of the world by a deluge: of the arbitrary choice of one people, as the favourites of heaven; and that people the countrymen of the author: of their deliverance from bondage by prodigies the most astonishing imaginable: I desire anyone to lay his hand upon his heart, and after a serious consideration declare whether he thinks that the falsehood of such a book, supported by such a testimony, would be more extraordinary and miraculous than all the miracles it relates; which is, however, necessary to make it be received, according to the measures of probability above established.

What we have said of miracles may be applied, without any variation, to prophecies; and indeed, all prophecies are real miracles, and as such only, can be admitted as proofs of any revelation. If it did not exceed the capacity of human nature to foretell future events, it would be absurd to employ any prophecy as an argument for a divine mission or authority from heaven. So that, upon the whole, we may conclude, that the *Christian religion* not only was at first attended with miracles, but even at this day cannot be believed by any reasonable person without one. Mere reason is insufficient to convince us of its veracity: and whoever is moved by *faith* to assent to it is conscious of a continued miracle in his own person, which subverts all the principles of his understanding, and gives him a determination to believe what is most contrary to custom and experience.

○ ○ ○   *49*

For the Possibility of Miracles
Richard Swinburne

· *I* ·

INTRODUCTION

IF A MAN concludes that it is probable that there is a God, it follows that he has a duty to worship and obey binding on him, and so he must investigate how best to fulfil it; and that involves investigating the claims of different creeds. However, I think that the expert or the person in a parental situation may still have a duty to compare creeds, even if on his evidence it is more probable than not that there is no God. For his duty is to show to others how best to attain goals of supreme worth. He must investigate whether non-theistic ways to salvation are likely to attain that salvation. And also those dependent on him need to know as surely as they can, even if it is probable that there is no God and non-theistic ways are unlikely to attain their goal, which is the way most likely to attain its goal. Even if the agricultural biochemist believes that on balance it is improbable that more food can be got out of the land, if the people are very short of food, he still has a duty to investigate which method of fertilizing, irrigation, or crop rotation is more likely to produce an increase of yield (in the hope that his inquiries will show that one method is much more likely than any others to be successful). By analogy, if the religious investigator, who is an expert or in a parental situation, judges the goals of religion to be very worthwhile, it follows that he has a duty to pursue religious investigation even if he believes that it is not probable with respect to any one way that it will attain the goals of religion. So in these various circumstances it is a duty or at any rate a very worthwhile thing to investigate the relative probability of creeds, in order to produce a rational belief about the relative probabilities of creeds, e.g., a belief that the Christian Creed is more probable than any rival creed which justifies a different religious way. The above conclusions about the duty to investigate the comparative probabilities of creeds hold, I urge, objectively for a man who has a certain belief about how probable it is that there is a God. If he does not support his beliefs about the comparative probabilities of creeds by proper investigation, they will not be rational. . . .

The process of showing the Christian Creed to be more probable than any rival creed which justifies a different religious way can be analyzed as needing three steps: first, a demonstration that it is probable to some degree on reasonably believed evidence that there is a God; secondly, a demonstration that it is more probable, if there is a God, that the other items of the Christian Creed are true than that the other items of some rival theistic creed are true; and thirdly, a demonstration that it is more probable that the Christian Creed as a whole is true than that any non-theistic religious creed is true.

The first task is the traditional task of natural theology and is far too big a subject to be discussed here. It was the subject of my earlier volume, *The Existence of God*. I concluded there that it is more probable than not that there is a God. But all that is necessary for weak belief in the Christian Creed is a much less probable belief—say, putting it loosely, that there is a significant probability that there is a God. For, given that, there is quite a chance that salvation may be had by pursuing one of the religious ways of theistic religions, since the attainment of salvation according to these religions consists in God providing that salvation (e.g., forgiveness and life after death). The next stage is to show that if there is a God it is more likely that the other items of the Christian Creed are true than that the other items of some rival creed are true. For given that there is a God, then if the other items of the Christian Creed are more probable than the other items of rival theistic creeds, the Christian Creed as a whole (item common with other theistic creeds plus different items) will be more probable than any other theistic creed as a whole (common item plus different items). We need to show that it is more probable that God became incarnate in Christ than that Muhammad was his chief prophet; that the way to worship regularly is by attendance at the Eucharist rather than by the five daily prayer-times, and so on. The choice between religious systems in these respects turns on a judgment about which is the true revelation of God. For the grounds for believing the other items of a theistic creed—that in this way God has intervened in history, that forgiveness is available in this way, that these are the fates for men in the after-life, that this is the way to live in this life—are normally that God has revealed these truths through the mouth of some human intermediary, whom we will call his prophet. I wish therefore now to discuss the kind of considerations which are relevant to assessing such claims to revelation. The discussion will be a brief discussion to indicate the kind of considerations which need to be investigated, rather than a thorough discussion of which is the true claim to revelation. I include the discussion to indicate the kind of investigation by which faith needs to be supported.

· II ·

THE EVIDENCE OF REVELATION

A theistic religion claims that its prophet is a special messenger of God and that what he says about the nature of reality and how men ought to live is to be believed because it comes from God. It is also sometimes claimed that the prophet and his actions have eternal significance because of his special status. The Christian claim that Jesus Christ was both God and man who by his sacrificial life redeemed the world is obviously such a claim—indeed it is by far the strongest claim for divine intervention in human history made by any of the great religions.

Theistic religions are normally prepared to allow that God has spoken to men in a limited way through prophets other than their own unique prophet. Thus Islam is prepared to allow that God spoke to men through Jesus Christ. But the point is that, according to each religion, there is truth and falsity mixed in the deliverances of prophets other than its own, and that where there is dispute the sayings of its own prophet take precedence—for what he says is true without qualification (and, perhaps also, what he does is of unrepeatable significance). If a religion claims that all prophets teach varying amounts of truth and falsity, and so purports to judge the worth of each prophet's teaching merely by considering what he says rather than the fact that he says it, that religion cannot be regarded in the traditional sense as a revealed religion, as teaching and supported by a revelation. For the grounds for believing any of what the religion asserts will not be that it has been revealed by God (for which in turn there is other evidence, including that other things which the prophet said are true); rather, the argument will always go the other way round—the grounds for believing that any of the things which a prophet teaches have been revealed by God are simply that they are true. A religion which claims a revelation in teaching claims that the prophet's message is to be believed, not because it can be known to be true independently of the prophet having said it, but because of the prophet's authority.

So then, what is the evidence for claims that some prophet is in this way a special messenger of God? The traditional view down the centuries, advocated among others by Aquinas, declared to be official Roman Catholic doctrine by the First Vatican Council and classically expounded by Paley, is that the evidence will be of various kinds but will include a central and crucial element of the miraculous.

In *Evidences of Christianity*, Paley argues that given that there is a God—who is, by definition, good—and that the human race lies in ignorance of things important for them to know, it is *a priori* to some extent to be expected that God would give a revelation to men. And what things are these important things? If the arguments of this book are correct, it is important for men to know the nature of the world and man's place in it, how they ought to live, how deep long-term happy well-being is to be achieved, how forgiveness is to be obtained from God, how God is to be worshipped and obeyed. A revelation such as the Christian revelation (as traditionally described) claims to provide knowledge on all these matters. Paley however stresses—to my mind totally disproportionately—the existence and nature of the after-life at the expense of all other elements of revelation.

Yet knowledge of all these things has great value, other than its value in preparing men for the after-life. It is good that man should understand the world, know how to live in it and how to obtain the deepest well-being this Earth can provide; it is good too that man should know how to worship and obey God and obtain forgiveness from him—all this quite independently of the consequences in an after-life for man of his doing these things. But it is also good that man know how to obtain his eternal well-being.

Men are capable of receiving such knowledge. But much of it could not to all appearances be obtained by mere reflection on the natural world. That God is three persons in one substance could hardly, if true, be known to be true by such human reflection. I claimed, in *The Existence of God*, that various phenomena, including chiefly very general and publicly observable ones such as the orderliness of nature, show the dependence of the world on a creator God. We must, I argued, suppose him to be very powerful, wise, etc., if he is to be able to bring about the existence and orderliness of the world; and considerations of simplicity involve us inferring from 'very powerful . . . etc.' to 'infinitely powerful . . . etc.' But it is hard to see how any further details of his nature could be read off from the world. I have no conclusive proof that this cannot be done. I simply appeal to the apparent impossibility of seeing how it can be done; and to the fact that nobody today thinks that it can be done, and that very few people in the past ever thought that it could be done. Likewise, mere reflection on the natural world could hardly show the details of how men ought to worship God, e.g. in the Eucharist on Sundays; or how forgiveness from God is to be obtained—through pleading the Passion of Christ. And so on.

Other such purported knowledge as is conveyed in revelations such as the Christian revelation, is purported knowledge of matters about which men produce arguments of a general philosophical character arising out of reflection on the natural world. That God is omnipotent, omniscient, etc., is, as we have seen, the subject of such argument. So too are the general principles or morality, such as that men ought to tell the truth, keep their promises, and show compassion. Now maybe all such arguments fail; it needs a detailed discussion of each case to show whether they do or not. However, I have argued in *The Existence of God* that arguments to show that there is a God omnipotent, omniscient, and perfectly free do work. And plausibly, reason can help to show claims about morality to be justified.

However, if such knowledge of the omnipotence, omniscience, etc. of God and the general principles of morality can be obtained by natural means, it is evident that some men are too stupid to obtain the knowledge—the savage argues only to a much more lowly God—and some men will never reach that knowledge because of the climate of contrary opinion in which they grow up, the climate of an atheistic authority. It is sometimes through men yielding to bad desires, either to teach things which they do not really believe (in the interests of their state or party, church or career), or not to investigate further things which they are told on authority (through fear or laziness), that men come to hold beliefs and climates of opinion develop. Hence sin plays a role in moulding belief.

So the detailed truths of creed will either not be known at all to men or (through men's stupidity, ignorance, and sin) be known only with difficulty. Yet these are the truths which are of crucial importance if men are to make themselves good men (true specimens of humanity), men worthy to obtain everlasting well-being. If there is a God (who is by definition good), he might to some degree be expected to intervene in history to reveal these truths which men could not discover for themselves and to give his authority to those to which reason pointed with insufficient force, for he has good reason to do this. There is also the reason to expect a revelation, not merely by teaching but by a human life, which the Christian tradition has always stressed but which Paley does not. Human sin and corruption need atonement. This is a primary reason why, on the traditional Christian doctrine, a revelation in the form of a person who lived a sacrificial life was to be expected.

So, given that there is good evidence that there is a God, there is some reason *a priori* to expect that there will be a revelation. What historical evidence would show that it had taken place on a certain occasion? It is a basic principle of confirmation theory that evidence confirms a hypothesis (i.e. adds to its probability) if and only if that evidence is more to be expected if the hypothesis is true than it would otherwise be. So given some prior probability that God would reveal himself in history, the evidence of history that he has done so will be such as is to be expected if the hypothesis is true, and not otherwise. The obvious kind of evidence, then, will be teaching such as God would be expected to give and actions such as God would be expected to do, of a kind and in circumstances in which they would not be expected to occur in the normal course of things.

What sort of teaching about the matters which man needs to know would God be expected to give through a prophet? Obviously teaching which is true and deep. Although the teaching itself must be true, it might however need to be embodied in the false historical and scientific presuppositions of the prophet's day if it is to be understood. For instance, suppose a prophet was teaching in a culture which believed that the world consisted of a flat and stationary earth surrounded by a heavenly dome in which Sun, Moon, planets, and stars moved. God wishes through the prophet to convey the message of the total dependence of the world on God. How is he to announce his message? There seem three possible ways. The prophet might say: 'It is God who holds the flat earth still and moves round it the heavenly lights.' Or he might say: 'Whatever the true scientific description of the world, it is God who brings about that state of affairs which that description describes.' Or he might begin by giving a true scientific account of the world and then say that God brings about that world. But if he is to announce his message in the third way, the religious truth can only be announced after a complete process of scientific education. And even if he is to announce it in the second way, the message will only be understood by a people who have done quite a lot of philosophical abstraction. They would have to have understood the possible falsity of most of their common-sense science, and have got used to the abstract concepts of states of affairs which might not be describable, and descriptions which might not apply to things. If the prophet's message is to be understood by a primitive culture, it is the first way of teaching which would have to be used. And unless one thinks that divine revelation can be given only to sophisticated peoples, that means that when a divine revelation is made to a primitive people, there is a distinction to be made between the prophet's message and the scientific and historical presuppositions in terms of which it is expressed. This distinction would need to be made by a later and less primitive society which knew a bit more about science and history, in order for it to see what was the religious message clothed in the false presuppositions. And of course if the later society was not sophisticated enough, it might fail to make the distinction, and so suppose the science and history to be part of the prophet's message. This could lead to its rejecting the message on the grounds that the science and history were false (the rational reaction); or, worse (the irrational reaction) adopting the old science and history (and rejecting the alleged advances here of more recent times) on the grounds that the prophet's message was true. It will, I hope, be unnecessary to give many historical examples of such reactions.

One all to sadly obvious modern one is the example of the different reactions to Darwin's theory of evolution. Christianity has regarded the Old Testament as in a sense and to a degree licensed by Christ. He took it largely for granted in his teaching, and the Church which he founded proclaimed it (with the exception of the laws about ritual and sacrifice) as God's message. The Old Testament in telling in Genesis 1 and 2 the Creation stories seems to presuppose that animal species came into being a few thousands years ago virtually simultaneously. The theory of evolution showed that they did not. So some rejected Christianity on the grounds that it taught what was scientifically false, and others rejected the theory of evolution on the grounds that it conflicted with true religion. But it seems odd to suppose that the religious message of what is evidently a piece of poetry was concerned with the exact time and method of animal arrival on the Earth, or that that was what those who composed it were attempting to tell the world. Their message concerned, not the details of the time and method of animal arrival, but the ultimate cause of that arrival. To make the point that there is a distinction between a prophet's religious message and its scientific and historical presuppositions is not to deny that it may not always be easy to disentangle the message from the presuppositions, or to express it in more modern terms. One obvious step in going about this task is for the investigator to inquire into the circumstances of the prophet's utterance and see what he was denying, and contrast this with the assumptions about more mundane matters shared by the prophet and his opponents.

So then, with this qualification, the prophet must teach what is true. Must he teach only what is true? Can there be falsity mixed with his teaching? No: the whole body of what the prophet announces as his message must be true, for the reaction given earlier: that it purports to be God's announcement to man of things beyond his power to discover for himself. However if a clear distinction could be made between the prophet's message and other things which he said but for which he did not claim any special authority, there is no reason to require that the latter be true.

The prophet's teaching must be, not merely true, but deep. Men need moral teaching and instruction about the nature of reality which is not readily available to them.

What would be the evidence that the prophet's teaching is true? First, none of what he teaches must be evidently false. His teaching on morality, for example, must not involve his telling men that they ought to do what is evidently morally wrong—the prophet who recommends cheating and child torture can be dismissed straight away. Likewise no factual teaching of the prophet must be proven false. If the prophet teaches that, whatever men do, the world will end in exactly thirty years time, and the world fails to end then; the prophet must be rejected. Secondly, such parts of the prophet's teaching as can be checked must be found to be true. Some of the prophet's moral teaching, for example, may coincide with our clear intuitions about morality. Thirdly, it may be that some parts of the prophet's teaching which do not appear obviously true to start with are found, through experience and reflection, to be true. One way in which subsequent experience could confirm a prophet's teaching would be if the sort of teaching about God, his nature, and action in history which the prophet gives makes sense of the investigator's own private and public experience, in the sense of making probable a course of experience which would not otherwise be probable. The course of a man's life, the answering of his prayers, and particular 'religious experiences' within that life might be such as the God proclaimed by the prophet would be expected to bring about. All that would be further evidence of the truth of the prophet's teaching.

All of this is independent evidence that some of what the prophet teaches is true. The fact that some of what the prophet teaches is seen to be true and deep is indeed some slight evidence that the other things which he said are true and deep. If a man says what is true on one deep matter, that is some evidence for supposing that he is a wise man, and so for supposing that what he says on other deep matters is true. But it is only slight evidence—many teachers who teach deep truths teach falsities also, and prophets who agree over one range of their teaching disagree over another range. That the moral teaching of Jesus Christ is true and deep is slender grounds for believing what he had to say about life after death.

Revelations include, and (as we have seen that Paley argued) can *a priori* be expected to include, things beyond human capacity independently to check. For example they typically assert the existence of a life after death; and they provide us with information about the sort of God who is to be worshipped in far more detail than a man could derive from examination of the created world, and they give us details of the way to worship him. Hence we need some evidence that what the prophet says is true when we cannot check independently whether it is or not. Analogy suggests the sort of evidence for which we ought to be looking. Suppose that in the days before wireless telephones, and fast travel, a man claims to have visited a king of a distant country and to have brought back a message from him. What would show that the message comes from the king? First, the message may contain some prediction of an event of the future occurrence of which the messenger could have learnt only from the king; e.g. that the messenger's arrival would be followed by the arrival of some of the king's ships (the messenger having to all appearances travelled by land and so not having been able to meet such ships en route). Secondly, the messenger may bring some token which a man could only have obtained from the king, e.g. a precious stone of a kind only to be found in the king's country, and which is mined by the king alone and kept by him. The token might be the sort of token which people of the culture of those days traditionally gave to authenticate messages. By analogy, evidence that the prophet has his revelation from God and so is to be believed on deep matters where we have no independent means of checking, would be given, first, by his ability to predict some future event which he would have no means of predicting otherwise, i.e. by mere human powers. But any event in accordance with natural laws could be predicted by mere human powers. So this evidence needs to be evidence of an ability to predict events not in accordance with natural laws; and that, in a basically deterministic world, means violations of natural laws. The evidence would need also to suggest that the violations were brought about by God, and so were miracles. Secondly, evidence that the prophet had his revelation from God would be provided if the prophet's life was accompanied by events which, evidence suggested, were violations of natural laws produced by God in circumstances where such violations would naturally and by local convention be interpreted as vindicating the prophet's teaching. Both these further sources of evidence thus involve the occurrence of miracles.

Before taking the argument further, I need to spell out what I understand by a miracle and what would be evidence that an event was a miracle in my sense. I understand by a miracle a violation of the laws of nature, that is, a non-repeatable exception to the operation of these laws, brought about by God. Laws of nature have the form of universal statements 'all *A*s are *B*,' and state how bodies behave of physical necessity. Thus Kepler's three laws of planetary motion state how the planets move. The first law states that all planets move in ellipses with the sun at one focus. If this purported law is to be a law of nature, planets must in general move as it states.

What however is to be said about an isolated exception to a purported law of nature? Suppose that one day Mars moves out of its elliptical path for a brief period and then returns to the path. There are two possibilities. This wandering of Mars may occur because of some current condition of the Universe (e.g. the proximity of Jupiter drawing Mars out of its elliptical path), such that if that condition were to be repeated the event would happen again. In this case the phenomenon is an entirely regular phenomenon. The trouble is that what might have appeared originally to be a basic law of nature proves now not to be one. It proves to be a consequence of a more fundamental law that the original purported law normally holds, but that under circumstances describable in general terms (e.g. 'when planets are close to each other') there are exceptions to it. Such repeatable exceptions to purported laws merely show that the purported laws are not basic laws of nature. The other possibility is that the exception to the law was not caused by some current condition, in such a way that if the condition were to recur the event would happen again. In this case we have a non-repeatable exception to a law of nature. But how are we to describe this event further? There are two possible moves. We may say that if there occurs an exception to a purported law of nature, the purported law can be no law. If the purported law says 'all As are B' and there is an A which is not B, then 'all As are B' is no law. The trouble with saying that is that the purported law may be a very good device for giving accurate predictions in our field of study; it may be by far the best general formula for describing what happens in the field which there is. (I understand by a general formula a formula which describes what happens in all circumstances of a certain kind, but does not mention by name particular individuals, times, or places.) To deny that the purported law is a law, when there is no more accurate general formula, just because there is an isolated exception to its operation, is to ignore its enormous ability to predict what happens in the field.

For this reason it seems not unnatural to say that the purported law is no less a law for there being a non-repeatable exception to it; and then to describe the exception as a 'violation' of the law. At any rate this is a coherent way of talking, and I think that it is what those who use such expressions as 'violation' of a law of nature are getting at. In this case we must amend our understanding of what is a law of nature. To say that a generalization 'all As are B' is a universal law of nature is to say that being A physically necessitates being B, and so that any A will be B—apart from violations.

But how do we know that some event such as the wandering of Mars from its elliptical path is a non-repeatable rather than a repeatable exception to a purported law of nature? We have grounds for believing that the exception is non-repeatable in so far as any attempt to amend the purported law of nature so that it predicted the wandering of Mars as well as all the other observed positions of Mars, would make it so complicated and *ad hoc* that we would have no grounds for trusting its future predictions. It is no good for example amending the law so that it reads: 'all planets move in ellipses with the Sun at one focus, except in years when there is a competition for the World Chess Championship between two players both of whose surnames begin with K.' Why not? Because this proposed law mentions properties which have no other place in physics (no other physical law invokes this sort of property) and it mentions them in an *ad hoc* way (that is, the proposed new law has the form 'so-and-so holds except under such-and-such circumstances,' when the only reason for adding the exceptive clause is that otherwise the law would be incompatible with observations; the clause does not follow naturally from the theory). What we need if we are to have a more adequate law is a general formula, of which it is an entirely natural consequence that the exception to the original law occurs when it does.

In these ways we could have grounds for believing that an exception to a purported law was non-repeatable and so a violation of a natural law. Claims of this sort are of course corrigible—we could be wrong; what seemed inexplicable by natural causes might be explicable after all. But then we could be wrong about most things, including claims of the opposite kind. When I drop a piece of chalk and it falls to the ground, every one supposes that here is an event perfectly explicable by natural laws. But we could be wrong. Maybe the laws of nature are much more complicated than we suppose, and Newton's and Einstein's laws are mere approximations to the true laws of mechanics. Maybe the true laws of mechanics predict that almost always when released from the hand, chalk will fall to the ground, but not today because of a slightly abnormal distribution of distant galaxies. However although the true laws of nature predict that the chalk will rise, in fact it falls. Here is a stark violation of natural laws, but one which no one detects because of their ignorance of natural laws. 'You could be wrong' is a knife which cuts both ways. What seem to be perfectly explicable events might prove, when we come to know the laws of nature much better, to be violations. But of course this is not very likely. The reasonable man goes by the available evidence here, and also in the converse case. He supposes that what is, on all the evidence, a violation of natural laws really is one. There is good reason to suppose that events such as the following if they occurred would be violations of laws of nature: levitation, that is, a man rising in the air against gravity without the operation of magnetism or any other known physical force; resurrection from the dead of a man whose heart has not been beating for twenty-four hours and who counts as dead by other currently used criteria; water turning into wine without the assistance of chemical apparatus or catalysts; a man growing a new arm from the stump of an old one.

Since the occurrence of a violation of natural laws cannot be explained in the normal way, either it has no explanation or it is to be explained in a different way. The obvious explanation exists if there is a God who is responsible for the whole order of nature, including its conformity to natural laws, and who therefore can on occasion suspend the normal operation of natural laws and bring about or allow some one else to bring about events, not via this normal route. We should suppose that events have explanations if suggested explanations are at all plausible. If there is quite a bit of evidence that there is a God responsible for the natural order, then any violations are plausibly attributed to his agency and so plausibly recognized as miracles—at least so long as those violations are not ruled out by such evidence as we may have from other sources about God's character. God's permitting a law of nature to be violated is clearly necessary for this to occur if he is the author of Nature; and in the absence of evidence that any other agent had a hand in the miracle, it ought to be attributed to God's sole agency. But if there is evidence, say, that it happens after a command (as opposed to a request to God) for it to happen issued by another agent, then the miracle is to be attributed to a joint agency.

I have not considered here the kind of historical evidence needed to prove the occurrence of an event which if it occurred would be a violation, but clearly it will be of the same kind as the evidence for any other historical event. There is the evidence of one's own senses, the testimony of others (oral and written) and the evidence of traces (effects left by events, such as footprints, fingerprints, cigarette ash, etc.). I see no reason in principle why there should not be evidence of this kind to show the occurrence of a levitation or a resurrection from the dead.

Now I claimed earlier that two further kinds of evidence for the genuineness of a prophet's revelation would be provided if there was evidence of the prophet's ability to predict miracles, and if there was evidence that his teaching was vindicated by miracles. Christian theology has traditionally claimed both these further sources of evidence for the truth of what Christ said.

The life of Christ was, according to the Gospels, full of 'miracles.' Some of the 'miracle' stories are perhaps not intended to be taken literally, some of them are ill-authenticated, and some of the 'miracles' were not violations of natural laws (e.g. perhaps certain cures of the mentally deranged come into this category). Yet some of the Gospel 'miracles,' in particular the stories of healings of the blind and dumb and lame, seem to me to be intended to be taken literally by the Gospel writers, to be moderately well authenticated, and to be violations of natural laws, if they occurred. But the story of one 'miracle' above all, of course, has dominated Christian teaching from the earliest days until the present—the story of the Resurrection of Christ. It seems to this writer that the writers of gospels and epistles intended their readers to believe that although Christ was killed on the Cross, he subsequently came to life (in a transformed body which left its tomb). If the events of the first Easter occurred in anything like the form recorded in the Gospels, there is a clear case of a violation of a natural law. As a violation of natural law, it would (for reasons already stated) be plausibly explained by the action of God intervening in human history.

Christian theology has claimed as evidence of the genuineness of Christ's revelation, his prophetic power in the sense of his ability to predict future events to be brought about by God, including Christ's crucifixion and resurrection, the establishment of the Church and the fall of Jerusalem. At any rate the resurrection, if it occurred, would have been, I have claimed, a miracle; and so if Christ had the ability to predict it, that would show some knowledge of God's purposes. I do not pronounce on the disputed issue of whether Christ did predict his Resurrection, or the other events, or whether there was anything miraculous in the latter.

Secondly, Christian theology has claimed that Christ's miracles, and above all the miracle of the Resurrection, marked God's vindication of Christ's teaching. The Resurrection meant that the sacrificial life of Jesus had not ended in disaster. If it occurred, it was the means of founding the Church and making the teaching of and about Jesus available to the world. Whatever is to be said about other purported miracles, the Resurrection (if it occurred) is for this reason reasonably interpreted as involving the divine judgement that it is good that the teaching of Jesus triumph. Since that teaching involves showing men the way to salvation, if it is good that it triumph, that must be because the way which it shows men does lead to salvation. For although God may have good reason for allowing evil to triumph, if it occurs through the free choice of men—because it is good that men should make a difference to the world through their free choice, or in accord with natural processes— as a warning to men as to the consequences of allowing such natural processes to continue; he would seem to have no reason to intervene in nature to make it triumph. Apparently, miraculous triumphing is not to be expected but for divine action and approval and therefore plausibly signifies divine action and approval. Also, Jews of the first century A.D. would, I suggest, readily interpret miraculous intervention to secure the triumphing of Jesus's life and teaching as evidence of a divine 'signature' on that teaching and so of its truth (and perhaps also, if Christ's death was an atoning sacrifice, as the acceptance of that sacrifice). If God gives a message to men, the right interpretation of the message is (in the absence of other considerations) the way in which it would naturally be interpreted by those who received it. For any giver of messages uses such devices as, given the conventions of his audience, will be interpreted in the right way.

Similar considerations to those about a revelation via a prophet's teaching are relevant for assessing any claim that the prophet's life was in some sense God's life, viz. that the prophet was in some sense God incarnate (although claims to such revelation are not our main concern in this chapter). A primary issue here is whether the concept of an incarnation is a coherent one at all—whether there is not some internal contradiction in the suggestion that the same individual was both God and man. If there is not, then to any claim that God has become incarnate on a particular occasion, there are relevant, first, *a priori* considerations about whether God is likely to become incarnate and under what circumstances. I noted earlier the *a priori* considerations put forward in favour of expecting God to bring about a Christian-type atonement. Then there will be evidence of two further kinds relevant to showing that God has on a particular occasion become incarnate. There will, first, be the quality of a certain prophet's human life—that it shows the kind of pattern which God would be expected to show if he accepted human limitations. It needs much argument to show what that pattern would be. But clearly, to make an atonement of the kind earlier referred to, a holy and sacrificial life is needed. Moral reflection and reflection on the prophet's life may help the investigator to see in its depths of holiness and sacrifice which are not in evidence at first sight. Yet there are many sacrificial lives lived by men on Earth. The evidence that a particular one was divine would be the testimony of the prophet himself (shown to teach true teaching by the criteria previously considered) or his accredited representative (e.g., a church); that the prophet himself could work miracles at will (not merely pray successfully for them to happen); and that his life began and ended in a way which violated natural processes. For if through the prophet's life God entered and left the world in response to the current human condition, this would require some interruption of the operation of natural processes which are concerned with the created world and planned by God from the beginning of the created world. For if the prophet's coming into the world was a natural consequence of natural laws operative throughout human history (even if made so to operate by God's original choice), his coming into the world (and so also his leaving it) would not be the result of God's spontaneous response to the mess which men had made of their lives and of the Earth. So for more than one reason, incarnation requires to be accompanied by miracle; and evidence for such miracles in connection with a holy and sacrificial life is evidence of incarnation. Claims of an incarnation typically need to be backed up by a claim to revelation in teaching (e.g. the prophet or his accredited representative—a church—teaching that the prophet was God incarnate); and there are major religions (e.g. Judaism and Islam) which claim no incarnation and yet are to be compared with Christianity in respect of a revelation in teaching.

· III ·

Brief though my discussion of revelation has been, I believe that it substantiates Paley's classical claim about revelation, especially revelation in teaching. Paley writes: 'In what way can a revelation be made, but by miracles? In none which we are able to conceive?' I have argued that Paley is right.

What a man needs to believe with respect to the claimed Christian revelation, if he is to pursue the Christian way is, we have seen, not that it is more probable than not that God revealed himself in Christ but that, if there is a God, it is more probable that he revealed himself in Christ than that he revealed himself through any other prophet with a conflicting message. If the argument of this chapter is correct, for another revelation to be more probable than the Christian revelation, it would have to be backed by a more evident miracle, or be backed by a miracle no less evident but containing more evidently true and deep teaching, or perhaps, be backed by a miracle somewhat less evident but containing teaching far more evidently true and deep. I shall come shortly to the question of how much investigation of comparative religion is necessary before a man can have a rational belief that this is so.

Paley's conclusion, after his investigation into this issue, was that no religion other than Christianity is backed by equally well-authenticated miracles. He claims that 'the only event in the history of the human species, which admits of comparison with the propagation of Christianity' is Islam. But he claims that 'Mahomet did not found his pretensions . . . upon proofs of supernatural agency, capable of being known and attested by others.'

I believe that, whatever the deficiencies of Paley's detailed historical arguments (and he wrote long before the great advances in biblical criticism in the late nineteenth century), the approach of the *Evidences* to these matters is correct. The evidence of a revelation is the plausibility to the reflective investigator of a prophet's teaching (and—if an incarnation is claimed—the holiness of his life); and some kind of miraculous divine signature symbolically affirming and forwarding the prophet's teaching and work. . . .

CHAPTER TWELVE

Life after Death

○

○   ○   ○   *50*

Immortality: An Absurd Supposition
Baron d'Holbach

1.   What Is the Soul? We Know Nothing about It. If this Pretended Soul Was of Another Essence from that of the Body, Their Union Would Be Impossible.

THE SUPERIORITY WHICH men arrogate to themselves over other animals is principally founded upon the opinion of possessing exclusively an immortal soul. But as soon as we ask what this soul is, they begin to stammer. It is an unknown substance; it is a secret force distinguished from their bodies; it is a spirit of which they can form no idea. Ask them how this spirit, which they suppose like their God, totally deprived of a physical substance, could combine itself with their material bodies? They will tell you that they know nothing about it; that it is a mystery to them; that this combination is the effect of the Almighty power. These are the clear ideas which men form of the hidden, or, rather, imaginary substance which they consider the motor of all their actions! If the soul is a substance essentially different from the body, and which can have no affinity with it, their union would be, not a mystery, but a thing impossible. Besides, this soul, being of an essence different from that of the body, ought to act necessarily in a different way from it. However, we see that the movements of the body are felt by this pretended soul, and that these two substances, so different in essence, always act in harmony. You will tell us that this harmony is a mystery; and I will tell you that I do not see my soul, that I know and feel but my body; that it is my body which feels, which reflects, which judges, which suffers, and which enjoys, and that all of its faculties are the necessary results of its own mechanism or of its organization.

2.   The Existence of a Soul Is an Absurd Supposition, and the Existence of an Immortal Soul Is a Still More Absurd Supposition.

Although it is impossible for men to have the least idea of the soul, or of this pretended spirit which animates them, they persuade themselves, however, that this unknown soul is exempt from death; everything proves to them that they feel, think, acquire ideas, enjoy or suffer, but by the means of the senses or of the material organs of the body. Even admitting the existence of this soul, one can not refuse to recognize that it depends wholly on the body, and suffers conjointly with it all the vicissitudes which it experiences itself; and however it is imagined that it has by its nature nothing analogous with it; it is pretended that it can act and feel without the assistance of this body; that deprived of this body and robbed of its senses, this soul will be able to live, to enjoy, to suffer, be sensitive of enjoyment or of rigorous torments. Upon such a tissue of conjectural absurdities the wonderful opinion of the immortality of the soul is built.

If I ask what ground we have for supposing that the soul is immortal: they reply, it is because man by his nature desires to be immortal, or to live forever. But I rejoin, if you desire anything very much, is it sufficient to conclude that this desire will be fulfilled? By what strange logic do they decide that a thing can not fail to happen because they ardently desire it to happen? Man's childish desires of the imagination, are they the measure of reality? Impious people, you say, deprived of the flattering hopes of another life, desire to be annihilated. Well, have they not just as much right to conclude by this desire that they will be annihilated, as you to conclude that you will exist forever because you desire it?

3.   It Is Evident that the Whole of Man Dies.

Man dies entirely. Nothing is more evident to him who is not delirious. The human body, after death, is but a mass, incapable of producing any movements the union of which constitutes life. We no longer see circulation, respiration, digestion, speech, or reflection. It is claimed then that the soul has separated itself from the body. But to say that this soul, which is unknown, is the principle of life, is saying nothing, unless that an unknown force is the invisible principle of imperceptible movements. Nothing is more natural and more simple than to believe that the dead man lives no more, nothing more absurd than to believe that the dead man is still living.

We ridicule the simplicity of some nations whose fashion is to bury provisions with the dead—under the idea that this food might be useful and necessary to them in another life. Is it more ridiculous or more absurd to believe that men will eat after death than to imagine that they will think; that they will have agreeable or disagreeable ideas; that they will enjoy; that they will suffer; that they will be conscious of sorrow or joy when the organs which produce sensations or ideas are dissolved and reduced to dust? To claim that the souls of men will be happy or unhappy after the death of the body is to pretend that man will be able to see without eyes, to hear without ears, to taste without a palate, to smell without a nose, and to feel without hands and without skin. Nations who believe themselves very rational, adopt, nevertheless, such ideas.

4.   Incontestable Proofs against the Spirituality of the Soul.

The dogma of the immortality of the soul assumes that the soul is a simple substance, a spirit; but I will always ask, what is a spirit? It is, you say, a substance deprived of expansion, incorruptible, and which has nothing in common with matter. But if this is true, how came your soul into existence? how did it grow? how did it strengthen? how weaken itself, get out of order, and grow old with your body? In reply to all these questions, you say that they are mysteries; but if they are mysteries, you understand nothing about them. If you do not understand anything about them, how can you positively affirm anything about them? In order to believe or to affirm anything, it is necessary at least to know what that consists of which we believe and which we affirm. To believe in the existence of your immaterial soul is to say that you are persuaded of the existence of a thing of which it is impossible for you to form any true idea; it is to believe in words without attaching any sense of them; to affirm that the thing is as you claim, is the highest folly or assumption. . . .

5. *It Is False that Materialism Can Be Debasing to the Human Race.*

Materialism, it is objected, makes of man a mere machine, which is considered very debasing to the human race. But will the human race be more honored when it can be said that man acts by the secret impulsions of a spirit, or a certain something which animates him without his knowing how? It is easy to perceive that the superiority which is given to mind over matter, or to the soul over the body, is based upon the ignorance of the nature of this soul; while we are more familiarized with matter or the body, which we imagine we know, and of which we believe we have understood the springs; but the most simple movements of our bodies are, for every thinking man, enigmas as difficult to divine as thought.

The esteem which so many people have for the spiritual substance appears to result from the impossibility they find in defining it in an intelligible way. The contempt which our metaphysicians show for matter comes from the fact that "familiarity breeds contempt." When they tell us that the soul is more excellent and noble than the body, they tell us nothing, except that what they know nothing about must be more beautiful than that of which they have some faint ideas.

6. *The Dogma of Another Life Is Useful but For Those Who Profit By It at the Expense of the Credulous Public.*

We are constantly told of the usefulness of the dogma of life hereafter. It is pretended that even if it should be a fiction, it is advantageous, because it imposes upon men and leads them to virtue. But is it true that this dogma renders men wiser and more virtuous? The nations where this fiction is established, are they remarkable for the morality of their conduct? Is not the visible world always preferred to the invisible world? If those who are charged to instruct and to govern men had themselves enlightenment and virtue, they would govern them far better by realities than by vain chimeras; but deceitful, ambitious, and corrupt, the legislators found it everywhere easier to put the nations to sleep by fables than to teach them truths; than to develop their reason; than to excite them to virtue by sensible and real motives; than to govern them in a reasonable way.

Theologians, no doubt, have had reasons for making the soul immaterial. They needed souls and chimeras to populate the imaginary regions which they have discovered in the other life. Material souls would have been subjected, like all bodies, to dissolution. Moreover, if men believe that everything is to perish with the body, the geographers of the other world would evidently lose the chance of guiding their souls to this unknown abode. They would draw no profits from the hopes with which they feast them, and from the terrors with which they take care to overwhelm them. If the future is of no real utility to the human race, it is at least of the greatest advantage to those who take upon themselves the responsibility of conducting mankind thither.

7. *It Is False that the Dogma of Another Life Can Be Consoling; And If It Were, It Would Be No Proof that This Assertion Is True.*

But, it will be said, is not the dogma of the immortality of the soul consoling for beings who often find themselves very unhappy here below? If this should be an illusion, is it not a sweet and agreeable one? Is it not a benefit for man to believe that he can live again and enjoy, sometime, the happiness which is refused to him on earth? Thus, poor mortals! you make your wishes the measure of the truth! Because you desire to live forever, and to be happier, you conclude from thence that you will live forever, and that you will be more fortunate in an unknown world than in the known world, in which you so often suffer! Consent, then, to leave without regret this world, which causes more trouble than pleasure to the majority of you. Resign yourselves to the order of destiny, which decrees that you, like all other beings, should not endure forever. But what will become of me? you ask! What you were several millions of years ago. You were then, I do not know what; resign yourselves, then, to become again in an instant, I do not know what; what you were then; return peaceably to the universal home from which you came without your knowledge into your material form, and pass by without murmuring, like all the beings which surround you!

○ ○ ○ **51**

Is Life after Death Possible?
C. J. Ducasse

THE QUESTION WHETHER human personality survives death is sometimes asserted to be one upon which reflection is futile. Only empirical evidence, it is said, can be relevant, since the question is purely one of fact.

But no question is purely one of fact until it is clearly understood; and this one is, on the contrary, ambiguous and replete with tacit assumptions. Until the ambiguities have been removed and the assumptions critically examined, we do not really know just what it is we want to know when we ask whether a life after death is possible. Nor, therefore, can we tell until then what bearing on this question various facts empirically known to us may have.

To clarify its meaning is chiefly what I now propose to attempt. I shall . . . state, as convincingly as I can in the space available, the arguments commonly advanced to prove that such a life is impossible. After that, I shall consider the logic of these arguments, and show that they quite fail to establish the impossibility. Next, the tacit but arbitrary assumption, which makes them nevertheless appear convincing, will be pointed out. . . .

Let us turn to the first of these tasks. . . .

I. The Arguments against Survival

There are, first of all, a number of *facts* which definitely suggest that both the existence and the nature of consciousness wholly depend on the presence of a functioning nervous system. [F1.] It is pointed out, for example, that wherever consciousness is observed, it is found associated with a living and functioning body. [F2.] Further, when the body dies, or the head is struck a heavy blow, or some anesthetic is administered, the familiar outward evidences of consciousness terminate, permanently or temporarily. [F3.] Again, we know well that drugs of various kinds— alcohol, caffeine, opium, heroin, and many others—cause specific changes at the time in their nature of a person's mental states. . . . [F4.] Again, the contents of consciousness, the mental powers, or even the personality, are modified in characteristic ways when certain regions of the brain are destroyed by disease or injury or are disconnected from the rest by such an operation as prefrontal lobotomy. . . .

That continued existence of mind after death is impossible has been argued also on the basis of *theoretical considerations*. [T1.] It has been contended, for instance, . . . that "consciousness" is only the name we give to certain types of behavior, which differentiate the higher animals from all other things in nature. According to this view, to say, for example, that an animal is conscious of a difference between two stimuli means nothing more than that it responds to each by different behavior. That is, the difference of *behavior* is what consciousness of difference between the stimuli *consists in*; and is not, as is commonly assumed, only the behavioral sign of something mental and not public, called "consciousness that the stimuli are different."

[T2.] Or again, consciousness, of the typically human sort called thought, is identified with the typically human sort of behavior called speech; and this, again, not in the sense that speech *expresses* or *manifests* something different from itself, called "thought," but in the sense that speech— whether uttered or only whispered— *is* thought itself. And obviously, if thought, or any mental activity, is thus but some mode of behavior of the living body, the mind cannot possibly survive death. . . .

II. The Arguments Examined

Such, in brief, are the chief reasons commonly advanced for holding that survival is impossible. Scrutiny of them, however, will, I think, reveal that they are not as strong as they first seem and far from strong enough to show that there can be no life after death.

[T1 and T2.] Let us consider first the assertion that "thought," or "consciousness," is but another name for subvocal speech, or for some other form of behavior, or for molecular processes in the tissues of the brain. As Paulsen and others have pointed out,[1] no evidence ever is or can be offered to support that assertion, because it is in fact but a disguised proposal to make the words "thought," "feeling," "sensation," "desire," and so on, denote facts quite different from those which these words are commonly employed to denote. To say that those words are but other names for certain chemical or behavioral events is as grossly arbitrary as it would be to say that "wood" is but another name for glass, or "potato" but another name for cabbage. What thought, desire, sensation, and other mental states are like, each of us can observe directly by introspection; and what introspection reveals is that they do not in the least resemble muscular contraction, or glandular secretion, or any other known bodily events. No tampering with language can alter the observable fact that thinking is one thing and muttering quite another; that the feeling called anger has no resemblance to the bodily behavior which usually goes with it; or that an act of will is not in the least like anything we find when we open the skull and examine the brain. Certain mental events are doubtless connected in some way with certain bodily events, but they are not those bodily events themselves. The connection is not identity.

[F2, F3, and F4.] This being clear, let us next consider the arguments offered to show that mental processes, although not identical with bodily processes, nevertheless depend on them. We are told, for instance, that some head injuries, or anesthetics, totally extinguish consciousness for the time being. As already pointed out, however, the strict fact is only that the usual bodily signs of consciousness are then absent. But they are also absent when a person is asleep; and yet, at the same time, dreams, which are states of consciousness, may be occurring.

It is true that when the person concerned awakens, he often remembers his dreams, whereas the person that has been anesthetized or injured has usually no memories relating to the period of apparent blankness. But this could mean that his

---

[1] F. Paulsen, "Introduction to Philosophy," 2nd ed., trans. F. Thilly. pp. 82–83.— C.J.D.

consciousness was, for the first time, dissociated from its ordinary channels of manifestation, as was reported of the co-conscious personalities of some of the patients of Dr. Morton Prince.[2] Moreover, it sometimes occurs that a person who has been in an accident reports lack of memories not only for the period of several hours *before* the accident, during which he had given to his associates all the ordinary external signs of being conscious as usual.

But, more generally, if absence of memories relating to a given period proved unconsciousness for that period, this would force us to conclude that we were unconscious during the first few years of our lives, and indeed have been so most of the time since; for the fact is that we have no memories whatever of most of our days. That we were alive and conscious on any long past specific date is, with only a few exceptions, not something we actually remember, but only something which we infer must be true.

III. Evidence from Psychical Research

[F1 and F2] Another argument advanced against survival was, it will be remembered, that death must extinguish the mind, since all manifestations of it then cease. But to assert that they invariably then cease is to ignore altogether the considerable amount of evidence to the contrary, gathered over many years and carefully checked by the Society for Psychical Research. This evidence which is of a variety of kinds, has been reviewed by Professor Gardner Murphy in an article published in the Journal of the Society.[3] He mentions first the numerous well-authenticated cases of apparition of a dead person to others as yet unaware that he had died or even been ill or in danger. The more strongly evidential cases of apparition are those in which the apparition conveys to the person who sees it specific facts until then secret. An example would be that of the apparition of a girl to her brother nine years after her death, with a conspicuous scratch on her cheek. Their mother then revealed to him that she herself had made that scratch accidentally while preparing her daughter's body for burial, but that she had then at once covered it with powder and never mentioned it to anyone.

Another famous case is that of a father whose apparition some time after death revealed to one of his sons the existence and location of an unsuspected second will, benefiting him, which was then found as indicated. Still another case would be the report by General Barter, then a subaltern in the British Army in India, of the apparition to him of a lieutenant he had not seen for two or three years. The lieutenant's apparition was riding a brown pony with black mane and tail. He was much stouter than at their last meeting, and, whereas formerly clean-shaven, he now wore a peculiar beard in the form of a fringe encircling his face. On inquiry the next day from a person who had known the lieutenant at the time he died, it turned out that he had indeed become very bloated before his death; that he had grown just such a beard while on the sick list; and that he had some time before bought and eventually ridden to death a pony of that very description.

---

[2] "My Life as a Dissociated Personality," ed. Morton Prince (Boston: Badger).— C.J.D.

[3] "An Outline of Survival Evidence," *Journal of the American Society for Psychical Research*, January, 1945.— C.J.D.

Other striking instances are those of an apparition seen simultaneously by several persons. It is on record that an apparition of a child was perceived first by a dog, that the animal's rushing at it, loudly barking, interrupted the conversation of the seven persons present in the room, thus drawing their attention to the apparition, and that the latter then moved through the room for some fifteen seconds, followed by the barking dog.[4]

Another type of empirical evidence of survival consists of communications, purporting to come from the dead, made through the persons commonly called sensitives, mediums, or automatists. Some of the most remarkable of these communications were given by the celebrated American medium, Mrs. Piper, who for many years was studied by the Society for Psychical Research, London, with the most elaborate precautions against all possibility of fraud. Twice, particularly, the evidences of identity supplied by the dead persons who purportedly were thus communicating with the living were of the very kinds, and of the same precision and detail, which would ordinarily satisfy a living person of the identity of another living person with whom he was not able to communicate directly, but only through an intermediary, or by letter or telephone.[5]

Again, sometimes the same mark of identity of a dead person, or the same message from him, or complementary parts of one message, are obtained independently from two mediums in different parts of the world.

Of course, when facts of these kinds are recounted, as I have just done, only in abstract summary, they make little if any impression upon us. And the very word "medium" at once brings to our minds the innumerable instances of demonstrated fraud perpetrated by charlatans to extract money from the credulous bereaved. But the modes of trickery and sources of error, which immediately suggest themselves to us as easy, natural explanations of the seemingly extraordinary facts, suggest themselves just as quickly to the members of the research committees of the Society for Psychical Research. Usually, these men have had a good deal more experience than the rest of us with the tricks of conjurers and fraudulent mediums, and take against them precautions far more strict and ingenious than would occur to the average skeptic.[6]

But when, instead of stopping at summaries, one takes the trouble to study the detailed, original reports, it then becomes evident that they cannot all be just laughed off; for to accept the hypothesis of fraud or malobservation would often require more credulity than to accept the facts reported.

---

[4] The documents obtained by the Society for Psychical Research concerning this case, that of the lieutenant's apparition, and that of the girl with the scratch are reproduced in Sir Ernest Bennett's "Apparitions and Haunted Houses" (London: Faber and Faber, 1945), pp. 334–337, 28–35, and 145–150 respectively.— C.J.D.

[5] A summary of some of the most evidential facts may be found in the book by M. Sage, entitled "Mrs. Piper and the Society for Psychical Research" (New York: Scott-Thaw Co., 1904); others of them are related in some detail in Sir Oliver Lodge's "The Survival of Man," sec. 4 (New York: Moffat, Yard and Co., 1909), and in A. M. Robbins' "Both Sides of the Veil," part 2 (Boston: Sherman, French, and Co., 1909). The fullest account is in the *Proceedings of the Society for Psychical Research*— C.J.D.

[6] Cf. H. Carrington, "The Physical Phenomena of Spiritualism, Fraudulent and Genuine" (Boston: Small, Maynard & Co., 1908).— C.J.D.

IV. The Initial Assumption behind the Arguments against Survival

We have now scrutinized . . . the reason mentioned earlier for rejecting the possibility of survival, and we have found them all logically weak . . . It will be useful for us to . . . inquire why so many of the persons who advance those reasons nevertheless think them convincing.

It is, I believe, because these persons approach the question of survival with a certain unconscious metaphysical bias. It derives from a particular initial assumption which they tacitly make. It is that *to be real is to be material.*[7] And to be material, of course, is to be some process or part of the perceptually public world, that is, of the world we all perceive by means of our so-called five senses.

Now, the assumption that to be real is to be material is a useful and appropriate one for the purpose of investigating the material world and of operating upon it; and this purpose is a legitimate and frequent one. But those persons, and most of us, do not realize that the validity of that assumption is strictly relative to that specific purpose. Hence they, and most of us, continue making the assumption, and it continues to rule judgment, even when, as now, the purpose in view is a different one, for which the assumption is no longer useful or even congruous.

The point is all-important here and therefore worth stressing. Its essence is that the conception of the nature of reality that proposes to define the real as the material is not the expression of an observable fact to which everyone would have to bow, but is the expression only of a certain direction of interest on the part of the persons who so define reality— of interest, namely, which they have chosen to center wholly in the material, perceptually public world. This specialized interest is of course as legitimate as any other, but it automatically ignores all the facts, commonly called facts of mind, which only introspection reveals. And that specialized interest is what alone compels persons in its grip to employ the word "mind" to denote, instead of what it commonly does denote, something else altogether, namely, the public behavior of bodies that have minds.

Only so long as one's judgment is swayed unawares by that special interest do the logically weak arguments against the possibility of survival, which we have examined, seem strong.

It is possible, however, and just as legitimate, as well as more conducive to a fair view of our question, to center one's interest at the start on the facts of mind as introspectively observable, ranking them as most real in the sense that they are the facts the intrinsic nature of which we most directly experience, the facts which we most certainly know to exist; and moreover, that they are the facts without the experiencing of which we should not know any other facts whatever— such, for instance, as those of the material world.

The sort of perspective one gets from this point of view is what I propose now to sketch briefly. For one thing, the material world is then seen to be but one among other objects of our consciousness. Moreover, one becomes aware of the crucially important fact that it is an object postulated rather than strictly given. What this

---

[7] This is to be interpreted as an identity claim. This x is real = x is material.— E.D.K.

means may be made clearer by an example. Suppose that, perhaps in a restaurant we visit for the first time, an entire wall is occupied by a large mirror and we look into it without realizing that it is a mirror. We then perceive, in the part of space beyond it, various material objects, notwithstanding that in fact they have no existence there at all. A certain set of the vivid color images which we call visual sensations was all that was strictly given to us, and these we construed, automatically and instantaneously, but nonetheless erroneously, as signs or appearances of the existence of certain material objects at a certain place.

Again, and similarly, we perceive in our dreams various objects which at the time we take as physical but which eventually we come to believe were not so. And this eventual conclusion, let it be noted, is forced upon us not because we then detect that something, called "physical substance," was lacking in those objects, but only because we notice, as we did not at the time, that their behavior was erratic— incoherent with their ordinary one. That is, their appearance was a *mere* appearance, deceptive in the sense that it did not then predict truly, as ordinarily it does, their later appearances. This, it is important to notice, is the *only* way in which we ever discover that an object we perceive was not really physical, or was not the particular sort of physical object we judged it to be.

These two examples illustrate the fact that our perception of physical objects is sometimes erroneous. But the essential point is that, even when it is veridical instead of erroneous, *all* that is literally and directly given to our minds is still only *some set of sensations*. These, on a given occasion, may be only color sensations; but they often include also tactual sensations, sounds, odors, and so on. It is especially interesting, however, to remark here in passing that, with respect to almost all the many thousands of persons and other "physical" objects we have perceived in a life time, *vivid color images* were the only data our perceiving strictly had to go by; so that, if the truth should happen to have been that those objects, like ghosts or images in a mirror, were actually intangible— that is, were *only* color images— we should never have discovered that this was the fact. For all we *directly* know, it *may* have been the fact!

To perceive a physical object, then, instead of merely experiencing passively certain sensations (something which perhaps hardly ever occurs) is always to *interpret*, that is to *construe*, given sensations as signs of, and appearances to us of, a postulated something other than themselves, which we believe is causing them in us and is capable of causing in us others of specific kinds. We believe this because we believe that our sensations too must have some cause, and we find none for them among our other mental states.

Such a postulated extramental something we call a physical object. We say that we observe physical objects, and this is true. But it is important for the present purpose to be clear that we "observe" them never in any more direct or literal manner than is constituted by the process of interpretive postulation just described— never, for example, in the wholly direct and literal manner in which we are able to observe our sensations themselves and our other mental states.

CHAPTER THIRTEEN

Religion and Ethics

○

○ ○ ○   **52**

Good and the Will of God
Emil Brunner

1. THERE IS NO general conception of ethics which would also include the Christian ethic. . . .

It is of course true that even the Christian ethic is concerned with the definition of conduct, which as "right" conduct has to be distinguished from conduct which is accidental or wrong; but this distinction or definition does not take place by means of an ultimate principle, which, as such, would be intelligible and valid. . . . The Christian conception of the Good differs from every other conception of the Good at this very point: that it cannot be defined in terms of principle at all.

Whatever can be defined in accordance with a principle—whether it be the principle of pleasure or the principle of duty—is legalistic. This means that it is possible—by the use of this principle—to pre-determine "the right" down to the smallest detail of conduct. We have already seen how this legalistic spirit corrupts the true conception of the Good from its very roots. The Christian moralist and the extreme individualist are at one in their emphatic rejection of legalistic conduct; they join hands, as it were, in face of the whole host of legalistic moralists; they are convinced that conduct which is regulated by abstract principles can never be good. But equally sternly the Christian moralist rejects the individualist doctrine of freedom, according to which there is no longer any difference between "right" and "wrong." Rather, in the Christian view, that alone is "good" which is free from all caprice, which takes place in unconditional obedience. There is no Good save obedient behaviour, save the obedient will. But this obedience is rendered not to a law or a principle which can be known beforehand, but only to the free, sovereign will of God. The Good consists in always doing what God wills at any particular moment.

This statement makes it clear that for us the will of God cannot be summed up under any principle, that it is not at our disposal, but that so far as we are concerned the will of God is absolutely free. The Christian is therefore " a free lord over all things,"[1] because he stands directly under the personal orders of the free Sovereign God. This is why genuine "Christian conduct"—if we may use this idea as an illustration—is so unaccountable, so unwelcome to the moral rigorist and to the hedonist alike. The moral rigorist regards the Christian as a hedonist, and the hedonist regards him as a rigorist. In reality, the Christian is neither, yet he is also something of both, since he is indeed absolutely *bound* and obedient, but, since he is bound to the *free* loving will of God, he is himself free from all transparent bondage

---

[1] Luther: *Of the Freedom of a Christian Man (Von der Freiheit eines Christenmenschen.).*—E.B.

to principles or to legalism. Above all it is important to recognize that even love is not a principle of this kind, neither the love which God Himself *has*, nor the love which He *requires*. Only God Himself defines love in His action. We, for our part, do not know what God is, nor do we know what *love* is, unless we learn to know God in His action, in faith. To be in this His Love, is the Commandment. Every attempt to conceive love as a principle leads to this result: it becomes distorted, either in the rigoristic, legalistic sense, or in the hedonistic sense. Man only knows what the love of God is when he sees the way in which God acts, and the only knows how he himself ought to love by allowing himself to be drawn by faith into this activity of God.

2. "To know God in His action" is only possible in faith. The action of God, in which He manifests Himself—and this means His love—is His revelation. God reveals Himself in His Word—which is at the same time a deed—in an actual event—in Jesus Christ; and He reveals Himself operatively in His living Word, which is now taking place—in the Holy Spirit. Because only conduct which takes place on the basis of this faith (and indeed in this faith in God's Word) can be "good conduct," in the sense of the Christian ethic, therefore, the science of good conduct, of ethics, is only possible within that other science which speaks of the Divine act of revelation, that is, within dogmatics. Reflection on the good conduct of man is only one part of more comprehensive reflection on the action of God in general. For human conduct can only be considered "good" when, and in so far as, God Himself acts in it, through the Holy Spirit. Hence just as this action is connected with the Divine action, so the Christian ethic is connected with dogmatics. . . .

3. The decisive point of view for ethics—even for Christian ethics—is conduct, not being, although even for the Christian ethic it is the being of man, "the person," which is the decisive point of view for conduct. The new being (*Sein*) of man, in so far as it is regarded only as the work of God, is the "new man" who is based on faith in justification. In so far as in the being of this new man the emphasis is laid on its manifesting itself in a "work," in actions towards others, it forms part of ethics. Yet this ethical element is not a second, independent element alongside of the dogmatic element, but it is simply the emphasis on a special "moment" within it. For just as the Christian Ethic is distinguished from natural ethics by the fact that in it God's action is always regarded as the basis of human action, so it is also characteristic of it that in all action, the *being* of the agent, as that which alone can be really good or evil, is kept in view.

Therefore, in spite of the fact that a uniform division of Christian doctrine into dogmatics and ethics can only take place with the greatest injury to both, there is always an external technical separation, which is forced upon us by necessity, and is indeed justifiable; that is, if this external separation does not denote an inner separation. These considerations may now be summed up in a sentence, in which the special subject of Christian ethics is defined: *Christian ethics is the science of human conduct as it is determined by Divine conduct.*

53

God and the Good
Kai Nielsen

IT IS THE claim of many influential Christian and Jewish theologians (Brunner, Buber, Niebuhr, and Bultmann—to take outstanding examples) that the *only* genuine basis for morality is in religion. And any old religion is not good enough. The only truly adequate foundation for moral belief is a religion that acknowledges the absolute sovereignty of the Lord found in the prophetic religions.

These theologians will readily grant what is plainly true, namely, that as a matter of fact many nonreligious people behave morally, but they contend that without a belief in God and his Law there is no *ground* or *reason* for being moral. The sense of moral relativism, skepticism and nihilism rampant in our age is due in large measure to the general weakening of religious belief in an age of science. Without God there can be no objective foundation for our moral beliefs. As Brunner puts it, "The believer *alone* clearly perceives that the Good, as it is recognized in faith, is the sole Good, and all that is otherwise called good cannot lay claim to this title, at least in the ultimate sense of the word." "The Good consists in always doing what God wills at any particular moment." This "Good" can only "take place in unconditional obedience" to God, the ground of our being. Without God life would have no point and morality would have no basis. Without religious belief, without the Living God, there could be no adequate answer to the persistently gnawing questions: What ought we to do? How ought I to live?

Is this frequently repeated claim justified? Are our moral beliefs and conceptions based on or grounded in a belief in the God of Judaism, Christianity, and Islam? More specifically still, we need to ask ourselves three very fundamental questions: (1) Is being willed by God the or even a *fundamental* criterion for that which is so willed being morally good or for its being something that ought to be done? (2) Is being willed by God the *only* criterion for that which is so willed being morally good or for its being something that ought to be done? (3) Is being willed by God the only *adequate* criterion for that which is so willed being morally good or being something that ought to be done? I shall argue that the fact that God wills something—if indeed that is a fact—cannot be a fundamental criterion for its being morally good or obligatory and thus it cannot be the only criterion or the only adequate criterion for moral goodness or obligation.

· I ·

By way of preliminaries we first need to get clear what is meant by a "fundamental criterion." When we speak of the criterion for the goodness of an action or attitude we speak of some *measure* or *test* by virtue of which we may decide which actions or attitudes are good or desirable, or, at least, are the least undesirable of the alternative actions or attitudes open to us. A moral criterion is the measure we use for determining the value or worth of an action or attitude. We have such a measure or test when we have some generally relevant considerations by which we may decide whether something is whatever it is said to be. A fundamental moral criterion is (a) a test or measure used to judge the legitimacy of moral rules and/or acts or attitudes, and (b) a measure that one would give up last if one were reasoning morally. (In reality, there probably is no *single* fundamental criterion, although there are fundamental criteria.)

There is a further preliminary matter we need to consider. In asking about the basis or authority for our moral beliefs we are not asking about how we came to have them. If you ask someone where he got his moral beliefs, he should answer that he got them from his parents, parent surrogates, teachers, etc.[1] They are beliefs which he has simply been conditioned to accept. But the validity or soundness of a belief is independent of its origin. When one person naively asks another where he got his moral beliefs, he is most likely not asking how he came by them; he is, in effect, asking: (1) On what authority does he hold these beliefs? or (b) What good reasons or justification does he have for these moral beliefs? He should answer that he does not and cannot hold these beliefs on *any authority*. It is indeed true that many of us turn to people for moral advice and guidance in moral matters, but if we *simply* do what we do because it has been authorized, we cannot be reasoning and acting as moral agents; for to respond as a moral agent, to treat a principle as one's moral principle, it must be something which is subscribed to by one's own deliberate commitment, and it must be something for which one is prepared to give reasons.

With these preliminaries out of the way we can return to my claim that the fact (if indeed it is a fact) that God has commanded, willed, or ordained something cannot, in the very nature of the case, be a fundamental criterion for claiming that whatever is commanded, willed, or ordained *ought* to be done.

· II ·

Some perceptive remarks made by A. C. Ewing can carry us part of the way.[2] Theologians like Barth and Brunner claim that ethical principles gain their justification simply because they are God's decrees. But as Ewing points out, if "being obligatory" *means* just "willed by God," it becomes unintelligible to ask why God wills one thing rather than another. In fact, there can be no *reason* for his willing one thing rather than another, for his willing it *eo ipso*[3] makes whatever it is he wills good, right, or obligatory. "God wills it because it ought to be done" becomes "God wills it because God wills it"; but the first sentence, even as used by the most ardent believer, is not a tautology. "If it were said in reply that God's commands determined what we ought to do but that these commands were only issued because it was good that they should be or because obedience to them did good, this would still make judgements about the good, at least, independent of the will of God, and we should not have given a definition of all fundamental ethical concepts in terms of God or made ethics

---

[1] P. H. Nowell-Smith, "Morality: Religious and Secular," *The Rationalist Annual* (1961), pp. 5-22.—K.N.

[2] A. C. Ewing, "The Autonomy of Ethics," in *Prospect for Metaphysics*, ed. Ian Ramsey (London: 1961).—K.N.

[3] Of itself.—E.D.K.

dependent on God."[4] Furthermore, it becomes senseless to say what the believer very much wants to say, namely, "He ought always to do what God wills" if "what he ought to do" and "what God wills" have the same meaning. And to say I ought to do what God wills because I love God makes the independent assumption that I ought to love God and *that I ought* to do what God wills if I love him.

Suppose we say instead that we ought to do what God wills because God will punish us if we do not obey him. This may very well be a cogent self-interested or prudential reason for doing what God commands, but we hardly have a morally good reason for doing what he commands since such considerations of self-interest cannot be an adequate basis for morality. A powerful being—an Omnipotent and Omniscient being—speaking out of the whirlwind cannot by his *mere commands* create an *obligation*. Ewing goes on to assert: "Without a prior conception of God as good or his commands as right God would have no more claim on our obedience than Hitler or Stalin except that he would have more power than even they had to make things uncomfortable for those who disobey him."[5] Unless we assume that God is morally perfect, unless we assume the perfect goodness of God, there can be no necessary" relation between being commanded or willed by God and being obligatory or good."[6]

To this it is perfectly correct to reply that as believers we must believe that God is wholly and completely good, the most perfect of all conceivable beings.[7] It is not open for a Jew or Christian to question the goodness of God. He must start with that assumption. Any man who seriously questions God's goodness or asks why he should obey God's commands shows by this very response that he is not a Jew or a Christian. Believers must indeed claim that God is wholly and utterly good and that what he wills or commands is of necessity good, though this does not entail that the believer is claiming that the necessity here is a *logical* necessity. For a believer, God is all good; he is the Perfect Good. This being so, it would seem that the believer is justified in saying that he and we—if his claim concerning God is correct—ought to do what God wills and that our morality is after all grounded in a belief in God. But this claim of his is clearly dependent on his assumption that God is good (a "given" for Jewish and Christian belief). Yet I shall argue that even if God is good, even if God is the perfect good, it does not follow that morality can be based on religion and that we can know what we ought to do simply by knowing what God wishes us to do.

· III ·

To see the rationale for these last "dark sayings" we must consider the logical status of "God is good." Is it a nonanalytic and in some way substantive claim, or is it analytic? (Can we say that it is neither?) No matter what we say, we get into difficulties.

Let us first try to claim that it is a nonanalytic, that is to say, that it is in some way a substantive statement. So understood, God cannot then be by *definition* good. If the statement is synthetic and substantive, its denial cannot be self-contradictory, that is,

---

[4] *Ibid.*, p. 39.—K.N.

[5] *Ibid.*, p. 40.—K.N.

[6] *Ibid.*, p. 41.—K.N.

[7] D. A. Rees, "Metaphysical Schemes and Moral Principles," *Prospect for Metaphysics*, p. 23.—K.N.

it cannot be self-contradictory to assert that *x* is God but *x* is not good. It would always *in fact* be wrong to assert this, for God is the Perfect Good, but the denial of this claim is not self-contradictory, it is just false or in some way mistaken. The "is" in "God is the Perfect Good" is not the "is" of identity, perfect goodness is being predicated of God in some *logically* contingent way. It is the religious experience of the believer and the events recorded in the Bible that lead the believer to the steadfast conviction that God has a purpose or vocation for him and guide him in every thought, word, and deed. Otherwise he will be like a man shipwrecked, lost in a vast and indifferent universe. Through careful attention to the Bible, he comes to understand that God is a wholly good being who has dealt faithfully with his chosen people. God is not *by definition* perfectly good or even good, but in reality, though not of logical necessity, he never falls short of perfection.

Assuming "God is good" is not a truth of language, how, then, do we know that God is good? Do we know or have good grounds for believing that the remarks made at the end of the above paragraph are so? The believer can indeed make a claim like the one we have make above, but how do we or how does he know that this is so? What grounds have we for believing that God is good? Naive people, recalling how God spoke to Job out of the whirlwind, may say that God is good because he is omnipotent and omniscient. But this clearly won't do, for, as Hepburn points out, there is nothing logically improper about saying "X is omnipotent and omniscient and morally wicked."[8] Surely in the world as we know it there is no logical connection between being powerful and knowledgeable, on the one hand, and, on the other, being good. As far as I can see, all that God proved to Job when he spoke to him out of the whirlwind was that God was an immeasurably powerful being; but he did not prove his moral superiority to Job, and he did nothing at all even to exhibit his moral goodness. (One might even argue that he exhibited moral wickedness.) We need not assume that omnipotence and omniscience bring with it goodness or even wisdom.

What other reason could we have for claiming that God is good? We might say that he is good because he tells us to do good in thought, word, and deed and to love one another. In short, in his life and in his precepts God exhibits for us his goodness and love. Now one might argue that children's hospitals and concentration camps clearly show that such a claim is false. But let us *assume* that in some way God does exhibit his goodness to man. Let us assume that if we examine God's works we cannot but affirm that God is good.[9] We come to understand that he isn't cruel, callous, or indifferent. But in order to make such judgments or to gain such an understanding, we must use our own logically independent moral criteria. On our present assumption in asserting "God is good" we have of necessity made a moral judgment, a moral appraisal, using a criterion that cannot be based on a knowledge that God exists or that he issues commands. We *call* God "good" because we have experienced the goodness of his acts, but in order to do this, in order to know that he is good or to have any grounds for believing that he is good, we must have an independent moral criterion which we use in making this predication of God. So if "God is good" is taken to be synthetic and substantive then morality cannot simply be based on a belief in God. We

---

[8] Ronald Hepburn, *Christianity and Paradox* (London: 1958), p. 132.—K.N.

[9] This is surely to assume a lot.—K.N.

must of logical necessity have some criterion of goodness that is not derived from any statement asserting that there is a Deity.

· IV ·

Let us alternatively, and more plausibly, treat "God is good" as a truth of language. Now some truths of language (some analytic statements) are statements of identity as in "puppies are young dogs" or "a father is a male parent." Such statements are definitions and the "is" is the "is of identity." But "God is good" is clearly not such a statement of identity, for that "God" does not equal "Good" or "God" does not have the same meaning as "good" can easily be seen from the following case: Jane says to Betsy, after Betsy helps an old lady across the street, "That was good of you." "That was good of you" most certainly does not mean "That was God of you." And when we say "conscientiousness is good" we do not mean to say "conscientiousness is God." To say, as a believer does, that God is good is not to say that God is God. This clearly indicates that the word "God does not have the same meaning oas the word good." When we are talking about God we are not simply talking about morality.

"God is the Perfect Good" is somewhat closer to "a father is a male parent," but even here "God" and "the Perfect Good" are not identical in meaning. "God is the Perfect Good" is like "a triangle is a trilateral" in some important respects. Though something is a triangle if and only if it is a trilateral, it does not follow that "triangle" and "trilateral" have the same meaning. Similarly, something is God if and only if that something is the Perfect Good, but it does not follow that "God" and "the Perfect Good" have the same meaning. When we speak of God we wish to say other things about him as well, though indeed what is true of God will also be true of the Perfect Good. Yet what is true of the evening star will also be true of the morning star for they both refer to the same object, namely Venus, but, as Frege has shown, it does not follow that the two terms have the same meaning if they have the same referent.

And even if it could be made out that "God is the Perfect Good" is in some way a statement of identity, (1) it would not make "God is good" a statement of identity, and (2) we could know that x is the Perfect Good only if we already knew how to decide that x is good.[10] Even on the assumption that "God is the Perfect Good" is a statement of identity, we need some independent way of deciding whether something is good, that is to say, we must have an independent criterion for goodness.

Surely it is more plausible to interpret "God is good" to be analytic in the way "puppies are young," "a bachelor is unmarried," or "unjustified killing is wrong" are analytic. These statements are not statements of identity; they are not definitions, though they all follow from definitions and to deny any of them is self-contradictory.

In short it seems to me correct to argue "God is good," "puppies are young," and "triangles are three-sided" are all truths of language; the predicates *partially* define their subjects. That is to say—to adopt for a moment a Platonic *sounding* idiom—goodness is partially definitive of Godhood, as youngness is partially definitive of puppyhood, and as three-sidedness is partially definitive of triangularity.

---

[10] Finally we must be quite clear that x's being good is but a necessary condition for x's being the Perfect Good, but what would be a sufficient condition? Do we really know? I don't think we do. We do not know how to identify the referent of "the Perfect Good." Thus in one clear sense we do not understand what such a phrase means.—K.N.

To admit this is not at all to admit that we can have no understanding of "good" without an understanding of "God," and the truth of the above claim about "God is good" will not show that God is the or even a fundamental criterion for goodness.

Let us first see how it does *not* show that we could not have an understanding of "good" without having an understanding of "God." We couldn't understand the full religious sense of what is meant by "God" without knowing that whatever is denoted by this term is said to be good, but, as "young" or "three-sided" are understood without reference to "puppies" or "triangles," though the converse cannot be the case, so "good" is also understood quite independently of any reference to "God," but again the converse cannot be the case. We can intelligibly say, "I have a three-sided figure here that is most certainly not a triangle" and "Colts are young but they are not puppies." Similarly, we can well say, "Conscientiousness, under most circumstances at least, is good even in a world without God." Such an utterance is clearly intelligible, to believer and nonbeliever alike. It is a well-formed English sentence with a use in the language. But here we can use "good" without implying anything about the reality of God. Such linguistic evidence clearly shows that good is a concept which can be understood quite independently of any reference to the Deity and that morality without religion, without theism, is quite possible. In fact quite the reverse is the case. Christianity, Judaism, and theistic religions of that sort could not exist if people did not have a moral understanding that was, logically speaking, quite independent of such religions. We could have no understanding of the truth of "God is good" or of the concept God unless we had an independent understanding of goodness.

That this is so can be seen from the following considerations. If we had no grasp of the use of the word "young," and if we did not know the criteria for deciding whether a dog was young, we could not know how correctly to apply the word "puppy." Without such a prior understanding of what it is to be young we could not understand the sentence "Puppies are young." "Similarly, if we had no grasp of the use of the word "good," and if we did not know the criteria for deciding whether a being (or if you will, a power or a force) was good, we could not know how correctly to apply the word "God." Without such a prior understanding of goodness we could not understand the sentence "God is good." This clearly shows that our understanding of morality and knowledge of goodness is independent of any knowledge that we may or may not have of the Divine. In fact the very converse is the case. Without a prior and logically independent understanding of "good" and without some nonreligious criterion for judging something to be good, the religious person could have no knowledge of God, for he could not know whether that powerful being who spoke out of the whirlwind and laid the foundations of the earth was in fact worthy of worship and perfectly good.

From the argument we have made so far we can conclude that we cannot decide whether something is good or whether it ought to be done simply from finding out (assuming that we can find out) that God commanded it, willed it, enjoined it, and the like. Furthermore, whether "God is good" is synthetic (substantive) or analytic (a truth of language), the concept of good must be understood as something distinct from the concept of God; that is to say, a man could know how to use "good" properly and still not know how to use "God." In fact quite the reverse is the case. A man could not know how to use "God" correctly unless he already understood how to use "good." An understanding of goodness is logically prior to and is, as such, independent of any understanding or acknowledgment of God.

. V .

In attempting to counter my argument for the necessary independence of morality—including a central facet of religious morality—from any beliefs about the existence or powers of the Deity, the religious moralist might begin by conceding that (1) there are secular moralities that are logically independent of religion, and (2) that we must understand the *meanings* of moral terms independently of understanding what it means to speak of God. He might even go so far as to grant that only a man who understood what good and bad were could come to believe in God. "Good," he might concede, does not mean "willed by God" or anything like that; and "There is no God, but human happiness is nonetheless good" is indeed perfectly intelligible as a moral utterance. But granting that, it is still the case that Jews and Christians do and must—on pain of ceasing to be Jews or Christians—take God's will as their final court of appeal in the making of moral appraisals or judgments. Any rule, act, or attitude that conflicts with what the believer sincerely believes to be the will of God must be rejected by him. It is indeed true that in making moral judgments the Jew or Christian does not always use God's will as a criterion for *what* is good or *what* ought to be done. When he says "Fluoridation is a good thing" or "The resumption of nuclear testing is a crime" he *need* not be using God's will as a criterion for his moral judgment, but *where any moral judgment whatsoever or where any other moral criterion conflicts with God's ordinances, or with what the person making the judgment honestly takes to be God's ordinances, he must accept them or he is no longer a Jew or a Christian.* Accepting this is a crucial test of his faith. In this way God's will is his fundamental moral criterion.

That orthodox Jews and Christians would reason in this way is perfectly true, but though they *say* that God's will is their most fundamental criterion (and in the way already referred to it is) it is still plain, from the very way the Christian must argue, that he has a yet more fundamental criterion which he *must use* in order to use God's will as a moral criterion. Such a religious moralist must believe and thus be prepared to make (be committed to) the *moral* claim that there exists a being whom he deems to be *perfectly good* or *worthy* of worship and whose will should always be obeyed. But to do this he must have a moral criterion (a standard for *what* is morally good) that is independent of God's will or what people believe to be God's will. In fact the believer's moral criterion—"because it is willed by God"—is in logical dependence on some *distinct* criterion in virtue of which the believer *judges that* something is *perfectly good*, is *worthy* of worship. And in making this very crucial judgment he cannot appeal to God's will as a criterion, for that there is a being *worthy* of the appellation "God" depends in part on the above prior moral claim. Only if it is correct we justifiably say that there is a God.

It is important to keep in mind that "A wholly *good* being exists who is *worthy* of worship" is *not* analytic, is not a truth of language, though "God is wholly good" is. It is rather a substantive moral statement (expressing a moral judgment) and very fundamental one indeed, for the believer's whole faith rests on it. Drop this and the whole works go.

It is tempting to reply to my above argument in this vein: "But it is *blasphemy* to *judge* God; no account of the logical structure of the believer's argument can be correct if it says that the believer must *judge* that God is good." Here we must beware of verbal magic and attend very carefully to exactly what it is we are saying. I did not—and could not on pain of contradiction—say, "God must be judged worthy of worship, perfectly good," for God by definition is worthy of worship, perfectly good. I said something quite different, namely that the believer and nonbeliever alike must decide for [themselves] whether there exists or could *conceivably* exist a force, a being ("ground of being"?) that is worthy of worship or perfectly good; and I further said that in deciding this one makes a moral judgment that can in no way be logically dependent on God's will. In fact it is exactly the reverse that is the case. The moral standard, "because it is willed by God," is dependent for its validity on the acceptance of the claim that there is a being worthy of worship. And, as our little word "worthy" indicates, this is unequivocally a moral judgment for believer and nonbeliever alike.

54

A Modified Divine Command Theory of Ethical Wrongness

Robert Merrihew Adams

· *I* ·

IT IS WIDELY held that all those theories are indefensible which attempt to explain in terms of the will or commands of God what it is for an act to be ethically right or wrong. In this paper I shall state such a theory, which I believe to be defensible; and I shall try to defend it against what seem to me to be the most important and interesting objections to it. I call my theory a *modified* divine command theory because in it I renounce certain claims that are commonly made in divine command analyses of ethical terms. (I should add that it is *my* theory only in that I shall state it, and that I believe it is defensible—not that I am sure it is correct.) I present it as a theory of ethical *wrongness* partly for convenience. It could also be presented as a theory of the nature of ethical obligatoriness or of ethical permittedness. Indeed, I will have occasion to make some remarks about the concept of ethical permittedness. But as we shall see (in Section IV) I am not prepared to claim that the theory can be extended to all ethical terms; and it is therefore important that it not be presented as a theory about ethical terms in general.

It will be helpful to begin with the statement of a simple, *un*modified divine command theory of ethical wrongness. This is the theory that ethical wrongness *consists in* being contrary to God's commands, or that the word 'wrong' in ethical contexts *means* 'contrary to God's commands'. It implies that the following two statement forms are logically equivalent.

(1)   It is wrong (for A) to do X.
(2)   It is contrary to God's commands (for A) to do X.

Of course that is not all that the theory implies. It also implies that (2) is conceptually prior to (1), so that the meaning of (1) is to be explained in terms of (2), and not the other way round. It might prove fairly difficult to state or explain in what that conceptual priority consists, but I shall not go into that here. I do not wish ultimately to defend the theory in its unmodified form, and I think I have stated it fully enough for my present purposes.

I have stated it as a theory about the meaning of the word 'wrong' in ethical contexts. The most obvious objection to the theory is that the word 'wrong' is used in ethical contexts by many people who cannot mean by it what the theory says they must mean, since they do not believe that there exists a God. This objection seems to me sufficient to refute the theory if it is presented as an analysis of what *everybody* means by 'wrong' in ethical contexts. The theory cannot reasonably be offered except as a theory about what the word 'wrong' means as used by *some but not all* people in ethical contexts. Let us say that the theory offers an analysis of the meaning of 'wrong' in Judeo-Christian religious ethical discourse. This restriction of scope will apply to my modified divine command theory too. This restriction obviously gives rise to a possible objection. Isn't it more plausible to suppose that Judeo-Christian believers use 'wrong' with the same meaning as other people do? This problem will be discussed in Section VI.

In Section II, I will discuss what seems to me the most important objection to the unmodified divine command theory, and suggest how the theory can be modified to meet it. Section III will be devoted to a brief but fairly comprehensive account of the use of 'wrong' in Judeo-Christian ethical discourse, from the point of view of the modified divine command theory. The theory will be further elaborated in dealing with objections in Sections IV to VI. In a seventh and final section, I will note some problems arising from unresolved issues in the general theory of analysis and meaning, and briefly discuss their bearing on the modified divine command theory.

· II ·

The following seems to me to be the gravest objection to the divine command theory of ethical wrongness, in the form in which I have stated it. Suppose God should command me to make it my chief end in life to inflict suffering on other human beings, for no other reason than that He commanded it. (For convenience I shall abbreviate this hypothesis to 'Suppose God should command cruelty for its own sake.') Will it seriously be claimed that in that case it would be wrong for me not to practice cruelty for its own sake? I see three possible answers to this question.

(1) It might be claimed that it is logically impossible for God to command cruelty for its own sake. In that case, of course, we need not worry about whether it would be wrong to disobey if He did command it. It is senseless to agonize about what one should do in a logically impossible situation. This solution to the problem seems unlikely to be available to the divine command theorist, however. For why would he hold that it is logically impossible for God to command cruelty for its own sake? Some theologians (for instance, Thomas Aquinas) have believed (a) that what is right and wrong is independent of God's will, *and* (b) that God always does right by the necessity of His nature. Such theologians, if they believe that it would be wrong for God to command cruelty for its own sake, have reason to believe that it is logically impossible for Him to do so. But the divine command theorist, who does not agree that what is right and wrong is independent of God's will, does not seem to have such a reason to deny that it is logically possible for God to command cruelty for its own sake.

(2) Let us assume that it is logically possible for God to command cruelty for its own sake. In that case the divine command theory seems to imply that it would be wrong not to practice cruelty for its own sake. There have been at least a few adherents of divine command ethics who have been prepared to accept this consequence. William Ockham held that those acts which we call 'theft,' 'adultery,' and 'hatred of

God' would be meritorious if God had commanded them.[1] He would surely have said the same about what I have been calling the practice of 'cruelty for its own sake.'

This position is one which I suspect most of us are likely to find somewhat shocking, even repulsive. We should therefore be particularly careful not to misunderstand it. We need not imagine that Ockham disciplined himself to be ready to practice cruelty for its own sake if God should command it. It was doubtless an article of faith for him that God is unalterably opposed to any such practice. The mere logical possibility that theft, adultery, and cruelty might have been commanded by God (and therefore meritorious) doubtless did not represent in Ockham's view any real possibility.

(3) Nonetheless, the view that if God commanded cruelty for its own sake it would be wrong not to practice it seems unacceptable to me; and I think many, perhaps most, other Jewish and Christian believers would find it unacceptable too. I must make clear the sense in which I find it unsatisfactory. It is not that I find an internal inconsistency in it. And I would not deny that it may reflect, accurately enough, the way in which some believers use the word 'wrong.' I might as well frankly avow that I am looking for a divine command theory which at least might possibly be a correct account of how I use the word 'wrong.' I do not use the word 'wrong' in such a way that I would say that it would be wrong not to practice cruelty if God commanded it, and I am sure that many other believers agree with me on this point.

But now have I not rejected the divine command theory? I have assumed that it would be logically possible for God to command cruelty for its own sake. And I have rejected the view that if God commanded cruelty for its own sake, it would be wrong not to obey. It seems to follow that I am committed to the view that in certain logically possible circumstances it would not be wrong to disobey God. This position seems to be inconsistent with the theory that 'wrong' means 'contrary to God's commands'.

I want to argue, however, that it is still open to me to accept a modified form of the divine command theory of ethical wrongness. According to the modified divine command theory, when I say, 'It is wrong to do X', (at least part of) what I *mean* is that it is contrary to God's commands to do X. 'It is wrong to do X' *implies* 'It is contrary to God's commands to do X.' But 'It is contrary to God's commands to do X' implies "It is wrong to do X' only if certain conditions are assumed—namely, only if it is assumed that God has the character which I believe Him to have, of loving His human creatures. If God were really to command us to make cruelty our goal, then He would not have that character of loving us, and I would not say it would be wrong to disobey Him.

But do I say that it would be wrong to obey Him in such a case? This is the point at which I am in danger of abandoning the divine command theory completely. I do abandon it completely if I say both of the following things.

(A)   It would be wrong to obey God if He commanded cruelty for its own sake.
(B)   In (A), 'wrong' is used in what is for me its normal ethical sense.

If I assert both (A) and (B), it is clear that I cannot consistently maintain that 'wrong' in its normal ethical sense for me means or implies 'contrary to God's commands.'

---

[1] Guillelus de Occam, *Super 4 libros sententiarum*, bk. II, qu. 19, 0, in vol. IV of his *Opera plurima* (Lyon, 1494–6; reimpression en fac-simile, Farnborough, Hants, England: Gregg Press, 1962). I am not claiming that Ockham held a divine command theory of exactly the same sort that I have been discussing.—R.M.A.

But from the fact that I deny that it would be wrong to disobey God if He commanded cruelty for its own sake, it does not follow that I must accept (A) and (B). Of course someone might claim that obedience and disobedience would both be ethically permitted in such a case; but that is not the view that I am suggesting. If I adopt the modified divine command theory as an analysis of my present concept of ethical wrongness (and if I adopt a similar analysis of my concept of ethical permittedness), I will not hold either that it would be wrong to disobey, or that it would be ethically permitted to disobey, or that it would be wrong to obey, or that it would be ethically permitted to obey, if God commanded cruelty for its own sake. For I will say that my concept of ethical wrongness (and my concept of ethical permittedness) would 'break down' if I really believed that God commanded cruelty for its own sake. Or to put the matter somewhat more prosaically, I will say that my concepts of ethical wrongness and permittedness could not serve the functions they now serve, because using those concepts I could not call any action ethically wrong or ethically permitted, if I believed that God's will was so unloving. This position can be explained or developed in either of two ways, each of which has its advantages.

I could say that by 'X is ethically wrong' I mean 'X is contrary to the commands of a *loving* God' (i.e., 'There is a *loving* God and X is contrary to His commands') and by 'X is ethically permitted' I mean 'X is in accord with the commands of a *loving* God' (i.e., 'There is a *loving* God and X is not contrary to His commands'). On this analysis we can reason as follows. If there is only one God and He commands cruelty for its own sake, then presumably there is not a *loving* God. If there is not a loving God then neither 'X is ethically wrong' nor 'X is ethically permitted' is true of any X. Using my present concepts of ethical wrongness and permittedness, therefore, I could not (consistently) call any action ethically wrong or permitted if I believed that God commanded cruelty for its own sake. This way of developing the modified divine command theory is the simpler and neater of the two, and that might reasonably lead one to choose it for the construction of a theological ethical theory. On the other hand, I think it is also simpler and neater than ordinary religious ethical discourse, in which (for example) it may be felt that the statement that a certain act is wrong is *about* the will or commands of God in a way in which it is not about His love.

In this essay I shall prefer a second, rather similar, but somewhat untidier, understanding of the modified divine command theory, because I think it may lead us into some insights about the complexities of actual religious ethical discourse. According to this second version of the theory, the statement that something is ethically wrong (or permitted) says something about the will or commands of God, but not about His love. Every such statement, however, *presupposes* that certain conditions for the applicability of the believer's concepts of ethical right and wrong are satisfied. Among these conditions is that God does not command cruelty for its own sake—or, more generally, that God loves His human creatures. It need not be assumed that God's love is the only such condition.

The modified divine command theorist can say that the possibility of God commanding cruelty for its own sake is not provided for in the Judeo-Christian religious ethical system as he understands it. The possibility is not provided for, in the sense that the concepts of right and wrong have not been developed in such a way that actions could be correctly said to be right or wrong if God were believed to command cruelty for its own sake. The modified divine command theorist agrees that it is

logically possible[2] that God should command cruelty for its own sake; but he holds
that it is unthinkable that God should do so. To have *faith* in God is not just to believe
that He exists, but also to trust in His love for mankind. The believer's concepts of
ethical wrongness and permittedness are developed within the framework of his (or
the religious community's) religious life, and therefore within the framework of the
assumption that God loves us. The concept of the will or commands of God has a
certain function in the believer's life, and the use of the words 'right' (in the sense of
'ethically permitted') and 'wrong' is tied to that function of that concept. But one of
the reasons why the concept of the will of God can function as it does is that the love
which God is believed to have toward men arouses in the believer certain attitudes of
love toward God and devotion to His will. If the believer thinks about the unthinkable
but logically possible situation in which God commands cruelty for its own sake, he
finds that in relation to that kind of command of God he cannot take up the same
attitude, and that the concept of the will or commands of God could not then have the
same function in his life. For this reason he will not say that it would be wrong to
disobey God, or right to obey Him, in that situation. At the same time he will not say
that it would be wrong to obey God in that situation, because he is accustomed to use
the word 'wrong' to say that something is contrary to the will of God, and it does not
seem to him to be the right word to use to express his own personal revulsion toward
an act against which there would be no divine authority. Similarly, he will not say that
it would be 'right,' in the sense of 'ethically permitted,' to disobey God's command of
cruelty; for that does not seem to him to be the right way to express his own personal
attitude toward an act which would not be in accord with a divine authority. In this way
the believer's concepts of ethical rightness and wrongness would break down in the
situation in which he believed that God commanded cruelty for its own sake—that is,
they would not function as they now do, because he would not be prepared to use them
to say that any action was right or wrong.

· *III* ·

It is clear that according to this modified divine command theory, the meaning of the
word 'wrong' in Judeo-Christian ethical discourse must be understood in terms of a
complex of relations which believers' use of the word has, not only to their beliefs
about God's commands, but also to their attitudes toward certain types of action. I
think it will help us to understand the theory better if we can give a brief but fairly
comprehensive description of the most important features of the Judeo-Christian
ethical use of 'wrong,' from the point of view of the modified divine command theory.
That is what I shall try to do in this section.

(1) 'Wrong' and 'contrary to God's commands' at least contextually imply each
other in Judeo-Christian ethical discourse. 'It is wrong to do X' will be assented to by
the sincere Jewish or Christian believer if and only if he assents to 'It is contrary to
God's commands to do X.' This is a fact sufficiently well known that the known
believer who says the one commits himself publicly to the other.

---

[2] Perhaps he will even think it is causally possible, but I do not regard any view on that issue as an integral
part of the theory. The question whether it is causally possible for God to act 'out of character' is a
difficult one which we need not go into here.—R.M.A.

Indeed 'wrong' and such expressions as 'against the will of God' seem to be used interchangeably in religious ethical discourse. If a believer asks his pastor, 'Do you think it's always against the will of God to use contraceptives?' and the pastor replies, 'I don't see anything wrong with the use of contraceptives in many cases,' the pastor has answered the same question the inquirer asked.

(2) In ethical contexts, the statement that a certain action is wrong normally expresses certain volitional and emotional attitudes toward that action. In particular it normally expresses an intention, or at least an inclination, not to perform the action, and/or dispositions to feel guilty if one has performed it, to discourage others from performing it, and to react with anger, sorrow, or diminished respect toward others if they have performed it. I think this is true of Judeo-Christian ethical discourse as well as of other ethical discourse.

The interchangeability of 'wrong' and 'against the will of God' applies in full force here. It seems to make no difference to the expressive function of an ethical statement in a Judeo-Christian context which of these expressions is used. So far as I can see, the feelings and dispositions normally expressed by 'It is wrong to commit suicide' in a Judeo-Christian context are exactly the same as those normally expressed by 'It is against God's will to commit suicide,' or by 'Suicide is a violation of the commandments of God.'

I am speaking of attitudes *normally* expressed by statements that it is wrong to do a certain thing, or that it would be against God's will or commands to do that thing. I am not claiming that such attitudes are *always* expressed by statements of those sorts. Neither am I now suggesting any analysis of the *meaning* of the statements in terms of the attitudes they normally express. The relation between the meaning of the statements and the attitudes expressed is a matter about which I shall have somewhat more to say, later in this section and in Section VI. At this point I am simply observing that in fact statements of the forms 'It is wrong to do X,' 'It is against God's will to do X,' 'X is a violation of the commandments of God,' normally do express certain attitudes, and that in Judeo-Christian ethical discourse they all typically express the same attitudes.

Of course these attitudes can be specified only within certain very wide limits of normality. The experience of guilt, for instance, or the feelings that one has about conduct of others of which one disapproves, vary greatly from one individual to another, and in the same individual from one occasion to another.

(3) In a Judeo-Christian context, moreover, the attitudes expressed by a statement that something is wrong are normally quite strongly affected and colored by specifically religious feelings and interests. They are apt to be motivated in various degrees by, and mixed in various proportions with, love, devotion, and loyalty toward God, and/or fear of God. Ethical wrongdoing is seen and experienced as *sin*, as rupture of personal or communal relationship with God. The normal feelings and experience of guilt for Judeo-Christian believers surely cannot be separated from beliefs, and ritual and devotional practices, having to do with God's judgment and forgiveness.

In all sin there is offense against a person (God), even when there is no offense against any other human person—for instance, if I have a vice which harms me but does not importantly harm any other human being. Therefore in the Judeo-Christian tradition reactions which are appropriate when one has offended another person are felt to be appropriate reactions to any ethical fault, regardless of whether another human being has been offended. I think this affects rather importantly the emotional connections of the word 'wrong' in Judeo-Christian discourse.

(4) When a Judeo-Christian believer is trying to decide, in an ethical way, whether it would be wrong for him to do a certain thing, he typically thinks of himself as trying to determine whether it would be against God's will for him to do it. His deliberations may turn on the interpretation of certain religiously authoritative texts. They may be partly carried out in the form of prayer. It is quite possible, however, that his deliberations will take forms more familiar to the nonbeliever. Possibly his theology will encourage him to give some weight to his own intuitions and feelings about the matter, and those of other people. Such encouragement might be provided, for instance, by a doctrine of the leading of the Holy Spirit. Probably the believer will accept certain very general ethical principles as expressing commandments of God, and most of these may be principles which many nonbelievers would also accept (for instance, that it is always, or with very few exceptions, wrong to kill another human being). The believer's deliberation might consist entirely of reasoning from such general principles. But he would still regard it as an attempt to discover God's will on the matter.

(5) Typically, the Judeo-Christian believer is a nonnaturalist objectivist about ethical wrongness. When he says that something is (ethically) wrong, he means to be stating what he believes to be a fact of a certain sort—what I shall call a 'nonnatural objective fact'. Such a fact is objective in the sense that whether it obtains or not does not depend on whether any human being thinks it does. It is harder to give a satisfactory explanation of what I mean by 'nonnatural' here. Let us say that a nonnatural fact is one which does not consist simply in any fact or complex of facts which can be stated entirely in the languages of physics, chemistry, biology, and human psychology. That way of putting it obviously raises questions which it leaves unanswered, but I hope it may be clear enough for present purposes.

That ethical facts are objective and nonnatural has been believed by many people, including some famous philosophers—for instance, Plato and G. E. Moore. The term 'nonnaturalism' is sometimes used rather narrowly, to refer to a position held by Moore, and positions closely resembling it. Clearly, I am using 'nonnaturalist' in a broader sense here.

Given that the facts of wrongness asserted in Judeo-Christian ethics are nonnatural in the sense explained above, and that they accordingly do not consist entirely in facts of physics, chemistry, biology, and human psychology, the question arises, in what they do consist. According to the divine command theory (even the modified divine command theory), in so far as they are nonnatural and objective, they consist in facts about the will or commands of God. I think this is really the central point in a divine command theory of ethical wrongness. This is the point at which the divine command theory is distinguished from alternative theological theories of ethical wrongness, such as the theory that facts of ethical rightness and wrongness are objective, nonnatural facts about ideas or essences subsisting eternally in God's understanding, not subject to His will but guiding it.

The divine command account of the nonnatural fact-stating function of Judeo-Christian ethical discourse has at least one advantage over its competitors. It is clear, I think, that in stating that X is wrong a believer normally commits himself to the view that X is contrary to the will or commands of God. And the fact (if it is a fact) that X is contrary to the will or commands of God is surely a nonnatural objective fact. But it is not nearly so clear that in saying that X is wrong, the believer normally commits himself to belief in any *other* nonnatural objective fact. (The preceding sentence presupposes the rejection of the Moorean view that the fact that X is wrong[3] is an objective nonnatural fact which cannot and should not be analyzed in terms of other facts, natural or nonnatural.)

(6) The modified divine command theorist cannot consistently claim that 'wrong' and 'contrary to God's commands' have exactly the same meaning for him. For he admits that there is a logically possible situation which he would describe by saying, 'God commands cruelty for its own sake,' but not by saying, 'It would be wrong not to practice cruelty for its own sake.' If there were not at least some little difference between the meanings with which he actually, normally uses the expressions 'wrong' and 'contrary to God's commands,' there would be no reason for them to differ in their applicability or inapplicability to the far-out unthinkable case. We may now be in a position to improve somewhat our understanding of what the modified divine command theorist can suppose that difference in meaning to be, and of why he supposes that the believer is unwilling to say that disobedience to a divine command of cruelty for its own sake would be wrong.

We have seen that the expressions 'It is wrong' and 'It is contrary to God's commands' or 'It is against the will of God' have virtually the same uses in religious ethical discourse, and the same functions in the religious ethical life. No doubt they differ slightly in the situations in which they are most likely to be used and the emotional overtones they are most apt to carry. But in all situations experienced or expected by the believer as a believer they at least contextually imply each other, and normally express the same or extremely similar emotional and volitional attitudes.

There is also a difference in meaning, however, a difference which is normally of no practical importance. All three of the following are aspects of the normal use of 'it is wrong' in the life and conversation of believers. (a) It is used to state what are believed to be facts about the will or commands of God. (b) It is used in formulating decisions and arguments about what to do (i.e., not just in deciding what one *ought* to do but in deciding *what to do*). (c) It expresses certain emotional and volitional attitudes toward the action under discussion. 'It is wrong' is commonly used to do all three of those things at once.

The same is true of 'It is contrary to God's commands' and 'It is against the will of God.' They are commonly used by believers to do the same three things, and to do them at once. But because of their grammatical form and their formal relationships with other straightforwardly descriptive expressions about God, they are taken to be, first and last, descriptive expressions about God and His relation to whatever actions are under discussion. They can therefore be used to state what are supposed to be facts about God, even when one's emotional and decision-making attitude toward those supposed facts is quite contrary to the attitudes normally expressed by the words 'against the will of God.'

In the case of 'It is wrong,' however, it is not clear that one of its functions, or one of the aspects of its normal use, is to be preferred in case of conflict with the others. I am not willing to say, 'It would be wrong not to do X,' when both my own attitude

---

[3] Moore took goodness and badness as primitive, rather than rightness and wrongness; but that need not concern us here.—R.M.A.

and the attitude of most other people toward the doing of X under the indicated circumstances is one of unqualified revulsion. On the other hand, neither am I willing to say, 'It would be wrong to do X,' when I would merely be expressing my own personal revulsion (and perhaps that of other people as well) but nothing that I could regard as clothed in the majesty of a divine authority. The believer's concept of ethical wrongness therefore breaks down if one tries to apply it to the unthinkable case in which God commands cruelty for its own sake.

None of this seems to me inconsistent with the claim that part of what the believer normally means in saying 'X is wrong' is that X is contrary to God's will or commands.

· *IV* ·

The modified divine command theory clearly conceives of believers as valuing some things independently of their relation to God's commands. If the believer will not say that it would be wrong not to practice cruelty for its own sake if God commanded it, that is because he values kindness, and has a revulsion for cruelty, in a way that is at least to some extent independent of his belief that God commands kindness and forbids cruelty. This point may be made the basis of both philosophical and theological objections to the modified divine command theory, but I think the objections can be answered.

The philosophical objection is, roughly, that if there are some things I value independently of their relation to God's commands, then my value concepts cannot rightly be analyzed in terms of God's commands. According to the modified divine command theory, the acceptability of divine command ethics depends in part on the believer's independent positive valuation of the sorts of things that God is believed to command. But then, the philosophical critic objects, the believer must have a prior, nontheological conception of ethical right and wrong, in terms of which he judges God's commandments to be acceptable—and to admit that the believer has a prior, nontheological conception of ethical right and wrong is to abandon the divine command theory.

The weakness of this philosophical objection is that it fails to note the distinctions that can be drawn among various value concepts. From the fact that the believer values some things independently of his beliefs about God's commands, the objector concludes, illegitimately, that the believer must have a conception of ethical right and wrong that is independent of his beliefs about God's commands. This inference is illegitimate because there can be valuations which do not imply or presuppose a judgment of ethical right or wrong. For instance, I may simply like something, or want something, or feel a revulsion at something.

What the modified divine command theorist will hold, then, is that the believer values some things independently of their relation to God's commands, but that these valuations are not judgments of ethical right and wrong and do not of themselves imply judgments of ethical right and wrong. He will maintain, on the other hand, that such independent valuations are involved in, or even necessary for, judgments of ethical right and wrong which also involve beliefs about God's will or commands. The adherent of a divine command ethics will normally be able to give reasons for his adherence. Such reasons might include: 'Because I am grateful to God for His love'; 'Because I find it the most satisfying form of ethical life'; 'Because there's got to be an objective moral law if life isn't to fall to pieces, and I can't understand what it would be if not the will of God.'[4] As we have already noted, the modified divine command theorist also has reasons why he would not accept a divine command ethics in certain logically possible situations which he believes not to be actual. All of these reasons seem to me to involve valuations that are independent of divine command ethics. The person who has such reasons wants certain things—happiness, certain satisfactions—for himself and others; he hates cruelty and loves kindness; he has perhaps a certain unique and 'numinous' awe of God. And these are not attitudes which he has simply because of his beliefs about God's commands.[5] They are not attitudes, however, which presuppose judgments of moral right and wrong.

It is sometimes objected to divine command theories of moral obligation, or of ethical rightness and wrongness, that one must have some reason for obeying God's commands or for adopting a divine command ethics, and that therefore a nontheological concept of moral obligation or of ethical rightness and wrongness must be presupposed, in order that one may judge that one ought to obey God's commands.[6] This objection is groundless. For one can certainly have reasons for doing something which do not involve believing one morally ought to do it or believing it would be ethically wrong not to do it.

I grant that in giving reasons for his attitudes toward God's commands the believer will probably use or presuppose concepts which, in the context, it is reasonable to count as nontheological value concepts (e.g., concepts of satisfactoriness and repulsiveness). Perhaps some of them might count as moral concepts. But all that the defender of a divine command theory of ethical wrongness has to maintain is that the concept of ethical wrongness which occurs in the ethical thought and discourse of believers is not one of the concepts which are used or presupposed in this way. Divine command theorists, including the modified divine command theorist, need not maintain that *all* value concepts, must be understood in terms of God's commands.

In fact some well-known philosophers have held forms of divine command theory which quite explicitly presuppose some nontheological value concepts. Locke, for instance, says in his *Essay*,

> Good and evil . . . are nothing but pleasure or pain, or that which occasions or procures pleasure or pain to us. *Morally good and evil*, then, is only the conformity or disagreement of our voluntary actions to some law, whereby good or evil is drawn on us from the will and power of the law maker. . . . (*Essay*, II.xxviii.5)[7]

---

[4] The mention of moral law in the last of these reasons may presuppose the ability to *mention* concepts of moral right and wrong, which may or may not be theological and which may or may be concepts one uses oneself to make judgments of right and wrong. So far as I can see, it does not *presuppose* the *use* of such concepts to make judgments of right and wrong, or one's adoption of them for such use, which is the crucial point here.—R.M.A.

[5] The independence ascribed to these attitudes is not a *genetic* independence. It may be that the person would not have come to have some of them had it not been for his religious beliefs. The point is that he has come to hold them in such a way that his holding them does not now depend entirely on his beliefs about God's commands.—R.M.A.

[6] I take A. C. Ewing to be offering an objection to this type on p. 112 of his book *Ethics* (London: English University Press, 1953).—R.M.A.

[7] I quote from John Yolton's edition of *An Essay Concerning Human Understanding*, 2 vols. (London and New York: Everyman's Library, 1967).—R.M.A.

Locke goes on to distinguish three laws, or types of law, by reference to which actions are commonly judged as to moral good and evil: '(1) The *divine* law. (2) The *civil* law. (3) The law of *opinion* or *reputation*, if I may so call it' (*Essay*, II.xxviii.7). Of these three Locke says that the third is 'the common *measure of virtue and vice*' (*Essay*, II.xxviii.11). In Locke's opinion the terms 'virtue' and 'vice' are particularly closely attached to the praise and blame of society. But the terms 'duty' and 'sin' are connected with the commandments of God. About the divine law Locke says,

> This is the only true touchstone of *moral rectitude*; and by comparing them to this law, it is that men judge of the most considerable *moral good* or *evil* of their actions: that is, whether, as *duties or sins*, they are like to procure them happiness or misery from the hands of the ALMIGHTY. (*Essay*, II.xxviii.8).

The structure of Locke's analysis is clear enough. By 'good' and 'evil' we *mean* (nontheologically enough) pleasurable and painful. By 'morally good' and 'morally evil' we *mean* that the actions so described agree or disagree with some law under which the agent stands to be rewarded or punished. By 'duty' and 'sin,' which denote the most important sort of moral good and evil, we *mean* (theologically now) actions which are apt to cause the agent good or evil (in the nontheological sense) because they agree or disagree with the law of God. I take it that the divine command theory advocated by Peter Geach,[8] and hinted at by Miss Anscombe,[9] is similar in structure, though not in all details, to Locke's.

The modified divine command theory that I have in mind does not rely as heavily as Locke's theory does on God's power to reward and punish, nor do I wish to assume Locke's analysis of 'good' and 'evil.' The point I want to make by discussing Locke here is just that there are many different value concepts and it is clearly possible to give one or more of them a theological analysis while giving others a nontheological analysis. And I do assume that the modified divine command theorist will give a nontheological analysis of some value concepts although he gives a theological analysis of the concept of ethical wrongness. For instance, he may give a nontheological analysis, perhaps a naturalistic one or a noncognitivist one, of the meaning of 'satisfactory' and 'repulsive', as he uses them in some contexts. He may even regard as *moral* concepts some value concepts of which he gives a nontheological analysis.

For it is not essential to a divine command theory of ethical wrongness to maintain that all valuing, or all value concepts, or even all moral concepts, depend on beliefs about God's commands. What is essential to such a theory is to maintain that when a believer says something is (ethically) *wrong*, at least part of what he means is that the action in question is contrary to God's will or commands. Another way of putting the matter is this. What depends on beliefs about God and His will is: not all of the religious person's value concepts, nor in general his ability to value things, but only his ability to appraise actions (and possible actions) in terms of their relation to a superhuman, nonnaturally objective, law. Indeed, it is obvious that Judeo-Christian ethics presupposes concepts that have at least ethical overtones and that are not essentially theological but have their background in human social relations and political institutions—such as the concepts of promise, kindness, law, and command.

---

[8] In *God and the Soul* (London: Routledge, 1969), ch. 9. [Reading XI.]—R.M.A.

[9] G. E. M. Anscombe, 'Modern Moral Philosophy', *Philosophy*, 33 (1958), pp. 1–19.—R.M.A.

What the specifically theological doctrines introduce into Judeo-Christian ethics, according to the divine command theory, is the belief in a law that is superior to all human laws.

This version of the divine command theory may seem *theologically* objectionable to some believers. One of the reasons, surely, why divine command theories of ethics have appealed to some theologians is that such theories seem especially congruous with the religious demand that God be the object of our highest allegiance. If our supreme commitment in life is to doing what is right just because it is right, and if what is right is right just because God wills or commands it, then surely our highest allegiance is to God. But the modified divine command theory seems not to have this advantage. For the modified divine command theorist is forced to admit, as we have seen, that he has reasons for his adherence to a divine command ethics, and that his having these reasons implies that there are some things which he values independently of his beliefs about God's commands. It is therefore not correct to say of him that he is committed to doing the will of God *just* because it is the will of God; he is committed to doing it partly because of other things which he values independently. Indeed it appears that there are certain logically possible situations in which his present attitudes would not commit him to obey God's commands (for instance, if God commanded cruelty for its own sake). This may even suggest that he values some things, not just independently of God's commands, but more than God's commands.

We have here a real problem in religious ethical motivation. The Judeo-Christian believer is supposed to make God the supreme focus of his loyalties; that is clear. One possible interpretation of this fact is the following. Obedience to whatever God may command is (or at least ought to be) the one thing that the believer values for its own sake and more than anything and everything else. Anything else that he values, he values (or ought to) only to a lesser degree and as a means to obedience to God. This conception of religious ethical motivation is obviously favorable to an *un*modified divine command theory of ethical wrongness.

But I think it is not a realistic conception. Loyalty to God, for instance, is very often explained, by believers themselves, as motivated by gratitude for benefits conferred. And I think it is clear in most cases that the gratitude presupposes that the benefits are valued, at least to some extent, independently of loyalty to God. Similarly, I do not think that most devout Judeo-Christian believers would say that it would be wrong to disobey God if He commanded cruelty for its own sake. And if I am right about that I thinks it shows that their positive valuation of (emotional/volitional pro-attitude toward) doing *whatever* God may command is not clearly greater than their independent negative valuation of cruelty.

In analyzing ethical motivation in general, as well as Judeo-Christian ethical motivation in particular, it is probably a mistake to suppose that there is (or can be expected to be) one thing only that is valued supremely and for its own sake, with nothing else being valued independently of it. The motivation for a person's ethical orientation in life is normally much more complex than that, and involves a plurality of emotional and volitional attitudes of different sorts which are at least partly independent of each other. At any rate, I think the modified divine command theorist is bound to say that that is true of his ethical motivation.

In what sense, then, can the modified divine command theorist maintain that God is the supreme focus of his loyalties? I suggest the following interpretation of the single-hearted loyalty to God which is demanded in Judeo-Christian religion. In this interpretation the crucial idea is *not* that some one thing is valued for its own sake and more than anything else, and nothing else valued independently of it. It is freely admitted that the religious person will have a plurality or motives for his ethical position, and that these will be at least partly independent of each other. It is admitted further that a desire to obey the commands of God (*whatever* they may be) may not be the strongest of these motives. What will be claimed is that certain beliefs about God enable the believer to integrate or focus his motives in a loyalty to God and His commands. Some of these beliefs are about what God commands or will (contingently—that is, although He could logically have commanded or willed something else instead).

Some of the motives in question might be called egoistic; they include desires for satisfactions for oneself—which God is believed to have given or to be going to give. Other motives may be desires for satisfaction for other people; these may be called altruistic. Still other motives might not be desires for anyone's satisfaction, but might be valuations of certain kinds of action for their own sakes; these might be called idealistic. I do not think my argument depends heavily on this particular classification, but it seems plausible that all of these types, and perhaps others as well, might be distinguished among the motives for a religious person's ethical position. Obviously such motives might pull one in different directions, conflicting with one another. But in Judeo-Christian ethics beliefs about what God does in fact will (although He could have willed otherwise) are supposed to enable one to *fuse* these motives, so to speak, into one's devotion to God and His will, so that they all pull together. Doubtless the believer will still have some motives which conflict with his loyalty to God. But the religious ideal is that these should all be merely momentary desires and impulses, and kept under control. They ought not to be allowed to influence voluntary action. The deeper, more stable, and controlling desires, intentions, and psychic energies are supposed to be fused in devotion to God. As I interpret it, however, it need not be inconsistent with the Judeo-Christian ethical and religious ideal that this fusion of motives, this integration of moral energies, depends on belief in certain propositions which are taken to be contingent truths about God.

Lest it be thought that I am proposing unprecedented theological positions, or simply altering Judeo-Christian religious beliefs to suit my theories, I will call to my aid on this point a theologian known for his insistence on the sovereignty of God. Karl Barth seems to me to hold a divine command theory of ethics. But when he raises the question of why we should obey God, he rejects with scorn the suggestion that God's *power* provides the basis for His claim on us. 'By deciding for God [man] has definitely decided not to be obedient to power as power.'[10] God's claim on us is based rather on His grace. 'God calls us and orders us and claims us by being gracious to us in Jesus Christ.'[11] I do not mean to suggest that Barth would agree with everything I have said about motivation, or that he offers a lucid account of a divine command theory. But he does agree with the positions I have proposed on this point, that the believer's loyalty is not to be construed as a loyalty to God *as* all-powerful, nor to God *whatever* He might

---

[10] Karl Barth, *Church Dogmatics*, Vol. II, Pt. 2, trans. G. W. Bromiley and others (Edinburgh: T. & T. Clark, 1957), p. 553.—R.M.A.

[11] Ibid., p. 560.—R.M.A.

conceivably have willed. It is a loyalty to God *as* having a certain attitude toward us, a certain will for us, which God was free not to have, but to which in Barth's view, He has committed Himself irrevocably in Jesus Christ. The believer's devotion is not to merely possible commands of God as such, but to God's actual (and gracious) will.

. *V* .

The ascription of moral qualities to God is commonly thought to cause problems for divine command theories of ethics. It is doubted that God, as an agent, can properly be called 'good' in the moral sense if He is not subject to a moral law that is not of His own making. For if He is morally good, mustn't He do what is right *because* it is right? And how can He do that, if what's right is right because He wills it? Or it may be charged that divine command theories trivialize the claim that God is good. If 'X is (morally) good' means roughly 'X does what God wills,' then 'God is (morally) good' means only that God does what He wills—which is surely much less than people are normally taken to mean when they say that God is (morally) good. In this section I will suggest an answer to those objections.

Surely no analysis of Judeo-Christian ethical discourse can be regarded as adequate which does not provide for a sense in which the believer can seriously assert that God is good. Indeed an adequate analysis should provide a plausible account of what believers so in fact mean when they say, 'God is good.' I believe that a divine command theory of ethical (rightness and) wrongness can include such an account. I will try to indicate its chief features.

(1) In saying 'God is good' one is normally expressing a favorable emotional attitude toward God. I shall not try to determine whether or not this is part of the meaning of 'God is good'; but it is normally, perhaps almost always, at least one of the things one is doing if one says that God is good. If we were to try to be more precise about the type of favorable emotional attitude normally expressed by 'God is good,' I suspect we would find that the attitude expressed is most commonly one of *gratitude*.

(2) This leads to a second point, which is that when God is called 'good' it is very often meant that He is *good to us*, or *good to* the speaker. 'Good' is sometimes virtually a synonym for 'kind.' And for the modified divine command theorist it is not a trivial truth that God is kind. In saying that God is good in the sense of 'kind,' one presupposes, of course, that there are some things which the beneficiaries of God's goodness value. We need not discuss here whether the beneficiaries must value them independently of their beliefs about God's will. For the modified divine command theorist does admit that there are some things which believers value independently of their beliefs about God's commands. Nothing that the modified divine command theorist says about the meaning of ('right' and) 'wrong' implies that it is a trivial truth that God bestows on His creatures things that they value.

(3) I would not suggest that the descriptive force of 'good' as applied to God is exhausted by the notion of kindness. 'God is good' must be taken in many contexts as

---

[12] The argument here is similar to one which is used for another purpose by Ninian Smart in 'Omnipotence Evil, and Superman', *Philosophy*, 36 (1961), reprinted in Nelson Pike, ed., *God and Evil* (Englewood Cliffs, N. J.: Prentice-Hall, 1964), pp. 103–12.
   I do not mean to endorse the doctrines of divine impassibility and theological determinism.—R.M.A.

ascribing to God, rather generally, qualities of character which the believing speaker regards as virtues in human beings. Among such qualities might be faithfulness, ethical consistency, a forgiving disposition, and, in general, various aspects of love, as well as kindness. Not that there is some definite list of qualities, the ascription of which to God is clearly implied by the claim that God is good. But saying that God is good normally commits one to the position that God has some important set of qualities which one regards as virtues in human beings.

(4) It will not be thought that God has *all* the qualities which are virtues in human beings. Some such qualities are logically inapplicable to a being such as God is supposed to be. For example, aside from certain complications arising from the doctrine of the incarnation, it would be logically inappropriate to speak of God as controlling His sexual desires. (He doesn't have any.) And given some widely held conceptions of God and His relation to the world, it would hardly make sense to speak of Him as *courageous*. For if He is impassible and has predetermined absolutely everything that happens, He has no risks to face and cannot endure (because He cannot suffer) pain or displeasure.[12]

Believers in God's goodness also typically think He lacks some human virtues which would *not* be logically inapplicable to a being like Him. A virtuous man, for instance, does not intentionally cause the death of other human beings, except under exceptional circumstances. But God has intentionally brought it about that all men die. There are agonizing forms of the problem of evil; but I think that for most Judeo-Christian believers (especially those who believe in life after death), this is not one of them. They believe that God's making men mortal and His commanding them not to kill each other, fit together in a larger pattern of harmonious purposes. How then can one distinguish between human virtues which God must have if He is good and human virtues which God may lack and still be good? This is an interesting and important question, but I will not attempt here to formulate a precise or adequate criterion for making the distinction. I fear it would require a lengthy digression from the issues with which we are principally concerned.

(5) If we accept a divine command theory of ethical rightness and wrongness, I think we shall have to say that *dutifulness* is a human virtue which, like sexual chastity, is logically inapplicable to God. God cannot either do or fail to do His duty, since He does not have a duty—at least not in the most important sense in which human beings have a duty. For He is not subject to a moral law not of His own making. Dutifulness is one virtuous disposition which men can have that God cannot have. But there are other virtuous dispositions which God can have as well as men. Love, for instance. It hardly makes sense to say that God does what he does *because* it is right. But it does not follow that God cannot have any reason for doing what He does. It does not even follow that He cannot have reasons of a type on which it would be morally virtuous for a man to act. For example, He might do something because He knew it would make His creatures happier.

(6) The modified divine command theorist must deny that in calling God 'good' one presupposes a standard of moral rightness and wrongness superior to the will of God, by reference to which it is determined whether God's character is virtuous or not. And I think he can consistently deny that. He can say that morally virtuous and vicious qualities of character are those which agree and conflict, respectively, with God's commands, and that it is their agreement or disagreement with God's commands

that makes them virtuous or vicious. But the believer normally thinks he has at least a general idea of what qualities of character are in fact virtuous and vicious (approved and disapproved by God). Having such an idea, he can apply the word 'good' descriptively to God, meaning that (with some exceptions, as I have noted) God has the qualities which the believer regards as virtues, such as faithfulness and kindness.

I will sum up by contrasting what the believer can mean when he says, 'Moses is good,' with what he can mean when he says, 'God is good,' according to the modified divine command theory. When the believer says, 'Moses is good,' (a) he normally is expressing a favorable emotional attitude toward Moses—normally, though perhaps not always. (Sometimes a person's moral goodness displeases us.) (b) He normally implies that Moses possesses a large proportion of those qualities of character which are recognized in the religious-ethical community as virtues, and few if any of those which are regarded as vices. (c) He normally implies that the qualities of Moses' character on the basis of which he described Moses as good are qualities approved by God.

When the believer says, 'God is good', (a) he normally is expressing a favorable emotional attitude toward God—and I think exceptions on this point would be rarer than in the case of statements that a man is good. (b) He normally is ascribing to God certain qualities of character. He may mean primarily that God is kind or benevolent, that He is *good to* human beings or certain ones of them. Or he may mean that God possesses (with some exceptions) those qualities of character which are regarded as virtues in the religious-ethical community. (c) Whereas in saying, 'Moses is good,' the believer was stating or implying that the qualities of character which he was ascribing to Moses conform to a standard of ethical rightness which is independent of the will of Moses, he is not stating or implying that the qualities of character which he ascribes to God conform to a standard of ethical rightness which is independent of the will of God.

· VI ·

As I noted at the outset, the divine command theory of ethical wrongness, even in its modified form, has the consequence that believers and nonbelievers use the word 'wrong' with different meanings in ethical contexts, since it will hardly be thought that nonbelievers mean by 'wrong' what the theory says believers mean by it. This consequence gives rise to an objection. For the phenomena of common moral discourse between believers and nonbelievers suggest that they mean the same thing by 'wrong' in ethical contexts. In the present section I shall try to explain how the modified divine command theorist can account for the facts of common ethical discourse.

I will first indicate what I think the troublesome facts are. Judeo-Christian believers enter into ethical discussions with people whose religious or anti-religious beliefs they do not know. It seems to be possible to conduct quite a lot of ethical discourse, with apparent understanding, without knowing one's partner's views on religious issues. Believers also discuss ethical questions with persons who are known to them to be nonbelievers. They agree with such persons, disagree with them, and try to persuade them, about what acts are morally wrong. (Or at least it is normally *said*, by the participants and others, that they agree and disagree about such issues.) Believers ascribe, to people who are known not to believe in God, beliefs that certain acts are morally wrong. Yet surely believers do not suppose that nonbelievers, in calling acts wrong, mean that they are contrary to the will or commandments of God. Under these circumstances how can the believer really mean 'contrary to the will or command-ments of God' when he says 'wrong'? If he agrees and disagrees with nonbelievers about what is wrong, if he ascribes to them beliefs that certain acts are wrong, must he not be using 'wrong' in a nontheological sense?

What I shall argue is that in some ordinary (and I fear imprecise) sense of 'mean,' what believers and nonbelievers mean by 'wrong' in ethical contexts may well be partly the same and partly different. There are agreements between believers and nonbe-lievers which make common moral discourse between them possible. But these agreements do not show that the two groups mean exactly the same thing by 'wrong.' They do not show that 'contrary to God's will or commands' is not part of what believers mean by 'wrong.'

Let us consider first the agreements which make possible common moral dis-course between believers and nonbelievers. (1) One important agreement, which is so obvious as to be easily overlooked, is that they use many of the same ethical terms— 'wrong,' 'right,' 'ought,' 'duty,' and others. And they may utter many of the same ethical sentences, such as 'Racial discrimination is morally wrong.' In determining what people believe we rely very heavily on what they say (when they seem to be speaking sincerely)—and that means in large part, on the words that they use and the sentences they utter. If I know that somebody says with apparent sincerity, 'Racial discrimination is morally wrong,' I will normally ascribe to him the belief that racial discrimination is morally wrong, even if I also know that he does not mean *exactly* the same thing as I do by 'racial discrimination' or 'morally wrong.' Of course if I know he means something *completely* different, I would not ascribe the belief to him without explicit qualification.

I would not claim that believers and nonbelievers use *all* the same ethical terms. 'Sin,' 'law of God,' and 'Christian,' for instance, occur as ethical terms in the discourse of many believers, but would be much less likely to occur in the same way in nonbelievers' discourse.

(2) The shared ethical terms have the same basic grammatical status for believers as for nonbelievers, and at least many of the same logical connections with other expressions. Everyone agrees, for instance, in treating 'wrong' as an adjective and 'Racial discrimination is morally wrong' as a declaration sentence. '(All) racial dis-crimination is morally wrong' would be treated by all parties as expressing an A-type (universal affirmative) proposition, from which consequences can be drawn by syllo-gistic reasoning or the predicate calculus. All agree that if X is morally wrong, then it isn't morally right and refraining from X is morally obligatory. Such grammatical and formal agreements are important to common moral discourse.

(3) There is a great deal of agreement, among believers and nonbelievers, as to what types of action they call 'wrong' in an ethical sense and I think that that agreement is one of the things that make common moral discourse possible.[13] It is certainly not complete agreement. Obviously there is a lot of ethical disagreement in the world. Much of it cuts right across religious lines, but not all of it does. There are things which are typically called 'wrong' by members of some religious groups, and not by others. Nonetheless there are types of action which everyone or almost everyone would call morally wrong—such as torturing someone to death because he

accidentally broke a small window in your house. Moreover any two people (including any one believer and one nonbeliever) are likely to find some actions they both call wrong that not everyone does. I imagine that most ethical discussion takes place among people whose area of agreement in what they call wrong is relatively large.

There is probably much less agreement about the most basic issues in moral theory than there is about many ethical issues of less generality. There is much more unanimity in what people (sincerely) say in answer to such questions as 'Was what Hitler did to the Jews wrong?' or 'Is it normally wrong to disobey the laws of one's country?' than in what they (sincerely) say in answer to such questions as 'Is it always right to do the act which will have the best results?' or 'Is pleasure the only thing that is good for its own sake?' The issue between adherents and nonadherents of divine command ethics is typical of basic issues in ethical and metaethical theory in this respect.

(4) The emotional and volitional attitudes normally expressed by the statement that something is 'wrong' are similar in believers and nonbelievers. They are not exactly the same; the attitudes typically expressed by the believer's statement that something is 'wrong' are importantly related to his religious practice and beliefs about God, and this doubtless makes them different in some ways from the attitudes expressed by nonbelievers uttering the same sentence. But the attitudes are certainly similar, and that is important for the possibility of common moral discourse.

(5) Perhaps even more important is the related fact that the social functions of a statement that something is (morally) 'wrong' are similar for believers and nonbelievers. To say that something someone else is known to have done is 'wrong' is commonly to attack him. If you say that something you are known to have done is 'wrong,' you abandon certain types of defense. To say that a public policy is 'wrong' is normally to register oneself as opposed to it, and is sometimes a signal that one is willing to be supportive of common action to change it. These social functions of moral discourse are extremely important. It is perhaps not surprising that we are inclined to say that two people agree with each other when they both utter the same sentence and thereby indicate their readiness to take the same side in a conflict.

Let us sum up these observations about the conditions which make common moral discourse between believers and nonbelievers possible. (1) They use many of the same ethical terms, such as 'wrong.' (2) They treat those terms as having the same basic grammatical and logical status, and many of the same logical connections with other expressions. (3) They agree to a large extent about what types of action are to be called 'wrong.' To call an action 'wrong' is, among other things, to classify it with certain other actions, and there is considerable agreement between believers and nonbelievers as to what actions those are. (4) The emotional and volitional attitudes which believers and nonbelievers normally express in saying that something is 'wrong'

---

[13] Cf. Ludwig Wittgenstein, *Philosophical Investigations*, 2nd ed. (Oxford: Blackwell, 1958), Pt. I, sec. 242: 'If language is to be a means of communication there must be agreement not only in definitions but also (queer as this may sound) in judgments.' In contemporary society I think it may well be the case that because there is not agreement in ethical definitions, common ethical discourse requires a measure of agreement in ethical judgments. (I do not mean to comment here more broadly on the truth or falsity of Wittgenstein's statement as a statement about the conditions of linguistic communication in general.)—R.M.A.

are similar, and (5) saying that something is 'wrong' has much the same social functions for believers and nonbelievers.

So far as I can see, none of this is inconsistent with the modified divine command theory of ethical wrongness. According to that theory there are several things which are true of the believer's use of 'wrong' which cannot plausibly be supposed to be true of the nonbeliever's. In saying, 'X is wrong,' the believer commits himself (subjectively, at least, and publicly if he is known to be a believer) to the claim that X is contrary to God's will or commandments. The believer will not say that anything would be wrong, under any possible circumstances, if it were not contrary to God's will or commandments. In many contexts he uses the term 'wrong' interchangeably with 'against the will of God' or 'against the commandments of God.' The heart of the modified divine command theory, I have suggested, is the claim that when the believer says, 'X is wrong,' one thing he means to be doing is stating a nonnatural objective fact about X, and the nonnatural objective fact he means to be stating is that X is contrary to the will or commandments of God. This claim may be true even though the uses of 'wrong' by believers and nonbelievers are similar in all five of the ways pointed out above.

Suppose these contentions of the modified divine command theory are correct. (I think they are very plausible as claims about the ethical discourse of at least some religious believers.) In that case believers and nonbelievers surely do not mean exactly the same thing by 'X is wrong' in ethical contexts. But neither is it plausible to suppose that they mean entirely different things, given the phenomena of common moral discourse. We must suppose, then, that their meaning is partly the same and partly different. 'Contrary to God's will or commands' must be taken as expressing only part of the meaning with which the believer uses 'wrong.' Some of the similarities between believers' and nonbelievers' use of 'wrong' must also be taken as expressing parts of the meaning with which the believer uses 'wrong.' This view of the matter agrees with the account of the modified divine command theory in Section III above, where I pointed out that the modified divine command theorist cannot mean exactly the same thing by 'wrong' that he means by 'contrary to God's commands.'

We have here a situation which commonly arises when some people hold, and others do not hold, a given theory about the nature of something which everyone talks about. The chemist, who believes that water is a compound of hydrogen and oxygen, and the man who knows nothing of chemistry, surely do not use the word 'water' in entirely different senses; but neither is it very plausible to suppose that they use it with exactly the same meaning. I am inclined to say that in some fairly ordinary sense of 'mean,' a phenomenalist, and a philosopher who holds some conflicting theory about what it is for a physical object to exist, do not mean exactly the same thing by 'There is a bottle of milk in the refrigerator.' But they certainly do not mean entirely different things, and they can agree that there is a bottle of milk in the refrigerator.

· *VII* ·

These remarks bring us face to face with some important issues in the general theory of analysis and meaning. What are the criteria for determining whether two utterers of the same expression mean exactly the same thing by it, or something partly different, or something entirely different? What is the relation between philosophical analyses, and philosophical theories about the natures of things, on the one hand, and the meanings of terms in ordinary discourse on the other hand? I have permitted myself the liberty of speaking as if these issues did not exist. But their existence is notorious, and I certainly cannot resolve them in this essay. Indeed, I do not have resolutions to offer.

In view of these uncertainties in the theory of meaning, it is worth noting that much of what the modified divine command theorist wants to say can be said without making claims about the *meaning* of ethical terms. He wants to say, for instance, that believers' claims that certain acts are wrong normally express certain attitudes towards those acts, whether or not that is part of their meaning; that an act is wrong if and only if it is contrary to God's will or commands (assuming God loves us); that nonetheless, if God commanded cruelty for its own sake, neither obedience nor disobedience would be ethically wrong or ethically permitted; that if an act is contrary to God's will or commands that is a nonnatural objective fact about it; and that that is the only nonnatural objective fact which obtains if and only if the act is wrong. These are among the most important claims of the modified divine command theory—perhaps they include the very most important. But in the form in which I have just stated them, they are not claims about the *meaning* of ethical terms.

I do not mean to reject the claims about the meanings of terms in religious ethical discourse which I have included in the modified divine command theory. In the absence of general solutions to general problems in the theory of meaning, we may perhaps say what seems to us intuitively plausible in particular cases. That is presumably what the modified divine command theorist is doing when he claims that 'contrary to the will or commands of God' is part of the meaning of '(ethically) wrong' for many Judeo-Christian believers. And I think it is fair to say that if we have found unresolved problems about meaning in the modified divine command theory, they are problems much more about what we mean in general by 'meaning' than about what Judeo-Christian believers mean by 'wrong.'[14]

---

[14] I am indebted to many who have read, or heard, and discussed versions of this essay, and particularly to Richard Brandt, William Frankena, John Reeder, and Stephen Stich, for helpful criticisms.—R.M.A.

CHAPTER FOURTEEN

Religion and the
Meaning of Life

○

○ ○ ○ *55*

The Dignity of Human Life
David F. Swenson

I. *The Need for a View of Life*

MAN LIVES FORWARD, but he thinks backward. As an active being, his task is to press forward to the things that are before, toward the goal where is the prize of the high calling. But as a thinking, active being, his forward movement is conditioned by a retrospect. If there were no past for a man, there could be no future; and if there were no future and no past, but only such an immersion in the present as is characteristic of the brute which perisheth, then there would be nothing eternal in human life, and everything distinctively and essentially human would disappear from our existence.

As a preparation for an existence in the present, the youth of a nation are trained in various skills and along devious lines, according to their capacities and circumstances, for the parts they are to play in existence; their natural talents are developed, some by extended periods of intellectual training, others for participation in various forms of business or technical training; but whatever be the ultimate end of the training, its purpose is to develop those latent powers they possess which will eventually prove of benefit to themselves or to others. But, in addition to this, which we may call a preparation for the external life, a something else is urgently needed, a something so fundamentally important that in its absence every other form of preparation is revealed as imperfect and incomplete, even ineffective and futile.

This so particularly indispensable something is a *view of life*, and a view of life is not acquired as a direct and immediate result of a course of study, the reading of books, or a communication of results. It is wholly a product of the individual's own knowledge of himself as an individual, of his individual capabilities and aspirations. A view of life is a principle of living, a spirit and an attitude capable of maintaining its unity and identity with itself in all of life's complexities and varying vicissitudes; and yet also capable of being declined, to use the terminology of the grammatical sciences, in all the infinite variety of cases that the language of life affords. Without this preparation the individual life is like a ship without a rudder, a bit of wreckage floating with the current to an uncomprehended destiny. A view of life is not objective knowledge, but subjective conviction. It is a part of man's own self, the source whence the stream of his life issues. It is the dominant attitude of the spirit which gives to life its direction and its goal. This is why it cannot be directly communicated or conveyed, like an article of commerce, from one person to another. If a view of life were a body of knowledge about life, or a direct and immediate implication from such knowledge, it would be subject to objective communication and systematic instruction. But it is rather a personal expression of what a man essentially is in his own inmost self, and this cannot be learned by rote, or accepted at the hands of some external authority. Knowledge is the answer or answers that things give to the questions we ask of them; a view of life is the reply a person gives to the question that life asks of him. We begin life by scrutinizing our environment, ourselves playing the role of questioners and examiners and critics; but at a later moment, when the soul comes of age and is about to enter upon its majority, it learns that the tables have been turned and the roles reversed; from that moment it confronts a question, a searching and imperative question, in relation to which no evasion can avail, and to which no shifting of responsibility is possible.

In discussing the problem of *a view of life which can give it meaning and dignity and worth*, I am well aware that no one can acquire a view of life by listening to a speech.[1] Nevertheless, a speech may serve the more modest purpose of stimulating a search, perhaps a more earnest search; and may render more articulate possibly the convictions of those who have already won some such conception, having made it their own by a heartfelt and spontaneous choice.

II. *One Approach*

All men are endowed by nature with a desire for happiness—a principle so obvious as scarcely to need any explanation, and certainly no defense. A human life without happiness or hope of happiness is not a life, but rather a death in life. Happiness is life's vital fluid and the very breath of its nostrils. Happiness and life are so much one and the same thing that the more profoundly any life discovers happiness, the more significant and abundant is that life itself. . . .

But for a thinking human being—and God made every man a thinker, whatever may be our estimate of that which men make of themselves—for a thinking human being, happiness cannot consist in satisfaction of momentary impulse, of blind feeling, of brute immediacy. A pleasant absorption in the present, oblivious of prospect or retrospect, careless of the wider relation or the deeper truth of life, can be called happiness only on the basis of frivolity and thoughtlessness. Just as life is not life unless it is happy, so happiness is not happiness unless it can be justified. In order really to be happiness it requires to be interpenetrated with a sense of *meaning, reason*, and *worth*.

For the quest of happiness, like every other human quest, faces a danger. The danger that confronts it is the possibility of error: the error of permitting oneself to be lured into promising paths that lead to no goal, and the error of coming to rest in hollow satisfactions and empty joys. It is possible to believe oneself happy, to seem happy to oneself and to others, and yet in reality to be plunged in the deepest misery; just as, on the other hand, it is possible to stand possessed of the greatest treasure, and yet, in thoughtlessness, to imagine oneself destitute, and through that very thoughtlessness not only neglect and ignore but actually deprive oneself of what one already has. The basic problem of life, the question in response to which a view of life seeks to propound an answer, may therefore be formulated as follows: What is that happiness which is also a genuine and lasting good? In what does it consist, and how may it be attained?

---

[1] This essay was originally presented as an address to an audience.—E.D.K.

There exists an ancient handbook, an *Art of Rhetoric*, compiled for the guidance and information of orators and other public speakers, written by one of the greatest of Greek philosophers. In this handbook the author formulates the commonly prevailing conceptions of happiness as among the things useful for public speakers to know. . . . Happiness is said to be commonly defined as independence of life, as prosperity with virtue, as comfortable circumstances with security, or as the enjoyment of many possessions, together with the power to keep and defend them. Its constituent elements are noble birth, wealth, many good and influential friends, bodily health and beauty, talents and capacities, good fortune, honors, and lastly virtue. We readily perceive how strange and old-fashioned these conceptions are, how foreign to all our modern and enlightened notions. I shall therefore subjoin a more up-to-date consideration of the same subject, derived from a very modern author writing in a journal of today. The author raises the question as to what circumstances and conditions have the power to make him feel really alive, tingling with vitality, instinct with the joy of living. He submits a long list including a variety of things, of which I shall quote the chief: the sense of health; successful creative work, like writing books; good food and drink; pleasant surroundings; praise, not spread on too thick; friends and their company; beautiful things, books, music; athletic exercises and sports; daydreaming; a good fight in a tolerably decent cause; the sense of bodily danger escaped; the consciousness of being a few steps ahead of the wolf of poverty. . . . So speaks our modern writer. And now that I have juxtaposed these two accounts, I have to confess to the strange feeling that, despite the interval of more than two thousand years between them, they sound unexpectedly alike. . . . How strange to find such a similarity! Can it be that after all that has been said and written about the revolutionary and radical changes introduced into life by modern science, modern invention, and modern industry, the influence of the steam engine and the printing press, the telegraph and the radio, the automobile and the airplane, together with the absolutely devastating discoveries of astronomers—can it be, in spite of all this, that the current conceptions of life and its meaning have remained essentially unchanged? . . .

III. Problems with that Approach

However that may be, I do not think that anyone will deny that such views as these are widely held, and constitute the view of life perhaps of the majority of men. . . . But there are serious difficulties in the way of constructing a view of life out of such considerations.

[1.] The constituents of happiness are in both cases a multiplicity of things. . . . But the self which sets its heart upon any such multiplicity of external goods, which lives in them and by them and for them, dependent upon them for the only happiness it knows—such a self is captive to the diverse world of its desires. It belongs to the world and does not own itself. It is not in the deepest sense a self, since it is not free and is not a unity. The manifold conditions of its happiness split the self asunder; no ruling passion dominates its life; no concentration gives unity to the personality and single-mindedness to the will. Its name is legion, and its nature is doublemindedness. . . .

[2.] Reflection discovers yet another difficulty in connection with such views of life. Whoever seeks his happiness in external conditions, of whatever sort, seeks it in that which is in its essential nature precarious. He presumes upon the realization of conditions which are not intrinsic to him, or within his control. This happiness is subject to the law of uncertainty, to the qualification of an unyielding, mysterious *perhaps*. Here lurks the possibility of despair. Give a man the full satisfaction of his wishes and ambitions, and he deems himself happy; withdraw from him the smile of fortune's favor, and disappoint his expectation and his hope, and he will be plunged into despair. The shift from happiness to unhappiness in such a life is every moment imminent. . . .

[3.] A third consideration. Wealth and power and the like, even bodily health and beauty of person, are not in the strictest sense intrinsic values, but rather representative and comparative, conditional and hypothetical. Money is good—if I have learned how to use it; and so with power and influence, health and strength. But in themselves these things are abstract and neutral, and no man can truthfully say whether the acquirement of them in any individual case will work more good than harm. . . .

[4.] Lastly, it must be pointed out that the conditions of happiness as conceived in all such views of life, inevitably imply a privileged status for the happy individual. They rest upon differential capabilities and exceptionally fortunate circumstances. To choose them as the end and aim of life constitutes an injury to the mass of men who are not so privileged. This one thought alone is of so arresting a quality as to give the deepest concern to every man who has the least trace of human sympathy and human feeling. I hope I have a soul not entirely a stranger to happy admiration; I know I feel moved to bend low in respect before exceptional talent and performance, and that I am eager to honor greatness and genius wherever I have the gift to understand it. And I am not so unfeeling as to refuse a tribute of sympathetic joy to those who rejoice in fortune's favors and bask in the smiles of outward success. But as the fundamental source of inspiration of my life, I need something that is not exclusive and differential, but inclusive and universal. I require to drink from a spring at which all men may refresh themselves; I need an aim that reconciles me to high and low, rich and poor, cultured and uncultured, sophisticated and simple; to the countless generations of the past as well as to the men and women of the future. I need a spiritual bond that binds me to all human beings in a common understanding of that which is fundamental and essential to human life. To have my life and happiness in that which is inaccessible to the many or to the few, seems to me an act of treason to humanity, a cowardly and pusillanimous attack upon the brotherhood of man; for without the inner spiritual tie of an essential aim which all can reach and all can understand, the concept of the human race as a spiritual unity is destroyed, and nothing is left of mankind but a biological species, only slightly better equipped than the other animals to cope with the present state of their physical environment.

The differences between man and man are indeed inseparable from this our imperfect temporal existence; but I cannot and will not believe that their development constitutes the perfection of life itself. Rather is this to be found in the discovery and expectation of *something underlying and absolute*, something that can be found by all who seek it in earnest, something to which our lives may give expression, subordinating to its unifying principle the infinite multitude of ends, reducing them to their own relative measure and proportion, and refusing to permit the unimportant to become important, the relative to become absolute. the possibility of making this discovery and of giving it expression is, so it seems to me, *the fundamental meaning of life, the source of its dignity and worth*. The happiness that is found with this discovery is not invidious and divisive, but unifying and reconciling; it does not abrogate the differences, but it destroys their power to wound and to harm, the fortunate through being puffed up in arrogance and pride, the unfortunate through being depressed in envy and disappointment. For this happiness is not denied to any man, no matter how insignificant and humble.

IV.   The Ethico-Religious View of Life

Our criticism has brought us to the threshold of an ethical view of life. That the essence of life and its happiness is to be sought in the moral consciousness alone is the conviction that animates this address, and gives it its reason for being. This view holds that *the individual human self has an infinite worth*, that *the personality has an external validity*, that *the bringing of this validity to expression in the manifold relations and complications of life is the true task of the self*, that *this task gives to the individual's historical development an infinite significance*, because it is a process through which the personality in its truth and depth comes its own. "Find your self," says the moral consciousness; "reclaim it in its total and in so far unworthy submergence in relative ends; dare to think the nothingness, the hollowness, the relativity, the precariousness, the lack of intrinsic meaning of that which constitutes the entire realm of the external and the manifold; liberate yourself from slavery to finite ends; have the courage to substitute the one thing needful for the many things wished for, and perhaps desirable, making first things first, and all other things secondary—and you will find that these other things will be added unto you in the measure in which you require them and can use them as servants and ministers of your highest good."

So speaks the voice within us, a still small voice, a soft whisper easily overwhelmed by the noise and traffic of life, but a voice, nevertheless, which no one can permit to be silenced except at the cost of acquiring restlessness instead of peace, anxiety instead of trust and confidence, a distracted spirit instead of harmony with one's self. The moral spirit finds the meaning of life in choice. It finds it in that which proceeds from man and remains with him as his inner essence rather than in the accidents of circumstance and turns of external fortune. The individual has his end in himself. He is no mere instrument in the service of something external, nor is he the slave of some powerful master; nor of a class, a group, or party; nor of the state or nation; nor even of humanity itself, as an abstraction solely external to the individual. Essentially and absolutely he is an end; only accidentally and relatively is he a means. And this is true of the meanest wage slave, so called, in industry's impersonal machine—precisely as true of him as it is of the greatest genius or the most powerful ruler.

Is there anyone so little stout-hearted, so effeminately tender, so extravagantly in love with an illusory and arbitrary freedom, as to feel that the glorious promise of such a view of life is ruined, its majestic grandeur shriveled into cramped pettiness, because the task which it offers the individual is not only an invitation, but also an obligation as well? Shall we confess that we cannot endure this "Thou must" spoken to ourselves,[2] even when the voice proceeds from no external power but from our inmost self, there where the human strikes its roots into the *divine*? Truly, it is this "Thou

---

[2] Suggested by Emerson's "So nigh is grandeur to our dust." *Voluntaries.*—D.F.S.

must" that is the *eternal* guarantee of our calling, the savior of our hope, the inspirer of our energy, the preserver of our aim against the shiftings of feeling and the vicissitudes of circumstance. It steels the will and makes it fast; it gives courage to begin after failure; it is the triumph over despondency and despair. For *duty is the eternal in a man, or that by which he lays hold of the eternal; and only through the eternal can a man become a conqueror of the life of time.* It is in the moral consciousness that a man begins truly to sense *the presence of God;* and every religion that has omitted the ethical is in so far a misunderstanding of religion, reducing it to myth and poetry, having significance only for the imagination, but not for the whole nature of man as concrete reality. The moral consciousness is a lamp, a wonderful lamp; but not like the famous lamp of Aladdin,[3] which when rubbed had the power to summon a spirit, a willing servant ready and able to fulfill every wish. But whenever a human being rubs the lamp of his moral consciousness with moral passion, a Spirit does appear. This Spirit is God, and the Spirit is master and lord, and man becomes his servant. But this service is man's true freedom, for a derivative spirit like man, who certainly has not made himself, or given himself his own powers, cannot in truth impose upon himself the law of his own being. It is in the "Thou must" of God and man's "I can" that the divine image of God in human life is contained, to which an ancient book refers when it asserts that God made man in his own image. That is the inner glory, the spiritual garb of man, which transcends the wonderful raiment with which the Author of the universe has clothed the lilies of the field, raiment which in its turn puts to shame the royal purple of Solomon. The lilies of the field[4] cannot hear the voice of duty or obey its call; hence they cannot bring their will into harmony with the divine will. In the capacity to do this lies man's unique distinction among all creatures; here is his self, his independence, his glory and his crown.

I know that all men do not share this conviction. Youth is often too sure of its future. The imagination paints the vision of success and fortune in the rosiest tints; the sufferings and disappointments of which one hears are for youth but the exception that proves the rule; the instinctive and blind faith of youth is in the relative happiness of some form of external success. Maturity, on the other hand, has often learned to be content with scraps and fragments, wretched crumbs saved out of the disasters on which its early hopes suffered shipwreck. Youth pursues an ideal that is illusory; age has learned, O wretched wisdom! to do without an ideal altogether. But the ideal is there, implanted in the heart and mind of man by his Maker, and no mirages of happiness or clouds of disappointment, not the stupor of habit or the frivolity of thoughtlessness, can entirely erase the sense of it from the depths of the soul. . . .

Let us but learn to perceive that no differential talent, no privileged status, no fortunate eventuality, can at bottom be worthwhile as a consummation; that all such things are quite incapable of dignifying life; and when the misunderstandings with respect to the nature of a moral consciousness have been cleared away, the road will be open to the discovery of man as man. A preoccupation with the secondary thoughts and interests of life is always exhausting and trivializing, and in the end bewildering.

---

[3] S. Kierkegaard, *Postscript*, p. 124.—D.F.S.
[4] S. Kierkegaard, *The Gospel of Suffering*, pp. 174–177.—D.F.S.

Our true refreshment and invigoration will come through going back to the first and simplest thoughts, the primary and indispensable interests. We have too long lost ourselves in anxious considerations of what it may mean to be a shoemaker or a philosopher, a poet or a millionaire; in order to find ourselves, it is needful that we concentrate our energies upon the infinitely significant problem of what it means simply to be a man, without any transiently qualifying adjectives. When Frederick the Great asked his Court preacher if he knew anything about the future life, the preacher answered, "Yes, Your Majesty, it is absolutely certain that in the future life Your Highness will not be king of Prussia." And so it is; we were men before we became whatever of relative value we became in life, and we shall doubtless be human beings long after what we thus became or acquired will have lost its significance for us. On the stage some actors have roles in which they are royal and important personages; others are simple folk, beggars, workingmen, and the like. But when the play is over and the curtain is rolled down, the actors cast aside their disguises, the differences vanish, and all are once more simply actors. So, when the play of life is over, and the curtain is rolled down upon the scene, the differences and relativities which have disguised the men and women who have taken part will vanish, and all will be simply human beings. But there is this difference between the actors of the stage and the actors of life. On the stage it is imperative that the illusion be maintained to the highest degree possible; an actor who plays the role of king as if he was an actor, or who too often reminds us that he is assuming a role, is precisely a poor actor. But on the stage of life, the reverse is the case. There it is the task, not to preserve, but to expose, the illusion; to win free from it while still retaining one's disguise. The disguising garment ought to flutter loosely about us, so loosely that the least wind of human feeling that blows may reveal the royal purple of humanity beneath. This revelation is the moral task; the moral consciousness is the consciousness of the dignity that invests human life when the personality has discovered itself, and is happy in the will to be itself.

Such is the view of life to which the present speaker is committed. He has sought to make it seem inviting, but not for a moment has he wished to deny that it sets a difficult task for him who would express it in the daily intercourse of life. Perhaps it has long since captured our imaginations; for it is no new gospel worked out to satisfy the imaginary requirements of the most recent fashions in human desire and feeling; on the contrary it is an old, old view. But it is not enough that the truth of the significance inherent in having such a view of life should be grasped by the imagination, or by the elevated mood of a solemn hour; only the heart's profound movement, the will's decisive commitment,[5] can make that which is truth in general also a truth for me.

---

[5] *Postscript*, p. 226.—D.F.S.

Living without Appeal:
An Affirmative Philosophy of Life[1]
E. D. Klemke

· I ·

FROM TIME TO time, philosophers get together at congresses and symposia in which some philosophers read papers and others criticize and raise questions. To the layman, I am sure, the topics which are discussed seem highly technical and inaccessible, and the vocabulary used is, doubtless, unintelligible. Indeed, if the ordinary man were to drop in on such meetings, he would, I suspect, find the proceedings to be either totally incomprehensible or the occasion for howling laughter. To give some indication of what I am referring to, I shall list the titles of some recent philosophical papers, many of which are acknowledged to be very important works:

The meaning of a word
Performative—constative
Negative existentials
Excluders
Reference and referents
Proper names
On referring
Parenthetical verbs
Bare particulars
Elementarism, independence, and ontology
The problem of counterfactual conditionals
Is existence a predicate?
Etc.

Upon hearing (or reading) papers such as these, the ordinary man would probably exclaim "What's this all got to do with philosophy?" And he would, no doubt, be in agreement with Kierkegaard, who once wrote:

> What the philosophers say about Reality is often as disappointing as a sign you see in a shop window which reads: Pressing Done Here. If you brought your clothes to be pressed, you would be fooled; for the sign is only for sale. (*Either/Or*, v. 1, p. 31.)

---

[1] This essay was first read in the Last Lecture Series, at DePauw University, and was repeated, by request, three times. In a revised form, it was read as the Top Prof lecture at Roosevelt University. It was again revised for this volume.—E.D.K.

Now I have no quarrel with what goes on at these professional gatherings. I engage in such activities myself. I believe that most philosophical problems are highly technical and that the making of minute distinctions and employment of a specialized vocabulary are essential for the solution of such problems. Philosophy here is in the same boat as any other discipline. For this reason, there is (and perhaps always will be) something aristocratic about the pursuit of philosophy, just as there is about the pursuit of theoretical physics or Peruvian excavation. The decriers of philosophy often overlook the fact that any discipline which amounts to more than a type of verbal diarrhea must proceed by making subtle distinctions, introducing technical terminology, and striving for as much rigor and precision as is possible. And the critics fail to see that, in philosophy as in other fields, by the very nature of the discipline, some problems will be somewhat rarified, and of interest mainly to the specialist.

On the other hand, I am inclined to think that the philosopher ought occasionally to leave the study, or the philosophical association lecture hall, or even the classroom, and, having shed his aristocratic garments, speak as a man among other men. For the philosopher is, after all, human too. Like other men, he eats, sleeps, makes love, drinks martinis (or perhaps cognac), get the flu, files income tax, and even reads the newspapers. On such more democratic occasions, he ought to employ his analytical tools as diligently as ever. But he should select as his topic some issue which is of concern to all men, or at least most men, at some time in their lives. It is my hope that I have chosen such a topic for this essay.

The problem which I wish to discuss has been formulated in a single sentence by Camus (in *The Myth of Sisyphus*), which I take as a kind of "text." The sentence to which I am referring is: "Knowing whether or not one can live *without appeal* is all that interests me."[2] I say that I take this as a *kind* of text because, as so often, Camus overstates the point. Thus I would not—and perhaps most of us would not—say that, knowing whether or not one can live without appeal is *all* that interests me. But I believe that most of us would say that it certainly is one of those crucial problems which each man must confront as he tries to make sense of his life in this wondrously strange existence.

· II ·

Prophets of doom and redemption seem to exist in almost every age, and ours is no exception. It is commonly held by many present-day thinkers, scholars, and poets, that the current state of the world and of many of the individuals within it is one of disintegration and vacuity. As they see it: Persons of our age grope for disrupting principles and loyalties, and often reveal a destructive tension, a lack of wholeness, or an acute anxiety. Whether or not this is a unique situation in history, as an account of the present state of things, such disintegration is commonly mentioned. And theorists in almost every discipline and pursuit have given analyses of the current predicament and offered solutions. For example, philosophers and theologians (Jaspers, Marcel, Swenson, Tillich, Schweitzer, Niebuhr), scientists and scientific writers (Einstein, DeNuoy), sociologists (Sorokin), historians (Butterfield), among others, have waved warning signs, sometimes in a last effort to "save civilization from utter destruction.

---

[2] A. Camus, *The Myth of Sisyphus*. Tr. by J. O'Brien (New York: Vintage Books, 1959), p.45.—E.D.K.

"I would like to consider some points which are held in common by many of these writers (and others whom I have not indicated) and then to comment about those views. In this section. I shall state the common core of this position. In the next section, I shall make my comments and show that there is another genuine alternative.

According to many of the above writers (and others whom I have not mentioned), our age is one in which a major catastrophe has taken place. This has been designated as an increasing lack of a determining principle, the severing of a determining bond, the loss of a determining passion, or the rejection of a determining ultimate. What is the nature of this ultimate? It has been described as a principle by which finite forces are held in equilibrium, a bond which relates all horizontally functioning powers vertically to a realm beyond the finite. It is said to be a unifying and controlling power by which the varied inclinations, desires, and aims of an individual may be kept in balance. It is characterized as an agency which removes those oppositions and dichotomies which tend to destroy human selfhood. It has been held, by writers such as the above, to be a *transcendent* and *unconditional ultimate*, the one indispensable factor for the attainment of a *meaningful* and *worthwhile* existence. In their view, in order to prevent the destruction of individuals and cultures, and to provide a sense of direction and wholeness, the awareness of and relationship to such an ultimate are absolutely necessary.

Many of the writers have noted that, not only in intellectual circles, but at a much wider level, many individuals are increasingly refusing to accept the reality of this controlling ultimate. As they see it, such individuals have either remained content with a kind of vacuum in "the dimension of the spiritual," or they have "transvaluated and exalted immanent, finite forces" into a substitute for the transcendent. Men have tried—say these writers—to find equilibrium and unity through "natural", non-authoritative, self-regulating, temporal aims and principles, which they hold to be capable of an innate self-integration which requires no outside aid. According to these writers, this hope is futile, for as soon as reliance upon the transcendent ultimate ceases, disintegration results. Only when finite relationships, processes, and forces are referred back to a transhistorical order can integration, wholeness, meaning, and purpose be achieved. As long as men lack confidence in, or sever the bond to, the transcendent, their accomplishments and goals, no matter how noble or worthy, can have no final consistency or solidity. Rather, their efforts are mere remnants of an "atrophied world," shut up within the realm of immanence, intoxicated with itself, lured by "phantasms and idolatrous forces."

According to this view, the integrity of the individual is today threatened by the loss of belief in the transcendent ultimate and its replacement by a "devitalized" and "perverse" confidence in the all-sufficiency of the finite. The only remedy, we are told, is the recognition of the determining regulation of a dimension beyond the fleeting pace of the temporal world, by which alone existence can have worth and value.

At this point, one might be tempted to ask several questions of these writers:

(1) "Even if the above characterization of the world has some truth, must one look to transcendentalism as the remedy? Cannot a 'natural' philosophy or principle help us?"

The usual answer is: No. All naturalistic views reduce existence to mere finite centers and relationships. But all of these finite agencies are conditioned by others. All are therefore transitory and unstable. None can become a determining ultimate. Only a transcendent ultimate is capable of sustaining the kind of faith which gives human existence meaning and value.

(2) "But isn't this supernaturalism all over again? And doesn't it (as usual) imply either an unbridgeable gulf between the finite and the infinite or an external control or suppression of the finite by the so-called infinite?"

The customary reply is that this view may indeed be called supernaturalism. But (we are told) this does not imply the impossibility of any association of the finite and the infinite. For the ultimate, according to these writers, is not transcendent in the sense of being totally isolated from the finite, but, rather, is operative within the natural world. Furthermore (so the reply goes), the existence of a transcendent order does not entail either external control or suppression of the finite. It merely implies a human receptivity to a non-natural realm. That is, human achievement and value result from the impingement of the infinite upon the finite in moments of *kairos*,[3] providing fullness and meaning but not at the price of denying the human activity which is involved. There always remains the awareness that the human subject is in a personal relation to another subject, a relation of supreme importance.

(3) "And how does one come to this relation?"

Perhaps mainly (say many of these writers) through suffering and sorrow, through a sense of sin and despair. When an individual sees that all finite centers and loyalties are fleeting and incapable of being lasting objects of faith, then he will renounce all previous efforts in despair, repent in humility, and gratefully make *the movement of faith* by which alone his life can become meaningful and worthwhile.

This, then, is the view which I propose to comment on. It is an all-or-nothing position. Its central thesis is that there exists a transcendent ultimate of absolute supremacy, which reigns over all finite things and powers, and *which alone is capable of providing meaning and worth to human existence.* Finite, historical centers can at best bring temporary assistance. They all wither with time and circumstances. Only when men turn from the finite to the infinite can they find (in the words of Kierkegaard) a hope and anticipation of the eternal which holds together all the "cleavages of existence."

· III ·

I shall refer to the above view (which I have tried to portray justly) as transcendentalism. It contains three component these. These are:

(1) There *exists* a transcendent being or ultimate with which man can enter into some sort of relation.

(2) Without such a transcendent ultimate, and the relation of faith to it, human life lacks *meaning, purpose,* and *integration.*

(3) Without such meaning, purpose, or integration, human life is not *worthwhile.*

It is necessary to comment upon all three of these points.

---

[3] In theology: a special event in which a transcendent being is said to make itself manifest to humans.— E.D.K.

(1) First, the thesis *exists* such a transcendent ultimate or power. I assume that those who assert the existence of a transcendent being intend their assertion to be a *cognitive* one. That is, they claim to be saying something which states a fact and which is capable of being either true or false. Thus they would not admit that their claim is merely an expression of feelings or attitudes. I also assume that those who make this assertion intend their statement to be interpreted *literally*. That is, they mean to say that the transcendent *really exists*. The transcendent presumably does not exist in the same sense in which Santa Claus may be said to "exist." These persons would, I assume, hold that the transcendent exists in actuality, although it may not exist in any empirical sense.

I ask: What *reasons* are there for holding that such an entity as the transcendent exists? I take it that I do not have to linger on such an answer as the testimony of a sacred book. The fact that the Bible or any other sacred writing asserts the existence of a transcendent is no more evidential to the existence of such a being than it is to the non-existence. All that a scriptural writing proves is that someone *believed* that a transcendent ultimate exists. And that is not at all the same as showing that such a being actually exists. The same may be said for the testimony of some unusual person—Moses, Jesus, Mohammed, etc. Furthermore, the fact that the testimony is made by a large number of persons does not substantiate the view. An impartial reading of history often shows that, on major issues, the majority is almost always wrong.

I also shall not linger on the traditional arguments for the existence of a god: The ontological, cosmological, teleological arguments, etc. Many theologians themselves now acknowledge that these are not so much arguments for the existence of such a being as they are explications of the affirmation of faith. Therefore, the fact that a certain segment of the universe is orderly, that it exhibits beauty, that it shows an adaptation of means to ends does not in any way provide evidence that there is one who orders, beautifies, and adapts, etc.

Arguments from religious experience are also unconvincing. Due to their lack of intersubjective testability, the most that such arguments can demonstrate is that someone has had an unusual experience. They do not provide any evidence that the *object* of such an experience exists. That object may, of course, exist. But the occurrence of such an experience does not verify the existence of an actual, rather than imaginary, object. Suppose that, while a dentist is drilling my tooth, I have an experience of a blinding light or an unusual voice. I do not take this to be an adequate reason for saying that I *know* that I have now communed with the Absolute. I trust that you do not do so either.

What evidence, then, is there for the existence of a transcendent? I submit that there is *none*. And my reading of religious writings and my conversations with many of those who maintain the existence of the transcendent lead me to affirm that they also would agree that there is none. For they hold that the existence of the transcendent (although a cognitive claim) is apprehended, *not* in a cognitive relationship but in the relationship of *faith*.

Thus in the usual sense of the term 'evidence,' there seems to be no evidence for the existence of a transcendent ultimate. Why, then, should I accept such a claim? After all, throughout the rest of my philosophical activity *and* throughout my normal, everyday activities, I constantly rely upon criteria of evidence before accepting a cognitive claim. I emphasize that this holds for my *everyday* life and not merely for any philosophical or scientific beliefs which I may entertain. Not only do I accept or reject (say) the Principle of Rectilinear Propogation of Light because of evidence. I also ask for evidence in order to substantiate such simple claims as 'The stylus in my stereo tone arm is defective,' or 'Jones eloped with his secretary.'

It is clear that both believers and non-believers share this desire for evidence with me. At least, believers agree up to the point of the transcendent-claim. If I reject this claim because of lack of evidence, I do not think that I can be justly accused of being an extremist. Rather, I should be commended for my consistency!

The transcendentalist will reply: "But the usual criteria do not apply in this case. They work only for natural entities. The transcendent is not a natural being." I answer: Then the only reasonable procedure seems to be that of suspending my judgment, for I do not know of any non-natural criteria. The transcendentalist replies: "No, merely suspending your judgment implies that you think that some evidence might eventually be found. We are in a different dimension here. An act of *faith* is required."

I reply with two points: (a) In its normal usage, the term 'faith' still implies evidence and reasons. Why do I have faith in Smith, but not in Jones? Obviously because of *reasons*. I do not have faith in people haphazardly and without evidence. (b) If I am told that faith in the transcendent is not faith in the normal sense, but a special act of commitment, then I can only honestly reply: *I have no need for such faith.* The transcendentalist retorts: "Ah, but you do, for only through faith in the transcendent can life have meaning; and surely you seek a life that is significant and worthwhile." And this leads us to the second thesis.

(2) The transcendentalist claims that without the transcendent and faith in the transcendent, human existence is without *meaning, purpose, integration.* Is this true? And if true in some sense, what follows?

(A) Let us take *meaning* first. Is there any reason to believe that without the existence of the transcendent, life has no meaning? That is, does the existence of meaning presuppose the existence of the transcendent?

It is necessary to distinguish between *objective* meaning and *subjective* meaning. An objective meaning, if there were such, would be one which is either structurally *part of* the universe, apart from human subjective evaluation; or dependent upon some *external agency* other than human evaluation. Two comments are in order: (i) *If* the notion of objective meaning is a plausible one, then I see no reason why it must be tied up with the existence of a transcendent being, for it certainly is not self-contradictory to hold that an objective meaning could conceivably exist even though a transcendent being did not. That is, the two concepts of 'transcendent being' and 'objective meaning' are not logically related in the way in which the two concepts 'three' and 'odd' (for example) are related. (ii) But, more fundamental, I find the notion of an objective meaning as difficult to accept as I do the notion of a transcendent being. Therefore I cannot rely upon the acceptance of objective meaning in order to substantiate the existence of the transcendent.

Further comment is needed on this point. It seems to me that there is no shred of evidence for the existence of an objective meaning in the universe. If I were to characterize the universe, attempting to give a complete description, I would do so in terms of matter in motion, or energy, or forces such as gravitation, or events, etc. Such a description is *neutral*. It can have no non-descriptive components. The same holds for a description of any segment of the universe. Kepler, for example, was entitled to say that the paths of the planets are elliptical, etc. But he was not entitled to say that this motion exhibits some fundamental, objective purpose more so than some other type of motion would. From the standpoint of present evidence, evaluational components such as meaning or purpose are not to be found in the universe as objective aspects of it. Such values are the result of human evaluation. With respect to them, we must say that the universe is valueless; it is *we* who evaluate, upon the basis of our subjective preferences. Hence, we do not discover values such as meaning to be inherent within the universe. Rather, we "impose" such values upon the universe.

When the transcendentalist holds that, without the transcendent, no objective meaning for human existence is possible, he assumes that the notion of an objective meaning is an intelligible one. But if one can show, as I believe one can, that the idea of objective meaning is an implausible one, then his argument has no point. In no way does it give even the slightest evidence for the existence of a transcendent ultimate.

However, it is possible that some transcendentalist would want to take a different position here. There are at least two alternatives which he might hold.

(i) The transcendentalist might *agree* that there is no *objective* meaning in the universe, that meaning *is* a function of human subjectivity. His point now is that *subjective* meaning is found if and only if there exists a transcendent. I reply with two points (1) This is a grandiose generalization, which might wow an imbecile but not anyone of normal intelligence, and, like most such generalizations, it is false. (I shall return to this point in connection with the transcendentalist's third thesis.) (2) The meaning which the transcendentalist here affirms cannot be subjective meaning, for it is dependent upon some external, non-human factor, namely, the existence of the transcendent. This sort of meaning is *not* a function of human subjectivity. Thus we are back where we were. The transcendentalist's views about meaning do not provide any evidence at all for the existence of a transcendent ultimate.

(ii) I mentioned that the transcendentalist may take a second alternative. He might want to hold: "Of course, the fact of meaning in human existence does not in any way prove, demonstratively or with probability, that there *is* a transcendent being. Therefore, I won't say that meaning in life is impossible unless the transcendent exists. I will merely say that one cannot find meaning unless *one has faith in* the transcendent. The fact of meaning testifies to the necessity of *faith*."

I reply again with two points. (1) This generalization is also false. I know of many humans who have found a meaningful existence without faith in the transcendent. (2) However, even if this statement were true—even if heretofore not a single human being had found meaning in his life without faith in the transcendent—*I should reject such meaning and search for some other kind*. To me, the price which the transcendentalist pays for his meaning is too dear. If I am to find any meaning in life, I must attempt to find it without the aid of crutches, illusory hopes, and incredulous beliefs and aspirations. I am perfectly willing to admit that *I may not find any meaning at all* (although I think I can, even if it is not of the noble variety of which the transcendentalist speaks). But at least *I must try* to find it on my own. And this much I know: I can strive for a meaning only if it is one which is within the range of my comprehension as an inquiring, rational *man*. A meaning which is tied to some transcendent entity—or to faith in such—is not intelligible to me. Again, I here maintain what I hold throughout the rest of my existence, both philosophically and simply as a living person. I can accept only what is comprehensible to me, i.e., that which is within the province of actual or possible experience, or that for which I find some sound reasons or evidence. Upon these grounds, I must reject any notion of meaning which is bound with the necessity of faith in some mysterious, utterly unknowable entity. If my life should turn out to be less happy thereby, then I shall have to endure it as such. As Shaw once said: "The fact that a believer is happier than a skeptic is no more to the point than the fact that a drunken man is happier than a sober one. The happiness of credulity is a cheap and dangerous quality."

(B) I shall not say much about the transcendentalist's claim that, without the transcendent, or without faith in it, human existence is *purposeless*. For if I were to reply in detail, I should do so in about the same manner as I did with respect to the matter of meaning. An objective purpose is as difficult to detect in the universe as an objective meaning. Hence, again, one cannot argue that there must be a transcendent or that faith in such is necessary.

(C) What about the transcendentalist's claim that, without the transcendent, or, without *faith* in the transcendent, no integration is possible?

(i) In one sense of the term, this assertion, too, is obviously false. There are many persons who have attained what might be called psychological integration, i.e., self-integration, integration of personality, etc., without faith in the transcendent. I know of dozens of people whose lives are integrated in this sense, yet have no transcendental commitments.

(ii) But perhaps the transcendentalist means something much more fundamental than this psychological thesis by his claim. Perhaps he is making some sort of metaphysical assertion—a statement about man and his place in the universe. Thus his assertion must be taken to mean that *metaphysical* integration is not achievable without the transcendent or without faith in it. Like Kierkegaard, he holds that the cleavages of existence cannot be held together without the transcendent. What shall we say to this interpretation?

I am not sure that I understand what such integration is supposed to be. But insofar as I do, it seems to me that it is not possible. I am willing to admit that, if such integration were achievable, it might perhaps be attained only by virtue of something transcendent. But I find no conclusive or even reasonable evidence that such integration has been achieved either by believers in the transcendent or by non-believers. Hence one cannot infer that there is a transcendent ultimate or that faith in such an entity is necessary.

What about the mystics? you ask. It would be silly for me to say that the mystics have not experienced something very unusual which they have *interpreted* as some sort of unity with the universe, or whatever it may be. They may, indeed, have *felt* that, at rare moments, they were "swallowed up in the infinite ocean of being," to quote James. But again, peculiar and non-intersubjectively testable experiences are not reliable evidence for any truth-claim. Besides, suppose that the mystics *had* occasionally achieved such unity with the universe. Still, this is somewhat irrelevant. For the point is, that *I*, and many beings like myself (perhaps most of you), have not been favored with such experiences. In fact, it appears that most people who have faith in the transcendent have not had such experiences. This is precisely *why* they have faith. If they had complete certainty, no faith would be needed. Thus faith itself does not seem to be enough for the achievement of integration; and if integration were obtained, faith would be unnecessary. Hence the transcendentalist's view that integration is achieved *via* faith in the transcendent is questionable.

But even if this last thesis were true, it does me no good. Once again, I cannot place my faith in an unknown X, in that which is incomprehensible to me. Hence I must accept the fact that, for me, life will remain without objective meaning, without purpose, and without metaphysical integration. *And I must go on from there*. Rather than crying for the moon, my task must be, as Camus said, to know whether or not one can live *without appeal*.

(3) This leads us to the transcendentalist's third (and most crucial) thesis: That without meaning, purpose, and integration, life is not *worthwhile*. From which he draws the conclusion that without a *transcendent* or *faith* in it, life is not worthwhile. I shall deal only with the claim that without *meaning*, life is not worthwhile. Similar comments could be made regarding purpose and integration.

If the transcendentalist's claim sounds plausible at all, it is only because he continues to confuse objective meaning with subjective meaning. It is true that life has no objective meaning. Let us face it once and for all. But from this it does not follow that life is not *worthwhile*, for it can still be subjectively meaningful. And, really, the latter is the only kind of meaning worth shouting about. An objective meaning—that is, one which is inherent within the universe or dependent upon external agencies—would, frankly, leave me cold. It would not be *mine*. It would be an outer, neutral thing, rather than an inner, dynamic achievement. I, for one, am *glad* that the universe has no meaning, for thereby is *man all the more glorious*. I willingly accept the fact that external meaning is non-existent (or if existent, certainly not apparent), for this leaves me free to *forge my own meaning*. The extent of my creativity and thereby my success in this undertaking depends partly on the richness of my own psyche. There are some persons whose subjectivity is poor and wretched. Once they give up the search for objective meaning, they may perhaps have a difficult time in finding life to be worthwhile. Such is the fate of the impoverished. But those whose subjectivity is enlarged—rationally, esthetically, sensually, passionally—may find life to be worthwhile by means of their creative activity of subjective evaluation, in which a neutral universe takes on color and light, darkness and shadow, becomes now a source of profound joy, now a cause for deep sorrow.

What are some ways by which such worthwhileness can be found? I can speak only for myself. I have found subjective meaning through such things as *knowledge, art, love, and work*. Even though I realize that complete and perfect knowledge of matters of fact is not attainable, this does not lessen my enthusiasm to know and to understand. Such pursuits may have no practical utility; they are not thereby any less significant. To know about the nature of necessary truth or the probable structure of the atom is intrinsically fascinating, to me. And what a wealth of material lies in the arts. A Bach fugue, a Vlaminck painting, a Dostoevsky novel; life is intensely enriched by things such as these. And one must not neglect mention of one's relationships of friendship and love. Fragmentary and imperfect as these often are, they nevertheless provide us with some of our most heightened moments of joy and value. Finally, of all of the ways which I listed, none is more significant and constantly sustaining to me than work. There have been times when I, like many others, no doubt, have suffered some tragedy which seemed unendurable. Every time, it has been my work that has pulled me through.

In short, even if life has no meaning , in an external, objective sense, this does not lead to the conclusion that it is not worth living, as the transcendentalist naively but dogmatically assumes. On the contrary, this fact opens up a greater field of almost infinite possibilities. For as long as I am *conscious*, I shall have the capacity with which to *endow* events, objects, persons, and achievements with value. Ultimately, it is through my *consciousness* and it alone that worth or value are obtained. Through consciousness, the scraping of horses' tails on cats' bowels (to use James' phrase) become the beautiful and melodic lines of a Beethoven string quartet. Through consciousness, a pile of rock can become the memorable Mount Alten which one has climbed and upon which one almost perished. Through consciousness, the arrangements of *P*s and *Q*s on paper can become the symbols of the formal beauty and certain truth of the realm of mathematical logic. Through consciousness, the gift of a carved little piece of wood, left at one's door by a friend, can become a priceless treasure. Yes, it is a *vital* and *sensitive consciousness* that counts. Thus there is a sense in which it is true, as many thinkers and artists have reminded us, that everything begins with my consciousness, and nothing has any worth except through my consciousness.

· *IV* ·

I shall conclude with an ancient story. "Once a man from Syria led a camel through the desert; but when he came to a dark abyss, the camel suddenly, with teeth showing and eyes protruding, pushed the unsuspecting paragon of the camel-driving profession into the pit. The clothes of the Syrian were caught by a rosebush, and he was held suspended over the pit, at the bottom of which an enormous dragon was waiting to swallow him. Moreover, two mice were busily engaged in chewing away the roots of the already sagging plant. Yet, in this desperate condition, the Syrian was thralled to the point of utmost contentment by a rose which adorned the bush and wafted its fragrance into his face."[3]

I find this parable most illuminating. We are all men hanging on the thread of a few rapidly vanishing years over the bottomless pit of death, destruction, and nothingness. Those objective facts are starkly real. Let us not try to disguise them. Yet I find it marvelously interesting that man's *consciousness*, his reason and his passion, can elevate these routine, objective, external events, in a moment of lucidity and feeling, to the status of a personally appropriated ideal—an ideal which does not annul those objective facts, but which *reinterprets* them and clothes them with the apparel of *man's subjectivity*.

---

[3] R. Hertz, *Chance and Symbol* (Chicago: University of Chicago, 1948), pp. 142–143.—E.D.K.

It is time, once again, to speak personally. What your situation is, I cannot say. But I know that I am that Syrian, and that I am hanging over the pit. My doom is inevitable and swiftly approaching. If, in these few moments that are yet mine, I can find no rose to respond to, or rather, if I have lost the ability to respond, then I shall moan and curse my fate with a howl of bitter agony. But *if* I can, in these last moments, respond to a rose—or to a philosophical argument or theory of physics, or to a Scarlatti sonata, or to the touch of a human hand—I say, if I can so respond and can thereby transform an external and fatal event into a moment of conscious insight and significance, then I shall go down *without hope or appeal* yet *passionately triumphant and with joy.*

Suggestions for Further Reading

○

I. General Books in the Philosophy of Religion[1]

Abernethy, George L., and Thomas A. Langford, eds. *Philosophy of Religion: A Book of Readings*. 2d ed. New York: Macmillan, 1968.

Alston, W. P., ed. *Religious Belief and Philosophical Thought*. New York: Harcourt Brace Jovanovich, 1963.

Bambrough, Renford. *Reason, Truth and God*. London: Methuen, 1969.

Bowden, John and James Richmond, eds. *A Reader in Contemporary Theology*. Philadelphia: Westminster Press, 1967.

Brody, Baruch A. *Readings in the Philosophy of Religion*. Englewood Cliffs, NJ: Prentice-Hall, 1974.

Burtt, E. *Types of Religious Philosophy*. rev. ed. New York: Harper & Row, 1951.

Cahn, S. *Philosophy of Religion*. New York: Harper & Row, 1970.

Campbell, C. A. *On Selfhood and Godhood*. London: Allen and Unwin, 1957.

Christian, W. *Meaning and Truth in Religion*. Princeton, NJ: Princeton University Press, 1964.

Collins, J. *God in Modern Philosophy*. Chicago: Henry Regnery, 1950.

Donnelly, J. *Logical Analysis and Contemporary Theism*. New York: Fordham University Press, 1972.

Edwards, R. B. *An Introduction to the Philosophy of Religion*. New York: Harcourt Brace Jovanovich, 1972.

Ferre, F. *Language, Logic and God*. New York: Harper & Row, 1961.

Flew, Antony. *God and Philosophy*. London: Hutchinson, 1966.

Flew, Antony, and Alasdair MacIntyre. *New Essays in Philosophical Theology*. London: SCM, 1955.

Gill, Jerry, ed. *Philosophy and Religion: Some Contemporary Perspectives*. Minneapolis: Burgess, 1968.

Hepburn, R. W. *Christianity and Paradox*. London: Routledge and Kegan Paul, 1969.

Hick, John, ed. *Classical and Contemporary Readings in the Philosophy of Religion*. 2d ed. Englewood Cliffs, NJ: Prentice-Hall, 1970.

Hick, John, ed. *Existence of God*. New York: Macmillan, 1964.

Hick, John. *Faith and the Philosophers*. London: Macmillan, 1964.

Hick, John. *The Philosophy of Religion*. 2d ed. Englewood Cliffs, NJ: Prentice-Hall, 1973.

Hook, S., ed. *Religious Experience and Truth*. New York: New York University Press, 1961.

---

[1] Some of these works are appropriate for Section II (p. 616) also.

Lewis, H. D. *Our Experience of God*. London: Allen and Unwin, 1959.

Lewis, H. D. *Philosophy of Religion*. London: English University Press, 1965.

MacIntyre, Alasdair C. *Difficulties in Christian Belief*. London: SCM, 1959.

Martin, C. B. *Religious Belief*. Ithaca, NY: Cornell University Press, 1959.

Mavrodes, George I. *Belief in God*. New York: Random House, 1970.

Mavrodes, George I. ed. *The Rationality of Belief in God*. Englewood Cliffs, NJ: Prentice-Hall, 1970.

Mavrodes, George I., and Stuart C. Hackett, eds. *Problems and Perspectives in the Philosophy of Religion*. New York: Harper & Row, 1970.

Miller, Ed, ed. *Classical Statements on Faith and Reason*. New York: Random House, 1970.

Miller, Ed. *God and Reason*. New York: Macmillan, 1972.

Miller, Ed, ed. *Philosophical and Religious Issues*. Belmont, CA: Dickenson, 1971.

Mitchell, Basil, ed. *Faith and Logic*. London: Allen and Unwin, 1957.

Mitchell, Basil. *The Philosophy of Religion*. London: Oxford University Press, 1971.

McPherson, T. *Philosophy of Religion*. London: Van Nostrand, 1965.

Neilsen, Kai. *An Introduction to the Philosophy of Religion*. London: Macmillan, 1982.

Penelhum, T. *Religion and Rationality*. New York: Random House, 1971.

Plantinga, Alvin, ed. *Faith and Philosophy*. Grand Rapids, MI: Eerdman, 1964.

Ross, J. F. *Introduction to the Philosophy of Religion*. New York: Macmillan, 1970.

Rowe, William. *Philosophy of Religion: An Introduction*. Belmont, CA: Wadsworth, 1978.

Rowe, William L., and William J. Wainwright, eds. *Philosophy of Religion: Selected Readings*. New York: Harcourt Brace Jovanovich, 1973.

Smart, N., ed. *Historical Selections in the Philosophy of Religion*. New York: Harper & Row, 1962.

Thomas, G. *Religious Philosophies of the West*. New York: Scribners, 1965.

II. The Existence of God[2]

A. General

Blackstone, William, ed. *The Problems of Religious Knowledge*. Englewood Cliffs, NJ: Prentice-Hall, 1963.

Davies, Brian. *An Introduction to the Philosophy of Religion*. Oxford: Oxford University Press, 1982.

Ducasse, C. J. *A Philosophical Scrutiny of Religion*. New York: The Ronald Press, 1953.

Ferre, Frederick. *Language, Logic and God*. New York: Harper & Row, 1969.

Flew, Antony. *God and Philosophy*. New York: Harper & Row, 1961.

Hepburn, Ronald W. *Christianity and Paradox*. London: C. A. Watts & Company Ltd., 1958.

Hick, John. *Arguments for the Existence of God*. New York: Herder and Herder, 1971.

Mackie, J. L. *The Miracle of Theism*. Oxford: Oxford University Press, 1982.

Mascall, E. L. *Existence and Analogy*. NY: Longman Group, 1949.

Matson, Wallace I. *The Existence of God*. Ithaca, NY: Cornell University Press, 1965.

Mavrodes, George I. *Belief in God*. New York: Random House, 1970.

Otto, Rudolf. *The Idea of the Holy*. Oxford: Oxford University Press, 1958.

Penelhum, Terrence. *Religion and Rationality*. New York: Random House, 1971.

---

[2] See also some of the titles in Section I (above).

Pike, Nelson. *God and Timelessness*. New York: Schocken Books, 1970.
Plantinga, Alvin. *God, Freedom, and Evil*. New York: Harper & Row, 1974.
Ross, James F. *Philosophical Theology*. New York: Bobbs-Merrill, 1969.
Rowe, William. *Philosophy of Religion: An Introduction*. Belmont, CA: Wadsworth, 1978.
Swinburne, Richard. T*he Existence of God*. Oxford: Clarendon Press, 1979.
Yandell, Keith. *Christianity and Philosophy*. Grand Rapids, MI: Eerdmans, 1984.

B. The Cosmological Argument

Burrill R. *The Cosmological Arguments*. Garden City, NY: Doubleday, Anchor Books, 1967.
Copleston, F. C. *Aquinas*. Baltimore: Penguin, 1955.
Craig, William. *The Cosmological Argument from Plato to Leibniz*. New York: Barnes and Noble, 1980.
Mascall, E. L. *He Who Is*. London: Longmans Green & Co., 1943.
Rowe, William. *The Cosmological Argument*. Princeton: Princeton University Press, 1975.

C. The Teleological Argument

McPherson, Thomas. *The Argument from Design*. London: Macmillan, 1972.
Salmon, Wesley. "Religion and Science: A New Look at Hume's Dialogue." *Philosophical Studies* 33 (1978): 145.
Swinburne, Richard. "The Argument from Design-A Defence." *Religious Studies* 8 (1972): 193–205.
Tennant, R. R. *Philosophical Theology*. Cambridge: Cambridge University Press, 1928–30.

D. The Ontological Argument

Adams, R. "The Logical Structure of Anselm's Argument." *Philosophical Review*, 1971.
Barnes, Jonathan. *The Ontological Argument*. London: Macmillan, 1972.
Hick, J., and A. McGill, eds. *The Many-Faced Argument*. New York: Macmillan, 1965.
Paton, H. J. *The Modern Predicament*. New York: Macmillan, 1955.
Plantinga, Alvin, ed. *The Ontological Argument from St. Anselm to Contemporary Philosophers*. Garden City, NY: Doubleday, 1965.
Plantinga, A. *God and Other Minds*. Ithaca, NY: Cornell University Press, 1967.

E. Mysticism and Religious Experience

Alston, W. P. "Ineffability." *Philosophical Review* (1956).
Baillie, John. *Our Knowledge of God*. New York: Scribners, 1962.
Gale, Richard. "Mysticism and Philosophy." *Journal of Philosphy* 57 (1960).
Inge, W. R. *Mysticism in Religion*. Chicago, IL: University of Chicago Press, 1948.
James, William. *Variety of Religious Experiences*. New York: Longmans, Green, 1902.
Lewis, H. D. *Our Experience of God*. New York: Macmillan, 1959.
Martin, C. B. *Religious Belief*. Ithaca, NY: Cornell University Press, 1959.
Nielsen, K. "Christian Positivism and the Appeal to Religious Experience." *Journal of Religion* (1962).
Stace, Walter T. *Mysticism and Philosophy*. New York: Macmillan, 1961.
Stace, Walter T. *The Teachings of the Mystics*. New York: New American Library, 1960.
Stace, Walter T. *Time and Eternity*. Princeton: Princeton University Press, 1952.
Underhill, E. *Mysticism*. New York: Macmillan, 1930.
Wainwright, William. "Mysticism and Sense Perception." *Religious Studies* 9 (1973).

III. The Attributes of God

David, Stephen T. *Logic and the Nature of God.* Grand Rapids, MI: Eerdmans, 1983.
Donnelly, J. "Creation ex nihilo." *Proceedings of the American Catholic Philosophical Association* (1970).
Geach, P. "Causality and Creation." *Sophia* (1962).
Geach, P. "God's Relation to the World." *Sophia* (1969).
Hartshorne, Charles. *The Divine Reality.* New Haven, CN: Yale University Press, 1948.
Kretzmann, Norman. "Omniscience and Immutability." *Journal of Philosophy* 63 (1966).
Pike, Nelson. *God and Time.* Ithaca, NY: Cornell University Press, 1970.
Ross, James. *Philosophical Theology.* Indianapolis: Bobbs-Merrill, 1969.
Stump, Eleonore, and Norman Kretzmann. "Eternity." *Journal of Philosophy* 78 (August 1981).
Swinburne, Richard. *The Coherence of Theism.* Oxford: Oxford University Press, 1977.
Urban, Linwood, and Douglas Walton, eds. *The Power of God.* Oxford: Oxford University Press, 1978.
Wolterstorff, Nicholas. "God Everlasting." In *God and the Good*, edited by C. Orlebeke and L. Smedes. Grand Rapids, MI: Eerdmans, 1975.

IV. Religious Belief

Crosson, Frederick, ed. *The Autonomy of Religious Belief.* Notre Dame: University of Notre Dame Press, 1981.
Delaney, C. F., ed. *Rationality and Religious Belief.* Notre Dame: University of Notre Dame Press, 1978.
Hick, J. *Faith and the Philosophers.* New York: Macmillan, 1964.
Kellenberger, J. *Religious Discovery, Faith and Knowledge.* Englewood Cliffs, NJ: Prentice-Hall, 1972.
Mackie, J. L. *The Miracle of Theism: Arguments for and against the Existence of God.* Oxford: Clarendon Press, 1982.
Mavrodes, George I. *Belief in God.* New York: Random House, 1970.
Mitchell, Basil. *The Justification of Religious Belief.* London: Macmillan, 1973.
Phillips, D. Z. *Religion without Explanation.* Oxford: Basil Blackwell, 1976.
Phillips, D. Z. "Religious Belief and Language-Games." *Ratio* (1970).
Price, H. H. "Belief in and Belief that." *Religious Studies* (1965).
Swinburne, Richard. *Faith and Reason.* Oxford: Clarendon Press, 1981.

V. Atheism

Angeles, Peter A., ed. *Critiques of God.* Buffalo, NY: Prometheus Books, 1976.
Angeles, Peter A. *The Problem of God: A Short Introduction.* Columbus, Ohio: Charles E. Merrill, 1974.
Baier, Kurt. *The Meaning of Life.* Inaugural lecture delivered at the Canberra University College on October 15, 1957. Canberra: Government Printer, 1957.
Baumer, Franklin L. *Religion and the Rise of Scepticism.* New York: Harcourt, Brace & World, 1960p.
Blackham, H. J., ed. *Objections to Humanism.* Philadelphia: Lippincott, 1963.
Blanshard, Paul. *Classics of Free Thought.* Buffalo, NY: Prometheus Books, 1976.
Cohen, Morris R. *A Dreamer's Journey.* Boston: Beacon Press, 1949.

Dewey, John. *A Common Faith*. New Haven: Yale University Press, 1960.

Ducasse, C. J. *A Philosophical Scrutiny of Religion*. New York: The Ronald Press Company, 1953.

Fabro, C. *God in Exile: Modern Atheism*. New York: Paulist-Newman, 1968.

Flew, Antony. *God and Philosophy*. New York: Dell, 1966.

Feuerbach Ludwig. *The Essence of Christianity*. New York: Harper & Row, 1953p.

Freud, Sigmund. *The Future of an Illusion*. Translated by W. D. Robson-Scott. Garden City, NY: Doubleday Anchor Books, 1957.

Gonzalez, J. M.-Ruiz. *Atheistic Humanism and Biblical God*. Milwaukee: Bruce, 1969.

Hawton, Hector. *Controversy: The Humanist-Christian Encounter*. Buffalo, NY: Prometheus Books, 1975.

Hook, Sidney, ed. *Religious Experience and Truth*. New York: New York University Press, 1961.

Huxley, Julian. *Religion without Revelation*, rev. ed. New York: New American Library, 1958.

Huxley, T. H. *Science and the Christian Tradition*. New York: Appleton & Company, 1894.

Ingersoll, Robert G. *The Gods, and Other Lectures*. Washington, D. C.: C. P. Farrell, 1882.

Ingersoll, Robert G. *Lectures and Essays*. London: Watts, 1904–1905.

Ingersoll, Robert G. *The Philosophy of Ingersoll*. Edited by V. Goldthwaite. New York: P. Elder, 1906.

Kaufmann, Walter. *Critique of Religion and Philosophy*. New York: Harper & Row, 1958.

Kaufmann, Walter. *The Faith of a Heretic*. Garden City, NY: Doubleday, 1961.

Knight, Margaret. *Honest to Man: Christian Ethics Re-examined*. Buffalo, NY: Prometheus Books, 1976.

Kolenda, Konstantin. *Religion without God*. Buffalo, NY: Prometheus Books, 1976.

Kurtz, Paul, and Albert Dondeyne, eds. *A Catholic/Humanist Dialogue*. Buffalo, NY: Prometheus Books, 1975.

Lamont, Corliss. *The Philosophy of Humanism*. New York: Frederick Ungar Co., 1965.

Lepp, Ignace. *Atheism in Our Time*. New York: Macmillan, 1964p.

MacIntyre, Alasdair C. *Difficulties in Christian Belief*. London: Student Christian Movement Press, 1959.

MacIntyre, Alasdair C. and P. Ricoeur. *The Religious Significance of Atheism*. New York: Columbia University Press, 1969.

Macy, Christopher, ed. *Science, Reason, and Religion*. Buffalo, NY: Prometheus Books. 1975.

Madden, E. H., R. Handy, and M. Farber, eds. *The Idea of God*. Springfield, Ill.: Thomas, 1968.

McPherson, Thomas. *The Philosophy of Religion*. London: D. Van Nostrand Co., 1965.

Mencken, H. L. *Treatise on the Gods*. New York: Vintage Books, 1958.

Nielsen, Kai. *Contemporary Critiques of Religion*. New York: Herder and Herder, 1971.

Nielsen, Kai. *Ethics Without God*. Buffalo, NY: Prometheus Books, 1973.

Nielsen, Kai. "In Defense of Atheism." In *Perspectives in Education, Religion, and the Arts* (127–56), edited by Howard E. Kiefer and Milton Munitz. Albany: State University of New York Press, 1970.

Nielsen, Kai. *Philosophy and Atheism*. Buffalo, NY: Prometheus Books 1985.

Nielsen, Kai. "Religion and Commitment." In *Religious Language and Knowledge*, edited by Robert Hyman Ayers and William T. Blackstone. Athens: University of Georgia Press, 1972.

Nielsen, Kai. *Scepticism*. New York: St. Martin's Press, 1973.

Robinson, Richard. *An Atheist's Values*. London: Oxford University Press, 1964.

Russell, Bertrand. *Religion and Science*. London: Oxford University Press, 1935.
Russell, Bertrand. *Why I Am Not a Christian*. New York: Simon & Schuster, 1967p.

VI. Religious Language

Ammerman, Robert R. ed., *Classics of Analytic Philosophy*. New York: McGraw-Hill, 1965.
Ayers, Robert H., and William T. Blackstone, eds. *Religious Language and Knowledge*. Athens: University of Georgia Press, 1972.
Blackstone, W. T. *The Problem of Religious Knowledge*. Englewood Cliffs, NJ: Prentice-Hall, 1963p.
Cell, E. *Language, Existence and God*. Nashville: Abingdon Press, 1971.
Donnelly, John, ed. *Logical Analysis and Contemporary Theism*. New York: Fordham University Press, 1972.
Downing, F. Gerald. "Games, Families, the Public, and Religion." *American Philosophical Quarterly* (April 1972).
Evans, Donald. *The Logic of Self-Involvement*. London: SCM, 1963.
Ewing, A. C. *Non-Linguistic Philosophy*. London: Allen and Unwin, 1968.
Ewing, A. C. "Religious Assertions in the Light of Contemporary Philosophy." *Philosophy* 32 (1957).
Ferre, Frederick. *Language, Logic and God*. New York: Harper, 1961.
Flew, Antony and Alasdair C. MacIntyre, eds. *New Essays in Philosophical Theology*. New York: Macmillan, 1955.
Gilkey, Langdon. *Naming the Whirlwind: The Renewal of God-Language*. Indianapolis: Bobbs-Merrill, 1969p.
Gill, Jerry. *The Possibility of Religious Knowledge*. Grand Rapids MI: Eerdmans, 1971.
Heimbeck. R. S. *Theology and Meaning*. Stanford: Stanford University Press, 1969.
Hepburn. R. W. *Christianity and Paradox*. London: Watts, 1958.
Hepburn, R. W. "Poetry and Religious Belief." In *Metaphysical Beliefs*, ed. Alasdair MacIntyre. London: SCM, 1957.
Hick, John. *Faith and Knowledge*. 2d ed. Ithaca, NY: Cornell University Press, 1966.
Hick, John. "The Justification of Religious Belief." *Theology* (1968): 100–107.
High, Dallas. *Language, Persons and Belief*. New York: Oxford University Press, 1967.
High, D. M., ed. *New Essays on Religious Language*. Oxford: Clarendon Press, 1969.
Hodges, H. A. *Languages, Standpoints and Attitudes*. Oxford: Clarendon Press, 1953.
Holland, R. F. "Religious Discourse and Theological Discourse." *The Australasian Journal of Philosophy* 34 (1956).
Kellenberger, James. *Religious Discovery, Faith and Knowledge*. New York: Prentice-Hall, 1972.
Macquarrie, John. *God-Talk*. New York: Harper & Row, 1967.
Miles, T. R. *Religion and the Scientific Outlook*. London: Allen & Unwin, 1959.
Mitchell, Basil, ed. *The Philosophy of Religion*. London: Oxford University Press, 1971.
Neilsen, Kai. *Contemporary Critiques of Religion*. New York: Herder and Herder, 1971.
Neilsen, Kai. "Eschatological Verification." *Canadian Journal of Theology* 9 (1963) 271–81.
Neilsen, Kai. "On Fixing the Reference Range of 'God'." *Religious Studies* 2 (1966).
Neilsen, Kai. "Wittgensteinian Fideism." *Philosophy* (1967).
Penelhum, Terrence. *Problems of Religious Knowledge*. New York: Herder and Herder, 1972.
Penelhum, Terrence. *Religion and Rationality*. New York: Random House, 1971.
Phillips, D. Z., ed. *Religion and Understanding*. Oxford: Blackwell, 1967.
Ramsey, Ian T. *Christian Discourse*. London: Oxford University Press, 1965.

Ramsey, Ian T. *Religious Language: An Empirical Placing of Theological Phrases*. London: SCM, 1957.

Ramsey, Ian T., ed. *Words About God*. New York: Harper & Row, 1971.

Richmond, James. *Theology and Metaphysics*. New York: SCM, 1970.

Santoni, Ronald E., ed. *Religious Language and the Problem of Religious Knowledge*. Bloomington: Indiana University Press, 1968p.

Schmidt, P. *Religious Knowledge*. New York: Free Press, 1961.

Vesey, G. N. A., ed. *Talk of God*. London: Macmillan, 1969.

Zuurdeeg, W. *An Analytical Philosophy of Religion*. Nashville: Abingdon Press, 1958.

VII. The Problem of Evil

Farrer, Austin. *Love Almighty and Ills Unlimited*. London: Fontana, 1961.

Flew, Antony. "Divine Omnipotence and Human Freedom." *New Essays in Philosophical Theology*. (144–69) eds. Flew and MacIntyre (q. v.), London: SCM, 1955.

Gilkey, Langdon. *Maker of Heaven and Earth*. New York: Doubleday, 1959.

Hick, John. *Evil and the God of Love*. New York: Macmillan, 1966.

James, John. *Why Evil? A Biblical Approach*. Baltimore, MD: Penguin, 1960.

Lewis, C. S. *The Problem of Pain*. London: Geoffrey Bles, 1940.

Mackie, J. L. "Evil and Omnipotence." *Mind* 64 (1955): 200–212.

Mackie, J. L. *The Miracle of Theism*. (Chap. 9) Oxford: Oxford University Press, 1982.

Mackie, J. L. "Theism and Utopia." *Philosophy* 37 (1962). Reprinted in *God and Evil*, ed. Pike.

Pike, N., ed. *God and Evil: Readings on the Theological Problem of Evil*. London: Prentice-Hall, 1964.

Plantinga, Alvin. *God and Other Minds*. Ithaca, NY: Cornell University Press, 1967.

Rowe, William. "The Problem of Evil and Some Varieties of Atheism." *American Philosophical Quarterly* 7 (1970): 335–41.

Schlesinger, George N. "Suffering and Evil." In *Contemporary Philosophy of Religion*, edited by Steven M. Cahn and David Shatz. Oxford: Oxford University Press, 1982.

Smart, R. N. "Omnipotence, Evil and Supermen." *Philosophy* 36 (1961). Reprinted in *God and Evil*, ed. Pike.

Swinburne, Richard. *The Existence of God*. (Chap. 11) Oxford: Oxford University Press, 1978.

Swinburne, Richard. "Natural Evil." *American Philosophical Quarterly* 15 (1978): 295–301.

Wainwright, William J. "God and the Necessity of Physical Evils." *Sophia* 11 (1972): 16–19.

Whale, J. S. *The Christian Answer to the Problem of Evil*. London: SCM, 1957.

Wisdom, J. "God and Evil." *Mind* 44 (1935).

VIII. Miracles

Broad, C. F. "Hume's Theory of the Credibility of Miracles." *Proceedings of the Aristotelian Society* 17 (1916–17).

Brummer, Vincent. *What Do We Do When We Pray?* London: SCM, 1984.

Dietl, Paul. "On Miracles." *American Philosophical Quarterly* 5 (1968): 130–34.

Flew, Antony. *God and Philosophy*. (Chap. 2) London: Hutchinson, 1966.

Flew, Antony. "Miracles." *Encyclopedia of Philosophy*, edited by Paul Edwards. New York: Macmillan, 1966.

Geisler, Norman L. *Miracles and Modern Thought*. Grand Rapids, MI: Zondervan, 1982.
Holland, R. F. "The Miraculous." *American Philosophical Quarterly* 2 (1965): 43–51.
Keller, E., and M. L. *Miracles in Dispute*. London: SCM Press, 1969.
Lewis, C. S. *Miracles*, rev. ed. London: Collins Fontana Books, 1955.
Nowell-Smith, Patrick. "Miracles." In *New Essays in Philosophical Theology*, edited by Antony Flew and Alasdair C. MacIntyre. London: Macmillan, 1955.
Rowe, William. *Philosophy of Religion*. (Chap. 9) Belmont: Wadsworth, 1978.
Smart, Ninian. "Miracles and David Hume." *Philosophers and Religious Truth*. (Chap. 2) London: SCM, 1964.
Swinburne, Richard. *The Concept of Miracle*. London: Macmillan, 1970.
Ward, Keith. "Miracles and Testimony." *Religious Studies* 21 (1985): 134–45.

IX. Life after Death

Ducasse, C. J. *A Critical Examination of the Belief in Life after Death*. Springfield, IL: Charles C. Thomas, 1961.
Flew, Antony. *Body, Mind, and Death*. New York: Macmillan, 1964.
Flew, Antony. "Immortality." *Encyclopedia of Philosophy*, edited by Paul Edwards. New York: Free Press, 1965.
Geach, Peter. *God and the Soul*. London: Routledge & Kegan Paul, 1969.
Lamont, Corliss. *The Illusion of Immortality*. New York: The Philosophical Library, 1965.
Penelhum, Terrence. *Survival and Disembodied Existence*. London: Routledge & Kegan Paul, 1970.
Perry, John. *Personal Identity and Immortality*. Indianapolis: Hackett, 1979.
Price, H. H. *Essays in the Philosophy of Religion*. London: Oxford University Press, 1972.
Purtill, Richard. *Thinking about Religion*. (Chaps. 9 and 10) Englewood Cliffs, NJ: Prentice-Hall, 1978.
Quinton, Antony. "The Soul." *Journal of Philosophy* 59 (1962): 393–409.

X. Religion and Ethics

Anscombe, G. E. M. "Modern Moral Philosophy." *Philosophy* (1958).
Brown, P. "Religious Morality." *Mind* (1963).
Helm, Paul, ed. *The Divine Command Theory of Ethics*. Oxford: Oxford University Press, 1979.
Kierkegaard, Soren. *Fear and Trembling*, translated by Howard V. Hong and Edna H. Hong. Princeton: Princeton University Press, 1983.
Nielsen, Kai. *Ethics without God*. London: Pemberton Books, 1973.
Nielsen, Kai. "On the Independence of Morality from Religion." *Mind* (1961).
Outka, Gene, and J. P. Reeder, eds. *Religion and Morality: A Collection of Essays*. New York: Anchor Books, 1973.
Phillips, D. Z. "Moral and Religious Conception of Duty." *Mind* (1964).
Quinn, Philip. *Divine Commands and Moral Requirements*. Oxford: Clarendon Press, 1978.

XI. Religion and the Meaning of Life

Althaus, Paul. "The Meaning and Purpose of History in the Christian View." *Universitas* 7 (1965): 197–204.
Barnes, Hazel E. *An Existentialist Ethic*. (98–115, passim) New York: Alfred A. Knopf, 1967.

Black, Algernon. "Our Quest for Faith: Is Humanism Enough?" In *The Humanist Alternative*, edited by P. Kurtz. Buffalo, NY: Prometheus Books, 1973.

Blackham, H. J. "The Human Programme." In *The Humanist Frame*, edited by J. Huxley. London: Allen and Unwin, 1961.

Britton, Karl. *Philosophy and the Meaning of Life.* Cambridge: Cambridge University Press, 1969.

de Saint-Exupery, Antoine. *Wind, Sand, and Stars.* (Chap. 9, passim) New York: Harcourt, Brace and World, 1939.

Fackenheim, E. L. "Judaism and the Meaning of Life." *Commentary* 39 (1965): 49–55.

Flew, Antony, "Tolstoi and the Meaning of Life." *Ethics* 73 (1963): 110–18.

Frankl, Victor. *Man's Search for Meaning.* New York: Beacon, 1963.

Fromm, Erich. *Man for Himself.* New York: Holt, Rinehart, and Winston, 1947.

Greene, T. M. "Man Out of Darkness." *Atlantic Monthly*, April 1949.

Hocking, W. E. "Meanings of Life." *Journal of Religion* 16 (1936).

Hollis, Christopher. "What Is the Purpose of Life?" *The Listener* 70 (1961): 133–36.

James, William. "Is Life Worth Living?" *The Will to Believe and Other Essays in Popular Philosophy*. New York: Longmans, Green, 1897.

Ketcham, Charles B. *The Search for Meaningful Existence.* New York: Weybright and Talley, 1968.

Klemke, E. D., ed. *The Meaning of Life.* New York: Oxford University Press, 1981.

Kurtz, Paul. *The Fullness of Life.* (Chap. 5) New York: Horizon, 1974.

Lamont, Corliss. "The Philosophy of Humanism." In *The Philosophy of Humanism.* (Passim) New York: Frederich Ungar, 1949.

Marcel, Gabriel. *The Mystery of Being.* Vol. 1 (199–215) Chicago: Henry Regnery, 1960.

Robinson, Richard. *An Atheist's Values.* (54–57, 155–57) Oxford: Oxford University Press, 1964.

Russell, L. J. "The Meaning of Life." *Philosophy* 28 (1953): 30–40.

Sartre, Jean-Paul. "Existentialism." In *Existentialism and Human Emotions*. New York: Philosophical Library, 1948.

Sanders, Steven, and David R. Cheney, eds. *The Meaning of Life: Questions, Answers, and Analysis.* Englewood Cliffs, NJ: Prentice-Hall, Inc., 1980.

Schopenhauer, Arthur. "On the Sufferings of the World." Translated by T. B. Saunders, Richard Taylor, ed., *The Will to Live: Selected Writings of Arthur Schopenhauer*. New York: Ungar, 1962.

Schopenhauer, Arthur. "On the Vanity and Suffering of Life." Translated by T. B. Sanders. Richard Taylor, ed., *The Will to Live: Selected Writings of Arthur Schopenhauer*. New York: Ungar, 1962.

Schopenhauer, Arthur. "The Vanity of Existence." Translated by T. B. Saunders. Richard Taylor, ed., *The Will to Live: Selected Writings of Arthur Schopenhauer.* New York: Ungar, 1962.

Stace, Walter T. "Man Against Darkness." *The Atlantic Monthly*, September 1948.

Copyrights and Acknowledgments

The editor and publisher gratefully acknowledge the kind permission of the authors, editors, and publishers that have enabled us to reprint the essays included in this book.

1. Saint Anselm, "The Ontological Argument for the Existence of God." From Anselm, *The Proslogion*, Chs. II–IV. Reprinted with permission of Macmillan Publishing Company from *The Many-Faced Argument* edited by Arthur C. McGill and John Hick. Translated by Arthur C. McGill. Copyright © 1968 John H. Hick and Arthur C. McGill.

2. St. Thomas Aquinas, "Five Ways to Prove the Existence of God (The Cosmological and Design Arguments)." From *The Basic Writings of St. Thomas Aquinas* (N.Y.: Random House, 1945). Translated by Anton C. Pegis. Reprinted by permission of the A. C. Pegis Estate and by permission of Burns and Oates, Ltd.

3. René Descartes, "The Ontological Argument Restated." From *The Philosophical Works of Descartes*, Vol. 1 (N.Y. 1911). Translated by Haldane and Ross. Reprinted with the permission of Cambridge University Press.

4. William Paley, "The Watch and the Human Eye: The Argument from Design." From Paley, *Evidence of the Existence and Attributes of the Deity* (1802).

5. Immanuel Kant, "God and Immortality as Postulates of Practical Reason." Reprinted with permission of Macmillan Publishing Company from Kant, *Critique of Practical Reason*. Translated by Lewis White Beck (pp. 114–115, 126–136). Copyright © 1956 by Macmillan Publishing Company.

6. William James, "Mysticism and Religious Experience." From James, *The Variety of Religious Experience* (1902). Lectures XVI–XVII.

7. W. T. Stace, "The Teachings of the Mystics." Reprinted with permission of the Jennifer Jean Stace Trust.

8. Gaunilo, "The Ontological Argument" with Anselm's Replies. From Anselm, *The Proslogian*, Chs. II–IV. Reprinted with permission of Macmillan Publishing Company from *The Many-Faced Argument* edited by Arthur C. McGill and John Hick. Translated by Arthur C. McGill. Copyright © 1968 John H. Hick and Arthur C. McGill.

9. David Hume, "The Cosmological Argument." From Hume, *Dialogues Concerning Natural Religion*. Parts IX.

10. David Hume, "The Design Argument." From Hume, *Dialogues Concerning Natural Religion*. Parts II, IV–VIII.

11. Immanuel Kant, "The Ontological, Cosmological, and Design Arguments." From *Immanuel Kant's Critique of Pure Reason*. Translated by Norman Kemp Smith. Copyright © 1933 by St. Martin's Press, Inc. Reprinted with permission of St. Martin's Press, Inc.

12. Søren Kierkegaard, "Against Proofs of God." From Kierkegaard, *Philosophical Fragments*. Copyright 1936 Princeton University Press. © 1962 renewed by Princeton University Press. Excerpt, pp. 31–36 reprinted with permission of Princeton University Press.

13. Søren Kierkegaard, "Truth Is Subjectivity." From Kierkegaard, *Concluding Unscientific Postscript*. Copyright 1941 Princeton University Press. © 1969 renewed by Princeton University Press. Excerpts, pp. 18–210 reprinted with permission of Princeton University Press.

14. Ludwig Feuerbach, "Religion as Illusion." From Feuerbach, *The Essence of Christianity*. Translated by George Eliot. Ch. 1, pp. 12–32.

15. Karl Marx, "The Opium of the People." From Marx, *Early Writings*. Translated and edited by T. B. Bottomore (N.Y.: McGraw Hill, 1963), pp. 43–44, 52–53, 58. Reprinted by permission of McGraw Hill Publishing Company.

16. Sigmund Freud, "Religious Ideas as Illusions." From Freud, *The Future of an Illusion*. Sigmund Freud Copyrights, The Institute of Psycho-Analysis and the Hogarth Press for permission to quote. Translated by W. D. Robson-Scott, 1928. Reprinted with permission of Chatto and Windus and The Hogarth Press.

17. Friedrich Nietzsche, "Attack on Christianity." From *The Portable Nietzsche*. Edited and translated by Walter Kaufmann. Copyright 1954 by the Viking Press, Inc. Copyright renewed © 1982 by Viking Penguin, Inc. Reprinted by permission of Viking Penguin, a division of Penguin Books USA, Inc.

18. Emile Durkheim, "The Social Foundation of Religion." From Durkheim, *The Elementary Forms of Religious Life*. Translated by Joseph Ward Swain. (N.Y.: The Free Press, 1965) Reprinted with permission of the Free Press, a Division of Macmillan, Inc.

19. John Stuart Mill, "Evil and a Finite God." From Mill, *Three Essays on Religion* (1875), "Attributes," Part II. Longmans Green & Co., Inc., 1974.

20. John Dewey, "Religion versus the Religious." From Dewey, *A Common Faith*, Ch. 1, pp. 1–28. Reprinted with permission of Yale University Press.

21. Ernest Nagel, "Philosophical Concepts of Atheism." In J. E. Fairchild (Ed.), *Basic Beliefs*. (N.Y.: Sheridan House, Inc. 1959.)

22. Bertrand Russell, "The Existence of God—A Debate." From Russell, *Why I Am Not a Christian* (N.Y.: Simon & Schuster), pp. 5–14. Copyright © 1957, 1985 by Allen and Unwin. Reprinted with permission.

23. Bertrand Russell and F. C. Copleston, "A Debate on the Existence of God." From Russell, *Why I Am Not a Christian*. Reprinted by kind permission of Unwin Hyman, Ltd. and by permission of Frederick C. Copleston.

24. Richard Taylor, "God: The Cosmological and Design Arguments." From Taylor, *Metaphysics*, 3/e, © 1983, pp. 90–105. Reprinted by permission of Prentice Hall, Inc., Englewood Cliffs, New Jersey.

25. J. B. Pratt, "Religious Knowledge and Mystical Experience." From Pratt, *Can We Keep the Faith*? Copyright 1941 by Yale University Press. Reprinted with permission of Yale University Press.

26. William Alston, "Religious Experience and Religious Belief." Reprinted by permission of the author and the editor of *Nous*, Vol. XVI, No. 1, (March 1982): 3–12. Copyright © 1982 by *Nous*, Indiana University.

27. C. S. Lewis, "The Basis of the Moral Law." From Lewis, *Mere Christianity*. Reprinted by permission of Collins Publishers.

28. Norman Malcolm, "Anselm's Ontological Arguments." From *The Philosophical Review* 69 (1960), pp. 41–62. Reprinted with the permission of the editor and the author.

29. A. J. Ayer, "The Elimination of Metaphysics." From Ayer, *Language, Truth, and Logic.* (N.Y.: Dover Publications, Inc. 1946). Reprinted with permission of Dover Publications.

30. A. J. Ayer, "Critique of Theology." From Ayer, *Language, Truth, and Logic.* (N.Y.: Dover Publications, Inc. 1946). Reprinted with permission of Dover Publications.

31. Antony Flew, R. M. Hare, and Basil Mitchell, "Theology and Falsification." From *New Essays in Philosophical Theology* by Antony Flew and Alasdair McIntyre (eds.). Copyright © 1955 by Antony Flew and Alasdair McIntyre. Reprinted with permission of Macmillan Publishing Company.

32. John Wisdom, "Gods." *Proceedings of the Aristotelian Society*, 1944–45. Copyright © The Aristotelian Society, 1944–45. Reprinted by courtesy of the Editor.

33. I. M. Crombie, "Theology and Falsification." From Crombie, reprinted with permission of Macmillan Publishing Company. Copyright © 1955 Antony Flew and Alasdair McIntyre.

34. R. B. Braithwaite, "An Empiricist's View of the Nature of Religious Belief." The Ninth Arthur Stanley Memorial Lecture, Nov. 1955, pp. 11–28, 30–35. Reprinted with permission of Cambridge University Press.

35. John Hick, "Theology and Verification." From *Theology Today* Vol. 17 (1960), pp. 1–22. Reprinted with the permission of the editor.

36. John Wisdom, "The Logic of God." From *Wisdom, Paradox and Discovery.* Reprinted with permission of the author.

37. E. D. Klemke, "Are Religious Statements Meaningful?" From *The Journal of Religion* Vol. XL, No. 1 (Jan. 1960) pp. 27–39. Reprinted with permission of the University of Chicago Press.

38. Ludwig Wittgenstein, "Lectures on Religious Belief." From Wittgenstein, *Lectures and Conversations on Aesthetics, Psychology, and Religious Belief.* (Berkeley: University of California Press, 1972). Translated and edited by Cyril Bairett. Copyright © 1966 Basil Blackwell. Reprinted with permission of the University of California Press.

39. John Hick, "Rational Theistic Belief without Proof." From Hick, *Arguments for the Existence of God.* (Macmillan, London and Basingstoke, 1971). Reprinted with permission of Macmillan Publishers.

40. Alvin Plantinga, "Religious Belief without Proof." From *Faith and Rationality*, VII. D.2. *Religious Belief without Evidence* by Alvin Plantinga © 1983 by the University of Notre Dame Press. Reprinted by permission of the editor and the author.

41. Philip Quinn, "In Search of the Foundation of Theism." *Faith and Philosophy* (Oct. 1985). Reprinted by permission of the editor.

42. Louis Pojman, "Can Religious Belief Be Rational?" From *Festschrift for John Macquarrie.* Reprinted with permission of the author.

43. H. J. McCloskey, "God and Evil." *The Philosophical Quarterly* Vol. 10, No. 39 (1960). Reprinted by permission of the author and Basil Blackwell Ltd.

44. John Hick, "The Irenaean Theodicy." From Hick, *Evil and the God of Love.* (N.Y.: Harper & Row, 1966) Ch. 13. Copyright © 1966, 1977 by John Hick. Reprinted by permission of Harper and Row, Publishers.

45. W. K. Clifford, "The Ethics of Belief." Part One of "The Ethics of Belief" in *Contemporary Review* (Jan. 1877). Reprinted in Clifford, Lectures and Essays (1879).

46. William James, "The Will to Believe." From James, *The Will to Believe and Other Essays* (1897).

47. John Hick, "Faith and Interpretation." From Hick, *Faith and Knowledge*. Ithaca, N. Y.: Cornell University Press, 1966. Reprinted with permission of the author.

48. David Hume, "Against Miracles." *An Enquiry Concerning Human Understanding* (Oxford: Oxford University Press, 1748).

49. Richard Swinburne, "For The Possibility of Miracles." *The Philosophical Quarterly* Vol. 18 (1968). Reprinted with permission.

50. Baron d'Holbach, "Immortality: An Absurd Supposition." From Jean Muslier (Baron d'Holbach), *Superstition in All Ages*. Peter Eckler, 1890.

51. C. J. Ducasse. "Is Life after Death Possible?" From Ducasse, *Is Life after Death Possible?* Foerster Lecture Series 2, (Berkeley: University of California Press, 1948) ten pages. Copyright © 1948 The Regents of the University of California. Reprinted with permission.

52. Emil Brunner, "Good and the Will of God." From Brunner, *The Divine Imperative*. Translated by Olive Wyon. Copyright © MCMXLVII, by W. L. Jenkins. Used by permission of Westminister/John Knox Press.

53. Kai Nielsen, "God and the Good." *Theology Today* Vol. 21 (1964). Reprinted with the permission of the editor.

54. Robert Merrihew Adams, "A Modified Divine Command Theory of Ethical Wrongness." From *Religion and Morality: A Collection of Essays* edited by Gene Outka and John P. Reeder, Jr. (N.Y.: Doubleday & Co., 1973) Copyright Gene Outka and John P. Reeder, Jr. Reprinted with permission.

55. David F. Swenson, "The Dignity of Human Life." From *Kierkegaardian Philosophy in the Faith of a Scholar*. (Philadelphia: Westminster Press, 1949) pp. 13–28.

56. E. D. Klemke, "Living without Appeal: An Affirmative Philosophy of Life." From Klemke, *Reflections and Perspectives: Essays in Philosophy*. West Berlin: W. de Gruyter/Mouton, 1974. pp. 98–109.

A 1
B 2
C 3
D 4
E 5
F 6
G 7
H 8
I 9
J 0